TESTIMONY AND TRADITION

Internationally recognised for his scholarship in the philosophy of religion and Christian Doctrine, and for his ecclesiastical connections as former Theological Secretary of the Geneva-based World Alliance of Reformed Churches, the Reformed theologian Alan Sell has an established reputation amongst theologians, church and intellectual historians, ecumenists, and ministers of religion.

This collection of Alan Sell's work on the Reformed and Dissenting traditions spans key doctrinal, philosophical, ethical, historical and ecumenical topics. The author illuminates central themes with the history and thought of the Reformed and Dissenting traditions including: the catholicity of the Church and danger of sectarianism, the importance of Church Meeting, the centrality of the Cross in Christian thought, the need for a viable Christian apologetic. Alan Sell also includes the only modern study of Henry Grove and papers on Andrew Fuller and P. T. Forsyth, in whose work there is currently a revival of interest. With growing interest world wide in the Reformed family, which is the third largest Christian world communion, this book offers an invaluable resource.

To my Aberystwyth friends and former colleagues and students

Testimony and Tradition

Studies in Reformed and Dissenting Thought

ALAN P. F. SELL

WIPF & STOCK · Eugene, Oregon

Wipf and Stock Publishers
199 W 8th Ave, Suite 3
Eugene, OR 97401

Testimony and Trandition
Studies in Reformed and Dissenting Thougth
By Sell, Alan P.F.
Copyright©2005 by Sell, Alan P.F.
ISBN 13: 978-1-62032-424-0
Publication date 7/31/2012
Previously published by Ashgate, 2005

Contents

Preface		vii
Acknowledgements		viii
1	Conservation and Exploration in Christian Theology Inaugural Lecture, The United Theological College, Aberystwyth, 1992	1
2.	The Worship of English Congregationalism Consultation on Reformed worship, Geneva, 2001	19
3.	Telling the Story: Then and Now *Festschrift* for Gabriel Fackre	37
4.	Doctrine, Polity, Liberty: What do Baptists Stand For? *Festschrift* for B. R. White	49
5.	The Life and Thought of Henry Grove Introduction to Alan P F Sell, ed., *Henry Grove: Religious and Ethical Writings*, 2000	91
6.	Andrew Fuller and the Socinians *Festschrift* for D. O. Thomas	119
7.	P. T. Forsyth as Unsystematic Systematician Quincentennial Colloquium, University of Aberdeen, 1993	139
8.	What Has P. T. Forsyth to do with Mercersburg? The Mercersburg Convocation, 1997	171
9.	A Renewed Plea for 'Impractical' Divinity University of Wales Theology and Religious Studies Staff Colloquium, 1994	211
10.	Reformed Theology: Whence and Whither? Reformed Studies Centre conference, Westminster College, Cambridge, 1999	233
11.	The Dissenting Witness: Yesterday and Today Annual Lecture to The Protestant Dissenting Deputies, 2001	253

12.	From Union to Church: Autobiographical Recollections of Congregational Ecclesiology in the 1960s *Festschrift* for Clyde Binfield	285
13	Reminiscence, Reflection, Reassurance The Davies Lecture, Presbyterian Church of Wales, 2001; The Annual Commemoration Lecture, Westminster College, Cambridge, 2001	317

Index of Persons — 353
General Index — 363

Preface

In this volume are gathered some of the papers I wrote during nine happy years' occupancy of the Chair of Christian Doctrine and Philosophy of Religion at The United Theological College, within the Aberystwyth and Lampeter School of Theology of the University of Wales. Appropriately enough, the first paper reprinted is my Inaugural Lecture; the last is the contribution I was honoured to make to the long line of Davies Lectures of the Presbyterian Church of Wales, under whose auspices I served whilst in Aberystwyth.

As well as being broadly concerned with the Reformed and Dissenting traditions, the collection, not surprisingly, affords evidence of my interests in ecclesiology, eighteenth-century thought, and ecumenism. It is characteristic of my method to seek to benefit from the wisdom of those who have gone before, as well as to engage with my contemporaries as appropriate. Some of the papers reveal my deep indebtedness to experiences gained while holding theological posts in England, Switzerland, Canada and Wales.

I have revised and updated the papers as necessary, and in some cases I have abbreviated them in order to reduce that undue repetition which is always a possibility when material originally prepared for different times and places is brought together. A measure of repetition remains, but I hope that by virtue of certain running themes the collection may constitute more of a unity than might otherwise have been the case.

I should like to thank those who invited me to prepare the papers: Elfed ap Nefydd Roberts (1), Lukas Vischer (2), Skye Fackre Gibson (3), Paul Fiddes and John Briggs (4), Martin Fitzpatrick (5), Rudi Thoemmes (6), Trevor Hart (7), Jeffrey Roth (8), Oliver Davies (9), Peter McEnhill (10), Geoffrey Roper (11), Timothy Larsen (12), and John Tudno Williams for the Trustees of the Davies Lecture (13). The page of Acknowledgements will indicate my gratitude to those who have cordially agreed that papers originally published under their auspices may be reprinted here.

Over the years I have been well served by several publishers, Sarah Lloyd and her colleagues at Ashgate Publishing being no exception: my thanks to them.

Alan P. F. Sell
Milton Keynes

Acknowledgements

The author and publisher are grateful to those named for permission to reprint the following papers:

Conservation and Exploration in Christian Theology, 1993: John Tudno Williams, The United Theological College, Aberystwyth.

'The worship of English Congregationalism,' in Lukas Vischer, ed., *Christian Worship in Reformed Churches Past and Present*, 2003: Jon Pott of Wm. B. Eerdmans Publishing Co., Grand Rapids.

'Telling the story: then and now,' in Skye Fackre Gibson, ed., *Story Lines: Chapters on Thought, Word and Deed for Gabriel Fackre*, 2002: Jon Pott of Wm. B. Eerdmans Publishing Co., Grand Rapids.

'Doctrine, polity, liberty: what do Baptists stand for?' in William H. Brackney and Paul S. Fiddes, with John H. Y. Briggs, eds., *Pilgrim Pathways: Essays in Baptist History in Honour of B. R. White*, 199 : Marc Jolley of Mercer University Press, Macon, Georgia.

'The life and thought of Henry Grove,' prefixed to *Henry Grove: Ethical and Theological Writings*, 2000: Rudi Thoemmes of Thoemmes Press, Bristol.

'Andrew Fuller and the Socinians,' *Enlightenment and Dissent*, XIX, 2000: Martin Fitzpatrick, editor.

'P. T. Forsyth as unsystematic systematician,' in Trevor Hart, ed., *Justice the True and Only Mercy: Essays on the Life and Theology of Peter Taylor Forsyth*, 1995: Ben Hayes of The Continuum International Publishing Group (T. and T. Clark).

'What has P. T. Forsyth to do with Mercersburg?' *The New Mercersburg Review*, XXII, Autumn 1997: Linden DeBie, editor.

'A renewed plea for "impractical" divinity,' *Studies in Christian Ethics*, VII no. 2, 1995: Esther D. Reed, editor.

The Dissenting Witness: Yesterday and Today, [2002] : Geoffrey H. Roper, for The Protestant Dissenting Deputies of the Three Denominations.

'From Union to Church: autobiographical recollections of Congregational ecclesiology in the 1960s,' in D. W. Bebbington and T. Larsen, eds., *Christianity and Cultural Aspirations since 1800*: Ulla Schnell of The Continuum International Publishing Group (Sheffield Academic Press).

Reminiscence, Reflection, Reassurance, 2002: Huw Owen and John Tudno Williams of the Davies Lecture Board.

The paper, 'Reformed theology: whence and whither?' has not previously been published.

CHAPTER 1

Conservation and Exploration in Christian Theology

Inaugural lectures are of various kinds. Some are highly technical, and give the newly inducted professor an opportunity to indulge in sufficient intellectual wizardry to justify the decision of the appointing board. At worst such lectures exemplify the remark of W. H. Auden that 'A professor is one who talks in someone else's sleep;'[1] and some such professors go on to earn the obituary euphemism, 'his (or her) gifts were not of the popular order' — which may simply mean, 'he or she managed to bore most of the people most of the time.' Then there is the kind of inaugural lecture in which the newly inducted scholar sets out to justify the place of his or her discipline in the university. That some such efforts have fallen on stony ground is evidenced by the devastation in the name of rationalisation which has overtaken certain departments in British higher education in recent years. I have elsewhere written in defence of theology in the curriculum of higher education, and I shall not repeat myself here.[2]

Rather, I wish to issue a call to action. There is much to be done in Christian theology broadly conceived, and every Christian has a part to play, and in fact plays a part. For no Christian is innocent of theological thoughts; and while professional theologians ought to be resource persons for the Church, skilled in the critical analysis of theological utterance, well versed in the Christian tradition, and competent to stand at the frontier between Church and world, they are by no means alone, and still less are they infallible. Indeed, in terms of Christian insight and wisdom (as distinct from theological expertise), and also from the point of view of sanctified living, they may well be left standing by Christians in other fields of endeavour, and not least by the unlettered. This, of course, is as it should be, given that we are saved by grace through faith, and not by our theological competence. However, if theologians need to be reminded of their lowly place, it is equally important that we do not encourage any to rejoice in avoidable theological illiteracy. The call to mine Scripture for the Word of God, to explore the faith once delivered with a view to testimony, to apply the

---

[1] W. H. Auden, quoted in Connie Robertson, ed., *The Wordsworth Dictionary of Quotations*, Ware, Hertfordshire: Wordsworth, 1996, no. 589.
[2] See Alan P. F. Sell, *Aspects of Christian Integrity*, Calgary: The University of Calgary Press, 1990, and Louisville: Westminster/John Knox Press, 1991; reprinted Eugene, OR: Wipf & Stock, 1998, ch. 1.

message in daily life, presents every Christian with an intellectual challenge. All I can do in this inaugural lecture is to erect some signposts in territory which urgently needs to be conserved, and which affords ample scope for exploration of the most exhilarating kind.

I

Before proceeding further we ought, perhaps, to consider the possible objection that theologizing is a fool's errand. How, it might be asked, can we speak of God — if, indeed, there is a God? The blunt answer is that Christians speak of God because they believe that in Christ God has both addressed humanity and acted for humanity — supremely in the Cross-Resurrection event. God speaks before we do, and Christ is the Word made flesh. But as soon as we say this, we have to go on at once to admit that we hear what we hear, and we can be notoriously selective in our hearing. This is one reason why our theologizing will always fall short of the reality we seek to worship and bear witness to. But the more important reason why we shall never fully succeed, and why the explorations must continue, lies in the nature of God himself. All Christians worth their salt have understood that while we may truly apprehend God, we shall never fully comprehend him. This inevitable Christian agnosticism must be distinguished from the modern agnosticism which some have derived from one side of Kant. According to this, and on the basis of the distinction between the noumenal and phenomenal realms, it is held that we cannot know anything at all about God, freedom and immorality, though we are intellectually obliged to postulate them.

However partial our grasp of the matter, Christians believe that we, by grace, have knowledge of the God who has made himself known in Christ. In Christ, we further believe, God has acted in a once-for-all way for the redemption of the world. This, I take it, is what lies at the heart of the message to be conserved. As P. T. Forsyth said, 'Revelation did not come in a statement, but in a person; yet stated it must be. Faith must go on to specify. It must be capable of statement, else it could not be spread; for it is not an ineffable, incommunicable mysticism.'[3] It is what has been passed on to us by the Church of the ages and it is what we are obliged to present in our time. We do not receive the message uninterpreted and, as I said, as individuals we hear it selectively. In order, therefore, to mitigate our own idiosyncratic hearing we need continually to test our reception of the message against the heritage of testimony out of which it comes, and to recognise that our theologizing is a communal matter: it is a churchly task. God addresses us by the Spirit, through the Word, discerned in

---

[3] P. T. Forsyth, *The Person and Place of Jesus Christ* (1909), London: Independent Press, 1961, 15.

fellowship; and if we separate Spirit, Word and fellowship we shall foster individualistic mysticism on the one side, and biblicist fundamentalism on the other; and we shall deprive ourselves of those ecclesial checks and balances — both historical and contemporary — which, humanly speaking, seem essential for the conservation of the apostles' doctrine. More seriously still, if we spurn the historical and the ecclesial dimensions we shall be implicitly adopting a stance which arrogantly denies that God was doing or saying anything of importance until we came on the scene: and that would be a huge slight upon God's providence through the ages, and upon the work of his ever-active Holy Spirit.

But even as we explore the Christian heritage and present-day Christian insights in order to see how to articulate what is to be conserved, we may not forget that we are not conservers of fossils for display in a museum, but communicators of a message which, we believe, holds the possibility of new life for all. For this reason our explorations must not be confined to the Christian tradition then and now. We must also investigate the intellectual and general human environment in which we are called to proclaim the message today.

It should by now be clear why the title of this lecture is conjunctive rather than disjunctive in character. In Christian theology we canot be *either* conservationists *or* explorers. In order to see what is to be conserved we have to explore the Christian heritage. In order to articulate our findings today we have to explore the circumstances of our time. If I had to state in one sentence what I think a truly contemporary theology would look like, I would say this: a truly contemporary theology will be fired by the Gospel, grounded in the Scriptures, nourished by the catholic faith of the ages, fertilised by Reformation emphases, tempered by Enlightenment critiques, and it will be applicable today. We are to be neither antiquarians on the one hand, nor, on the other, people who give the impression that a novel theology needs to be invented each new morning.[4]

The temptation to antiquarianism on the one hand and theological 'ad hoc-ery' on the other is strong, however, and some yield one way or the other. Thus, on the one side, instead of being conservationists in the sense I have described, some Christians fall into a hard, narrow, exclusivist conservatism. Examples of this are not unknown in the Reformed family. Overlooking the time-bound character of all confessional statements, forgetting that some of those who composed the confessions wrote introductions in which they expressed their willingness to amend their text if it could be shown to be unbiblical, these Christians so elevate their forms of words as to suggest that here is the statement of God's truth for all time. If they then proceed to unchurch all those who see things differently, you have the ugly phenomena of sectarianism and secession

---

[4] To strike the right balance to the satisfaction of all is easier said than done.

with which the history of the Reformed family is cluttered. The body of Christ is divided, subordinate standards become new idols, doctrinal matters are fixed once and for all, and you have the implicit denial of the ongoing illuminative work of the Holy Spirit.

Analagous conservatism can result from the elevation of particular codes of ethics or ways of doing theology into quasi-absolute norms for all time. As to ethics, Robert Mackintosh noted the paradox concerning the heirs of Puritanism, namely, that 'doctrinally and emotionally [a person] was to live by grace, but his conduct was to be exactly the same *as if he expected to be justified by works* ...'[5] In this way Christianity is converted into a new legalism: 'Believe on the Lord Jesus Christ — and do not play cards, go dancing, wear make-up, etc., etc. — and you shall be saved.' It may well be that having begun the Christian pilgrimage a person will adjust his or her lifestyle in a number of ways. But the adjustments are repsonses to grace, not conditions of grace — otherwise we have landed in a doctrine of works.

Where theology is concerned the shibboleths are many. I recall the exasperation of the Baptist Thomas Crosby in the eighteenth century. Having been spurned by his fellow-Baptist, the high Calvinist John Gill, he expostulated, 'It is *Christ* that must be followed, and not *Calvin*, or *Arminius* ... Are the peculiar distinguishing doctrines of *Calvin*, or *Arminius*, essential to a Christian? If not, why are they made essential to communion with one another? ... What praise can they expect from Christ their divine master, who make the door to a profession of his religion *straiter* [that is, narrower], than he has left it?'[6] A course of modern movements in theology would swiftly undeceive any who may be tempted to think that theological sectarianism died with the eighteenth century — or have you never encountered a *certain kind of* biblical inerrantist, feminist, liberation theologian, Barthian, or Thomist?[7]

On the other side some, instead of being theological explorers who mine the heritage and communicate it to a closely investigated contemporary situation, seem to loosen their grip on the heritage and, in a laudable desire to reach modern people, capitulate to the thought forms of the age and emasculate the Gospel in the process. Forsyth rightly warned that 'There must surely be in every positive religion some point where it may so change as to lose its identity

---

[5] Robert Mackintosh, *The Insufficiency of Revivalism as a Religious System*, 8. This pamphlet is bound with his *Essays Towards a New Theology*, Glasgow: Maclehose, 1889. See further, Alan P. F. Sell, *Robert Mackintosh: Theologian of Integrity*, Bern: Peter Lang, 1977.

[6] Thomas Crosby, *The History of the English Baptists*, London, 1740, IV, 15, 16 (spelling modernised).

[7] On ethical and theological sectarianism see further Alan P. F. Sell, *Commemorations. Studies in Christian Thought and History*, Calgary: The University of Calgary Press and Cardiff: University of Wales Press, 1993; reprinted Eugene, OR: Wipf & Stock, 1998, ch. 2.

and become another religion.'⁸ If he did not embrace another religion, D. F. Strauss thought himself out of Christianity in the mid-nineteenth century, for example. On the basis of his distinction between the facts of history and the mythological expressions of the Christian Idea he concluded that the Cross-Resurrection event was a parable of the fact that humanity dies and rises again. He eventually concluded that he was no longer a Christian.⁹ Henry Jones, an early teacher of philosophy in the University College of Wales, Aberystwyth, was another whose explorations were, in the opinion of some, inadequately anchored. Having preached a favourably-received sermon at Llanfair P. G., Anglesey, he was promised a return visit, but no invitation came. On asking John Morris Jones why this was, the latter replied, 'They are told that you deny the divinity of Christ.' 'I! I deny the divinity of Christ!' said Jones, 'I do not deny the divinity of any man!'¹⁰ Among contemporary explorers who have caused some to express concern are Hans Küng, Charles Curran and Leonardo Boff,¹¹ who are not currently permitted to teach under the auspices of the Roman Church, and Don Cupitt of the Church of England. Whereas the latter has not been subjected to formal ecclesiastical censure, the former have. This underlines the fact that the discipline of churchly bodies varies in relation to the question of authority, and such bodies have to find their own way on this matter. If, as I have suggested, theology is a churchly matter, this is as it should be. No doubt the question of the different ways in which it may be appropriate to treat babes in Christ on the one hand and official teachers of the Church on the other when divergence from the received doctrinal position is detected is never easy to resolve. My own inclinations are to recognise the positive benefits of those whose explorations have led them into what the majority have deemed to be heresy: at the very least they have prompted critical thought on the part of the Church; to invoke formal church discipline as a last resort only; to make it clear that we are not saved by subscription to specific doctrinal formulae but by God's grace in Christ; and to suggest that it is a moot point whether more harm has been done to the cause of Christ by explorers of the faith who have lost the compass of their heritage, or by conservers of the faith who have unwarrantably hedged about God's free grace with their narrow doctrinal definitions and new ethical legalisms.

---

⁸ P. T. Forsyth, *The Principle of Authority* (1913), London: Independent Press, 1952, 219.

⁹ See further, Alan P. F. Sell, *Theology in Turmoil. The Roots, Course and Significance of the Conservative-Liberal Debate in Modern Theology*, (1986), Eugene, OR: Wipf & Stock, 1998, ch. 2.

¹⁰ See H. J. W. Hetherington, *The Life and Letters of Sir Henry Jones*, London: Hodder & Stoughton, 1924, 42–3.

¹¹ For the way in which the question of the locus of authority in the Church is currently raised see Alan P. F. Sell, *Commemorations*, ch. 1.

Ideally theological conservationists will not become antiquarian conservatives, and theological explorers will not degenerate into theological freewheelers. Rather, conservation and exploration will go hand in hand. The heritage will be explored to see what is to be conserved, and the manner and the content of the resulting contemporary communication will be sensitive to the prevailing climate of thought and conditions of life. The importance of this balance is seen not dramatically when theological 'red alert' situations arise. I think of Athanasius standing against the world in the cause of the full humanity and divinity of Christ; of Luther rediscovering the grand theme of justification by grace through faith; of the authors of the Barmen Declaration of 1934; of the theological stand taken against apartheid in more recent time. On these occasions the Gospel was deemed to be at risk, and a stand had to be taken. But the stands taken in every case both drew resources from the Christian heritage and ultimately from Scripture, and were thoroughly alive to the challenges of the time. Dramatic occasions of the kind noted are, no doubt, few and far between; but they highlight the work of theological conservation and exploration which, in less spectacular times, is no less needed if the message which has been committed to the Church is to be heard in each successive generation.

II

Having, I trust, shown sufficiently the way in which conservation and exploration are necessarily related in the theological enterprise, I now wish to turn in greater detail to the question, 'Who are the conservers and the explorers?' As I suggested earlier, they are Christians — all of them. Insofar as believers reflect upon, and seek to articulate their faith, they are theologizing. It must be emphasised that all constructive theologizing presupposes faith. As the distinguished nineteenth-century Reformed theologian and historian Philip Schaff wrote, 'A theologian without faith is like a sky without a star, a heart without a pulse, a light without warmth, a sword without an edge, a body without a Soul.'[12] And if we ask what is true faith, the Heidelberg Catechism will remind us: it is 'not only a certain knowledge by which I accept as true all that God has revealed to us in his Word, but also a wholehearted trust which the Holy Spirit creates in me through the gospel.'[13] In those last words we have the claim that even the faith with which we respond to God's grace is itself a gift to

---

[12] Quoted by George H. Shriver, *Philip Schaff. Christian Scholar and Ecumenical Prophet*, Macon, GA: Mercer University Press, 1987, 12.
[13] Heidelberg Catechism, Q. 21.

us — and that is why we cannot boast about it, as Paul told the Ephesians.[14] Moreover, this faith issues in grateful obedience — in what our forebears would have called 'a godly walk' under the inspiration of the same Holy Spirit. 'To commend a Saviour one has no love for,' wrote John Brown of Haddington, 'to preach a Gospel one does not believe; to point out the way to heaven, and never to have taken a step that way; to enforce a saving acquaintance with religion and to be an entire stranger to it oneself, how sad, how preposterous!'[15]

To say that theologizing is the task of the whole Church is not to say the professional theologians have no particular part to play. Ideally they will be the theological advance party, committed to the Church but permitted by the ecclesial authorities to engage in their exploratory tasks; accountable to the institutions in which they work for the rigour of their scholarship and the vitality of their teaching. Professional theologians, as I have suggested, are people of faith; but they have less right than anyone else illegitimately to use faith as the ace up their sleeve when the way of argument becomes tough. Their calling to reflect upon their faith and that of the Church in such a way as to obey the injunction to love God with all their mind requires them to address technical questions in doctrine, ethics and philosophy which will not occupy the majority of Christians. In 1923 Harnack complained to his former pupil Karl Barth that Barth was turning theology into a form of preaching, and neglecting the scientific aspects of the discipline. I believe that there is a proper place for both the presentation of systematic reflection upon the Christian faith which, since it is written by believers will necessarily have something of the character of proclamation about it, and for the detailed attention to specific technical points. When the technical questions — sometimes called 'scientific' — become all-consuming idols, however, and when theologians gnostically retreat from the churches — as some did in Germany in the nineteenth century, and as others did in America in the 1960s, then it is time for them to take stock. For they have practically denied the importance of the earthen vessel, the Church, which nevertheless carries Christ to humanity and which was, in the vast majority of cases, the vehicle through which they themselves heard the Gospel.

Theologians may or may not be ministers of the Gospel, but ministers of the Gospel ought to be theologians. They comprise a second category of theological conservationists and explorers. I wish to dwell upon them in view of a major objective of this College. A century and a half ago Robert Vaughan was contemplating becoming the first President of my own theological college. He wrote, 'My impression has long been, that our own progress, and even our

---

[14] Ephesians 2: 9.
[15] Robert Mackenzie, *John Brown of Haddington* (1918), London: The Banner of Truth Trust, 1964, 138.

reputable existence as a denomination ... will depend in a very special degree on the prosperous state of our collegiate institutions — on their prosperous state I mean as sending forth a large number of men of deep piety, of solid acquisition, and of real pulpit power.'[16] That we need such men — and women - still cannot be denied. We need men and women who will conserve and explore the faith — not only in their preaching, but in their entire approach to their ministry. If they do not see all of the activities of the church in a theological perspective, how will they be able to help the church members to view matters in this light? It is a question of the presuppositions and motivations of mission and service. It is a question of what we preach on Sundays, of how we teach the young, of what we say to the dying and to the bereaved. What preparation ought such persons to receive?

Most people would agree that there are certain things about which prospective ministers ought to be informed. Indeed, one of our current problems is the very proliferation during this century of possible subjects of study. We have traditionally valued biblical, historical, theological and pastoral studies; but before our eyes have blossomed psychology of religion, sociology of religion, world religions, ecumenical studies, liturgical studies, Christian education, church administration, courses on spirituality, church growth and mission; and pastoral counselling has become a veritable industry in some quarters. Since in most cases the overall length of the course has not increased, it is hardly surprising that there are urgent questions to be addressed concerning core disciplines. Are we to have more and more 'surveys' and 'outlines', and less and less progression and depth in basic theological education? Are we to innoculate students for life against learning, by giving them such small quantities of this and that that they never see the point of any of it, still less enjoy it? If not, what are the implications for required, probationary in-service training following a core course?

In addition to the matter of information, there is that of formation. Is there a sharp line to be drawn between subjects which are informative and those which are formative, between the so-called 'academic' subjects and the so-called 'practical' ones? There is in most subjects, whether linguistic or philosophical, a certain basic grind of grammar or terminology or the mastery of techniques before real progress can be made. But at their best the several subjects should both inform and form. The first thing about pastoral theology, for example, is that it is theology; and as for New Testament exegesis, my happy experience under T. W. Manson and Owen Evans was that this could be as academically rigorous as it was devout.

---

[16] Joseph Thompson, *Lancashire Independent College, 1843–1893*, Manchester: Cornish, 1893, 72.

But as with the mastery of material, so with the formation of persons: time is required. In these days students have marital commitments which were not permitted in my student days; some, especially in North America, maintain themselves by working at as many as three part-time jobs; many commute — for as little as one day per week. How different was the experience of John Brown of Haddington (1722–1787), whom I quoted earlier. He not only knew where all his students were, he was in the habit of visiting their lodgings between six and eight in the morning. We read, 'Not a few were startled out of their slumbers by a loud and peremptory challenge, that was occasionally helped by a poke from the pastoral staff.'[17] It was a different world. Such a professor would today risk litigation in respect of invasion of privacy and common assault.

We need not, indeed, be too starry-eyed about the past: when James Martineau participated in a presbytery examination *circa* 1830, he noted that some of the fathers and brethren 'sat through the ordeal gravely holding their Hebrew Bibles upside down.'[18] The facts now are that we have a welcome diversity of age-range and ability in our present-day theological student bodies; that, owing to adverse economic factors, few have a preliminary degree before commencing theological studies; and that in some seminaries and the theological colleges almost fifty per cent of the students are second-career people. All of this is potentially enriching as far as the ministries of the several churches are concerned. But one thing in particular disturbs me. I believe that we face a crisis in high-calibre theological leadership in many churches in the West.

With reference to a similar situation in 1865, Dr. Falding of Rotherham [Independent] College told delegates at a conference on theological education that 'the higher attainments are not *likely* to be made, that in fact, in present circumstances, they *cannot* be made by all, but that there are special and urgent reasons why what cannot be done by all should yet be done by *some*.' He proceeded to note that 'the class of men from which tutors are selected ... is not large. Certainly there has never been anything like a strong contest for our vacant tutorships.'[19] With the passage of time matters improved, and within Falding's own denomination theological students were taught by such luminaries as A. M. Fairbairn, J. Vernon Bartlet, P. T. Forsyth, A. E. Garvie, W. F. Adeney, W. H. Bennett, Robert Mackintosh, Sydney Cave, Robert Franks, H. F. Lovell Cocks, John Marsh, Geoffrey Nuttall, John Whale and others. But now,

---

[17] R. Mackenzie, *John Brown of Haddington*, 143.
[18] Quoted by H. McLachlan, *Essays and Addresses*, Manchester: Manchester University Press, 1950, 181.
[19] F. J. Falding, *Minutes of the Proceedings of a Conference of Delegates from the Committees of the Theological Colleges and Institutes connected with the Congregational Churches of England*, London: Jackson, Walford and Hodder, [1865], 15, 17.

for reasons which I cannot now stay to enumerate,[20] many denominations find themselves in the situation described in 1865 by Falding. If we still believe that it is important that those educating our ministers should normally themselves have had good pastoral experience as well as the opportunity of advanced study, we must recognise that it takes time to grow such a person, and we must encourage by all possible means those in our shrunken pools of younger candidates who may hear this specific call and rise to this arduous yet exciting challenge. I make no plea for theological élitism. I never cease to thank God for three of his ministers, none of whom had a university degree, and one of whom had been a non-collegiate ministerial candidate. There were no better or more faithful preachers or pastors. My point is simply that while the diverse gifts of all are to be valued and nurtured, we must urgently pray that God will raise up some whose gifts include that of competence for theological leadership. Such people are for the benefit of the whole church. But, to repeat, every minister is called to be a theological leader in his or her place.

The third category of theological conservationists and explorers comprises the rest of the church members. Certainly theological reflection is too important to be left to the theologians and ministers. When Paul wrote to the Philippians he reminded them that they shared his privilege of defending the Gospel, and he prayed that 'your love may grow ever richer in knowledge and insight of every kind.'[21] Every Christian believer who reflects at all upon God and the Gospel is, after his or her fashion, a theologian. But, as with theologians and ministers, so with everybody else: they need the checks and balances supplied by the heritage and the contemporary Church. Theology is a churchly activity. This is why it is so sad if church members have come to think, or have been encouraged to believe, that they have nothing to contribute when theological, ecumenical, ethical documents are referred to them from wider churchly circles. 'We leave discussions of this sort to the experts,' I have heard them say. But this is not why we had a Reformation! Moreover, if theological convictions do not hold a church together and sustain it, what will? There have always been those who have thought it impolite to mention doctrine over much; they have preferred to regard genial fellowship and common service as a glue which binds

---

[20] The reasons include the decline in membership of some Western churches, and with it the decrease in the overall number of candidates for the ordained ministry; the expansion of higher education during this century and the laicising of theological education, which have produced many career opportunities in theology and religious studies, so that budding academics in these fields do not need to be ordained or to seek employment in ecclesiastical institutions in order to fulfil their vocations; and the change in the balance of student bodies of theological colleges, whereby up to 50% of ministerial candidates are second-career people, with the consequence that the pool of those who will have time to obtain good pastoral experience and develop as scholars is much reduced.

[21] Philippians 1: 7, 9.

the church together. Over a hundred years ago some of these heard the retort of Principal D. W. Simon: 'No communities fall to pieces so quickly as those which have no tie but sentiment, whereas communities which are welded together by convictions as well as by feelings, resist attack alike from within and from without.'[22] (The convictions may not always be laudable, of course; people may be glued together by quite the wrong convictions; and convictions can be wielded as swords of sectarianism. But we may take Simon's main point that sentiment alone will not suffice to sustain the churches.)

We must face the fact that some feel at sea in theological waters, and we must make every effort to teach them to swim. The people need to be built up in the faith. It is as unsatisfactory to serve Christ's babes the dregs of the latest theological fashion as it is to force-feed them on the hard rusks of five-point Calvinism. They have a language to learn and not merely to parrot; they have experiences to develop and ideas to grasp. And they need help in these matters.

A Baptist from the Ottawa Valley recalled his upbringing in the middle of the nineteenth century. He wrote, 'Every dinner table was a theological class, and with the pork and potatoes went the Calvinism and Arminianism in due course. The Bible was the family hand-book, and handled reverently, it was the arbiter of the daily discussion.'[23] Here were people who, if they did but know it (and perhaps they did), were living in the spirit of the injunction of the *Westminster Larger Catechism.* to the question, 'What is required of those that hear the word preached?' the answer is, 'It is required of those that hear the word preached, that they attend upon it with diligence, preparation, and prayer; examine what they hear by the scriptures; receive the truth with faith, love, meekness, and readiness of mind, as the word of God; meditate and confer of it; hide it in their hearts, and bring forth the fruit of it in their lives.'[24] There have always been some who have done these things, but relatively few today in the West have the experience of the Ottawa Valley Baptist; and after more than one hundred years of popular education in England and Wales, with religion as a required subject, we cannot be certain that the major biblical themes have been grasped, or even that the major biblical characters are recognised by vast numbers in our population. How vital the theological role of the church members is. How else than through them will a theological perspective be brought to bear upon the issues of the day, the concerns of the workplace, the drawing room conversation of the retirement home? And how will ministers and theologians understand the environmental territory to be explored for the sake of the Gospel unless the

---

[22] D. W. Simon, 'Theological training,' in *Memorial of the Opening of the New and Enlarged Buildings of Lancashire Independent College*, Manchester: Tubbs and Brook, 1878, 91.
[23] Quoted by David B. Marshall, *Secularizing the Faith. Canadian Protestant Clergy and the Crisis of Belief, 1850–1940*. Toronto: University of Toronto Press, 1992.
[24] *Westminster Larger Catechism*, Q. 160.

church members act as their antennae in places where life is lived and death is feared, work is done and fun is had, marriages are made and homes are broken?

III

What are the areas which cry out for theological exploration with a view to the lively communication of the Christian message? The list is long, and I shall very briefly indicate a few themes which, as I see it, clamour for attention. The themes will exemplify the closeness of the relationship between churchly conservation and exploration of the Christian heritage, and the Church's engagement with contemporary culture.

I am sure I am not alone in having noticed a return in much recent theological writing to the doctrine of the Trinity. I welcome this, because the activity of the triune God is *the* context of Christian theology and life. But what is the notion of God that is actually operative in Christian circles? Here and there I have found a thoroughly domesticated God, who is so friendly and loving and forgiving that you would hardly think a Cross necessary to satisfy a holiness outraged by that wilful human rebellion which we call sin. The worship of this God is led by ever so jolly persons to whom the grand doctrinal hymns of the faith are an encumbrance to be banished in favour of ditties which are often sentimental in the extreme, and sometimes almost blasphemously self-serving. I do not advocate worship which is dull and boring; and as a reaction against worship which is precisely that — sterile and cold and too frequently Reformed — what I have just described is explicable. But there is a place for godly reverence before one who is holy and righteous. Before the majesty of God I can no more bound into the pulpit in a 'Wake up happy campers' kind of way, than I can refer to Christianity's personal God as 'it'. In such explorations of the non-churchly environment which I have undertaken I have discovered that seekers expect God to be God-like, and that those who do not or will not believe would feel thoroughly patronised by the candyfloss divinity who sometimes seems to be on offer.

What shall we say of God the Son? There are theologians who do not feel happy with this traditional language for Jesus Christ. They prefer to think of Jesus as the first among men; our exemplar. Accordingly, where the Cross is concerned what we have is an object lesson — perhaps the greatest object lesson, to teach us how God suffers alongside suffering humanity. What is missing from this presentation is the conviction that in the Cross-Resurrection event God in Christ acted in such a way as to bridge the sin-caused gulf between himself and us, and is victorious. Where the suffering world is concerned it does not seem to me that we have good news to offer if the most we can say is that in the Son God is suffering too.

But this is not all. What especially concerns some theologians when they reflect upon the classical ways of viewing the Incarnation is the scandal of particularity which is involved in it. They are conscious, and rightly so, that we live in a pluralist world, and they wish to find common ground with others where they can — again, rightly so. But for them the idea that God has acted once and for all, and for all, in Christ is disturbing because it seems to slight those of other faiths. However, if we believe God has acted thus, albeit for inclusive and not exclusive reasons, we abuse the integrity of dialogue if we remain silent on the point; we cheat our partners. They will expect us to speak from the heart, and they will wish to do so also. We need neither trim our own faith nor malign the faith of others. There is, let us never forget, a very important distinction to be drawn between the scandal of the Cross and scandalous behaviour on the part of Christians.[25]

Concerning the third person of the Trinity it might be supposed that the Holy Spirit has had more than sufficient attention paid to him by Christians in recent years. We have burgeoning Pentecostalism and a widespread charismatic movement which is no respecter of denominations. However, it seems to me that some of the attention paid to the Holy Spirit is of an unfortunately truncated kind. The Christian tradition has been explored in a selective way, and not in a way which would encourage the Christians concerned to be active at the intellectual frontier with the world. In some circles I hear much about healings and glossolalia, but little about the Spirit and creation, the Spirit and the Word, the Spirit and the Church, the Spirit and the world. Does God the Holy Spirit address the Church through the Bible discerned in fellowship, or not? If so, in what terms should we address the clamant ethical issues of the day, for example? How often a Christian's final ethical resort is, 'So long as you are not hurting anybody else …'[26] This is Enlightenment individualism at its blandest and least effective. As Bonhoeffer wrote long ago, 'It is not our heart that determines our course, but God's Word … How often we hear innumerable arguments "from life" and "from experience" put forward as the basis for the most crucial decisions, but the argument of Scripture is missing. And this authority would perhaps point in exactly the opposite direction.'[27]

Turning from the Trinity, I take a second example from another field of doctrine, that of the Church. Much could be said, but I shall make three brief assertions. First, despite ecumenical set-backs in many places, I continue to believe that God in Christ has made his people one, and that this given unity is

---

[25] Concerning this and the preceding paragraph see further Alan P. F. Sell, *Aspects of Christian Integrity*, chs. 2, 5.
[26] See further, ibid., ch. 3.
[27] D. Bonhoeffer, *Life Together*, London: SCM Press, 1954, 45.

to be manifested by them. Some people say 'In the name of the Gospel, we must not mingle with those who disagree with us certain doctrinal or institutional points. Unity must be in the truth.' No doubt; but our grasp of God's truth is always partial, and our formulations of it are always imperfect. Hence any attempt to treat such formulations as utterly sacrosanct is blasphemous idolatry, and any attempt to wield them as principles of exclusion is blatant sectarianism.[28] Over against all of this I say, 'Because I believe the Gospel declares that God has broken down barriers between those who are in Christ, I dare not withhold myself from all who name Christ as Saviour Lord, no matter how odd some of their beliefs and practices may seem to me to be.' What denies this unity is the sectarian spirit, and this, I believe, must be countered wherever it rears its head. We can argue about Christian doctrines until the cows come home, or the parousia intervenes — whichever is the sooner; we can worship and conduct ourselves in a variety of ways in accordance with ' our several traditions and cultural inheritances; but until we cordially and *mutually* welcome one another at the Lord's table we are dividing what God in Christ has made one, and we need not expect the world around to be over-impressed by our Gospel of reconciliation.

Secondly, what of the Church's ordained ministry? I believe that the concept of ministerial vocation needs urgent exploration in relation to our heritage and the needs of the world around. Under God, ministers must be teachers and shepherds of the flock; the flock must be equipped to disperse. Is this what is happening? I sometimes suspect that at this point in some churchly circles we have listened to the world too much. The world is hurting, so ministers must be therapists. The church is a quasi-corporation, so ministers must be managers. The church is a business, so they must know their product. This in turn influences the way we speak about ministry — 'the hiring and firing pastors,' 'ministerial career structures,' 'the minister as salesman', and so forth; and it affects the theological curriculum — sometimes drastically. But is it right? I do not say that we have nothing to learn from secular counsellors, or from the world of business, or from elsewhere. But our hearing of the world must be tempered by our hearing of the tradition.[29] It might be no bad thing for us to reflect upon some of our modern talk about ministerial professionalism and the like in relation to these words of John Robinson, pastor to the Pilgrims:

> the bond between the minister, and people is the most strait, and near religious bond that may be, and therefore not to be entered but with mutual consent, any more than the civil bond of marriage between the husband, and wife... It makes much, both for the provocation of the minister unto all

---

[28] See further, Alan P. F. Sell, *Commemorations*, ch. 2.
[29] See further idem, *Aspects of Christian Integrity*, ch. 6.

diligence and faithfulness: and also for his comfort in all the trials and temptations which befall him in his ministry, when he considereth how the people, unto whom he ministereth, have committed that rich treasure of their souls, in the Lord, yea, I may say, of their very faith, and joy, to be helped forward unto salvation, to his care, and charge, by their free and voluntary choice of him.[30]

What, thirdly, of the ministry of the whole people of God? We hear much about this at the present time, but what do we really mean by it, and what steps do we take to render the idea practicable? When I analysed the responses of Reformed churches around the world to the World Council of Churches document, *Baptism, Eucharist and Ministry* (1982), I found that there was widespread pleasure that at the opening of the chapter on ministry the 'calling of the whole people of God' was affirmed; and widespread dismay that so soon it was displaced by the all-too-familiar question of the threefold, ordained ministry.[31] Can it be said, however, that the Reformed have always acted consistently with their words? Have we not known of autocratic princes of the pulpit who have ruled with a rod of iron; or of oligarchies or elders or deacons who have revelled in the role of ecclesiastical fixer? And is it not odd that in some Presbyterian circles church members are permitted an annual, often brief, meeting in which they approve the budget and elect one or two elders, but are never consulted throughout the rest of the year concerning the mission and service of their local church? We have more than enough reason to engage in fresh explorations concerning the ministry of the whole people of God in relation to our heritage and the context in which we are called to witness today.[32]

I have attempted in my examples from trinitarian doctrine and ecclesiology to show that our reflections are not simply in-house matters. Our conservationist role is with a view to confessing Christ today. There can be no question that this is the objective where my last illustration is concerned, for here the impetus frequently comes from outside the circle of believers. I refer to our apologetic task. Here we seek directly to engage with the intellectual climate of our day with a view to giving a reason for the hope that is in us. Or do we? I have a distinct impression that some theologians shun the apologetic task. This may be done for a variety of reasons. They may feel that since the Enlightenment the rug has been pulled from under the entire apologetic enterprise. The traditional arguments for God's existence have been undermined from various points of view; since Hume we cannot easily adduce miracles as evidence of

---

[30] John Robinson, *A Justification of Separation from the Church of England: Against Mr. Richard Bernard his Invective* (1610), in *The Works of John Robinson*, London: John Snow, 1851, II, 396–397.
[31] See further Alan P. F. Sell, 'Some Reformed responses to *Baptism, Eucharist and Ministry*,' *The Reformed World*, XXXIX, no. 3, September 1986.
[32] See further idem, *Commemorations*, ch. 14.

God's existence and activity in the world; and accordingly there is no future for apologetics. Again, some theologians may feel that because we are in receipt of a Word from God there can be no argument about this, and our role is simply that of articulating what we have seen and heard. Yet others may have persuaded themselves that since in religion we opt for one of a number of possible language games which logically cannot overlap or conflict with others, the question of truth as between the several options cannot be raised. Because I am now in the realm of one of my special enthusiasms I must take particular pains to be brief.[33] I shall content myself by making three blunt observations.

First, I believe that there is something philosophically and theologically autocratic about appearing to tell those around us who ask for a justification of the faith, or for a response to sincere and serious questions, that they have no right to raise such matters. People do ask these persistent questions whether we like it or not. They will not be helped by philosophical or theological embargoes, or by that creeping anti-intellectualism, signs of which may be detected in many main-line Western churches, in which the current emphasis is so much upon the allegedly practical and the professional. In reality, there is nothing more practical or more pastoral than the attempt to address people's agonising questions.

Secondly, whereas in the middle years of this century relatively few professional philosophers in the English-speaking world were discussing substantive theological questions (though a number were offering analytical critiques of theological discourse)[34] an encouragingly large number of today's professional philosophers are doing precisely this. I have in mind such writers as Michael Dummett, Basil Mitchell and Richard Swinburne in this country, William Alston, Alvin Plantinga and Richard Gale in the United States, and Terence Penelhum, Hugo Meynell and Kai Nielsen in Canada. But all too frequently theologians seem content to proceed in innocence of the questions raised and the contributions made, contenting themselves with dogmatic utterances within the circle of faith, or with historical studies, or with domestic ecclesiastical questions. There is, of course, a proper place for this dogmatic, historical and domestic work. For example, some of the Church's domestic questions are very important. Consider the ordination of women. I can see no good theological grounds for not ordaining women, and I have sought to put

---

[33] Elsewhere I have been less brief. Indeed, this paper was written when I was about one third of the way through a fifteen-year project concerned with Christian apologetic method. This has resulted in a trilogy published by the University of Wales Press, Cardiff: *Philosophical Idealism and Christian Belief*, 1995; *John Locke and the Eighteenth-Century Divines*, 1997; *Confessing and Commending the Faith: Historic Witness and Apologetic Method*, 2002.

[34] See further Alan P. F. Sell, *The Philosophy of Religion 1875–1980*, (1988) Bristol: Thoemmes Press, 1996.

my case to churches around the world. The fact remains, however, that secular philosophers who were among my former colleagues in the University of Calgary never once asked me about the propriety or otherwise of ordaining women. Their questions were quite otherwise, and concerned the rationality or otherwise of faith, the idea of the supernatural, the concept of revelation. Yet so often the apologetic task is either avoided or else, in more popular, usually very conservative, Christian literature apologetics degenerates into wanton cult-bashing. One of my more distressing findings when I attempted a critical analysis of the theological contribution of the World Alliance of Reformed Churches and its predecessor bodies from 1875 to 1982 was the fact that whereas until about 1930 both the Presbyterians and the Congregationalists were tackling the challenges posed by the intellectual environment of their day, from that time onwards the amount of time given to apologetic concerns shrank almost to vanishing point.[35] If theologians neglect this territory, how can we expect ministers to assist their members who will face the challenges I have described in the work-place and wherever they go? No doubt nobody has ever been argued into the faith, and I am not pleading that we try to imprison the Gospel within a new rationalism; but it is equally certain that some have had intellectual obstacles removed by careful apologetic discussion (and what is to prevent the Holy Spirit from working through such discussion?); and it is utterly undeniable that to refuse a sincere question on grounds of theological policy represents a profound pastoral failure. Such a failure to respond reaps its reward in that apathy which always greets an intellectually introverted Church.

Thirdly, although, as I said at the outset, the theologian is a person of faith, as soon as he or she publishes by means of the spoken or written word that content is available for public scrutiny. There are theological texts and papers which are available for study and may be subjected to free and open critical analysis. Were it not so theology would have no justification in a place of higher learning. You will see why I was somewhat concerned by a sentence in an interesting book by Joel Beeke on the subject of assurance. He writes, 'saving faith is essential to the true study of Christian theology.'[36] The problematic word here is 'study'. No doubt constructive theology is written by people of faith, but let it be *studied* by all. It has its public content no less than philosophy, the sciences and other academic, disciplines and, like them, it has its appropriate tools: in its case these are linguistic, philosophical and historical. If in addition the student who does not profess the Christian faith can also bring some imaginative insight to the

---

[35] See Alan P. F. Sell, *A Reformed, Evangelical, Catholic Theology. The Contribution of the World Alliance of Reformed Churches 1875–1982*, (1991), Eugene, OR: Wipf & Stock, 1998, ch. 5.

[36] Joel R. Beeke, *Assurance of Faith. Calvin, English Puritanism and the Dutch Second Reformation*, New York: Peter Lang, 1991, 361.

proceedings which will facilitate some grasp of what it might be like to believe, so much the better. All of which brings us right to where we are: in a theological college which operates academically under the auspices of a Church and a secular university. Here, at least as much as anywhere else, conservation and exploration of the faith should be our daily bread and butter; and the exploration must and will be undertaken by people within and without the Christian faith. This will and ought to influence the manner of our proceedings lest we censor the enquirer and unwarrantably cocoon the believer — neither of which is kind.

IV

The challenge of exploring the Christian heritage with a view to seeing what it is which must be conserved, and of exploring the current intellectual and cultural environment with a view to addressing it relevantly is one which should engage and excite all Christians. Theologians and ministers of religion have their part to play, but the task is not theirs alone: it belongs to the whole Church.

Who is sufficient for these things? It is good to recognise that we are not — but that recognition applies to every aspect of Christian witness and service. On the one hand we must not down tools because of our inadequacy; on the other hand, we must not become frantic because of any apparent lack of success. While those who have received the Gospel are charged to be good stewards of it, they may not regard themselves as those who guard the ark of God — as if God's mission would fail if they were to advance a fallacious argument. Christians are under obligation to testify to what they have seen and heard; but in the deepest sense the faith is conserved and Christians are kept by the God Holy Spirit, to whom we owe any truth, and any ability to articulate the truth, which we have. Our incompetence unaided underlines the importance of Karl Barth's observation that theological work 'takes place in a realm which not only has open windows ... facing the surrounding life of the Church and world, but also and above all has a skylight.'[37] While communion with God will not render our theologizing infallible, it will most certainly fertilize and motivate it, and keep it humble.

---

[37] K. Barth, *Evangelical Theology*, London: Collins Fontana, 1965, 150.

CHAPTER 2

The Worship of English Congregationalism

In this paper I hope to show (a) that over the 450 years of its life the English Congregational tradition has manifested considerable variety in attitudes towards, and the practice of, public worship; and that although appeal has frequently been made to the Bible for the authorization of particular liturgical practices, the circumstances of the times have played their part in suggesting how the scriptures may legitimately be interpreted; and (b) that from this story there emerge some 'matters arising' which have wider than Congregational implications.

I

At a time when the authorities in the land sought civil order cemented by legally required religious comprehension, those who sought a fuller reform, and who believed that it was not the prerogative of the monarch or government of the day to legislate upon matters of worship and church order were necessarily Separatists from the Church 'by law established', and members of underground movements. While we know of their existence, their records are, for obvious reasons, scanty. We do, however, have news of a group of Christians meeting in London in 1567. They were members of Richard Fitz's 'privie [that is, private] church,' and what is especially interesting about them, having regard to some within later Congregationalism who did not give the sacraments their due, is that among the objectives of Fitz's church was 'To haue the Sacraments mynistred purely, onely and all together according to the institution and goode worde of the Lorde Jesus, without any tradicion of inuention of man.'[1] To the Separatist mind (and in a delightful mirror image of nineteenth-century Anglo-Catholic attitudes towards the allegedly 'invalid' sacraments of the Nonconformists) true sacraments are to be found only in the true church; the Church of England is Antichrist, and hence there are no true sacraments there. As the Separatist lawyer, Henry Barrow put it, 'A false churche cannot have

---

[1] Champlin Burrage, *Early English Dissenters*, 1912, II, 13, quoting *State Papers Domestic, Elizabeth I, Addenda* xx, 107. I.

trewe sacraments, neither iz there trewe substance or promise of blessinge to false sacraments.'[2] Another Separatist, Robert Harrison, declared that by baptism we are received into God's house, while the Lord's Supper, 'which we are often to receyue', is 'the foode wherewith our soules are nourished.'[3] No Separatist expressed more clearly than Robert Browne the relation between the church as the saints gathered and the Lord's Supper as the means and expression of churchly unity:

> The Lords supper is a Sacrament or marke of the apparent Church, sealing vnto vs by the breaking and eating of breade and drinking the Cuppe in one holie communion, and by the worde accordinglie preached, that we are happilie redeemed by the breaking of the bodie and shedding of the bloud of Christ Iesus, and we thereby growe into one bodie, and church, in one communion of graces, whereof Christ is the heade, to keepe and seake agreement vnder one lawe and gouernement in all thankefulness & holy obedience.[4]

From a deposition lodged against a Barrowist church in 1588 we learn something of their worship and use of Sunday, though there is no reference to the Lord's Supper:

> In the somer tyme they mett together in the fields a mile or more about london. there they sit down vppon A Bank & divers of them expound out of the bible so long as they are there assembled. In the winter tyme they assemble themselves by 5. of the clocke in the morning to that howse where they make there Conventicle for that Saboth daie men & women together there they Continewe in there kind of praier and exposicion of Scriptures all that daie. They dyne together. After dinner make collection to paie for their diet & what mony is left somme one of them carrieth it to the prisons where any of their sect be committed. In their praier one speketh and the rest doe groane, or sob. or sigh, as if they would ring out teares... there prayer is extemporall. In there conventicles they vse not the lordes praier, nor any forme of sett praier.[5]

---

[2] H. Barrow, *Reply to Dr. Some's A Godly Treatise*, in *The Writings of Henry Barrow 1587-1590*, ed. Leland H. Carlson, London: Allen and Unwin, 1962, 157. For the ecclesiology of Congregationalism and its Separatist harbingers see Alan P. F. Sell, *Saints:Visible, Orderly and Catholic. The Congregational Idea of the Church*, Geneva: World Alliance of Reformed Churches, and Allison Park, PA: Pickwick Publications, 1986.

[3] R. Harrison, *Three Formes of Catechismes*, (1583), in *The Writings of Robert Harrison and Robert Browne*, ed. A. Peel and L. H. I. Carlson, London: Allen and Unwin, 1953, 140.

[4] R. Browne, *A Booke which sheweth the life and manners of all true Christians*, (1582), in *The Writings of Robert Harrison and Robert Browne*, 279, 280.

[5] C. Burrage, *Early English Dissenters*, II, 27. See further, Stephen H. Mayor, *The Lord's Supper in Early English Dissent*, London: Epworth Press, 1972. Barrow, together with his Separatist colleague, John Greenwood, was martyred in 1593. See Alan P. F. Sell, *Commemorations. Studies in Christian Thought and History*, Calgary: University of Calgary Press and Cardiff: University of Wales Press, 1993; Eugene, OR: Wipf & Stock, 1998, ch.5.

What is interesting here is the insistence on extempore prayer as evidence, negatively, of the determination not to be bound to a prayer book composed by men, and, positively, to be open to the Spirit. The Separatists were among the charismatics of their day, and this emerges also in their predilection for prophesying during worship – albeit they did not expect the Holy Spirit to extend the gift of prophecy to women. As for singing, the Psalms only were approved, and certainly not what Henry Barrow called 'the apocryphal erroneous ballads in time-song' prescribed in the *Book of Common Prayer* of the Church of England.

The Separatists comprised the radical wing of Puritanism, Puritans being those who sought pure worship and church order according to the Word of God. Whether radical or not, all Puritans throughout the seventeenth century gave great place to the preaching of the Word, and to the observance of what they called the Lord's Day. Though by no means the humourless pious prigs of caricature (at least the majority of them were not), they nevertheless repudiated traditional festivals and saints' days because of their associations with Rome, their superstitious aspects, and their overlooking the fact that the saints are all those whom God gathers into his Church. As already hinted, the *Book of Common Prayer* was weighed and found wanting, not least because it was deemed to uphold the hated doctrine of baptismal regeneration, and this further dissuaded the Dissenters from adopting set forms of prayer. Nevertheless in 1645 the Westminster Assembly (the members of which included some Independent or Congregational representatives) did produce its *Directory*, which, though not containing set liturgies, did offer guidance on the order of worship to those called to lead it. Such guidance notwithstanding, the form and content of Congregational worship varied considerably. When Robert Kirk of the Scottish Episcopal Church visited London shortly after the passing of the Toleration Act of 1689, which for the first time legalized non-Anglican worship – but only that of orthodox protestant Dissenters (that is, not Roman Catholics, Unitarians or Jews), he attended a service conducted by the Congregationalist, George Cockain. Kirk records that there were,

> no psalms before or after sermon. The people heard sermon with heads covered, and stood at prayer…The preacher prayed not for the Protestant Churches, nor English, nor any Churchmen, only barely for the King and High Council, without naming the Queen. he did plead vehemently with God for a young man at the grave's mouth…saying, 'Lord, 'tis rare to find a good man, more a good young man. Thou sparest 10,000ds of debauched youths, may not this dry but tender and fruitful branch escape the blast of thy displeasure. Save his soul. Spare his body. Sanctify all to the parents seeing though dost it, not theirs nor ours, but thy will be done.' He had not the blessing at the end. The minister vested in a black coat.[6]

---

[6] D. Maclean, *London at Worship*, 1689-1690, quoted by A.G. Matthews (see next note), 180.

The narrowly-focussed pastoral concern in the prayer is noteworthy here, as is the absence of singing, especially considering that many Puritans happily used metrical psalms in worship.[7] It is more than likely that this reluctance to sing resulted from the belief that since the apostolic exhortation was to sing with grace in one's heart, it would be wrong for the grace-less in a 'promiscuous' congregation to join in.

Thus far we see, speaking generally, that in the worship of the Congregationalists and their Separatist harbingers, the preaching of the World is central, the sacraments are given due place, metrical psalms are sung, extempore prayers are used, and set liturgies are despised as cramping the spirit, preventing earnest prayer relevant to local needs, leading to formalism in worship and, when officially imposed, denying that freedom under Christ which is an essential gift of God to his Church. Creeds are not used in worship on the grounds that assent to them may be made a test of membership; they are 'man-made', whereas Scripture is the Word of God; Christians are expected to make their own confessions of faith; creeds can fossilize the faith and over-emphasize its intellectual aspects.[8] Separatists and Puritans alike sought a form of worship in accordance with Christ's will and with apostolic practice, and there would have been widespread agreement with John Owen that the 'chiefest acts and parts' of worship are *'preaching of the word, administration of the sacraments, and the exercise of discipline; all to be performed with prayer and thanksgiving'*.[9] While it would take us too far afield to pursue the theme of church discipline here, we should note that the quest of a pure church inspired both the fencing of the Lord's table so that church members only were permitted to receive what was, after all, a sacrament of the Church.

The gradual transition from exclusive metrical psalmody to paraphrases and thence to full-blown Christian hymns enabled the Congregationalists of the eighteenth century to offer some of their best gifts to the world Church. I refer,

---

[7] See further on Puritan Worship, A.G. Matthews, 'The Puritans', in Nathaniel Micklem, ed., *Christian Worship. Studies in its History and Meaning by Members of Mansfield College*, London: OUP, 1936, 172-88; Horton Davies, *The Worship of the English Puritans*, London: Dacre Press, 1948; and for the period 1690 to the present, Horton Davies, *Worship and Theology in England*, 4 vols., Princeton: Princeton University Press, 1961 etc. For the Lord's supper see Bryan D. Spinks, *Freedom or Order? The Eucharistic Liturgy in English Congregationalism 1645-1980*, Allison Park, PA: Pickwick Publications, 1984.

[8] See further, Geoffrey F. Nuttall., *Congregationalists and Creeds*, London: Epworth Press, 1966; Alan P.F. Sell, *Dissenting Thought and the Life of the Churches. Studies in an English Tradition*, Lewiston, NY: Edwin Mellen Press, 1990, 57-8.

[9] J. Owen, *A Discourse concerning Liturgies and their Imposition*, in his *Works*, ed. W. H. Goold, (1850-1853), London: The Banner of Truth Trust, 1966, 10. Congregational teaching on these matters is summarized in *The Savoy Declaration of Faith and Order*, 1658, itself patterned closely upon the Westminster Confession of 1647, though with modifications of varying degrees of significance.

of course, to the hymns of Isaac Watts and Philip Doddridge, 'When I survey the wondrous Cross', and 'My gracious Lord, I won Thy right to every service I can pay' among them. Isaac Watts also produced *A Guide to Prayer*, in which he advocates biblically-grounded, orderly free, or conceived, prayer, the parts of which he summarizes in verse thus:

> Call upon God, adore, confess,
> Petition, plead, and then declare
> You are the Lord's, give thanks and bless,
> And let Amen confirm the prayer.[10]

For an example of a service of worship in eighteenth-century London we may turn to the Bury Street Independent meeting:

> In the morning we begin with singing a psalm, then a short prayer follows to desire the Divine Presence in all the following parts of worship; after that, about half an hour in the exposition of some portion of Scripture, which is succeeded by singing a psalm or an hymn. After this the minister prays more at large, for all the variety of blessings, spiritual and temporal, for the whole congregation, with confession of sins, and thanksgiving for mercies; petitions also are offered up for the whole world, for all our rulers and governors, together with any particular cases which are represented. Then a sermon is preached, and the morning worship concluded with a short prayer and the benediction.[11]

When the Lord's Supper was kept at Bury Street it followed the sermon, though elsewhere, as recommended by Philip Doddridge, there was a gap between what we would later learn to call the liturgy of the catechumens and the liturgy of the table. It may well be that in Doddridge's mind was the desirability of ensuring that church members only partook of the Supper. But by the twentieth century the gap between the two services had become the occasion for wrapping up and distributing flowers and counting the offering – abominations from which that century's liturgical renewal did much to deliver us.

It cannot be denied that the sermon gained increasing prominence during the eighteenth century, and to some it took precedence over all other parts of the service, which came to be regarded as preliminaries. Indeed, some people absented themselves from the lengthy prayer preceding the sermon, and if one cannot agree with this practice, one can at least understand it, when such prayers were, as Horton Davies remarked 'occasionally Pentecostal', but 'more

---

[10] I. Watts, *A Guide to Prayer*, (1715), abridged and edited by Harry Escott, London: Epworth Press, 1948, 50.

[11] *Transactions of the Congregational Historical Society*, VI, 334.

frequently Purgatorial'.[12] Consider Samuel Brewer of Stepney Meeting, London. We are told that he 'was remarkable for great particularity in prayer', and that:

> Having many seafaring people among his hearers, when a merchant ship was going to sail, he specified the captain, the mate, the carpenter, the boatswain, and all the sailors with great affection; and, it is said, that impressed with a belief of the benefit of his prayers, they frequently brought him home, as a token of gratitude, something of the produce of the country to which they went.[13]

Perhaps not surprisingly in view of such pastoral prolixity, a number of moves were made during the nineteenth century to tidy up worship. Thus in 1812 *A New Directory for Nonconformist Churches Containing Remarks on Their Mode of Public Worship, and a Plan for the Improvement of it* was published, and as the century progressed numerous other liturgical handbooks followed. Not the least of the motives in all of this activity was the hope of making worship more palatable to the mercantile classes, from amongst whom the Congregationalists were increasingly drawing members. Robert Vaughan (1795–1868) was not untypical in explaining that 'Distinguished laymen who take their place frankly among protestant dissenters, need not be apprehensive that the respect shown to their civil rank elsewhere, will be wanting on the part of their new friends.'[14] There was also the influence of Anglo-Catholicism, with whose ritualistic extravagances (from their point of view) the Congregationalists had no patience at all, but from which they derived inspiration to seek liturgical propriety in their own way; and, under the influence of Romanticism, a greater concern for that which was aesthetically sensitive and pleasing – a motive which influenced congregational chapel architecture away from the meeting house style towards Georgian 'opera house' and Victorian Nonconformist Gothic.[15] Even the Unitarians, under the distinguished leadership of James Martineau, were reforming their worship – could trinitarians do less?

In 1856, with all of these influences swirling around him, Thomas Binney, one of Congregationalism's most distinguished ministers, reminded his co-

---

[12] H. Davies, 'Liturgical reform in nineteenth-century English Congregationalism', *Congregational Historical Society Transactions*, XVII no.3, August 1954, 75.

[13] David Bogue and James Bennett, *The History of Dissenters from the Revolution to the Year 1898*, London: Frederick Westley and A.H. Davis, 2nd edn., 1833, II, 634.

[14] R. Vaughan, *Congregationalism: or, the Polity of Independent Churches viewed in relation to the State and Tendencies of Modern Society*, 2nd rev. ed., 1842, 181.

[15] Concerning the Gothic, John Huxtable lamented that 'Those who planned such places of worship did not consider carefully enough the question whether the building in which the Church gathers should be designed principally for hearing God's Word read and preached or for seeing the drama of the Mass enacted.' See his 'Worship in contemporary Congregationalism', in *Proceedings of the Ninth Assembly of the International Congregational Council*, London: Independent Press, 1962, 130.

religionists (whilst overlooking some negative examples) that their Nonconformist forebears 'had no objection to a Liturgy as such, but only wished some changes to be made in that which was in use, – that is should not be exclusively enforced, that there should be the means of giving variety to the services, and the opportunity afforded for free prayer.'[16] In 1847 an anonymous work, *The Congregational Service Book* was published in which, while the *Te Deum* was admitted a creed was not because it was deemed unnecessary. Also absent are printed prayers, on the ground that free prayer is more biblical and more ancient. A number of nineteenth-century directories[17] accord no place to the Lord's Supper – this possibly in reaction against Anglo-Catholic ritualism. The *Declaration of Faith, Church Order and Discipline* adopted by the Congregational Union of England and Wales in 1833 specified that baptism was to be administered to all converts and their children, and that the Lord's Supper was 'to be celebrated by Christian Churches as a token of faith in the Saviour, and of brotherly love'. This meagre anthropocentrism (which was to be rebuked by a Union Commission exactly one hundred years later[18]) fostered an increasingly 'memorialist' understanding of the Lord's Supper, so that R. W. Dale of Birmingham regretted that 'There is little doubt that modern Congregationalists, in their extreme dread of high sacramental doctrines, have drifted into pure Zwinglianism.'[19]

In further reaction against ritualism and sacerdotalist ideas of priesthood, some Congregationalists emphasized the priesthood of all believers in such a way as to permit what (somewhat unfortunately) we nowadays call the lay celebration of the sacrament – something which their forebears of earlier periods would by no means have sanctioned. They further chirpily proclaimed that they were as catholic – if not more so – as anyone else, not least because they did not bar professed believers from the Lord's table. As for baptism, the individualism flowing down from the Evangelical Revival of the eighteenth century, with its emphasis upon conversion as the way into the saved community, devastated the concept of the local covenanted church comprising believers and their children, and the creation by larger churches of 'mission stations', while they undoubtedly permitted many to hear the Gospel, did little to foster the

---

[16] Preface to Binney's edition of Charles Baird's *Eutaxia*, entitled, *A Chapter on Liturgies: Historical Sketches*, London: Knight, 1856, ix-x.

[17] For the variety of such directories see Bryan D. Spinks, 'The liturgical revival amongst nineteenth-century English Congregationalists,' *Studia Liturgica*, XV nos. 3-4, 1982–1983, 178–87.

[18] See *The Report of the Commission on the Sacraments of Baptism and the Lord's Supper*, London: Congregational Union of England and Wales, [1933], 11.

[19] R. W. Dale in H. R. Reynolds, ed., *Ecclesia*, London, 1870, 371. On the other hand the celebrated leader J. Guinness Rogers was among many who were quite unperturbed by memorialism. See his 'Sacramentalism,' *The Congregationalist*, XIII, 1884, 980-89.

Congregational church order with its emphasis upon the baptized community and the centrality of Church Meeting.[20] Hence Robert Mackintosh's sardonic observation that infant baptism 'stands as the one bulwark against the destruction of the Church in favour of the evangelistic committee.'[21] In connection with evangelism we should note that from the nineteenth century until well into the twentieth, many Congregational churches held a more formal or traditional service on Sunday mornings, and a more evangelistic service in the evenings. Further dissuasives to liturgical fulness include biblical higher criticism, which persuaded some ministers that Jesus had not after all instituted baptism and the Lord's Supper,[22] and the rise of a genial universalism which not only drew the sting of 'hellfire and damnation' preaching, but also blurred the distinction between those who are 'in Christ' and those who are not – the very distinction upon which Congregational ecclesiology turns.

Among those who spoke out against the subjectivism of memorialism was R. W. Dale, whose oft-reprinted Congregational Lecture on The Atonement first appeared in 1875 and, in the next generation, P. T. Forsyth, whose book, Lectures on the Church and the Sacraments was first published in 1917.[23] The latter work, which contained the declaration that 'mere memorialism' is 'a more fatal error than the Mass, and a far less lovely,'[24] did more than any other theological work to prepare a number of Congregationalists for the liturgical renewal of the twentieth century. Also of considerable significance in this respect was John Hunter's widely circulated book of *Devotional Services,* which was first published in 1890. An order for the Lord's Supper was included in the third edition of 1886.

In 1933 the Council of the Congregational Union of England and Wales received *The Report of the Commission on the Sacraments of Batism and the Lord's Supper*. The commissioners included the liberal theologian C. J. Cadoux, the middle of the road Principal Sydney Cave, the historian Albert Peel, and the 'Genevan' Congregationalist, Bernard Lord Manning, another historian. They make no secret of the differences of opinion among them, some being more

---

[20] For the dramatic decline in local covenants after 1820 see Alan P. F. Sell, *Dissenting Thought and the Life of the Churches*, ch. 1.

[21] R. Mackintosh, *The Insufficiency of Revivalism as a Religious System*, bound with *Essays Towards a New Theology*, Glasgow: Maclehose, 1889, 28.

[22] Robert Mackintosh felt that a stronger case could be made for Jesus's institution of the Lord's Supper than of baptism, but held that 'a certain element of doubt exists whether Jesus literally founded either of the two New Testament sacraments.' See his paper, 'The living church...Its Scaraments', *Proceedings of the International Congregational Council*, London: Congregational Union of England and Wales, 1930, V, 139. See further, Alan P. F. Sell, *Robert Mackintosh, Theologian of Integrity*, Bern: Peter Lang, 1977, ch.3.

[23] In subsequent reprintings the words 'Lectures on' were dropped from the title.

[24] P.T. Forsyth, *The Church and the Sacraments*, London: Independent Press, 1947, xvi.

certain than others that Jesus instituted the sacraments; some being content with a memorialist view of the Lord's Supper – though not a *mere* memorialist view, for it is the Lord who is remembered; others keener to emphasize 'the Christ Who is present with us, the risen Lord, Who gives Himself anew to those who come to His table in humble faith.'[25] Of them all, Peel was perhaps the most radical in holding that:

> 1. No one today would claim categorically that the two Sacraments were instituted by Christ and that He ordered them to be perpetually observed. 2. No one can claim that the Sacraments are indispensable, in so far as the like grace can be otherwise mediated. 3. No one will deny that Christians have lived faithful and devout lives without the use of the two sacraments ... 4. No one will deny that our Lord stresses the spirit and not the letter, principles on which to act rather than acts themselves ... 5. No one will claim that it accords with the mind of Christ to exclude from His Church believers on Him, on the ground that they do not accept the perpetual obligation of sacraments and make no use of them ... Are the outward symbols essential? Has not the experience of the Friends and others shown there is proved religious value in worship without symbols ...? ... Let us claim that there is a baptism of the Spirit which all Christ's followers must have, but that does not necessarily include baptism by water.[26]

The significance of Peel's words is that they represent a Quaker-Anabaptist-influenced strand of Congregationalism which has been present from the beginning, and they come from the most distinguished Congregational historian of his day. Looking forward, Peel cautioned, 'If a reunited Church were to be formed which was to rule out the Friends because they did not use the Sacraments, may Free Churchmen, certainly I for one, would range myself with the Friends – outside a man-made Church, yet within the spacious freedom of the Church of God'.[27]

By now, however, more international breezes were beginning to be felt. There is no doubt that Barth's theology of the Word made an impact upon such

---

[25] *The Report of the Commission*, 21. I have reason to think that this latter view was held by my teacher of Christian Doctrine, the greatly loved George Phillips, a member of the Commission. At this point we are far removed from that 'liturgicial fusspottery' which overtook some of those influenced by the liturgical renewal of the twentieth century, and finds a number today in many-hued vestments whose relation to the heritage is not altogether clear. George, raised among the Strict and Particular Baptists, would have greeted this with benign amusement ('Bless my soul!' was one of his favourite expostulations), but would never have fallen for it. W.E. Orchard was a Congregational minister who tended ever Romewards and, indeed, reached that destination. His book of prayers, *The Temple*, appealed to a wider circle of Congregationalists than did his liturgies, for which see Bryan D. Spinks, *Freedom or Order?* ch. 7. His Romish rite may have been permissible by the Congregational polity, but it was far removed from the Congregational tradition.
[26] A. Peel, *Christian Freedom*, London: Independent Press, 1938, 79-83.
[27] Ibid., 84.

Congregationalists as H. F. Lovell Cocks, John Marsh, Hubert Cunliffe-Jones, W.A. Whitehouse and Daniel Jenkins,[28] while the more home-grown influence of Forsyth left its mark upon B. L. Manning, John Huxtable and, above all, Lovell Cocks.[29] John Whale's particular contribution was the recovery for Congregationalism of its Reformation heritage. On 12 March 1939 a letter was addressed *To the ministers of Christ's Holy Gospel in the Churches of the Congregational Order.* It was drafted by Manning and revised by Nathaniel Micklem and Whale. The other signatories were J. D. Jones of Bournemouth, Principals Lovell Cocks and E. J. Price, and John Short. It was a call to a deeper understanding of the Church and of its life as utterly dependent upon the Gospel of God's free grace. Because of their recourse to the faith of the ages, and especially because of their renewed emphasis upon the Reformed tradition, this group and their associates attracted the label, 'Genevan'.

The burgeoning of the modern ecumenical movement, to which the Genevan party was committed, broadened liturgical horizons and cut a channel through which flowed continental liturgical influences.[30] The Church Order Group was formed in 1946 to stimulate liturgical renewal and a concern for good church order within Congregationalism, and while only a minority of ministers became active members of it, the Group's influence was more widely beneficial in fostering the view that Word and sacrament belong together, and that the pattern of approach, ministry of the Word, and response to the Word in the offertory and prayers of thanksgiving, or in the Lord's Supper, should be the norm as far as the local church's full diet of public worship was concerned.[31]

---

[28] 'Though none of them swallowed Bath whole, some being especially critical of his hostile attitude towards natural theology. See further, my paper, 'The theological contribution of Protestant Nonconformists in the twentieth century: some soundings,' in Alan P. F. Sell and Anthony R. Cross, eds., *Protestant Nonconformity in the Twentieth Century*, Carlisle: Paternoster Press, 2003, 42-6.

[29] For this unduly neglected theologian see Alan P. F. Sell, *Commemorations*, ch. 13.

[30] Not indeed that all ecumenists were necessarily Barthians. To one of Congregationalism's pioneer ecumenists, A. E. Garvie, the Barthian theology was 'a minor evil product of the war.' See his 'Fifty years' retrospect,' *Congregational Quarterly*, VII, 1929, 21.

[31] In his paper, '"Austere ritual": the reformation of worship in inter-War English Congregationalism,' in R. N. Swanson, ed., *Continuity and Change in Christian Worship*, Woodbridge, Suffolk: The Boydell Press, 436, Ian M. Randall finds me 'restrictive in interpreting the process by which the Genevans "shunned the individualistic nineteenth century, and exalted Owen and others" in ecclesiological terms.' He refers to my *Saints: Visible, Orderly and Catholic. The Congregational Idea of the Church*, Geneva: World Alliance of Reformed Churches and Allison Park, PA: Pickwick Publications, 1986, 97, and points out that 'in the mid-1930s Micklem and Whale were using every opportunity to raise the profile of preaching.' Far from denying this, I affirm it. My point was that the Genevans strongly held the view that Word and sacraments belong together, and that what was needed in Congregationalism was the restoration of the latter to their rightful place. This, too, cannot be denied. See *Saints*, 99.

One way of registering the changing attitude is by comparing service books. The book with which I was presented on leaving my home church for college was *A Manual for Ministers*, first published in 1936. This was the successor to the *Book of Congregational Worship* of 1920. It draws upon a number of sources, though its general theological cast is mildly liberal; it includes suggestions for the several parts of worship, as well as services of baptism and the Lord's Supper. It acknowledges much, but not all, of the Christian Year (no Advent, no Trinity Sunday), compensating with services for Hospital Sunday, Peace Sunday, Choir Sunday and the like. Of this book John Huxtable somewhat saucily remarked that it 'had few redeeming features. Its liturgical formlessness found compensation in an appendix full of information about ministerial insurance; and there was an excellent order for the opening of a sale of work.'[32] With this book may be contrasted *A Book of Public Worship Compiled for the Use of Congregationalists* by John Huxtable, John Marsh, Romilly Micklem and James Todd (1948). This reveals the degree to which liturgical lessons had been learned, and the term 'sale of work' is nowhere to be found. However, Geoffrey F. Nuttall, Congregationalism's leading historian of the Separatists and Puritans, and himself not influenced by the Quaker/Anabaptist strand of the Congregational heritage, observed in his review of this book that 'Throughout Dr. Marsh's Introduction our traditional repudiation of such books is not discussed, while dependence on the Spirit's leadings is not mentioned at all.'[33] Few strove more resolutely to hold the balance than W. Gordon Robinson, who chaired the committee appointed by the Congregational Union of England and Wales to produce *A Book of Services and Prayers* (1959), which appeared just in time for my ordination. In the contents the heritage of faith of the ages is acknowledged, the services are shaped in an orderly way, but space is left for *Our Heritage of Free Prayer* – the title of a pamphlet anonymously prepared by Gordon Robinson for the Union in the 1950s.[34]

Not all of public worship takes it cue directly from service books, however ill- or well-prepared they may be. I have in mind especially the children of the church and the way in which the traditional (that is, post-late-eighteenth-century) Sunday School gave way from the middle of the twentieth century onwards so family worship in various permutations. In this matter the Congregationalists were pioneers, and the leadership given by H. A. Hamilton and his colleagues at Westhill College, Selly Oak, Birmingham, was widely influential. Increasingly, whole families gathered for the opening parts of the

---

[32] J. Huxtable, 'Worship in contemporary Congregationalism,' 131.
[33] G. F. Nuttall, review in *The Congregational Quarterly*, XXVI no.4, 1948, 367.
[34] This was Isaac Watts for the mid-twentieth century. *A Book of Services and Prayers* is not accurately described by Bryan Spinks as a 'neo-orthodox' book. See his *Freedom or Order?* 189. To my knowledge some 50% of the committee members would have declined to be so labelled.

service, the children leaving at a certain point for worship and instruction appropriate to their several age-groups. Sometimes they would return either to witness (or, more rarely and more recently, to partake in) the Lord's Supper. I shall return to this important segment of the Church's membership in due course.

In 1972 the majority of the English and English-speaking Welsh Congregationalists united with the Presbyterian Church of England to form the United Reformed Church, and with this union my story ends. There could hardly have been a more fitting climax than the paragraphs on worship in the *Declaration of Faith* published by the Congregational Church in England and Wales in 1967. The first paragraph of this section is as follows:

> God calls the Church into renewed love and obedience to himself through its worship. The worship of the Church is expressed in many ways: through prayer and praise, through the reading of the Bible and the proclamation of Christ in preaching, through the sacraments of Baptism and the Lord's Supper, through many and varied acts of devotion and Christian ordinances, and through the fellowship and decisions of the Church. In all worship, God is present in his Word of Grace. Our part is to respond, in adoration and fidelity, by hearing and obeying him.[35]

I fear that I have been able only to distil the essence of a vast literature extending over 450 years. I trust, however, that it has become clear that the English Congregationalists, though always intending to ground themselves in Scripture, have been significantly influenced in their interpretation of the Bible by the ecclesiastical, intellectual and socio-political environment in which the have lived. In the early decades they saw themselves as over against the Church of England, and there was a psychological tendency to do things differently on principle. The same thing happened during the Anglo-Catholic hey-day in the nineteenth century. With the advent of modern biblical scholarship there has been less of a desire to adopt the earlier restorationist attitude to worship and church order; and in the twentieth century, openness to other Christian traditions at home and abroad lessened the fear of utilizing liturgical material form elsewhere. After a somewhat patchy period during much of the nineteenth century the sacraments have been restored to their former prominence, and, more often than not, are related in the liturgy to the preaching of the Word – an activity which has never declined, however much it may from time to time have been abused (and even from time to time replaced among the *avant garde* by spontaneous dialogues, dramatic presentations, liturgical dance, and suchlike).

---

[35] *A Declaration of Faith*, reprinted in Lukas Vischer, ed., *Reformed Witness Today: A Collection of Confessions and Statements of Faith issued by Reformed Churches*, Bern: Evangelische Arbeitsstelle Oukumene Schweiz, 1982, 142.

In the last sixty years much more though has been paid to the place of children in worship than hitherto. But for all the general increase of orderliness, there still linger (in my view rightly) echoes of the view that a minister who cannot pray without a book is somehow less than a complete pastor. And now that many churches have resorted to one service per Sunday only, the attempt in some quarters to marry the more formal liturgy with the more evangelistic type of meeting in such a way that the Te Deum rubs shoulders with banal jingles projected on the wall, and stockbrokers find themselves liberally bestowing the kiss of peace upon people from whom they hide behind the *Financial Times* on the train on Mondays to Fridays, may well offend the liturgically correct, confuse the babes in Christ, and vastly irritate the old hands.

II

I turn now, and briefly, to some matters arising from the foregoing account. I suspect that some at least of these will have a bearing upon the entire Reformed family, and not only upon those from the Congregational part of it.

First, the case study of Congregational worship shows that in different periods recourse has been had to the Bible for guidance on worship, but that what has been discovered has to a considerable extent depended upon the ecclesiastical and socio-political circumstances of the seekers, and the attitude taken towards the question of biblical authority. If public worship is to be our own, it cannot be simply that of a previous age, neither can it be something we invent anew each morning as we kick over the traces of all that has gone before. There are proper issues of the heritage of praise on the one hand and liturgical adventurousness on the other, and these need to be held in balance, ot least on the pastoral ground of the proper security of the flock. The rhythm of the familiar is not altogether to be despised. But if pastoral sensitivity is to be prized, so is intellectual integrity, and this is a perennial challenge both in ordering worship and in preaching. I should, nevertheless, need a lot of persuading before I could agree that the full diet of Christian worship (and worship does not have always to be the 'full diet' – it can take many forms) should be anything other than the holding together of World and Lord's Supper in a liturgy in which the rhythm of approach, ministry of the Word, and response at the table are clearly preserved. As the Congregational Union's Commission reported., 'Our classic position is Calvinistic, and involves the belief that there is no difference of meaning between the preaching of the Word of God and the Sacraments; both of them alike "hold forth and offer Christ to us, and in Him the treasures of heavenly grace."'[36] What seems quite clear is that the distinction

---

[36] *The Report of the Commission on the Sacraments of Baptism and the Lord's Supper*, 20.

between liturgical churches and non-liturgical churches is quite misplaced. 'Liturgy' means service, and there are simply more and less adequate liturgies. Lest that sound elitist, let me hasten to point out that by 'adequate' I do not mean in the first place 'having liturgical propriety'. That may well be a bonus, but by an adequate liturgy I mean one which enables people in diverse times and places to offer their praise to God and to hear and respond to his Word. It is possible to be too liturgically precious – as if the kingdom will not come if the *epiklesis* is misplaced; it is possible on the other hand to be abysmally careless, as when we forget what it is God with whom we have to do. In this latter connection I recall an incident concerning the Jesuit theologian, Avery Dulles. It is said that during a service of worship he was horrified to see a banner hanging on the wall of the church proclaiming the sentimental heresy, 'God is other people.' When he could bear it no longer he went out to the vestry and returned with a marker pen, went to the banner and inserted a comma, so that it now read, 'God is other, people.'

Secondly, at their best the Congregationalists strove for freedom within order. In their origins they were charismatic in the sense of being open to the Spirit's prompting, and in freely addressing God in extempore prayers. May it be that, for all the benefits to be derived from drawing upon the liturgical inheritance of the ages, the pendulum has nowadays swung too far in the direction of liturgical scriptedness? In this connection I should like to pay tribute to the skill in conceived prayer of W. Gordon Robinson, author of the booklet, *Our Heritage of Free Prayer*, to which I referred earlier. He was my college Principal, and it was liturgically inspiring to experience six years of his prayers in college chapel. The prayers were biblically grounded, orderly, rhythmically phrased, and ever fresh. One soon learned that what comes out in free prayer is directly related to what has previously gone on in terms of Bible study and personal meditation. There is nothing haphazard or 'off the cuff' about it.

Again, freedom within order comes into view in connection with the attempt in some circles to marry the more traditional order of worship with the more evangelistic. I have already referred to this challenge, but now I add the though that when the focus is on ever larger congregations, and when church growth methods and the corporate model are employed to this end, the question arises, Can a worshiping group be so large as to be a church no longer? In the nineteenth century, during the period of expansion when Nonconformists were building ever larger chapels, one writer declared that a church building which seats more than two thousand people goes against Nonconformist principles. What did he mean? He had in mind the traditional understanding, now so frequently lost, that those who gather under the preaching of the Word and receive the bread and wine together at the Lord's table, proceed to Church Meeting, where, under the guidance of the Spirit, their primary task is the credal one of confessing the Lordship of Christ over all the work and witness of their church, and seeking his will in that matter. It is a Christocratic assembly where unanimity in Christ is sought (which does not mean that all agree with everything), not a democratic one in which we have one person, one vote, and government by the majority; and it should be conducted by the one called to lead the saints to the throne of grace, and not by some managerial type who is 'good at meetings'. Least of all should it be called the church's 'business meeting'. The critic of large buildings was therefore unable to conceive how one could have a church meeting of 2,000 people. How much more would he have boogled at churches where five or ten thousand gather? You will recall that in the opening paragraph of the section on worship in the Congregational *Declaration of Faith* of 1967 it is stated that one of the ways in which worship is expressed is 'through the fellowship and decisions of the Church'. The point is heavily underlined in the immediately following section on 'Membership'. The connection between the Sunday worship and the Church Meeting, though frequently obscured by Congregationalists themselves, is, I continue to believe, one of the tradition's great gifts to the Church at large. It is also the point at which the Congregational tradition completes the Reformation on the side of polity, for whereas Calvin stopped at elders and deacons, the Congregationalists have sought to involve the whole people of God in ministry, and it seems odd, and possibly an indication of an individualistic understanding of ministry, that such a document as *Baptism, Eucharist and Ministry*, whilst emphasizing the importance of the ministry of the whole people of God, does not recommend changes of church polity which would facilitate the common seeking of God's will by the corporate holy priesthood.[37]

Those whose polity does incorporate Church Meeting face a particular challenge at the present time. It used to be the case that a person's confession of faith, made at 'years of discretion' – generally between sixteen and eighteen – would be followed by reception as a church member, admission to the Lord's table, and immediate participation in Church Meeting. Nowadays, with children receiving the Lord's Supper in many churches on the ground that they are baptized members of the Church, and with professions of faith occurring at earlier ages, attendance at Church Meeting as part of the discipline of membership is delayed, and in some cases never honoured at all.[38]

---

[37] See further, Daniel Jenkins, *The Church Meeting and Democracy*, London: Independent Press, 1944; Alan P. F. Sell, *A Reformed Evangelical Catholic Theology. The Contribution of the World Alliance of Reformed Churches, 1875-1982*, (1991), reprinted Eugene, OR: Wipf & Stock, 1998, 99-100; idem., *Commemorations*, ch. 14.

[38] Cf. *A Reformed, Evangelical Catholic Theology*, 155; *Liturgical Group Report*, Congregational Union of England and Wales, 1965, 16.

This leads to the third point. Every church order is open to abuse because the Church comprises saints who are also sinners. And it must be confessed that Congregationalists have from time to time given the impression, and actually believed, that in the Church anyone can do anything. In fact, of course, their position really is that in the Church those called to specific tasks are appointed thereto by the church, following whatever testing of the call and training of the person may be required. Their experience in the nineteenth century, when they were setting themselves over against Anglican ritualism and sacerdotalism, does, however, raise the question, Who may preside at the Lord's table? This question in turn raises that of the meaning of ordination. I believe that at this point some sorting out needs to be done. On the one hand we have learned from the liturgiologists that Word and Sacrament belong together, yet often we permit all and sundry to preach, whilst prohibiting lay persons from presiding at the table. But this seems to sunder Word and Sacrament once more. (I am not advocating laxity in this matter; all who conduct the Lord's Supper should be appointed to do so by the church). Again, while most Christian traditions will accept baptism with water in the name of the Trinity, even if performed by a lay person, some will not permit lay celebration of the Lord's Supper; and this seems to drive a wedge between the sacraments. I suspect that we may be holding to very un-Reformed doctrine if we think that God will not meet with his people if the Lord's Supper is conducted by a faithful lay person who has been called by the Church to officiate. To say this is not to denigrate the ordained ministry; but it is to honour the ministry of all who are called by God to serve, and to remind the ministers that they, along with all other members, are part of the *laos* of God, and not members of a priestly caste.[39] Finally, we have seen that the Congregationalists took steps to ensure that children were welcome at the church's worship. They had always been welcome as candidates for infant baptism, and the propriety of the baptism of children of the covenant has never been in question. However, unless there is a strong grasp of the covenant idea, and a real attempt to teach and receive as members parents who have not professed their faith, it would seem that the justification that baptism provides an evangelical opportunity for outreach to unchurched parents rings hollow. As for the presence of children in worship, great strides have been made in this direction, but there are still divergent views as to what should happen liturgically while they are present. The advice of the Congregational Union's Liturgical Group in 1965 was as follows:

> We regard an attempt to make the part of the service in which all share 'suitable for the children' as mistaken. All are present to join in the church's corporate worship, not in a short children's service before adult worship

---

[39] See further, *A Reformed, Evangelical Catholic Theology*, 170-72.

begins. The service ought not to give the impression of beginning all over again after the children have left. What the church family has done together need not be repeated in the church or in the children's services.[40]

It is, nevertheless, in some circles a brave minister who will banish the children's address.

Underlying the entire practice of worship in the Congregational tradition is the presupposition that we know who the gathered saints are; they have passed from death to life, made their profession of faith, and had their children baptized; they join in Church Meeting, and are under the church's kindly Gospel discipline. Ever since the Evangelical Revival question marks have been played against some aspects of this catalogue. Today, with increasingly mobile populations, with Congregational churches (or their united heirs) serving as *quasi*-parish churches in some areas, and with the consumerist spirit which inclines many people to join in worship on grounds more aesthetic or emotional – or even on grounds of geographical convenience or the availability of ancillary facilities – rather than on ecclesiologically principled grounds, the question 'Who are the church?' is sharply posed.

On the narrower question of the shape of the liturgy, the moral I draw from studying the worship of the English Congregational tradition is that one of the most important terms in the liturgiolgist's vocabulary is the blessed word 'normally'. This word, we may hope, both restrains the legalistic and leaves open a window for the Spirit.

---

[40] *Liturgical Group Report*, 6-7.

CHAPTER 3

Telling the Story: Then and Now

> Had you all the refined science of Plato or Socrates, all the skill in morals that ever was attained by Zeno, Seneca or Epictetus; were you furnished with all the glowing oratory of Cicero, or the thunder of Demosthenes...you could have no reasonable hope to convert and save one soul in Great Britain...while you lay aside the glorious gospel of Christ, and leave it entirely out of your discourses.[1]

With this paper I am pleased to honour a theologian who has never lost his foothold in the Church and who, to a greater extent than many, has sought to locate his theological endeavours in the realities of the pastoral situation. Indeed, he is producing a multi-volume 'pastoral systematics', at the heart of which is the good news of God's redeeming love in Christ. This is the story, as evangelical as it is catholic, which Gabriel Fackre has delighted to tell to diverse churches, to industrial workers in Pittsburgh, to students in Lancaster and Andover Newton seminaries, and, through his many writings, to a much wider constituency.

It is no secret that 'telling the story' has been a central feature of the Reformed family's life. Truth to tell, the sermon has sometimes been so elevated in importance that other components of the liturgy have been demoted to 'mere preliminaries'. Again, the Reformed have contributed considerably to the literature of homiletics, and that there is still work to be done in this field is exemplified by a remark made to me: 'His sermons are just a lot of hot air, but doesn't he do a wonderful "pause for profile"?' But my concern here is not with the place of the sermon in the liturgy, or with the techniques of preaching. I simply wish to ask, How has the privilege of preaching been viewed in the Reformed family, and what have our forebears in the faith to teach us on the matter? I propose to limit this vast subject by summoning two principal witnesses from the English Reformed heritage: Richard Baxter (1615–1691) and P. T. Forsyth (1848–1921). In the case of each of these a caveat must be entered. Although Baxter is the seventeenth century's Reformed pastor *par excellence*, we should remember that in a period of ecclesiological fluidity devoid of denominations in our modern sense, he regarded 'Presbyterian' as 'the odious name' and, in the interests of Christian unity, was not averse to 'moderate

---

[1] Isaac Watts, *An Humble Attempt towards the Revival of Practical Religion among Christians*, in *The Works of the Reverend and Learned Isaac Watts, D.D.*, 6 vols., London: J. Barfield, 1810, III, 15.

Episcopacy'.² In 1681 he declared, 'You could not (except a Catholick Christian) have trulier called me than an Episcopal-Presbyterian-Independent.'³ As for Forsyth, I annex this Scot to England only because his five pastorates and his principalship of Hackney College, London, were all on English soil, and because his contribution to English Congregationalism, and through it to the wider Church, was of great significance.⁴

I

In the wake of a period of civil and religious unrest, and with toleration under the law denied to Dissenters until two years before his death, Richard Baxter returned time and again in his writings to the solemn responsibility and awesome privilege of proclaiming the Gospel, the heart of which he construed in these terms:

> By sin we have all forfeited our right to heaven; but Eternal love hath given us a Redeemer, who is God and man, who as our surety became a sacrifice for our sins, and by his merits hath purchased a conditional grant of free forgiveness, and of renewing grace, and endless glory ... Man is not now put upon satisfying God's justice, or purchasing his salvation by a price. Christ hath done these, and made a free gift of grace and glory to all that will but accept it ... To acquaint men with this, is our ministerial office; we are charged to set before them the great salvation which Christ hath procured, and importunately to beseech them to mind it, believe it, and accept it, that it may be theirs for ever ....⁵

It is no light task to proclaim such a Gospel: 'All our sermons must be fitted to change men's hearts, from carnal into spiritual, and to kindle in them the love of God';⁶ and 'You cannot break men's hearts by jesting with them, or telling them a smooth tale, or patching up a gaudy oration.'⁷ The problem is that 'Multitudes have such dead and hardened hearts, that, when we tell them that they must

---

² See *Reliquiae Baxterianae*, ed. M. Sylvester, 1696, I.ii.373, para. 242; I.ii.281, para. 120. See further, Alan P. F. Sell, *Commemorations. Studies in Christian Thought and History*, Calgary: Univesity of Calgary Press and Cardiff: University of Wales Press, 1993; reprinted, Eugene, OR: Wipf & Stock, 1998, ch. 3.

³ R. Baxter, *Third Defence of the Cause of Peace*, 1681, I, 110.

⁴ For the welcome revival of interest in Forsyth's theology see Trevor Hart, ed., *Justice the True and Only Mercy. Essays on the Life and Theology of P. T. Forsyth*, Edinburgh: T. & T. Clark, 1995; Leslie McCurdy, *Attributes and Atonement. The Holy Love of God in the Theology of P. T. Forsyth*, Carlisle: Paternoster Press, 1999; Richard L. Floyd, *When I Survey the Wondrous Cross. Reflections on the Atonement*, San Jose, CA: Pickwick Publications, 2000; Alan P. F. Sell, ed., *P. T. Forsyth: Theologian for a New Millennium*, London: The United Reformed Church, 2000.

⁵ R. Baxter, *Reasons for Ministers using the greatest Plainness and Seriousness Possible*, in Works, XV, 535.

⁶ Idem, Knowledge and Love Compared, in Works, XV, 229.

⁷ Idem, *Gildas Salvianus: The Reformed Pastor*, in Works, XIV, 225.

shortly be in heaven or hell, as they are here prepared, we speak almost as to blocks, or men asleep: they feel not what we say, as if they did not hear us.'[8] Hence the urgency of preaching – an urgency which emerges in the often-ailing Baxter's oft-repeated words,

> I Preach'd as never sure to Preach again
> And as a dying man to dying men.[9]

Baxter was concerned, however, not only with the content of the message, but with the condition of the preacher:

> When your minds are in a heavenly, holy frame, your people are likely to partake of the fruits of it ... They will feel when you have been much with God ... We are the nurses of Christ's little ones. If we forbear our food, we shall famish them ... If we let our love go down, we are not likely to raise up theirs.[10]

One further point of importance should be noted: for Baxter, preaching was grounded upon, and presupposed, consistent catechetical instruction. He exhorted church members to 'Learn first your catechisms at home, and the great essential points of religion, contained in the creed, the Lord's prayer, and the ten commandments ... You can scarce bestow too much care and pains in learning these great essential points.'[11] He did not, however, stop at exhortation. He summoned those of his people who lived in the town of Kidderminster to his home, or to that of his assistant, and he despatched his colleague to the homes of those who lived further afield – and all of this with pastoral and catechetical intent:

> I set two Days a Week apart for this Employment: my (faithful unwearied) Assistant and my self, took fourteen Families every Week ... First, they recited the Catechism to us (a Family only being present at a time, and no Stranger admitted); after that I first helped them to understand it, and next enquired modestly into the State of their Souls, and lastly, endeavoured to set all home to the convincing, awakening and resolving of their Hearts according to their several Conditions; bestowing about an Hour (and the Labour of a Sermon) with every Family.[12]

---

[8] Idem, *Reasons for Ministers using Plainness with their People*, in *Works*, XV, 537.
[9] From Baxter's *Poetical Fragments*, 1681; cf. *Reliquiae Baxterianae*, I.i, paras. 137, 32; I.i, para. 114.
[10] Idem, *Gildas Salvianus: The Reformed Pastor*, in *Works*, XIV, 223.
[11] Idem, *Christian Directory*, in *Works*, IV, 253.
[12] *Reliquiae Baxterianae*, I.ii, para. 41.

II

Between the death of Baxter and the working life of Forsyth there intervened a number of significant intellectual and ecclesiastical movements. There was the Enlightenment which, insofar as it encouraged the individual's quest of conscientious and reasonable religion over against untoward authorities whether biblicist or ecclesiastical, and fostered the moral critique of a scholastic theology which in some hands had perpetrated the blasphemous view that the Father had to be cajoled into being gracious by the death of his Son (a false 'gospel' which may still be heard in some quarters to this day), by no means merits the blanket denunciations which have been pronounced against it of late by some prolific but insufficiently discriminating theologians. This is not at all to deny that from the Enlightenment there also flowed an individual*ism* which adversely affected Church and society alike. Indeed, from one point of view the Evangelical Revival is Enlightenment individualism gone pious. This diagnosis is confirmed with particular clarity in the Congregational branch of the Reformed family. From about 1820 onwards the local covenant was in decline,[13] and with it Church Meeting – that Christocratic, credal assembly of the saints, in which Christ's Lordship over the church's life was proclaimed and God's will for its mission was sought, unanimity in Christ being the objective (this was no democratic assembly with one person, one vote, and government by the majority). Baptism was a further casualty. In some quarters it was demoted and even regarded as optional, for the great thing now was a prospective member's experience of conversion. Like other evangelicals, whether Arminian or Calvinist, the Congregationalists began to establish 'mission stations' in both rural and rapidly expanding industrial areas. No doubt it is better that people hear and respond to the Gospel than that they do not, but it cannot be denied that in all of this activity the covenant-based polity was, here and there, well nigh obliterated.

Concurrently there was the rise of modern biblical criticism and the explosion of evolutionary thought, and these elicited Christian responses on a continuum from the petrified to the incautious.[14] There was also the question of Catholic emancipation, perceived as a threat by many Nonconformists, and the growth within the Church of England of an Anglo-Catholicism which in some cases seemed more Roman than the Roman, and which propelled numerous Nonconformist pamphleteers into anti-sacerdotalist mode. Some of the

---

[13] For the evidence see Alan P. F. Sell, *Dissenting Thought and the Life of the Churches. Studies in an English Tradition*, Lewiston, NY: The Edwin Mellen Press, 1990, ch. 1.

[14] See further, Alan P. F. Sell, *Theology in Turmoil. The Roots, Course and Significance of the Conservative-Liberal Debate in Modern Theology*, (1986), Eugene, OR: Wipf & Stock, 1998.

Congregationalists among these, seeking to beat the devil at his own game, trumpeted their conviction that in view of their acknowledgment of the sole Headship of Christ over the Church (sub-text: not Christ plus the Pope or the monarch of the day) *they* were the true high churchpeople.

III

Into this context stepped Forsyth, a Congregational high churchman if ever there was one, and one whose language is of particular interest. He takes the terms of the ecclesiastical 'opposition' and rebaptizes them into his own ecclesiology. Thus he emphasizes the *priestly* role of the minister, and the *sacramental* nature of preaching, even utilizing such words as 'host' and 'transubstantiation':

> No wonder the ministry is lightly treated if it is viewed as a mere convenience, like a chairman, as the proposer of the adoption of the divine report. And in some quarters it is so viewed. Some preaching is like proposing the health of the gospel. Some prayer is like moving a vote of thanks to the Almighty, with a request for favours to come ... That is all wrong. The minister is much more than a leading brother as the Church itself is more than a fraternity. He is neither the mouthpiece of the Church, nor its chairman, nor its secretary. He is not the servant, not the employee, of the Church. He is an apostle to it, the mouthpiece of Christ's gospel to it, the servant of the Word and not of the Church; he serves the Church only for that sake. The ministry is a prophetic and sacramental office; it is not a secretarial, it is not merely presidential. It is sacramental and not merely functional. It is the outward and visible agent of the inward gospel Grace. It is more sacramental than the elements. It is a living host, produced by a conversion which goes deeper than transubstantiation. It is the trustee of the one sacrament of the Word, the Word of New Creation.[15]

Elsewhere he underlines the point:

> You perceive what high ground I take. The preacher's place in the Church is sacramental. It is not sacerdotal, but it is sacramental. He mediates the word to the Church ... He is a living element in Christ's hands (broken, if need be) for the distribution and increment of grace. He is not a mere reporter, nor a mere lecturer, on sacred things. He is not merely illuminative, he is augmentive. His work is not to enlighten simply, but to empower and enhance ... We spend our polemic upon the Mass, and fitly enough in proper place. But the Catholic form of worship will always have a vast

---

[15] P. T. Forsyth, *The Church and the Sacraments*, (1917), London: Independent Press, 1953, 132–3. In the very year in which this book was first published Constance Mary Coltman became the first woman to be ordained to the Congregational ministry in England. Thereafter masculine personal pronouns were no longer appropriate when referring to those on that ministerial role as a whole.

advantage over ours so long as people come away from its central act with the sense of something done in the spirit-world, while they leave ours with the sense only of something said to this present world. In true preaching, as in a true sacrament, more is done than said.[16]

As if to encourage the faint-hearted, he immediately adds, 'And much is well done which is poorly said.'

What is more, it is the Church, as the community of those living the new life, that is the preacher: 'The one great preacher in history, I would contend, is the Church. And the first business of the individual preacher is to enable the Church to preach.'[17] Again, 'The ministry ... has not to be directly effective on the world so much as to make a Church that is. It has not to reform the world, but to create a Church for the world's reformation.'[18]

As to the content of preaching, Forsyth, the erstwhile liberal, set his face against the gospel of brotherhood, the gospel of love-gone-sentimental, any gospel in which God's holiness had been extruded from his love. He trounced any doctrine of the atonement which suggested that the Cross was exclusively to do with humanity, its sin and need. On the contrary,

> The Holy Father's first care is holiness. The first charge on a Redeemer is satisfaction to that holiness. The Holy Father is one who does and must atone. As Holy Father he offers a sacrifice rent from his own heart. It is made to him by no third party, but by himself in his Son ... [19]

Hence, 'The Gospel of Christ is the Gospel of HOLY LOVE and its victory.'[20] Conversely,

> So long as the chief value of the Cross is its value for man, so long as its first effect is upon man and not upon God, so long as its prime action is not upon reality but upon our feeling about reality, then so long shall we be led away from direct contact with reality at our religious centre; and we shall be induced to dwell more upon our experience of reconciliation than on the God by whose self-reconciliation we are reconciled.[21]

Not surprisingly, therefore, Forsyth had no patience with the idea of Christ as the first Christian. On the contrary, 'A Christ that differs from the rest of men only in saintly degree and not in redeeming kind is not the Christ of the New Testament nor of a Gospel Church.'[22] Fearing that 'The homely may have

---

[16] Idem, *Positive Preaching and the Modern Mind*, (1907), London: Independent Press, 1964, 53-4.
[17] Idem, 53.
[18] Idem, *The Church and the Sacraments*, 131.
[19] Idem, *God the Holy Father*, London: Independent Press, 1957, 4.
[20] Idem, *Congregationalism and Reunion*, London: 1952, 40.
[21] Idem, *Positive Preaching and the Modern Mind*, 121.
[22] Idem, *The Church, the Gospel and Society*, London: Independent Press, 1962, 99.

belittled the holy,' he was equally concerned to pose a further question: 'The dear Christ of the Gospels – has He not obscured the great Christ of Ephesians? The prophet of the Kingdom has hidden the Founder of the Kingdom on the Cross.'[23] Above all, he could not tolerate the way in which, in some quarters, the Gospel was being pared down so that it suited the modern mentality. While enunciating the prescription, 'Reduce the burden of belief we must. The old orthodoxy laid on men's believing power more than it could carry;'[24] and while in no way an enemy of biblical criticism as such, he nevertheless protested that 'Too many are occupied in throwing over precious cargo; they are lightening the ship even of its fuel.'[25] In face of all reductionism, trivializing, sentimentalizing, he reminded preachers in no uncertain terms that

> The solution of the world ... is what destroys its guilt. And nothing can destroy guilt but the very holiness that makes guilt guilt. And that destruction is the work of Christ upon His Cross, the Word of Life Eternal in your hands and in your souls.[26]

IV

'Telling the story : then' – but 'now'? Perhaps the most prudent course would be to invite readers to ponder Baxter and Forsyth and draw their own conclusions. But since that might also be the cowardly course, I shall venture a few modest observations.

First, I value Forsyth's emphasis upon the fact that just as it is the Church (and not the ministry) which celebrates the sacraments, so it is the Church which is called to proclaim the Gospel. In this connection it is worth pondering the Greek terms used in Acts 8: 4,5. The church members, persecuted out of their homes following the death of Stephen, 'went through the country preaching ('telling the good tidings') the word'; whereas Philip, the appointed evangelist, went to Samaria and 'began proclaiming (heralding – something official) the Messiah there.' Acts 11: 9–11 records the expansion of the Church in the wake of the testimony of the 'ordinary' church members. Or come to seventeenth-century Wales. The Civil War is raging, and Walter Cradock of Llanvaches is among other ministers who flee to London for relative safety. Following a return visit to Wales he delivers a sermon in London in which he reports as follows:

---

[23] Idem, *The Charter of the Church*, London: Alexander & Shepheard, 1896, 47.
[24] Idem, *Positive Preaching and the Modern Mind*, 84. Though see his qualification on p. 97.
[25] Idem, *The Principle of Authority. Its Relation to Certainty, Sanctity and Society*, (1913), London: Independent Press, 1952, 261.
[26] Idem, *Positive Preaching and the Modern Mind*, 228.

> I have observed, and seen, in the Mountains of Wales [that] the Gospel is run over the Mountains between Brecknockshire and Monmouthshire, as the fire in the thatch; and who should doe this? They have no ministers: but some of the wisest say, there are about eight hundred godly people, and they goe from one to another. They have no ministers, it is true; if they had, they would honour and blesse God for them: and shall we raile at such, and say they are Tubpreachers, and they were never at the University? Let us fall downe, and honour God ... They were filled with good newes, and they tell it to others.[27]

It is a humbling thing for ministers to reflect upon how much good can be done when they are nowhere in sight![28]

Secondly, I propose that we who are called to preach examine ourselves (wholesomely, not morbidly) in the light of Baxter's remarks concerning our own spiritual condition. It is not a matter of clearing our diaries so that we can accommodate a week at Iona or a fortnight at Taizé, or even a one-day course on spirituality. Hear Baxter once more:

> O brethren, watch, therefore, over your own hearts! Keep out sinful passions and worldly inclinations; keep up the life of faith and love; be much at home; and be much with God. If it be not your daily, serious business to study your own hearts, and subdue corruptions, and live as upon God; if you make it not your very work which you constantly attend, all will go amiss, and you will starve your auditors; or if you have but an affected fervency, you cannot expect such a blessing to attend it: above all, be much in secret prayer and meditation. There you must fetch the heavenly fire that must kindle your sacrifices. Remember, you cannot decline and neglect your duty to your own hurt alone; many will be losers by it as well as you. For your people's sake, therefore, look to your hearts.[29]

For a blunter and more concise word along the same lines we may invoke a Baptist (albeit he was raised in Congregationalism and converted in a Primitive Methodist service). Said Charles Haddon Spurgeon (1834–1892) to his budding preachers: 'We may not be butchers at the block chopping off for hungry ones the meat of which we do not partake.'[30]

Thirdly, I suggest that we have much to learn from Baxter's way of supplying the pastoral and catechetical foundations for preaching. As Baxter's Congregational contemporary, John Owen (1616–1683), said, 'It is the duty of a shepherd to know the state of his flock; and unless he do so he will never feed

---

[27] Walter Cradock, *Glad Tidings from Heaven to the Worst Sinners on Earth*, 1648.
[28] This is, of course, a testimony to God's providence, not an inducement to ministerial laziness.
[29] R. Baxter, *Gildas Salvianus: The Reformed Pastor*, in *Works*, XIV, 224.
[30] C. H. Spurgeon, *An All-Round Ministry*, (1900), London: The Banner of Truth Trust, 1960, 66.

them profitably.'³¹ What then are we to make of such a present-day ministerial designation as, 'Minister for preaching and Christian administration?' Incredible as it may seem, such persons exist; can they truly preach? 'The pastor's work,' said Forsyth, 'is not merely to go about among the people with human sympathy and kindly help, [but to carry] Christ to the people individually, sacramentally [there is that word again] ... The pastor is only the preacher in retail.'³²

And how is it with the catechetical task in an age in which, in so many Western churches, pastoral visitation and Christian education are vitiated by members' personal and family time-tables, and when enormous pressure is put on the one hour per week which is all some are able to allow for churchly concerns? What are the implications of this for the size of our local churches? I was recently informed that in the Presbyterian Church USA 50% of the churches have fewer than two hundred members, while 60% of the total membership dwell in churches having more than five hundred members. If we take the relations of preaching-catechizing-pastoring seriously the latter statistic may be ecclesiologically more problematic than the former.

Fourthly, may not Baxter and Forsyth together recall us to the solemnity and urgency of the preacher's task? This is not the place for one more diatribe against 'feel good' religion; but let us at least heed Forsyth: 'There are crowds and crowds of even Christian people who are sympathetic for every human ache ... who have a heart for every plea of man, but they are entirely heartless for the affliction of the God of a prodigal race with the iniquity of it all laid upon His holy Soul.'³³ How dare any preach half a doctrine of atonement – as if the sacrifice of Christ were for humanity alone?

Fifthly, in their different ways both Baxter and Forsyth understood the distinction which Isaac Watts drew for preachers in these terms:

> Let your hearers know that there is a vast and unspeakable difference betwixt a saint and a sinner, one in Christ, and one out of Christ ... Let them know that this distinction is great and necessary; and it is not made (as some have imagined) by the water of baptism, but by the operations of the word and Spirit of God on the hearts of men, and by their diligent attendance on all the appointed means and methods of converting grace. It is a most real change, and of infinite importance ....³⁴

It is not too much to say that the entire Congregational polity turns upon this distinction. What are the implications of this for our churches' present bearing in

---

³¹ *The Works of John Owen*, ed. Wiliam Goold, (1850–1853), London: The Banner of Truth Trust, 1968, IV, 511.
³² P. T. Forsyth, *The Church and the Sacraments*, 145.
³³ Idem, *Faith, Freedom and the Future*, (1912), London: Independent Press, 1955, 282–3.
³⁴ Isaac Watts, *Works*, III, 18.

society? Undeniably, churches and Christians can be 'different' in obnoxious ways which are a woeful hindrance to the Gospel. But may they not also be so identified with the world around that any distinctiveness is lost, and with it the challenge of the Gospel, the rigour and exhilaration of the 'godly walk', and the ability to utter a prophetic word?

This uncritical blending may even be revealed in our language. We saw how Forsyth took the terms of others and rebaptized them to his own use. May it not be that we in the West have poached the terms of the corporate world and shown no inclination to rebaptize them (were that even possible)? Can we imagine that Baxter or Forsyth would think of the ministry as a 'job', that they would be impressed by talk of 'ministerial career patterns' or the 'hiring and firing' of pastors; that they would rate the person in a four-point charge lower than one in a 'tall steeple church', or think of the latter as having been 'promoted'? By their language ye shall know them.[35] And where in all of this has gone the doctrine of vocation? It may be that the introduction of the corporate model is to some extent a function of congregational size, to which reference has already been made. But this simply raises again the questions, Can local churches be too large? May we not have lost more than we have gained in our carving up of ministerial functions into 'specialisms' – even granted that an individual minister may not be equally competent in all aspects of the work?

Finally, it must be granted that Baxter and Forsyth cannot do all our work for us. However it may have been in their own preaching, in their writings on preaching they do not have much to say concerning the need to ensure that the major themes of the Christian faith are regularly enunciated from the pulpit. Perhaps they could take it for granted. I have good reason to think that we cannot. Too many worshippers are deprived of the eschatological note; Pentecost can be transmogrified into Animal Sunday; and in itinerant situations the situation can be even more haphazard. While I should not wish to belong to a church which required the slavish use of a lectionary, it is not too much to ask that preachers at least heed the Christian Year, and treat their hearers to biblical expositions which will acquaint them with the main arteries of that 'body of divinity' about which some of our forebears unburdened themselves at such great length.

Baxter, and even Forsyth to a lesser degree, could make the assumptions of Christendom whereas we can no longer do so. Thus Baxter specifies the matters which the minister is obliged to teach to the people, and these matters assume the existence of God, the viability of natural theology, and the pre-critical

---

[35] See further, Alan P. F. Sell, *Aspects of Christian Integrity*, Calgary: University of Calgary Press and Louisville: Westminster/John Knox Press, 1990; Eugene, OR: Wipf & Stock, 1998, ch. 6.

recourse to biblical evidences.[36] While our sermons should not become disquisitions on apologetics, we should certainly be aware that many faithful church members harbour doubts concerning basic Christian doctrines which they may feel inhibited from articulating, either because they feel the minister's reply will not rise above banalities or platitudes, or because the godly will pronounce them lacking in faith, or both. In too many cases such people, having looked up and not been fed, drift elsewhere, or worship nowhere.

Although they were both staunchly trinitarian, neither Baxter not Forsyth related this aspect of their faith in detail to their remarks on preaching. They were, like Paul and Augustine before them, occasional writers rather than Barth-like systematicians.[37] For my part, however, I should like to express my opinion that, no matter how varied the cultural, intellectual, socio-political contexts of Christian preaching may be, *the* context of preaching is the gracious work of the triune God who, on the ground of the Son's saving work at the Cross, calls out a people by his Holy Spirit, who shall praise and serve their heavenly Father now and eternally.

It is a happy thought that both streams of the English Reformed tradition[38] – the Presbyterian and the Congregational – were involved in the Westminster Assembly. That Assembly's *Larger Catechism* contains the question, 'How is the word of God to be preached by those that are called thereunto?' The answer is:

> They that are called to labour in the ministry of the word, are to preach sound doctrine, diligently, in season and out of season; plainly, not in the enticing words of man's wisdom, but in demonstration of the Spirit, and of power; faithfully, making known the whole counsel of God; wisely, applying themselves to the necessities and capacities of the hearers; zealously, with fervent love to God and the souls of his people; sincerely, aiming at his glory, and their conversion, edification, and salvation.

More than 350 years on, that answer remains as challenging as it is comprehensive.

---

[36] See R. Baxter, *Christian Directory*, in *Works*, V, 120–30.
[37] See further, ch. 7 below.
[38] I do not, of course, deny that among the Anglicans and the Baptists there are those who have swallowed gallons of Reformed doctrine in eager gulps. Here I refer to the Reformed family as such, in distinction from the Anglican and the Baptist.

CHAPTER 4

Doctrine, Polity, Liberty:
What do Baptists Stand For?

> In writing upon the theological beliefs for the English Baptists of this century, I do not intend to pen a word as the advocate of a party, or set down a sentence with a grain of personal bias.[1]

If John Clifford felt it necessary to introduce his 1888 study of Baptist theology in this vein, how much more ought a friendly Reformed observer of Baptists to endorse such words—especially since I am ambitious enough to rove over four centuries, not one. The operative word is, of course, 'intend', and it is always possible for results to belie intentions. Be that as it may, it is not my purpose to produce one more tract of 'The Dippers Dipp'd' variety. Indeed, baptism is not the main focus of this paper, for until the harvest of the dialogues between Baptists, Reformed and others is safely gathered in, there is not much more to be said upon that hoary topic.[2] The concern here is not with Baptists *vis-à-vis* other Christian traditions; rather, I am interested in the attitudes and antics of Baptists among themselves regarding three of their historic concerns: doctrine, polity, and liberty. Were this not such an auspicious volume my contribution might have been adorned with the title 'Baptists through the Keyhole.' As it is, the second part of my heading suggests that, as in other communions (for I am the last to adopt a 'more-ecciesiastically-pure-than-thou' posture), Baptist trumpets have on

---

[1] John Clifford, 'Baptist Theology,' *Contemporary Review* 53 (1888): 503. For Clifford (1836–1923), see the *Oxford Dictionary of National Biography* (hereinafter ODNB).

[2] Only the most daring ecumenist would predict when the harvest referred to will be in. For while, when responding to the World Council of Churches' document, *Baptism, Eucharist, and Ministry*, the Council of the Baptist Union of Great Britain and Ireland declared, 'It would seem that any further work on baptism could usefully be done only in the wider context of Christian initiation'—the very suggestion proposed in the international Baptist-Reformed dialogue of the 1970s—Ernest A. Payne's restrained words of fifty years ago have subsequently lost none of their force: 'Since the formation of the Baptist World Alliance, it is the stricter wing of the Baptist movement which has, on the whole, been dominant.' The continuing positive work of such Baptists as W. M. S. West, and J. H. Y. Briggs, and such thoughtful contributions as that of M. J. Quicke should not, however, be overlooked. See *Baptism, Eucharist, and Ministry. The Response of the Baptist Union of Great Britain and Ireland to the Faith and Order Paper No. 111 of the World Council of Churches'* London: Baptist Union of Great Britain and Ireland, 1985, 3, cf. 13; *Baptists and Reformed in Dialogue*, Geneva: World Alliance of Reformed Churches, 1984; Ernest A. Payne, 'Baptist-Congregational Relationships,' *The Congregational Quarterly* XXXIII no. 3, July 1955, 225; M. J. Quicke, 'Baptists and the Current Debate on Baptism,' *The Baptist Quarterly* (hereinafter BQ) 29/4 (October 1981): 153–68.

occasion, on the issues under review, made not uncertain sounds, but a number of different certain sounds, some of them discordant. On one issue, however—establishment—Baptist trumpets, like those of others in the line of Old Dissent, are nowadays decidedly muted, if not altogether silent. This is my justification for turning Henry Cook's bold title, *What Baptists Stand For* (1947), into a question.

This preamble may conclude with one procedural point and one statement of the obvious. First, we shall have more than enough material to consider if we confine ourselves to soundings taken within the English Baptist heritage, and no disrespect to Baptists elsewhere is implied by this restriction. Secondly, there 'is unavoidable artificiality in attempting to treat doctrine, polity and liberty *seriatim*, for Baptist polity has been determined by the Baptist doctrine of the Church, doctrine which has required liberty for its articulation and expression, and implies a theory of church-state relations. In fact, the organs of polity—Church Meeting, Association—have stated those doctrines commonly believed and, in some instances, required to be believed. Nevertheless, in the interests of clarity of exposition, I shall attempt to deal with one matter at a time.

I

We may permit a Congregationalist to erect the poles between which our discussion of Baptist doctrine will oscillate. In one place P. T. Forsyth declares, 'There must surely be in very positive religion some point where it may so change as to lose its identity and become another religion.'[3] Elsewhere he warns, 'Where you fix a creed you flatten faith.'[4] Here was aptly posited that tension between clearly defined doctrinal identity and liberty of conscience which Baptists of various stripes have experienced through the centuries. Thus, for example, on the one hand those General Baptists who devised *An Orthodox Creed* (1678) declared that 'The three creeds, viz. Nicene creed, Athanasius's creed, and the Apostles creed, as they are commonly called, ought thoroughly to be received, and believed.'[5] On the other hand, the Western Association, which at its inception embraced a few General Baptist churches, entrusted 'every church to their own liberty, to walk together as they have received from the Lord.'

However, in the wake of the debates over the Trinity and subscription fueled by both Anglican Samuel Clarke's *The Scripture Doctrine of the Trinity* (1712) as

---

[3] P. T. Forsyth, *The Principle of Authority* (1913), London: Independent Press, 1952, 219.

[4] P. T. Forsyth, *Positive Preaching and the Modern Mind* (1907), London: Independent Press, 1964, 141.

[5] *An Orthodox Creed, or a Protestant Confession of Faith, Being an Essay to Unite and Confirm All True Protestants in the Fundamental Articles of the Christian Religion, against the Errors and Heresies of Rome*, London, 1697, art. XXXVIII; in William L. Lumpkin, ed., *Baptist Confessions of Faith*, rev. ed., Valley Forge PA: Judson Press, 1969, 326.

well as the Salters' Hall conference of 1719, the Association, subsequent to its reformation in 1722, heeded a letter prepared by Bernard Foskett, from the Broadmead church, Bristol. This letter urged that every member church would 'in their Letter every year signify their approbation of' the *Second London Confession* of 1689, and requested members to affirm the Trinity and to deny 'the destructive and corrupt principles of the Arminians...and of the Antinomians.'[6] With reference to the same confession, the Particular Baptist John Collett Ryland signed a Circular Letter to the Northamptonshire Baptist Association in 1777 in which the ministers and messengers remarked, 'Our confession of faith, and our catechism for the instruction of our young people, are published to the world; and from these glorious principles we hope you will never depart: if you should, you will not longer be churches of Christ, but synagogues of Satan.'[7]

These random examples drawn from the two major classical streams of English and Welsh Baptist witness will suffice to justify E. A. Payne's remark, 'It is a mistake to suggest that [the earliest Baptists] eschewed credal statements or objected to creeds and confessions.'[8] It remains only to add that in addition to proclaiming their doctrines and indicating to churches and members what the doctrinal parameters were, the early confessions served the apologetic purpose of countering those who maliciously attributed to Baptists view which they did not hold and Münster-like aspirations which they did not share, and of demonstrating Baptist loyalty to the faith of the ages. Thus, the Particular Baptists' London Confession of 1644 was:

> Presented to the view of all that feare God, to examine by the touchstone of the Word of Truth: As likewise, for the taking off those aspersions which are frequently both in Pulpit and Print, (though unjustly) cast upon them.[9]

Similarly, the General Baptist *Standard Confession* of 1660 was:

---

[6] Caleb Evans, "Records of the Western Association," MSS at Bristol Baptist College, 7; J. G. Fuller, *A Brief History of the Western Association, from Its Commencement, about the Middle of the Seventeenth Century, to Its Dvision into Four Smaller Ones—the Bristol, the Western, the Southern, and the South Western—in 1823*, Bristol: I. Hemmons, 1845, 30. See further, Roger Hayden, 'The Particular Baptist Confession of 1689 and Baptists today,' BQ XXXII no. 2, 1988, 403-17. For Foskett (1685–1758), see Norman Moon, *Education for Ministry. Bristol Baptist College 1679–1979* (Bristol: Bristol Baptist College, 1979) 108; Roger Hayden, 'The contribution of Bernard Foskett,' in William H. Brackney and Paul S. Fiddes, with John H. Y. Briggs, eds., *Pilgrim Pathways. Essays in Honour of B. R. White*, Macon, GA: Mercer University Press, 1999, 189-206; Alan P. F. Sell, *Philosophy, Dissent and Nonconformity 1689-1920*, Cambridge: James Clarke, 2004, ch. 3.

[7] *The Beauty of Social Religion; or, the Nature and Glory of a Gospel Church, Represented in a Circular Letter from the Baptist Ministers and Messengers, Assembled at Oakham, in Rutlandshire, May 20, 21, 1777*, 7. For Ryland (1723–1792), see ODNB.

[8] Ernest A. Payne, *The Fellowship of Believers, Baptist Thought and Practice Yesterday and Today*, enlarged ed., London: Carey Kingsgate Press, 1952, 103.

[9] Lumpkin, *Baptist Confessions of Faith*, 153.

> Set forth by many of us, who are (falsely) called Ana-Baptists, to inform all Men (in these days of scandal and reproach) of our innocent Belief and Practise; for which we are not only resolved to suffer Persecution, to the loss of our Goods, but also Life itself, rather than to decline the same.[10]

Apologetics apart, what happened when, as in other traditions, some Baptists deemed others to have overshot the rigorist or libertarian doctrinal markers? Let us recall some incidents drawn from the several streams of Baptist witness, all of which will encourage reflection upon the ever-present question of the permissible degrees of doctrinal tolerance within the church.

Although there is a long prehistory of unorthodoxy—especially Socinian—concerning the Trinity and person of Christ,[11] and although John Smyth 'flirted with Anabaptist Melchiorite Christology that Christ received his second flesh but not His first flesh from Mary'[12]—a position repudiated by Thomas Helwys and his supporters[13]—we may set out from the General Baptist Matthew Caffyn (1628–1714).[14] Sent down from Oxford circa 1624 for advocating Baptist views, he farmed at Horsham, where he joined the General Baptist movement. He was cordially welcomed by the minister, Samuel Lover, whom he succeeded in 1748,[15] and was instrumental in founding a number of other churches in Sussex and Kent. Alexander Gordon writes:

> Caffyn was an intrepid man in the advocacy of Baptist views, but in the expression of his own peculiar sentiments he was exceedingly cautious; he published nothing which could be laid hold of, and I believe I must add that the was purposely ambiguous when attempts were made to bring him to book.[16]

It appears that until 1653 Caffyn maintained orthodox trinitarian convictions, but thereafter he embraced an unorthodox Christology. Gordon came across Christopher Cooper's scarce volume, *The Vail Turn'd Aside* (1701), which recounts Caffyn's addressing a large assembly in London, declaring that the second person of the Trinity was changed into flesh and literally died. This, said

---

[10] Ibid., 224.

[11] E.g., see H. John McLachlan, *Socinianism in Seventeenth-Century England*, London: Oxford University Press, 1951.

[12] James R. Coggins, 'The Theological positions of John Smyth,' BQ XXX no. 6, April 1984, 255.

[13] See Lonnie D. Kliever, 'General Baptist Origins: The Question of Anabaptist Influence,' *Mennonite Quarterly Review* XXXVI, 1962, 293.

[14] For Caffyn, see *DNB*. This article, by Alexander Gordon, is supplemented by his "Matthew Caffyn and General Baptist latitude," *The Christian Life and Unitarian Herald*, 5 Nov. 1892, 531-2.

[15] John J. Evershed, 'A Short Account of the Free Christian Church, Billingshurst,' repr. from *Transactions of the Unitarian Historical Society*, October 1949, 2–3.

[16] A. Gordon, 'Matthew Caffyn and General Baptist latitude,' 531(c).

Caffyn, had been taught to him by a man wearing a leathern doublet, who approached him at Horsham Fair. Whereas Cooper, casting his net wide, supposed that "some evil spirit in human shape appeared to deceive him, or else the craft of some intriguing Jesuit or popish friar, or one of the Arian stamp sent by the whore of Babylon." This is on the basis that Caffyn adopted in 1661 the anthropomorphic line that God takes human, or similar, form and is not omnipresent. Gordon conjectured that the teacher was a Muggletonian. Gordon ruled out the possibility that Caffyn was influenced by Socinianism on the ground that he expressed no sympathy with that party; and sought to convert its members to his own position.[17] Rather, his Christology had a Melchiorite ring to it, which appealed to a number of General Baptists as it had already done to the continental Anabaptists.

Melchior Hoffman argued that 'the whole seed of Adam ... is cursed and delivered to eternal death.' Accordingly, if Jesus Christ took on this accursed flesh, then 'redemption has not yet happened.' That is to say, 'if it should be established that Christ's flesh was Mary's natural flesh and blood, we would all have to wait for another redeemer, for in such a one we could get no righteousness.' Rather, it was the eternal Word who became incarnate.[18]

How do such views measure up against the Christology of the *Standard Confession*?

> We Believe ... III. That there is one Lord Jesus Christ, by whom are all things, who is the only begotten Son of God, born of the Virgin Mary; yet as truly *David's* Lord and *David's* root, as *David's* Son, and *David's* Offspring, Luke 20.44., Revel. 22.16, whom God freely *sent into the world* (because of his great love unto the World) who *as freely gave himself a ransom for all*, I Tim. 2.5,6. *Tasting death for every man*, Heb. 2.9. *a propitiation for your sins; and not for ours only, but also for the sins of the whole World*, 1 John 2.2.[19]

Here is a tapestry of selected biblical texts which clearly sound the note of general redemption and are but vaguely Christological in any technical sense. William Lumpkin, noting that 'In clarity and definiteness of statement it hardly matches the Particular Baptist Confession of 1644,' generously suggests that 'The poor arrangement of subjects might indicate that the document was drawn up hurriedly'[20]—certainly the drafters were urgently wishing to remove grounds of persecution. The fact remains that, since little concerning Christ's nature was specified, or precluded, a General Baptist of Caffyn's persuasion enjoyed, a good

---

[17] Ibid., 531(c)-32(a).
[18] See Walter Klaassen, ed., *Anabaptism in Outline*, Kitchener ON: Herald Press, 1981, 27-8; translated from F. O. zur Linden, *Melchoir Hoffman: Ein Prophet der Wiedertaufer*, Haarlem: De Erven F. Bohn, 1885, 441-3.
[19] Lumpkin, *Baptist Confessions of Faith*, 225.
[20] Ibid., 221.

deal of doctrinal freedom, while devotees of heresy trials were deprived of effective ammunition. So it proved. At Aylesbury in 1672 Caffyn was charged with blasphemy by the General Baptists of Buckinghamshire.[21] He agreed that saying the eternal Word could die was blasphemous, and confessed his puzzlement concerning Christ's person. Utterly dissatisfied with Caffyn's prevarications on the matter, Thomas Monk, the messenger for Buckinghamshire and Hertfordshire, published *A Cure for the Cankering Error of the New Eutychians: Who (concerning the Truth) Have Erred; Saying That Our Blessed Mediator Did Not Take His Flesh of the Virgin Mary* in the same year. At the Assembly of 1673 Caffyn sought to clip Monk's wings by bringing a charge— apparently ethical—against him, but this failed; neither was there a further attempt to denounce Caffyn's teaching. Monk was undeterred. In fact, along with a group of fifty-four, like-minded General Baptists from Buckinghamshire, Hertfordshire, Bedfordshire, and Oxford, he published the *Orthodox Creed* in 1679.[22] Echoing biblical and patristic authors, they declared:

> We confess and believe, that the Son of God, or the eternal word, is very and true God, having his personal subsistence of the father alone, and yet for ever of himself as God; and of the father as the son, the eternal son of an eternal father; not later in the beginning. There was never any time when he was not, not other in substance ... not a metaphorical, or subordinate God; not a God by office, but a God by nature, coequal, coessential, and coeternal, with the father and the holy ghost ... [T]he second person in the sacred Trinity, took to himself a true, real, and fleshly body, and reasonable soul, being conceived in the fulness of time, by the holy ghost, and born of the virgin Mary, and became very and true man ... [23]

In article XXXVIII they reproduced the Apostles, Nicene, and Athanasian Creeds in full, and expressed their wish that these be 'catechistically opened, and expounded in all Christian families, for the edification of young and old, which might be a means to prevent heresy in doctrine, and practice, these creeds containing all things in a brief manner, that are necessary to be known, fundamentally, in order to our salvation.'[24]

---

[21] As early as 1659 Caffyn had been one of George Fox's targets in *The Great Mistery of the Great Whore Unfolded*, published during that year.

[22] For Monk and the other signatories, see Arnold H. J. Baines, "The signatories of the Orthodox Confession of 1679, *BQ* 18, 1957–1958, 35-42, 74-86, 122-8, 170-8.

[23] Lumpkin, *Baptist Confessions of Faith*, 299-300.

[24] Ibid., 326. In which connection A. C. Underwood has a curious phrase. Having noted the inclusion of the creeds in the Orthodox Confession, and the injunction that they be taught, as something which 'would surprise most Baptists', he continued, 'There is a return to true Baptist principles in the article on Liberty.' See A. C. Underwood, *A History of the English Baptists*, London: Baptist Union Publication Department [Kingsgate Press], 1947, 107. This would appear by implication to sanction that leap from the New Testament to the Reformation, which would deprive Baptists of a good deal of their doctrinal inheritance.

At the General Baptist Assembly of 1691 Caffyn, his orthodoxy challenged by Joseph Wright, the messenger from Maidstone, renewed his subscription to the 1660 Confession, but two years later Wright brought a charge of heresy against him at the Assembly in London. The allegation now was that he was a follower of John Weller, who taught that the Word was a creature and Christ's body the created Word 'turned into flesh, —a Melchiorite-cum-Arian concoction. As put by the churches of the Northern Association (that is, by churches of the Buckinghamshire, London, and Essex areas), the question's being 'Audibly read was universally owned to be an error in the Terms stated.' Whereupon 'Bror Smart charging Bror Caffin with owneing the last aforemenconed Ques. Bror Caffin was acquitted by far the greater part of the Assembly.'[25] The more orthodox General Baptists of Buckinghamshire and Northamptonshire continued to agitate for a further trial, and at the Assembly of April 15, 1698, the questions of:

> Whether the father Distinct or Seperate from the Word and the Holy Host [sic] is the Most High God ... our Lord Jesus Christ is a God only by Deputation as Magistrates and Judges are ... the body of our Lord Jesus Christ Consisting of flesh blood and bones is not of the same substance as ours (to Wit) Mankind[26] were answered in the negative. The same Assembly heard a communication from Northamptonshire as well, one accusing Caffyn of holding that 'the Son of God or the word was not of the Uncreated Nature & substance of the Father neither of the Created Nature & substance of his Mother.' The representatives agreed, with one exception, that such teaching was erroneous, and determined that 'Matthew Caffin shall be admitted to a faire Tryall in our Next Assembly And in the meantime that timely notice thereof be given unto him.'[27]

The trial took place at the Assembly in May 1700. A group of messengers laid the following statement before the Assembly:

> That Christ as he was the word is from the Beginning But in Time that word tooke not on him the Nature of Angells but he took on him the Seed of Abraham & as such is Emmanuell God with us or God manifest in the flesh & he is the word is one with the ffather & the Holy Ghost & as he was God manifest in the flesh so is he Jesus that Tasted Death for Every Man And further whereas that have been & yett are Debates about the most High God wee Conceive he is one Infirmative Unchangable & Eternall Spiritt & Incomprehensable Godhead & doth Subsist in the father ye word & the Holy Ghost.[28]

---

[25] W. T. Whitley, ed., *Minutes of the General Assembly of the General Baptist Churches in England*, London: Baptist Historical Society, 1909, 40.
[26] Ibid., 53.
[27] Ibid., 53-4.
[28] Ibid., 66-7.

During the course of the meeting, it was 'Agreed that the Defence Bror Matthew Caffin made in the Assembly and his Acknowledgment was in the satisfaccon of the Assembly.'[29] Once again, as Gordon noted with pleasure, 'the General Assembly deliberately endorsed latitudinarian opinions in the article of the Trinity and the Incarnation.'[30] It passed 'the very first formal resolution of tolerance for heterodox opinions on the subject of the Trinity, that was ever passed by any Nonconformist union of congregations, in other words, by any cooperating religious body in this country.[31] *The Moderate Trinitarian* (1699)—a plea for doctrinal tolerance by Daniel Allen, Caffyn's friend—was influential in securing this result. Meanwhile, in 1696, a more orthodox General Association had been constituted over against the General Assembly—not, indeed, that it was so orthodox as to risk Calvinism. On the contrary, it disciplined and dismissed Joseph Stennett of Paul's Alley church, London, for erring in that direction, whereupon he associated with Particular Baptists.[32] In 1704 the breach between Association and Assembly was temporarily healed on the basis of a book entitled *The Unity of the* Churches as well as six agreed articles. But when at the following Assembly all representatives were required either to assent to the contents of the book without question or forfeit the right to membership of the Assembly, a breach ensued and another Assembly was constituted.[33]

From the orthodox side, as Robert Torbet points out, the ministers Richard Allen, Benjamin Keach, Mark Key, and Shad Thames had deserted the General for the Particular Baptists between 1679 and 1689.[34] Churches as well as individuals were affected: the General Baptists were excluded by the Particulars at Smarden, Kent, in 1706;[35] at Cranbrook there were three varieties of Baptist causes in 1716; while in 1728 a group of General Baptists of the Folkestone-Hythe church seceded to form a Particular church, which associated with fellow

---

[29] Ibid., 67.

[30] Gordon, 'Matthew Caffyn and General Baptist Latitude,' 532(b).

[31] Alexander Gordon, *Addresses Biographical and Historical*, London: Lindsey Press, 1922, 141. Cf. idem, *Heads of English Unitarian History*, London: Philip Green, 1895, 30. Gordon notes that the Assembly's significant stand for tolerance 'is very often forgotten. It is sometimes forgotten by Baptists, as well as by those who are not Baptists,' *Addresses*, 141. Whether or not they forgot it, Whitley, Underwood, and Torbet, authors of standard Baptist histories, do not mention it.

[32] For Stennett (1633–1713) see *DNB*.

[33] See Whitley, ed., *Minutes of the General Assembly of the General Baptist Churches in England*, xx-xxiii.

[34] Robert G. Torbet, *A History of the Baptists*, Valley Forge PA: Judson Press, 1950, 64. For Keach (1640–1704) see *DNB*. See further Raymond Brown, *The English Baptists of the Eighteenth Century*, London: Baptist Historical Society, 1986, ch. 2.

[35] See Brian A. Packer, *The Unitarian Heritage in Kent*, London: London District and South Eastern Provincial Assembly of the Unitarian and Free Christian Churches [Incorporated], 1991, 10. Anon., 'Baptists in the Weald,' *BQ* 2 (1924–1925): 374. Those described as 'semi-unitarians' of Biddenden, Frittenden, and Headcorn seceded from the Smarden church in 1677.

believers in Canterbury. Michael Bligh left Bessels Green General Baptist Church to form a Particular cause at Sevenoaks in the 1740s, while in 1762 Henry Booker, influenced by George Whitefield's teaching, began to preach in such a way as to displease the General Baptists of Ditchling, with the result that he was ejected and founded in 1763 a Particular Baptist church, Wivelsfield (where he was born). In the following year a former minister at Ditchling, John Simmonds, was called as pastor.[36] He soon disputed with his fellow preacher, Booker, and appeared to take an Arian line. He brought a case against booker to the Church Meeting in March 1767, but the church sided with Booker, and in June, 'Agreed to silence John Simons from preaching in our meetings by the Consent of the Church untill Such time as Reconciled with the Church.'[37] Conversely, in October 1793, nineteen members of the Particular Baptist church at Bond Street, Brighton, who had been led by one of their number, William Stevens, to embrace the views of the Universalist Elhanan Winchester, were excommunicated, constituted a General Baptist church, and eventually opened their own building in New Road in August 1820.[38]

With the passage of time the General Baptists—apart from those evangelical Arminians who joined Dan Taylor's New Connexion of 1770[39]—inclined more and more to Unitarianism, so that by the year 1846 Beard could note twenty-four Unitarian Baptist churches among the 'Anti-Trinitarian Congregations and Ministers in England and Scotland', and five in Wales. The majority of these were in Kent and Sussex.[40] Such a doctrinal change played into the hands of C. H. Spurgeon who, with a flourish of splendidly ironical rhetoric, declared:

---

[36] Frank Buffard, *Kent and Sussex Baptist Associations* (privately published, 1963) 2728; Ralph F. Chambers, *The Strict Baptist Chapels of England. II. The Chapels of Sussex*, privately printed, n.d., 15-16.

[37] *A Transcription of the Church Book of Wivelsfield, 1763–1817*, by Leonard J. Macguire, privately published, 1984, 10-11. It would appear that R. F. Chambers, *Sussex*, 16, errs in dating this dispute 1765. The minutes make clear that the church was in close touch with Dr. John Gill throughout its several early upsets.

[38] Philip Huxtable Bliss, 'A Brief History of the Six Member Churches of the Sussex Unitarian Union', presidential address to the General Baptist Assembly, 1968, typescript, 11; *The Unitarian Heritage*, Sheffield, 1986, 58; John Rowland, *The Story of Brighton Unitarian Church*, London: the Lindsey Press, 1972, 5. The historian of the Strict Baptist chapels simply records that Thomas Vine, called to the pastorate of Salem, Bond Street, in 1790 'proved unfaithful, and after three years the church asked him to resign, which he did, and left, taking with him some of the members and weakening the church.' Chambers, *The Strict Baptist Chapels of England. II. The Chapels of Sussex*, 19.

[39] For Taylor (1738–1816), see ODNB. The New Connexion severed its link with the General Baptist Assembly when in 1802 the latter body admitted a universalist church having unbaptized members in its midst. See 'Baptists in the Weald,' 380.

[40] J. R. Beard, ed., *Unitarianism Exhibited in Its Actual Condition*, London: Simpkin, Marshall, 1846, 330-37. For the parallel story of Presbyterianism in England, see Alan P. F. Sell, *Dissenting Thought and the Life of the Churches. Studies in an English Tradition*, Lewiston NY: Edwin Mellen Press, 1990, ch. 5.

> Now, we know, at the present time, certain ancient chapels shut up, with grass growing in the front of them, and over the door of them is the *name Unitarian Baptist Chapel*. Although it has been said that he is a benefactor of his race who makes two blades of grow where only one grew before, we have no desire to empty our pews in order to grow more grass. We have in our eye certain other chapels, not yet arrived at that consummation, where the spiders are dwelling in delightful quietude, in which the pews are more numerous than the people, and although an endowment keeps the minister's mouth open, there are but few open ears for him to address.[41]

It is more than likely that Spurgeon here committed the fallacy of incomplete enumeration, for very rarely is doctrinal change alone sufficient to decimate a church; it is even possible that it had nothing to do with the decline in the church concerned, in which case he has committed the fallacy of the false cause. Moreover, the implication that only churches in the Arminian-Arian-Unitarian line could flounder (and some of them did not, while new General Baptist chapels were opened at Cranbrook in 1807, Headcorn in 1819 and Dover in 1820[42]) needs seriously to be questioned. J. M. Cramp's mournful eulogy, 'The loss *of life* followed the obscuration *of light*', can be shown to apply equally (and just as misleadingly) to some Particular Baptist causes.[43] As a Baptist writer has said, 'if the General Baptist churches were often liable to heresy, the Particular Baptists were liable to immorality, and again and again ministers gave scandal.'[44] Thus the church which Daniel Gillard began at Hammersmith 'had to dissolve, owing to his conduct.'[45] Underwood, among others, have named the doctrinal cause 'antinomianism',[46] and for practical antinomianism David Crosley reigned supreme in Baptist demonology (though he did manage—or, rather, was enabled—to end his days as 'a trophy of grace').[47]

Less morally scandalous heresy also beset Particular Baptists. A fairly mild, yet significant form of this is seen in the *Somerset Confession* of 1656, whose principal architect, Thomas Collier, was the lay apostle to the West country.[48]

---

[41] C. H. Spurgeon, *An All-Round Ministry. Addresses to Ministers and Students* (1900), London: The Banner of Truth Trust, 1960, 94-5. For Spurgeon (1834–1892), see ODNB. It will be noted that I speak of 'doctrinal change,' not of 'declension' or 'development' – still less do I refer to what some branded 'the Socinian blight'.

[42] See Brian A. Packer, *the Unitarian Heritage in Kent*, 15.

[43] J. M. Cramp, *Baptist History: From the Foundation of the Christian Church to the Present Time*, London: Elliot Stock, 1871, 434.

[44] Anon., 'Baptists in East Kent,'186. One could wish, however, for more evidence to justify the 'again and again.' Cf. my comment against W. T. Whitley in *The Great Debate. Calvinism, Arminianism, and Salvation*, (1982), Eugene, OR: Wipf & Stock, 1998, 46.

[45] Ibid., 187.

[46] A. C. Underwood, *A History of the English Baptists*, London: Baptist Union, 1947), 128.

[47] See further Frederick Overend, *History of the Ebenezer Baptist Church Bacup*, London: Kingsgate Press, 1912, pt. 2, ch. 1; cf. W. T. Whitley, *Baptists of North-West England*, London: Kingsgate Press, 1913, 83.

[48] For Collier (fl. 1691) see ODNB.

Under challenge from the Quakers, the Baptists wished to demonstrate that their doctrine was Calvinistic and not out of accord with that of the framers of the *London Confession* of 1644, as well as to dissuade those who forsook sound doctrine 'under glorious notions of spiritualness and holiness.'[49] Noting that 'The Calvinism of the Western Association was not of a rigid type', Lumpkin suggested that a further objective may have been to enable Particular and General Baptists of the region to stand together, the first Baptist confession to attempt this.[50] Alexander Gordon declared:

> [I]t is remarkable that this confession, while strongly affirming the Calvinistic doctrine of election , is absolutely silent on the Trinity, the eternal sonship, the co-equality of the Father and Son, and the satisfaction of divine justice by the death of Christ.[51]

These points must be conceded, though Gordon does not wish to build an argument on silence. He further records that at first he was disinclined not to take the omissions as implying denials on the ground that the Confession does affirm in article XIII, 'We believe that Jesus Christ is truly God. ... ' But Gordon, following William Grigge, came to the conclusion that these words refer to Christ's office, not to his essence, and hence, 'The confession is one which, so far as its Christology goes, an Arian might subscribe. ... We must now add to the tale of Baptist heretics not alone Collier himself, but the sixteen churches whose representatives pledged themselves to his confession.'[52] I see no necessity to follow Gordon's reading of article XIII, but am convinced that there are doctrinal silences at the places specified which could only hinder the objective of demonstrating agreement with the London Confession, and might indicate either inner-Baptist ecumenical concern or doctrinal hesitancy at crucial points, or both.

Particular Baptist Associations, no less than those of the General Baptists, reveal a propensity for division on doctrinal grounds. The Norfolk and Suffolk Association of Baptist Churches, founded in 1771, entrusted to George Wright of Beccles the task of writing its 1829 'Circular Letter.' Wright's Letter was discussed at the Annual Meeting of the Association at Stradbroke in June of the same year, and a controversy erupted. Wright feared that Arminian teaching was infiltrating the churches, and that this led to 'the concealing of the discriminating doctrines of the Gospel in the public ministry.' While Wright did not point a finger in any specific direction, it became clear that he and his followers could no longer live within the original Association. Accordingly, at

---

[49] Epistle dedicatory.
[50] Lumpkin, *Baptists Confessions of Faith*, 201-202.
[51] A. Gordon, 'Unitarian Baptists,' *The Christian Life*, 28 January 1988, 45(a).
[52] Ibid.

Grundisburgh in September 1829, the New Suffolk, and Norfolk Association (now the Suffolk and Norfolk Association of Strict Baptist Churches) was constituted in order "To preserve in an Association of Baptist Churches in this County, the doctrine of the Cross, uncorrupted by a system which can rest on no basis but that of General Redemption and Universal Salvation."[53] By contrast the New Association staunchly denied, "that saving faith is the duty of all men."[54]

But with the reference to universal salvation and duty of faith, we come to one of two further inner-Baptist doctrinal disputes—one coming down from the eighteenth century, the other from the nineteenth. The first concerned the obligation to, and the manner of, preaching the Gospel, and the question of whether all hearers of the Word have a duty to receive Christ. The second concerned the doctrine of the eternal generation of the Son. In both cases, it is the Calvinistic Baptists who were involved.

Evidence has already been adduced to show that both Particular and General Baptist churches could suffer decline. Such statistics as are available suggest that, whereas there were some 220 Particular causes in England in 1715, by 1750 the number had dwindled to about 150. As with General Baptists and other Old Dissenters, the causes of this decline were various: local factions and party spirit, demographic changes, torpor after the heady pre-Toleration days of struggle for Baptist identity among them. Nor can we rule out the possibility that scholastic Calvinism purveyed in sufficiently deadening ways may stifle zeal. We must not, however, commit Spurgeon's fallacies in reverse. That there was decline—and that many Particular Baptist pastors lamented "the decay of practical and vital godliness"[55]—cannot be denied. Happily, by 1798 Particular Baptist churches numbered 361, and of these, 320 had pastors.[56] Why the reversal of the downward trend? In a word, evangelization. Though we should

---

[53] See S. Wolstenholme, *These Hundred and Fifty Years. A Commemorative Momento* [sic] *of the Suffolk and Norfolk Association of Strict Baptist Churches, 1830–1980* (1980) 3; John Doggett, 'Having obtained help of God ... ,' *Grace Magazine* no. 140, January 1983, 1.

[54] W. Reynolds et al., *Circular Letter to the Baptist Churches of Suffolk and Norfolk*, Grundisburgh, 1829, 2.

[55] Benjamin Wallin, *The Christian Life. In Divers of Its Branches, Described and Recommended*, London, 1746, 2:ix. Perhaps, therefore, Kenneth Dix exaggerates the contrast between the Particular Baptists and others: 'For the PBs the eighteenth century was not at any point a period of disaster, as it was for both the General Baptists and the English Presbyterians.' See his 'Particular Baptists and Strict Baptists. A Historical Survey,' *The Strict Baptist Historical Society Annual Report and Bulletin*, 13, 1976, 4-5.

[56] See K. Dix, 'Particular Baptists and Strict Baptists,' 5, citing John Rippon, *The Baptist Annual Register*, 1798, 1-40. See further on the declension and the statistics, Michael A. G. Haykin, '"A Habitation of God, though the Spirit," John Sutcliff (1752–1814) and the Revitalization of Calvinistic Baptists in the Late Eighteenth Century,' *BQ* XXXIV no. 7, July 1992, 304-19; idem, 'The Baptist Identity: A View from the Eighteenth Century,' *Evangelical Quarterly* LVII, 1995, 137-52.

dishonor the memory of Alvery Jackson, Benjamin Beddome, and others who in the earlier years of the eighteenth century were no strangers to revival in their pastorates if we were to a paint too gloomy of those decades, it cannot be denied that when Baptists—like others—caught the missionary spirit, their strength at home increased and their theology underwent a subtle change. That some resisted the change is clear from the disputes of the time.

To a considerable extent the disputes revolved around the question of the free offer of the Gospel, and the question of to what extent sinners had a duty to respond positively to it. A focal point of the Baptist debate in the mid-eighteenth century was the teaching of John Brine and John Gill, both of whom had been influenced by John Skepp's book of 1722 (behind which stood the Independent Joseph Hussey's *God's Operations of Grace but No Offers of Grace* [1707], which Gill republished in 175 l):[57] *The divine energy: or the efficacious operations of the Spirit of God in the soul of man, in his effectual calling and conversion: stated, proved and vindicated. Wherein the real weakness and insufficiency of moral persuasion, without the super-addition of the exceeding greatness of God's power for faith and conversion to God, are fully evinced. Being an antidote against the Pelagian plague.*

In the meantime, Matthias Maurice of Rothwell had published *The Modern Question* (1737), in which he proclaimed the duty of those who heard the Word preached to close with Christ. Gill and Brine stoutly denounced this teaching, fearing the encroachment of Arminian universalism. Gill was widely understood not 'to address unconverted sinners, nor to enforce the invitations of the gospel,'[58] and Spurgeon, while noting that some of Gill's utterances on practical godliness had prompted an hyper-Calvinist to charge him (of all people!) with Arminianism, nevertheless declared that this theology, together with that of Brine, 'chilled many churches to their very soul, for it has led them to omit the free invitations of the gospel, and to deny that it is the duty of

---

[57] Skepp had preceded Brine at Curriers' Hall. See further on this entire subject, Alan P. F. Sell, *The Great Debate*, ch. 3. For Gill (1697–1771) and Brine (1703–1765) see ODNB. For Hussey (1659–1726) see Geoffrey F. Nuttall, 'Northamptonshire and the Modem Question: a Turning Point in Eighteenth-Century Dissent,' *Journal of Theological Studies*, n.s. VII, 1965, 101-23; idem, 'Cambridge Nonconformity 1660–1710: from Holcroft to Hussey,' *The Journal of the United Reformed Church History Society* I no. 9, 1977, 241-58; Sell, *The Great Debate*, 52-54.

[58] Walter Wilson, *The History and Antiquities of Dissenting Churches and Meeting Houses in London, &c.*, London, 1808, IV, 222. Cf. Cramp, *Baptist History*, 443: Gill 'abstained from personal addresses to sinners, by inviting them to the Saviour, and satisfied himself with declaring their guilt and doom, and the necessity of a change of heart. It is not surprising that the congregation declined under such a ministry.' Gill, however, did rather more than Cramp suggests but, no doubt, not as much as he would have liked. For Maurice (1684–1738) see *The Dictionary of Welsh Biography*, London: Honourable Society of Cymmrodorion, 1959; Thomas Rees, *History of Protestant Nonconformity in Wales*, London: Snow, 1883, 302-305; G. F. Nuttall, 'Northamptonshire and the Modem Question'; Sell, *The Great Debate*, 59, 78-79.

sinners to believe in Jesus.'[59] Some recent Baptist scholars have sought to temper this doleful estimate of Gill. Thomas J. Nettles has gone so far as to claim that Gill believed that all people were under obligation to repent of sin, and that all hearers of the gospel had a duty to believe it.[60] But this would seem to allow the pendulum to swing too far in the opposite direction, for while Gill could insist that, 'The gospel of salvation ... declares ... that whoever believes in [Christ] shall be saved: this is the gospel every faithful minister preaches, and every sensible sinner desires to hear,'[61] on other occasions, especially when in polemical, anti-Arminian, mood—against Whitby, for example—Gill wrote in terms which are too definite to admit of misinterpretation: 'I know of none [i.e. texts of Scripture], that exhort and command all men ... to repent, and believe in Christ for salvation.' Again, he denied that, 'God calls all those to faith and repentance, and conversion, who have a knowledge of the divine will, a sense of sin, a dread of punishment, and some hopes of pardon: for the devils have all these but the last, whom he never calls to faith and repentance.'[62] Positively, he contended for prevenient, enabling grace: 'Men are required to believe in Christ, to love the Lord with all their heart ... to keep the whole law of God; but it does not follow that they are able of themselves to do all these things.'[63]

Whatever the final judgment on Gill and his fellow High Calvinists (and we should not assume either that they saw exactly eye-to-eye on all points of doctrine,[64] or that their views necessarily precluded cooperation with ministers on the opposite side of the argument[65]), there can be no doubt that many felt that

---

[59] Susannah Spurgeon and J. W Harrald, eds., *C. H. Spurgeon's Autobiography*, London: Passmore and Alabaster, 1899–1900, I, 310.

[60] Thomas J. Nettles, *By His Grace and for His Glory. A Historical, Theological, and Practical Study of the Doctrines of Grace in Baptist Life*, Grand Rapids MI: Baker Book House, 1986, 107. Timothy George is somewhat more cautious. See his paper on Gill in Timothy George and David S. Dockery, eds., *Baptist Theologians*, Nashville TN: Broadman Press, 1990, 93.

[61] John Gill, *A Complete Body of Doctrinal and Practical Divinity* (1839), Grand Rapids MI: Baker Book House, 1978, II, 668.

[62] John Gill, *The Cause of God and Truth*, repr., Grand Rapids MI: Sovereign Grace Publishers, 1971, 167(a), 179(a).

[63] Ibid., 35(a). For a study of Gill's preaching, see Peter Naylor, *Picking up a Pin for the Lord. English Particular Baptists from 1688 to the Early Nineteenth Century*, London: Grace Publications, 1992, ch. 11. For Daniel Whitby (1638–1726), see ODNB.

[64] Indeed, John Johnson's hyper-Calvinism was too much even for Brine. Johnson, raised a General Baptist, became minister at Byrom Street Particular Baptist chapel, Liverpool, in 1741, seceding with his followers in 1747 to form a new denomination, the Johnsonian Baptists, which were represented in northwest England in East Anglia. For Johnson (1706–1791) see ODNB; Raymond Brown, *The English Baptists of the Eighteenth Century*, 86.

[65] E.g., as Kenneth Dix properly reminds us, Joseph Stennett sat with both Brine and Gill on the Baptist board. See 'Particular Baptists and Strict Baptists,' 3. On the other hand, John Stevens, author of the anti-Fuller work, *Help for the True Disciples of Immanuel* (1803), made his witness in noncooperative isolation. See anon., *Memoirs of Mr. John Stevens*, London, 1848, 3 1; Robert Oliver, 'John Stevens. A Forgotten Leader,' *Grace Magazine* no. 149, November 1983, 2-7.

the gospel was being proclaimed in a stultifying manner. This was unquestionably Andrew Fuller's view, and he expected a far from easy ride in challenging the practice of his elders. As he confided to his diary in October 1784, 'I feel some pain at the thought of being about to publish on the obligations of men to believe in Christ, fearing I shall hereby expose myself to a good deal of abuse, which is disagreeable to the flesh.'[66] But publish he eventually did, and in the *Gospel Worthy of All Acceptation* (ca. 1785), he countered the opinions of Gill and Brine on duty faith,[67] and boldly proved, 'that faith in Christ is the duty of all men who hear, or have opportunity to hear, the gospel.'[68] He thereby gave impetus both to the modem missionary movement, and also that gradual softening of the sharper edges of scholastic Calvinism which was eventually to facilitate the union of the majority of the Particular Baptists with the evangelical Arminians of the New Connexion to form the Baptist Union.[69]

That the Strict and Particular Baptists who could not take this road were not immune to internal doctrinal differences is clear from the continuing strife engendered by the 'duty faith' question.[70] The line derived from Gill, Brine, and others, reinforced by the powerful views of such an Independent as William Huntington,[71] was, as we have seen, evidenced in the declaration of the New Association of Norfolk and Suffolk of 1829, and reached its terminus (I say neither 'nemesis' nor 'fruition') among the Gospel Standard Baptists, whose leaders were William, Gadsby; John Warburton; John Kershaw; the erstwhile Anglican, J. C Philpot; and James Wells of the Surrey Tabernacle.[72] The comment on Gadsby is applicable to them all: 'Mr. G. always considered, and often stated

---

[66] John Ryland, *The Work of Faith, the Labour of Love and the Patience or Hope Illustrated in the Life and Death of Andrew Fuller*, London, 1816, 206. For Fuller (1754–1815) see ODNB; Sell, *The Great Debate*, 83-87, 93-94, 130-33.

[67] See *The Complete Works of the Rev. Andrew Fuller*, London: Holdsworth and Ball, 1831, II, 26, 50-59, 67.

[68] Ibid., 22ff.

[69] See Ernest A. Payne, *The Baptist Union. A Short History*, London: Carey Kingsgate Press, 1958.

[70] See Robert Oliver, 'The significance of Strict Baptist attitudes towards duty faith in the nineteenth century,' *Strict Baptist Historical Society Bulletin* 20, 1993; Sell, *The Great Debate*, 93-94, 129-30, 133; Kenneth Dix, *English Strict and Particular Baptists in the Nineteenth Century*, Didcot: Baptist Historical Society for the Strict Baptist Historical Society, 2001, *passim*.

[71] For Huntington (1745–1813), see ODNB; W. Huntington, *The Kingdom of Heaven Taken by Prayer* (1784), Redhill: Sovereign Grace Union, 1966; T. Wright, *The Life of William Huntington, S.S.*, London: Farncombe, 1909; K. Dix, op.cit., ch 1.

[72] For Gadsby (1773–1813) see ODNB; Sell, *The Great Debate*, passim. For Warburton (1776–1857) see *Mercies of a Covenant God. Being an Account of Some of the Lord's Dealings in Providence and Grace with John Warburton, Minister of the Gospel, Trowbridge* (1837) (Schwengel PA: Reiner Publications, 197 1). For Kershaw (1792–1870) see *John Kershaw. The Autobiography of an Eminent Lancashire Preacher* (1870), Sheffield: Gospel Tidings Publications, 1968. For Philpot (1802–1869) see J. H. Philpot, *The Seceders*, 2 vols., 1930–1932; for Wells (1803–1870), see *A Concise Account of the Experience of James Wells*, London: C. J. Farncombe, 1840. For all of these see K. Dix, op.cit.

publicly, that Andrew Fuller was the greatest enemy the church of God every had, as his sentiments were so much cloaked with the sheep's clothing.'[73] Not surprisingly, article XXVI of the Gospel Standard Baptists stated, 'We deny duty faith and duty repentance—these terms signifying that it is very man's duty to spiritually and savingly repent and believe. ... [W]e reject the doctrine that men in a state of nature should be exhorted to believe in or turn to God.' In 1878, after lively discussion, four new articles (XXXII–XXXV) were added, the burden of which was:

> That for ministers in the present day to address unconverted persons, or indiscriminately all in a mixed congregation, calling upon them savingly to repent, believe, and receive Christ, or perform any other acts dependent upon the new creative power of the Holy Ghost, is on the one hand, to imply creature power, and, on the other, to deny the doctrine of special redemption. (article XXXIII)

A fresh lease of life was given to the controversy when, in 1921, William Wileman (1848–1944), who had been associated with the *Gospel Standard* committee and magazine at the time the added articles were devised, published a critique of the articles and of the motives of those who framed them. J. K. Popham, editor of the *Gospel Standard*, reprinted his earlier defense of the articles, and pieces on either side of the argument still appear from time to time.[74]

Turning with some relief from the Baptists' anxieties over duty of faith and the free offer of the Gospel, we come to our second example of an inner-Calvinistic-Baptist doctrinal dispute: that concerning the eternal generation of the Son; and we may be brief. From time to time during the eighteenth century, the doctrine surfaced that Christ's Sonship is a function of his human nature, not his divine; hence, the second person of the Trinity is not eternally Son (though, oddly, the first person is eternally Father). In the early years of the nineteenth century the Calvinistic Baptist pastor John Stevens embraced this teaching, to

---

[73] *A Memoir of the late Mr William Gadsby*, in Gadsby's Works I, 1870, 33n.

[74] See further, S. F. Paul, *Historical Sketch of the Gospel Standard Baptists*, London: Gospel Standard Publications, 1945; B. A. Ramsbottom, *The History of The Gospel Standard Magazine, 1835–1985*, Carshalton, Surrey: Gospel Standard Societies, 1985, 60-61; J. K. Popham, 'Preaching the Gospel.' *The Gospel Standard*, December 1906; idem, 'An Address to the Unconverted and Such as Have No Distinct Knowledge of God or of Themselves,' *The Gospel Standard*, January 1908; idem, 'An opening word,' *The Gospel Standard*, January 1926, wherein he defends the view that the Gospel Standard Baptists 'are a definite, distinct, and separate body, or denomination,' 9; William Wileman, 'The Secret History of the Four 'Added' Articles: 32, 33, 34, 35,' *The Christian's Pathway* XXVI, November 1921: 206-10; B. J. Honeysett, 'The Ill-fated Articles,' *Reformation Today* no. 2 (Summer 1960): 23-30, repr. as *How to Address Unbelievers* (n.d.). For James Kidwell Popham (1847–1937), see B. A. Ramsbottom, *The History of The Gospel Standard Magazine, 1835–1985*, 191-204.

the consternation of other pastors. He further taught that, Christ's human soul existed prior to the incarnation, and that any reference to a preexistent Son must refer to Christ's humanity as yet to be enfleshed.

These and opposing views began to spread, but it was J. C. Philpot who brought the debate out into the open with an article in the *Gospel Standard for 1844*. In the previous year Charles Waters Banks had founded *The Earthen Vessel* and while he himself upheld the doctrine of the eternal generation of the Son, he permitted alternative views to be published in his journal, and his successor editors either did not accept the doctrine or did not declare themselves upon it. In a subsequent article, Philpot set out to refute the view that the doctrine was (in words drawn from *The Earthen Vessel* of November 1860) 'a piece of twaddle', 'a metaphysical conceit,'etc., etc.—'as if the true and proper Sonship of Jesus, as the only begotten of the Father, were a lying tale.'[75] The longevity and disruptiveness of the dispute is shown in the fact that in 1926 J. K. Popham could say regarding Philpot's case, 'From that day to this the breach has remained open, and the two parties have been known as the *"Gospel Standard"* Churches and the *"Earthen Vessel"* Churches, respectively, and as holding the exact opposite views on that fundamental doctrine.'[76]

So concerned were the Gospel Standard leaders to preserve the purity of proclamation of their denomination that in 1926 they determined that only those preachers who upheld the agreed doctrinal petitions and submitted a satisfactory account of their call to preach should have the pulpits of *Gospel Standard* churches opened to them. This policy drew fire from a number of quarters, not least from some pastors and preachers sympathetic to *Gospel Standard* views. Alfred Dye, for example, strongly objected to a list of approved preachers:

> To me a Committee in London or elsewhere proposing Rules and deciding cases belonging to any Church or minister is too near a relation to *a Jewish Sanhedrim* [sic].And indeed there must be something radically wrong when *more* than *three* parts out of the four of Churches and ministers in the G. S. Connection are not seen upon the List of Supplies; and the fact is, so many stringent Rules betray *weakness* and not *strength*.[77]

The illustrations provided of inner-Baptist doctrinal debate, though necessarily selective, invite a few reflections. First, it has become clear that within the English Baptist tradition(s) a variety of positions have been adopted on fundamental Christian doctrines. If the old General Baptists emerged from the Caffyn case as

---

[75] Repr. in J. C. Philpot, *The True, Proper and Eternal Sonship of the Lord Jesus Christ, the Only-Begotten Son of God*, (1861), Harpenden: Gospel Standard Baptist Trust, 1962, 84.

[76] Philpot, 'An Opening Word,' 13. See further on this doctrinal (and journalistic) maze, Paul, *Historical Sketch of the Gospel Standard Baptists*, ch. 5.

[77] A. Dye, letter to the editor, *The Christian's Pathway* XXXI, 1926, 42. See further Alan P. F. Sell, *Alfred Dye, Minister of the Gospel*, London: Fauconberg Press, 1974, ch. 5.

those most tolerant of views they would not formally endorse, the Gospel Standard Baptists exemplified the most rigorist posture *vis-à-vis* doctrines and interpretations deemed by them essential. To recall Forsyth's poles from which I set out, if the Arminians were keenest not to flatten faith, the Gospel Standard leaders were most anxious not to forsake the faith for 'another gospel.'

Secondly, we have seen that in Baptist circles, the 'faith once delivered' has, as far as its doctrinal expression is concerned, undergone changes in a number of directions. Not only did many General Baptists become Unitarians, and many Particulars become hyper-Calvinists (if those proclaiming at least doctrinal antinomianism, or denying "duty faith," may thus be designated), but the converging center parties, which came together in the Baptist Union, could do so only on the basis of a measure of Calvinist-Arminian accommodation. The extent of this is clearly seen if we juxtapose examples of regional and national affirmations. In 1779 the Kent and Sussex Association of Particular Baptist Churches declared:

> We, the ministers and messengers of the Baptist denomination representing our respective churches, holding the Doctrines of personal election, particular redemption, effectual vocation and the final perseverance of the Saints, being met together at Ashford in Kent this second day of March 1779 have entered the several churches we represent into an Association.

In 1904, following the union nationally of the Particular with the New Connexion Baptists, the Kent and Sussex Association revised its terms of membership in doctrinally significant ways, providing:

> That this Kent and Sussex Association consist only of Evangelical Churches practising believer's baptism, and whose doctrinal basis includes the Divine authority of the Holy Scripture, the Doctrine of the Trinity, the Divine abhorrence and punishment of sin, the deity and the atoning sacrificial death of Christ, regeneration by the Holy Ghost, justification by faith and the obligation to live a righteous and godly life.[78]

As for the national General Union itself, although its founding doctrinal basis of 1813 had been Calvinistic in tone, its revised constitution of 1832 specified its first objective thus: 'To extend brotherly love and union among the Baptist ministers and churches who agree in the sentiments usually denominated evangelical.' This facilitated the entry of the New Connexion churches into the Union. As Ernest Payne remarked, '"Fullerism" had provided a bridge between the Particular Baptist churches and those of the New Connexion of the General Baptists.'[79]

---

[78] See Frank Buffard, *Kent and Sussex Baptist Associations*, 50: 123-24; E. Bruce Hardy, 'Association life in Kent and Sussex, 1770-1950,' BQ XXVII no. 4, 173, 181.

[79] Payne, *The Baptist Union*, 61.

I cannot find, however, that English Baptists have engaged in corporate reflection upon what might be called a doctrine of doctrinal development, which would do more than simply assert the fact of doctrinal modification (even if only of expression rather than of substance—a big 'if'), but seek to explain it and consider what possible criteria there might be for justifying it. In this Baptists are by no means alone, and I shall revert to this point in the conclusion of this paper. Similarly, the status of confessions of faith might be thought to require theological consideration. For example, there is on the face of it a great gulf separating the position of the Gospel Standard Baptists from Henry Cook, who declared, 'Membership in the Church of Christ is not restricted to those who worship in a specified way or accept a detailed theological creed; it is available for all who look to Christ as their Saviour and, like Peter, make to Him the great Confession.'[80] The operative word, of course, is 'detailed', and Cook seemed to have the New Testament on his side with his implication that church members comprise those who are babes on milk and older hands on strong doctrinal meat.

But what of those who speak officially in the name of the Gospel? This was a particular concern of the Gospel Standard Baptists, and it is a question which many mainline denominations answer in a vague way, if at all. To pose the question in another way, did Ernest Payne sufficiently guard his flank when, with reference to the growth of Fullerism between 1780 and 1830, he asserted that apart from the Strict Baptist churches,

> The main stream of Baptist life was ... to be found in those fellowships which had learned the dangers of heresy hunting and had come to believe in a more liberal and tolerant attitude, fellowships which had recognized that a profession of orthodoxy in belief is no guarantee of the fruits of the Spirit?[81]

Of course, to profess orthodoxy is not necessarily to display the fruit of the Spirit. No doubt heresy hunting is a messy pursuit, and tolerance within the Church is essential, but Payne raised the question, which he did not there address, of the permissible degrees of tolerance within the Church. He appeared to be sailing close to Forsyth's liberal pole, and perhaps needs to be balanced by the protest of Joseph Angus: 'We must have beliefs or we are not Christians. We must have beliefs—great principles of truth and life—or we cannot have Christian churches.[82] Or, as Forsyth himself put it, '[A] Christianity which would exclude none has no power to include the world.'[83]

---

[80] H. Cook, *What Baptists Stand For*, (1947), London: Carey Kingsgate Press, 1964 60.
[81] Payne, *The Fellowship of Believers*, 104.
[82] J. Angus, *Freeman*, 13 April 1885.
[83] P. T. Forsyth, *The Work of Christ*, London: Independent Press, 1938, 62.

Thirdly, it is interesting to note a matter over which Baptists *en bloc* have *not* seceded from one another, namely, the authority of Scripture. It may be that those who might have seceded on this issue were already in one of the more conservative groupings of Baptists. However that may be, we do not have in England the situation which prevails in Canada, for example, where the *raison d'être* of the Fellowship Baptist denomination over against the Baptist Convention of Ontario and Quebec is the former's requirement of belief in biblical inerrancy.[84] Conversely, there is some evidence to show that if a secession did not occur among the most numerous body of Baptists, conservative attitudes to Scripture, which came to the fore within the Baptist Union during the Downgrade Controversy of the 1870s, coupled with the strength of Unitarian views among the old General Baptists of Kent and Sussex, thwarted the attempts of Henry Solly and his New Connexion colleagues John Clifford and Dawson Burns to bring the old General Baptists into the Baptist Union.[85]

Finally, we have seen that Baptists of all persuasions have historically been more than willing to state the belief commonly held among them in confessional form, and they have at times required subscription to their confessions. They have not, however, spoken in terms of the utility of confessions as 'guardians' of the faith. In this connection Robert Hall's outburst against an Anglican author enshrined the Baptists' typical position:

> It is with peculiar effrontery that this author insists on subscription to articles as a sufficient security for the purity of religious instruction, when it is the professed object of his work to recall his contemporaries to that purity.... A long course of experience has clearly demonstrated the inefficacy of creeds and confessions to perpetuate religious belief. Of this the only faithful depository is, not that which is 'written with ink', but on the 'fleshly tables of the heart.'[86]

We have further seen that Baptists have been willing to dissent from those deemed to be in error, and on occasion have disciplined them. It must, however, be said that Baptists do not seem to have propounded a clear theology of the practice of doctrinal discipline as it concerns the relations between assemblies or associations, local churches and individuals. Time and again the practical result of doctrinal difference has been secession—as if to say that when the doctrinal

---

[84] See James A. Beverley, 'Tensions in Canadian Baptist Theology, 1975–1987,' in Jarold K. Zeman, ed., *Costly Vision. The Baptist Pilgrimage in Canada*, Burlington ON: Welch Publishing Co., 1988, 223-4.

[85] See Ian Sellers, 'The Rev. Henry Solly and the General Baptists,' *Transactions of the Unitarian Historical Society* XIX no. 3, April 1989, 195-6.

[86] Olinthus Gregory, ed., *The Works of Robert Hall, A.M.*, London: Henry G. Bohn, 1850, IV, 62. Hall here reviews *Zeal without Innovation* (1808). For Hall (1764–1831), see ODNB.

crunch comes, the will of the disaffected concerning doctrine takes precedence over the obligation of maintaining wider fellowship. But this brings us to polity.

II

It would be a serious mistake to suppose that among Baptists (or among heirs of Old Dissent generally) polity is to doctrine as rules are to constitution. On the contrary, the polity is doctrinal; it is ecclesiology. In particular, it is a churchly working out of such interrelated themes as the covenanted saints of God, the regenerating power of the Spirit, and the Lordship of Christ. General, no less than Particular Baptists have classically been in accord on this matter. Thus to John Smyth, Jesus Christ was, 'the only King, Priest, & Prophet of his Church',[87] and Smyth's repeated citing of Matthew 18:20, 'For where two or three are gathered together in my name, there am I in the midst of them', clearly indicated his understanding of the saints as visibly gathered by and under Christ. This lofty theme has been transposed into a lower key by the time we reach Joseph Angus in the nineteenth century. Admittedly, he was replying to Thomas Chalmers's defense of church establishments, but at the head of a chapter, 'Of the principles and prospects of the voluntary system', he invoked Locke on the church as, 'a voluntary society of men, joining themselves together of their own accord, in order to the public worshipping of God, in such a manner as they judge acceptable to him and effectual to the salvation of their souls', and argued that voluntaryism is consistent with Scripture, and 'sufficient under the blessing of the Divine Spirit, to secure the maintenance and ultimate diffusion of truth.'[88] However, in a subsequent work Angus denied that Christian voluntaryism is 'the authority of self will', and argued for the theocratic nature of the Church, whose members are 'the sons and daughters of the Lord Almighty.'[89]

In the mid-twentieth century we find Arthur Dakin asserting the Lordship of Christ in no uncertain terms: 'The true head of the church is the Lord Jesus Himself, who through the Holy Spirit makes His will known as the members seek it.'[90] Henry Cook concurred: 'The Church ... is 'the holy society of believers in our Lord Jesus Christ which He founded.' But its relation to Him is more than historical; it is experimental, and He still is what He always was, the Church's

---

[87] W. T. Whitley, ed., *The Works of John Smyth*, Cambridge: Cambridge University Press, 1915, II, 471.

[88] J. Angus, *The Voluntary System*, London: Jackson and Walford, 1839, 178-79. It should not be overlooked—though it often is—that Locke was not unaware of the divine initiative in calling out the church. See Alan P. F. Sell, *John Locke and the Eighteenth-Century Divines*, Cardiff. University of Wales Press, 1997, ch. 5. For Angus (1816–1902), see ODNB.

[89] Idem, *Christian Churches*, London: Ward, 1862, 19.

[90] A. Dakin, *The Baptist View of the Church and Ministry*, London: Baptist Union 1944, 21.

Founder, Guide, and Controller.'[91] Never one to pull his punches, Cook proclaimed that 'Baptists are High Churchmen in the best and truest sense of that much-abused term.'[92] Against this background, let us briefly investigate the place of church meeting and associations in Baptist life and experience.

Consistently with the intention of honouring, 'the crown's rights of the Redeemer' in his Church, both Strict Baptists and those in fellowship with the Baptist Union of Great Britain have, in recent years, made clear statements concerning the nature of Church Meeting. For the former, 'When the church meets to make decisions, the object is not primarily to discover the majority opinion, but rather to discover the mind of Christ.'[93] The Baptist Union adopts trinitarian phraseology: 'The church meeting is the children of the Father; meeting together in the presence of the Spirit; and seeking together the mind of Christ.[94] Many older writers concur. Dakin, for example, asserted that 'the [church] meeting is emphatically a meeting under God',[95] but at the same time he declared that, 'it is clear that the government of a Baptist church is on democratic lines.' He went on to point out that, 'the democratic government in a Baptist church is very different from all forms of democracy which visualize nothing beyond purely human judgment and debate, not to say contention.'[96] For this reason a number of writers warn of the danger which lurks in the term 'democratic'—as if the objective were simply 'one person, one vote—and government by the majority.' Thus, in a statement of 1948, the Baptist Union Council affirmed that:

> The church meeting, though outwardly a democratic way of ordering the affairs of the church, has deeper significance. It is the occasion when, as individuals and as a community, we submit ourselves to the guidance of the Holy Spirit and stand under the judgments of God that we may know what is the mind of Christ.[97]

This seems strikingly different in tone—and far less anthropocentric—than H. Wheeler Robinson's exposition of 1927, which was reissued two years before the Council's document was published: In church meeting 'all the members of the Church are at liberty to speak on matters affecting its common welfare, but the control of the meeting is naturally in the hands of the "deacons" and the

---

[91] Cook, *What Baptists Stand For*, 34.
[92] Ibid., 32.
[93] *We Believe. A Guide for Church Fellowship*, Devizes, Wilts: National Assembly of Strict Baptist Churches, 1974, 40.
[94] John Weaver, *Baptist Basics. The Church Meeting*, Didcot, Berks.: Baptist Union, n.d. col. ii.
[95] A. Dakin, *The Baptist View of the Church and Ministry*, 23.
[96] Ibid., 25.
[97] *The Baptist Doctrine of the Church*, London: Carey Kingsgate Press, 1948, 3.

minister who presides.'[98] From the other side of the Atlantic, Robert G. Torbet waxed lyrical about Baptist democracy: 'The democratic principle is at the heart of Baptist polity and largely explained the tremendous popularity and appeal of the denomination in the development of the religious life of the United States.'[99] Well might the saints tremble, as many of them are doing. The cautionary word uttered by John W. Grant to Congregationalists applies: 'Congregationalists have been under constant pressure to apply to their Church life the secular forms of their own ideas. The original desire to spiritualize the nation has tended to secularize the Church.'[100] Small wonder that A. Gilmore bluntly declared, 'The Church is not, and must never be regarded as, a democracy, for the power is not in the hands of the *demos* but of the *christos*: it is a Christocracy.'[101]

Who are they who thus gather? The classical confessions have been interestingly ambiguous on the matter. According to the London Confession of 1644, the

> Church, as it is visible to us, is a company of visible Saints, called & separated from the world, by the word and Spirit of God, to the visible profession of the faith of the Gospel, being baptized into that faith, and joyned to the Lord, and each other, by mutuall agreement, in the practical enjoyment of the Ordinances, commanded by Christ their head and King.[102]

The Particular Baptist *Somerset Confession* of 1656 agreed that, 'it is the duty of every man and woman, that have repented from dead works, and have faith towards God, to be baptized.' By so doing, they are 'planted in the visible church or body of Christ ... who are a company of men and women separated out to the world by the preaching of the gospel.'[103] In its rambling and more polemical way, the General Baptist *Standard Confession* of 1660 concurred:

---

[98] H. Wheeler Robinson, *The Life and Faith of the Baptists*, London: Carey Kingsgate Press, 1946; 1927, 88.

[99] Torbet, *A History of the Baptists*, 487. There is a lament concerning the more baneful influence of the corporate model on church life, as well as a defense of Church Meeting, in Alan P. F. Sell, *Commemorations. Studies in Christian Thought and History*, Cardiff: University of Wales Press and Calgary: University of Calgary Press, 1993; Eugene, OR: Wipf & Stock, 1998, ch. 14. There is even, at note 4, a mild rebuke on a different matter addressed to the recipient of this *festschrift*. How grace prevails!

[100] John W Grant, *Free Churchmanship in England, 1870–1940*, London: Independent Press, n.d., 87.

[101] A. Gilmore in *The Pattern of the Church. A Baptist View*, London: Lutterworth Press, 1963, 143.

[102] Lumpkin, *Baptist Confessions of Faith*, 165.

[103] Ibid., 209.

> XI. That the right and only way, of gathering Churches ... is first to teach, or preach the Gospel ... then to *Baptise* (that is in English to *Dip*) in the name of the Father, Son and Holy Spirit, or in the name of the Lord Jesus Christ;[104] such only of them as profess *repentance towards God, and faith towards our Lord Jesus Christ.* ... And as for all such who preach not this Doctrine, but instead thereof, that Scriptureless thing of Sprinkling of Infants (*falsely called Baptisme*) whereby the pure word of God is made of no effect, and the New Testament way of bringing in Members, into the church by regeneration, cast out ... all such we utterly deny. ...
>
> XII. That it is the duty of all such who are believers Baptized, to draw nigh unto God in submission to that principle of Christs Doctrine, to wit, Prayer and Laying on of Hands. ...
>
> XIII. That it is the duty of such who are constituted as aforesaid, to *continue stedfastly in Christs and the Apostles Doctrine, and assembling together, in fellowship, in breaking of Bread, and Prayer.* ...[105]

These three Confessions agreed that the way into the company of the visible saints—God's covenanted churches[106]—was by baptism, and to this the General Baptists added prayer and the laying on of hands. But, strangely, in the *London* [Particular] *Confession* of 1677 the link between baptism and church membership was not clearly established. Chapter XXVI contained fifteen paragraphs 'Of the Church' in which baptism is not mentioned, while Chapters XXXVIII and XXXIX on baptism required believers to be baptized as a sign of their engrafting into Christ, but did not relate the ordinance to church membership.

A century later, in a context in which they were convinced that 'there is a very criminal inattention to [church fellowship] amongst professors of Christianity, and even among Protestant Dissenters of our own denomination', John Collett Ryland and his Northamptonshire colleagues declared in 1777 that

> A Church of Christ is a peculiar society of gracious souls, who are called out of a state of sin and misery by the almighty Spirit of God, associated by their own free consent to maintain the doctrines of grace—to perform gospel worship, and celebrate gospel ordinances, with the exercise of holy discipline to the glory of the divine perfections, and to promote their own usefulness and happiness in time and eternity. ... They are, or ought to be, real believers in the Lord Jesus Christ, with the exercise of true repentance towards God. They are distinguished from all other men by three great characteristics, (viz.) Their convictions, their faith, and their new and divine nature.[107]

---

[104] An alternative, this, which did not escape the notice of the Unitarian Alexander Gordon. See his 'Matthew Caffyn and General Baptist latitude,' 531(c).

[105] Lumpkin, *Baptist Confessions of Faith*, 228-9.

[106] For the theology of, and examples of, local covenants see Charles W Deweese, *Baptist Church Covenants*, Nashville TN: Broadman Press, 1990.

[107] *The Beauty of Social Religion*, 2, 3.

We thus have oscillations in Baptist circles between those, like the Strict Baptists, who would make believer's baptism a term of membership and of communion, and fence the Lord's Table against all not thus baptized; those who, like eighteenth century Benjamin Wallin, believed that believer's baptism and congregational church fellowship were 'necessary to [Christianity's] Growth or Continuance in any Place; so that every Method taken to promote or revive it, which doth not include and insist on a Conformity to this Gospel Institution, is essentially deficient';[108] those like H. Wheeler Robinson who can say that 'Entrance into the Church is regarded as distinct from baptism, though in practice it is usually combined with it';[109] and those who with John Clifford denied that the acceptance of candidates for baptism had anything to do with the church.[110]

Into the tangled web of Baptist history concerning the debates over open versus closed membership and (which is not the same) open or closed communion we cannot here enter. Suffice it to say that in their most recent statements on the matter, Baptist Union writers are not, perhaps, as consistent as an interested enquirer might wish. Thus, while Paul Beasley-Murray boldly affirms that, 'Baptism is the normal way of entry into the church. ... Baptism is God's way for you to join the church', David Coffey, while noting that 'For some people it is a natural progression to move from commitment to Christ confessed in believer's baptism to commitment to Christ expressed in membership in the local church', and while answering those who do not or cannot see the connection between the two, does not explicitly justify the connection theologically along the lines that to be baptized is to be a member of the church. W. M. S. West has reassured Baptists that there is 'a growing body of opinion which recognizes that [the procedure of baptismal classes and the place of church meeting in decisions concerning those who are to be baptized] must have a basic principle for action that baptism makes a person a member of the Church,'[111] the optional possibility continues to hover. One wonders whether Baptists are tempted to believe that baptized non-members (to me a contradiction in terms) can be catholic Christians 'in general' without the requirement and the challenge of anchorage within a local group of visible saints,[112] or whether there is an implied concession to open membership—perhaps on ecumenical grounds—in which case there needs to be a follow

---

[108] Benjamin B. Wallin, *The Folly of Neglecting Divine Institutions. An Earnest Address to the Christian, Who Continues to Refrain from the Appointments of the Gospel*, 2nd ed., London, 1758, v.
[109] Robinson, *The Life and Faith of the Baptists*, 84n.2.
[110] See Briggs, *The English Baptists of the 19th Century*, 136.
[111] West in Gilmore, ed., *The Pattern of the Church*, 34; cf. 36.
[112] Paul Beasley-Murray, *Baptist Basics: Believers' Baptism*, col. iv; David Coffey, *Baptist Basics. Church Membership*, col. i.

through regarding the several 'moments' of Christian initiation, of which the baptism of infants might be one.

Lest it be thought that Strict Baptists alone may appear to be the rigorists of the Baptist family where matters of church membership are concerned, we may note in passing that, as their *Standard Confession* made plain, the old General Baptists required new members to receive the laying on of hands. They were more restorationist at this point and others than some of their contemporary Particular Baptists were concerning believer's baptism as a prerequisite of membership and communion. Thus, for example, the Horsham General Baptist church was founded as a 'Six-principle' cause, membership of which required (in accordance with Hebrews vi: 1,2) repentance from dead works, faith towards God, baptism, the laying on of hands, and belief in the resurrection of the dead as well as eternal judgment. When in 1818 it was

> Resolved that the Church return to its original mode of admitting members; viz., by baptism and the Laying on of hands, henceforth no person shall be admitted to the church without complying with his mode; and that those friends who have hitherto been admitted without the Laying on of Hands ... can no longer be considered as members unless they choose to submit to the rite ...

a rift developed between the Horsham members and those who lived at Billingshurst. The latter protested against the dismission of thirteen members of their branch 'without any charge being made against their moral conduct', and the result was that they constituted themselves as a separate church.[113] Other issues could cause similar disturbances. When John Stanger arrived among the General Baptists of Bessels Green in 1769 (where the rite of foot washing was observed until 1785), he caused a split in the church, not least because 'he was a Calvinist, in favor of Singing and Catholic Communion.' The fact that his preaching was 'tedious and tautological' may also have had something to do with the breach.[114]

In all parts of the English Baptist tradition, the duties of Church Meeting are similar: members are to be received and, where necessary, disciplined; ministers are to be called and officers appointed; the needy are to be supported, premises maintained, relationship with like-minded believers elsewhere developed, and specific questions such as the introduction of singing and organs, or the anointing of the sick determined. In the early days members would sign the covenant, and the question of relations with the state would sometimes loom large. In 1764 the Yorkshire and Lancashire Association of Particular Baptists

---

[113] Emily Kensett, *History of the Free Christian Church Horsham from 1721 to 1921*, Horsham: Free Christian Church Public Library, 1921, 103-105.
[114] Packer, *The Unitarian Heritage in Kent*, 31.

gave advice concerning matters with which church meetings might deal: the truths of the gospel, specific passages of Scripture, cases of conscience, the discussion of sermons—but none of this in such a ways to 'glide into a light and frothy conversation' or beget dullness.[115] Latterly, questions concerning mission, education, and ecumenism have found their way onto the agenda of church meetings. Underlying all has been the doctrine of the priesthood of all believers—at its best rightly construed to denote the corporate priesthood of the gathered saints, not the sanctification of the aspirations, whims, or prejudices of every individual member.[116]

But for all the theory, in practice church meeting is admitted to have declined in attendance and significance in many churches. R. C. Walton lamented that, 'In the great majority of our churches [the] exalted view of the nature of the church meeting has been almost entirely lost, and with it has gone one of the most important characteristics of the Baptist community.'[117] All through this century writers have been speculating upon why this might be. H. Wheeler Robinson spoke of 'the rivalry of other forms of organization ... Christian Endeavour Societies, Young People's Guilds, and the like, together with the very large number of special organizations not linked to any one Church, yet drawing their supporters almost exclusively from the Churches.'[118] Henry Cook questioned 'whether our present system is really suited to some conditions. It does wonderfully well in suburban districts where get a good community of middle-class people. But what about the mission field? What about slum areas?'[119] Ernest Payne observed that 'Changed social conditions and habits have made it more difficult to secure a large attendance of members at a midweek meeting. The two World Wars accentuated these developments. So did the growth of a more centralized denominational organization.'[120] For his part, B. R. White, 'calling a spade a spade', has pointed to the dissuasion that in church meeting and Association alike, 'the "boredom quotient" is about 95%'—a view endorsed by Alistair Campbell.[121] The latter, though not opposed to Church Meeting as such, questions whether the institution should any longer be deemed 'the test of loyalty and the badge of identity.' It is not simply that many local churches are finding other ways of expressing, 'the Scriptural principle of every member ministry', it is, *inter alia*, that, 'The Church Meeting cannot be proved from

---

[115] See Raymond Brown, *English Baptists of the 18th Century*, 88-9.
[116] Cf. West in Gilmore, ed., *The Pattern of the Church*, 46-47; N. Clark in ibid., 106.
[117] R. C. Walton, *The Gathered Community*, London: Carey Press, 1946, 130.
[118] Robinson, *The Life and Faith of the Baptists*, 90.
[119] Cook, *What Baptists Stand For*, 82-3.
[120] Payne, *The Fellowship of Believers*, 105.
[121] B. R. White in David Slater, ed., *A Perspective on Baptist Identity*, Kingsbridge: Mainstream, 1987, 25; cf. ibid., 35.

Scripture to have existed in any form recognizable to us, let alone be shown to have obtained everywhere or have been laid down by the Apostles.'[122]

Clearly, the questions of the locus of authority and the validity of restorationism lie beneath this remark, which appears in a discussion pamphlet offered by conservative evangelical Baptists. I should simply enquire, 'Is there a more fitting way for those called to be saints to pray about, and deliberate upon, their witness and mission than to gather regularly and expectantly for this purpose?' While agreeing with Brian Haymes that, 'It is [Christ's] presence and not the specific organization that makes the Church the Church,'[123] we may nevertheless ask, did not Baptist (and Congregational) forebears do something of value when they 'completed' Reformed ecclesiology by including the ministry of the whole people of God in their deliberative aspect; and could not this experience put flesh on the bones of an ecumenical ecclesiology which affirms the importance of this ministry, to which some polities pay little more than lip service?[124] These questions press if Baptists still intend to regard the local church as comprising called, regenerate, baptized, covenanted saints who, by virtue of their local enrolment, are members of the Church catholic.[125]

I do not suggest that the perceived inadequacies of Church Meeting are the only counterproductive factors in facilitating the offering of the Baptists' ecclesiological gift. We may ask, for example, how are Baptists to relate convictions on polity still shared by many of them to the predilection shared by some of them for church growth? This may be especially a problem for Baptists in North America and Korea, where local Baptist churches of twenty to forty thousand members are not unknown, whose ministers know personally only a number of the deacons. One can, no doubt, have evangelical meetings—even worship—on such a scale, but can one have gathered churches of like size? It would seem that a Church Meeting of such numbers is impossible to organize if not fearful to contemplate—certainly if the words of Thomas Helwys' confession are still thought to have significance:

---

[122] A. Campbell in *A Perspective on Baptist Identity*, 35. It would be utterly undiplomatic—even evidence of an unsanctified mind—to mutter, '*A fortiori*, neither can Southern Baptist boards!'

[123] In Keith Clements et al., *A Call to Mind. Baptist Essays towards a Theology of Commitment*, London: Baptist Union, 1981, 59.

[124] E.g., see the opening paragraphs of the chapter on 'Ministry' in *Baptism, Eucharist, and Ministry*, Geneva: World Council of Churches, 1982.

[125] Covenanted' is perhaps the operative word at this point. One suspects a situation among (at least) British Baptists similar to that manifested by Congregationalists, namely, that in the wake of the Evangelical Revival the emphasis in many places switched from 'covenant' to 'conversion', so that the church came to be regarded not so much as God's corporate election of grace, but as an aggregate of saved individuals. In Congregationalism there is a decided tailing off of local covenants from about 1830. See Sell, *Dissenting Thought and the Life of the Churches*, ch. 1.

> The members off everie Church or Congregacion ought to knowe one another, that so they may performe all the duties off love towards another both to soule and bodie. ... And therefore a Church ought not to consist off such a multitude as cannot have particular knowledg one off another.[126]

Long before the modern church growth movement was launched, a correspondent in *The Patriot* in January 1866 declared that 'a chapel of over a thousand seats was a denial of basic nonconformist principles.'[127]

While taking full account of these points, may it not also be that, just as secular democratic ideas have done their eroding work, so, too, has a feeling of embarrassment felt in many quarters. Is there an, unease about the clash between the inherited doctrine on which so much Baptist polity turns, namely, that there is a distinction of eternal significance between those who are in Christ and those who are not, and the perceived need to reach out to other Christian traditions, and to do right by members of other faiths and of none? It is not only members of established churches who need to ask, 'Who is A Christian?' Robert Hall drew the distinction plainly enough: 'Congregations are the creatures of circumstances; churches the institution of God.'[128] What Charles Deweese has written of Baptists in the United States would appear to have wider application: 'A dilemma facing contemporary Baptists in America is how to reconcile mounting trends toward an uncommitted membership with doctrinal statements that require a committed membership.'[129]

I cannot claim to have read every piece of Baptist writing on the Church Meeting, but in what I *have* read, the connection between church meeting and worship has only rarely been drawn. There is, for example, the suggestion by A. Gilmore that 'the chief responsibility of the church meeting is to complete the liturgy by planning the social life of the church (*koinonia*), together with the church's witness (*marturia*) and service (*diakonia*),'[130] but the worship-Church meeting relationship merits fuller exposition, for the idea that the saints who sit under the Word and gather at the Lord's Table then become the church *meeting*, under the Lordship of Christ, in order to determine how the gospel received is to be proclaimed where God has placed them, is too important to be played down.

---

[126] Lumpkin, *Baptist Confessions of Faith*, 121. The insistence that 'the belief that Jesus Christ is not only Lord over all the congregation, but exercises his reign through that whole community, not just certain designated members of it' is said to be a conviction 'which cannot be jettisoned without a radical departure from the meaning of "Baptist" in this country.' See Paul S. Fiddes et al., *Bound to Love. The Covenant Basis of Baptist Life and Mission*, London: Baptist Union, 1985, 7. In the same volume is found Roger Hayden's defense of church meeting, 34-5. For Helwys (?1550–/1616, see ODNB.
[127] See Briggs, *The English Baptists of the 19th Century*, 13.
[128] Gregory, ed., *The Works of Robert Hall, A.M.* IV, 296.
[129] Deweese, *Baptist Church Covenants*, vii.
[130] Gilmore in *The Pattern of the Church*, 148; cf. Clark in ibid., 108-109.

The idea facilitates witness to the fact that just as in worship Christ is proclaimed as Lord, so too is he proclaimed in Church Meeting, which then takes on its true character as a credal assembly. A related point is that the one presiding at Church Meeting should normally be the minister—not a businessperson 'good at meetings'—for just as he or she is called to lead the church to the throne of grace in worship, so the minister is charged to lead the church to seek the mind of Christ in church meeting.[131]

Experience suggests that if there is not a strong sense of church locally, it is difficult to see how there can be mutuality between the local church and the wider denominational associations, since the latter will find an ecclesiological void, and attempts to develop relationships will be vitiated. On the other hand, there may be a strong, but narrow sense of local church autonomy of the kind which justifies B. R. White's useful observation: 'Across three and a half centuries, if Baptists have had to choose between the independence of the local church and cooperation in fellowship with an association, they have chosen independence.'[132] Arthur Dakin, while granting that the idea of setting out from the local church is 'fundamental to Baptist polity and cannot be departed from without abandoning the essential Baptist position', had to admit that 'this it is that creates some of our present difficulties.'[133] Among these are the parochialism and isolationism against which Henry Cook warned.[134] Such is the force of the individualism flowing down from the nineteenth century that Baptists who have fallen into these traps would, no doubt, be surprised to be told by William Lumpkin that 'Baptists were never independents, strictly speaking,'[135] and they would find it hard to accept Whitley's assertion that, 'Baptists from the beginning sought to maintain sisterly intercourse between local churches; they never thought that one church was independent of others.'[136] There can be no doubt that the classical confessions, both Particular and General, bear Whitley out—and Ernest Payne, too:

---

[131] I was therefore surprised to read the following in the statement on church government of a Reformed Baptist church (even though a plurality of elders, each having different gifts, is envisaged) 'The elders or church officers call all meetings of the church. ... They will also appoint a chairman for each meeting.' See *Reformation Today*, no. 82, November–December 1984, 37. For a discussion of church meeting in Congregationalism and its heirs, see Alan P. F. Sell, *Commemorations*, ch. 14.

[132] White in Slater, ed., *A Perspective on Baptist Identity*, 20.

[133] Dakin, *The Baptist View of the Church and Ministry*, 5. Beware N. G. Wright's significant misquotation of Dakin: 'Baptists start all their organization from the local church and it is this which causes our difficulties.' See his '"Koinonia" and Baptist Ecclesiology,' *BQ* XXXV no. 8, October 1994, 365.

[134] Cook, *What Baptists Stand For*, 79-80.

[135] Lumpkin, *Baptist Confessions of Faith*, 172.

[136] W. T. Whitley, *A History of British Baptists*, London: Charles Griffin, 1923, 86.

> [F]rom the seventeenth century Baptists have regarded the visible Church as finding expression in local communities of believers who constitute themselves by the election of officers, the observance of Baptism and the Lord's Supper, and Christian discipline, and who find an extension and expression of their life in free association, first, with other churches of their own faith and order, but also with all other groups of Christians loyal to the central truths of the apostolic Gospel. This, in outline, is the Baptist doctrine of the Church as visible. it is something very different from the exaggerated independence, self-sufficiency and atomism which have sometimes been favored of recent days.[137]

The Baptist Council statement of 1948 underlined the point: 'Gathered companies of believers are the local manifestation of the one Church of God on earth and in heaven.'[138] All of this in line with the *London Confession*'s assertion that

> although the particular Congregations be distinct and severall Bodies, every one a company and knit Citie in it selfe; yet are they all to walk by one and the same Rule, and by all means convenient to have the counsell and help one of another in all needfull affaires of the Church, as members of one body in the common faith under Christ their onely head.[139]

The *Second London Confession* agrees that the local churches 'ought to hold communion amongst themselves for their peace, increase of love, and mutual edification.' It then proceeds immediately to say, however, that messengers to assemblies 'are not entrusted with any Church-power properly so called; or with any jurisdiction over the Churches themselves, to exercise any censures either over any Churches, or Persons; or to impose their determination on the Churches, or Officers.'[140]

The General Baptists who composed the *Orthodox Creed* of 1678 were even clearer that at assemblies 'the churches appearing there by their representatives, make but one church, and have lawful right, and suffrage in this general meeting, or assembly, to act in the name of Christ.' Then, in a manner consistent with the rigorism concerning polity which we earlier noted, they stated,

> To such a meeting, or assembly, appeals ought to be made, in case of any injustice done, or heresy, and schism countenanced, in any particular congregation of Christ, and the decisive voice in such general assemblies is the major part, and such general assemblies have lawful power to hear, and determine, and also to excommunicate.[141]

---

[137] Payne, *The Fellowship of Believers*, 36-37; cf. West in Gilmore, ed., *The Pattern of the Church*, 42-3.
[138] *The Baptist Doctrine of the Church*, 2.
[139] Lumpkin, *Baptist Confessions of Faith*, 168-9.
[140] Ibid., 289.
[141] Ibid., 327.

If it appears that these General Baptists did less than justice to Church Meetings, the Particular Confessions seem to have left the associations toothless. They had no church power. Indeed, Ryland and the Northamptonshire ministers and messengers did not mention them at all in their Circular Letter of 1777. But, according to B. R White, fellowship was an obligation: 'Fellowship is the lifestyle of the gospel. *Inter*dependence is the mark of the converted—the search for independence was Adam's sin.'[142] The question thus presses: If local church power leads to a breach of fellowship, how are matters to be restored? It would seem that Baptists have not always clearly articulated the practical ways by which the mutuality which they profess as between local church and wider association is actually to be achieved.[143] Doctrinally, the point may be expressed in terms of pneumatology. Can it be supposed that the Holy Spirit who addresses the local Church Meeting through the Word is powerless to fulfil a similar function in assemblies? If not, then in cases in which the local church and the assembly are out of accord, and on the assumption that the Spirit does not speak with a forked tongue, there needs to be a process of mutual discussion in a spirit of humility and prayer, in the hope that differences may be resolved. Certainly there is something worryingly casual about H. Wheeler Robinson's matter-of-fact assertion that 'local Churches join or withdraw from [associations] as they see fit,'[144] especially if there is truth in the Orthodox Creed's declaration that churches represented at assemblies 'make but one church.' A more recent writer, Brian Haymes, is quite clear on the matter: 'When we gather as local congregations, Associations or in Denominational Assembly we meet as those whom God has gathered together in communion with Christ.'[145]

III

I turn finally to liberty. We have seen that on matters of doctrine and polity, Baptists have believed a number of different things, and that there have been varying degrees of tolerance amongst them. Some have sailed closer to rigorism, others to a freewheeling liberty of thought, but all would agree that the church, as Church, possesses God-given liberty as over against any powers which would curtail or stifle its spiritual freedom. The negative implication of freedom for Christ, is freedom from the world (in Separatist parlance), and from a coercive state (in the language of Old Dissent). The conviction was classically

---

[142] White in Slater, ed., *A Perspective on Baptist Identity*, 29.
[143] Even Gilmore is deficient at this point. See *The Pattern of the Church*, 149-54.
[144] Robinson, *The Life and Faith of the Baptists*, 91.
[145] Haymes in Clements et al., *A Call to Mind*, 67.

expressed by the General Baptists. In the one hundred *Propositions and Conclusions* (1612) of the Smyth party in Amsterdam, the draft of which had been written by its recently deceased leader, we read:

> 84. That the magistrate is not by virtue of his office to meddle with religion, or matters of conscience, to force or compel men to this or that form of religion, or doctrine: but to leave Christian religion free, to every man's conscience, and to handle only civil transgressions (Rom. Xiii), injuries and wrongs of man against man, in murder, adultery, theft, etc., for Christ only is the king and lawgiver of the church and conscience (James iv.12).[146]

Thomas Helwys was even more pointed:

> our lord the King is but an earthly King, and he hath no authority as a King but in earthly causes, and if the Kings people be obedient and true subjects, obeying all humane lawes made by the King, our lord the King can require no more: for mens religion to God is betwixt God and themselves; the King shall not answer for it, neither may the King be iugd betwene God and man. Let them be heretikes, Turcks, Jewes or whatsoever, it apperteynes not to the earthly power to punish them in the least measure.[147]

In succession, and on similar lines, came Leonard Busher's *Religion's Peace* (1614), John Murton's *Objectives Answered* (1615) and *An Humble Supplication* (1626), and Roger Williams's *The Bloody Tenent of Persecution* (1644). In making this protest, the early seventeenth-century Baptists stood alone among what might (anachronistically) be called the mainline Old Dissenters.[148]

Although the early English Baptist confessions are unanimous on the necessity of spiritual freedom, they were nevertheless couched interestingly varied terms. The authors of the *London Confession*, while granting that 'a civill Magistrate is an ordinance of God set up by God for the punishment of evill doers, and for the praise of them that doe well', nevertheless reserved the right to continue witnessing faithfully should magistrates turn adverse, 'And thus wee desire to give unto God that which is Gods, and unto Caesar that which is Caesars.'[149] The *Second London Confession* followed the same general line, though the absence of a declaration of intent to stand against erring magistrates is noteworthy, and was probably owing to the desire of the authors not to incite

---

[146] Lumpkin, *Baptist Confessions of Faith*, 140.

[147] Helwys, *A Short Declaration of the Mistery of Iniquity* (1612), 69.

[148] The Independents were quite happy to be the established church in Massachussetts, and in England they did not turn their thought seriously towards toleration until it became clear during the Westminster Assembly that if they did not they would lose out to Presbyterianism. See farther, Robert S. Paul, *The Assembly of the Lord. Politics and Religion in the Westminister Assembly and the 'Grand Debate'*, Edinburgh: T. & T. Clark, 1985, 31, 467. Some Presbyterians hoped for an establishment along their favored lines of polity as late as the early years of the eighteenth century.

[149] Lumpkin, *Baptist Confessions of Faith*, 169-71.

further persecution and to encourage thoughts of toleration in their opponents. The General Baptists' *Standard Confession* of 1660 showed no such inhibitions—and this is surprising in view of their desire to demonstrate that all rumours aligning them with Munster and other disturbing agents are wide of the mark. They granted that there ought to be civil magistrates—and that they were to be submitted to—but they gave notice that

> in case the Civil Powers do, or shall at any time impose things about matters of Religion, which we through conscience to God cannot actually obey, then we with *Peter* also do say, that we ought (in such cases) to obey God rather than men; *Acts* 5.29 and accordingly do hereby declare our whole, and holy intent and purpose, that (through the help of grace) we will not yield, nor (in such cases) in the least actually obey them; yet humbly purposing (in the Lords strength) patiently to suffer whatsoever shall be inflicted upon us, for our conscionable forebearance.[150]

On the basis of the foundations laid, it will now suffice if we take soundings in subsequent centuries. When in 1772 a bill to repeal the law requiring nonconformist subscription to Anglican articles was defeated in the House of Lords, one bishop only voting in favor, Robert Robinson apostrophized thus:

> Christian liberty! Thou favorite offspring of heaven! Thou firstborn of Christianity! I saw the wise and pious servants of God nourish thee in their houses, and cherish thee in their bosoms! I saw them lead thee into public view; all good men hailed thee; the generous British Commons caressed and praised thee, and led thee into an upper house, and there ... there didst thou expire in the holy laps of spiritual lords![151]

Five years later, Ryland and his Northamptonshire colleagues made it clear that those who comprise the Church were

> Very much distinguished from the merely civil and political societies of this world, by the spiritual nature of their constitution, the privileges they enjoy, the officers they appoint, the worship they perform, the rules they observe, the head they obey, and the great and noble ends they pursue, which are abundantly superior to all the designs of the political societies of this world.[152]

Increasingly, Baptist heat was turned upon the establishment principle as such: 'Turn a Christian society into an established church', warned Robert Hall, 'and it is no longer a voluntary assembly for the worship of God; it is a powerful corporation, full of such sentiments and passions, as usually distinguish those

---

[150] Ibid., 233.
[151] *Miscellaneous Works of Robert Robinson, Late Pastor of the Baptist Church and Congregation of Protestant Dissenters, at Cambridge*, Harlow: B. Flower, 1807), II, 182-3. For Robinson (1735–1790), see ODNB.
[152] *The Beauty of Social Religion*, 3,

bodies; a dread of innovation, an attachment to abuses, a propensity to tyranny and oppression.'[153] He elsewhere argued that, 'A full toleration of religious principles, and the protection of all parties in their respective modes of worship, are the natural operations of a free government; and everything that tends to check and restrain them, materially affects the interests of religion.'[154]

In 1843 the Kent and Sussex Particular Baptist Association rather missed the point as they glanced north to Scotland. They unanimously resolved to endorse the action of those Free Church people who had seceded from the Church of Scotland in that year, but seem not to have grasped the fact that the Free Church of Scotland staunchly maintained (and its remnant still maintains) the establishment principle, regarded itself as the Church of Scotland (Free), and believed that the *Church* "came out"—mainly over the question of the patronage system which permitted the intrusion of nonevangelical ministers into pulpits against the will of the people. But at least the Kent and Sussex Baptists reaffirmed their own view of church-state relations.

By the end of the nineteenth century, the cry was 'a free Church in a free state', and Baptists and others worked for this, their ardour increased by perceived injustices in the field of education—a long story which cannot now detain us. Suffice it to say that none worked harder for what he regarded as the proper freedoms of both Church and state than John Clifford:

> Our fathers suffered and fought for what they described as "the crown rights of King Jesus." This is—be it believed or be it scorned—this is the real force at the heart of the agitation for Disestablishment or Disendowment. In that unselfish and sublime aim lies its unsubduable strength; from thence it draws its patience, its quenchless enthusiasm, and its assurance of final success.[155]

From Clifford's day to the 1950s, the case was made in these terms with some, but by no means all, remembering what Clifford here seems to have forgotten, namely that in addition, 'our fathers'—consistently with their view of a regenerate church—had serious reservations concerning the established Church, to whose communion services regenerate and unregenerate alike could come on nonbiblical grounds.

At the end of the nineteenth century, Principal William Edwards adduced no fewer than fifty arguments favor of Nonconformity, many of hem standard, but some of them idiosyncratic, for example: 'As the Welsh especially are a nation of

---

[153] Gregory, ed., *The Works of Robert Hall, A.M.*, 3:145. Cf. Sell, *Dissenting Thought and the Life of the Churches*, 63 8-39. This is from *An Apology for the Freedom of the Press and for General Liberty* (1793; repr. 1831).
[154] Ibid., 12
[155] Clifford in *The Contemporary Review* LXVII, March 1895, 454-5.

Nonconformists, the presence of the Establishment is an anomaly and a grievous injustice.'[156] The Welsh Non-Conformists have their reward.

The middle years of the twentieth century saw a flurry of literary activity by Baptists on the establishment question. The classical position n the matter was reiterated, though in modem accents, but as to what should be done about the problem, some were more cautious than others. In 1944 Arthur Dakin explained that:

> The gathered church distinguishes itself sharply from every form of national or state church, and from every sort of church where the basis of membership is birth privilege of any kind. Those who adhere to the gathered-church idea cannot allow that a person is of necessity a member of the Christian Church because he happens to be born in a so-called Christian country, or for that matter in a Christian family.[157]

As he reflected on the establishment issue, Henry Cook concluded hat the underlying vital question is:

> What is the Church? And how is it constituted? The State Church or Church State assumes that membership in the one is coterminous with the other, and 'converts' are made by the fact that they are born and then baptized. But this is fundamentally wrong. The Church, Baptists believe, is a society freely constituted by the free acceptance on the part of men and women of the free grace of God, and unless there be a 'willing covenant' there cannot be the entrance into the holy society we call the Church. (op. cit., 202–3)

Freedom from an unregenerate Church was implicit only in the remarks of both Dakin and Cook.

Four years later the Baptist Council expressed itself on the general question of Church and state, without reference to the establishment, thus:

> Our conviction of Christ's Lordship over His Church leads us to insist that churches formed by His will must be free from all other rule in matters relating to their spiritual life. Any form of control by the State in these matters appears to us to challenge the "Crown Rights of the Redeemer." We also hold that this freedom in Christ implies the right of the church to exercise responsible self-government. This has been the Baptist position since the seventeenth century.
>
> This freedom, however, has not led to irresponsibility in our duties as citizens. We believe it is a Christian obligation to honour and serve the State and to labour for the well-being of all men and women.[158]

---

[156] William Edwards, *A Handbook of Protestant Nonconformity*, Bristol, 1901, 226. See further Sell, *Dissenting Thought and the Life of the Churches*, 646-8.
[157] Dakin, *The Baptist View of the Church and Ministry*, 15-16.
[158] H. Townsend. *The Claims of the Free Churches*, London: Hodder and Stoughton, 1949, 196.

By far the most sustained and perceptive treatment of the entire question of Church and state was that by Henry Townsend, principal of Manchester Baptist College, which was published in 1949. He set out from the assertion that 'The Bible ascribes absolute authority to the transcendent Lawgiver, Who revealed to Moses, the prophets, and finally through Jesus of Nazareth, the ethical standards of righteousness and love. In the New Testament Jesus Christ is Lord—a term signifying His unique ethical authority over his followers.'[159] Townsend pointed out that Jesus distinguished sharply between God's kingdom and that of earthly governments, and taught that, as citizens, his followers should 'obey authority except when it clashed with loyalty to Himself.' It was a sad day for the Church when the Empire of Constantine entered into official relations with it, for

> The World entered the Church as it had never done for three hundred years; and ever since the fourth century its presence in the church has been the bane of the Christian religion. It was, and is still, a departure from the spiritual independence of the Church. ... When it has suited their mutual interests, mostly financial and entirely worldly, the Church and State have flirted with each other, and both have suffered; the betrayal of Christ and the Gospel lies at the Church's door, and such betrayal cannot be divorced from the demonic forces which have swept over the world in these latter days.[160]

These forthright words did not, however, imply the absolute ignoring of the church by the state, and *vice versa*. On the contrary, 'The State makes the laws, must administer justice and restrict evil doers. The function of the Church is to preach the gospel in the State, to leaven society, and to educate the people in Christian principles, until they elect men to rule who will make laws approximating to the Christian ethical ideal.'[161]

Townsend is unflinching: 'National Churches have arrested the universal ideas of the New Testament, and have thereby de-Christianised the idea of God which was revealed by Jesus.'[162] We shall not expect him to endorse the arguments of those in the Church of England who appeal to the utility of the establishment, and he does not: 'The whole argument from Free Church history is a protest against the complacency of the principle of the utility of the Establishment.'[163] He allies himself with the Puritans, who, 'regarded the alliance of Church and State as a betrayal of the Gospel and a hindrance to the spiritual growth of the nation', declaring that 'the dread of the loss of endowments keeps the Church in bondage to the State: the proposals for her

---

[159] H. Townsend. *The Claims of the Free Churches*, London: Hodder and Stoughton, 1949, 196.
[160] Ibid., 197.
[161] Ibid., 199.
[162] Ibid., 200.
[163] Ibid., 208.

independence confirm this statement.'[164] In answer to Archbishop Garbett's claim that the Church of England, 'has in practice freedom which is hardly equaled by any other church or sect', Townsend points to the way in which the church cannot without recourse to Parliament legally determine its worship, appoint its senior officers, change its statement of doctrine, or amend its constitution.[165]

Three years later, as if to dampen down any seditious thoughts which Townsend's robust argument might engender, Ernest Payne was found reaffirming the classical position on *the Free Churches and the State*, but he advised that the time was not ripe for the Free Churches to press for the disestablishment of the Church of England (a) because 'We are obviously in a dangerous transitional period in regard to the theory and activity of the State' ; (b) because 'A sharp church conflict would seriously endanger' growing inter-Church confidence; and (c) because 'it would be disastrous at the beginning of a new reign to embark upon a religious controversy which would inevitably be complicated, prolonged and embittered, and which would, equally inevitably, involve the status and powers of the Crown.'[166] Payne denied that his position entailed repudiating '"he historic witness of the Free Churches.' Rather, he appealed for Anglicans and others, 'to think a little more, and learn a little longer, before we commit ourselves to an entirely new religious settlement in this country.'[167]

As already hinted, fifty years on the situation is significantly changed. To use the words of the 1593 Act Against Puritans, if Baptists are not (necessarily!) 'seditious sectaries and disloyal persons',[168] it is equally clear that such relative youngsters in our land as Methodists and Muslims, Sikhs and secularists—and many others—are not so to be labeled either. But their presence calls into question any lingering establishment theology to the effect that to be English is to be a member of the Church of England, and that not so to belong implies subversion at best and treachery at worst. Moreover, many parish churches are *de facto* gathered (and often highly eclectic gatherings at that), while many gathered churches, as we have seen, sit more loosely to the principle of the regenerate saints than once they did.

---

[164] Ibid., 2 10-11.
[165] Ibid., 211. He quotes, C. Garbett, *The Claims of the Church of England*, London: Hodder and Stoughton, 1947, 182.
[166] E. A. Payne, *The Free Churches and the State*, London: Independent Press, 1952, 28. Repr. in idem., *Free Churchmen Unrepentant and Repentant*, London: Carey Kingsgate Press, 1965, ch. 5.
[167] Ibid., 29.
[168] Henry Gee and William John Hardy, *Documents Illustrative of the History of the English Church*, London: Macmillan, 1896, 492.

Further, at a time when the monarchy is under review—by everyone from the royal household to writers in the tabloid press;[169] and when nationalisms are rapidly developing across Europe—some of them highly dangerous—the churches might be thought to have a prophetic and a genuinely ecumenical word to speak. The fact that older religious disabilities have almost entirely vanished, and that Nonconformists are no longer thrown into prison or killed, should make it easier for the underlying theological questions to be amicably discussed, and for the necessary reconciliation of memories to take place. We do not need to be so blunt as Forsyth, from whom I set out: 'What we protest against is not the abuses but the existence, the principle, of a national Church.'[170] We need not sound so complacent as H. Wheeler Robinson who, in 1927, wrote, 'While Baptists still feel that the "establishment" of one religious denomination above all others is an anomaly under present conditions [what an astounding qualification!], they are probably less disposed today to promote political action for its removal, and prefer to leave this, in the interests of religion, to the more or less inevitable course of events, within and without the Anglican Church.'[171] And we ought not to sound as triumphalist as Henry Cook:

> [T]he Free churches are a recognized power in the religious life of the nation. The Church of England itself is conscious of the chains that bind it, and the Liberty and Life movement under the late Dr. Temple has done much to create a desire for a larger freedom. That cannot, however, fully come until the gilded bonds of the Establishment are broken, and the Church of England itself becomes a Free Church.[172]

It is not necessary for the Free Churches to agitate for disestablishment[173] that will come about, if at all, when the Church of England itself seeks it. But all the pertinent issues might be raised in a wide-ranging ecumenical discussion in England and in Europe (for the Lutheran and Reformed establishments, though different, are also being urged to examine themselves) of the theological basis of

---

[169] The tabloid breast-beating over the question whether Prince Charles, because of his divorce, his flirtation with New Age thought, and the like, is fit to be the next temporal head of the Church of England represents a sublime missing of the point.

[170] P. T. Forsyth, 'The Evangelical basis of Free Churchism,' *The Contemporary Review* LXXXI, January–June 1902, 693.

[171] Robinson, *The Life and Faith of the Baptists*, 134.

[172] Cook, *What Baptists Stand For*, 209.

[173] And republicanism has never been regarded by most Dissenters as the necessary consequence of their theological stance. On the contrary, time and again they have professed loyalty to successive (not always very helpful) monarchs. Consider this, for example, from a John Collett Ryland and his Northamptonshire colleagues: '[We] do not judge ourselves independent of civil government, as we are members of society: no, sirs! We are so far from assuming independence on [sic] the good old British constitution, that we will dare to affirm, no men in England, or in the world, are better friends to such civil government that we are, and desire always to be.' See *The Beauty of Social Religion*, 7.

church-state relations as Christianity's third millennium approaches. There are signs that such a discussion is already in its early stages,[174] and one wonders how much part Baptists (and, indeed, other Old Dissenters) will wish to play in it.[175]

To end, as I began, with some poles: at the 250th anniversary of the Great Ejectment of 1662, the Baptist Alexander Maclaren bequeathed agenda, begged questions, and implied rebukes in all directions:

> The future of England will be to that Church which shall know how to reconcile most perfectly the rights of the individual and the power of society; the claims of free thought and the claims of dogmatic truth. A Church on the so-called multitudinist theory will not do it; for of the two terms of the antithesis it reduces one, the element of dogmatic truth, practically to zero. An Established church, be-articled, and be-liturgied, and be-bishoped, will not do it. Narrow Dissenterisms will not do it. But Churches which take the Bible for their creed, and Christ for their sole master, and all their members for brethren, ought to do it. They may do it if they will be true to themselves, to their principles, to their ancestry. Shame on them if they fail.[176]

IV

From this necessarily selective consideration, of varied Baptist positions on doctrine, polity, and liberty, there arise three urgent questions of ecumenical significance: How are we to understand the development of doctrine in relation to degrees of tolerance within the Church? How may we best articulate a theology which will clearly relate the several foci of churchly life? Which theology of Church-state relations will most adequately facilitate the Church's mission as Christianity's third millennium dawns? Is it too much to hope that Baptists will be among those who will urge these questions upon us?

If and when the churches pay substantial ecumenical attention to these questions, in relation both to their several heritages and to what our forebears

---

[174] See Sell, 'Called to be one: Decision Making in Our Churches, Including Matters of Faith. A Report,' *One In Christ*, XXXII no. 1, 1996, 82-83.

[175] I have no means of predicting what role the Free Churches Group within Churches Together in England might play in such discussions. It is surely concerned with Church-state relations, but its membership is diverse, and its young members did not, for the most part, find their origin in matters ecclesiological, neither have they the stimulus of martyrs, or such long memories of civil and religious disabilities. Since I should not wish to encourage others to do what I am not prepared to do myself, I may, perhaps, mention a few attempts made to increase the visibility of a question the consideration of which I believe to be an urgent matter: *Dissenting Thought and the Life of the Churches*, ch. 22; *Commemorations. Studies in Christian Thought and History*, ch. 4; ch. 11 below.

[176] Alexander Maclaren, 'Fidelity to Conscience,' in *The Ejectment of 1662 and the Free Churches*, London: National Council of Evangelical Churches, 1912, 34. For Maclaren (1826-1910), see ODNB.

would have called 'the needs of the hour', they would do well to have the devoutly majestic words of the 'Epistle Dedicatory' to the Particular Baptist Confession of 1644 ringing in their ears:

> [W]e confesse that we know but in part, and that we are ignorant of many things which we desire and seek to know: and if any shall doe us that friendly part to shew us from the word of God that we see not, we shall have cause to be thankful to God and them.[177]

---

[177] Lumpkin, *Baptist Confessions of Faith*, 149.

CHAPTER 5

The Life and Thought of Henry Grove[1]

The Life of Henry Grove

Henry Grove came of good Dissenting stock. The Groves of Wiltshire and, on his mother's side, the Rowes of Devonshire were 'remarkable for several generations, for strict piety, and a steady attachment to religious liberty.'[2] His grandfather, Edward Grove, Vicar of Pinhoe, Devonshire, was deprived of his living on 23 September 1662;[3] his father, a Taunton upholsterer, married a sister of John Rowe, who forfeited his lectureship at Westminster Abbey in 1660.[4] Edward Grove and John Rowe were among some two thousand clergymen and schoolmasters who, on conscientious grounds, could not meet the requirements of the Act of Uniformity of 1662 by giving their 'unfeigned assent and consent' to the *Book of Common Prayer* of the Church of England. To have done so would have been to agree that it was the prerogative of the monarch and Parliament to prescribe particular forms of liturgy and church order, and this they denied. They therefore became subject to the provisions of the Clarendon Code which, although unequally enforced across the country, represented a serious threat to Dissenters, excluded them from the universities and public life, and rendered

---

[1] Abbreviations used in the notes: CR : A. G. Matthews, *Calamy Revised. Being a Revision of Edumund Calamy's Account of the Ministers and Others Ejected and Silenced, 1660-2*, Oxford: Clarendon Press, 1934 (reissued 1988); ODNB: *The Oxford Dictionary of National Biography*; DSCBP/DECBP: *Dictionary of Seventeenth/Eighteenth-Century British Philosophers*, Bristol: Thoemmes Press, 2000, 1999 respectively; PDM : *The Protestant Dissenter's Magazine*.

[2] 'Memoirs of the Rev. Henry Grove,' PDM, III, March 1796, 81. This is an abbreviated version of Thomas Amory's account of his uncle, which is prefixed to Grove's posthumous *Works*, for which see below. For Grove see further DNB; DECBP; Alan P. F. Sell, *Dissenting Thought and the Life pf the Churches. Studies in an English Tradition*, Lewiston, NY: Edwin Mellen Press, 1990, ch. 6; idem, *Philosophy, Dissent and Nonconformity 1689–1920*, Cambridge: James Clarke, 2004. For the academies see further 'An Account of the Dissenting Academies from the Restoration of Charles the Second,' Doctor Williams's Library, London, MS, 24.59.25; Irene Parker, *Dissenting Academies in England*, Cambridge: CUP, 1914; H. McLachlan, *English Education under the Test Acts*, Manchester: Manchester University Press, 1931; J. W. Ashley Smith, *The Birth of Modern Education: The Contributon of the Dissenting Academies 1600–1800*, London: Independent Press, 1954; David L. Wykes, 'The contribution of the Dissenting academy to the emergence of Rational Dissent,' in Knud Haakonssen, ed., *Enlightenment and Religion. Rational Dissent in Eighteenth-Century Britain*, Cambridge: CUP, 1996, 99–139

[3] See CR, 237.

[4] Ibid., 419.

their religious gatherings strictly illegal, and their early academies ever at risk of closure.[5]

With the passing of the Toleration Act in 1689 liberty of worship was accorded to doctrinally orthodox Protestant Dissenters (which is to say that Roman Catholics, Jews and unitarians were excluded from the provisions of the Act). Apart from the immediate benefit to Congregationalists, Presbyterians, Baptists and Quakers, the long-term significance of the Act was that for the first time in England worship outside the Established Church was deemed lawful. This measure of toleration was granted in a delightfully English way: none of the earlier legislation was repealed; it was simply determined that its adverse provisions would no longer apply to the favoured groups and individuals. During the next twenty years the Dissenters established about one thousand places of meeting, and their academies, though not always long-lived, were conducted in relative calm: 'relative' calm because on more than one occasion – notably in 1714, when the Schism Bill failed to reach the statute books only because Queen Anne died on the day she was to have signed it (a singular providence in the eyes of the Dissenters) – attempts were made to remove the rights of Dissenters to educate their young in their own institutions. While some academies confined themselves to providing a theological education for intending ministers, many offered a general education, including biblical and theological subjects. The education provided was in some cases of such a quality that Anglican as well as Dissenting youths availed themselves of it. The academies with which Grove was connected were of the open kind.

Henry Grove was born on 4 January 1684, some five years before toleration was enacted, and he died on 27 February 1738, roughly three months before John Wesley's heart was 'stragely warmed' in Aldersgate Street on 24 May, and the Arminians of the Evangelical Revival (in the wake of their Calvinistic precursors, the Baptist Benjamin Beddome, the Congregationalist Philip Doddridge, and the Welsh Anglicans Howel Harris and Daniel Rowland) set about their work in earnest.[6] As we shall see, Grove, the temperate Presbyterian, was as opposed to Calvinism as he was to enthusiasm (the Civil War and the excesses of the radical Commonwealth sects were not easily forgotten, and some feared a recurrence of civil unrest). He was, however, troubled by the decline in the Dissenting interest which set in a generation after the initial burst of post-Toleration activity. This he attributed not to theological disputes and

---

[5] See further Michael R. Watts, *The Dissenters from the Reformation to the French Revolution*, Oxford: Clarendon Press, 1978, ch. 3; Alan P. F. Sell, *Commemorations. Studies in Christian Thought and History*, Calgary: Univesity of Calgary Press and Cardiff: University of Wales Press, 1993, reprinted Eugene, OR: Wipf & Stock, 1998, ch. 5.

[6] For some of the doctrinal issues see Alan P. F. Sell, *The Great Debate. Calvinism, Arminianism and Salvation*, (1982), Eugene, OR: Wipf & Stock, 1998, especially ch. 3.

philosophical challenges, of which there were not a few, but to some extent to lukewarm ministers, but also to the people:

> Let those that are concerned lay their hands on their hearts, and say, whether they have not grown cold and indifferent to Nonconformity, and in some company been ashamed to be known for Dissenters, only because the favours and preferments, of the world, and publick fashion are not on this side; and whether they do not think that others have forsaken us quite, for no other reason than this? The duty of such persons is to mortify their love of the world ... [7]

Grove was the youngest of fourteen children, a number of whom died young, and he himself did not enjoy robust health. It was said of him that 'In him the life of reason and religion seemed to have commenced together.'[8] He early developed a fondness for the classical poets, historians and philosophers and, as the numerous allusions in his writings demonstrate, this interest remained with him throughout his life. From Taunton Grammar School, where he especially enjoyed Latin and Greek, he proceeded to the Dissenting academy in the town in 1698, and found himself under the congenial instruction of Matthew Warren (1642-1706).[9] It appears that Warren, educated at Oxford, though unbeneficed (and therefore not ejectable) at the time of the passing of the Act of Uniformity of 1662, was nevertheless silenced by the Act.[10] By 1671 he was tutor of the academy in Taunton, where he also gathered a Dissenting congregation in 1687, under the Declaration of Indulgence. Joshua Toulmin (1714-1858), a Presbyterian divine who moved from Calvinism to Socinianism, has this to say of Warren and his academy:

> Convinced of the great importance, and even necessity, for the conduct of future life, of furnishing the youthful minds with principles of morality, he directed his particular attention to his pupils' understandings in that part of learning ... He had been himself educated in the old logic and philosophy, and was little acquainted with the improvements of the new; yet it was expressive of liberality of mind and good sense, that he encouraged his pupils in freedom of enquiry, and in the study of those authors who were better suited to gratify the love of knowledge and truth, even though they differed from the writers on whom he had formed his own sentiments. While Burgersdicius or Derodon, and in ethics Eustacius, were used as text-books in the lecture-room; Locke, Le Clerc, and Cumberland were guides to just thinking, close reasoning, and enlightened views, in their closets ... He was

---

[7] H. Grove, *Works*, I, 535-6; cf. IV, 341-2. All the references to Grove's *Works* are to *Henry Grove: Ethical and Theological Writings*, Bristol: Thoemmes Press, 2000.

[8] PDM, 81.

[9] For Warren see ODNB; DSCBP; Alexander Gordon, *Freedom After Ejection. A Review (1690-1692) of Presbyterian and Congregational Nonconformity in England and Wales*, Manchester: Manchester University Press, 1917, 376.

[10] See CR, 511.

> reckoned among the moderate divines of the day: ever studious of the things that make for peace, and promote christian harmony and love ... The name of Mr. Grove, whose genius, character, and talents were formed in his seminary, is alone sufficient to do honour to its president.[11]

The Congregational historians, Bogue and Bennett explain that:

> From that disposition of mind, which would compel every student to think in every thing like his tutor, he was far removed. But, while he wished them to form their own judgment, so that their system might be the result of conviction, he was careful to guard them against those errors which undermine the foundations of religion ... [12]

In 1703 Henry Grove went on to the important Moorfields academy in London, the principal of which was his cousin, the Independent divine, Thomas Rowe (1657–1705), son of the ejected John Rowe, and brother of Benoni (c. 1658–c. 1706), also a minister.[13] Rowe was probably educated at Theophilus Gale's academy at Newington Green, and he certainly succeeded him there as pastor and tutor on Gale's death in 1678.[14] He was thus a student contemporary of Daniel Defoe, and among his own more distinguished pupils were Daniel Neal, the historian of the Puritans; John Evans theological writer and statistician of Nonconformity; the learned 'rational preacher' Jeremiah Hunt; Samuel Say and John Wilson, Independent and Presbyterian ministers respectively; the poet John Hughes; and Josiah Hort, who conformed to the Established church and became archbishop of Tuam, Ireland. Without doubt the most widely known of Rowe's pupils was Isaac Watts, Independent minister, hymn writer and philosopher. He was Grove's contemporary in the academy, and the two became lifelong friends; indeed, on 4 September 1706,

---

[11] J. Toulmin, *An Historical View of the State of the Protestant Dissenters in England, and the Progress of Free Enquiry and Religious Liberty, from the Revoluton to the Accession of Queen Anne*, Bath, 1814, 231–2.

[12] David Bogue and James Bennett, *The History of Dissenters from the Revolution to the year 1808*, 2nd. edn. by James Bennett, London: Frederick Westley and A. H. Davis, 1833, I, 302.

[13] For Rowe see ODNB; DSCBP; Alfred W. Light, *Bunhill Fields*, London: C. J. Farncombe, 1913, I, 35; A. Gordon, *Freedom After Ejection*, 343; Walter Wilson, *History and Antiquities of Dissenting Churches and Meeting-houses in London, Westminster and Southwark*, London: printed for the author, sold by W. Button et al., 1808–1814, III, 168–72. It will be noted that Grove the Presbyterian was in no way inhibited from attending an Independent (Congregational) academy. This exemplifies the general truth that there was in Grove's time a degree of 'denominational' fluidity which should caution us against reading subsequent institutionalized denominations back into the early eighteenth century. Benoni Rowe's son, Thomas (1687–1715), like his father, uncle Thomas and grandfather John, was also a Dissenting minister. He married the writer Elizabeth Singer (1674–1737), who was the inspiration and encourager of Grove the poet. See Grove's *Works*, IV, 393–4.

[14] For Gale (1628–1678) see ODNB; DSCBP.

after leaving the academy, Grove addressed some gently teasing verse to Watts, exhorting him to

> be cautious how you use
> To transports so intensely rais'd your Muse,
> Lest, whilst th' ecstatic impulse you obey,
> The soul leap out, and drop the duller clay.[15]

In later years the genial and mild-mannered Grove did not decline to offer Watts some further hymnological advice:

> The Rev. Samuel Palmer states, that he heard from Dr. Amory [Grove's nephew and successor at Taunton] a conversation which took place between Mr. Grove and Watts ... Mr. Grove remarked, that several of the hymns laid the stress of our redemption on the compassion of Christ, rather than on the love of God; and expressed his wish that he would alter them in this respect, and make them more conformable to the scripture doctrine.[16]

Among Watts's verses is one 'To the much honoured Mr. Thomas Rowe, the director of my youthful studies,' which includes the following stanza:

> I hate these shackles of the mind
> Forg'd by the haughty wise;
> Souls were not born to be confin'd,
> And led, like Sampson, blind and bound;
> But when his native strength he found
> He well aveng'd his eyes.
> I love thy gentle influence, Rowe,
> Thy gentle influence like the sun,
> Only dissoves the frozen snow,
> Then bids our thoughts like rivers flow,
> And choose the channels where they run.[17]

With the sentiments here expressed Grove was in complete sympathy. Indeed from the point of view of their desire to encourage the independent thought of their students Grove's main mentors, Warren and Rowe, were two of a kind. Of Rowe it was more prosaically said that he 'possessed a noble and generous mind, free from the shackles of a party, and utterly averse to all impositions in the concerns of religion. It was this that made him a decided Nonconformist. To all his pupils he allowed the most enlarged freedom of enquiry, and it is well known that some of them followed a path in controversy very different to that of

---

[15] H. Grove, *Works*, IV, 392.
[16] Thomas Milner, *The Life, Times and Correspondence of the Rev. Isaac Watts*, London, 1834, 281.
[17] I. Watts, *Horae Lyricae. Poems, Chiefly of the Lyric Kind*, in Watts's *Works*, reprinted with an Introduction by Andrew Pyle, Bristol: Thoemmes Press, 1999, 151.

their tutor.'[18] The same could not have been said of all divines who followed in Calvin's doctrinal footsteps, as did Rowe.

According to Alexander Gordon, Rowe, a keen student of philosophy, was 'the first to desert the traditional text-books, introducing his pupils, about 1680, to what was known as "free philosophy." Rowe was a Cartesian at a time when the Aristotelian philosophy was dominant in the older schools of learning; and while in physics he adhered to Descartes against the rising influence of Newton, in mental science he became one of the earliest exponents of Locke.'[19] As to Rowe's general demeanour, 'To extensive learning, he united great urbanity of manners, and a most amiable conciliating disposition. These gained him the affections of his pupils, and rendered their path to knowledge the more easy as it was the more pleasing.'[20]

During his two years at Rowe's academy Grove made strenuous and successful efforts to master Hebrew in order that he might read the Old Testament in the original. He also took the opportunity of sitting under the preaching of the Anglican Richard Lucas, Prebendary of Westminster, whose *Enquiry after Happiness* (1685) and *Practical Christianity or an account of the Holiness which the Gospel enjoins* (1690) greatly impressed him; and the ejected John Howe, who had been ministering to the Presbyterian congregation at Haberdasher' Hall, Cheapside, since 1675.[21] To these divines Grove's preaching style owed much.

His training completed, Grove returned to Somerset in 1705, and soon became known as an acceptable preacher: 'His voice,' we are informed, 'though not strong, was sweet, and well governed.'[22] On 14 June 1706 Matthew Warren died, and the Presbyterians of Somerset met to determine the future of the Taunton academy. Although Grove was twenty-two years of age only, they appointed him to teach ethics and pneumatology, while divinity was placed in the hands of the Reverend Stephen James, and natural philosophy and mathematics were assigned to the Reverend Robert Darch.[23] On Darch's resignation Grove assumed his teaching duties, and when James died in 1725

---

[18] W. Wilson, op.cit., III, 171.
[19] A. Gordon, *Addresses Biographical and Historical*, London: The Lindsey Press, 1922, 203–204.
[20] W. Wilson, op.cit., III, 170–171.
[21] For Lucas (1648–1715) and Howe (1630–1705) see ODNB. For Howe see also DSCBP.
[22] PDM, 82.
[23] For James (d. 1725) see A. Gordon, *Freedom After Ejection*, 291–2; T. S. James, *The History of Litigation and Legislation respecting Presbyterian Chapels and Charities inEngland and Ireland between 1816 and 1849*, London: Hamilton Adams, 1867, 676; H. McLachlan, *English Education under the Test Acts*, 72–5, 275–6. For Darch (d. 1737) see H. McLachlan, op.cit., 72–5. On James's and Darch's deaths, Grove delivered funeral sermons with dedications to their wives. See *Works*, I, 107–137; 315–317.

divinity came Grove's way also – but so did a new colleague, Thomas Amory (1701–1774), Grove's nephew and former student, who had also attended Moorfields academy under the learned John Eames (1686–1744). He relieved his uncle of classics and mathematics.[24]

Like Warren before him, Henry Grove

> confined himself to no system in divinity, but the scriptures, directing his pupils to the best writers on the several subjects of enquiry, recommending an impartial examination of the arguments, on all sides, in controversial matters, and talking over with them, in the freest manner, the subjects of each lecture; hearing and answering their doubts and objections, with the greatest candour, and constantly exhorting them to the love of truth, and the exercise of moderation and charity towards all who honestly sought it, how widely soever they might differ from him.[25]

Grove's most significant curriculum innovation was the separation of ethics, his favourite subject, from dogmatics, under which umbrella it had traditionally travelled – though, as we shall see, this by no implies that God was excluded from his ethical system.[26] This helped to pave the way for subsequent debates in ethics on the question how far religion and morality are necessarily related. Of Grove's educational contribution in general, Gordon aptly remarks that he 'made a very deep mark on the ministry of the so-called Presbyterian dissent. He taught no heresies; but he illuminated the ethical side of Christianity, and placed its "reasonableness" in the suasiveness of its perfect moral purity.'[27] In all, more than one hundred students passed through Grove's hands.[28] In addition to Thomas Amory, their number included William

---

[24] For Amory and Eames see ODNB; DECBP. For Amory see further W. Wilson, op. Cit., II, 385–393. The manuscript of Henry Grove's lectures on pneumatology is at the Huntington Library, California. I am grateful to Professor M. A. Stewart for advising me of this fact.

[25] PDM, 83. Stephen James had, however, devised a theological system, albeit one biblically based. See the three volumes of his lectures in the Congregational Library, MS I h 1–3, at Dr. Williams's Library.

[26] See further Alan P. F. Sell, *Dissenting Thought*, ch. 6.

[27] A. Gordon, *Heads of English Unitarian History*, London: Philip Green, 1895, 36. A tangled history lies behind Gordon's use of the adjective 'so-called'. Unable to practise their synodical polity after 1662, and notwithstanding the ministerial associations which were established in some parts of the country, the Presbyterian churches became *de facto* independent congregations. Doctrinally, some eighteenth-century Presbyterians – Richard Price, for example – became Arian, while others, like Joseph Priestley, ended in Unitarianism. See further Alan P. F. Sell, *Dissenting Thought*, ch. 5.

[28] The extant lists of students are neither complete nor entirely reliable: Walter Wilson MS D*, 53–4, at Dr. Williams's Library lists 95 students who studied under Grove and a further 23 who studied under Amory. See also MS 24. 59, 73–7. See also the Joshua Wilson MS L54/1/19–20 in the New College, London, archives at Dr. Williams's Library; cf. *Transactions of the Congregational Historical Society*, IV, 239–240. I am grateful to Dr. David L. Wykes for supplying these references.

Cornish[29] and the cousins Micaijah and Stephen Towgood, who became prominent Arian divines in Exeter.[30] That Grove was concerned with the morals of his students as well as with their intellects is clear from his first publication, *The Regulation of Diversions; Designed principally for the Benefit of Young Persons*, 1808.[31]

In addition to his teaching commitments Grove, together with his former students James Strong of Ilminster and William Cornish, served the nearby churches at Bishops Hull and West Hatch for eighteen years. There were two hundred hearers at Bishops Hull and one hundred at West Hatch.[32] For his services here Grove received the less than princely sum of £20 p.a., but nevertheless 'he went on cheerfully, in the service of his Master and immortal souls ... '[33] On the death of Stephen James he resigned his joint charge and assumed responsibility for James's church of 250 hearers at Fullwood/Pitminster.[34] Of Grove's pulpit ministry in general it is recorded that:

> Though his great modesty and love of retirement, kept him greatly out of the way of public notice, when he occasionally preached in some of the more considerable congregations, he had many admirers, and he received invitations from Exeter, and other places of note, which he refused through a strong attachment to quiet, liberty, and independence.[35]

Grove was happily married, though sorely afflicted by loss. Of their thirteen children eight predeceased him, which, declares his memorialist, 'gave him opportunities for manifesting great resignation.'[36] For one of them he wrote a moving funeral oration, as he did for Mrs. Grove, who died in 1736 following a protracted period of painful mental sickness. Grove himself suffered regularly from fevers and headaches, and in 1718, in the wake of a life-threatening illness,

---

[29] Cornish served the churches at Bishops Hull and West Hatch, and was then at Sherborne from 1744 until his death in 1763. He was an Arian, and during his Sherborne ministry more evangelical members of the congregation seceded and joined with others to form an Independent church at Milborne Port. Meanwhile the Sherborne meeting house was halved in size. When in 1753 the evangelical 'Star of the West', Risdon Darracott, came to Sherborne and stayed with Benjamin Vowell, one of Cornish's prominent members, Cornish refused to open his pulpit to him, whereupon more withdrew, never having been 'satisfied with the mild morality of Mr. Cornish's preaching,' and began to worship in private houses. See W. Densham and J. Ogle, *The Story of the Congregational Churches of Dorset*, Bournemouth: W. Mate, 1899, 256-7. And see note 31 below.

[30] See the lists in the Wilson papers in the New College, London, MSS at Dr. Williams's Library. For Micaijah Towgood see DNB; Alan P. F. Sell, *Dissenting Thought*, ch. 7.

[31] H. Grove, *Works*, II, 473-512.

[32] See T. S. James, op.cit., 676-7. Bishop's Hill is here given for Bishops Hull.

[33] PDM, 82.

[34] See T. S. James, op. Cit, 676.

[35] PDM, 83.

[36] PDM, 82. This, no doubt, is intended as a matter-of-fact statement, not a dry, still less a cynical, one.

he composed 'An Ode on the Author's Recovery from Sickness.'[37] In 1738, during his last illness Grove was restless, but not impatient. 'Divine Providence has wise and good reasons for this discipline,' he said: 'The designs of God are large: in the next state we shall comprehend them, and see that all was right ... I have no uneasy fears of dying, the religion of Jesus hath taught me to conquer death.'[38]

Henry Grove 'was seiz'd with a violent fever, Lord's-day night, Feb. 19. Having preach'd that day with uncommon spirit, and the fever continuing without intermission, he died the 27th, in the morning.'[39] He was buried in Taunton. Funeral sermons were delivered by James Strong and William May of London. Of these the first only was published. Said Strong, 'A very great person is now remov'd from us.'[40]

Henry Grove's writings and thought

Henry Grove's publications appeared in various permutations from his earliest tract in 1708 to 1773, when his sermon on *The Reasonableness of Religion* (Job 21: 15) appeared in volume two of *The English Preacher*. This present reprint comprises the four volumes of works published during his lifetime (1747), together with his most significant philosophical work, the posthumous two-volume *A System of Moral Philosophy* (1749). The latter was prepared for the press by Thomas Amory, who also contributed the concluding eight chapters. Amory had earlier gathered and edited six volumes of *Sermons and Tracts; being the posthumous works of Henry Grove* (1740–1741), to which collection are prefixed Amory's account of Grove's life, writings and character, and an elegy on Grove's death by N. Munckley, a physician of Exeter.[41] The first four volumes were revised and the whole republished in 1741–1742 under the title, *Sermons on the following Subjects, etc.* The works now reprinted amply convey the main lines of Grove's thought.

---

[37] H. Grove, Works, IV, 419–24.

[38] PDM, 84.

[39] James Strong, *The Suddenness of Christ's Coming, Consider'd and Improv'd*, a funeral oration for Grove, London, 1738, 22–3 n. For Strong (1686–1738) see Jerom Murch, *A History of the Presbyterian and General Baptist Churches in the West of England*, London: R. Hunter, 1735, 231, 234, 235–6.

[40] Ibid., 22. Less than three months later, on 21 May 1738, Strong himself died. His funeral sermon was delivered by Thomas Amory: *The Character and Blessedness of those to whom to live is Christ, and to die Gain; at Ilminster in the Counrty of Somerset, May 25 1738, on the Death of the Rev. James Strong, aet. 53*, London: R. Hett and J. Gray, 1738.

[41] There were connections between the Munckley and Rowe families of Devonshire. For example, the Reverend John Munckley married into the Rowe family. See W. Wilson, op.cit., III, 380.

As with most eighteenth-century divines, the classification of Grove's thought is not easy. Into the most pastoral sermon he will introduce an ethical topic; into the most philosophical work he will introduce biblical exposition. More particularly, the line between theology and philosophy is notoriously difficult to draw: the disciplinary lines of demaraction (not absolute to this day) with which we are so familiar had yet to be drawn, and the widespread laicizing of philosophy which has proceeded apace only during the last century was a thing of the future. Nevertheless some attempt may be made to indicate the general tendencies of Grove's thought.

(a) The Christian ministry

Grove was first and foremost a Christian minister, and from a number of his works we can derive some indication of his view of ministry and the pastor's function. As we might expect, this theme is to the fore in the ordination charges he delivered. Thus, for example, at the ordination service of Thomas Amory and William Cornish held at Taunton on 7 October 1730 he exhorted the young men to emulate the industry, fidelity and persistence in difficulties which the early apostles evinced, their sole motivation being 'their love to the blessed Jesus.'[42] Ministers must set before the people the evidences of the Christian religion and preach 'the pure uncorrupted doctrine of Jesus Christ.'[43] In this latter connection they must beware lest 'while we tie ourselves down to any human Creeds and Confessions, and Catechisms, it is very possible that some part of what we are building upon the common foundation may be only hay and stubble, not, what we take it for, gold and silver.'[44] Preaching must be in plain speech, and be undertaken in such a way as to prove that 'no man who makes a right use of his Reason can refuse his assent to the Christian Revelation, or find fault with it ... '[45]

As to the other parts of public worship, ministers must take care that these are conducted in a proper, orderly manner, special attention being paid to prayer and the sacraments. The following words from Grove's treatise on the Lord's Supper[46] contain the gist of his memorialist view: 'To perpetuate the memory of his dying love, our blessed Saviour instituted his Supper, to be observed till his second coming, commanding his disciples to do it in

---

[42] H. Grove, Works, I, 511.
[43] Ibid., 520.
[44] Ibid., 522.
[45] Ibid., 526.
[46] The Discourse on the Lord's Supper ran to eleven editions, including two published in America.

remembrance of him.'[47] He also supplied church members with devotional exercises which they might use prior to, and following, attendance at communion services.[48] This exemplifies his desire to equip his people for the devotional habits which he inculcated from the pulpit. He offered further assistance in his two-part sermon and two essays on private prayer, in which he urges the rationality of prayer;[49]

In his ordination charge addressed to Daniel Harson at Moreton Hampstead, Devonshire, on 27 July 1737, Grove discusses the minister's pastoral motivation:

> Social affections are a credit to human nature. There is a pleasure in the exercise of them, where only some inferior good is to be procured; but the divinest satisfaction is when we befriend others in respect of their highest, their eternal, interests ... [The minister is obliged] to do his utmost to prevent the misery and ruin of his fellow-christians; those especially of whom he hath a more particular charge, and to direct, and quicken, and assist them in their pursuit after everlasting happiness.[50]

Something of Grove's own pastoral sensitivity emerges from the funeral orations and dedications he published, of which Volume I includes no fewer than six.[51] He thus writes to Mrs. Mullins, whose son, Samuel, died aged seventeen:

> They that know the heart of a Parent [and we may here recall Grove's own bereavements], will easily apprehend, that the loss of a Beloved Child is no small Trial; and that of an Only Son, in the Spring of his Days, and with the lovely Blossoms of his Wisdom, Goodness, and Piety upon him, still greater. And yet, even this trial is not so great, but that the comforts which flow from the glorious discoveries of the Gospel, its precious Promises and its divine Assistances, are more than equal to it.[52]

In his funeral oration for Samuel on the theme of Christ's having abolished death, he seeks to comfort the mourners:

> How little reason hath the true christian to be afraid of Death. Why should he shrink and tremble at its approach, when it only wears a frightful vizor? Why decline its summons, when it is sent on the kindest message, to bring his Soul into the Presence of his Lord?[53]

---

[47] Ibid., 320. Grove makes only a passing reference to baptism, maintaining that it is a divinely appointed ordinance of initiation, and that it is not be be repeated. Ibid., 296–7, 383.

[48] Ibid., 417–69.

[49] Ibid., II, 159–291. This reached its sixth edition in 1752.

[50] Ibid., IV, 202.

[51] Not, indeed, that Grove's thoughts on death were offered only at funerals. See his sermon to young men, Works, I, 65–103.

[52] Ibid., I, 174.

[53] Ibid., 197–198.

Something of the impact of Grove's sermons on death is revealed in the following anecdote:

> It is recorded of the celebrated Mr. Henry Grove, who had published a sermon on the fear of death,[54] in which the subject was treated in so masterly a manner, that a person of considerable rank in the learned world declared, that, after reading it, he could have laid down his head and died, with as much readiness and satisfaction as he had ever done anything in his life.[55]

(b) Doctrinal themes

Henry Grove touched on many Christian doctrines in his sermons and tracts, but he was reticent on some of them. In particular, we look in vain for 'Trinity' in the index to the works published during his lifetime; and while the entry for 'God' contains references to God's providence[56] and moral attributes, his goodness, eternity, freedom and wisdom there is, again, no reference to God as triune. As to 'Christ', the index entries concern his death, resurrection, kingly power and second coming, but do not, for example, refer to his pre-existence or to the two-nature doctrine of his person. All of this is significant, given that Grove's career spanned the Salters' Hall controversy of 1719, where the issue was ostensibly the Trinity, but, more crucially, that of confessional subscription.[57] Grove took no part in these proceedings – not for him the heat of doctrinal battle; but from his remarks on confessions, to which I have already alluded, and which we shall return shortly, we may infer that he would have been on the side of the non-subscribers, most of whom subsequently affirmed their belief in the Trinity.[58] Those, like Martin Tomkins,[59] who did not sign the

---

[54] Ibid., 209–262.
[55] W. Wilson, op. cit., III, 171.
[56] See especially *Works*, I, 33–61.
[57] A series of influential works reaching back into the late seventeenth century lay behind the debates on the Trinity. Notable among these was the Anglican Samuel Clarke's *The Scripture-Doctrine of the Trinity*, London: James Knapton, 1712. For Clarke (1675–1729) see ODNB; DECBP; J. P. Ferguson, *An Eighteenth-Century Heretic, Dr. Samuel Clarke*, Kineton, Warwickshire: The Roundwood Press, 1976; T. C. Pfizenmaier, *The Trinitarian Theology of Dr. Samuel Clarke*, Leiden: Brill, 1997; and the papers and bibliography in *Enlightenment and Dissent*, no. 16, 1997 – an issue devoted entirely to Clarke.
[58] See *An Authentick Account of Several Things Done and Agreed upon by the Dissenting Ministers lately assembles at Salters-Hall*, 1719. For the Salters' Hall controversy see A. Gordon, *Addresses, Biographical and Historical*, ch. 5; F. J. Powicke, 'The Salters' Hall controversy,' *Congregational Historical Society Transactions*, VII, 110–24; R. Thomas in C. G. Bolam et al., *The English Presbyterians. From Elizabethan Puritanism to Modern Unitarianism*, London: Allen and Unwin, 1968, 151–74; idem, 'The non-subscription controversy amongst Dissenters in 1719: the Salters' Hall debate,' *Journal of Ecclesiastical History*, 1953, 162–186; M. R. Watts, *The Dissenters*, 371–382; Alan P. F. Sell, *Dissenting Thought*, passim.
[59] For Tomkins (d. 1755?) see ODNB.

affirmation were Arians or Semi-Arians who, on biblical grounds, denied the co-eternity of the Son with the Father and hence the full divinity of Christ. They, and others like them, became increasingly suspect in the eyes of high Calvinists, some of whom possessed doctrinal antennae so sensitive as to be analogous to the political antennae of a Senator McCarthy. Not to declare oneself on the Trinity was to be suspect.

Of Grove's general attitude towards doctrinal disputation we are informed that:

> His aversion to engage in those angry disputes, which, in the year 1719, and following, unhappily divided the dissenters, was another thing that made him the fonder of his retirement. He often applied to the warm dealers in controversy, those lines of Mr. Baxter,
>
> We croud about a little spark,
> Learnedly striving in the dark;
> Never so bold as when most blind,
> Run fastest when the truth's behind.
>
> His moderate conduct drew on him the censures of some, as if he were indifferent to the truths of the gospel; but these could not induce him to alter. He did not believe that the wrath of man would ever work the righteousness of God, or that interposing the authority of fallible mortals was the proper way to end controversies, or establish divine truth.[60]

As Grove said to Farnham Haskoll in his ordination charge of 1733, the good minister, 'studiously avoids entering into party-quarrels, is very sensible of his being himself frail and fallible, takes not upon himself to judge the hearts of men, and considers that it is not so much the knowledge as the love of the truth; and not so much faith as the good disposition of mind whence it flows, that renders a man acceptable to God ... '.[61] These words epitomize Grove's general disposition.

However, Grove was less reticent in his opposition to Calvinism, not least in connection with the desire of some to elevate 'the authority of fallible mortals' above Scripture. With reference to such bodies as the Westminster Assembly and its notable *Confession*, he asks – publicly during Haskoll's ordination service:

> Did these Assemblies pretend Authority to decree Articles of Faith, or did they not? If they did, it will be time enough to submit to their decrees, when they have satisfied the world, who gave them this authority ... In vain are we referred to the Scriptures, if after all we must not search the Scriptures, to

---

[60] PDM, 83.
[61] H. Grove, *Works*, IV, 182.

see whether these things are so, but be obliged to receive the Scripture with their interpretation of it.[62]

Liberty of judgement, he contends, is endorsed by Scripture and reason alike – his text is 'Study to shew thyself approved unto God' (II Tim. 2 : 15); the sole authority is that of 'the only Head and Lawgiver of the Church,' Jesus Christ; and he regrets that 'whoever does not express a like reverence for human Creeds as for the Word of God, is sure to be censured by almost every party, though there is no party but would give him leave to have as little respect as he pleased for every other Creed and Catechism, as far as it differed from their own.'[63] By contrast, as he told Daniel Harson at his ordination in 1737, 'Honest men that think for themselves, will value you the more for doing what they themselves have done [that is, they have searched the Scriptures], though the consequence should be your differing from them in some opinions; and as for the censures of others, who want honesty, or whose notions are not properly their own, but their party's from whom they have taken them, they are not worth regarding.'[64]

Grove's most pointed remarks against Calvinism are to be found in notes accompanying the printed version of his charge at Harson's ordination. He here repudiates on moral grounds the idea that whereas the Bible teaches that God is no respecter of persons, the Calvinist doctrine of election teaches that God deals with people not in accordance with their behaviour, but because they are from eternity predestined for heaven or hell. 'Upon the whole,' he declares, 'the peculiar principles of this odd scheme of doctrine are evidently repugnant to the first principles of natural and revealed Religion professedly embraced by all Christians, and therefore must needs be false; and those places of Scripture that seem to favour them ought to be taken in another and milder sense, of which they are easily capable ...'[65] He further charges that Calvinism with its absolute decrees removes free agency from human beings, and also denies God's love by supposing that he would treat people arbitrarily in ways which we would not approve in lesser beings. He concludes,

> when we believe the mercies of God to be over all his works, and his intention to save all who, by their obstinate continuance in sin, do not exclude themselves from the common salvation, the thoughts of such a glorious design naturally dilate the heart in love to God and man, and place all men in the most amiable point of view, as good, or capable of being so, and our companions in bliss for ever.[66]

---

[62] Ibid., IV, 168.
[63] Ibid., 172–3.
[64] Ibid., 213.
[65] Ibid., 215 n.
[66] Ibid., 220 n.

None of which would have satisfied John Ball, the venerable high Calvinist Presbyterian of Honiton.[67] In 1736, six years after Grove's sermon on the occasion of the ordination of Amory and Cornish was published, Ball published *Some remarks on a new way of preaching propos'd in an ordination sermon preach'd at Taunton*. The new way is the way of the rationalists, and the major culprits are Socinus and Locke. On his own admission, says Ball, Socinus 'did not believe a Thing, because he found it in the Scriptures; but first consulted whether the Thing was agreeable to his Reason, and then believed what was written, otherwise not … '.[68] As for Locke, he blunts the edge of such texts as 'Thou shalt surely die' by holding that after death the wicked have no sensation or being. By contrast, Christ's own preaching, he avers, was 'dogmatical'. The new preaching, he continues, does not work and, what is more it would have been repudiated by Grove's pious parents, whom Ball had known:

> They were indeed no Philosophers, but they thought it the highest Reason that Men should obey his Commands, who after he had killed, was able to destroy both Body and Soul in Hell-fire. But the wise Doctor says, this is to please Children with Sugar-Plums, and to fright 'em with Whips, and not likely to do any Good, because they did not form their Minds to a rational Sense of Good and Evil, or give 'em a Taste and Relish for Virtue.[69]

Jesus himself, says Ball, 'taught by Precepts, Promises and Threatenings' – 'Wo to our Saviour when he falls into the Hand of Philosophers and rational Divines!'[70]

Not even the peaceable Grove could restrain himself. Of Ball he writes,

> He mistakes, he accuses, he rails, he exclaims and laments; and that's all. This, indeed, must be said for him, that he is a bright example of the dogmatical and mechanical way of writing, and of that aversion to Reason in Religion, with which it seems to be one principal part of his aim to possess his Readers.[71]

Grove cannot subscribe to Ball's 'inhuman' and 'unchristian' view that God damns the heathen without mercy; he denies that those who take a more generous view are fellow-travellers with freethinkers and atheists; against Ball's contention that Jesus Christ was a dogmatical person Grove retorts that Jesus did not deduce his moral instruction from a theological system, and frequently

---

[67] For Ball (1655?–1745) see ODNB where, however, his father is said to have been the ejected Nathaniel Ball of Barley, Hertfordshire. In fact he was William Ball. See CR, 25; Alan P. F. Sell, *Dissenting Thought*, 360.
[68] J. Ball, *Some Remarks on a new way of Preaching propos'd in an Ordination Sermon preach'd at Taunton*, 1736, 9.
[69] Ibid., 19.
[70] Ibid., 20.
[71] H. Grove, *Works*, IV, 256.

gave reasons for his commands. Furthermore, in the absence of rational consent, a person's conversion would be nothing more than an arbitrary action of the Holy Spirit: 'I make the change of the heart in conversion, under the influences of divine Grace, to be the effect of rational conviction, and that of serious consideration, and suppose that it is by means of this latter, and not so directly, or immediately, that the promises and threatenings of the Gospel produce their intended effect ... '[72]

To Ball's 'Woe!' Grove returns two of his own: 'Woe to the most Reasonable religion in the whole world, when it falls into the hands of men that are the avowed enemies of Reason; the Goths and Vandals of the Christian Church! Woe to the Rational Divines should they fall under the power of blind and merciless bigots!'[73]

Turning from expostulation, Grove points out to Ball that in his ordination sermon he did not, as charged, fail to rebuke Locke for his view that 'the wicked after death shall have no Sense or Being.' On the contrary, he spent several pages refuting the notion while not naming the man.[74]

Grove thanks Ball for the 'honourable' reference to his parents 'whose memory will be ever precious to me, with whatever sinister reason you might do it;' but he points out that although his parents were not philosophers, they showed their lack of aversion to philosophy by giving their son a liberal education.[75]

The upshot is that Ball's pamphlet confirms Grove in his resolution 'not tamely to submit my Faith or Practice to the haughty dictates of any man, or party of men whatsoever; and in my notion of the necessity of mens making more use of their Reason in religious matters, than they ordinarily do ...'[76]

If Grove said little on some major Christian doctrines, he said a good deal on the Cross and Resurrection of Christ: 'The death of Christ may be considered as a demonstration of the most astonishing love that ever was, both of the Father and of the Son; of the Father in giving his Son to die for us, and of the Son of God who freely offered himself.'[77] If this were all he said we should be justified in attributing a 'moral influence' theory of the atonement to Grove, of a kind generally associated with the name of Abelard: in view of the demonstration of God's love at the Cross we are constrained to love him in return. But Grove has more to say: 'The death of Christ may be considered as that of a sacrifice, by

---

[72] Ibid., 273–4.
[73] Ibid., 275.
[74] Ibid., 283. Grove had in 1730 – the year of the offending sermon – published a substantial pamphlet on the future state, in which he repudiated the annihilationist view.
[75] Ibid., 285–6.
[76] Ibid., 287.
[77] Ibid., II, 319.

which the displeasure of God was atoned, and the sin of man expiated.'[78] Of God's love in Christ the Resurrection is, for Grove, the vindication, and he has three sermons which, taken together, comprise a fairly substantial treatise on the subject.[79] The Resurrection, he insists, is 'a fundamental doctrine of Christianity. Take away this article, the whole frame of our religion falls to the ground.'[80] He proceeds to state, and to counter objections to the doctrine and, in the third sermon, he draws out the implications of the Resurrection for the Christian's life and future hope.

As for the believer in this life, Grove writes at length on saving faith,[81] his discussion turning on his proposed definition: 'Faith is such a firm and lively persuasion of the truth of the Gospel, and of the great things therein contained, those especially that concern man as a sinner, and this upon the testimony of God the revealer, as ingages the Christian to chuse and act suitably to the nature and importance of the things he believes.'[82] As he proceeds we see that for Grove faith is not, in later evangelical (or earlier Pauline) fashion, construed in terms of personal trust (*fiducia*). Rather, 'the object of this Faith is divine truth, and the immediate reason and foundation of it, is the divine veracity ... '.[83] It may well be that at this point Grove's mode of expression is influenced by the fact that he has 'enthusiasts' in view. He is convinced that they are in thrall to a spirit which' renders all those, that are possessed by it, very unfit to be soberly reasoned with.' Certainly he can later say that to receive Christ is the same as to believe his words.[84] Christians are engaged to a life of holiness and obedience, and hence 'Faith stands for the sum of Practical Christianity.'[85] Again, faith is the condition of the great salvation promised in the Gospel, and the exercise of it is 'a sober and virtuous act of the mind.'[86] The doctrine is then applied to the believer's life, and Christians are exhorted to walk by faith. Five meditations are appended to the discourse.

Grove says relatively little about the nature of the Church, though he did address an assembly of ministers on the text, 'My kingdom is not of this world' (John 18: 17) in 1735.[87] He equates Kingdom and Church (in a way which some modern scholars would decline to do), argues that Christ alone is Head of the Church, and hence that the Church of Rome, with its papal authoritarianism is

---

[78] Ibid., 325.
[79] Ibid., I, 361–465.
[80] Ibid., 371.
[81] Ibid., III, 3–170.
[82] Ibid., 13.
[83] Ibid., 33.
[84] Ibid., 50.
[85] Ibid., 71.
[86] Ibid., 121.
[87] Ibid., II, 109–56.

without a basis in Scripture. Although the Church's foundation is eternal, the true Church visible may be in a minority on earth. It is not Rome alone which is at fault: 'among Protestants whoever make the Christian Religion, or any part of it, an engine of State, seem either to mistake, or not duly consider, the nature of Christ's Kingdom ... '.[88] There follows a critique of papal infallibility into which we need not delve. The address concludes with a characteristic exhortation to the listening ministers: 'The less fond we shew ourselves of worldly power and dominion, the greater influence shall we be likely to have over the minds of men ... [and this] will furnish us with a capacity and opportunity of doing more good in the world.'[89]

As we have already seen, Grove's more theological writings are permeated by respect for, and confidence in, reason. This theme comes to the fore in his *Queries proposed to the consideration of all such as think it an Injury to Religion to shew the Reasonableness of it*.[90] These queries were stimulated by objections voiced against certain passages in Grove's Amory-Cornish ordination sermon. Reason, Grove declares, is a gift of God; it is one of two ways in which God speaks to us, the other being through revelation. Those who judge Christianity to be excellent are those who most clearly discern its reasonableness. If people in the early Christian centuries had used their Bibles and their reason, and judged for themselves, instead of blindly following blind guides, there would not have been as many gross corruptions of doctrine and worship. Grove upholds the right of rational enquiry into Scripture and among his justifying reasons is one to the effect that if reason be banished from religion, how shall we be able to repudiate the Roman Catholic avoidance of Scripture? In the preface to the sermon which occasioned the Queries Grove proposes a moral test of doctrine: 'Are there any Doctrines then, the obvious tendency of which, instead of inspiring and cherishing the love of God, is to damp the flame of that divine affection, and to beget a servile tormenting fear, which that love was intended to cast out ... ?'. Are there 'Doctrines which ... harden the heart against the more generous and humane passions ... which lead [those who espouse them] astray from God while they think they are imitating him?' Any such doctrines must be questioned, 'For truth is ever uniform and consistent with itself, truth in the understanding with truth in the will, affections, and practice.'[91] With this emphasis upon the importance of reason we may pass to Grove's more philosophical writings.

---

[88] Ibid., 128.
[89] Ibid., 155.
[90] Ibid., IV, 227–51.
[91] Ibid., I, 493.

(c) Philosophy

As early as 1708 Henry Grove corresponded with Samuel Clarke. He raised certain queries concerning Clarke's theistic arguments, but was entirely sympathetic to his general Newtonian stance, and 'thought it the grossest perversion of natural philosophy to separate it from its relation to Deity, whose perfections and works it was his delight to explore.'[92]

Grove's first significant philosophical work concerns the immateriality of the soul.[93] By 'soul' Grove means 'that in every man which reasons, deliberates, resolves, feels pleasure, or pain, &c. all which when we would express by a single term, we make use of the word thought.'[94] As to the shape of his argument, whereas many have argued from the soul's immateriality to its immortality, Grove intends to do the reverse. From the perfection of the infinitely wise, just and good God, and from the human being's nature as a reasonable agent, he concludes to the immortality of the soul. He then argues for its immortality on the ground that if the soul is naturally immortal it cannot be a system of matter. This leads him in passing to counter Locke's supposition that had he so chosen, God might have endowed matter with the power of thought:

Matter cannot have a power of thinking superadded to it. I do not say that a substance having this power cannot be settled in matter; on the contrary, if this be a proper sense of superadding, I own God hath superadded a power of thinking to matter by substantially uniting the soul to the body. But my meaning ... is that a power of thinking cannot be made to inhere immediately in matter, or that matter cannot be the next and immediate subject of a power of thinking.[95]

To his own satisfaction Grove thus demonstrates 'Mr. Locke not to have been infallible.'[96]

Like a number of other divines, Grove was fearful that to transfer the soul's property of thinking to matter would make the soul redundant, and land one in outright materialism, thereby threatening the being of God himself.[97] Indeed, as he tells us in his Preface, his major objective in this essay is 'to prove the existence of spiritual substances against the materialists.'[98] But he does not wish

---

[92] PDM, 82–83.
[93] H. Grove, *Works*, III, 173–237.
[94] Ibid., 187.
[95] Ibid., 210; cf. 229–31. See John Locke, *An Essay concerning Human Understanding*, ed. Peter H. Nidditch, Oxford: Clarendon Press, 1975, IV.iii.6.
[96] Ibid., III, 210–11.
[97] See further Alan P. F. Sell, *John Locke and the Eighteenth-Century Divines*, Cardiff: University of Wales Press, 1997, 258–62. For a full study of the topic see John Yolton, *Thinking Matter: Materialism in Eighteenth Century Britain*, Oxford: Blackwell, 1984.
[98] H. Grove, *Works*, III, 176.

to fall into the opposite trap of denying the existence of the external world. Hence his prefatory critique of Arthur Collier's *Clavis Universalis: or, a New Inquiry after Truth. Being a Demonstration of the Non-existence, or Impossibility of an External World* (1713).[99] Collier holds that matter has no existence independently of its being perceived. Grove thinks it is as unnecessary to rebut Collier in detail as it would be 'to give one's self the trouble of cutting off every toe or finger from a monster, whom we could dispatch with one solid knock on the head.'[100] He agrees with Collier that the world, the immediate object of perception, is not external: our knowledge of the visible world is by idea, not intuition. But why should Collier claim that the external world is an utter impossibility? Grove sets out to prove that 'if the world serves all the same ends both of contemplation and action, tho' knowable only by idea, as it would if it were visible, or the immediate object of perception, then its invisibility can be no reason against its existence.'[101]

But, to repeat, Grove's concern in the discourse itself is, to rebut materialism. Hence his argument for the view that it is

> altogether unreasonable to suppose the soul is matter, even tho' by the omnipotent Will of the Creator a system of matter were capable of becoming a cogitative Being. Thinking belongs not essentially to matter, neither is it a mode of some other power originally in matter, but must, in order to have a place in it, be superinduced by creative power, and exerted by matter, not considered as matter, but by a faculty quite foreign to its original nature and capacity.[102]

Moreover, 'God is a Spirit, and thinking doth essentially and necessarily belong to his Being.'[103] It is not incredible that God should 'communicate a copy of his essence [to human beings], as he hath done of his attributes;'[104] and in both cases this can be achieved without blurring the distinction between the finite and the infinite. After all of which Grove concludes with a prayer.

In 1730 Grove entered the lists against a fellow Dissenting divine, Joseph Hallett, Jr., on the question of the future state.[105] Hallett had argued that it was impossible to prove a future state from the light of nature. In so doing he had, thought Grove, undermined the admirable views of Howe, Clarke, and Wollaston, and Grove set out to redress the balance.[106]

---

[99] For Collier (1680–1732) see ODNB; DECBP.
[100] H. Grove, *Works*, III, 177.
[101] Ibid., 179.
[102] Ibid., 231.
[103] Ibid., 233.
[104] Ibid., 234.
[105] For Hallett (1691?-1744) see ODNB.
[106] For William Wollaston (1660–1724) see ODNB; DECBP.

He begins by setting down the three possible options: 'that reason affords no proof at all of a future state, whether of rewards or punishments. The second, that a future state is capable of being proved, but not of rewards. The third, that Reason leads men to believe a life after this, in which they shall receive according to what they have done in the body, whether it be good or evil.'[107] Hallett adopts the first position and argues that apart from the Gospel we have no proof of a future state. But the most charitable implication of this position, retorts Grove, would be the annihilation of those who have never heard the Gospel. Grove cannot stomach this, though it is, he thinks, preferable to the second alternative, according to which the heathen would be 'necessarily miserable.' His favoured position is the third, because it is 'more agreeable to the doctrine of holy scripture, better fitted to wipe off all aspersions from the Perfections and Providence of God, and of greater service in disputing with the enemies of our Religion.'[108]

In opposition to deists, he contends that both reason and revelation teach a future state, and both inculcate the same duties, to which the same rewards and punishments are annexed. However, revelation has the advantage over reason in that 'it gives a plainer and fuller representation of the whole duty of man than was ever done by unassisted Reason ... .'[109] Against the annihilationists, he proceeds to argue for the future state from the natural immortality of the soul and the universal desire for immortality. He advances the further ground that since God wills people to believe in a future state that belief cannot be false. Despite human imperfections, reason conveys the idea of future rewards, while revelation proposes nothing which destroys the arguments for future recompense from the light of nature.[110] He almost concludes with a lengthy consideration, replete with biblical and classical illustrations, of the advantages regarding this life and the life to come which Christians enjoy by the Gospel revelation, but then spills over into an appendix of further thoughts, of which the last is this:

> Happy we who have the benefit of the Gospel-Revelation, for which we cannot be too thankful, while we pity wretched mistaken mortals wandring in the mists of Paganism! ... [L]et us not ... argue, that Reason can afford no proof of a Future State; but thus (which is very true) that Reason set wrong in the beginning, and accustomed to false principles is not so well qualified to separate truth from error, to point out the best arguments in defence of the truth, and to urge them with the same strength and advantage, as when it

---

[107] H. Grove, *Works*, III, 241.
[108] Ibid., 243–4.
[109] Ibid., 245–6.
[110] Note Grove's important statement on self-interest in relation to divine rewards and punishments, ibid., I, 486–7.

hath everything to assist, and nothing to obstruct and pervert its operations.[111]

During the 1730s there was a flurry of pamphleteering concerning the first spring of action in the Deity. In 1730 John Balguy opted for the moral principles of *Divine Rectitude*; in the following year Thomas Bayes chose *Divine Benevolence*, and depicted a God with utilitarian proclivities, ever seeking the happiness of all; and in 1734 Henry Grove entered the lists with his tract, *Wisdom the first spring of Action in the Deity*.[112] Grove's case, argued at some length and with reference to Descartes, Hobbes and others, is that it is absurd to think of God as motivated by natural inclinations, or as possessing unbounded liberty. We may not lose sight of God's moral attributes, of which we have clear and distinct, though not adequate, ideas. Thus, God's goodness is not so flexible as to countenance moral evil – indeed, in the only example of the kind known to us, Christ's sufferings and obedience and ensuing glory clearly reveal God's abhorrence of sin; and sin is at the root of all evil:

> God made everything good, but, for wise reasons, not immutably so. He saw fit to make his reasonable creatures free, and to suspend both their future highest happiness, and the continuance of the present, upon the right use of their freedom. This freedom they abuse, this abuse is a moral evil, and productive of pain, both of body and mind, which is natural evil.[113]

Grove proceeds to reinforce his arguments and to counter objections to them. He elaborates upon the divine-human relationship, and concludes,

> Upon the whole; since we can have no reason to doubt of the truth of that notion which best consults the honour of the divine perfections, best agrees with the universal sense of mankind, and is best adapted to promote the cause of Virtue and Religion, and to answer the most difficult questions on the subject of Creation and Providence, I take leave to conclude that Wisdom (and not arbitrary will or blind inclination) is the first spring of action in the Deity.[114]

Of his uncle, Thomas Amory wrote, 'Truth in every form had charms for him, but moral truth the most, because it immediately improves the heart.'[115] Without question, wherever we look in Grove's writings we can detect his ethical, practical and apologetic interest. This is manifest in his three sermons on some 'Errors and imperfections in the conduct of Christians, by which they

---

[111] H. Grove, *Works*, III, 482–3. Hallett replied to Grove in *A Defense of a Discourse on the Impossibility of proving a Future State by the Light of Nature. With an Answer to the Reverend Mr. Grove's Thoughts on the same Subject*, London: J. Noon, 1731.
[112] For Balguy (1686–1748) and Bayes (1702–1761) see ODNB; DECBP.
[113] H. Grove, *Works*, IV, 73.
[114] Ibid., 141.
[115] PDM, 82.

lessen both their own reputation and that of religion.'[116] Again, he prefaces his Amory-Cornish ordination sermon with twenty-five pages of reasoning designed to show that 'morality is originally founded in the nature and relations of reasonable Beings; and that it is one great excellency and commendation of the Religion of our blessed Saviour, that it hath given us a scheme of the purest, the most useful, and the most perfect morality that ever was.' This one sentence encapsulates apologetic, practical and ethical concerns. In the same Preface he announces the supreme moral obligation, love to God: 'We are obliged to love God not merely because he hath commanded us to love him, but because he hath made us capable of loving him, and both by his perfections and his benefits challenges our love.'[117] But Grove's most substantial offering in moral philosophy is his *System*, edited and completed by Amory, and posthumously published in 1749.[118]

Grove defines morality as the knowledge and practice of those things that concern human beings as moral agents. The pursuit of the moral path leads to happiness, which is man's chief end.[119] Light is shed on the path by revelation, which enables us to see out duty clearly; but reason also has its role in investigating the foundations of moral goodness and distinguishing the several virtues. Reason further guards us against false ideas of God and illegitimate appeals to Scripture, and it enables us to demonstrate the Gospel's coherence with itself. We cannot attain absolute happiness here below, but God will reward the virtuous hereafter, however adverse their earthly circumstances may have been.

In the course of his argument Grove repudiates Hobbes's materialism, and his reduction of the natural law to a law of self-preservation. Though in broad agreement with Locke on many matters, Grove also challenges Locke, not least in connection with the freedom of the will. He agrees with Locke that liberty is a power to act or not to act, but takes exception to Locke's additional clause: 'according to the preference of the mind,' because in respect of that, Locke more than once or twice says that human beings are not free.[120] Grove replies that if a man prefers to stay locked in a room with a harlot and the preference of his mind is not free, he is guilty of no wrong, for free actions only can be culpable. But 'If he be free, then it follows, that he has a power to will or not to will his

---

[116] H. Grove, *Works*, II, 3–105.

[117] Ibid., I, 470–471.

[118] For a fuller account of Grove's *System*, set in the broader context of eighteenth-century ethical discussion, see Alan P. F. Sell, *Philosophy, Dissent and Nonconformity*, ch. 3.

[119] Cf. H. Grove, *Works*, IV, 327: 'the end for which [God] designed his reasonable offspring is the contemplation of his works, the injoyment of himself, and in both to be happy, having, to this purpose, endowed them with correspondent faculties and desires.'

[120] H. Grove, *A System of Moral Philosophy*, London: J. Waugh, 1749, I, 198.

stay; in other words, that he is free as willing.'¹²¹ On the question of human agency in relation to divine foreknowledge Grove contends that God foreknows human actions as free. How God does this, Grove does not presume to say, somewhat lamely adding that God 'may have ways of knowing things wholly inconceivable by us.'¹²²

In Part II of his *System* Grove discusses conscience. The external, supreme and ultimate law is God's law, but conscience is 'the internal, subordinate, and immediate Rule of every man's actions ... '.¹²³ It is not a power or faculty distinct from reason, but is 'the reasoning or judicative faculty of the Mind.'¹²⁴ God's will, discerned by reason and revelation, is the only rule which immediately binds the conscience. Moral obligation is 'a moral Necessity of doing actions, or forbearing them.'¹²⁵ He strongly resents Hobbes's idea that irresistible power is the source of God's sovereignty, for his, he argues, would mean that God has a right to do whatever he has the power to do: he could, for example, damn innocent creatures, and in this way other attributes of God would be flouted. Grove proceeds to discuss the law of nations, canon law and civil law, and finally embarks upon a consideration of virtues: prudence, sincerity, fortitude, sobriety, temperance, justice, truth and faithfulness. With faithfulness Grove's own writing ends, and Amory completes the volume.

In his DNB article on Grove, Alexander Gordon describes Grove's *System* as 'a mild Christian stoicism.' Readers may judge the matter for themselves, but in fairness to Grove we ought to note what he has to say elsewhere than in the volumes now reprinted:

> It has been thought by many learned men, that the Stoic philosophy comes the nearest of any to the christian religion, both in its principles and precepts. But I must own, I can hardly be of this opinion, were it only for this reason, that they differ so widely in their very foundations; one of them having its original in pride, the other in humility; one of them robbing God of his glory to adorn man, the other representing man in his true meanness, and weakness, and guilt, in order to exalt the glory of God, and the honour of divine grace.¹²⁶

While it is true that some Stoic sayings are similar – even identical – to Christian teachings,

---

¹²¹ Ibid., 199.
¹²² Ibid., 217.
¹²³ Ibid., II, 2.
¹²⁴ Ibid., 7.
¹²⁵ Ibid., 66.
¹²⁶ H. Grove, 'Of the obligation upon Christians to give thanks in every Condition, even the most afflicted,' (I Thess. 5: 18), in *The Protestant System: containing Discourses on the Principal Doctrines of Natural and Revealed Religion*, London: R. Griffiths, 1758, II, 188.

when we come to examine things, we shall find this great disparity in the case, that many of the Stoical maxims are really extravagancies, inconsistent with the present frame of human nature, and in no way suited to the present state of human life; whereas Christianity advances nothing but what is truly practicable, and what the grace of God has enabled great numbers to exemplify in real life. The Stoic philosophy had no consideration of the weakness of nature, but required of men to divest themselves of their natural appetites and passions, and to do and suffer things utterly beyond their own strength, without directing them, at the same time, where they might have the strength which they wanted; whereas the gospel makes allowance for the weakness of nature ... [127]

(d) Miscellaneous writings

It remains to note Grove's contributions to two journals. In 1714 four of his essays appeared in *The Spectator*, and in 1722 a further six were published in the *St. James's Journal*. Written for a general readership, these contributions reveal Grove's skill as a popularizer.

In his *Spectator* essays we see something of his underlying optimism. Thus, against Hobbes he muses, 'Hitherto I always imagined that kind and benevolent propensions were the original growth of the heart of man, and, however checked and overtoped by counter inclinations that have since sprung up within us, have still some force in the worst of tempers, and a considerable influence on the best.'[128] Again, 'It is a property of the heart of man to be diffusive; its kind wishes spread abroad over the face of creation; and if there be those, as we may observe too many of them, who are all wrapt up in their own dear selves, without any visible concern for their species, let us suppose that their good-nature is frozen ... '[129] We see also, in his essay 'On Novelty', his capacity to employ homely illustrations:

> When I have seen young Puss playing her wanton gambols, and with a thousand antick shapes express her own gaiety at the same time that she moved mine, while the old Grannum hath sat by with a most exemplary gravity,unmoved at all that past, it hath made me reflect what should be the occasion of humours so opposite in two creatures, between whom there was no visible difference but that of age; and I have been able to resolve it into nothing else but the force of novelty.[130]

---

[127] Ibid., 189.
[128] H. Grove, *Works*, IV, 305.
[129] Ibid., 312.
[130] Ibid., 319.

Of this essay no less a critic than Samuel Johnson declared that it was 'one of the finest pieces in the English language ... '.[131] In the fourth essay, 'On the large capacities of the human soul, and the perfection of happiness for which it is designed', Grove pays tribute to Newton: 'How doth such a genius as Sir Isaac Newton, from amidst the darkness that involves human understanding, break forth, and appear like one of another species!' Yet, 'alas, how narrow is the prospect even of such a mind!' So Grove looks forward to the time when he, who knows 'so small a portion of the works of the Creator, and with slow and painful steps creep up and down on the surface of this globe, shall e'er long shoot away with the swiftness of imagination' and comprehend the workings of the vast universe.[132]

The last of his essays in the *St. James's Journal* is also 'On the immortality of the soul.' It takes the form of a popular defence of his view that matter cannot think. In his first essay to the *Journal* he defends the Presbyterians against the charge of the Whig politician, John Trenchard,[133] that of all the Dissenters the Presbyterians take the least favourable view of the Anglican clergy. Grove replies that this may once, in more tempestuous times, but now a broader view prevails. He agrees with the protagonist that Presbyterian numbers are insufficient to make his denomination a threat, but adds that in any case Presbyterians do not wish to be a threat to the Established Church.

In his second and third essays Grove discusses the limitations of civil power. In overturning Hobbes's 'imaginary state of nature, in which every man hath a right to every thing,' he argues that it is God's will that individuals should pursue their own ends only in so far as these are 'reconcileable with the general good of mankind.'[134] Grove can be sardonic: 'I am sensible that in our enlightened Age, and among many of my fellow subjects, such a supposition as this – That their Governors standing upon higher ground than they, may sometimes see further – is hardly to be made,'[135] but at the same time reveals his commitment to the idea of the orders of society which was characteristic of much of eighteenth-century culture. Indeed, 'we are become a Nation of Politicians; every three half-penny author, of Coffee-house orator, is fit to be of the Privy Council, and, if he were advised with, would quickly set matters upon a better foot.'[136] They are like the apes who tried to sail the ship in the tale which

---

[131] J. Boswell, *Life of Johnson*, eds. G. B. Hill and L. F. Powell, Oxford: Clarendon Press, 1934, III, 33, entry for 10 April 1776; cf. ibid., IV, 32. See further, Frances Hodgess Roper, '"One of the finest pieces in the English language": Henry Grove, a note,' *Journal of the United Reformed Church History Society*, II no. 5, May 1980, 147–9.
[132] H. Grove, *Works*, IV, 329–330.
[133] For Trenchard (1662–1723) see ODNB. He was MP for Taunton.
[134] H. Grove, *Works*, 351.
[135] Ibid., 355.
[136] Ibid., 355–6.

Grove, with some glee, borrows.[137] Against those who think that political power originates in the people, Grove insists that it derives from God.

The fourth essay is 'A defence of the liberty of the will,' in which Grove at his liveliest recapitulates the position he elsewhere more formally states.

(e) Conclusion

In doctrinally and philosophically turbulent times Henry Grove was a peacemaker. He lived by the rule he commended to Daniel Harson: 'Love, follow, and make peace. It is the happiest temper, the most divine imployment. Besides the reward immediately attending a state of tranquillity, you will have an opportunity of doing more good ... '.[138] However, Grove's recognition of the other side of the coin emerges in such an injunction as this: 'We may not sacrifice truth to peace.'[139] We have seen that, despite his dislike of controversy, he was not averse to standing his ground when occasion arose. Presumably we must take James Strong's funeral pronouncement as a testimony to Grove's equability: 'I never knew him earnest and zealous for, or against, any particular principles.'[140] We may certainly believe that any criticism from Grove was offered in the spirit of one of his prayers, in which he asks to continue 'in the regular and uniform discharge of the duties of piety towards God, and charity towards man ... '.[141]

We need not expect that Grove will satisfy us on all the philosophical and theological points he touched. As for his verse, whether or not we applaud the sentiments expressed, we may feel that much of it rises little above doggerel:

> But 'tis enough that Heav'n's my Home,
> And th'Earth while passing thro',
> Tho' trackless spaces lie between,
> My Home I have in view.[142]

For all that, it has been a pleasure to introduce this tolerant, equable, kindly divine.

As Grove lay dying he said 'I cannot express it, it is unutterable.' When asked to what he referred, he replied, 'The goodness of God.'[143] A tablet inscribed with

---

[137] Ibid., 356–8.
[138] Ibid., 209.
[139] Ibid., I, 23.
[140] J. Strong, *The suddenness of Christ's Coming*, 26.
[141] H. Grove, *Works*, II, 290.
[142] Ibid., IV, 425.
[143] PDM, 84.

forty-two lines in Latin by the Gresham professor of rhetoric, John Ward,[144] was erected in Paul's Meeting, Taunton. Part of the tribute reads thus: 'Sincere and studious of the Truth, He recommended to the Approbation of All, as the most important points in religion, Piety toward God, Charity to men, and Restraint of the Passions.'[145]

James Strong may have the last word. Grove, he says, was 'a burning and a shining light ... [H]e had a remarkable vivacity, and penetration of thought, a fine imagination, and a profound judgment ... [He possessed] sweetness of temper, and modesty ... He was very charitable in his sentiments of those that were of different opinions from himself ... He [had] frequently been heard to say, "the older I grow, the less inclined I am to quarrel with men for different opinions," adding, that "where there's an honest heart, God will overlook a thousand mistakes of the head." [He did not make] religion look disagreeable, by unsociable rigours, and sour austerities. [He happily joined] the agreeable humour of a considerable wit, with the decent deportment of a serious divine. [He led an exemplary life, was good to his family and kind to the needy, even though] his worldly income was not great.'[146]

---

[144] For Ward (1679?-1758) see ODNB. He was the son of a Dissenting minister of the same name.
[145] See *Transactions of the Congregational Historical Society*, IV, 238–9.
[146] J. Strong, op.cit., 23–4, 26–7.

CHAPTER 6

Andrew Fuller and the Socinians[1]

Near the beginning of the eighteenth century, the Puritan divine, Matthew Henry (1662–1714), remarked, 'It was a pleasure to Socinus, that arch-heretick, that he had no master: we wish it had been his fate to have had no scholars.'[2] Henry would, no doubt, have been dismayed by the number of Socinus's 'scholars' who were vigorously propagating their 'heresy' in the last quarter of the same century. Theophilus Lindsey, Thomas Belsham and, above all, Joseph Priestley, were all found advocating what their opponents branded 'Socinianism', and what they preferred to designate 'Unitarianism'. Among their sturdiest opponents was the evangelical Calvinist Baptist, Andrew Fuller (1754–1815).[3]

Best known for his advocacy of mission, and for his leadership of the Baptist Missionary Society (1792), Fuller was, albeit self-taught, the leading Baptist theologian of his generation, and a formidable polemicist to boot.[4] He took on deists,[5] universalists, Sandemanians and Socinians, and it is with these last that we are here concerned. In his diary for 1791 Fuller wrote, 'I have lately been reading several Socinian writers; viz. *Lindsey, Priestley, Belsham, &c.*, and have

---

[1] I count it an honour to have been invited to contribute to this *festschrift* for my good friend, Dr. D. O. Thomas. My subject brings together the two traditions, Baptist and Unitarian, with which he has been most closely associated.

[2] J. B. Williams, *Memoirs of the Life, Character, and Writings of the Rev. Matthew Henry*, (1828), Edinburgh: The Banner of Truth Trust, 1974, 181.

[3] For Fuller see *The Oxford Dictionary of National Biography* (hereinafter ODNB); Donald M. Lewis, ed., *The Blackwell Dictionary of Evangelical Biography 1730–1860*, Oxford: Blackwell, 1995; Phil Roberts, 'Andrew Fuller,' in Timothy George and David S. Dockery, eds., *Baptist Theologians*, Nashville, TN: Broadman Press, 1990, ch. 6.

[4] Fuller's polemical works do not appear to have received much attention of late. Phil Roberts declines to discuss them on the ground that they are not theological treatises, op.cit., 138; but Fuller's polemics are intensely theological, as we shall see. Fuller is not mentioned by J. C. D. Clark, *The Language of Liberty 1660–1832. Political Discourse and Social Dynamics in the Anglo-American World*, Cambridge: CUP, 1994. Rachel Eckersley has reported Clark as saying that 'Socinian and Deist were equally synonymous with Unitarian ... '. I cannot find that Clark says this, and since (p. 15) he distinguishes the parties by the Socinians' recourse to revelation, and in view of the importance of revelaiton to the Unitarians, he hardly could. See R. Eckersley, 'John Cartwright: radical reformer and Unitarian?', *Transactions of the Unitarian Historical Society*, XXII no. 1, April 1999, 39.

[5] See Alan P. F. Sell, '*The Gospel its Own Witness*: deism, Thomas Paine and Andrew Fuller,' in R. Glenn Wooden, Timothy R. Ashley and Robert S. Wilson, *'You Shall Be My Witnesses'. A Festschrift in Honour of the Reverend Dr. Allison A. Trites on the Occasion of his Retirement*, Macon, GA: Mercer University Press, 2003, 188–229.

employed myself in penning down thoughts on the moral tendency of their system. I felt an increasing aversion to their views of things, and feel the ground on which my hopes are built more solid than heretofore.'[6] It would thus seem that Fuller, at least, benefited from his own polemics. But what was it about Socinianism that prompted his pamphleteering on the issue? We may for convenience take our bearings from some remarks of Priestley.

Priestley develops his position in the light of his study of what he understands as the progressive corruption of Christianity. Whereas the Christianity of the apostles consisted of 'few doctrines, and those perfectly rational and intelligible, and of few rites, and those as simple as can well be imagined,' a dramatic change subsequently occurred, which grossly perverted teachings and rites alike. Indeed, 'This departure from simplicity and truth will ever be one of the most memorable things in the history of the human mind.'[7] Among the misfortunes is the replacement of the one God of the apostles by the three supreme deities of Athanasius. Thus,

> we see how a just and merciful God, freely pardoning all sins that are repented of and forsaken, who expresses the most earnest desire that all would repent and live, came to be regarded as the most unreasonable of tyrants; not only requiring an infinite satisfaction for the slightest offences, but dooming the greater part of his creatures to everlasting torments; a catastrophe foreseen, and intended by him before they were born.[8]

If this change is extraordinary, 'The recovery of genuine Christianity from this deplorably corrupted state to the rational views we now entertain of it, is no less extraordinary; and the contemplation of it cannot but impress the thoughtful and pious mind with sentiments of wonder and gratitude.'[9] In this recovery, John Biddle, 'a man of great piety, who, without having read any of the writings of the Unitarians, but from the study of the Scriptures, embraced their sentiments,'[10] played a significant part.

When Priestley takes pains to mention that Biddle had not read the Unitarians but simply studied the Bible, he is implicitly objecting to the bestowal upon himself and his co-religionists of the label, 'Socinian', and upholding the principle of the sufficiency of Scripture. He is convinced that the early Christians believed in one God only – indeed, Jesus himself prayed to the Father as 'the only true God' (John 17: 3); Paul agrees (I Tim. 2: 5); and there is one Mediator

---

[6] Andrew Gunton Fuller's *Memoir* of Fuller in *The Complete Works of the Rev. Andrew Fuller*, London: Holdsworth and Ball, 1831, I, lxxxvii.

[7] J. T. Rutt, ed., *The Theological and Miscellaneous Works of Joseph Priestley*, 25 vols. 1817–31, X, 532.

[8] Ibid., 533.

[9] Ibid.

[10] Ibid.,VIII, 360.

between humanity and God, 'the man Christ Jesus.'[11] On the basis of such texts, Priestley is able to rule out, to his own satisfaction, that Arianism in which, from his point of view, some of his fellow divines – not least his friend Richard Price – unfortunately lingered: 'the Arian hypothesis, which makes Christ to have been a great pre-existent spirit, the maker of the world, and the giver of the law of Moses, was ... unknown to the learned and to the unlearned, till the age of *Arius* himself.'[12] In a letter to the biblical critic Alexander Geddes, Priestley repudiates the 'inferior' God of the Platonizing early theologians – a god whom contemporary Arians seemed bent on restoring. For his own part he will not call Jesus God: 'I believe Christ to be *a prophet mighty in word and deed*, a man whom God sent, by whom God spake, whom God raised from the dead, and who will come again in the glory and power of God his Father, to raise the dead, to judge the world, and to give to every man according to his works.'[13] As for the Trinity, Priestley thinks the doctrine as absurd as, and more mischevious than, that of transubstantiation.[14]

Especially in Priestley's recourse to revelation, and his convictions concerning the after-life, we see the distance between him and his fellow Unitarians and the deists – a gap which Fuller and others were concerned to narrow. But Priestley insists that it is a slander to equate deism with Unitarianism: 'where freedom of thinking is joined to real piety, and a sense of the value of revelation, as that alone which can give us any assurance of a future state, the difference between Socinianism and Deism (which is now seen to be intimately connected with Atheism) will appear to be infinitely greater, and of a much more serious nature, than any of the differences of opinions preceding it ... '.[15]

Priestley is particularly concerned to deny that commitment to Unitarianism leads to a loosening grip upon morality. Thus he challenges the Reverend Edward Burn of Birmingham to show him which of the Ten Commandments the Unitarians habitually violate, and contends that a person 'who is persuaded that our very hearts are constantly open to the Divine inspection ... will not be a bad man, or a dangerous member of society.'[16] But it was with particular reference to the moral tendency of Unitarianism that Andrew Fuller entered the lists, and to him we now turn.

---

[11] Ibid., XVIII, 553.
[12] Ibid., VI, 473.
[13] Ibid., XVIII, 443. For Geddes (1737–1802) see ODNB; Nigel M. de S. Cameron, *et al.*, *Dictionary of Scottish Church History and Theoogy*, Edinburgh: T. & T. Clark, 1993.
[14] Ibid., 550–51.
[15] Ibid., XVII, 99; cf. XVIII, 553–5.
[16] Ibid., XIX, 340.

I

In 1793 Fuller published his substantial tract, *The Calvinist and Socinian Systems Examined and Compared, as to their Moral Tendency*. A second edition appeared in 1802, in the Preface to which Fuller declares that the fact that Dissenters of varying doctrinal hues had recently combined to press for the repeal of the Test and Corporation Acts does not imply that doctrinal differences are of no importance; the cause was a civil one, and the united front was to achieve a civil objective. He also corrects the impression, conveyed in part by the multitude of Socinian writings, that the bulk of Dissent has embraced Socinianism. Next, he explains why he speaks of Socinians rather than of Unitarians. He grants that the latter term is preferred by his opponents, but deems such usage unfair. For no Christians worship a multiplicity of gods, and trinitarians no less than Unitarians profess belief in one God. Finally, he points out that his anti-Socinian letters were written prior to the Birmingham riots of 1791, and he regrets the suffering meted out to Priestley and others by those who were not true trinitarians, but quite unprincipled people. At the same time, the detestable riots do not 'render the religious principles of Dr. Priestley less erroneous, or less pernicious; or an opposition to them, upon fair ground of argument, less necessary.'[17]

Fuller recognizes that much has been written on Socinianism, but a detailed comparison of the influence of Calvinism and Socinianism on the heart and life has not appeared; and this is the gap he proposes to fill. He welcomes the fact that Calvinists and Socinians agree that 'the value or importance of religious principles is to be estimated by their influence on the morals of men.'[18] Neither adversion to a few good individuals on either side, nor zeal in defence of principles will suffice to make the case. The question at issue is the general tendency of each system. To estimate such a tendency we can both compare a system's principles with the nature of holiness, and, by referring to plain and acknowledged facts, judge the nature of causes by their effects. As compared with Socinians, Calvinists take a more serious view of sin and the need of repentance, and of faith as trust in Jesus Christ for salvation. Not surprisingly, therefore, Socinian congregations do not abound in conversions from profanity to holiness and devotion to God, while such conversions are a regular feature of Calvinistic religious life in Britain and North America. Even Priestley has accepted that Methodists have 'civilized and Christianized a great part of the uncivilized and unchristianized part of this country,'[19] though he avers that

---

[17] A. Fuller, *The Calvinistic and Socinian Systems Compared*, in Works, I, 153–4.
[18] Ibid., 157.
[19] Ibid., 169.

since Socinians have generally been brought up in virtuous habits of life, conversion is not so necessary for them. Fuller is at a loss to account for the fact that, on Priestley's own admission, the Methodists have had such a beneficial effect, whilst proclaiming doctrines – including salvation by Christ's atonement – which are, according to Priestley, erroneous. As for the conversion of unbelievers as a result of Christian mission – can Socinians show that their system produces like effects? Fuller does not deny that Socinianism is gaining ground among 'speculating individuals', but many of their congregations are in decline. Insofar as such individuals are virtuous, this has little to do with their religious principles, for Priestley himself has said concerning the simple humanity of Christ that 'the connexion between this simple truth and regular Christian life is very slight.'[20]

While all agree that we are to love God with all our heart, and our neighbour as ourselves, the Socinians pay much more heed to the social virtues than to love of God. When Priestley says that we shall at the last be judged by our good works, not by our opinions, he overlooks the fact that what makes a work good is that it originates in a good principle. To Priestley's objection that on Calvinistic principles people have no incentive to attend to moral conduct because the unregenerate are necessarily sinful and believers are entirely passive in regeneration, Fuller retorts that where vice predominates (that is, where regeneration is needed) a person cannot but be passive 'in the first change of his mind in favour of virtue;'[21] and as for election, 'Dr. Priestley cannot consistently maintain his scheme of necessity without admitting it.'[22] For on Priestley's view virtue, like everything else, is necessary; but whence this necessity? It is not self-originated or accidental, and hence, it is ordained by God. Thus, Priestley's necessarian principles lead to Calvinism, and if he denies this he is self-contradictory.

As for the moral effects of Socinianism and Calvinism, Priestley cannot prove that 'a loose, dissipated, and abandoned life is a more general thing among the Calvinists than among their opponents;'[23] indeed, the evidence points the other way, and Fuller quotes Priestley himself as saying that 'a great number of the Unitarians of the present age are only men of good sense, and without much practical religion.'[24] By contrast, lands where Calvinism prevails have been noted not for immorality, but for the reverse. As for the Dissenters, were not the Puritans and Nonconformists of the last two centuries exemplars of holiness, piety and devotion?

---

[20] Ibid., 188.
[21] Ibid., 201.
[22] Ibid., 202.
[23] Ibid., 206.
[24] Ibid., 207.

To the charge that Calvinists believe in a vindictive God, whereas the God of the Socinians is a father, Fuller replies that God does not punish for the sake of it, but his wrath against sin is a function of his righteousness, and it is exercised not as personal vengeance, but by one who is the universal moral governor. Priestley is equally mistaken in thinking that God's first concern, his own glory, militates against the objective of the general happiness of all his creatures – excepting those who are finally impenitent. Finally, when the Socinians accuse the Calvinists of detracting from the worship of the one God by their worship of Christ, Fuller replies that the first Christians worshipped Christ, and that Christ is worshipped 'not on account of that wherein he differs from the Father, but on account of those perfections which we believe him to possess in common with him.'[25] The upshot is that Calvinists, who have been forgiven much, have a more compelling motive for loving God than Socinians.

Fuller next considers Priestley's charge that the Calvinistic system is inconsistent with 'perfect candour and benevolence to man.' He points out that much of what is called candour and benevolence is nothing more than indifference to all religious principle, and that good will towards people does not entail approval of their opinions or practices. Candour towards adversaries is a matter of fair treatment: it has nothing to do with indifference to religious principle. If Socinians advert to Calvin's persecution of Servetus, Fuller will invoke Lindsey's acknowledgment of Faustus Socinus's hostility towards Francis David of Transylvania. As for humility, here again Calvinism scores over Socinianism – the Unitarian Joshua Toulmin's remark to the effect that those who maintain the two-nature doctrine of the person of Christ are to be pitied 'as being under a debility of mind in this respect,'[26] being cited in evidence. As for the complaint that Calvinists lack charity and are bigots, Fuller protests that 'If the proper deity of Christ be a divine truth, it is a great and a fundamental truth in Christianity,'[27] and it is not bigotry to proclaim and defend it. Similarly, 'If the doctrine of atonement by the cross of Christ be a divine truth, it constitutes the very substance of the gospel; and, consequently, it essential to it.'[28] His point is that these, in the way in which Calvinists construe them, are indeed divine truths, and that Socinians are guilty of reductionism in regarding the Cross merely as evidencing the fact that Christ truly died. Fuller does not deny that Calvinists may be bigots, but he contends that there is no more bigotry in denying that Socinians are Christians than there is on their part when they accuse Calvinists of idolatry for their worship of Christ. Further, Socinians are

---

[25] Ibid., 223.
[26] Ibid., 237.
[27] Ibid., 251.
[28] Ibid., 252.

bigots in denying the name of Unitarian to Calvinists, who believe in the divine unity as much as they do. He concludes this part of his case by quoting Priestley as allowing all he himself pleads for: 'The man whose sole spring of action is a concern for lost souls, and a care to preserve the purity of that gospel which alone teaches the most effectual method of their recovery from the power of sin and Satan unto God, will feel an ardour of mind that will prompt him strenuously to oppose all those whom he considers as obstructing his benevolent designs.'[29]

Fuller proceeds to show to his own satisfaction that Calvinism scores over Socinianism in promoting love to Christ, whereas the Socinian system has little use for him. Christ is the animating soul and centre of the Calvinist system:

> Take away Christ; nay, take away the deity and atonement of Christ; and the whole ceremonial of the Old Testament appears to us little more than a dead mass of uninteresting matter: prophecy loses all that is interesting and endearing: the gospel is annihilated, or ceases to be that good news to lost sinners which it professes to be; practical religion is divested of its most powerful motives; the evangelical dispensation of its peculiar glory; and heaven itself of its most transporting joys.[30]

With their views on human depravity the Calvinists have much more to be grateful to Christ for than the Socinians, and as for the Bible, Calvinists venerate is much more than Socinians, the latter construing its inspiration in terms of stimulation rather than as yielding the rule of faith and practice. As for the charge that Calvinism is gloomy and tending to misery and melancholy: it is true that levity is no part of Calvinism; but from a true recognition of our state and trust in God's gracious provision there flows a happiness which is much deeper than the Socinian's 'calmness of mind.' The root of the Socinian's problem is that 'The Socinian scheme, by rejecting the deity and atonement of Christ, rejects the very essence of that which both supports and transports a Christian's heart.'[31] From this root, neglected by Socinians, arise those motives of gratitude, obedience and hevenly-mindedness which Calvinism typifies.

Fuller next seeks to demonstrate his claim that Socinianism leads to infidelity. The infidelity he has principally in mind here is deism – the very phenomenon from which Priestley and other Unitarians were most anxious to distance themselves. Like the deists, says Fuller, Socinians elevate the principle of the sufficiency of human reason. He grants that Socinians do appeal to revelation, but the conclusions they reach are governed by a reason deemed sufficient. They do not reject as much as the deists, but this is only a difference of degree, not of

---

[29] Ibid., 261.
[30] Ibid., 266.
[31] Ibid., 293.

principle. Again, like the deists the Socinians hold to *'the non-importance of principle ... in order to the enjoyment of the divine favour.'*[32] In this connection Fuller associates Priestley and other Unitarians with the view expressed by the deist Thomas Paine, that 'it matters not what religion we are of, if we be but sincere in it.'[33] Socinians share with deists the prejudices that the religion of the vulgar is superstitious and false; that they themselves are wiser than the rest of humanity; and that it is appropriate to sneer at Christ the carpenter's son. Both Socinianism and deism appeal to those of a speculative turn of mind, and these are prominent in denying the plenary inspiration of the Bible, in reading the Scriptures selectively, and in holding degrading notions of the person of Christ. Fuller cites a number of alleged instances of Socinians who have proceeded to infidelity, and then concludes that that system which is friendly to the deity and atonement of Christ is representative of the saving Gospel, whereas that which denies those doctrines is shown by its fruit to be inadequate.

Having now summarized Fuller's argument, we must turn to his Unitarian respondents.

II

Joshua Toulmin (1740–1815) was educated at Hoxton Dissenting academy (1701–85), an institution supported by the Congregational Fund Board and, from 1738, by the Coward Trust – two Calvinistic bodies, with whose doctrine Toulmin, to the distress of his parents, disagreed even whilst a student. He became minister of the Presbyterian church at Colyton, Devonshire, but on embracing baptist views he removed to the Taunton pastorate, where he supplemented his income by running a school. In 1803 he was called to the New Meeting, Birmingham, and became John Kentish's colleague there in 1804. With the bulk of his many writings, which include historical works of continuing interest, we are not here concerned. It is as a defender of Socinianism against Fuller's charges that he appears before us.[34]

It would seem that other Unitarian respondents held back from replying immediately to Fuller in the hope that Priestley himself would enter the lists. To

---

[32] Ibid., 310.
[33] Ibid., 311.
[34] For Toulmin see ODNB. Toulmin's tutors at Hoxton were David Jennings and his relative, Samuel Morton Savage, for both of whom see ODNB. Among his Taunton pupils was J. T. Rutt, the editor of Priestley's *Works*. Since this paper was written David L. Wykes has published, 'Joshua Toulmin (1740–1815) of Taunton: Baptist minister, historian and religious radical,' *The Baptist Quarterly*, XXXIX no. 5, January 2002, 224–3. Though partly concerned with doctrinal issues, Dr. Wykes makes no reference to the Toulmin-Fuller exchange. Our papers thus complement one another.

Toulmin's regret he did not, hence Toulmin's offering.[35] He first sets down the fundamental principles of those whom Fuller [36] calls Socinians: 'there is but one God, the sole former, supporter, and governor of the universe, the only proper object of religious worship; and that there is but one mediator between God and man, the Man Christ Jesus, who was commissioned by God to instruct men in their duty, and to reveal the doctrine of a future life.' With an implicit appeal to the principle of the sufficiency of Scripture, Toulmin continues, 'We think it, Sir, a just ground of boast over our fellow-christians who hold different tenets from us, that we can express our fundamental opinions in the *words* of scripture.'[37]

Toulmin proceeds through the Acts of the Apostles with a view to demonstrating his claim that the apostles preached Unitarian doctrine. For example, he notes that at Pentecost Peter did not preach depravity, the deity and atonement of Christ, justification by the imputation of Christ's righteousness, and, unlike the Moravian missionaries to Greenland, he did not mention Christ's dying for our sins. Paul is presented as following in Peter's line on his missionary journeys.

But Toulmin realizes that he must not simply list doctrinal lacunae; he must demonstrate the efficacy and sufficiency of Unitarian doctrine. He therefore appeals to John Flavel, Richard Baxter and John Howe, all of whom wrote large portions of their works without reference to the doctrines deemed essential by Fuller; so did John Smith the Cambridge Platonist, John Rogers and Samuel Bold. Yet all of these were apprised of the necessity of vital religion. Hence, 'the Calvinistic system is not essential for devotion.'[38] Toulmin then presents a roll-call of non-Calvinists who were people of eminent piety: Faustus Socinus, the Polish Brethren, Biddle, Emlyn, Hopkins, Lardner, Jebb and Price. Thus, if modern Unitarians are less pious than they ought to be, it is not, contra Fuller, because of deficient principles, for those principles are identical with those of the early Church. It is indeed for this reason that Toulmin resents the reproachful designation 'Socinian'. Modern Unitarians do not derive their views from Socinus – in fact most of them are unaquainted with his works – but from primitive truth.

As for Fuller's attempt to equate Unitarianism with deism, this 'implies that to *receive* the divine mission of Jesus has a resemblance to considering him as a deceiver: that to take him as my master, the resurrection and the life has a tendency to the rejection of him: that to learn of him is to deny him: that to

---

[35] J. Toulmin, *The Practical Efficacy of the Unitarian Doctrine considered, in a Series of Letters to the Rev. Andrew Fuller: occasioned by his Publication entitled 'The Calvinist and Socinian Systems examined and compared, as to their Moral Tendency* ... (1796), London: J. Johnson, 1801, 2 n.
[36] Ibid., 4.
[37] Ibid., 5. He cites I Corinthians 8: 6 and I Timothy 2: 3.
[38] Ibid., 71.

profess to obey him resembles disobedience: and that to hope for the mercy of God in him will lead me to cast off this hope.'[39] When Fuller chides Socinians for boasting of their increase in followers, Toulmin retorts that Calvinists are equally prone to such boasting, and Fuller is guilty of it with his reference to hundreds of ministers and congregations whose existence, he declares, proves the efficacy of Calvinism.

In a Postscript to his first edition, Toulmin commends Kentish's reply to Fuller as being more complete and more detailed than his own.

III

John Kentish (1768–1853) was educated at Daventry Dissenting academy under Thomas Belsham. He left that academy in 1788 following the Coward Trustees' prohibition of read prayers, and completed his studies at Hackney College (1786–96), Hoxton's successor, under Abraham Rees, Thomas Belsham and Andrew Kippis. In 1790 Kentish became minister of the new Unitarian cause at Plymouth Dock; he proceeded to Treville Street, Plymouth in 1794, and to London in the following year. In 1803 he accepted the call to the New Meeting, Birmingham. He resigned his charge in 1832, but continued to preach regularly there until 1844.[40]

On 6 July 1796 Kentish addressed the West of England Society of Unitarian Christians at Bow Meeting-house, Exeter, on *The Moral Tendency of the Genuine Christian Doctrine*. This is his direct reply to Fuller. Like Toulmin, Kentish begins by stating the Unitarian positions, namely, that God is strictly one being, and that Jesus of Nazareth was 'simply of the human race, though greatly exalted above every former prophet.'[41] His case will be that reliance upon these doctrines makes for godliness, that is they inculcate the duties we owe to God and to general virtue. While recognizing that if it is difficult to judge the conduct even of individuals, it is so much more difficult to judge that of whole denominations of Christians, he will nevertheless inquire into the moral tendency of Unitarian doctrine.

First, Kentish contends that the virtues which we are under obligation to cherish and express with reference to God are of primary importance in

---

[39] Ibid., 87.
[40] For Kentish see ODNB.
[41] J. Kentish, *The Moral Tendency of the Genuine Christian Doctrine. A Discourse, written with to Mr. A. Fuller's examination of the Calvinistic and Socinian Systems, and delivered at Exeter, July 6th, 1796. Before the Society of Unitarian Christians, established in the West of England for promoting Christian Knowledge and the practice of Virtue by the distribution of Books*, London: J. Johnson, 2nd edn. 1798, 6.

Christian morals and, indeed, 'in every rational system of ethics.'[42] In his view, 'Love to God is no enthusiastic fervour, no offspring of a licentious imagination.'[43] It flows from a lively appreciation of the divine mercies. God's justice, truth and holiness are all construed in terms of his love, and he is glorified as happiness, the object of his works, is diffused. Indeed,

> By the goodness of the Almighty exhibited in the works of nature, in the dispensations of providence, and in our temporal comfort, we are as much impressed, I presume, as any class of Christians. And if we neither think nor speak exactly like some of them, concerning the divine love manifested in the gift of Jesus Christ, it must not hence be inferred, that we are less attentive to its magnitude and extent.[44]

The love that Unitarians feel for God is 'a powerful motive to the most willing obedience.'[45] Such a depth of love can be expressed only towards one person, not to a plurality of deities, as is advanced by the trinitarian scheme. This is not to deny that Jesus's 'love to the human race, a love which even death could not destroy, calls for every tribute of affection, which is consistent with the supreme thankfulness and love we owe to "his Father, and our Father, to his God, and our God."'[46] Like Toulmin, Kentish produces a catalogue of Unitarians who have lead pious lives.

It is not true, Kentish continues, that belief in the simple humanity of Jesus detracts from 'the respect and obedience we render to him as a moral instructor.'[47] Unitarians of integrity know that they rely upon divine mercy alone for the forgiveness of their sins, and they know that 'repentance and amendment of life are essential to a participation in the divine favour.'[48] Further, since Unitarian doctrines are scriptural, they are able to supply 'all the aid and comfort to the rational and virtuous mind, which frail humanity requires.'[49] It is wrong to charge Unitarians with impotence where the conversion of profligates and unbelievers is concerned, for many Unitarians have 'found the plain, simple, yet the despised Gospel of Christ "the power of God unto salvation."'[50] Looking ahead, we may be confident that 'that representation of Christianity which has Scripture and antiquity for its basis' will 'everywhere prevail.'[51] Finally, Kentish takes strong exception to Fuller's equating Unitarians with

---

[42] Ibid., 9.
[43] Ibid., 10.
[44] Ibid., 12.
[45] Ibid., 13.
[46] Ibid., 18. The reference is to John 20: 17.
[47] Ibid., 27.
[48] Ibid., 28.
[49] Ibid., 35.
[50] Ibid., 36.
[51] Ibid., 37.

deists, for the teaching of the former is consonant with that of the earliest Christians.

IV

The efforts of Toulmin and Kentish failed to silence Fuller. In 1797 he published an answer to them: *Socinianism Indefensible on the Ground of its Moral Tendency*. He first replies to Toulmin, making it clear that in his earlier work he focused upon the moral tendency of the two systems under review partly because the doctrinal questions had been much debated, and partly because there was no point in reasoning on the basis of biblical texts with those who disallowed Scripture's meaning. He also observes that to judge a tree by its fruit is to employ a biblical principle.

Toulmin, he declares, has not so much as looked his arguments in the face. Instead, he turns to other matters, and Fuller complains thus:

> I attempted to prove that the apostolic and Calvinistic doctrines are nearly similar, from the similarity of their effects; and that the apostolic and Socinian doctrines are dissimilar, from the dissimilarity of their effects. To have answered this reasoning, Dr. Toulmin should have proved, either that the effects of the Calvinistic doctrine are *not* similar to those which attended the doctrine of the apostles, and that the efferct of the Socinian doctrine *are* so; or else that a similarity of effects in not a proper ground from which to infer a similarity in the nature of the doctrines. His attempting to prove the practical efficacy of the Unitarian doctrine by assuming that the apostles were Unitarians, in his sense of the term, is nothing better than *begging the question*; and his endeavouring to screen himself from this reproach, by labouring to prove the point in dispute from a review of the Acts of the Apostles, let his reasonings be ever so just, is foreign to the purpose: it is *shifting the ground of the argument*: it is declining to meet the inquiry on the ground of moral tendency, and substituting, in its place, *observations on the meaning of Scripture testimony*, which, to all intents and purposes, is relinquishing the practical efficacy of modern Unitarianism as indefensible.[52]

Fuller proceeds to point out that while Unitarians and Calvinists appeal to the same passages of Scripture, the latters' problem with the former is that the Unitarians put their own unwarrantable glosses upon the words of the Bible. This is exemplified by their question-begging choice of the title 'Unitarian'. Fuller's concern is that

> We must either admit every pretender into communion with us, and so acknowledge him as a fellow-christian, or we shall be accused of judging the hearts of men. The rule by which we admit to fellowship is a *credible*

---

[52] A. Fuller, *Works*, I, 341–2.

profession of Christianity. There are two things which render a profession credible: First: That the thing professed be Christianity; Secondly: That the profession be accompanied with a practice correspondent to it.[53]

To acknowledge those as fellow-Christians whose doctrines are defective would be to act hypocritically. In an appendix, Fuller queries Toulmin's interpretation of the Acts of the Apostles, arguing that for the apostles, 'the deity and atonement of Christ were comprehended in the great doctrines of his Sonship and Messiahship.'[54]

In Fuller's opinion, Kentish is the only respondent to have attempted to meet his argument. Nevertheless, he accuses him of begging the question in his title, *The Moral Tendency of the Genuine Christian Doctrine*. In the course of addressing Kentish's preliminary points, Fuller agrees that it is difficult to judge the tenor of whole denominations of people, but nevertheless maintains that 'It is not impossible to discover who in general are serious, conscientious, and pious men, and who they are that indulge in dissipation and folly.'[55]

Turning to the heart of Kentish's case, Fuller notes that in extolling God's love, Kentish entirely overlooks the doctrine of the atonement. Further, genuine love of God is 'shed abroad in the heart *by the Holy Spirit*,' but Kentish has no need of the Spirit: to him it is natural to love God. Again, Kentish's claim that to elevate Christ is to diminish God is untenable, for on the divine authority Calvinists believe that Christ and the Father are one. Kentish is further silent on the idea of trusting in Christ; and as for his catalogue of pious Unitarians: to single people out in this way is invidious, and beside the point, for Fuller's concern was not with individuals, but with the general moral tendency of the Socinian system.

Fuller next finds Unitarianism wanting in respect of assistance, support and consolation in the time of temptation, affliction and death, and in respect of the conversion of profligates and unbelievers. He repudiates Kentish's claim that Unitarians venerate the Scriptures, because they do not pay heed to the profession of the sacred writers. For his part, Fuller declares, 'it is with sacred satisfaction I anticipate the time when all that exalteth itself against Christ, let it affect whose systems it may, shall utterly fall, and nothing shall be left standing but the simple unadulterated doctrine of the cross.'[56]

Toulmin returned to the fray in the 1801 edition of his tract on *The Practical Efficacy of the Unitarian Doctrine*. In a lengthy footnote he charges Fuller with

---

[53] Ibid., 357.
[54] Ibid., 364.
[55] Ibid., 370.
[56] Ibid., 397.

sectarianism. Fuller, he notes, wishes to exclude from fellowship those who do not agree with his interpretation of doctrine:

> But on the principles of protestants, of dissenters, among whom Mr. Fuller classes himself, and of christianity, no individual christian, no body of christians hath a right of so modelling the christian profession and worship, as to make it inconsistent with any sincere christian to join in it, or to bring themselcves under a sense of obligation to exclude such ... [On Fuller's approach] Each community excludes only those, whose sentiments they consider as subversive of the gospel. Each community, in these cases, sets up a standard of christianity, of its own framing. If this be not to become lawgivers and masters in the church of Christ, I know not what can answer the character ... It is surprising, that men can thus deceive themselves with an affectation of disclaiming, with a *verbal* renunciation of infallibility, when their *conduct* can be justified on no other principle than really possessing it. It gives one concern to have occasion to remonstrate, on this subject, with a gentleman, who is *Dissenting* and a *Baptist* Minister.[57]

In a new appendix to his tract Toulmin denies that he has side-stepped Fuller's argument, and cites others who have found him very much to the point. More substantively, he refers to the decline in some Calvinistic churches, and says that Fuller would no doubt find causes for this. For example, the parable of the sower shows that the divine seed is not always productive of fruit. But if such reasoning applies to Calvinist causes, why not to those where Unitarians are defective in piety or virtue – especially when under Unitarian principles a thousand were born in one day [presumably a further disputed reference to Pentecost, though with the number of converts reduced by two thousand]?

Fuller wrongly supposes that he is employing a mode of argument used by Unitarians against Calvinists, for 'The falsehood of Calvinistic doctrines has been inferred, not from the *lives* of Calvinists, but from the nature of the tenets themselves.'[58] Toulmin follows up with a catalogue of Calvinism's falsehoods:

> Calvinism is the system, which represents the Divine Being as placing the eternal interests of the whole human race upon the hazard of the first man's obedience to a single injunction. It clothes the Deity with power and justice, but it allows not the display of mercy, till an infinite satisfaction has answered the demands of justice ... Here virtuous desires, holy efforts, are enervated by an apprehension, that the fall of Adam has introduced into our frame a total impotence, and inability to do what is good.[59]

As for Fuller's attempt to liken Unitarianism to deism: if the Unitarians are like the deists, so were the apostles, and 'The Socinian may reflect with pleasure

---

[57] Ibid., 98, 101.
[58] J. Toulmin, *The Practical Efficacy of the Unitarian Doctrine*, 155.
[59] Ibid., 163.

on the affinity.'⁶⁰ Furthermore, the comparison regarding a like attraction to men of a speculative turn of mind will not hold. For the truth and excellence of Unitarian or other sentiments is not estimated by their adherents, but by 'their conformity to good sense and scripture.'⁶¹ Toulmin concludes in the confidence that truth, whether it be with Fuller, or with himself, or with neither of them, will finally prevail.

In 1798 Kentish published some *Strictures upon the Reply of Mr. A. Fuller to Mr. Kentish's Discourse, entitled "The Moral Tendency of the Genuine Christian Doctrine.* On this occasion his tone seems rather more impatient, as if he is tiring of what he regards as a dialogue with the deaf. He repeats many of his arguments, but now explains that his neglect of the atonement was owing to the fact that that doctrine had no place among the principles the moral tendency of which he was attempting to illustrate. Fuller, in turn, has been less than forthcoming too: 'Upon the question, whether it be reconcileable with our conceptions of an infinitely powerful, wise and good Being to suppose, that from all eternity, and for no actual crime, he has doomed the larger part of mankind to eternal misery, Mr. Fuller has been profoundly and discreetly silent.'⁶² Kentish persists in being unable to understand how a godhead comprising three distinct, infinite, minds can be other than a plurality of deities; neither has Fuller shown how we can love two such minds with all our heart and soul.

Kentish concludes by saying that in his previous tract he granted that the truth of Unitarian claims was to be determined by evidence other than that of the morality of Unitarians, but, standing on Fuller's ground, he addressed the question of the moral tendency of Socinianism over against that of Calvinism. But now he has had to respond to misrepresentations concerning doctrine.

It remains only to add that in a twelve-page Postscript which Fuller appended to the 1802 edition of his examination of the Calvinistic and Socinian systems, he declines to say anything further to Kentish; accuses Toulmin of further irrelevancies; and does nothing more than reiterate his by now familiar positions.

Not surprisingly, nothing said by Fuller dissuaded Toulmin and Kentish from zealously propagating Unitarianism to their dying days.⁶³

---

⁶⁰ Ibid., 165.
⁶¹ Ibid., 167. Note the order here.
⁶² J. Kentish, *Strictures upon the Reply of Mr. A. Fuller, to Mr. Kentish's Discourse, entitled, The Moral Tendency of the Genuine Christian Doctrine,* London: J. Johnson, 1798, 12.
⁶³ See, for example, J. Toulmin, *The Injustice of classing Unitarians with Deists and Infidels. A Discourse written with reference to some Reflections from the Pens of Bishops Newton, Hurd, and Horsley, Doctors White, Knox, and Fuller, Mrs. Piozzi, and Others: and delivered at Tiverton, July 5, 1797, before the Society of Unitarian Christians, established in the West of England, for Promoting Christian Knowledge, and the Practice of Virtue, by the Distribution of Books,* London: J. Johnson, 1797;

As a footnote to the pamphlet skirmish we have been reviewing, we should be reminded that the Socinian/Calvinist debate, like other theological tussles in the eighteenth century, was by no means simply an arm-chair affair. The issues affected people's lives, not least their church allegiance. This emerges in the contretemps at Soham, Cambridgeshire, which involved Fuller and the prominent Unitarian Robert Aspland (1782–1845), editor of the *Monthly Repository*.[64] Local connections played a part: Aspland came from Wicken, near Soham, where Fuller was born and held his first pastorate. During that ministry, Fuller had drawn up a doctrinal statement to which every church member was required to assent. The refusal to comply of Fuller's former assistant and successor, John Gisburne, the Wesleyan-turned-Baptist-turned-Unitarian, coupled with Gisburne's statement of the Nonconformist principle in unduly blunt terms (since the Church of England has two Heads, King Jesus and King George, it is a monster), prompted a dispute concerning doctrine and the ownership of the chapel property. Both Fuller and Aspland intervened. Fuller published a *Narrative of Facts* concerning the case,[65] and Aspland replied in his pamphlet of 1811, *Bigotry and Intolerance Defeated*. Into the details we need not probe, but what relevant to our theme are some remarks of Aspland concerning Fuller himself. He is pleased that in the *Narrative* Fuller no longer calls his opponents Socinians – 'judging, no doubt, that it is unjust to class people under a leader whom they do not follow, and whom they have renounced; and that to force a name upon them which in reason does not belong to them, and which they are known to disapprove, is reproach, and, as far as language goes, persecution.'[66] He hopes that Fuller's brethren will follow his lead, 'and the epithet Socinian will then be speedily banished to the same oblivion to which the good sense and liberality of the religious world have long doomed the not more incorrect and reproachful term, Anabaptist.'[67]

---

dem, *The Unitarian Doctrine Stated, and the Objections to it Obviated, on the Ground of Christ's Declaration: A Sermon, Preached before the Devon and Cornwall Association, at Plymouth, on the 6th of July, 1814; and on the 13th, before the Western Unitarian Society, at Yeovil, Somersetshire*, Birmingham: O. and H. Smith and J. Belcher, 1814; J. Kentish, *A Review of Christian Doctrine: a Sermon preached at St. Thomas's, Southwark, December 26th, 1802, and at the Gravel-Pit, Hackney, January 2d, 1803, on resigning the Office of a Minister in those Societies*, London: J. Johnson, 1803; idem, *Christian Truth Stated, Vindicated, and Recommended*, Birmingham: J. Belcher, 1807.

[64] For Aspland see ODNB; Alan P. F. Sell in *Dictionary of Nineteenth-Century Philosophers*, eds. W. J. Mander and Alan P. F. Sell, Bristol: Thoemmes Press, 2002.

[65] See the Memoir in Fuller's Works, I, cxxxv-cxxxvi, though the *Narrative* is not to be found in the five volumes; R. Brook Aspland, *Memoir of the Life, Works and Correspondence of the Rev. Robert Aspland, of Hackney*, London: Edward T. Whitfield, 1850, 207-15, 221-2.

[66] R. Aspland, *Bigotry and Intolerance Defeated: or, an Account of the late Persecution of Mr. John Gisburne, Unitarian Minister of Soham, Cambridgeshire: with an Exposure and Correction of the Defects and Mistakes of Mr. Andrew Fuller's Narrative of that Affair: in Letters to John Christie, Esq. Treasurer of the Unitarian Fund*, Harlow: B. Flower, 1811, 3.

[67] Ibid.

V

How shall we evaluate this debate upon which the dust of two hundred years has now settled? Leaving on one side such 'tit-for-tatting' name-calling as 'You are bigots/No, you are', it must first be granted that Fuller's chosen ground of argument is shaky indeed. His opponents clearly point out that to seek to judge the moral tendency of an entire denomination is a hazardous epistemological undertaking; and in the event neither they nor Fuller himself can avoid the temptation of citing virtuous *individuals* from their respective parties. It transpires that much of Fuller's case consists not in his finding Unitarians to be immoral, but in his failure to find exactly the kind of pious experiences and practices, or religious language, that he seeks. The alleged experiential and language deficiencies thus become parallels to the alleged doctrinal deficiencies, to which we shall shortly refer.

While it is no doubt ideally the case that virtue follows the sincere commitment to worthy principles, Fuller wisely does not attempt to establish that, empirically, virtue always flows from adherance to correct religious principles. On the contrary, both he and his opponents admit that there are rotten apples in every theological-ecclesiastical barrel. Moreover, when Fuller charges Toulmin with changing the ground of argument, it must be admitted that in view of Fuller's talk of doctrinal principles, Toulmin was sorely tempted.

Fuller's attempt to tar the Unitarians with the deist brush is loaded and unfair. The Unitarians' appeal to Jesus Christ, their recourse to special revelation, and their insistence upon the reality and importance of the after-life distinguish them from those commonly labelled 'deist' (however different from one another they were). However, Fuller's justifiable rejection of Paine's view that 'it matters not what religion we are of, if we be but sincere in it,' clamantly raises the question of truth.

Fuller rightly points out to Toulmin that while Unitarians and Calvinists can quote the same texts of Scripture, their interpretations of the words differ significantly. Moreover, it does seem that Toulmin is selective in the verses he chooses to employ, and from our present vantage-point both he and Fuller seem to have, if one may speak anachronistically, a 'fundamentalist', proof-texting approach to the words of the Bible which, in the light of modern biblical criticism would be repudiated by scholars of many theological complexions.

There is little doubt that, the element of caricature in their portrayals of 'morbid' Calvinism notwithstanding, the Unitarians' moral challenge to more gruesome ways of articulating Christian doctrine helped to pave the way for such nineteenth-century writers as Thomas Erskine of Linlathen and John McLeod Campbell, who reminded those who would listen that the first word of the Gospel is grace, not sin, and who fostered the view that the atonement did not procure grace, it flowed from it.

When Fuller charges Kentish with omitting the atonement from his statement of principles, it is nothing more than an evasion on Kentish's part to reply that he omits it because it is not a Unitarian conviction. The question is, whether it ought to be, and if so, in which sense? From Kentish's day to our own there have been varieties of liberal theology which – often in justifiable recoil from 'immoral' presentations of atonement theory – have taken a less than radical view of God's holiness and humanity's sinfulness, have hence managed with an understanding of the Cross as exemplary only, and have, unsurprisingly, found that what others regard as a reduced Christology will meet their need.[68]

Fuller is not on strong ground when he applies his *tu quoque* argument to the effect that, as a necessarian, Priestley ought to find Calvinism to his liking. Calvinists may be well advised to understand predestination and election as religious concepts rather than as equivalent or related to philosophical determinism. For example, it would appear that for Paul these religious ideas arise out of his grateful retrospective testimony that he has not been brough to his present stand by his own efforts: it is all of grace, and in the purpose of God. To press these ideas in a deterministic way and, still more, to encumber them with appeals to God's inscrutable will (about which, it would seem, some believers have known a good deal) makes for disastrous theology, and prevents Calvinists from being variously libertarians or determinists in ethics, for example – which they may perfectly well be.[69]

While it cannot be said that all doctrinal issues as between Unitarians and Calvinists – or trinitarians at large – have by now been resolved, it may be suggested that neither side is, either attitudinally or doctrinally, in exactly the same position as its forebears of the eighteenth century. It also seems to be the case that the specific doctrinal issues which concerned Fuller and his opponents are scarcely discussed at the present time. This may be partly because of liberalizing tendencies within many trinitarian folds, and partly because Unitarians have been marginalized by many ecumenical bodies. But this reference to ecumenism raises the question which undelies the old debate, and still haunts us today: Who is a Christian? Fuller's criteria are a commitment to

---

[68] See further, Alan P. F. Sell, *Aspects of Christian Integrity*, (1990), Eugene, OR: Wipf & Stock, 1998, ch. 2.

[69] See William Cunningham's judicious paper, 'Calvinism and the doctrine of philosophical necessity,' in his *The Reformers and the Theology of the Reformation*, (1862), London: Banner of Truth trust, 1967. He writes, 'Predestination implies that the end or result is certain, and that adequate provision has been made for bringing it about. But it does not indicate anything as to what must be the nature of this provision in regard to the different classes of events which are taking place under God's government, including the volitions of rational and responsible beings,' 508–9.

Christ and a confession of Christ's deity and atoning work. Toulmin, reacting against this, accuses Fuller of placing a formula above a simple commitment to Jesus our Mediator. Now on the one hand it is undeniable that Christians of many communions may and do fall into sectarianism if, having equated God's truth with their formulations of it, they proceed to unchurch those who view matters differently. On the other hand, what are we to make of such a claim as that of P. T. Forsyth: 'There must surely be in every positive religion some point where it may so change as to lose its identity and become another religion'?[70] Thus is set the continuing ecumenical problem which the old debate between Fuller and the Socinians illustrates so clearly. The road to the solution of this problem is long and arduous. We may, perhaps, draw some consolation from the fact that even Matthew Henry, from whose sardonic remark concerning Socinians I set out, could also say:

> Those I call Christians, not who are of this or that party, but who call upon the name of Jesus Christ our Lord: those, whatever dividing name they are known by, who live soberly, righteously, and godly in this world. The question by and bye will not be – in what place, or what posture we worshipped God; but, did we worship in the spirit.[71]

Until we are faced by that question we may take further comfort from the likelihood that we shall not meet exact replicas of either Fuller or his Unitarian opponents in any dark alley. What the discussion topics of the heavenly fraternal will be remains to be seen.

---

[70] P. T. Forsyth, *The Principle of Authority*, (1913), London: Independent Press, 1952, 219. For a caution against sectarianisms ancient and modern see Alan P. F. Sell, *Commemorations. Studies in Christian Thought and History*, Cardiff: University of Wales Press, 1993 and Eugene, OR: Wipf & Stock, 1998, ch. 2.

[71] J. B. Williams, *The Life of Matthew Henry*, 182.

CHAPTER 7

P. T. Forsyth as Unsystematic Systematician

If ever a theologian deserved to be treated under a paradoxical title, that theologian is P. T. Forsyth. His pages are peppered with paradoxes, enlivened by epigrams and they abound in antitheses. All of these devices assail the mind and challenge the heart. I shall be content if the paradox in my title stimulates thought on the themes of one whose message is, to a high degree, as fresh and as pertinent as when he uttered it, and whose theological method is systematically unconventional, and this to surprisingly good effect.

I set out from the verdict of H. F. Lovell Cocks who, until his death in 1983, was among the last surviving students of Forsyth.[1] Although Lovell Cocks held his teacher in the highest regard ('I shall never cease to regard it as a signal act of Divine Providence that it was to Dr Forsyth that I was led to be instructed'),[2] he nevertheless had to open his assessment of Forsyth's *The Person and Place of Jesus Christ* with the words, 'Peter Taylor Forsyth was far from being a systematic theologian.'[3] The emphasis upon the term 'systematic' is clear from the context. It is not being said that Forsyth was more the historical or the philosophical theologian; still less that he was not a theologian at all — how could that be suggested in the case of one who believed that 'non-theological religion can do but a coasting trade'?[4] J. K. Mozley who, as much as any other Anglican of his generation saw Forsyth's point, some reservations notwithstanding, declared in a half-sentence redolent of understatement that 'Systematic is not a word that one would naturally apply to Dr Forsyth.'[5] What grounds have been offered in support of this widely-echoed judgement?

---

[1] For Lovell Cocks, see Alan P. F. Sell, 'Theology for all: The contribution of H. F. Lovell Cocks,' in Sell, *Commemorations: Studies in Christian Thought and History*, Calgary: University of Calgary Press, 1993; Eugene, OR: Wipf & Stock, 1998, ch. 13.
[2] Cocks, 'Ordination Statement', in the Lovell Cocks papers at Dr Williams's Library, London.
[3] Idem, 'P. T. Forsyth's *The Person and Place of Jesus Christ*,' *The Expository Times*, LXIV no. 7, April 1953, 195.
[4] P. T. Forsyth, *The Person and Place of Jesus Christ*, (1909), London: Independent Press, 1961, 262.
[5] J. K. Mozley, *The Doctrine of the Atonement*, London: Duckworth, 1915, 182.

I

First, it has been said that Forsyth's writings are insufficiently scholarly. He is sparing with references, most of his works lack indices. Unlike Samuel Morton Savage (1721–91; D. D., Marischal College, Aberdeen, 1767)[6] Congregational tutor at the first Hoxton Academy, who 'was apt to take from the interest of his lectures by entering into learned minutiae',[7] Forsyth seldom deals in detailed biblical exegesis or takes special pains to provide full evidence for his often rapier-like and accurate assessments of Christian thought ancient and modern.

Where the Bible was concerned, some found Forsyth unbalanced in more than one way. To T. Hywel Hughes, Forsyth's God was too much of the Old Testament sort: 'The God of Forsyth seems to be more concerned with Himself, with His holiness, His judgement, His satisfaction, than with the sinner, whereas in the Gospel the supreme object of interest is not law, judgement, not even sin, but the sinner.'[8] Forsyth's younger colleague, A. E. Garvie, Principal of New College, London, likewise lamented that Forsyth put more emphasis upon God's holiness than upon his love.[9] My own reading is that Forsyth, as few others, conjoined the terms 'holy love' and could scarcely think of the one without the other. And as for the 'Old Testament God' charge, it is interesting to observe that on another wicket and on an earlier occasion, the same Hughes contrasted Forsyth favourably with Barth-to-1934 in these terms: 'Barth is unwilling to apply the term "Father" to God .... We should speak of him as "Sovereign" or "Judge". To Forsyth, however, fatherhood is basal, and the result is that whereas Barth's God is much akin to the *Old Testament* conception, Forsyth's God is the God of Jesus.'[10]

More serious was the charge that Forsyth neglected, or gave inadequate place to, the ministry of Jesus. The context of the charge was the desire of some to flee what they regarded as grotesque doctrines of the atonement, and to turn instead to the quest of the historical Jesus. To them Jesus' words and deeds were crucial, even if some of his miracles caused them embarrassment. Thus, Joseph

---

[6] The University of Aberdeen, for whose quincentenary this series of lectures was prepared, has not been ungenerous to theologians of the Congregational Way. The centenary of the award of its degree of Doctor of Divinity to P. T. Forsyth fell on 30 March 1995, and he is our main concern. However, in the course of my paper, I shall refer to other Congregationalists who have been similarly honoured by Forsyth's *alma mater*.

[7] *Protestant Dissenter's Magazine*, III, May 1796, 162.

[8] T. Hywel Hughes, 'Dr Forsyth's View of the Atonement' *The Congregational Quarterly*, XVIII, 1940, 37; cf., 36. Cf. his *The Atonement: Modern Theories of the Doctrine*, London: Allen & Unwin, 1949, 38–46. Hughes was Principal of the Scottish Congregational College from 1922 until his death in 1936. He was succeeded by Lovell Cocks (1937–41), who in the latter year became Principal of Western College, Bristol, until his retirement in 1960.

[9] A. E. Garvie, 'A Cross-Centred Theology.' *The Congregational Quarterly*, XXII, 1944, 325.

[10] Hughes, 'A Barthian before Barth?' ibid., XII, 1934, 311.

Warschauer, who transferred to the Congregational ministry from the Unitarian, and who was an implacable foe of Calvinism, objected to the way in which Forsyth opted for Paul's understanding of the fall and of total depravity. He pointed to the importance Jesus himself attached to 'these words of mine' (Mt 7.24–27). Nowhere, observed Warschauer, did the words of Jesus include references to the fall or to total depravity.[11] A weightier opinion was that of A. S. Peake, who would not go so far as to say that Forsyth dwelt too much upon Christ's death, but thought that he was 'in danger of concentrating on it too exclusively'.[12] In Garvie's view, Forsyth's 'absorption in the Cross made him insensitive and unresponsive to the truth and grace which [the ministry of Jesus] disclosed. He depreciated any attempt to understand the inner life of Jesus, especially His relation as Son to God as Father'.[13] Forsyth's antitheses, thought Garvie, were instruments too blunt for useful service in this field of enquiry. If we do not have data concerning the inner relations of Son and Father, how, asked Garvie, could Forsyth defend the antithesis, 'Jesus was more engrossed with the will of God than the needs of men in his last hours'?[14] Garvie did not deny that 'the relation to God must be primary, and to man secondary, yet His love for God need not be contrasted with His love for man'.[15]

Forsyth did not become more exegetical, but neither did he wilt under criticism levelled during his lifetime. He was content to assert his position positively. In so doing, he revealed himself to be a thoroughly biblical theologian — not in the sense of a systematic exegete, not in the sense of a seeker of the 'Jesus of history', not in the sense of a 'word-study' scholar of the 1950s, but in the sense of one saturated by what he took to be the Bible's fundamental message.

Forsyth's point is that the 'ethical, cosmic, eternal estimate of Christ cannot be based on his biography alone, or chiefly, but upon his cross, as we shall again find when we have surmounted the present fertile obsession by "the historical Jesus"'.[16] Indeed, as he elsewhere remarks, satisfaction concerning 'the historic evidence for every fact recorded in the New Testament' would not necessarily yield the certainty that we were 'amidst time, on the Rock Eternal'.[17] If he

---

[11] J. Warschauer, '"Liberty, limited": A Rejoinder to Dr P. T. Forsyth,' *The Contemporary Review*, CI, 1912, 834.

[12] A. S. Peake, *Recollections and Appreciations*, ed. W. Howard, London: Epworth, 1938, 193.

[13] A. E. Garvie, 'Placarding the Cross: The Theology of P. T. Forsyth', *The Congregational Quarterly*, XXI, 1943, 352.

[14] Garvie, 'Placarding the Cross', 352, quotes Forsyth's annotations to Robert Mackintosh's paper of 1906, 'The Authority of the Cross,' reprinted ibid., XXI, 1943, 216.

[15] Garvie, 'Placarding the Cross', 352. We should note Garvie's (and Hughes's) temperate interest in the then ascendant 'new psychology'. Moreover, Garvie had published a book in 1907 under the title, *Studies in the Inner Life of Jesus*.

[16] P. T. Forsyth, 'The Insufficiency of Social Righteousness as a Moral Ideal,' *The Hibbert Journal*, VII no. 3, April 1909, 611.

[17] Idem, 'A Rallying Ground for the Free Churches: The Reality of Grace' (1906): 831.

focuses much more on Paul than on the Gospels, it is not because of scepticism concerning the major details of the life of Jesus; it is not because the life of Jesus is unimportant; it is not because he was 'a latter-day Marcion distinguishing between an inspired Paul and a mistaken Twelve'.[18] After all, 'what Jesus preached was but part of the whole Gospel';[19] indeed, 'in the teaching of Christ nothing was done, in the strict sense of that word'.[20] Moreover, to concentrate exclusively upon Christ's precepts is to make him a legislator, 'a finer Moses'. All the precepts are to be read, and if necessary, to be revised, in the light of the Cross.[21] What must carry weight with us is the view of Christ's place and person which pervades the New Testament.[22] Hence, for example, while it is true that 'the Cross was not central to Christ's teaching as the kingdom was, . . . it was central to what is more than His teaching — to His healing, to His Person, work, and victory . . . Christianity spread, not as a religion of truth, but of power, help, healing, resurrection, redemption'.[23] No doubt one less fond of antitheses would have paused at the realization that Christianity claims to be a word of truth as well as of redemption; but Forsyth's intention to deny that we have exhausted Christianity's meaning when we have gathered and presented its teachings is sound. As if echoing some of his critics, Forsyth could write, 'To preach only the atonement, the death apart from the life, or only the person of Christ, the life apart from the death, or only the teaching of Christ, His words apart from His life, may all be equally one-sided, and extreme to falsity.'[24] More bluntly still, he declares, 'You cannot sever the death of Christ from the life of Christ.'[25] But that the scales were weighted in the direction of the comprehensive 'fact of Christ' is undeniable. This is because,

> the real evidence that Christ is risen is something I can verify, who am little skilled in handling documents and assessing evidence. It is that I have had dealings with Him. It is like the evidence for the whole Bible. It is laymen's evidence, not scientific but moral. It is the witness of the evangelical conscience, and of Christian experience to a risen Redeemer. The essential thing is not historic belief in the Resurrection of Jesus (which devils might believe and tremble), but moral faith is a risen Saviour.[26]

---

[18] J. K. Mozley, *The Heart of the Gospel*, London: SPCK, 1927, 80. Mozley did not, of course, think that Forsyth was a latter-day Marcion.
[19] Idem, *The Person and Place of Jesus Christ*, 101.
[20] Idem, *The Christian Ethic of War*, London: Longmans, 1916, 52.
[21] Idem, 'A Holy Church the Moral Guide of Society' (1905), reprinted in idem, *The Church, the Gospel and Society*, London: Independent Press, 1962, 16.
[22] Idem, *The Person and Place of Jesus Christ*, 181.
[23] Idem, *Missions in State and Church*, London: Hodder and Stoughton, 1907, 11.
[24] Idem, *The Cruciality of the Cross*, (1909), London: Independent Press, 1948, 42.
[25] Idem, *The Work of Christ*, (1910), London: Independent Press, 1958, 153.
[26] Idem, *The Church, the Gospel and Society*, 82. Cf. for example, 'The Evangelical Churches and the Higher Criticism,' *The Contemporary Review*, LXXXVIII, 1905, 578.

Summoning Paul as a witness, Forsyth avers, he 'would seem to have had something like a constitutional inability to respond to Christ the parablist or even the character till the Cross broke for him access to Christ's person. I cannot think Paul was ignorant of Christ's words or biography. But they did not *find* him'.[27] All of which reinforces Forsyth's conviction that 'in the Gospels Christ appears as acting, in the Epistles the same Christ interprets His own action'.[28] Again, and now more broadly still, 'It is the whole Biblical Christ that is the truly and deeply historic Christ.[29]

It is not without significance that despite his failure to provide systematic exegesis, and much as we should have wished to hear him at greater length on such important biblical concepts as covenant and creation,[30] Professor A. M. Hunter, sometime of the University of Aberdeen, could nevertheless write an article entitled, 'P. T. Forsyth Neutestamentler', in which he showed that Forsyth was in advance of subsequent biblical scholars in his emphasis upon the historic, redemptive deed rather than upon truth as propositional; in his adumbration of the *kerygma*, in his anticipation of realized eschatology; and in his understanding of the one Church as being manifested in various places.[31] As the same writer elsewhere said, 'One of the supreme strengths of Forsyth's theology is that it is biblically based as few modern theologies are.'[32]

As with the Bible, so with his observations upon thought through the Christian ages: Forsyth does not trouble us with apparatus; indeed, he does not supply the grounds of his assertions as often as we should like. It is not surprising that a reviewer of *The Church and the Sacraments* should regret the absence of detailed discussion of the patristic witness on the matter — especially given Forsyth's determination to question certain aspects of it.[33] Forsyth's often unsupported summary judgements of persons and movements can sound gnomic — for example, his rejection of 'a Monism which is rather the

---

[27] Idem, Annotations to Mackintosh, 'The Authority of the Cross,' 213.
[28] Idem, 'The Evangelical Churches and the Higher Criticism', 584.
[29] Idem, *The Person and Place of Jesus Christ*, 169.
[30] John H. Rodgers regrets these omissions in his *The Theology of P. T. Forsyth*, 263. But for creation see 'Veracity, Reality and Regeneration,' *The London Quarterly Review*, CXXIII, April 1915, 208ff., where Forsyth relates creation to the new creation in Christ.
[31] See A. M. Hunter, 'P. T. Forsyth Neutestamentler,' *The Expository Times*, LXXIII no. 4, January 1962, 100-106.
[32] Hunter, *P. T. Forsyth. Per Crucem ad Lucem*, London: SCM Press, 1974, 31. Cf. Mozley, preface to P. T. Forsyth, *The Church and the Sacraments*, (1917), London: Independent Press, 1947, vii: 'Forsyth was not primarily, like Hoskyns, a New Testament scholar, but he was not less resolved than the younger man to bring his teaching to the test of that word of God which was declared and expounded by evangelists and apostles.'
[33] See Harold Hamilton, review of *The Church and the Sacraments*, in *The Journal of Theological Studies*, XIX no. 73, October 1917, 93–4.

absolutising of the immanent than the incarnation of the transcendent'[34] — and to this extent he is a dangerous model to any who would 'sound off' in similar fashion, but without having done their homework. Theology is not free of such to this day: to refer to them pejoratively as 'theological journalists' is to slander a noble profession. Forsyth was not of their number. He declared that 'it really takes a great deal of theology to revolutionise theology'.[35] He knew of what he wrote in shorthand, and those who have themselves travelled the ground can see that this is so. They can see too that Forsyth seldom regurgitates, and that he generally qualifies the insights of those from whom he has learned most, recasting their contributions in his own terms. The words he used of others apply to himself. 'There is an amplitude and an atmosphere about the great dogmatists of theology which is absent from the dogmatists of research.'[36]

The indebtedness of Forsyth to others is considerable.[37] 'What have I that I have not received?' he asks in one place, immediately citing Rothe, Kähler, Seeberg, Grützmacher, Wernle, Schmiedel and Zahn as being among those from whom he has learned.[38] But, to repeat, he is no scissors-and-paste eclectic. Everything has been processed by a sharp, critical mind. If he leaves us with positive conclusions unsystematically bereft of the stages through which he has passed on the way to them, this only serves to underline his conviction that theology is a practical business of some urgency; and it is consistent with the fact

---

[34] P. T. Forsyth, *Faith, Freedom and the Future*, (1912), London: Independent Press, 1955, 342.

[35] Idem, *The Person and Place of Jesus Christ*, 264. Forsyth is here rebuking Harnack, who is 'a great historian, and a valuable apologist; but as a theologian he is – not so great.' Forsyth's aversion to wanton 'sounding off' on theological matters is consistent with his quest of rigour in rigour he sought the theological curriculum. In this latter connection he remarked, 'My complaint as to the education of our ministry is that most of the students who come to us have to take up academic subjects after a quadrennium of routine business, following straight on a defective elementary education; so that they are mostly devoid of knowledge of men, habits of study, taste for accuracy or power of concentration...They are without what a universal religion requires – a historical background, a cosmopolitan horizon, the atmosphere of serious culture for conscience or imagination, which lifts piety to faith. It is pitiably hard for them to buckle down to accurate subjects.' Quoted by Sydney Cave (a pupil of Forsyth, and Principal of Hackney and New – latterly New – College, London, 1933–1953) in his 'Dr. P. T. Forsyth. The man and his writings,' *The Congregational Quarterly*, XXVI no. 2, April 1948, 111. Cave cites Forsyth's paper, 'Reconstruction and religion' in Fred A. Rees, *Problems of Tomorrow: Social, Moral and Religious*, London: James Clarke, 1918, 19. In the interest of balance the following should also be quoted. 'Gentlemen,' said Forsyth to his students, 'you are *not* here to graduate in the University of London. You may or may not do that. You are here to graduate in Christ and His ministry.' Quoted by his daughter, Jessie Forsyth Andrews, 'Memoir' prefixed to her father's *The Work of Christ*, 1958, xix.

[36] P. T. Forsyth, *The Person and Place of Jesus Christ*, 263.

[37] On this matter, see further 'Ministerial Libraries: V. Principal Forsyth's Library at Hackney College' (1904); W. L. Bradley, *P. T. Forsyth: The Man and His Work*, ch. 3. I am grateful to Dr Leslie McCurdy for drawing the 'Ministerial Libraries' article to my attention.

[38] P. T. Forsyth, *The Person and Place of Jesus Christ*, vi–vii.

that as with Paul so with Forsyth: the majority of his writings were occasional in nature.

Among easily detectable and personally acknowledged influences upon Forsyth is F. D. Maurice: 'I owe a great deal to Maurice; in some respects I owe him everything.'[39] The Anglican is approved for his view of church and sacraments, though not of ministry; and he is an important stimulus towards Forsyth's view of the solidarity of the race and the consequent necessity of an atonement universal, and not merely individual, in scope — a position also advanced by R. W. Dale in his Congregational Lecture, *The Atonement* (1857). 'It was a race that Christ redeemed,' thunders Forsyth, 'and not a mere *bouquet* of believers.'[40] Forsyth was encouraged to read Hegel's *Logic* by A. M. Fairbairn,[41] and he later bore witness that 'no books have done more for my mind than Hegel's "Logic", or for my insight than his "Aesthetik"'.[42] But he remained unsatisfied by Hegel's system which he deemed more intellectualist than moral, and by Fairbairn's metaphysical rather than moral approach to kenotic theory.[43] While welcoming the emphasis of Kant and the Neo-Kantians (and of T. H. Green, who seems now more Kantian, now more Hegelian) upon the primacy of the will in the appropriation of reality, Forsyth found their understanding of history as the theatre of God's activity deficient. Learning of the primacy of faith from Pascal and Kierkegaard, valuing the life philosophers' view of reality as organic, he nevertheless objected to the way in which von Hartmann, for example, while seeing the need of redemption, placed humanity in an impersonal process rather than faced it with the grace and judgement of a personal, redemptive act. That revelation is supremely in a historic act Forsyth learned from Herrmann, though while indebted to the Marburg scholar for theological and religious insight, he distanced himself from Herrmann's philosophical position.[44] For this he gave no reasons — a fact the more

---

[39] Quoted in 'Ministerial Libraries', 268.

[40] Idem, *The Church and the Sacraments*, 43.

[41] Idem, *Positive Preaching and the Modern Mind*, 195 n. Forsyth wrote a tribute to Fairbairn in *British Weekly* (1912). One of the most puzzling things about Forsyth is that, having vanquished the post-Hegelian immanentism of the New Theology of 1907, he could so readily utilize Hegelianism in *Christ on Parnassus: Lectures on Art, Ethic and Theology*, London: Hodder and Stoughton, [1911]. See the papers by Jeremy Begbie and Stanley Russell in Trevor Hart, ed., *Justice the True and Only Mercy. Essays on the Life and Theology of P. T. Forsyth*, Edinburgh: T. & T. Clark, 1995. See also my remarks below on the 'Hegelian drag' which is occasionally felt in Forsyth's other writings.

[42] Quoted in 'Ministerial Libraries', 269.

[43] He could nevertheless say, 'After Ritschl I think I owe most to Dr Fairbairn', 'Ministerial Libraries', 269.

[44] Idem, 'Revelation and the Person of Christ,' in *Faith and Criticism*, London: Sampson Low Marston, 2nd edn., 1893, 97 n. This article is commonly regarded as marking Forsyth's final break from the liberal theology which he had espoused during the first part of his ministry.

surprising in view of Hermann's espousal of a Kantian voluntarism generally acceptable to Forsyth. If Forsyth followed Kähler in replacing the two-nature theory of Christ's person with his account of two personal movements within Christ's personality, he almost certainly derived his conviction that atonement theory must do something to satisfy God's holiness (and not simply do something for human beings) from the Puritan Thomas Goodwin, whom he called 'the apostle and high priest of our confession'.[45]

As might be expected in one who took his stand on morality, Forsyth regarded Schleiermacher's elevation of the conscience as a theological breakthrough of the greatest importance. He was generous in praise of his older contemporary, the Unitarian Martineau, for his fidelity to conscience. But he could not rest in Schleiermacher's experimentalism. The elevation of human experience could only detract from the significance of that which we experience — namely, God's grace revealed and active in history at the cross. Accordingly, Schleiermacher must be corrected by Ritschl'.[46] 'From the nettle danger in the Tübingen treatment of the historic Bible [Ritschl] plucked the flower of safety in a historic Gospel,'[47] he declared. In perceiving that faith is an act of judgement and of obedience, Ritschl did well; but he too stands in need of correction. Believing that justification was forgiveness, he was weak on the need of an atonement which could satisfy holy love. The juristic note was insufficiently sounded by Ritschl: 'The chief defect of the great revolution which began in Schleiermacher and ended in Ritschl has been that it allowed no place to that side of Christ's work.'[48] Correct in pointing to the pitfalls of pietism — self-engrossment, withdrawal from the world, the acquisition of 'more religious taste than weight'[49] — Ritschl wrongly depreciated the inward aspects of the kingdom. In embracing kenoticism, Forsyth stood at a considerable remove from his Göttingen teacher.

Much more could be said of the materials on which Forsyth went to work. I have not mentioned such literary persons as Carlyle, for example; but I have said enough to indicate that however unsystematic his writings from the point of view of demonstrated arguments from history, close textual criticism, and the provision of scholarly apparatus, Forsyth was a thoroughly biblical theologian

---

[45] Idem, *Faith, Freedom and the Future*, 118.

[46] Idem, 'The Place of Spiritual Experience in the Making of Theology' (1906) in *Revelation Old and New*, 68.

[47] Ibid., 74. It would therefore seem that Marvin Anderson goes too far (or has unhelpfully imbibed the antithetical habit) in writing, 'Martin Kähler, not Albrecht Ritschl, was the source of Forsyth's insight intothe world, the Christ, and the Cross.' See his, 'P. T. Forsyth: prophet of the Cross,' *The Evangelical Quarterly*, XLVII no. 3, July-September 1975, 161.

[48] P. T. Forsyth, *The Work of Christ*, 228–9.

[49] *The Church and the Sacraments*, 91.

who knew his history of thought and who, brooding on the whole territory with systematic intensity, emerged with something fresh and incisive to say.

II

Secondly, it has been suggested that Forsyth is unsystematic not only in his refusal to behave in scholarly fashion, but also in his willingness to leave loose ends in argumentation, and in his proneness to declaim rather than to dissect. I shall offer some random examples.

It cannot be denied that at times Forsyth's antithetical style trips him up. Edward Caird might almost have had him in mind when he wrote, 'While . . . an antithetic writer . . . is likely to bring out certain aspects of life and history with a vividness and force which could not be attained in any other way, he is likely at the same time to fall into an over-estimate of these aspects, and an under-estimate of other aspects, which by this method are necessarily thrown into the background.'[50] It would be tedious to record at length the many occasions on which Forsyth's antitheses prompt the responses, 'Why may we not "both . . . and?"' or 'May it not be partly one and partly the other?' Thus, to take one example, he declares that 'the mighty thing in Christ is his grace and not His constitution'.[51] Are his grace and his constitution thus separable? As he is towards us, so he is in himself. Granted, Forsyth's context here is the primacy and facticity of the evangelical experience over intellectual construction and forms of thought. But the antithesis nevertheless hinders rather than helps.

On the substantive point concerning the person of Christ, Forsyth, though stimulating, leaves us with puzzles at certain points. Of course the final mystery can never be probed by us, and Forsyth rightly recognizes the place of a proper agnosticism: 'If we ask *how* Eternal Godhead could make the actual condition of human nature His own, we must answer, . . . that we do not know.'[52] But this does not excuse human confusions. Thus, in a number of writings he conducts a running battle against the Chalcedonian formula. In the formula, he declares, the two natures of Christ are united miraculously, not morally: 'The person was the resultant of the two natures rather than the agent of their union.'[53] His complaint is that the underlying thought is metaphysical rather than ethical, and the terms employed were material rather than personal and ethical.[54] More generally, he contends that 'the Roman or the Chalcedonian type of doctrine

---

[50] Edward Caird, 'St Paul and the Idea of Evolution', *Hibbert Journal*, II no. 1, October 1903, 2.
[51] P. T. Forsyth, *The Person and Place of Jesus Christ*, 10.
[52] Ibid., 320.
[53] Ibid., 223.
[54] Ibid., 331.

begins with the Incarnation, beyond experience but believed on authority, and then it descends on the Atonement; instead of beginning with the Atonement, in a moral departure, and going on from that experience to the Incarnation, since God only could atone'.[55]

Forsyth does recognize the service performed by the formula in blocking the exit routes into a variety of heresies, but I feel he might have been more generous in his appreciation than he is. No doubt the early theologians used terms which lay to hand — what else could they do? But their intention was undoubtedly to maintain the unity of Christ's person, and to be as agnostic as to the 'how' of it as was Forsyth himself. When he elsewhere avers that 'Chalcedonism means the substitution for experience of truth, and metaphysical truth, on the external authority of a Church over the intelligence',[56] we may suspect that he is attempting truth by definition. Moreover, Forsyth's suggested replacement-theory is not without its difficulties. He recommends that we think in terms of two modes of being in Christ: 'it might be better to describe the union of God and man in Christ as the mutual involution of two personal movements raised to the whole scale of the human soul and divine'.[57] But when he proceeds to indicate what this means in terms of our salvation, he comes perilously close to an antithesis which threatens the mutuality he has just advocated: 'Our Redeemer must save us by his difference from us, however the salvation get home to us by his parity with us. He saves because he is God and not man.'[58] The matter is further complicated by Forsyth's reiterated view that the offering of the cross is made by God and to God. Thus when Forsyth observes that 'when we find God actually reconciling us in [Christ] we cannot help inferring some more substantial unity between him and God than between God and ourselves', it is possible to divine his meaning, though I think the term 'substantial' is problematic. But when he immediately adds, 'The inner life of Jesus could not really reveal to man the inner life of God if at his centre he was not more God than man, and doing the redeeming thing which God alone can do',[59] it is impossible not to see the chasm of docetism opening up before us as Forsyth by implication resists synergism. No doubt God alone can save, but he does it through the Son who is fully human. Another mode of Forsythian expression is that on the cross, Jesus obediently says 'Amen' on behalf of humanity to God's holy judgement upon sin.[60] It is not that the Saviour was punished, 'but He took

---

[55] Idem, *The Church and the Sacraments*, 197.
[56] Idem, *The Justification of God*, (1917), London: Independent Press, 1948, 94.
[57] *The Person and Place of Jesus Christ*, 333; cf. 307.
[58] Ibid., 342.
[59] 'Faith, Metaphysic and Incarnation,' *Methodist Review*, XCVII, September 1915, 718–19.
[60] See, for example, *The Cruciality of the Cross*, 102.

the penalty of sin, the chastisement of our peace'.[61] Many have felt that the ground of Forsyth's claim that the sinless one (and he is insistent that Christ was sinless) could both bear the penalty and not be punished is presented in a manner which is less than fully clear.

Christ's atonement is for the race: Forsyth insists upon this. More than one friendly critic has noted the impersonal, metaphysical ring to the concept of racial solidarity.[62] This would seem to be born out by Forsyth's claim that 'the first charge upon Christ and His Cross was the reconciliation of the race, and of its individuals by implication'.[63] In so far as Forsyth wished to counter the individualistic — even atomistic — understanding of salvation which was current in some circles in his day, he was in the right; but at times his language is problematic. The problem arises because of Forsyth's use of the term 'cross'. He is frequently, according to taste, comprehensive or slippery. 'Cross' characteristically functions as shorthand for a constellation of ideas including the actual cross of Calvary, the Cross eternally in the heart of God, the lamb slain from the foundation of the world, the Son's voluntary, obedient, juristic, victorious work. In this way, numerous soteriological strands are entwined in Forsyth's language. It is not that they are improper in themselves; the difficulty is that it is not always easy to determine which he has in mind in a given instance. Furthermore, when Forsyth claims that 'it is Christ that works out His own redemption and reconciliation, from God's right hand, throughout the course of history'- and this with reference to 'His whole celestial life from the beginning',[64] the question of the relation of the eternal cross to Calvary's Cross is raised but not fully resolved. Given the intellectual climate of Forsyth's day, and with reference to the eternal Cross motif, there are times when I am tempted to think that there is in operation what might be called a post-Hegelian-idealistic drag, momentarily tempting him in the direction of the idealized Cross remote from the historic Cross, the importance of which had so strongly been impressed upon him by Ritschl.

On the question of our appropriation of God's redemption, Forsyth is ambiguous. On the one hand, the Christian experience of salvation is given; but, on the other hand, when considering the accusation that Christians, in adverting to their experience, are guilty of psychologism, Forsyth replies that what we have in Christ is not an impression but a life-change which places us within a community of experience, the church; and this experience is the product of a 'venture of faith' which believers make. The relation between God's gracious

---

[61] Ibid., 103.
[62] For example, Bradley, *P. T Forsyth: The Man and His Work*, 272.
[63] P. T. Forsyth, *The Work of Christ*, 199; cf. *Missions in State and Church*, 340–1.
[64] Idem, *The Work of Christ*, 154, 153.

immediately received gift and the Christian community's venturing is far from clear.[65]

Forsyth's antitheses are frequently inspired by the horrors he wishes to avoid. So concerned is he, for example, to avoid any suggestion that grace is a mysterious, manually-communicable substance conferring *potestas* upon members of the priestly caste that his doctrine of ordination is not as 'high' as the rest of his churchmanship, seems to require. He writes, 'The grace conferred at ordination is but the formal and corporate *opportunity* provided by the Church to minister [the] Gospel; it is not a new spiritual gift belonging to an order and its canonical entry ... . Our ordinations are acts of denominational order and worship. If they do not convey grace they do impart public authority, corporate responsibility, and representative opportunity.'[66] The first puzzle here is that within thirty pages, Forsyth declares that ordination does and does not confer or convey grace. The second puzzle is that the last sentence quoted may be taken as implying that God's grace is operative everywhere except in ordination. Surely those of Forsyth's tradition may deny what they deem to be untoward notions of priestly caste while at the same time maintaining that ordination is more than the formal and corporate bestowal of an opportunity of representative service. May they not believe that God hears the ordination prayer and bestows the grace sought in it? As to grace itself, in one memorable phrase, Forsyth announces that 'it is not mercy to our failure, or pity for our pain, but it is pardon for our sins!'.[67] As a protest against sentimental understandings of the divine Fatherhood this may have some point; but as a definition of grace it is needlessly disjunctive, for while we ought certainly to place the pardon of sinners (and what has been done to secure it) at the heart of our understanding of grace, we surely cannot exclude from it the Father's mercy and pity. A similar comment seems to be called for in relation to the Lord's Supper. Forsyth asserts, 'In the Supper Christ is present not to bless a religious coterie, but as having suffered and conquered in history for a sinful people, to whom His Passion brings the saving gift of forgiveness and regeneration.'[68] He is right in what he affirms, and (passing over the tendentious term 'religious coterie') wrong in what he denies. If Christ is present the people are blessed: we may not appear to divide the presence of Christ from his benefits.

---

[65] For further discussion along these lines, see Arthur Boutwood's review of *The Person and Place of Jesus Christ*, in *The Hibbert Journal*, VIII, 1909-10, 686–90.

[66] P. T. Forsyth, *Congregationalism and Reunion*, (1917), London: Independent Press, 1952, 32, 59.

[67] Idem, 'The Church's One Foundation' *The London Quarterly Review*, CVI, October 1906, 197.

[68] Idem, *The Church and the Sacraments*, 253.

III

I turn from my random and by no means exhaustive list of Forsythian loose ends — many of them linguistically inspired — to two areas where his failure to follow through both exemplifies his unsystematic ways and bequeathes us tasks of the greatest importance.

I refer first to Forsyth on the Trinity. There is no question but that Forsyth was a convinced trinitarian, or that 'Unitarian' was on his lips something akin to a term of abuse. His Congregational forebear Thomas Ridgley (1667?–1734; D.D., King's College, Aberdeen, 1738), would have agreed with Forsyth that 'the triune God ... is what makes Christianity Christian',[69] though, because of Forsyth's conviction that 'where you fix a creed you flatten faith,'[70] I cannot imagine that he would have joined Ridgley among the subscribers at the Salters' Hall in 1719.[71] But while his writings are replete with trinitarian references, Forsyth takes no special pains to anchor his major theological concerns in a fully-fledged doctrine of the Trinity. I do not say he is culpable here — I am not so insubordinate! An unsystematic theologian may write on whatsoever he pleases; and it is understandable that one who sets such store by the order of Christian experience should have written as he did — how many *begin* their Christian pilgrimages from a fully-fledged articulation of the doctrine of the Trinity? It is the last thing we come to — and this is reflected in the Christian Year. As he said, 'any belief in either a Trinity or an Incarnation can only flow from a final experience of grace by the sinful soul'.[72] Or again, 'Paul in Romans, when he wants to condense Christian doctrine into a compendium, does he philosophise about the mysteries of the Trinity, or the method of incarnation, or an active and a passive creation? He does nothing of the kind. He speaks of law, sin and grace; of conscience, guilt and salvation.'[73] On the other hand, Forsyth recognizes that 'The Father who *spoke* by his prophets must *come* to save in the Son and must *occupy* in the Spirit.'[74] In other words, redemption is the work of the triune Godhead.[75] Accordingly, however it may be in the order of our

---

[69] Idem, *Faith, Freedom and the Future*, 263.
[70] Idem, *Positive Preaching and the Modern Mind*, 141.
[71] It will be recalled that at the Salters' Hall the question of subscription was paramount, though the Trinity was ostensibly the point at issue. The non-subscribers denied that they were Arian, and declared that 'we ... sincerely believe the Doctrine of the Blessed Trinity'. See *An Authentick Account of Several Things Done and agreed upon by the Dissenting Ministers Lately assembled at Salters-Hall* (1917), 15; Sell, *Dissenting Thought and the Life of the Churches*. Lewiston, NY: Edwin Mellen Press, 1990, 137-8.
[72] P. T. Forsyth, *The Person and Place of Jesus Christ*, 325.
[73] Ibid., 221.
[74] Ibid., 327.
[75] Cf. idem, *The Work of Christ*, 152; *The Cruciality of the Cross*, 101.

experience, for *theology* the activity of the triune God is both the base and the context of reflection. As he puts it:

> All the metaphysic of the Trinity ... is at bottom but the church's effort to express in thought the incomparable reality and absolute glory of the Saviour whom faith saw sitting by the Father as man's redeeming and eternal Lord, to engage the whole and present God directly in our salvation, and found the soul in Christ on the eternal Rock .... A doctrine of the Trinity may be, so far as the crude individual goes, a piece of theological science, but for the church it is part of its essential faith.[76]

In view of this, I respectfully suggest that some who embrace Forsyth's fundamental concerns for an objective atonement provided by the God of holy love should show more clearly than he did how (and not merely declare that) the entire Godhead is implicated in the work and reception of redemption.

With Forsyth's observation that 'it is impossible with due reverence to speak in any but the most careful and tentative way of the relations in the Godhead'[77] none may reasonably quarrel. But here as elsewhere he is sometimes more opaque than is strictly necessary. He strongly asserts that 'the idea of an Eternal Father is unthinkable without an Eternal Son of equal personal reality and finality',[78] but when writing of the subordination of wives to husbands he refers to the Son's obedience and declares that 'obedience is not conceivable without some form of subordination. Yet in His very obedience the Son was co-equal with the Father .... Therefore, in the very nature of God, subordination implies no inferiority'.[79] It is difficult not to believe that we have here a mauling of concepts which is prompted by something other than a proper agnosticism before mystery.

Again, Forsyth does not hesitate to couch the motivating force of Christian mission in trinitarian terms: 'The first missionary was God the Father, who sent forth His Son in the likeness of sinful flesh.'[80] The second missionary was the Son, and the third was the Spirit, sent forth by the Saviour into all the earth. But then we are told that the fourth missionary is the church. Is not this different in kind from the others — especially given Forsyth's insistence that the church is not and cannot be the extension, or continuation, of the incarnation, for 'that which owes itself to a rebirth cannot be a prolongation of the ever sinless'?[81] Again, what is the precise meaning, and what happens to the Trinity when we

---

[76] Idem, 'Faith, Metaphysic, and Incarnation', 707.
[77] Idem, *The Person and Place of Jesus Christ*, 283.
[78] Ibid., 116.
[79] Idem, *Marriage, its Ethic and Religion*, London: Hodder and Stoughton, 70.
[80] Idem, *Missions in State and Church*, 270.
[81] Idem, The Church and the Sacraments, 83.

are told that the Holy Spirit is inseparable from the work of Christ?[82] Yet again, what are we to make of the claim that 'Detached from the Word [meaning here, the Bible] the supernatural action of the Holy Spirit becomes gradually the natural evolution of the human spirit'?[83] Forsyth rightly protests against those who claim a mystic 'hot-line' to God which bypasses, claims to supplement, or even contradicts, the Bible. But does he really mean to say that the third person is ineffectual apart from the sixty-six books of the Bible? There is much more to be said concerning Forsyth and the Trinity, but I trust that the evidence supplied will suffice to justify my conviction that Forsyth's treatment of this foundational doctrine is not rigorously systematic.

IV

The second territory in which activity is called for is that of apologetics. On the one hand, Forsyth is by no means as hostile to traditional apologetics as were some who came after him. He accords a place to natural theology, although he does not produce a systematic apologetic himself. As with the Trinity, so here: we need not fault a theologian for failing to do what he did not set out to do. But on the other hand, some of Forsyth's utterances seem to preclude apologetics. There is thus an ambivalence in his corpus on this matter which needs to be exposed. When this is done I think he emerges as more in favour of apologetics than not, and this I find enormously encouraging given the present situation in many mainline Western churches which are losing and not replacing minds at an alarming rate, and which here and there are displaying signs of a most disturbing anti-intellectualism — sometimes in the name of what are alleged to be pastoral practicalities.

Forsyth's attitude towards apologetics, natural theology, general revelation, was shaped by his struggle against what he took to be the question of the hour: liberalism within the church. 'The greatest issue for the moment,' he writes, 'is within the Christian pale; it is not between Christianity and the world. It is the issue between theological liberalism (which is practically unitarian) and a free but positive theology, which is essentially evangelical.[84] 'He insists that:

> Christianity does not peddle ideas; it does things .... What cries to be done is to make the spiritual world a moral reality. To do that we must present it as an atoning Gospel adjusted to our peculiar moral extremity. We shall never get what we want by coquetting with the higher physics, nor by psychical

---

[82] Idem, *Faith, Freedom and the Future*, 13.
[83] Ibid., 95.
[84] Idem, *The Person and Place of Jesus Christ*, 84. See further, Alan P. F. Sell, *Theology in Turmoil. The Roots, Course and Significance of the Conservative-Liberal Debate in Modern Theology*, (1986), Eugene, OR: Wipf & Stock, 1998.

research, nor by theosophic religion, nor by undiluted Hegel, nor by mystical, fanciful, sermonic, and unhistoric treatment of the Bible. We can get it only by the moral power and effect of a historic Gospel, one that draws us from the belly of hell.[85]

It is well known that Forsyth had himself imbibed liberalism in his early days; and we have it on his own testimony that he was 'turned from a Christian to a believer, from a lover of love to an object of grace'.[86] The change was radical — it even took sartorial effect, so that he came to rebuke preachers who wore tweeds and bright ties, as he himself had once done. But no more than Newman utterly shook off the evangelical piety in which he was reared did Forsyth completely break free of liberalism. 'The service rendered to Christianity by the great critical movement is almost beyond words,' he declared.[87] He was no 'conservative' obscurantist, tied to revelation-in-propositions, and he regretted the way in which the Bible had, following the Reformation, become regarded as the infallible source of pure doctrine which yielded a quasi-Aristotelian system grounded in medieval logic.[88] To him revelation was God's supreme redemptive *act* in Christ. Furthermore, since 'humanity ... is an organism, with a history', God's treatment of us must be by a historic redemption: 'its compass is cosmic; its sphere is human history, actual history'.[89] None of which, of course, was intended as denigrating the Bible. On the contrary, 'I do not believe in verbal inspiration. I am with the critics in principle. But the true minister ought to find the words and phrases of the Bible so full of spiritual food and felicity that he has some difficulty in not believing in verbal inspiration.'[90] 'Revelation is not a statement,' he declared, 'but it must be capable of statement.'[91] The fact remains that 'the Gospel of God's historic act of grace is the infallible power and authority over both Church and Bible'.[92]

Forsyth's fundamental objection to what he calls liberalism is methodological. I suggest that because of his desire to shun this method he is dissuaded from pursuing the apologetic path, the legitimacy of which in principle he admits. He believes that in liberal circles of the philosophical kind

---

[85] Idem, 'The Grace of the Gospel as the Moral Authority in the Church,' in *The Church, the Gospel and Society*, 95, 97.

[86] Idem, *Positive Preaching and the Modern Mind*, 193. Cf. Robert McAfee Brown, 'The "Conversion" of P. T. Forsyth', *The Congregational Quarterly*, XXX no. 3, 1952, 236-44.

[87] P. T. Forsyth, *The Person and Place of Jesus Christ*, viii.

[88] Idem, *The Church and the Sacraments*, 305. Cf. *The Principle of Authority*, 53. See further, Garvie, 'Placarding the Cross', 343-6.

[89] P. T. Forsyth, 'Revelation and Bible,' *The Hibbert Journal*, X no. 1, 1911, 241.

[90] Idem, *Positive Preaching and the Modern Mind*, 26.

[91] Idem, *Faith, Freedom and the Future*, 239.

[92] Idem, 'The Evangelical Churches and the Higher Criticism,' *The Contemporary Review*, LXXXVIII, July-December 1905, 574.

scholasticism is the order of the day, and while Hegel, or another, takes the place of Aristotle, everything which the Christian wishes to say has to be articulated under the favoured, albeit extraneous, systematic rubric.[93] In fact the gospel of moral redemption by a historic act cannot be thus contained or constricted. When the attempt is made we reach an intellectualism which is either mystical or aesthetic in tone.[94] Hence, for example, Forsyth's strong opposition to R. J. Campbell and the so-called New Theology, whose proponents 'become as much the doctrinaire victims of a speculative theology as our forefathers were the victims of an orthodox theology'.[95]

Alternatively, everything, as with Harnack, must be made to conform to modern historical method, so that if the miracles are by this criterion awkward, they must be dispensed with. In either case, the gospel is pared down to suit prevailing intellectual fashions, and this with a view to persuading modern human beings that the gospel was only what they had always thought. 'Reduce the burden of belief we must,' says Forsyth, for 'the old orthodoxy laid on men's believing power more than it could carry.'[96] Not for him any reversion to Calvinistic scholasticism. But the problem now was that 'too many are occupied in throwing over precious cargo; they are lightening the ship even of its fuel'.[97] He would thus have the immanentist evolutionists learn that 'any theology that places us in a spiritual *process*, or native movement between the finite and the infinite, depreciates the value of spiritual *act*, and thus makes us independent of the grace of God'.[98] He would have the historians understand that the exemplar Christ, Christ the first Christian — these were Christs who, on Forsyth's reckoning, were almost worse than no Christ at all, for 'with the person of Jesus comes a new religion, of which he is the object, and not simply the subject as its saint or sage'.[99] The underlying problem was that 'the liberal theology finds Christ's centre of gravity in what He has in common with us, a positive theology in that wherein He differs'.[100] His general affirmation, made with reference to pointedly-chosen names is that 'there is no greater division within religion than that between Emerson and Kierkegaard, between a religion that but consecrates the optimism of clean youth, and that which hallows the tragic note, and deals

---

[93] Idem, *Positive Preaching and the Modern Mind*, 143.
[94] See *Faith, Freedom and the Future*, 99.
[95] P. T. Forsyth, 'The Distinctive Thing in Christian Experience,' *The Hibbert Journal*, VI no. 3, April 1908, 485.
[96] Idem, *Positive Preaching and the Modern Mind*, 84.
[97] Idem, *The Principle of Authority*, 261. Cf. *Theology in Church and State*, London: Hodder and Stoughton, 1915, 25: 'We must not empty the Gospel in order quickly to fill the Church.'
[98] Idem, *Positive Preaching and the Modern Mind*, 146.
[99] Idem, *The Person and Place of Jesus Christ*, 114.
[100] Ibid., 163.

with a world sick unto death. We choose the latter'.[101] Neither the heart nor the reason can stand in judgement over God's redemptive revelation.[102] Indeed 'if we had theology brought entirely up to date in regard to current thought, we should not then have the great condition for the Kingdom of God. It is the wills of men, and not their views, that are the great obstacle to the Gospel, and the things most intractable'.[103] This is why truths as such will not save, but only God's redeeming act.[104]

As we have seen, a large part of Forsyth's work is in the form of an inner-ecclesial apologetic. He is out to confront Christians with the gospel they have denied or overlooked, and to expose counterfeits of the gospel. He believed the crucial battle of the moment to be within the church and not between it and the world. He wished to hammer the gospel home to those who should have known it all along: hence his crusade against that then current variety of religion which 'seeks rather to commend the Gospel to the natural man than to set the natural man in the searchlight of the Gospel.'[105] While I think it true to say that Forsyth was not of the patiently-argumentative kind, and that he was temperamentally disinclined to the apologetic enterprise in its more technical form, he does not altogether shun the apologetic task of defending the faith against its cultured despisers from without. He does somewhat more than indicate the lines along which such an apologetic might travel. At its heart is natural man's conscience which affirms human culpability. Conscience is the bar before which we all stand. It is the Word of God within us, and we cannot flout it with impunity.[106] As he elsewhere says, 'At the heart of man you will find divine symptoms, but not a divine salvation.'[107] Expecting the answer 'Yes,' he asks, 'Is not all illumination revelation — the light of nature, of reason, of the heart? Is there no revelation in earth's daily splendour around us, in heaven's mighty glory above us, in the heart's tender or tragic voice within us?' True, they reveal what he calls 'a borrowed light' which comes from the Saviour, but they do reveal it.[108] Forsyth can thus commend the Quakers for holding to 'the light that lighteth

---

[101] Idem, *The Principle of Authority*, 203.
[102] Idem, 'Revelation and the Person of Christ', 107, 109.
[103] Idem, *Positive Preaching and the Modern Mind*, 197.
[104] Idem, 'Revelation and the Person of Christ', 102.
[105] Idem, 'Lay Religion,' *The Constructive Quarterly*, III, December 1915, 779.
[106] Idem, *The Cruciality of the Cross*, 62–5. For reservations concerning the unqualified identification of conscience with the Word, or voice, of God, see my remarks on James Martineau in *Commemorations*, 20-26. It is odd that John Rodgers can say that according to Scripture the witness of conscience 'is not heard by natural man.' See his *The Theology of P. T. Forsyth*, 254. Paul's point in Romans 1 – and Forsyth's – is that it is heard, and that it is wilfully suppressed and repudiated. Hence natural man's 'conduct ... is indefensible' (Romans 1: 20).
[107] P. T. Forsyth, *The Church, The Gospel and Society*, 112.
[108] Idem, 'Revelation, Old and New' (1911), in *Revelation Old and New*, 14–15.

every man'.[109] Thus, while 'nature cannot of itself culminate in grace, at least it was not put there without regard to grace'.[110] Indeed, 'nature, if not the mother, is the matrix of Grace'.[111] Nowhere does Forsyth concede so much to general revelation as in his aesthetics: 'The great Christian truths are not truths of a church or of a book, but of the human spirit in its very nature and constitution. They are the exposition of that Reason which constitutes the unity of God, man, and nature. They are truths which are at the foundation of Science, Religion, Art.'[112] No doubt these sentiments must be set against such an assertion as this: 'The sole content of Revelation ... is the love, will, presence and purpose of God for our redemption';[113] and it is this sentence and others like it which mislead John Rodgers into thinking that Forsyth has rejected all natural theology'.[114] Rather, here is the ambivalence of which I warned.

On the one hand Forsyth, the undeserving recipient of God's gracious revelation, can protest, 'We do not review God's claims and then admit Him as we are satisfied.'[115] That is, we are in no position to judge the Word of the holy God by the use of our reason. Nor, with 'the religion of Monism', can we posit a God-humanity rational continuity whereby 'to be glorified we have but to be amplified'.[116] On the other hand 'we must own the justice of that demand for some *a priori* in the soul to which the revelation comes, and on which it strikes its proper note'.[117] But this *a priori* is 'not in the region of the reason but of the will. Its function is not criticism but obedience ... We do not accept [Christ] on His credentials; we fall down dead before Him'.[118] Once again the antithesis is unhelpful. Forsyth is no irrationalist, and he knows that there can be no legitimate, non-idolatrous 'falling down' before one whose credentials have not in some sense been judged by us: why, otherwise, would he repeat the scriptural

---

[109] Idem, *The Church and the Sacraments*, 91.
[110] Idem, *This Life and the Next*, (1918), London: Independent Press, 1948, 69.
[111] Idem, *The Christian Ethic of War*, London: Longmans, Green, 1916, 171.
[112] Idem, *Religion in Recent Art*, London: Hodder and Stoughton, 1901, 147. In 'Christ on Parnassus: P. T. Forsyth among the liberals,' *Journal of Literature and Theology*, II no. 1, March 1988, 83-95, Ralph C. Wood finds Forsyth to be a true Victorian liberal in seeking 'a society founded upon the moral life that springs from the redemption wrought in Christ.' This, he feels, makes Forsyth more a harbinger of Niebuhr than of Barth (92). However, to describe Forsyth as 'a true Hegelian' (86) obscures much more than it reveals, notwithstanding the occasional 'Hegelian drag' in his writings to which I have referred.
[113] Idem, 'Revelation and the Person of Christ', 102.
[114] Rodgers, *The Theology of P. T. Forsyth*, 253. Similarly, Bradley is 'inclined to question' Hughes's assertion that 'in Forsyth there is not "the radical dualism between truth from revelation and truth by man's unaided reason".' See Bradley, *P. T. Forsyth: The Man and His Work*, 168; Hughes, 'A Barthian before Barth?' 314–15.
[115] P. T. Forsyth, *The Principle of Authority*, 146.
[116] Ibid., 170.
[117] Ibid., 168.
[118] Ibid., 168, 173.

injunction that 'we must prove the spirits whether they are of God'.[119] No doubt religious faith is not simply rational assent to propositions: it is a life-commitment. But propositions are never far away, as Forsyth realized when he insisted that 'God's own act of redeeming is not completed without its self-interpretation. That is *His Word*'.[120] His entire approach is that of one whose faith seeks understanding — an understanding which can be commended to others on the basis of the shared common ground of reason and conscience: 'A philosophy can bring us to no security of a revelation; but a revelation develops a philosophy, or a view of the world.'[121] In developing a Christian view of the world, Forsyth is supremely concerned to preserve the revealed *fact* inviolate. Hence his complaint that 'rationalism, whether orthodox or heterodox, consists in measuring Revelation by something outside itself'.[122] A similarly grave mistake is made along affective lines, for 'to make the heart the judge of Revelation is to raise sentiment and individualism to the control of Revelation, and so to make them the real Revelation'.[123]

To repeat: Forsyth is no irrationalist, and he does not deny the existence of epistemological and moral common ground as between Christians and others. Hence his protest against the empiricist reductionists that 'you are doing to religion what you fiercely resent that religion should do to art or science. You are limiting its freedom by a foreign dogma'.[124] He contends against historicism, the dissolution of the objective of faith into a handful of facts, and psychologism, the resolution of religion into subjective processes or symbols, insisting that 'for a religion the first requisite is an objective reality... which we either reach or receive. According as we receive it we have it as revelation and by the way of living faith; according as we reach it we have it by way of discovery, of thought, of metaphysic'.[125] If historicism and psychologism successfully vanquish metaphysic then, he is convinced, 'the sense of a real and objective God fails; the note of reality goes out of such religion as we have left, and with that in due course all fails'.[126] Lacking metaphysical anchorage, religion would survive for a time only because suspended by traditionalism, constitutionalism and nationalism.[127]

---

[119] Ibid., 39.
[120] Idem, 'Revelation and Bible,' *The Hibbert Journal*, XI, 1911-12, 243.
[121] Idem, *Positive Preaching and the Modern Mind*, 170. The gospel, he argues, has to be distilled from the Bible; ibid., 251.
[122] Idem, 'Revelation and the Person of Christ', 109.
[123] Ibid., 107.
[124] Idem, 'Theological Liberalism v. Liberal Theology,' *The British Weekly*, 17 February 1910, 557.
[125] Idem, 'Faith, Metaphysic, and Incarnation', 697.
[126] 'Faith, Metaphysic, and Incarnation', 697.
[127] 128 Ibid., 698.

Again, running through Forsyth's work is his quoted concurrence with Butler, confirmed by Kant,[128] that 'morality is the nature of things'[129] Such a conviction cannot be annexed by any one religion, nor would Forsyth wish it otherwise. The sphere, though not the source, of morality is human consciousness.[130] It is true that in Forsyth's hands the moral is construed as personal, active, holy love, its task being that of redeeming a sinful race; but this is because metaphysic, by which he means the ordered articulation of what one has perceived, cannot but reflect upon what has been given in experience.[131] 'Our theological capital,' he declares, 'is not ideas we arrive at but experience we go through ... . The theologian is not a syllogist but an experient, an observer.'[132] Paul, indeed, had 'to coin a new metaphysic' in order to convert, rather than to develop an intellectual heritage which gave no place to 'the experienced redemption of a ruined world'.[133] Similarly, 'what we have to ask about Christ then, is this, what account of him is demanded by that work, that new creation of us, that real bringing of us to God, not simply in nearness but in likeness?'[134] No doubt 'it is by no metaphysic that we come to the faith of Christ's Godhead; but, having come there, some metaphysic is inevitable wherever religion does not mean mental poverty, the loss of spiritual majesty, and a decayed sense of the price of the soul and the cost of sin'.[135] The upshot is that 'it is not to metaphysic that we need ever object, but to archaic metaphysic made final and compulsory'.[136] Furthermore, 'since Kant opened the new age must it not be a metaphysic or ethic?'[137]

But once again comes the warning that 'notions' will not suffice (compare the Quakers once more): 'We cannot start with a view of God reached on speculative or other similar grounds, and then use Christ as a mere means for confirming it or giving it practical effect.'[138] 'It takes a sound education to get rid of that notional religion' which thinks 'that faith rests finally on any truth or synthesis of truths.'[139] Indeed, 'in a strict use of words, there is no such thing as saving truth'.[140] The ultimate choice is between 'a rational Christianity and a

---

[128] Idem, *The Principle of Authority*, 4.
[129] Cf. 'Veracity, Reality, and Regeneration,' 206.
[130] Idem, *The Principle of Authority*, 75.
[131] See *Positive Preaching and the Modern Mind*, 255. Cf. 170; *The Principle of Authority*, 6, 8, 44.
[132] Idem, *The Principle of Authority*, 93. Presumably 'theologian' here needs to be qualified by 'constructive'.
[133] Ibid., 80. Cf. *The Church, The Gospel and Society*, 80–1.
[134] Idem, *The Person and Place of Jesus Christ*, 346.
[135] Idem, 'Faith, Metaphysic, and Incarnation', 708.
[136] Ibid., 701.
[137] Ibid., 702.
[138] Idem, *The Principle of Authority*, 353.
[139] Idem, *Theology in Church and State*, 203.
[140] Idem, 'Authority and theology,' *The Hibbert Journal*, IV, 1905-06, 69.

redemptive'[141] — an antithesis which on Forsyth's own terms seems to be too strong: he is not for irrationalism or anti-rationalism. We can, however, sympathize with a bluntness which probably derives in part from experiences which called forth this remark: 'The bulk of the questions with which the amateur critic poses faith, and the illiterate heretic delights the public, are as unanswerable as if it were asked — what is the difference between London Bridge and four o'clock?'[142] There could hardly be a greater contrast than that between such trivializing and Forsyth's understanding of prayer according to which 'all the meditation of Nature and of things sinks here to the rear, and we are left with God in Christ as His own Mediator and His own Revealer'.[143]

V

I hope that I may have persuaded you that Forsyth is not a systematic exegete or historian of thought — though he has done all of the required homework in those fields; he does not systematically ground arguments or pursue them wheresoever they lead; and there are loose ends in his work, some of them inspired by his fondness for antithesis. In particular, he bequeaths to those who follow him the tasks of attending to trinitarian foundations and to apologetics (which he does not rule out).

But I have not so far mentioned the most blatantly obvious way in which Forsyth is unsystematic. He simply does not set out from the doctrine of God or, like the *Westminster Confession*, for example, from the doctrine of Scripture, and take us step by step through the so-called 'departments' of theology in sequence. In this, he contrasts dramatically with his Dissenting forebear Thomas Ridgley, whose two-volume *Body of Divinity* comprises a thorough-going progression through the *Westminster Larger Catechism*; and who, staunch trinitarian though he was, fell foul of the high Calvinist Baptist, John Gill – another of Aberdeen's D.D.s (1748) – who found his Congregationalist contemporary wanting on the eternal generation of the Son. Or consider Forsyth's colleague, A. E. Garvie, a master of thorough exegesis and patient exposition, whose major works are replete with numbered sections, ample references, and copious indices.

However, to say that Forsyth is unsystematic in all the ways described is, in the end, to say one of the less important things about him, and to express a judgement which would probably not have disturbed him in the slightest. It may even be said that his formally unsystematic approach highlights his ever-reverberating themes and makes him appear less dated than might otherwise

---

[141] Idem, *The Person and Place of Jesus Christ*, 96.
[142] Ibid., 312.
[143] Idem, *The Soul of Prayer*, (1916), London: Independent Press, 1949, 30.

have been the case. There is, after all, something to be said for a theologian of his generation who is not consumed by the felt need to engage in incessant blow-by-blow refutations of Herbert Spencer, or by an insatiable desire to pulverize repeatedly the higher critics, or by the conviction that theological salvation is to be found in a marriage with absolute idealism. To what is most important about Forsyth, I now turn.

At the outset I quoted his pupil, Lovell Cocks, as declaring that, Forsyth was not a systematic theologian, and in support I summoned half a sentence of the Anglican, J. K. Mozley. But the second half of Mozley's sentence is of great importance, and I now quote him in full: 'Systematic is not a word that one would naturally apply to Dr Forsyth; yet I know of no theologian of the day who has fewer loose ends to his thought.'[144] I claim to have shown that there are loose ends, but Mozley clarifies his point by further remarking that, at every point which he reaches in the gradual development of a position, or by some bold *coup de main*, one knows that there is a straight line back, as from any point on the circle's circumference to its centre, to that which is the moral and therefore the only possible centre of the world — the Cross of Christ'.[145] Here we approach the heart of the matter, provided that we understand 'cross' as encompassing a cluster of convictions: God's fatherly love as holy and victorious; grace as judgement; Christ as having wrought once and for all at Calvary an atonement for the race, by virtue of which penitent sinners receive new life in the Spirit, are engrafted into the church, and are in fellowship with God and the communion of saints eternally. For all of this, at least, 'Cross' is shorthand in Forsyth. Sustained reflection having brought him to this point, these themes become refrains which permeate all his post-1893 writings. We know that no matter what the ostensible subject of a discourse, these themes will underlie it and reverberate through it. Here is a highly sytematic — in the sense of sustained and consistent – application of central convictions to the whole range of human concerns. Forsyth's complex of fundamental convictions are his controlling passion; they dictate his method and motivate his testimony. What he coveted for the whole church he manifested in his own work: 'The faith of the evangelized Church must suffuse its mind .... The Church's experience of its revelation must not only be stated but it must be organized by its own principle in the manifold wisdom of God and riches of Christ.'[146]

To underscore points which have already emerged: Forsyth centres in the cross, which is the place where, once and for all, something is not merely shown, but done, by God: 'The cross does not in the New Testament exhibit God as

---

[144] J. K. Mozley, *The Doctrine of the Atonement*, 182.
[145] J. K. Mozley, *The Doctrine of the Atonement*, 182.
[146] P. T. Forsyth, *Theology in Church and State*, 47.

accepting sacrifice so much as making it.'[147] Indeed, God being supremely holy and just, he alone could move in love to redeem. The testimony to Christ's divinity flows from the realization that 'no half-God could redeem the soul which it took the whole God to create';[148] hence the claim that 'a Christ that differs from the rest of men only in saintly degree and not in redeeming kind is not the Christ of the New Testament nor of a Gospel Church'.[149] The 'holy God could be satisfied by neither pain nor death, but by holiness alone. The atoning thing is not obedient suffering but suffering obedience'.[150] 'It was [Christ's] holiness, with which the Holy Father was perfectly pleased and satisfied.'[151] Hence, 'Christ is more precious to us by what distinguishes Him from us than by what identifies Him with us.'[152] Not surprisingly, Forsyth insisted that 'only the Atonement gives the Incarnation its base and value in any moral and religious sense. Without it, it is but a philosophic theme';[153] but he had no time for atonement theories which he deemed immoral: 'The atonement did not procure grace, it flowed from grace ... . We must renounce the idea that [Christ[was punished by the God who was ever well pleased with His beloved Son.'[154]

Inspired and motivated by this constellation of convictions, Forsyth treats themes as various as theodicy, socialism, pacifism and ecclesiology. I can only briefly indicate his procedure by way of illustration.

Thus, the Cross judges the then (and in some quarters still) popular religion of humanity for its failure to reconcile ethic and religion in the supreme moral idea of holiness, and its contentment with the worship of our better slaves.[155]

---

[147] Idem, *The Cruciality of the Cross*, 92; cf. *The Work of Christ*, 24, 92, 93, 99. During the Aberdeen Forsyth Colloquium of 1993 it was occasionally remarked that Forsyth does not pay great heed to the resurrection of Jesus. As far as the resurrection narratives in the gospels are concerned, this is true. But that the idea of resurrection permeates his theology – supremely, perhaps, his theodicy, cannot be denied. Holy love is victorious at the Cross. With Paul, Forsyth rejoices in the Cross (not, of course, in the crucifixion, and not in the Incarnation conceived apart from the Cross); and he understands that the most satisfactory route to Christology is *via* soteriology. On this last point see further, Alan P. F. Sell, *Aspects of Christian Integrity*, (1990), Eugene, OR: Wipf & Stock, 1998, ch. 2.

[148] Idem, *The Person and Place of Jesus Christ*, 86; cf. 'Faith, Metaphysic, and Incarnation', 703.

[149] Idem, *The Church, The Gospel and Society*, 99.

[150] Idem, *The Work of Christ*, 205.

[151] Idem, *The Person and Place of Jesus Christ*, 235.

[152] Idem, 'The Distinctive Thing in Christian Experience', 486.

[153] Idem, *The Church, The Gospel and Society*, 120. Forsyth had considerable grounds for this judgement in view of the widely-prevalent post-Hegelian idealism of his day, and that variety of Anglican incarnational theology, exemplifed in *Lux Mundi*, which came near to regarding incarnation as evolution 'Christologized'. Cf. *The Cruciality of the Cross*, 50; *Positive Preaching and the Modern Mind*, 216; *Missions in State and Church*, 68.

[154] Idem, *The Cruciality of the Cross*, 4 1. See further, Alan P. F. Sell, *Philosophical Idealism and Christian Belief*, Cardiff: University of Wales Press and New York: St. Martin's Press, 1995.

[155] P. T. Forsyth, *The Principle of Authority*, 66.

Neither will sophisticated versions of monism suffice. For here 'the fundamental relation is one of identity. To be glorified we have but to be amplified.'[156] While conceding that 'we are all Monists in the sense of striving to introduce unity of conception into our view of life and things ... we do not all think that the principle of the world is wholly within the world .... Beware of a juggle, however honest, by which a homogeneous and singular identity is slipped in to meet our need for a manifold and solidary universal.'[157] Revelation requires a dualism of giver and receiver; a God conceived on monistic and immanentist lines could not reveal himself for he would have no other; hence God must be regarded as for ever distinct from the world.[158] What is required is 'a Dualism with a unity of Reconciliation, and not a Monism with a unity of Identity as real in the sin as in the Saviour.'[159]

Forsyth speaks not on the authority of the Bible or the church, but of the redeeming gospel which called forth both. Those regenerated by the Spirit and called by grace under the proclamation of the gospel comprise the church. With reference to the cross he declares, 'It is that thing *done* that makes a Church at last, and gives dynamic both to preaching and hearing.'[160] The church is 'a new creation of God in the Holy Spirit'.[161] Moreover, the church is inescapable, for while 'salvation is personal ... it is not individual ... it is personal in its appropriation but collective in its nature'.[162] To be a believer is to be of the gathering of saints.

It follows from Forsyth's understanding of the Cross that true liberty is not freedom from, but for and under the gospel.[163] It is not the liberty of individualists — and the doctrine of the unlimited right of private judgement derives more from the Renaissance than the Reformation;[164] it is the liberty of those who stand under 'the authoritative Word of an evangelical Church'.[165] Hence his determined opposition to those of his own Congregational family who, in those theologically free-wheeling days, behaved as if Christian liberty conferred the right to believe and do as one pleased. On the contrary, 'there

---

[156] Ibid., 170.
[157] 'Monism', a paper read before the London Society for the Study of Religion, 2 February 1909; printed for the use of members, 14, 15.
[158] Ibid., 7, 8, 9.
[159] Ibid., 12.
[160] Idem, 'Church, Ministry and Sacraments,' printed with J. Vernon Bartlet and J. D. Jones, *The Validity of the Congregational Ministry*, London: Congregational Union of England and Wales, 1916, 39.
[161] P. T. Forsyth, *The Church and the Sacraments*, 34.
[162] Idem, *The Work of Christ*, 119. Cf. *The Church and the Sacraments*, 43; *The Charter of the Church*, London: Alexander and Shepheard, 1896, 41.
[163] Idem, *The Principle of Authority*, 219; cf. *Faith, Freedom and the Future*, 216–17.
[164] Idem, *The Principle of Authority*, 283.
[165] Ibid., 224.

must surely be in every positive religion some point where it may so change as to lose its identity and become another religion'.[166] Christianity can never legitimately slip its anchorage in redemption by holy love. As he repeatedly insists, the freedom of Congregationalists is a 'founded freedom'[167] — it is freedom created and founded and reared by an authority which cannot be either evaded or shaken; and which creates our emancipation ... by the eternal redemption at the heart of all history in Christ's Cross'.[168] In the interests of the Lordship of Christ over the church, and in opposition to the heresy that Free Church polity is democratic, he thunders, 'Between a Church and a democracy is this eternal gulf, that a democracy recognises no authority but what arises from itself, and a Church none but what is imposed on it from without. The one founds on self-help, the other on Redemption'.[169]

All of this, however, is more than Congregationalist, it is catholic; and on the basis of it Forsyth has a word for others — not least the Church of England. Since 'the Church stands on eternal certainty, the State on public security',[170] the church cannot be legitimated by, or regarded as co-terminus with, the state; for 'it is the adoption as sons that gives us the fellowship of brothers'.[171] Further, since Christ is the only Lord of the Church, no monarch can assume that role. As he said, in the patient tones of one explaining things to uncomprehending infants, 'what we protest against is not the abuses but the existence, the principle, of a national Church'.[172] 'Christianity is not national in spirit,' he averred. 'Its conception is catholic and universal ... "elect from every nation, yet one o'er all the earth".'[173] We may surmise that Forsyth would have approved of the earlier Aberdeen graduate, Savage, who was urged by friends to enter the ministry of the national church, within which he would have the advantages of the patronage of a relative who was the Irish Primate. In the event, 'this scheme was dropt in deference to his own judgment, which determined him for nonconformity'.[174] None of which is to deny that Church and state have mutual responsibilities the one towards the other, for the gospel is entrusted to the church for the whole of society. Forsyth sought a 'deepening of the real distinction between Church and State in the interests of the true function of each part, and its complementary service to the social whole. It is not a severance so

---

[166] Ibid., 219.
[167] Idem, *Faith, Freedom and the Future*, 290, 293, 336, 347.
[168] Ibid., 347.
[169] Idem, *The Principle of Authority*, 253.
[170] Idem, *Theology in Church and State*, 211.
[171] Idem, *Congregatioanlism and Reunion*, 47. Cf. *Missions in State and Church*, 80.
[172] Idem, 'The Evangelical Basis of Free Churchism,' 693. Cf. *The Charter of the Church*, 32.
[173] Idem, *The Charter of the Church*, 49.
[174] Walter Wilson, *The History and Antiquities of Dissenting Churches and Meeting Houses*.London, 1808, 1: 321.

much as a moving of the two far enough apart to give them room to act, and to grow, and to be themselves.'[175]

If God's action in the Cross is the supremely authoritative event, on the ground of which the church is called out by the Spirit, the grace revealed in the redemptive act, and not the ministry and the sacraments as such, is what constitutes the church and makes it one: 'In our view the unity of the Church is founded in the creative act of our moral redemption which creates our faith today and which created the Church at first; it is not in the traditional polity, creed or cultus we inherit. If unity is in polity Christ died in vain. Unity is in the Gospel, it is not in orders or sacraments, valuable as these are.'[176] Hence Forsyth's conviction that any doctrine of ministerial orders and any sacerdotal view of the sacraments is divisive and anti-Catholic because it erects barriers between those who have been made one in Christ. To use his own word, it is 'monopolist': 'The correct name of the Church which limits the true Church to a particular community is not the Catholic, but the *Monopolist* Church. No Church has a right to name Catholic if it insists on unchurching all others which are not episcopal or established by the State.'[177] After all, 'what the Gospel created was not a crowd of Churches but the one Church in various places'.[178]

None of this is to depreciate either the ministry or the sacraments: on the contrary, Forsyth takes a 'high' view of both. But it is to understand both as authorized by, and as witnessing to, the gospel. Accordingly, the crucial question is not whether the church has a threefold ministry of bishops, priests and deacons; it is what is believed about such ministers — especially *vis à vis* the sacraments, and whether the doctrine is wielded in a monopolist, sectarian manner.

Positively, Forsyth affirms that 'the ministry is a prophetic and sacramental office; it is not a secretarial, it is not merely presidential. It is sacramental and not merely functional. It is the outwards and visible agent of the inward gospel Grace'.[179] How sad, then, that 'the pulpit has lost authority because it has lost intimacy with the Cross, immersion in the Cross. It has robbed Christ of Paul'.[180] He is convinced that 'no pastoral, social, theological work will ever atone for defect in [preaching]. Nothing will atone for neglect or inability to feed the flock in the plentiful pasture of Scripture, or to speak to the world the word of God so that they shall either love or hate, trust or fear, and shall listen either unto their

---

[175] P. T. Forsyth, 'The Evangelical Basis of Free Churchism', 681.
[176] Idem, *Congregationalism and Reunion*, 21.
[177] Idem, *The Charter of the Church*, 39; cf. *The Church and the Sacraments*, 46.
[178] Idem, *The Church and the Sacraments*, 68; cf. *Theology in Church and State*, 124.
[179] Idem, *The Church and the Sacraments*, 133.
[180] A. E. Garvie did not consider that the loss or the robbery were as complete as Forsyth supposed. See his 'Placarding the Cross', 345.

perdition or unto their life'.[181] But as well as speaking to the people in the name of God as a prophet, the minister must 'also speak to God as priest in the name of the people. He must pray as well as preach; and in private as in public he must carry his people into the presence of God'.[182] Concerning the sacraments, Forsyth is in no doubt that they 'are not emblems but symbols, and symbols not as mere channels, but in the active sense that something is done as well as conveyed'.[183] They are acts not of the ministers, but of the Church. In somewhat polemical tones inspired by his opposition to monopolism, he refers to the sacraments in his own communion, affirming that 'our Sacraments as acts of the Church, and of Christ's indwelling in the Church by His Spirit, there offering Himself crucified to us anew, are at least equal to any sacrament where the virtue is in the elements or in the canonical succession'.[184]

Forsyth's vision of the church's task is wide but, once again, it is grounded in the Cross: 'we shall never worship right nor serve right till we are more engrossed with our God than even with our worship, with His reality than our piety, with His Cross than our service'.[185] The church's work is determined by Christ's work on the Cross, which secured 'once for all the Kingdom of God in the real world unseen, by an ethical and spiritual victory'.[186] Accordingly, 'the prime duty of the Church is not to impress, or even to save, men, but to confess the Saviour, to confess in various forms the God, the Christ, the Cross that does save'.[187] Indeed, 'our missions will escape from chronic difficulties when our Church recovers the ruling note of the redeeming Cross and the accent of the Holy Ghost ... A Church cold to missions is a Church dead to the Cross'.[188]

When we turn to the ethical obligation of the church towards society as a whole we find, once again, that the Cross is central. 'The source of the new life must be also its norm'; and this is to be found neither in the affections nor the intuitions of the individual heart, but in Christ. And it is not in Christ's conviction and teaching, nor in His example, but in His great creative and crucial Act behind all His teaching and beneficence. It is in the Cross, where is the one all comprehensive gift of a holy God, and the one constant source and

---

[181] P. T. Forsyth, 'The Ideal Ministry,' in *Revelation Old and New*, 107.
[182] Ibid., 99. Forsyth was writing before the first woman, Constance Mary Coltman, was ordained into the Congregational ministry in 1917. Many have now become aware of good theological reasons for unease with the masculine pronouns he uses in this connection, and would nowadays cast such sentences in the plural.
[183] P. T. Forsyth, *The Church and the Sacraments*, xv.
[184] Idem, 'Church, Ministry and Sacraments', 52.
[185] Idem, *The Church and the Sacraments*, 25.
[186] Idem, *The Church, The Gospel and Society*, 10.
[187] Idem, *Faith, Freedom and the Future*, 220.
[188] Idem, *Missions in State and Church*, 23, 250.

principle of the new life.'[189] The Christian ethic is paralyzed by 'a demoralized Christian religion which is more concerned to consecrate a natural ethic than to create a new ethic from the fountain of a New Humanity in the Cross'.[190] It follows that 'if we bring a Gospel whose first charge . . . is not the honouring of God's holiness, then the moral demand must slowly slacken; whole tracts of life will be exempted from it; the soul's worth will decline with our conception of God's requirement and the soul's price; and men will be more easily treated as tools in a great concern, or as pawns in a great game'.[191] What does this mean in practical terms? I give one example:

> Christian ethics cannot be satisfied with calling on . . . people to glorify God in their station. It must go on to promote such a reorganization of industry as may give the worker freedom to live and hope as a man should, to keep a secure home and property, and become, in some sense, a responsible partner in the industry of which he is so great a part. This cannot be done simply by the goodwill of certain employers; it involves a gradual change of the whole system, under the ethical influences which it is the business of a Church that understands its business, its Gospel, and its world, to foster.[192]

In the last decade of his life, Forsyth wrestled as determinedly as most with the societal upheaval occasioned by the First World War. The need of a theodicy was clamant, and Forsyth produced one which was by no means to the liking of all of his contemporaries. The War showed that bland humanism would no longer suffice: its roots were shallow and its remedies ineffectual. The prevailing mentality 'is not used to first-class crisis. And in its shock it can find no theodicy in the course of history, no conduct of things by God worthy of a God — worthy of its kind of God, whose Cross was but a kindly boon to crippled men, and not chiefly an honour done to the Holy Name, and the foundation of the Holy Realm'.[193] When many were asking, 'How can there be a love of God if all of this destruction is permitted?' it took a particular kind of courage to declare that in view of God's righteous, holy love 'the scandal and the stumbling block would have been if such judgments did not come'.[194] His consolation is that since 'our faith did not arise from the order of the world; the world's convulsion, therefore, need not destroy it'.[195] Our faith arose from the once-for-all victory of Christ's cross. The last enemy is destroyed; the final victory won: 'The thing is done, it is not to do. "Be of good cheer, I *have* overcome the world" .... The evil world will

---

[189] Idem, *The Christian Ethic of War*, 136; cf. 133; *The Church, The Gospel and Society*, 24.
[190] Idem, 'Veracity, Reality, and Regeneration', 202.
[191] Idem, *The Church, The Gospel and Society*, 29.
[192] Ibid., 54.
[193] Idem, *The Justification of God*, 36.
[194] Ibid., 119.
[195] Ibid., 57.

not win at last, because it failed to win at the only time it ever could. It is a vanquished world where men play their devilries. Christ has overcome it. It can make tribulation, but desolution it can never make.'[196] In that confidence believers continue their pilgrimage, remembering that 'the Christian idea is not happiness and it is not power, but it is perfection — which is the growth of God's image and glory as our destiny'.[197]

VI

The inscription on the tomb of Thomas Goodwin, Forsyth's Puritan hero, includes words, translated from the Latin by another of Aberdeen's Congregational D.D.'s, Thomas Gibbons (1720–85; D. D., King's College, 1764), which may, perhaps with a slight hesitation over the word 'clearly', be applied to Forsyth himself,

> None ever entered deeper
> Into the mysteries of the gospel,
> Or more clearly unfolded them
> For the benefit of others.[198]

Of Goodwin another wrote words which most certainly describe Forsyth: 'He appears to have been specially raised up for great purposes.'[199] By announcing the gospel of victorious holy love, Forsyth served such purposes then, and he continues to serve them now.

As I have shown, Forsyth was unsystematic in a variety of ways. If by 'systematic theologian' is meant one whose biblical foundations are displayed with exegetical thoroughness, whose judgements on thinkers and movements are supported by copious apparatus, whose linguistic challenges and argumentative loose ends are few, and whose method is to take us stage by stage through the several Christian doctrines with more or less equal thoroughness, then Forsyth fits the description less than adequately. Accordingly, he cannot be our *intellectual* refuge. However, that is not our

---

[196] Ibid., 166–7, 223. Cf. *Work*, 160.

[197] *This Life and the Next*, 87.

[198] Quoted by Walter Wilson, *The History and Antiquities of Dissenting Churches and Meeting Houses*, III, 431. The third line here may give some pause: much has been written concerning Forsyth's alleged obscurity. It must be granted that this style and urgency can cause him to tumble along to the puzzlement of most readers at times; on the other hand, there are none so deaf as those who will not hear. For Forsyth's own remarks on the matter see *Positive Preaching and the Modern Mind*, 23–4. See also Thomas D. Meadley, 'The "Obscurity" of P. T. Forsyth,' *The Congregational Quarterly*, XXIV no. 4, October 1946, 308–17.

[199] An unnamed 'late eminent minister', quoted in J. A. Jones, ed., *Bunhill Memorials: Sacred Reminiscences of Three Hundred Ministers and Other Persons of Note who are Buried in Bunhill Fields* (London: 1849), 67.

greatest need. Forsyth proclaims an eternal refuge, in the victory of whose holy love we may trust. 'What he said of Independency characterizes his own founded, systematic, reflection: 'Its note has not been theological system but theological footing, not an ordered knowledge of divine procedure but an experienced certainty of divine redemption.'[200] In proclaiming the holiness and victory of God's love (at Calvary something is done for God and for us, not merely shown); in insisting upon the authority of grace and upon the inescapability and catholicity of the church; and, above all, in making the umbrella term 'cross' central and determinative for Christology and all else, Forsyth sounded notes which must never be absent from the score of Christian theology. Indeed, apart from these notes there would be no score at all. Because he realized this, and because he viewed everything from the vantage-point of the cross in a sustained, passionate, urgent, practical, and (to a high degree) consistent manner, he may be deemed a systematic theologian *par excellence*. Small wonder that the Scottish Congregationalist Charles Duthie (1911–81; D.D., Aberdeen, 1952), who was the last in Garvie's line as Principal of New College, London, testified, 'One page of Forsyth can do more to stir the conscience and inflame the heart than a dozen pages of some thinkers of quite high repute.'[201] Not surprisingly, on the occasion of the closing of New College, London, in 1977, Lovell Cocks bore witness: 'During my lifetime I have learned much from many teachers but it is to Peter Forsyth that I owe my theological soul and my footing in the Gospel.'[202]

Students who had the good fortune to sit under both Garvie and Forsyth were inclined to say that while Garvie got them through their B. D. examinations, Forsyth gave them a gospel to preach. Be that as it may, both Principals would without question have joined in the words of Aberdeen's most widely-sung Congregational D.D., Philip Doddridge (1702–51; D.D., Marischal College, 1736; King's College, 1737):

> Grace, 'tis a charming sound,
> Harmonious to my ear;
> Heaven with the echo shall resound,
> And all the earth shall hear.

---

[200] P. T. Forsyth, *Faith, Freedom and the Future*, 139.

[201] Charles S. Duthie, 'Fireworks in a Fog?', 'The Faith of P. T. Forsyth,' *The British Weekly*, 17 December 1964, 9. Duthie, who also held the M.A. and B.D. of the University of Aberdeen, trained at the Scottish Congregational College, and was Principal of it from 1944–64. He was Principal of New College, London, from 1964 to 1977, when the College closed.

[202] H. F. Lovell Cocks, 'New College', an MS address delivered on 16 June 1977. In the H. F. L. Cocks Papers, Dr William's Library, London.

CHAPTER 8

What Has P. T. Forsyth to do with Mercersburg?

Born in 1848, P. T. Forsyth was a Congregational minister who served five pastorates prior to becoming Principal of Hackney College, London, from 1901 until his death in 1921. If we compare his dates with those of the formative Mercersburg years we can see that in a literal historical sense, Forsyth and Mercersburg have nothing whatever to do with one another. Nevin, born forty-five years before Forsyth, died in 1886, some years before Forsyth's 'conversion' from liberal theology to his theology of the Cross. Schaff died in 1893, when Forsyth was emerging from what he had come to regard as a defective and inadequate theology. In his own celebrated words, he was turned 'from a Christian to a believer, from a lover of love to an object of grace.'[1] Further, since most of Forsyth's works were not published until the first two decades of the twentieth century, the Mercersburg pioneers could hardly have been familiar with them; nor, as far as I am aware, did Forsyth publish any remarks upon the Mercersburg theology. But ideas know no temporal or spatial boundaries, and I did not cross the ocean simply in order to inform you that the answer to my title's question is 'Nothing.' On the contrary, I believe that if we place Forsyth and the Mercersburg theologians side by side we shall discover that here they are in hearty accord, there they interestingly complement one another, while occasionally the sparks fly in lively fashion. More than this, I hope to show that Forsyth usefully corrects Mercersburg at certain points, just as he is corrected by it; and I shall even presume to suggest that not only the United Church of Christ but the Church at large could with profit own these joint and mutually correcting contributors to the Reformed heritage.

Partly because of the delightfully British habit of picking up the ideas of others fifty years after they have been discarded in their places of origin, Forsyth's intellectual inheritance was not altogether dissimilar to that of Nevin. For just as the latter, under the tutelage of F. A. Rauch, imbibed Hegelianism

---

[1] P. T. Forsyth, *Positive Preaching and the Modern Mind*, (1907), London: Independent Press, 1964, 193. For Leslie McCurdy's comprehensive bibliography of works by, and on, Forsyth see Trevor Hart, ed., *Justice the True and Only Mercy. Essays on the Life and Theology of P. T. Forsyth*, Edinburgh: T. & T. Clark, 1995.

even if it did not drown him,[2] so by the time Forsyth was at the University of Aberdeen, post-Hegelian idealism was beginning to find its way across the English Channel. It was in 1865 that the Scot James Hutchinson Stirling published the first significant British work on Hegel, *The Secret of Hegel*, a work concerning which a waggish reviewer declared that 'if Mr. Hutchinson Stirling knew the secret of Hegel he had managed to keep it to himself.'[3] Be that as it may (and it is not entirely fair to Stirling), there followed a succession of philosophers – some more Kantian like T. H. Green, others more strictly Hegelian like John and Edward Caird – but all of them influenced by post-Hegelian immanentism, and prone to assert the fundamental human-divine continuity, and to rebaptize evolutionary thought in terms of a Pauline 'dying and rising' teleology.[4]

But although Forsyth could confess that 'No books have done more for my mind than Hegel's "Logic," or for my insights than his "Aesthetik,"'[5] and call Hegel 'the greatest philosopher the world ever saw,'[6] the influence of another German, Albrecht Ritschl (whose work Schaff ignored[7]), under whom Forsyth studied for a year in Göttingen, was, on his own admission, more significant than that of any other theologian.[8] While distancing himself from Ritschl's view that justification is primarily a matter of forgiveness received in faith, he thoroughly endorsed Ritschl's emphasis upon the supreme importance of God's historic act in Christ for a redemption which was truly moral; this, for Forsyth, was all important. Ritschl secured the objective, evangelical base for religion and theology in 'a positive act of revelation.' He made it clear that faith entails a

---

[2] Louis H. Gunnemann notes the importance of Nevin's embracing of the *Heidelberg Catechism*, Schaff's importation of the best German thought of the day, and the quest of cultural identity on the part of German immigrants. See *The Shaping of the United Church of Christ. An Essay in the History of American Christianity*, New York: United Church press, 1977, 177–9.

[3] Quoted by J. H. Muirhead, *The Platonic Tradition in Anglo-Saxon Philosophy*, London: Allen & Unwin, 1931, 171. For the provenance of British post-Hegelian idealism see Alan P. F. Sell, *Philosophical Idealism and Christian Belief*, Cardiff: University of Wales Press and New York: St. Martin's Press, 1995.

[4] For detailed discussions of T. H. Green and Edward Caird see Alan P. F. Sell, *Philosophical Idealism and Christian Belief*, Cardiff: University of Wales Press and New York: St. Martin's Press, 1995; for John Caird see Alan P. F. Sell, *Defending and Declaring the Faith. Some Scottish Examples 1860–1920*, Exeter: Paternoster Press and Colorado Springs: Helmers and Howard, 1987, ch. 4.

[5] 'Ministerial libraries. V. Principal Forsyth's library at Hackney College,' *The British Monthly*, May 1904, 268. The nouns are important.

[6] P. T. Forsyth, *The Work of Christ*, (1910), London: Independent Press, 1938, 60.

[7] So Klaus Penzel, ed., *Philip Schaff, Historian and Ambassador of the Universal Church*, Macon, GA: Mercer University Press, 1991, lxvii.

[8] 'Ministerial libraries. V,' 269.

judgment involving the whole person, and was at the same time an act of obedience.⁹ It is from this standpoint that he criticises Hegel.¹⁰

In thinking their thoughts in an intellectual environment permeated to a greater or lesser degree by Hegelianism, Nevin and Forsyth were also reacting against certain characteristic features of the Enlightenment. (Even as I say this I recognize what an elastic term 'Enlightenment' is; and I find it necessary from time to time to caution those who seem to think that there was but one Enlightenment. In fact, there were several: the English was not exactly the same as the Scottish, and neither was so anti-clerical as the French). Like some theologians at the present time, Nevin was not particularly discriminating in this matter: indeed, he was positively impolite. With reference to Bacon, Locke and the Scottish common sense philosophy (which he uncritically lumps together) he declares, 'The general character of this bastard philosophy is, that it affects to measure all things, both on earth and in heaven, by the categories of the common abstract understanding, as it stands related simply to the world of time and sense.'¹¹ In The Mystical Presence (1846) he had already lamented that 'The eighteenth century was characteristically infidel. As an age, it seemed to have no organ for the supernatural ... The views of rationalism may be said to infect the whole theology of this period ... '.¹² Since he seems to have overlooked Jonathan Edwards's 'new spiritual sense,' Wesley's theology, and a goodly amount of Dutch and German pietism – to mention no more – a modicum of rhetorical exaggeration may be suspected. In the same year Schaff likewise declared that 'Rationalism ... sets itself in hostile array against the substance of the orthodox theory [of history], and against Christianity itself, reducing it to the character of a mutable and transient system.'¹³ Forsyth is

---

⁹ P. T. Forsyth, *Revelation Old and New*, ed. John Huxtable, London: Independent Press, 1962, 74.

¹⁰ Though it should be noted that there is what I have elsewhere called 'a post-Hegelian-idealistic drag' at some points in Forsyth's writings – especially in *Christ on Parnassus: Lectures on Art, Ethic, and Theology*, London: Hodder & Stoughton, [1911]. See further ch. 7 above. See also Jeremy Begbie, 'The ambivalent rainbow: Forsyth, Art and Creation,' and Stanley Russell, 'Spoiling the Egyptians: P. T. Forsyth and Hegel,' in T. Hart, ed., op.cit.; and Ralph C. Wood, 'Christ on Parnassus: P. T. Forsyth among the liberals,' *Journal of Literature and Theology*, 2, no. 1, March 1988, 83–95. Forsyth's indebtedness to Herrmann's emphasis upon the importance history as the supreme locus of revelation should also be noted.

¹¹ J. W. Nevin, *Human Freedom and a Plea for Philosophy: Two Essays*, Mercersburg: P. A. Rice, 1850, 42. For a full discussion of Locke and some reference to the common sense tradition, see Alan P. F. Sell, *John Locke and the Eighteenth-Century Divines*, Cardiff: University of Wales Press, 1997.

¹² J. W. Nevin, *The Mystical Presence*, (1846), Philadelphia: United Church Press, 1966, 134.

¹³ P. Schaff, *What is Church History? A Vindication of the Idea of Historical Development*, Philadelphia: J. B. Lippincott, (1846), in Charles Yrigoyen, Jr. And George M. (sic) Bricker, eds., *Reformed and Catholic. Selected Historical and Theological Writings of Philip Schaff*, Pittsburgh: The Pickwick Press, 1979, 76.

equally opposed to rationalism, though he is more temperate – and hence perhaps more effective – though no less decisive in his mode of expression. Lessing, he explains, introduced a rational and ethical humanity in Germany, Rousseau a sentimental humanity in France, as the standard by which religion was to be judged. 'The Illumination,' he declares, 'was the rational counterpart of Pietism. It was the reference of Christianity, not now to a supernatural experience of guilt and salvation, but to a logical sense of truth, and to a natural experience of justice and kindness ... Religion became a flush on the face of philosophy or idealism ... '[14] As far as the world of thought was concerned, the Lisbon earthquake of 1755 delivered the death blow to this 'cheery creed,' but 'it did not die on the day it was killed. It is not dead yet.'[15] It takes various forms – not least Hegelian. Indeed, 'modernism is the latter-day scholasticism, where Hegel, or some other recent philosopher, takes the normative place of Aristotle. It is intellectualism, either mystic or aesthetic in tone ... '[16]

That there is a Ritschlian aversion to some forms of mysticism in Forsyth's writings cannot be denied; but there is also a strong conviction that in raising the moral question, Kant had performed a most valuable task. Indeed, as far as the concept of law is concerned, Forsyth testifies that if Hooker was his first teacher, and Burke his second, 'my greatest was the father of modern thought – Kant.'[17] Thus he can say,

> With Kant came a new order of things. The ethical took the place that had been held by the intellectual. The notion of reality replaced that of truth.

---

[14] P. T. Forsyth, 'Lay religion,' *The Constructive Quarterly*, 3, 1915, 775.

[15] Ibid., 776. It should be remembered that much of Forsyth's critique of post-Hegelian immanentism was fuelled by the activities of such a prominent minister as R. J. Campbell of the City Temple, whose *The New Theology*, one of theology's nine-day wonders, appeared in 1907. H. F.Lovell Cocks recalled that on the appearance of one of Campbell's books, Forsyth opened his lecture for the day with the words, 'He's done it again, gentlemen! Froth, gentlemen; froth!! Champagne froth, I grant you; but froth, gentlemen, all the same.' Quoted by John Huxtable, 'P. T. Forsyth: 1848–1921,' *The Journal of the United Reformed Church History Society*, 4 no. 1, October 1987, 73. For Campbell, who subsequently turned Anglican, see Alan P. F. Sell, *Theology in Turmoil: The Roots, Course and Significance of the Conservative-Liberal Debate in Modern Theology*, (1986), Eugene, OR: Wipf and Stock, 1998, 35–6, 105, 154. For Lovell Cocks see idem, *Commemorations. Studies in Christian Thought and History*, (1993), Eugene, OR: Wipf and Stock, 1998, ch. 13.

[16] Idem, *Faith, Freedom and the Future*, (1912), London: Independent Press, 1955, 99.

[17] Idem, 'Law and atonement: Dr. Forsyth and Dr. W. L. Walker: Dr. Forsyth's rejoinder,' *The Christian World*, 24 September 1908, 9. Of course, Forsyth's appreciation of Kant is qualified by his understanding of the authority of grace in the Gospel. Thus, for example, he distances himself from Kant in writing, 'conscience is not a legislator, it is a judge. It does not give the laws either for action or belief, it receives them; it recognizes the authority of laws from another source, and administers them to the occasions which arise. It does not emit authority, it owns it.' See *The Problem of Authority in relation to Certainty, Sanctity and Society*, (1913), London: Independent Press, 1952, 300.

Religion placed us not in line with the rationality of the world but in *rapport* with the reality of it. And the ethical was the real.[18]

But the main point for the moment is that Forsyth is more open to the dangers of Hegelian rationalism than Nevin appears to have been (though even Nevin can say that before the article, 'I believe in the holy catholic church,' 'The logic of Hegel ... becomes no better than a spider's web').[19] The situation between them will become clear if we consider their views of history.

Nevin is the apostle of historic continuity. He takes an organic view of history, and understands the Gospel itself as being always in a state of historical development The following passage from 'Early Christianity' (1851/2) will serve as representative of many places in his writings where the point is made:

It is the theory of historical development, which assumes the possibility and necessity

> of a transition on the part of the church through various stages of form ... for the very purpose of bringing out more and more fully always the true inward sense of its life, which has been one and the same from the beginning ...
>
> We are shut up ... to the idea of *historical development,* as the only possible way of escape from the difficulty with which we are met in bringing the present here into comparison with the past. If the modern church must be the same in substance with the ancient church, a true continuation of its life as this has been in the world by divine promise from the beginning, while it is perfectly plain at the same time that a wide difference holds between the two systems as to form, the relation binding them together can only be one of living progress or growth. No other will satisfy these opposite conditions.
>
> Each part of the process ... is regarded as necessary and right in its own order and time; but still only as *relatively* right, and as having need thus to complete itself, passing ultimately into a higher form.[20]

The Hegelian notes are unmistakeable, and they are echoed by Philip Schaff:

> Development is properly identical with history itself; for history is life, and all life involves growth, evolution and progress. Our bodily existence, all our mental faculties, the Christian life, and the sanctification of every individual,

---

[18] Idem, *The Problem of Authority*, 4. This is by no means to imply that Forsyth was an *irrationalist*. See further ch. 8 above.

[19] J. W. Nevin, 'Early Christianity,' (1851-2), in *Catholic and Reformed*, 228. See further on Nevin's philosophical inheritance, William DiPuccio, 'Nevin's idealistic philosophy,' in Sam Hamstra, Jr., and Arie J. Griffioen, *Reformed Confessionalism in Nineteenth-Century America. Essays on the Thought of John Williamson Nevin*, Lanham, MD: The Scarecrow Press, 1995; W. DiPuccio, 'Mercersburg and contemporary thought: the incarnation as meta-narrative,' *The New Mercersburg Review*, 20, Autumn 1996, 29–52; Lawrence S. Stepelevich, 'Eucharistic theory: Hegelianism and Mercersburg theology,' ibid., 3–16.

[20] Ibid., 197, 288–9, 294.

constitute such a process of development from the lower to the higher. Why should not the same law hold, when applied to the whole, the communion which is made up of individuals?[21]

Not surprisingly, Klaus Penzel has referred to Schaff's 'sincere belief that he had found the key to the meaning of the history of Christianity in the principle of historical development as moulded by the romantic-idealistic currents of early nineteenth-century German culture.'[22]

Interestingly, as we shall see, Forsyth would have queried Schaff's understanding of the Church as a 'communion which is made up of individuals' – he would have thought this too atomistic and not organic enough. But for the present we must focus upon his critique of the idea of development. We may even say that Philip Schaff gives Forsyth his entrée, for Schaff insists that 'The right application of the theory of development depends altogether on having beforehand a right view of positive Christianity, and being grounded in it, not only in thought, but also in heart and experience.'[23] In a nutshell, the burden of Forsyth's complaint is that if we make humanity's or the Church's progress too automatic (as we would if we were to become imprisoned in an Hegelian dialectic, or in a Romantic understanding of organic process),[24] we skirt the historic redemptive act, minimise humanity's moral need, and open the door to salvation by education or social improvement rather than by radical rescue. He bluntly asks,

> Are we regenerate by the Word or fortified by the sacraments? Is the Christian life a continual moral conversion or a continual mystic feeding? Is Christ in the last resort the eternal Redeemer of a wrecked race or the steady Perfecter of a race merely defective? That will be the difference in principle between the Evangelical and the Catholic type of Christianity ... [25]

---

[21] P. Schaff, 'German theology and the Church question,' *The Mercersburg Review*, 5, January 1855, extracted in Klaus Penzel, *Philip Schaff*, 109. Long after his Mercersburg days, Schaff seriously qualified this statement. Recognizing that the Church is ever an earthen vessel, he declared, 'The true theory of development must be both conservative and progressive, and provide for what is good and valuable in all ages and divisions of Christendom.' See *Theological Propaedeutic: A General Introduction to the Study of Theology*, New York: Charles Scribners, 1892, 241.

[22] K. Penzel, ibid., 297. Cf. John B. Payne, 'Philip Schaff: Christian scholar, historian and ecumenist,' *Historical Intelligencer*, II no. 1, 1982, 20–22; ibid., 'Schaff and Nevin, colleagues at Mercersburg: the Church question,' *Church History*, LXI no. 2, June 1992, 171.

[23] P. Schaff, *History of the Apostolic Church, with a General Introduction to Church History*, trans. Edward D. Yeomans, 1853, in K. Penzel, op.cit., 33.

[24] K. Penzel says that Schaff eclectically fused these. See *Philip Schaff*, xliv.

[25] P. T. Forsyth, *Congregationalism and Reunion*, London: Independent Press, 1952, 20. We may well feel that here Forsyth overstates his case by disjunction – a characteristic pitfall in his style. At crucial points 'both ... and' do not come easily to him. Cf. ch. 7 above.

Not, indeed, that the Catholic type alone is at risk. Forsyth declares that while both Hegel and Ritschl, in their differing ways, proclaimed reconciliation, 'they both united to obscure the idea of atonement or expiation.' The whole world, said Hegel,

> was a movement or process of the grand, divine idea; but it was a process. Now please to put down and make much use of this fundamental distinction between a process and an act. A process has nothing moral in it. We are simply carried along on the crest of a wave. An act, on the other hand, can only be done by a moral personality.

Forsyth fears lest fusion or absorption in the organic whole replace the moral and spiritual reconciliation of persons, which makes for communion.[26] He insists that 'The Gospel stands with the predominance of intervention, it falls with the predominance of evolution.'[27] Again,

> Any theology that places us in a spiritual *process*, or native movement between the finite and the infinite, depreciates the value of spiritual *act*, and thus makes us independent of the grace of God. Its movement is processional spectacular, aesthetic, it is not historic, dramatic, tragic or ethical. If it speak of the grace of God it does not take it with moral seriousness.[28]

'Evolution,' he elsewhere stated, 'becomes the unfolding of a Divine Immanence and not the coming of a Divine Redeemer.'[29]

Forsyth reiterated the point in a variety of ways in many places. He fears the loss of God 'in a Monism which is rather the absolutising of the immanent than the incarnation of the transcendent.'[30] Again, while 'we are all Monists in the sense of striving to introduce unity of conception into our view of life and things ... we do not all think that the principle of the world is wholly within the world.' Certain it is that 'revelation is ... an impossible idea except on a dualist base of He and You, giver and receiver ... For a God conceived as above all things monistic and immanent to the world cannot reveal Himself, because he has no recipient Other.' Forsyth therefore crusaded for 'a Dualism with a unity of Reconciliation, and not a Monism with a unity of Identity as real in the sin as in the Saviour.' In other words, he affirms not a unity of material substance, or of

---

[26] P. T. Forsyth, *The Work of Christ*, 66–9.

[27] Ibid., 'The distinctive thing in Christian experience,' *The Hibbert Journal*, 6 no. 3, April 1908, 486.

[28] Ibid., *Positive Preaching and the Modern Mind*, 146; cf. 150, 161, and 229, where he regrets that so many follow 'in the wake of the great cosmic processionist, Hegel, with his staff of subordinate evolutionists.'

[29] Idem, *Missions in State and Church. Sermons and Addresses*, London: Hodder & Stoughton, 1908, 83. Cf. Idem, Revelation Old and New, 58.

[30] Idem, *Faith, Freedom and the Future*, 342.

intellectual system, but of moral soul. Where Hegel envisages a reconciling process, Christ performs a reconciling act.[31] Again, but now in more theological terms, Forsyth declares that 'It is ... not a case of rational continuity as in Monistic Idealism, where we test the revelation or absorb it ... We do not realise ourselves in Christ so much as submit ourselves.'[32] Such a personal transaction is impossible in Hegelianism, for the individual imbued with power, because 'In Hegel's system there is no room left for such an individual, and that was the defect which brought down [Hegelianism's] grand flight.' Hence there can finally be no genuinely moral relations or moral control in that system: 'There is no control in Monism with its force, law and efficiency, but only in Monotheism with its will, conscience, and love.'[33] For this reason no source for revelation may be found in philosophical idealism – or, for that matter, in the principle of divine sonship severed from the person of Christ, or in the aesthetic Christ:

> The active contents of Revelation, it must be reiterated, are not truths, ideas, or even principles. That is the fatal error shared also by the vicious notion of an orthodoxy or saving system. The sole content of Revelation ... is the love, will, presence and purpose of God for our redemption.[34]

While rationalism, whether orthodox or heterodox, 'consists in measuring Revelation by something outside itself,' thereby making human reason the control of revelation, revelation, properly understood, is a religious idea, the appropriate response to which is not knowledge or poetry, but faith.[35]

Enough has been said, I think, to indicate the broad reactions of Nevin, Schaff and Forsyth to the philosophical environment in which they were called to work. We may already begin to suspect that when we turn to those doctrinal matters which are our primary concern we shall hear echoes of these reactions. For the present it would seem that the Mercersburg men were more sympathetic to post-Hegelian immanentism than was Forsyth. This may be partly because Forsyth was writing in the heyday of liberal theology, from which he regarded himself as a refugee, while Schaff, but especially Nevin, had plenty of other bogeymen in their sights – revivalists, New England 'Puritans' and Reformed-Christians-perceived-as-recalcitrant among them. This contextual reference

---

[31] Idem, 'Monism,' A paper read before the London Society for the Study of Religion, 2 February 1909, printed for members only, 14, 7, 8, 12, 15. The paper is at The Congregational Library, Dr. Williams's Library, London. See further his 'Faith, metaphysic and incarnation,' *Methodist Review*, 97, September 1915, 696–719.

[32] Idem, *The Principle of Authority*, 172–3.

[33] Idem, *The Justification of God. Lectures for War-Time on a Christian Theodicy*, (1917), London: Independent Press, 1948, 51, 132; cf. 70–71.

[34] Idem, 'Revelation and the purpose of Christ,' in *Faith and Criticism. Essays by Congregationalists*, London: Sampson Low Marston, 2nd edn. 1893, 102.

[35] Ibid., 109, 107.

reminds us that, like Paul and Augustine before them, neither Forsyth nor Nevin were systematic in the sense of producing rounded doctrinal systems covering all the *loci* from God to eschatology. On the contrary, many of their writings were occasional – even controversial – and if they did not write 'off the cuff' (for this would quite wrongly suggest casualness) they certainly wrote and thought, as it were, 'on the hoof.' Nevertheless in a deeper sense they were thoroughly systematic, with Nevin ranging back and forth from his standing-ground in the mystical presence, and Forsyth from his in the Cross. All of this will become clear as we proceed. But how to select from the many topics which fell within our authors' purview? I shall take my cue from Nevin's own list of the characteristic features of the Mercersburg theology (though in the interest of the flow of my paper I very slightly reorder them): it is Christological, or Christocentric; objective, historical and credal; churchly and liturgical.[36] Let us, then, view Mercersburg and Forsyth through these lenses.

I

No reader of Nevin's works who is even half awake could miss his strongly Christocentric thrust. He is at pains to distinguish Christ from all other teachers and leaders, and at this point he and Forsyth are in complete accord. Listen first to Nevin:

> Christ ... was not the founder simply of a religious school – of vastly greater eminence, it might be, than Pythagoras, Plato, or Moses, but still a teacher of truth only in the same general sense. Christianity is not a *doctrine*, to be taught or learned like a system of philosophy or a rule of moral conduct. Rationalism is always prone to look upon the gospel in this way. As Moses made known more of the divine will than the world had understood before, so Christ is taken to be only a greater prophet in the same form. But this is to wrong his character altogether.[37]

Now hear Forsyth: 'A Christ that differs from the rest of men only in saintly degree and not in redeeming kind is not the Christ of the New Testament nor of a Gospel Church.'[38] 'No faith born in true repentance could speak of our all being "sons of God" like Christ.'[39] 'Christ is more precious to us by what distinguishes Him from us than by what identifies Him with us.'[40]

---

[36] See J. W. Nevin, *Vindication of the Revised Liturgy, Historical and Theological*, Philadelphia: Jas. B. Rodgers, 1867, in *Catholic and Reformed*, 365. Nevin places 'Ruled by the Apostles' Creed' before 'Objective and Historical.'

[37] Idem, *The Mystical Presence*, 216.

[38] P. T. Forsyth, The Church, *The Gospel and Society*, London: Independent Press, 1962, 99.

[39] Idem, *The Person and Place of Jesus Christ*, 55–6.

[40] Idem, 'The distinctive thing in Christian experience,' 486; cf. *The Person and Place of Jesus Christ*, 342.

As is well known, Nevin's Christocentrism is rooted in the incarnation. For Nevin,

> The incarnation ... is the key that unlocks the sense of all God's works, and brings to light the true meaning of the universe ... Nature and revelation, the world and Christianity, as springing from the same Divine Mind, are not two different systems joined in a merely outward way. They form a single whole, harmonious with itself in all its parts...The mystery of the new creation must involve in the end the mystery of the old, and the key that serves to unlock the meaning of the first must serve to unlock at the same time the inmost secret of the last.

The incarnation forms thus the great central *fact* of the world.[41] Here, clearly stated or implicit, are the great Mercersburg themes of incarnation, divine-human continuity, the mystical union, and the summing up of all things in Christ. Nevin proceeds to elaborate upon these themes with considerable reference to the Johannine writings and Hebrews. Not, indeed, that Paul is forgotten, for Nevin incorporates the apostle's discussion of the old Adam and the new, Christ, as a significant strand in his argument.[42] Thus he can write,

> The fall of Adam was the fall of the race. Not simply because he represented the race, but because the race itself was comprehended in his person ... When Christ died and rose, humanity died and rose at the same time in his person; not figuratively, but truly; just as it had fallen before in the person of Adam.[43]

---

[41] J. W. Nevin, *The Mystical Presence*, 201–2.

[42] At this point I may perhaps be permitted to raise an eyebrow at David Layman's denial that Nevin's incarnationalism plays down the novelty of the new creation 'as Alan P. F. Sell contends.' See David Wayne Layman, 'Nevin's holistic supernaturalism,' in Sam Hamstra and Arie J.Griffioen, *Reformed Confessionalism in Nineteenth-Century America*, 205. The reference is to my paper, 'J. H. A. Bomberger (1817–1890) versus J. W. Nevin: a centenary reappraisal,' *The New Mercersburg Review*, 8, Autumn 1990, 16; reprinted in Alan P. F. Sell, *Commemorations*, ch. 11, where I gently ask, 'If much Reformed theology has had too little regard to the old creation, may not Mercersburg play down the novelty of the new?' I raised a question for consideration, I did not 'contend' for this point – though perhaps I will now! I think that there is a trap here (which is more than linguistic) that Mercersburg devotees need to avoid, and it may be that in spoiling for a fight on this matter David Layman indicates that I have touched a vulnerable point. It is the question of mystical union cashed in terms which sometimes appear to skirt the historic atoning act. Or again, it is the question whether, on the ground of the incarnation = the coming of Christ as God-man, humanity (all of it) is already united to Christ, as when Nevin says, 'The object of the incarnation was to couple the human nature in real union with the Logos, as a permanent source of life,' (*The Mystical Presence*, 162); or whether, as Nevin himself perhaps more carefully says, 'Christianity is grounded in the living union *of the believer* with the person of Christ.' See ibid., 27 (my italics). Again, 'The union of Christ *with believers* is wrought by the power of the Holy Spirit,' ibid., 173 (my italics). Moreover, the believers's new life 'includes degrees, and will become complete only in the resurrection,' (ibid., 175). These seem to be significant checks upon the incarnational-automaticism which some Mercersburg phrases seem to imply, even to articulate. I shall return to this theme below.

[43] J. W. Nevin, *The Mystical Presence*, 160, 163.

Here are strong declarations of the cosmic significance of Christ, and with this motif Forsyth is in hearty accord. For him, reconciliation is by atonement, and 'this means a change of relation between God and man – man, mind you, not two or three men, not several groups of men, but man, the human race as a whole.'[44] Why? Because 'as a race we are not even stray sheep, or wandering prodigals merely; we are rebels taken with weapons in our hands.'[45] Furthermore, the salvation wrought is 'universal not by the addition of all units, but in a solidary sense.'[46] But to a much greater degree than Nevin, Forsyth views the cosmic victory in the light of the atoning Cross (though we should always remember that for him 'Cross' is shorthand for many things, including the sacrifice once-for-all made, the resurrection, the cosmic victory, the reign of Christ.[47]) Thus, 'the cross of Christ, the greatest absurdity in history, is the centre and solution of history.'[48] And again: 'Only if [a person] hold that in the atoning cross of Christ the world was redeemed by a holy God once for all, that there, and only there, sin was judged and broken, that there and only there the race was reconciled and has its access to the face and grace of God – only then has he the genius and the plerophory of the Gospel.'[49]

It must be said that at this point both Forsyth and Nevin seem to be under post-Hegelian influence. That is to say, the idea of racial solidarity, and of a race already redeemed may seem to encourage a universalistic 'automaticism' of salvation, or a by-passing of the individual which Forsyth, in particular, was elsewhere concerned to avoid. That is to say, we here seem to be more in the realm of the metaphysical and ontological than of the moral. The problem takes ecclesiological form too, as we shall see. On occasion, however, Forsyth makes what appears to be a necessary qualification. The Gospel, he declares, 'Is an objective power and historic act of God in Christ, decisive for humanity in time and eternity, and altering for ever the whole relation of the soul to God *as it may be rejected or believed.*'[50]

Although Nevin and Forsyth are at one in their grasp of the cosmic significance of Christ, we need to press the question, what is the place of the atoning Cross in Nevin's thought? Like Calvin before him – and like Forsyth too – Nevin views the entire life and ministry of Christ as having saving intent. He certainly would not wish to assert that 'Jesus came to die' – as if that were all;

---

[44] P. T. Forsyth, *The Work of Christ*, 57; cf. 96, 114.
[45] Idem, *Positive Preaching and the Modern Mind*, 38.
[46] Ibid., 116; cf. 'The distinctive thing in Christian experience,' 495; *The Cruciality of the Cross*, (1909), London: Independent Press, 1948, 18; The Justification of God, 19, 78.
[47] See further ch. 7 above.
[48] P. T. Forsyth, *God the Holy Father*, London: Independent Press, 1957, 84.
[49] Idem, *The Cruciality of the Cross*, 39.
[50] Idem, 'A rallying ground for the Free Churches. The reality of grace,' *The Hibbert Journal*, 4 no. 4, July 1906, 826 n. My italics.

and neither would Forsyth: 'You cannot sever the death of Christ from the life of Christ.'⁵¹ The redemption wrought by Christ upon the Cross, declares Nevin, is not 'something abstracted from his life ... It simply represents the form, under which specifically the life comprehended in Christ's person for the benefit of a dying world, becomes fully effective towards this end.'⁵² Elsewhere he argues that 'the true ground principle of Christianity ... is not Christ's death, but His incarnation; which not only comes before the atonement, but forms the basis also of its universal possibility and power.'⁵³ It would seem that the reference here is to both temporal and logical priority. This is confirmed elsewhere, where he declares, 'The Saviour must come into the world, before He could die in the world ... More than ... mere chronological priority, however; it is no less plain that the incarnation carries in it the antecedent necessary *conditions* of the atonement ... [I]t is not to be viewed as a mere outward device for making the Atonement possible.'⁵⁴ Clearly, what Nevin wishes to guard against is the notion that the entire worth of Christ is instrumental on a particular occasion only – at Calvary. For this reason he declares that while the death and resurrection of Christ are crucial, nevertheless the 'original root' of salvation lay 'in the constitution of his own glorious person.'⁵⁵ Clearly there is nothing that human beings can do about this – it either is, or is not, the case; and it may be that Nevin's emphasis here was fuelled by his despair at those 'new measures' revivalists who led people to understand – or misled them into thinking – that their salvation depended entirely upon their decision for Christ crucified and raised. By contrast, Nevin's plea may be construed as a plea for the prevenience of grace – the sovereign God graciously acts before we do. However, Nevin does seem to have been frightened into both relative silence upon the response which we are *enabled* to make by that same grace, and into playing down the significance of the atoning Cross. He argues that the death of Christ is not the centre of the Gospel as if all that preceded and followed it were subordinate to it; and he points out that 'The key-note of the Gospel is ... "Christ declared to be the Son of God with power according to the Spirit of holiness, by the resurrection from the dead." We hear but little of the atonement directly; it is taken up into the glorious exaltation of the Redeemer at the right hand of

---

[51] Idem, *The Work of Christ*, 153.
[52] J. W. Nevin, *The Mystical Presence*, 246–7.
[53] Idem., *Weekly Messenger*, 8 April 1868.
[54] Idem, *Liturgical Discussion. Answer to Professor Dorner*, 69–70.
[55] Idem, *Weekly Messenger*, 29 April 1868.

God.'⁵⁶ Four pages later, however, he is somewhat more positive concerning the atonement. The New Testament, he declares,

> makes the death of Christ the necessary medium of our salvation ... But the atonement itself ... is not an abstraction; it is immanent, or as we may say, resident throughout, in the person of Christ, and derives all its force thus continually from the power of his indestructible life.⁵⁷

More characteristically, he declares in a letter to Dr. Henry Harbaugh, 'Christ saves the world, not ultimately by what he teaches or by what he does, but by what he is in the constitution of his own person.'⁵⁸

Forsyth would be the first to agree that Christ can only do what he does because he is who he is – 'No half-God could redeem the soul which it took the whole God to create';⁵⁹ but he would still place the emphasis differently from Nevin: since, in view of God's holiness and humanity's sinfulness, a moral redemption is needed if we are ever to know him as he is, the focus must be upon the historic, saving act. This is why Forsyth insists 'We begin with facts of experience, not with forms of thought.' Accordingly, he declares, as if in direct opposition to Nevin, 'The mighty thing in Christ is his grace and not His constitution ... '⁶⁰ Again, 'It was not the rank or power of the Redeemer that made his death precious for redemption, but his worth.'⁶¹ These, however are among many occasions on which Forsyth is needlessly disjunctive, for grace is grace because of the one whence it flows, and Christ's constitution is with a view to grace to a sinful race. What Forsyth intends is that the point at which our moral need is dealt with, and from which we then begin to see who he is, is grace – in the experience of the redeemed atoning grace is the first thing, not the two natures. This is why, whilst recognising the moral plight in which a sinful race is found, he opposes any preaching which would rest content with ethical

---

⁵⁶ J. W. Nevin, *Liturgical Discussion. Answer to Professor Dorner*, Philadelphia: S. R. Fisher, 1868, 76–7. Nevin's apparent playing down of the centrality of the atonement was one of the bones of contention between him and J. H. A. Bomberger of Ursinus College. The latter accused Nevin of dividing the work from the person of Christ, and found this to be entirely opposed to the teaching of the Heidelberg Catechism. See, for example, his 'Dr. Nevin on the Church Movement,' *The Reformed Church Monthly*, 1, July 1868, 302–5; 'What they mean by development,' ibid., 6, 1873, 521–5; 'Mercersburg errors,' ibid., 8, 1875, 126–35. Cf. Alan P. F. Sell, *Commemorations*, ch. 11.
⁵⁷ Ibid., 81.
⁵⁸ Idem, 'Letter to Dr. Henry Harbaugh,' in *Catholic and Reformed*, 408.
⁵⁹ P. T. Forsyth, *The Person and Place of Jesus Christ*, (1909), London: Independent Press, 1961, 86. Cf. Ibid, 257: 'In Christ we have the whole of God, but not everything about God, the whole heart of God but not the whole range of God.'
⁶⁰ Ibid., 10.
⁶¹ Idem., *The Person and Place of Jesus Christ*, 235.

exhortation. Along this line, he is convinced, 'Sin is treated more thoughtfully than thoroughly. It is rinsed with water rather than cleansed with blood.'[62] Because of this debasement, and with the rise of a liberal theology for which Jesus is our master, elder brother, leader, teacher, rather than saviour, he declares that

> it means little to the purpose now to say that we concentrate on Christ. A Christocentric Christianity was the ideal of the late nineteenth century, but it is already out of date ... Men are very willing to gather about Christ as their brother and captain but not as their salvation, not as absolute King. But we must not empty the Gospel in order quickly to fill the Church.'[63]

Indeed, the churches are languishing because of the watered-down Gospel to which they have been treated: 'With an ideal or a fraternal Christ they dwindle and the power goes out of them.'[64]

By the same token, Forsyth strongly objected to any attempt, especially from catholic quarters, to construe 'The unsearchable riches of Christ' in terms of his nature rather than of his grace:

> So utterly foreign is it to the Gospel when we sing, how grotesque it is when Protestants sing, the theosophy of the mass.
>
> And that a higher gift than Grace
> Should flesh and blood refine,
> God's presence, and His very self,
> And essence all divine.

He is not more Himself in His essence (which we know nothing about) than in His grace (which we know intimately).[65]

From the evidence already presented I think we can say with confidence that if Nevin complained at the way in which revivalists were abstracting the death of Christ from the life of Christ, Forsyth would query Nevin's confining of the atonement to the death of Christ.[66] The Cross, as I said, is for him a comprehensive term, and atonement entails life, death, resurrection, ascension, and final triumph. Moreover, he would suspect talk of an immanent atonement as skirting the historic act, and tending in an intellectualist rather than a moral

---

[62] Idem., *Revelation Old and New*, 105.
[63] Idem., *Theology in Church and State*, Longon: Hodder & Stoughton, 1915, 24–5.
[64] Idem, *The Person and Place of Jesus Christ*, 15.
[65] Idem, *The Church and the Sacraments*, 290; cf. 41 n., 238; idem, Congregationalism and Reunion, 27.
[66] Nevin argues that Peter's confession at Caesarea Phillipi was none the less significant because it was not centred in the atonement. See *Liturgical Discussion. Answer to Professor Dorner*, 75. But can we say that Peter really grasped the full significance of his own words on that side of the Cross? If so, by analogy, why does not Nevin rest content with the Last as distinct from the *Lord's* Supper in his sacramental theory?

direction. But I need not find words for Forsyth: he has more than enough of his own, and very pungent they are, as the following collage will show:

> Doubtless for thought, for theological science, Incarnation is the logical *prius*. It is at the rational base of Atonement, of Redemption, which was God's offering up of Himself in Christ. But that is to say it was God's Act in Christ more than his mere presence. The metaphysic is one of ethic, of action, not of being; it is of will rather than thought.[67]

Hence,

> Christ came to redeem, which he could only do by his Incarnation; He did not come to be incarnate, and incidentally to redeem.

> The Roman or the Chalcedonian type of doctrine begins with the Incarnation, beyond experience but believed on authority, and then it descends on the Atonement; instead of beginning with the Atonement, in a moral departure, and going on from that experience to the Incarnation, since God only could atone. But between this and the evangelical position there is sought a *via media* which claims to be both evangelical and catholic ... [It is] taken by those who are engrossed with the Person of Christ as the Son of God in Whom we mystically live, but who do not give a first and crucial place to the New creation in the Cross as the source of our life and the sum and crown and key of all the Person was. Christ is our food rather than our new Creator.[68]

In fact, the incarnation

> central as many find it, has not such centrality as the principle of atoning forgiveness. The doctrine of the Incarnation did not create the Church; it grew up (very quickly) in the Church out of the doctrine of the cross which did create it – in so far as that can be said of any doctrine, and not rather of the act and power which the doctrine tries to state.[69]

For this reason, 'Our approach to Christology is through the office of Christ as Saviour. We only grasp the real divinity of His person by the value for us of His Cross.'[70] With this we come to our second theme: objectivity, history and creed.

II

For Forsyth everything in religion and theology turns upon the objective, atoning, act of God's holy love, performed in Christ once-for-all on the stage of

---

[67] P. T. Forsyth, *The Justification of God*, 90.
[68] Idem, *The Church and the Sacraments*, (1917), London: Independent Press, 1953, 197; cf. *God the Holy Father*, 39–40; *The Preaching of Jesus and the Gospel of Christ* (articles reprinted from *The Expositor*, 1915), Blackwood, South Australia: New Creation Publications, 1987, 120–1.
[69] Idem, *The Cruciality of the Cross*, 50 n.
[70] Idem, *The Church and the Sacraments*, 33.

human history at Calvary. This alone is the locus of authority for the Christian: it is the authority of the Gospel, which the Bible proclaims[71] and to which Church, sacraments and creeds bear witness. In his own words:

> Our final authority is our new Creator. The authority cannot, therefore, be either a Church or a Book – both of which are historically the products of such communion with God ... The only final authority for Christian faith is ... God asserting His holy Self in Christ's historic and regenerative work, and in its perpetual energy in the soul.[72]

Again, the 'authority is not the Church, but it is the effectual Word of God in the preaching of the cross, to which the conscience owes its life.'[73] Yet again, 'Protestant theology is founded upon authority as much as Catholic. It starts from something given. It is not the discovery of new truth so much as the unfolding of old grace.'[74] What has this grace done?

Forsyth, following Paul, underlines the fact that at the Cross it is God in Christ reconciling the world to himself: 'It was not human nature offering its very best to God. It was God offering His very best to man.'[75] Again, 'The real objectivity in the atonement is not that it was made to God, but by God.'[76] Moreover, the God who thus acts is the God of holy love. At this point the contrast with Nevin becomes clear. Forsyth makes much more of the dire consequences of sin – supremely its affront to God's holiness – than does Nevin. The ethical thrust of his theology is nowhere clearer than at this point. 'The more we grasp this function of the Cross,' he declares, 'the more we ethicize it.'[77] I do not say that Nevin had no place for the holiness of God, but holy love was not the fulcrum of his theology as it was for Forsyth's. Forsyth insists that 'It is the holiness of God which makes sin guilt. It is the holiness of God that necessitates the work of Christ, that calls for it, and that provides it.'[78] God's holy love could not be further removed in Forsyth's mind from liberal ideas of love gone sentimental. Indeed, against those who say we have no need to be afraid of God because God is love, he thunders, 'But there is everything in the love of God to be afraid of. Love is not holy without judgment. It is the love of holy God that is

---

[71] Idem, *The Church, The Gospel and Society*, 68: 'It is more true that God's great Word contains the Bible than that the Bible contains the Word. The Word in Christ needed exposition by the bible. The Gospels find their only central interpretation in the Epistles.'

[72] Idem, *The Principle of Authority*, 53.

[73] Idem., *Rome, Reform and Reaction. Four Lectures on the Religious Situation*, London: Hodder & Stoughton, 1899, 136.

[74] Idem., 'Authority and theology,' *The Hibbert Journal*, 4 no. 1, October 1905, 65.

[75] Idem., *The Work of Christ*, 24. Here, as elsewhere, Forsyth is needlessly disjunctive.

[76] Ibid., 92.

[77] Idem., *Positive Preaching and the Modern Mind*, 214; cf. 221.

[78] Idem., *The Work of Christ*, 79; cf. *The Principle of Authority*, 7; *The Cruciality of the Cross*, ix, 24; *The Justification of God*, 128.

the consuming fire.'⁷⁹ It follows that 'If the real is the holy, its treatment of sin is the *locus* for our contact with reality, and our footing for all eternal things. And that *locus* is the cross of Christ in history and experience, as the crisis of existence both human and divine.'⁸⁰ In other words, 'The seat of revelation is in the cross, and not in the heart. The precious thing is something given, and not evolved.'⁸¹ Nothing could be clearer to Forsyth than that God's act in Christ alone saves, not our feelings about it: 'We are not saved by the love we exercise, but by the Love we trust.'⁸² Nevin would have been the first to agree. Against Taylorism and Finneyism he complained that 'The ground of the sinner's salvation is made to lie at last in his own separate person.' That is to say, 'Justification is taken to be in fact by *feeling*, not by faith; and in this way falls back as fully into the sphere of self-righteousness as though it were expected from works under any other form.'⁸³ He would surely also have agreed with Forsyth that while 'Reality must ... be real for me ... it makes much difference whether it have its source in my consciousness as well as its *sphere* ... '.⁸⁴

Inherent in his statement of the objectivity of the holy God's saving act is Forsyth's critique of individualistic subjectivism. Thus he insists that 'Salvation is personal, but it is not individual.' He denies that the Reformation stood for religious individualism, private judgment and individual independence. The Reformers were not individualists: 'They were as strong as their opponents about the necessity of the Church for the soul – though as its home, not its master.'⁸⁵ He laments that 'We have become, first, individualists, and then denominationalists, at the cost of the great corporate Church mind which so ruled our Puritans and fed their Puritanism.'⁸⁶ At this point he is entirely at one with Nevin (though it is a pity that for all the respect he shows to John Owen,⁸⁷ the latter uses the term 'Puritan' pejoratively to designate the very phenomena that Forsyth presents as degenerate Puritanism). However, if Forsyth's

---

⁷⁹ Ibid., 85; cf. *God the Holy Father*, 5. Forsyth elevates the ethical in all 'departments' of theology. For example, on the Trinity he writes, 'the unity of a trinity of persons is a moral unity rather than a metaphysical. It is a *Holy* Trinity.' See *The Church, The Gospel and Society*, 20.

⁸⁰ Idem., *The Principle of Authority*, 191.

⁸¹ Idem, *The Person and Place of Jesus Christ*, 193.

⁸² Idem, *God the Holy Father*, 122; cf. *Positive Preaching and the Modern Mind*, 121; 'The reality of grace,' *The Hibbert Journal*, 4 no. 4, July 1906, 839; *The Person and Place of Jesus Christ*, 193.

⁸³ J. W. Nevin, *The Anxious Bench*, (1844), in Catholic and Reformed, 98, 99.

⁸⁴ P. T. Forsyth, *The Principle of Authority*, 75. Cf. Idem, *The Work of Christ*, 49 '[Y]ou cannot preach a Cross to any purpose if you preach it only as an experience.'

⁸⁵ Idem, *The Work of Christ*, 119–20.

⁸⁶ Idem, *The Church and the Sacraments*, 43. Interestingly, he elsewhere avers that 'What saved the Reformation religiously was the rise of Pietism, which rescued faith both from the politicians and the theologians.' See *The Person and Place of Jesus Christ*, 21.

⁸⁷ J. W. Nevin, *The Mystical Presence*, 181–2. Cf. Deborah Rahn Clemens, 'Principles of antagonism, or The mystical nuisance,' *The New Mercersburg Review*, 9, Spring 1991, 33–53.

immediate context was liberal theology gone sentimental, Nevin's was a non-ecclesial individualism which ransacked the Bible for what it wished to find, and then, in sectarian fashion, unchurched all who found something else. As he wrote, 'However much they may differ among themselves in regard to what it teaches, sects all agree in proclaiming the Bible the only guide of their faith.'[88] To this they add an appeal to private judgment. But both Bible and private judgment are in reality controlled by 'a scheme of notions already at hand, a certain system of opinion and practice, which is made to underlie all this boasted freedom in the use of the Bible, leading private judgment along by the nose, and forcing the divine text always to speak in its own way.'[89] Nevin elsewhere contrasts the supernaturalism of the early Fathers favourably with the hermeneutic of the sects.[90] For his part, Schaff shows that he could be a blunt as Forsyth was after him: 'Sectarianism is one-sided practical religious subjectivism and has found its classic ground within the territory of the Reformed Church, in the predominantly practical countries, England and America.'[91] Forsyth draws an important distinction between sectarianism as just described, and 'sect' as a sociological description of a Christian church which may be catholic in its ecclesiology (as he himself understood Congregationalsm to be). Indeed, he writes, 'It was [the] true Churchliness of the sects that took effect in their invention of modern missions at the beginning of the nineteenth century. Foreign missions was the Church in them saving itself from the sects, the world note saving them from the note worldly and bourgeois.'[92]

We must now turn to Nevin's understanding of the locus of authority. Forsyth, as we have seen, locates authority supremely in the Cross, in the redemptive act of holy love, in the Gospel. Nevin appeals to the Bible, to the Church's creeds, and to the heritage of Christian testimony. For him objectivity resides supremely in the incarnation and, in consequence of that, in the union of believers with Christ and with others in the fellowship of the Church. We do not find in Nevin's writings such an intense concern with sin and the moral need of redemption by rescue which, as we have seen, characterises Forsyth's approach. Rather, we have a more ontological concern with divine-human continuity – a continuity realised in history in the incarnation of Christ, and enjoyed by Christian believers. This union is not simply legal or moral. On the contrary, 'we must be incorporated with his blood, in order that we may have part truly at the

---

[88] J. W. Nevin, 'The Sect System', (1849) in *Catholic and Reformed*, 137.
[89] Ibid., 141; cf. 165, and 'Early Christianity,' (1851), in *Catholic and Reformed*, 243–5. For a fuller exposition of Nevin's position on the sects see Martin L. Cox, Jr., 'To be the Church: John Williamson Nevin's critique of sectarianism,' *The New Mercersburg Review*, 3, Spring 1987, 23–9.
[90] Idem, 'Early Christianity,' in *Catholic and Reformed*, 203.
[91] P. Schaff, *The Principle of Protestantism*, (1845), in K. Penzel, Philip Schaff, 87; cf. 101, 143–4.
[92] P. T. Forsyth, *The Justification of God*, 10 n.

same time in all the blessings he has procured, as though "we had in our own persons suffered and made satisfaction for our sins unto God."'[93] Spiritually, nor carnally, the believer feed on the body and blood of Christ, who was 'born of Mary, and hung upon the cross, and is now enthroned in heaven'; and, by the Holy Spirit, the believer becomes '"flesh of his flesh and bone of his bone," even as limb and head are filled and ruled with the same life in the body physically considered.'[94] The benefits of Christ are sealed to the believer in the Lord's Supper.

It is Nevin's emphasis here upon the work of the Spirit, and upon the incarnation as clearly entailing the sacrifice of the Cross that prevents a slide into that pantheistic immanentist automaticism which was ever the peril of those in Hegel's wake. If this is Nevin's peril, Forsyth's is relative neglect of the birth, life and teachings of Christ. That neither of them intended to fall into their respective traps is clear; but in the heat of controversy the pendulum can swing, and incautious remarks are from time to time made. It seems to me that this is a cardinal point at which Nevin and Forsyth – each concerned with religious and theological objectivity – need to balance one another.

Like Forsyth, Nevin finds his Gospel in the Bible, but to a greater degree than Forsyth he appeals to the historic witness of the Church of the ages – a witness which is for him supremely encapsulated in the Apostles' Creed. According to Nevin, this Creed is 'the most comprehensive of all Christian symbols.' It is not so much a summary of Christian doctrine as 'the necessary form of the Gospel, as this is first apprehended by faith ... '[95] That is to say, 'As there is but one method of the objective movement of the Gospel in Christ Himself, so can there be only one method for the apprehension of it on the part of believers. That method we have in the Apostles' Creed.'[96] It is not that every doctrine is contained in the Creed, but all doctrines are properly developed only within the orbit of the Creed. He continues, 'The historical character of the Gospel, objectively considered, meets us, first of all, in the Person and Work of Christ Himself ... ' and if he had stopped there, Forsyth would have agreed with him. But he closes his sentence with the words, 'as they are exhibited to us in the Creed.'[97] At this point Forsyth would demur; but before I explain why, and in order to show that this is not simply a solitary lapse on Nevin's part, let me quote him further: contrasting what he calls 'The Gospel of the Creed' with the subjectivism of what he rudely calls 'Puritanism', he declares that the former 'is, throughout, Christological, concentrates itself in Christ, throws itself, in full,

---

[93] J. W. Nevin, *The Mystical Presence*, 73.
[94] Ibid., 74.
[95] Idem, *Vindication of the Revised Liturgy*, in *Catholic and Reformed*, 370.
[96] Ibid., 372.
[97] Ibid., 377.

upon the incarnation, and sees in the objective movement of this Mystery of Godliness, as St. Paul calls it, the whole process of grace and salvation on to the resurrection of the dead and the life everlasting.'[98] 'The whole process of salvation?' Listen to Forsyth: 'There is far too much said ... about the Creeds and their simplicity and the way they keep to the Christian facts. Yes, and all but ignore the one fact on which Christianity rests – the fact of redemption by grace alone through faith. It is the supreme Catholic error.'[99] But if there is a Catholic error, there is a liberal one too: 'That which is distinctive of the life-principle of Christianity is not what is common to the creeds of all the Churches, as a false liberalism has it, but what is the marrow of the Gospel and the core of its historic revelation – which is redemption.'[100] Forsyth, therefore, would probably have charged Nevin with being strangely ahistorical in his views on the creeds – and that in two ways. First, he overlooks the fact that the crucial, historic, redemptive act at the Cross in its saving significance has to be inferred from them: 'The doctrine of Redemption is signally absent from the creeds, yet the Church has a more direct connection with Redemption than with Incarnation,' he thunders;[101] and secondly, he pays insufficient attention to the context of the creed-makers, which is of great significance for their content. If docetism is the enemy the key points in the life of Jesus the real man must be emphasised – and this is what the Apostles' Creed does. Moreover, claims Forsyth, 'The object of redemption in the creed-making age was less to forgive man than to immortalise him, less to convert him than to deify him. It was not a work of grace in the sense of mercy, in the sense of destroying mortal guilt, but in the sense of destroying a fatal disease.'[102]

It would be quite wrong to suggest that Forsyth's reservations concerning the creeds imply that he favoured an easy believe-as-you-please-ism. On the contrary, he has little patience with 'those free lances of the genial heart and sterile mind, who face theology as a bull greets scarlet, and regard positive views as a tramp does four walls ... '[103] True Christian freedom is a 'founded freedom' – a freedom in the Gospel which sets people free. Moreover,

> Not freedom alone is our genius; for freedom alone is but caprice, atomism, and anarchy in the end. But it is freedom created and founded and reared by an authority which cannot be either evaded or shaken; and which creates our

---

[98] Ibid., 386.
[99] P. T. Forsyth, *The Church, The Gospel and Society*, 124.
[100] Idem, 'The evangelical basis of Free Churchism,' *The Contemporary Review*, 81, January-June 1902, 689 n.
[101] Idem, *The Church and the Sacraments*, 83.
[102] Idem, *The Person and Place of Jesus Christ*, 331.
[103] Ibid., 215.

emancipation, in the very depth and crisis of our soul, by the eternal redemption at the heart of history in Christ's cross.[104]

Rooted in the Gospel, faithful to the living Word, guided by the Holy Spirit, the messages can be articulated freshly in each succeeding age – and must be: 'A cohesive Church must have a coherent creed,' he writes; 'But it must be a dogma the Church holds, not one that holds the Church. The life is in the body, not in the system. It must be a dogma revisible from time to time to keep pace with the Church's growth as a living body in a living world.'[105] After all, 'Truths about Christ are really sure to the Church only as they arise out of its experience of Christ.'[106] It all comes to this: 'The one article, or dogma, of a standing or falling Church is the statement, but not the exposition, of God's act of justifying grace in Christ and Him crucified.'[107] The implication is that if we insist upon peddling our expositions as if they were conditon of salvation or terms of fellowship, we have landed once more in sectarianism. Remember Nevin's warning that those who claim sectarian freedom have simply made a new yoke for themselves, for 'The man who puts his conscience in the keeping of a sect, is no longer free. It might as well be in the keeping of a Roman priest.'[108]

As we have already seen, for both Nevin and Forsyth the Gospel is inescapably social, and the Church, therefore, an utter necessity. To their ecclesiologies I now turn.

III

Nevin, Schaff and Forsyth were deeply committed churchmen, and it is pleasant to record that their ecclesiologies are in agreement at a number of points. In the first place, they agree that the Church is a divine society called out by God. It is, of course also human; but as Schaff points out,

> Though the church is ... a society of men, yet it is by no means on that account a production of men, called into existence by their own invention and will, like free-masonry, for instance, temperance societies, and the various political and literary associations. It is founded by *God* himself through *Christ*, through His incarnation, His life, His sufferings, death, and resurrection, and the outpouring of the *Holy Ghost*, for His own glory, and the redemption of the world.[109]

---

[104] Idem, *Faith, Freedom and the Future*, 347; cf. 289, 336.
[105] Idem, *The Person and Place of Jesus Christ*, 213.
[106] Idem, *The Principle of Authority*, 64.
[107] Idem, *Theology in State and Church*, 34.
[108] J. W. Nevin, 'The Sect System,' *in Catholic and Reformed*, 159.
[109] P. Schaff, *History of the Apostolic Church with a General Introduction to Church History*, Edinburgh: T. & T. Clark, 1854, 165. Cf. Idem, What is Church History? in Reformed and Catholic, 31.

Secondly, both Forsyth and the Mercersburg theologians have in view the entire heritage of the Church, though the latter speak much more of the Church's history in terms of a doctrine of development. For Forsyth the occasion of reflection is the claim of the Church of England, despite its break with Rome, solely to represent the catholic Church of the ages in England. Against this he protests vigorously:

> The whole history of the Church up to the Reformation at least is as much ours as theirs. We believe in a church, and in one common inheritance in the historic Church of the West ...
>
> It is the greatest mistake either to claim, or to allow the claim, that the Established Church is the sole continuation of the great Mediaeval Church in this country. Principles which we alone have vindicated lay as deep there as some which they assert, and especially one.
>
> In that great Church there were two principles in particular – *unity and autonomy*, organic unity and spiritual independence, or self-government under Christ. These were ruined, indeed, in practice by the relations between the Mediaeval Church and the temporal power ...
>
> [I]f the Established Church has preserved the idea of unity it has not kept the idea of continuity. For it is the Nonconformists that have continued, even at the cost of unity, the far more vital principle of the autonomy of faith, the independence of the Church, its responsibility to Christ alone, that self-government of the Church which was, and is, a real and true principle asserted with vast consistency always by the Roman Church.[110]

Thirdly, both Forsyth and the Mercersburg theologians uphold the importance – indeed the inescapability for Christians – of the Church.[111] As Forsyth says, *'the same act which sets us in Christ sets us also in the society of Christ.'*[112] They express their convictions, however, in interestingly different ways. With the serried – even ecclesiastically disorderly – ranks of Finney's individualists before his gaze, Nevin insists that the Church is the place where, and medium through which, the mystical union of Christ with believers occurs. Over against the Anxious Bench – a term which frequently functions as shorthand for the several 'new measures' introduced by revivalists and abhorred by Nevin, he sets the catechism, and the role of the Church as mother and nurturer. The Church is not properly viewed as 'an aggregate of parts mechanically brought together,' but

---

[110] P. T. Forsyth, *The Charter of the Church. Six Lectures on the Spiritual Principle of Nonconformity*, London: Alexander & Shepheard, 9, 11, 13.

[111] For the socio-political background to Nevin's ecclesiology see, for example, Walter H. Conser, Jr., *Church and Confession. Conservative Theologians in Germany, England, and America 1815–1866*, Macon, GA: Mercer University Press, 1984, ch. 7; James D. Bratt, 'Nevin and the Antebellum cultural wars,' and Richard E. Wentz, 'Nevin and American nationalism,' in *Reformed Confessionalism in Nineteenth-Century America*, chs 1 and 2.

[112] P. T. Forsyth, *The Church and the Sacraments*, 61. His italics.

rather 'as an organic life ... [T]he Church is truly the mother of all her children. They do not impart life to her, but she imparts life to them.' The Church exists prior to the individuals who comprise it; indeed, 'Christ lives in the Church, and through the Church in its particular members.'[113] All within the family of the Church are to be nurtured by the Church, and Nevin proceeds to extol Richard Baxter, the English *Puritan*, whose catechetical ministry he finds exemplary – as, indeed, it was.[114] All of which is consistent with Nevin's understanding of catholicity – the totality and *wholeness* of believers in organic union with Christ.

However, it must be said that at times what appears to be an Hegelian legacy skews his thought, as when he pits what he regards as the incorrect idea of saved aggregates of individuals over against 'The idea of the true necessary wholeness of humanity ... ;'[115] for this would seem to raise the unanswered questions, What is the difference, if any, between humanity's being whole, and believers being in union with Christ? Christ having become incarnate, is there a difference of eternal significance between between those who are 'in Christ' and those who are not? Reformed – and especially Congregational – ecclesiology has traditionally assumed that there is; and it is not a foregone conclusion that ecumenical discomfort at the possibility suffices by itself to invalidate the doctrine. Interestingly, the same questions can be posed to Forsyth, who here, perhaps, succumbs to what I have called the 'post-Hegelian drag.' He writes, '[I]t was a race that Christ redeemed, and not a mere bouquet of believers. It was a Church He saved, and not a certain pale of souls.'[116] Once again it is the apparent equating of the human race with the Church that is problematic.

Be all this as it may, for Nevin, the place *par excellence* where the union of believers with Christ is realised and their faith nourished is at the Lord's table. As they partake of the life of Christ, 'Christians are vitally related and joined together as one great spiritual whole; and this whole is the Church. The Church, therefore, is His Body, the fulness of Him that filleth all in all. The union by which it is held together, through all ages, is organic.'[117]

As we might by now expect, Forsyth is absolutely clear on the foundation of the Church:

---

[113] J. W. Nevin, *The Anxious Bench*, in *Catholic and Reformed*, 110–11. Elsewhere Nevin charges the German theologian Dorner with espousing the view he here counters. See *Liturgical Discussion. Answer to Professor Dorner*, 45.

[114] See further ch. 3 above.

[115] Idem, 'Catholicism,' *The Mercersburg Review*, 3, 1851, 10.

[116] P. T. Forsyth, *The Church and the Sacraments*, 43.

[117] Quoted by Jack Martin Maxwell, *Worship and Reformed Theology. The Liturgical Lessons of Mercersburg*, Pittsburgh: The Pickwick Press, 1976, 21, citing Nevin's 'Catholic unity,' appended to Schaff's *The Principle of Protestantism*, German Reformed Church, 1845.

> It was the atoning death of Christ that founded the Church; it was no ordinance of His life, or injunction of His teaching ... The Church's one foundation is Christ crucified, and risen, and bringing forth judgment unto love's victory. To lose that element in faith is to dissolve any Church in time.[118]

Far from this atoning work being of concern to individuals only, 'As a matter of fact, the historic effect of Christ's holy work was social at once. It was to create a Society. It crystallized in a Church.'[119] Negatively, therefore,

> A Church is not made by Christian sympathies or affinities. Rather are these made by a Church. A Church is made by the Christian Gospel, its creative Word of the Cross, its Holy Spirit. The religion that makes a Church is not temperamental but evangelical ... The Church ... is no creature either of humane sympathy or of voluntary association, even though these give it local and practical form ... It is a new creation of God in the Holy Spirit, a spiritual organism [mark the word] in which we find our soul. Men unite with the Church because already united with Christ, and because they are, in that very act of union with Him, already in spirit and principle organised into the great Church he created, and whose life He is.[120]

The foundation of the Church's catholicity is the Gospel, for 'What the Gospel created was not a crowd of Churches but the one Church in various places.'[121] But, of course, the catholicity of the Church is not, according to Forsyth, a matter of the beatific vision and aesthetics; it concerns the evangelical note of the kingdom of God; it is moral; it has to do with the power of grace rather than with the beauty of holiness.[122]

We thus see that although they make the point in significantly different ways, Forsyth, Nevin and Schaff set their faces against sectarian individualism, they regard the Church as the creation of God by the Spirit through the Word, and they understand it to be catholic in an evangelical sense. But at one point they seriously part company. Nevin happily speaks of the Church as the continuation of the incarnation; Forsyth abominates such language. Let us approach this thorny issue in stages.

First, Nevin makes an ontological claim, where Forsyth would prefer a moral one. Nevin writes,

> Christianity ... is a *life*, not only as revealed at first in Christ, but as continued also in the church. It flows over from Christ to his people, always in this form. They do not simply bear his name, and acknowledge his doctrine. They are so united with him as to have part in the substance of his

---

[118] P. T. Forsyth, *Missions in State and Church*, 80.
[119] Idem, *The Church, The Gospel and Society*, 31.
[120] Idem, *The Church and the Sacraments*, 25, 34.
[121] Ibid., 68; cf. 7.
[122] Idem, Faith, *Freedom and the Future*, 183–4.

life itself. Their conversion is a new *birth*; 'not of blood, nor of the will of the flesh, nor of the will of man, but of God' (John 1: 13).[123]

From this is it but a short step to Nevin's conviction that the Church is, 'in very deed, the depository and continuation of the Saviour's theanthropic life itself, and as such a truly supernatural constitution.'[124] Philip Schaff concurs. To him the Church is 'the depository and continuation of the earthly human life of the Redeemer, in his threefold office of prophet, priest, and king.'[125] Forsyth would agree that the constitution of the Church is supernatural – it is by the grace of God in the Gospel; but his question would arise over the use, by both Nevin and Schaff, of the words 'depository and continuation' of the Church *vis à vis Christ*.

Against this usage Forsyth lodges a number of objections. He grants that the idea of the Church as a prolongation of the incarnation is 'an attractive imagination.' But 'It is the Catholic form of the engaging fallacy of liberalism that Christ is but the eternal God-in-man, supremely revealed and carried to a luminous heat in him, but forming always the spirit of Humanity and looking out in every great soul.' Forsyth queries whether such a Church can be the body of Christ, 'For when Christ became incarnate, His soul took a material body (the talk of a spiritual or astral body inside it is mere theosophy); whereas the Church in which Christ dwells is not a material body, but an organism of spirits ... [I]n the Church He passes into living souls capable of moral reciprocity of which the body of his Incarnation was incapable.' Again, it is not the case that human nature conceived in psychological terms is the body of Christ, for 'It is a regenerated human nature in which Christ dwells. But that cannot be the prolongation of His Incarnation, wherein there was no regeneration. His great spiritual work was not the result of regeneration, but the source of it, as the Church cannot be.'[126] Hence, 'The Church is not the continuation of Christ, but His creation and His response.'[127] Interestingly, Dorner had earlier remarked that Nevin's concentration upon 'the mystical communication of the life of Christ, on the expansion of the theanthropic life' is misguided, because 'the Church can thus be identified with Christ only by ignoring the work of atonement and justification ...'[128] It seems to me that the Mercersburg theologians and Forsyth are nowhere farther apart than here.

---

[123] J. W. Nevin, *The Mystical Presence*, 222.
[124] Ibid., 256.
[125] P. Schaff, *The Principle of Protestantism*, in *Philip Schaff, Historian and Ambassador of the Universal Church*, 81. Cf. The exposition of George W. Richards in his article, 'The Mercersburg Theology, its purpose and principles,' *Church History*, 20 no. 3, 1951, 43.
[126] P. T. Forsyth, *The Church and the Sacraments*, 82.
[127] Ibid., 83.
[128] J. [sic = I.] A. Dorner, *The Liturgical Conflict in the Reformed Church of North America*, reprinted from *The Reformed Church Monthly*, 1, 1868, 27–8.

Despite their view of the Church as a prolongation of the incarnation, the Mercersburg theologians were only too aware of the imperfections of the empirical Church. Schaff, for example, declares that '[w]here God builds a temple, the devil is sure to have a chapel alongside.'[129] All of which exacerbates rather than resolves Forsyth's problem, for Christ is the ever sinless. The Mercersburg theologians distinguish between the invisible Church and the Church visible.[130] Do they wish us to understand that Christ is incarnate only in the invisible Church – the Church of believers known only to God – or in that earthen vessel which is the Church we know? Schaff declares that 'As the body of Christ, the church is the dwelling-place of Christ, in which He exerts all the powers of His theanthropic life ... ' but then comes a significant qualification which suggests that he has the empirical, visible, church in view: 'We may justly say ... that the church is the continuation of the life and work of Christ upon earth, though never, indeed, so far as men in their present state are concerned, without a mixture of sin and error.'[131] How does the identification of the incarnate Christ with the sinful empirical Church square with the sinlessness of Christ?

For his part Forsyth has no difficulty in speaking of Christ's indwelling of the Church: indeed, Congregational polity turns upon the fact that he does so indwell the Church:

> Is the Church simply a messenger of Christ to men? Does Christ not do more than send it? Does He not dwell in it? Does He not act from the midst of it? Is it not His chief and chosen organ on earth? And is not His great action based on the perpetual sacrifice of Himself for the world? ... Is not the great sacrifice of Christ, both to God and to man? And does the Church not offer this spiritual sacrifice in manifold ways continually?[132]

To all of these questions Forsyth answers with a resounding 'Yes.'

It is precisely because he believes that Christ indwells his people and that they are one in him that he emphasizes the importance of Church polity to a greater degree than the Mercersburg theologians. The Church comprises all who are Christ's; by the Holy Spirit they are gathered in fellowship around the Word and the sacraments, and as a corporate priesthood of believers they are charged with owning the Lordship of Christ in their midst. Hence that Congregational catholicity of which Forsyth was so powerful an advocate. Hence the importance of Church Meeting – that credal assembly where those who have sat under the Word and received the bread and wine gather, under the Lordship of

---

[129] Quoted by K. Penzel in *Philip Schaff*, 126.
[130] See, for example, P. Schaff, *What is Church History? in Reformed and Catholic*, 34.
[131] P. Schaff, *History of the Apostolic Church, in Reformed and Catholic*, 165, 166.
[132] P. T. Forsyth, *Rome, Reform and Reaction*, 215.

Christ, to seek – not majority rule – but unanimity in Christ concerning their witness and mission. It is a travesty to present Congregationalism as democratic – whatever some Congregationalists may have done with it.[133] As Forsyth declared, 'no society which gives Christ the regal place the Church does can be a democracy. It is an absolute monarchy.'[134] Again, '[T]he democracy will recognise no authority but what it creates, the Church none but what creates it; and the collision is sharp.'[135] Nevin, on the other hand, writes, that in Congregationalism, 'The people are the fountain of right. Congregationalism completes itself in full Independency. All thus comes to the platform of common sense; all goes by popular judgment and popular vote.'[136] I do not say that Nevin had no cause to write as he did, but he might have acknowledged that what he was rebuking was a travesty of Congregationalism. Hear Forsyth on New Testament Christianity:

> New Testament Christianity is a priestly religion or it is nothing. It gathers about a priestly cross on earth and a Great High Priest Eternal in the heavens. It means also the equal priesthood of each believer. But it means much more. That belief by itself is ruinous individualism. It means the great collective priesthood of the Church as one.[137]

These are the ideals of Congregationalism. Those who have inherited the Forsythian emphasis which runs through that variety of Reformed Christianity may well ask others of the Reformed family – not least Mercersburg theologians – why they have not done more to realise catholicity locally in Church Meeting. Why does polity effectively stop at elders, or lapse from them into corporate boards? Did the Congregational Christian Churches offer their Evangelical and Reformed partners in the United Church of Christ a vibrant experience of locally covenanted catholicity, or had they lost it themselves? Lest I appear as an unduly prickly guest, I remind you that not dissimilar questions were posed by your own Robert S. Paul and Louis H. Gunnemann.[138] And did not even the

---

[133] See further Alan P. F. Sell, *Saints: Visible, Orderly and Catholic. The Congregational Idea of the Church*, Allison Park, PA: Pickwick Publications and Geneva: World Alliance of Reformed Churches, 1986; idem, *Commemorations*, ch. 14; and this volume, passim.
[134] P. T. Forsyth, *The Church and the Sacraments*, 12–13.
[135] Idem, *Faith, Freedom and the Future*, 192; cf. 209; *The Principle of Authority*, 253.
[136] J. W. Nevin, 'Early Christianity,' in *Catholic and Reformed*, 233.
[137] P. T. Forsyth, *The Person and Place of Jesus Christ*, 12.
[138] See Robert S. Paul, *Freedom with Order. The Doctrine of the Church in the United Curch of Christ*, New York: United Church Press, 1987, 56, 58; Louis H. Gunnemann, *United and Uniting. The Meaning of an Ecclesial Journey*, New York: United Church Press, 1987, 137. If Nevin's remarks upon Congregationalism are undiscriminating, the remarks of the later Schaff, by now personally acquainted with the challenges to Church unity posed by the realities of the American ecclesial scene, are almost embarrassingly fulsome: 'The Congregational Church is a glorious Church: for she has taught the principle, and proved the capacity, of congregational independence and self-government based upon a living faith in Christ, without diminishing

later Schaff say that 'the Protestant idea of the general priesthood of all believers, if true at all, must lead to a certain degree of congregational independence or self-government, and to an active cooperation of the laity with the ministry.'[139]

But with the mention of the term 'ministry' we come to a further area in which interesting comparisons and contrasts may be drawn between the Mercersburg theologians and Forsyth. To begin on a note of profound agreement: for neither Nevin nor Forsyth is the ministry, in its deepest reaches, a merely natural phenomenon. Rather, says Nevin, the ministry 'proceeds directly and altogether from a new and higher order of things brought to pass by the Spirit of Christ in consequence of his resurrection and ascension.'[140] By contrast, he laments,

> Puritanism makes the ministers of religion to be much like county or town officers, or sees in them at best only good religious counsellors and teachers, whom the people create for their own use and follow as far as to themselves may seem good. It spurns the whole idea of a divinely established hierarchy, drawing its rights and powers from heaven, and forming in its corporate character the bond of unity for the church, the ground of its perpetual stability, the channel of all communications of grace to it from Him who is its glorified head.[141]

When P. T. Forsyth was inducted to the pastoral charge at Cheetham Hill, Manchester, in 1885, he declared, 'You have called me and I have answered gladly. But it is not your call that has made me a minister. I was a minister before any congregation called me. My election is of God.'[142] Nevin concurs. But where Forsyth says, 'The Church is the product of the Incarnation, and the

---

the effect of voluntary co-operation in the Master's service ...' See his *The Reunion of Christendom*, 1893, in K. Penzel, ed., *Philip Schaff*, 338. In the twentieth century some Congregationalists, many now in united churches, have discovered that co-operation with wider Congregational institutions – at county or regional level, for example – is not only useful but right; and therefore is not voluntary but mandatory. They generally, and in my view rightly, need the reassurance, however, that the *episcope* as between these several foci (I do not say 'levels') of churchly life – Church Meeting-District-General Assembly – will be genuinely mutual, for all alike are under the one Lord of the Church. See further Alan P. F. Sell, *Commemorations. Studies in Christian Thought and History*, Calgary: University of Calgary Press and Cardiff: University of Wales Press, 1993; Eugene, OR: Wipf & Stock, 1998, 349–61; and ch. 12 below.

[139] P. Schaff, *Christianity in America*, in *Reformed and Catholic*, 381. Cf. Deborah Rahn Clemens, 'Principles of antagonism,' passim.

[140] J. W. Nevin, 'The Christian ministry,' The Mercersburg Review, 7, 1865; reprinted in James H. Nichols, The Mercersburg Theology, New York: OUP, 1966, 356.

[141] Idem, '*Early Christianity*,' in *Catholic and Reformed*, 235–6.

[142] Quoted by W.L. Bradley, *P. T. Forsyth: The Man and His Work*, London: Indepednent Press, 1952, 38. For an account of Forsyth's pastoral ministry see Clyde Binfield, 'P. T. Forsyth as Congregational minister,' in Trevor Hart, ed., *Justice the True and Only Mercy*.

ministry is a gift to the Church,'[143] Nevin would identify Church and ministry in ontological fashion; indeed, 'they are so joined together that they cannot be severed from one another.'[144] What, then, are we to make of Sam Hamstra's exposition of Nevin: 'Logically ... the ministry preceded the Church and there would be no Church without it.'[145]

Be that as it may, Forsyth would agree with Nevin that the minister is not on a par with a social worker. Forsyth returns to this theme in many places, not least when he has the burgeoning institutional churches, with their very worthy soup kitchens and manifold social agencies, in mind:

> The ministry is not meant to be a social and philanthropic instituton, to organise and run all kinds of movements and campaigns for the external reform of mankind. It is intended to be the soul of the world, not its arms and feet; an inspirer, a teacher, a healer, not an engineer.[146]

Again:

> [I]n the present state of the Church ... theology is a greater need than philanthropy. Because men do not know where they are. They are only steering by dead reckoning – when anything may happen. But theology is 'taking the sun.' And it is wonderful – it is dangerous – how few of our officers can use the sextant for themselves. Yet what is the use of captains who are more at home entertaining the passengers than navigating the ship?[147]

Not surprisingly, Forsyth regretted that 'There is some tendency [among ministers] to be acting directly on the world with the Church for a platform, instead of acting directly on the Church, and on the world through it. The ministers are tempted to exchange slow deep influence on the world for swift power over it.'[148] So important does Forsyth consider the action of the ministry upon the Church to be that he emphasises the corrollary of this much more than Nevin: 'The effectiveness of the ministry is not possible without the people. A sacrament is a sacrament to faith, to a real recipient.'[149]

Notwithstanding his high view of the ministry, Forsyth would stoutly object to some of Nevin's phrases. He would not speak in terms of 'a divinely established hierarchy,' and as for Nevin's account of the role of the corporate ministry as comprising 'the bond of unity for the church' and as being 'the

---

[143] P. T. Forsyth, *The Church and the Sacraments*, 139.
[144] J. W. Nevin, 'The Christian ministry,' in *The Mercersburg Theology*, 354.
[145] S. Hamstra, 'Nevin on the pastoral office,' in *Reformed Confessionalism in Nineteenth-Century America*, 175.
[146] Ibid., 186.
[147] Idem, *Positive Preaching and the Modern Mind*, 101.
[148] Idem, *The Church and the Sacraments*, 131.
[149] Ibid., 147.

channel of all communications of grace to it' he would surely protest that the Church is held in Gospel unity by the Holy Spirit, and that God's grace is not exclusively channelled to the Church by the corporate ministry. Listen to his carefully qualified understanding of priestly ministry:

> It is priesthood that saves the world- the priesthood of Christ, and the real fellowship of the Church which His priestly act founded, and in whose action its High priest lives for ever. The Church which the Great High priest inhabits and inspires must be a priestly Church.
>
> The confusion is caused when we cease to think that the Church *is* a priesthood, and begin to think that it *has* a priesthood. It is like the error the evangelicals make (so full of practical mischief to religion) when they say that man *has* a soul, instead of saying man *is* a soul.[150]

What, then, of ordination? Nevin grounds in the apostolic succession and, as he construes this, ordination becomes 'the veritable channel through which is transmitted mystically, from age to age, the supernatural authority in which this succession consists.'[151] In the Service of Ordination which Nevin prepared for the Provisional Liturgy of 1857, he regards ordination as 'a tactual communication of heavenly powers' – a use of language which Forsyth would find positively dangerous. Further, ordination according to Nevin is

> the actual investiture with the very power of the office itself, the sacramental seal of a heavenly commission, and a symbolic assurance from God that [the ordinands'] consecration to the service of Christ is accepted, and that the Holy Spirit will be with them in the faithful discharge of their official duties.[152]

Forsyth would have no difficulty with this latter claim – and, interestingly, Nevin invoked Forsyth's father in the faith, John Owen, when countering Dorner on this very matter.[153] But as for the mystical transmission of grace – at this point Forsyth would surely demur. He does not deny that grace is conferred

---

[150] Idem, *Rome, Reform and Reaction*, 183. Nevin's mode of speech calls to mind a phrase in the final report of the first round of the international Anglican-Roman Catholic dialogue. Of ordained ministers it is said that 'their ministry is not an extension of the common Christian priesthood but belongs to another realm of the gifts of the Spirit.' See *The Final Report*, London: Catholic Truth Society and SPCK, 1982, 36. I have elsewhere dared to say that this sentence 'wins my prize for the naughtiest sentence in the whole of ecumenical literature!' See Alan P. F. Sell, 'The role of bilateral dialogues in the one ecumenical movement,' *Ecumenical Review*, 46 no. 4, October 1994, 459 n. 11. It is difficult not to agree with J. H. Nichols that 'Nevin's views on the ministry are, from an historic Reformed basis, his widest deviation.' See the letter of J. H. Nichols to Miss Elizabeth Clarke Kieffer, 16 December 1959, Library of the Evangelical and Reformed Historical Society, Lancaster Theological Seminary. Quoted by Jack Martin Maxwell, *Worship and Reformed Theology*, 39.

[151] J. W. Nevin, 'The Christian ministry,' in *The Mercersburg Theology*, 361.

[152] Idem, 'The ordination of ministers,' in *The Mercersburg Theology*, 347.

[153] Idem, *Liturgical Discussion. Answer to Professor Dorner*, 99–100.

at ordination, but this grace 'is but the formal and corporate *opportunity* provided by the Church to minister [the] Gospel; it is not a new spiritual gift belonging to an order and its canonical entry.'[154] He elaborates upon the point thus:

> The Apostles appointed no canonical succesors. They could not. They were unique ... [T]he Apostolate ... was by its nature incommunicable. Christ gave no canon for its perpetuation ... The Apostles could not send as they had been sent by Christ.
>
> The ministry is, therefore, not the canonical prolongation of the Apostolate any more than the Church is the prolongation of the Incarnation. The Church is the product of the Incarnation, and the ministry is a gift to the Church ... The prolongation of the Apostolate and the legatee of its unique authority ... is the New Testament, as the precipitate of the apostolic preaching at first hand ... The apostolic continuity is ... in the Eternal Word proclaimed, not in the unbroken chain prolonged...Christ chose the Apostles directly, the ministers He chose and chooses through the Church ... The Apostolate was not perpetuated, and certainly not self-perpetuated ... [155]

Not far below the surface here is Forsyth's distaste for that ecclesiastical sectarianism, which exalts one understanding of ministry over all others, which requires a lineal apostolic succession, and which entertains serious doubts regarding the validity of non-episcopal ministries. Writing in the wake of the heyday of Anglo-Catholicism, and as a member of a Dissenting denomination, Forsyth thunders: 'We hear the question raised whether our ministry is a *valid* ministry. It is absurd. God alone can really know if a ministry is valid ... Only that gospel validates the ministry which created it.'[156] This unfortunate, monopolist rather that truly catholic, attitude vitiates the manifestation of the Church's unity.[157] Forsyth stoutly opposed any notion of 'polity as a condition of Church unity.'[158] He would certainly have endorsed the later Schaff's view that 'The non-episcopal Churches will never unchurch themselves and cast reproach on their ministry.'[159] After all, 'We are in the apostolic succession rather than the ecclesiastic.'[160] And again, in more pungent tones, 'I do not find

---

[154] P. T. Forsyth, *Congregationalism and Reunion*, 32; cf. *Revelation Old and New*, 96.
[155] Idem, *The Church and the Sacraments*, 138–9.
[156] Ibid., 140; cf. Idem, *Congregationalism and Reunion*, 24.
[157] See ibid., 57.
[158] P. T. Forsyth, *The Church and the Sacraments*, 46.
[159] P. Schaff, *The Reunion of Christendom*, in K. Penzel, *Philip Schaff*, 321.
[160] P. T. Forsyth, *The Principle of Authority*, 127. Nevin has adverse remarks to make upon the Church of England too, though from a somewhat different standpoint. He finds it incongruous that a Church should place so high a value of episcopacy as linking it with the Church of the ages, and at the same time break the unity of the Church and replace the pope with the monarch. See 'Early Christianity,' in *Catholic and Reformed*, 199. Cf. Forsyth's indictment, 'It was a national church that slew the universal Christ.' *The Charter of the Church*, 10.

the ministry's authority to be canonical, but evangelical. It is not patristic, but apostolic; and the apostles were neither modern bishops nor sacrificing priests.'[161]

With this rather terse reference to sacrificing priests we come to Nevin's final Mercersburg characteristic: the sacraments and liturgy.

IV

Forsyth and the Mercersburg theologians are in hearty agreement that, in Nevin's words, the sacraments 'become, for faith, seals also of the actual realities themselves, which they exhibit ... '[162] He contrasts his definition of 'sacrament' with that of the 'Puritans' thus:

> [W]hat is a sacrament? The visible exhibition of an invisible grace – a mystery ... where the visible and invisible are brought together, and held together, not simply in man's thought, but in God's power, by a bond holding beyond nature altogether in the supernatural order of grace. Does Puritanism believe this? Not at all. It will know no sacrament, save in the intelligible form of a sign, which simply represents and calls to mind what God does for men spiritually, and on the outside of the sacrament altogether.[163]

Forsyth is clearly on Nevin's side:

> A seal is something distinctive of the person who uses it, and of an act of his. It is not simply a sign or relic of him, which might be unconscous, unmeant, like his footprint or the smoke of his fire. It means an act in which he intends to convey *himself*, his mind, his will, his act.
>
> The Sacraments are not only signs or symptoms, but deliberate seals of the loving will and work of Christ for us.[164]

Negatively, therefore, a sacrament 'is no mere memorial. How can you have a mere memorial of One who is always living, always present ... ?[165]

Forsyth immediately proceeds to point out that 'The Sacraments are not primarily *individual* acts. They are corporate acts, acts *of the Church*'[166] – and neither Nevin nor Schaff would disagree.

However, when Forsyth applies this insight to the Lord's Supper, he speaks in a way which would not, perhaps, commend itself so readily to the

---

[161] Idem, *Congregationalism and Reunion*, 57.
[162] J. W. Nevin, 'Theological Vindication of the New Liturgy,' in *Catholic and Reformed*, 380; cf. The Mystical Presence, 33–4, 109.
[163] Ibid., 402.
[164] P. T. Forsyth, *The Church and the Sacraments*, 176.
[165] Idem, *Positive Preaching and the Modern Mind*, 55.
[166] Idem, *The Church and the Sacraments*, 177.

Mercersburg theologians: '[T]he cardinal thing in the Sacraments is the reality of the Church's act (and of Christ's act in it), and the comparative indifference of the elements.'[167] He further explains: 'the centre of gravity lies not in the material element but in the communal act. That is the site of Christ's real presence. It is not metaphysical but moral and personal.'[168] This is consistent with his view, expressed elsewhere, that 'the fundamental Catholic note is neither the sacramental nor the institutional. It is the evangelical.'[169] And, as we know, for him the evangel centres in the Cross. He therefore regrets that 'There is a whole type of piety represented by the Fourth Gospel, which detaches the Eucharist from the atoning death of Christ and connects it with the spiritual appropriation of His person, regarding Him as food rather than Redeemer.' He finds this unfortunate tendency in Catherine of Genoa, and also in latter day High Church Anglicans and Quakers, of whom he declares, 'In the theology of both ... a real atonement is not the key to the person [of Christ], nor is it the marrow of the Cross. Their Key to the incarnation is not Christ's work but His birth or excellence.'[170] His recommendation, therefore, is, 'Let us begin rather from the work of Christ, which is the effective thing both in Him and in His Sacraments, the point where all begins and all takes order. Let us begin with the New Covenant, with which Christ was more concerned than with either Church or Sacrament.'[171]

For his part, Nevin finds the Lord's Supper central to Christian doctrine and devotion because it concerns that union with Christ which is more than legal or moral; it is a matter of a communion with Christ which 'involves a real participation in him as the principle of life' under the form of his humanity. What is received is 'the substantial life of the Saviour himself.'[172] Here is ontology once more, though we should note the qualification that 'the participation of Christ's life in the sacrament, is in no sense corporeal, but altogether spiritual, as the necessary condition of its being real,' but it must affect the whole person.[173] But such participation in Christ's life in the sacrament does seem to be essential to Nevin. Expounding with approval the old Reformed understanding of the Lord's Supper, he declares that Christ's

---

[167] Idem, 'Church, ministry and sacraments,' in J. Vernon Bartlet and J. D. Jones, eds., *The Validity of the Congregational Ministry*, London: Congregational Union of England and Wales, [1916], 45; cf. *The Church and the Sacraments*, 234.
[168] Idem, *Positive Preaching and the Modern Mind*, 56.
[169] Idem, 'Church, ministry and sacraments,' 34; cf. The Church and the Sacraments, 47.
[170] Idem, *The Church and the Sacraments*, 235 n.
[171] Ibid., 198.
[172] J. W. Nevin, *The Mystical Presence*, 40. See further, Arie J. Griffioen, 'Nevin on the Lord's Supper,' in *Reformed Confessionalism in Nineteenth-Century America*.
[173] Ibid., 185.

humanity forms the medium of his union with the church. The life of which he is the fountain, flows forth from him only as he is the Son of Man. To have part in it a all we must have part in it as a real human life; we must eat his flesh and drink blood; take into us the substance of what he was as man; so as to become flesh of his flesh and bone of his bone.[174]

Here, as before, lies the significant difference of emphasis as between Forsyth and Mercersburg; but what is quite clear is that both emphasise the objectivity of the means of grace. Whilst eschewing the *opus operatum*, Nevin insists that 'The signs are bound to what they represent, not subjectively simply in the thought of the worshipper.'[175] Similarly, among Schaff's list of the defects of contemporary Protestantism is 'an undervaluation of the sacraments as objective institutions of the Lord, independent of individual views and states.'[176] For Forsyth this becomes especially clear in connection with baptism:

> It is our individualism that has done most to ruin the sacrament of Baptism among us. We get a wrong answer because we do not ask the right question. We ask, What good does Baptism do me or that child? Instead of, What is the active witness and service the Church renders to the active Word of Christ's Gospel in the Baptism of young or old? Baptism is not there primarily for the individual, nor for the family, but for the Church, to confess before God and man the Word of Regeneration. It is not a domestic occasion but an ecclesiastical.[177]

Baptism, he continues, is not necessary for an individual's salvation, for regeneration is from Christ, not the sacraments. But 'It marks off the people of the New Covenant from the world in virtue of their corporate union with its Creator in a higher creation.'[178] Moreover, infant baptism testifies primarily to 'God's changeless will of salvation in Christ and the Church.'[179] Accordingly, 'Baptism is wrong, not when applied to children, but when separated from the other means of grace, from the nurture of the Church, and especially from the Word of the Gospel whose vehicle it is.'[180] That Nevin and Schaff would have agreed is clear at many points in their writings.[181] For example, one of Nevin's serious charges against conversion as understood by the new breed of revivalists was precisely that 'as a matter of course baptism becomes a barren

---

[174] Ibid., 113.
[175] Ibid., 185; cf. Nevin in *The Weekly Messenger of the German Reformed Church*, 12 no. 51, 1847, 2490.
[176] P. Schaff, *The Principle of Protestantism*, in K. Penzel, *Philip Schaff*, 88.
[177] P. T. Forsyth, *The Church and the Sacraments*, 178; cf. 190–1, 208, 274.
[178] Ibid., 206; cf. 210, 220.
[179] Ibid., 216.
[180] Ibid., 223.
[181] See further, John B. Payne, 'Nevin on Baptism,' in *Reformed Confessionalism in Nineteenth-Century America*.

sign, and the children of the Church are left to grow up like the children of the world under general most heartless, most disastrous neglect.'[182] His understanding of infant baptism, coupled with his commitment to catechetical training were advanced as bulwarks against this unhappy outcome. The objective of the latter is to prepare the way for the subjective appropriation by faith of the objective grace of baptism, such a personal response being 'the natural and suitable close of the baptismal act itself.'[183]

Both the Mercersburg theologians and Forsyth agree that since baptism and the Lord's Supper are sacraments of the Church, their normal place is within the regular worship of the Church. What is the nature of this worship, and of what constituents is it made up? At this point I can be brief, for since Nevin devoted much more time to technical liturgical matters than Forsyth, the points of comparison and contrast are relatively few. But this much may be said: First, that consistently with their understanding of the objectivity of God's gracious dealings with us – whether couched in terms of the Cross or of the mystical union – they both endeavour to move worship from an anthropological to a Christocentric base. Forsyth insists that 'The greatest product of the Church is not brotherly love but divine worship. And we shall never worship right nor serve right till we are more engrossed with our God than even with our worship, with His reality than our piety, with His Cross than our service.'[184] It would seem, in passing, that those words, written against a theological liberalism gone sentimental, are not entirely without application to those circles in our own time where the view abounds that the objective of worship is to make us *feel better!*

As to the hoary debate as to whether set liturgical forms should be used in preference to free forms, Nevin and Schaff, on grounds of objectivity and continuity with the Church of the ages argue for the former at length. Noting that texts of Scripture, the Creed, the Lord's Prayer, and verses of hymns are lovingly recalled in believers' devotions, Nevin asks against opponents of set liturgies, 'Do *they* lose their force by repetition? ... These simple formularies are powerful for the purposes of devotion and faith, just because they echo in the same words always, from childhood to old age, and from one century onward to another, what has been the universal worship of the one Catholic Church through all times.'[185] By contrast, 'No thoughtful mind turned toward the subject, can well help seeing and feeling, that there is in some way an ominous affinity between free worship and free thinking in religion, both in its fanatical

---

[182] J. W. Nevin, *The Anxious Bench*, in *Catholic and Reformed*, 112.
[183] Idem, 'Review of Noel's "Essay on Christian Baptism,"' *The Mercersburg Review*, 2, 1850, 263.
[184] P. T. Forsyth, *The Church and the Sacraments*, 25.
[185] J. W. Nevin, *The Liturgical Question*, 12–13.

and in its rationalistic polar extremes.'[186] (Though it must be said that most users of free liturgies have been doctrinally orthodox, while some Unitarians have used set liturgies, and some Anglicans, the *Book of Common Prayer* notwithstanding, have been Arians at best).

Forsyth is much kinder to free prayer than Nevin – but Nevin was set among numerous ranters. Forsyth regrets that free prayer is all too often undisciplined, but insists that it need not be so.[187] There is ample evidence that Nevin would heartily have endorsed Forsyth's view that 'I would rather have a liturgy reflecting the conscience of the Church than one reflecting the idiosyncracy of an individual.'[188] But Forsyth regards intercessory prayer as very much part of the minister's priestly function; the people have called the minister to speak for them to God;[189] he believes that if 'condemned to an exclusive choice,' the evangelical free churches would have to opt for free prayer. But he recognises that in changed circumstances there are problems:

> Perhaps the exclusive use of free prayer descends to us from a time when the worshipping congregation was almost identical with the church of believers, who hada real spiritual experience, and whose soul of faith the minister found it easy to utter through his own. Whereas now the church is but a minority of the congregation, and a power so sympathetic as free prayer cannot do its mighty work because of unbelief.[190]

But where Forsyth and the Mercersburg theologians would most seriously part company in liturgical matters is over the balance between the Word and the Sacrament. Nevin insists that Christian liturgy must be an 'altar' liturgy rather than a 'pulpit' liturgy. This is consistent with his view that 'the last ground of all true Christian worship [is] the mystical presence of Christ in the Holy Eucharist.'[191] For this reason the Lord's Supper must be restored to its rightful, regular, place in Christian worship. But it is clear that Nevin wishes to do more than redress the balance as between preaching and Lord's Supper: the Provisional Liturgy of the German Reformed Church, he tells us, 'was intended to be prevailingly a liturgy for the altar, and not simply a pulpit liturgy;'[192] and this despite his occasional affirmation of the importance of preaching.[193]

---

[186] Ibid., 15.
[187] Ibid., 20–21.
[188] P. T. Forsyth, *Congregationalism and Reunion*, 76.
[189] Idem, *The Church and the Sacraments*, 145–6.
[190] Idem, *Intercessory Prayers for aid in Public Worship*, Manchester: John Heywood, [1896], 4.
[191] J. W. Nevin, *The Liturgical Question*, 23.
[192] Ibid., 38. As Sam Hamstra has reminded us, 'Nevin exhausted more time in his pastoral theology class lecturing his students on the style of preaching than on its content.' See 'Nevin on the pastoral office,' *Reformed Confessionalism in Nineteenth-Century America*, 182.
[193] See, for example, J. W. Nevin, 'Education,' Mercersburg Review, 18, 1871, 11.

We can imagine what Forsyth would reply to this – but we do not have to. He can thunder for himself:

> The Word and the Sacraments are the two great expressions of the Gospel in worship. The Sacraments are the acted Word – variants of the preached Word. They are signs, but they are more than signs. They are the Word, the Gospel itself, visible, as in preaching the Word is audible. But in either case it is an act. It is Christ in a real presence giving us anew His Redemption.[194]

Indeed, for Forsyth, 'The sacrament which gives value to all other sacraments is the Sacrament of the living Word.'[195] This is why, in a cheeky reference to a leading Anglo-Catholic, Forsyth declared, 'Were there no other alternative, Bishop Gore's gospel would make many put up, for a time at least, with his view of the ministry.'[196]

But, to end on a note of harmony: Forsyth and the Mercersburg theologians would be in thorough concord on the point that the Church's primary task and joy is to worship God. Hence Forsyth's swingeing criticisms of those churches with their bulging programmes, where 'You have bustle all the week and baldness all the Sunday. You have energy everywhere except in the Spirit ... Suppose [Christ] had measured His success by His supporters! Suppose His great and first object had been conversions!'[197]

V

As I explained at the outset, in writing this paper I have allowed Mercersburg to set the agenda, and I have viewed Forsyth in relation to it. Consequently Forsyth's writings on eschatology, theodicy, prayer, freedom, marriage, war, and art have not come under consideration. Nevertheless the points of coalescence are surely of great importance, and I believe that through the comparisons and contrasts with which we have been occupied, we may be encouraged, challenged, cautioned and instructed.

Arising from their common indebtedness to post-Hegelian immanentist thought, both the Mercersburg theologians and Forsyth were inclined at times to relapse into an 'automaticism' of salvation. Nevin, however, did this from the standpoint of the incarnation (and did it more frequently than Forsyth), Forsyth from his starting-point in the Cross (understood as a portmanteau term). Forsyth was able to guard himself against the pitfall more easily than the Mercersburg men because he focused upon the moral rather than upon the

---

[194] P. T. Forsyth, The Church and the Sacraments, 176.
[195] Idem, *Positive Preaching and the Modern Mind*, 4.
[196] Idem, *The Principle of Authority*, 224.
[197] Idem, *Positive Preaching and the Modern Mind*, 117.

ontological and metaphysical, and because he insisted upon the importance of the holy God's loving, redemptive, once-for-all *act* in Christ on the stage of history. It may be suggested, however, that the Mercersburg emphasis upon the incarnation, provided that it can be disentangled from those process and divine-human continuity features of which Forsyth was so suspicious, serves as a useful corrective to Forsyth who, although he knew quite well that the whole earthly experience and ministry of Jesus is of significance, did not dwell upon the life and ministry very much.[198] Since a comparable charge may be levelled against Nevin in relation to the atoning death, we have a paramount instance here of the way in which Forsyth and the Mercersburg theology may mutually balance one another.

Both the Mercersburg theologians and Forsyth are convinced that salvation is not in the first place a matter of subjective response, or of the believer's feelings, but of an objective work of grace. For Forsyth, however, this work is encapsulated in the Cross, which is, for him, the heart of the Gospel and the supreme locus of authority. Nevin and Schaff appeal much more to the historic witness of the creeds, and at this point they correct Forsyth's *tendency* at times to play down the Spirit's work through the ages. But this playing down is to be understood, and at least partially excused for being, a strong expression of confidence in the Spirit's prompting of Christian confession in every age. In other words, it is not simply that Forsyth weighs the ancient creeds and finds them wanting as far as the articulation of the Gospel is concerned – though he does do this, and not without good cause.

Forsyth and the Mercersburg theologians are in complete accord on the Church as a divine society called out by God. They further agree that the Church's heritage of faith and witness is to be received as a whole: the Church did not begin in the New Testament and then vanish until the Reformation, as some ardent Protestants seemed to suppose. Neither party can understand Christian faith apart from Christian fellowship, for Christianity, though personal, is not private and individualistic. The Church is inescapable for Christians. But at times both the Mercersburg theologians and Forsyth appear to blur the distinction between the Church and 'the world' with their references to a racial salvation. To all of them the Church is catholic, though for Forsyth it is grounded in a moral redemption, whereas Nevin speaks rather in terms of ontological union with Christ. The most significant disagreement between the two parties is over the notion that the Church is the continuation or

---

[198] For this he was criticised by, among others, A. E. Garvie, his Congregational colleague at New College, London. See the latter's *The Christian Certainty amid the Modern Perplexity: Essays Constructive and Critical, towards the Solution of Some Current Theological Problems*, London: Hodder & Stoughton, 1910, 460–74.

prolongation of the incarnation. While in no way denying that the risen and exalted Christ lives in his people by the Spirit, and they in him, I endorse Forsyth's criticisms of what is at best an unguarded way of speaking, and at worst a heresy as far as the empirical Church is concerned.

In relation to church order and polity I find Forsyth much more realistic than the Mercersburg theologians. Does Christ dwell with his people? Are they truly one in him? Very well – let them gather as a holy priesthood not only in worship but also in Church Meeting, which, like worship, is a credal assembly where the Lordship of Christ is acknowledged and his will for witness and service sought. Here is a word for all who, in these ecumenical times, exalt – on paper – the ministry of the whole people of God, whilst perpetuating polities which exclude the bulk of the holy priesthood from those deliberations which are the proper concern of every local-cum-catholic church. It would, for example, do nothing but good if the United Church of Christ could really fuse and express in lively ways its twin heritage of representative church government and local Church Meeting. There is, after all, no catholicity which does not begin where the saints gather.

As for the ministry, both Forsyth and the Mercersburg theologians insist that the minister's call is from God, and that the first charge upon ministers is to lead the people to the throne of grace. Forsyth, however, would, in my view rightly, not agree with Nevin that the ministry comprises the bond of unity of the Church; nor would he endorse language which appears to elevate the ministry above the Holy Spirit. We are saved from such lapses, he thinks, by remembering that the Church, founded in the act of its great High priest, *is*, rather than *has* a priesthood. Similarly, he eschews the Mercersburg tendency to speak in terms of ordination as entailing 'a tactual communication heavenly powers' or the mystical transmission of grace. This is because, for him, the apostolic succession is a succession in the Gospel, and not a prolongation of the original apostolate. He is particularly alive to the sectarian spirit which the latter claim can foster in those inclined to annexe the term 'catholic.'

Mercersburg and Forsyth are at one in holding that the sacraments are signs but also seals of the covenant of grace – not for them 'memorialism.' But, once again, Forsyth's teaching on the sacraments is couched in moral and personal rather than metaphysical terms. For him the key to the sacraments, as to all else, is the new covenant ushered in by the work of Christ.

As to liturgy, there is agreement that the worship of God is the Church's primary obligation, and that truly Christian worship is Christocentric. Nevin is more inclined towards set forms of worship than Forsyth, though the latter by no means sanctions liturgical disorder. Forsyth, though well aware of possible abuses, is much kinder to free prayer than is Nevin; and, above all, Forsyth elevates preaching to a degree that Nevin does not. He could never agree that

Christian liturgy must be an altar *rather than* a pulpit liturgy. For him Word and Sacrament belong together and, under the Spirit, the former is the interpreter of the latter.

If we could substitute 'Gospel' for 'creed', I do not think Forsyth would have much difficulty in assenting to the following words of Nevin:

> A theology which is truly Christocentric must follow the Creed, must be objective, must be historical; with this, must be churchly; and, with this again, must be sacramental and liturgical.[199]

However, the fact that Forsyth would construe some of these clauses in a way significantly different from that of Nevin, substantiates my case that either needs the other, and the Church needs both.

---

[199] J. W. Nevin, 'The theology of the New Liturgy,' *Mercersburg Review*, 1867; quoted by Jack Martin Maxwell, *Worship and Reformed Theology*, 41.

CHAPTER 9

A Renewed Plea for 'Impractical' Divinity

In the early 1990s two literary anniversaries slipped by without comment. The tercentenary of Thomas Watson's *A Body of Practical Divinity* might have been observed in 1992, but as far as I know it was not. Watson's work is a patient, still illuminating exposition of the *Westminster Shorter Catechism* by an ejected Presbyterian divine who elsewhere declared, 'There are two things which I have always looked upon as difficult. The one is. to make the sinner sad; the other is, to make the godly joyful.'[1] Since the aim of his 'practical divinity' is to meet this need, Watson expounds both the doctrinal foundations of the faith as a dissuasive against what he calls 'feathery Christians' who are blown all over the place,[2] and the Beatitudes, the Lord's Prayer and the Ten Commandments. With Watson, as for Puritan divines in general, doctrine and ethics go hand in hand. In the middle of the following century the high Calvinist Baptist, John Gill, concurred. In the Introduction to his *Complete Body of Doctrinal and Practical Divinity* (1767, 1770) he writes, 'Where there is not the doctrine of faith, the obedience of faith cannot be expected ... And on the other hand, doctrine without practice ... is of no avail ...'[3]

The second bypassed literary anniversary is of considerably less significance: indeed, it is of scarcely any importance at all. The fact is, however, that 1993 saw the thirtieth anniversary of the publication of my first academic paper. It occasioned such a resounding silence that ever since, apart from the solace provided by the collection of papers, *Christian Ethics and Moral Philosophy* (1966) and the continuing labours of a few philosophers who are Christians — among whom Basil Mitchell is prominent, I have been tempted to feel like 'a voice crying in the wilderness'. My article was entitled, 'Christian ethics and moral philosophy: some reflections on the contemporary situation'.[4] The burden of my message was that there was inadequate commerce between moral philosophers and Christian ethicists, and that this was likely to continue unless and until the latter devoted themselves with some enthusiasm to those metaethical tasks which to many of the former were in those days the sole concern of ethics. By

---

[1] Thomas Watson, Preface to *A Divine Cordial* (1663), Grand Rapids: Sovereign Grace Publishers, 1971, 6.
[2] Idem, *A Body of Divinity*, rev. edn, London: The Banner of Truth Trust, 1965, 1.
[3] John Gill, *Complete Body of Doctrinal and Practical Divinity*, reprinted by Baker Book House, Grand Rapids, 1978, from the 1839 edn, vii.
[4] See *Scottish Journal of Theology*, XVI, no. 4, December 1963, 337–51.

way of illustrating the need I referred to the then relatively recently published book by G. F. Thomas, *Christian Ethics and Moral Philosophy* (1955) — a hopeful title indeed. But on consulting the index I discovered that whereas the author referred to Bradley, Broad, Moore, Ross, Sidgwick and Taylor, there was no mention of Hare, Toulmin, Nowell-Smith, Prior or others who had by 1955 made significant contributions to moral philosophy.[5]

Among more recent works on Christian ethics is Philip Wogaman's *Christian Ethics. A [sic] Historical Introduction* (1993). Although Wogaman clearly sees the importance for Christian Ethics of secular philosophy in the early Christian centuries and in the medieval period, his engagement with it in the eighteenth century (a crucial period for ethics) is slight, and in the twentieth century is almost entirely non-existent. Like G. F. Thomas, Wogaman makes no reference to moral philosophers of the past forty-five years; unlike Thomas, he does not mention the succession from Bradley to Taylor either.[6]

I take no comfort from this, and feel that today the situation is even more desperate than it was thirty years ago. Hence, although I should not necessarily wish to be tied to every statement in my early article, I do feel constrained to utter a *renewed* plea for 'impractical' divinity. I am entirely with Watson, Gill and many others in holding together what they called doctrinal and practical divinity. It seems to me altogether consonant with the shape of the Decalogue and of many of Paul's letters that doctrine and life belong together and that the former should influence the latter. Did they not do so we could not be hypocrites — which we often are. To put the point in another way: I think that a good case can be made for saying that Christian ethics are theological ethics, that the imperative flows from the indicative, that the Christian's way of life is a response to revealed and appropriated grace. It is with divinity that we have to do in Christian ethics. But none of this requires us to shirk, or exonerates us from shirking, the hard task of 'impractical' divinity. I place 'impractical' within inverted commas because that is how my concerns are sometimes branded; in fact, I believe, they are integral to the study of Christian ethics, and while not every practitioner need major in every aspect of the discipline, theoretical Christian ethical reflection which is broader than, though not innocent of, linguistic analysis, should not be as scarce as it is, and no writings in the field should be entirely devoid of it. That way lie wanton moralizing and that thoughtless jumping upon passing ethical bandwagons of which we have so much at the present time. While not arguing for antisocial ethics or even for

---

[5] Ibid., 349–50.
[6] See further my review of Wogaman's book in *Modern Believing*, xxv No. 2, April 1994, 64–6. For an attempt to redress the balance as far as the eighteenth century, and English and Welsh Dissent, are concerned, see Alan P. F. Sell, *Philosophy, Dissent and Nonconformity 1689–1920*, Cambridge: James Clarke, 2004, ch. 3.

asocial ethics, I do feel that some move far too quickly to socio-ethical prescriptions. We can see where they have arrived, but since we cannot make out the route by which they have travelled, their conclusions are offered for acceptance only on their own authority. Whether those advocating them are theologically conservative or liberal these new authoritarian legalisms are ethically unacceptable.

Ironically, the continued evaporation of theoretical ethics from Christian ethics results in part from the boom in the discipline. I call it a discipline, but it is one of the more undisciplined of disciplines in that it runs everywhere. Traversing as it does biblical ethics, the history of ethics, casuistry and morals, social ethics, and touching upon the territories of ascetic and pastoral theology, the comprehensive Christian ethicist would be a polymath indeed.[7] As if this were not enough, Lonnie D. Kliever has referred to the 'mixed bag of technical labels found in [the literature of Christian ethics] — situation ethics, contextual ethics, circumstance ethics, relational ethics, non-principled ethics, pure act-*agapism*, mixed act-*agapism*, faith-doing ethics, response ethics, Christomorphic ethics, theonomic ethics, and the jaw-breaking *cathekontological* ethics'.[8] (I recite this list partly in order to terrify you, but mostly by way of pointing out that Christian metaethics is conspicuous by its absence from this list.) To repeat: Christian ethics is a veritable growth industry — so much so that Professor Robin Gill is quite bullish about it. In his book, *Christian Ethics and Secular Worlds* he properly notes the increasingly complicated ethical issues which are posed as new scientific developments occur and, equally rightly, he welcomes the fact that Christian ethicists are increasingly being called upon to consult with those of other relevant disciplines. He is not altogether clear as to the basis upon which they do this — now appearing to think in terms of natural law, now in terms of Christian values which have permeated society as if by osmosis. Nevertheless, he declares that it would be what he calls 'patent nonsense' for Christian ethicists to ignore the world around them, for 'The secular world is the

---

[7] The variety within the discipline of Christian ethics was ably described by my own teacher of Christian ethics, the late Ronald Preston, in his 'Christian ethics and moral theology, 1939–1960 — II', *Theology*, LXIV, February 1961, 46–57. The variety continues to this day though, of course, Professor Preston's illustrations of it could now be multiplied. I should like to take this opportunity of paying tribute to Professor Preston, who not only pioneered Christian ethics at the University of Manchester, developing the post there from a part-time lectureship to a Chair, but who also in wider circles did as much as any to advocate the study of the subject. Many have reason to be grateful for the way in which, in his own writings and in a spirit of ecumenical openness, he has combined biblical and theological sensitivity with alertness to the challenge of empirical circumstances and constraints.

[8] Lonnie D. Kliever, 'Moral argument in the new morality,' *Harvard Theological Review*, LXV, January 1972, 53.

very *raison d'être* of Christian ethics'.⁹ Writing as I am in the pantomime season, I am tempted to retort, 'Oh no it isn't!' But instead I shall more soberly suggest that Gill here begs a huge question. Thomas Watson, for example, with the *Catechism* before him, might say that the glorifying and eternal enjoying of God is the *raison d'être* of Christian ethics; Barth might opt for the Word of God, Paul Ramsey for *agape*, and I for the atonement as the ground of new life in the Spirit and of the restoration of all things in God.¹⁰

While in no way objecting to the outreach on the part of Christian ethicists to those of other professions; while agreeing with Professor Gill that 'Not the least of our difficulties is acquiring sufficient secular expertise,'¹¹ I should like to observe that one of the greatest difficulties at the moment is that of equipping Christian ethicists with ethics understood as the ability rigorously to examine Christian ethical presuppositions and closely to analyse Christian ethical discourse — and to undertake these tasks in relation to the heritage of moral philosophy. There are many reasons for what maybe called this flight from the theoretical, and I shall offer some at random.

The most obvious dissuasive is the proliferation and urgency of practical issues which need to be addressed. Such issues arise in medicine, law, economics, social work, and elsewhere. We need not dissent from Professor Gill's claim that '[If] they are to avoid naiveties, ethicists have no choice but to stray into any number of academic areas which are not properly their own.'¹² My point is that they need first to have strayed into — even to have tabernacled in — the field of ethics. There is a real danger that under the pressure of the times Christian ethicists and those they teach will make straight for the issues of the day, doing obeisance to the god Relevance, and that hard theoretical, wrestling will go by the board. I fear that this is more likely to happen today than in the past because, with the demotion, under financial and other pressures of the taught B.D. to a first degree in many universities, the vast majority of those taking courses in Christian ethics will not possess a first degree in which they have pursued logic and philosophy — not least moral philosophy. I fully accept that even when the B.D. was a further degree it could be taken by those with no philosophical — or, indeed, humanities — background at all. But this in no way invalidates my point that it is desirable that *some* studying Christian

---

⁹ Robin Gill, *Christian Ethics and Secular Worlds*, Edinburgh: T. and T. Clark 1991, xvii. It is perhaps necessary to caution readers that Professor Gill oddly classes Luther and Bonhoeffer among Reformed theologians, p 6–8, 10.

¹⁰ See further, Alan P. F. Sell, '*Agape*, atonement and Christian ethics,' *The Downside Review*, XCI, April 1973, 83–100; idem, *Aspects of Christian Integrity*, Louisville: Westminster/John Knox and Calgary: University of Calgary Press, 1990; Eugene, OR: Wipf & Stock, 1998, ch. 3.

¹¹ R. Gill, *Christian Ethics and Secular Worlds*, xi.

¹² Ibid., p. xv.

ethics, and that *all* teaching it, shall have mastered the relevant philosophical and theological disciplines.

I do not overlook the fact that a possible cause of the flight of some from the theoretical may be found in the house of moral philosophy itself. In the mid-century heyday of linguistic analysis it was possible to hear ethicists congratulating themselves on the practical uselessness of their discipline, despising the history of philosophy as being a non-philosophical pursuit, and contenting themselves with the deployment of linguistic counters on an ethereal board. But this was not a necessary consequence of analytical zeal, and such analytically-trained philosophers as R. M. Hare, Basil Mitchell and Jonathan Harrison have devoted themselves to substantive ethical issues of perennial significance. Others, among them Dorothy Emmet and A. C. Ewing, while never ranged against metaphysics as such, as were some in the analytical (and especially the positivist) ascendency, wrote perceptively on ethics with considerable analytical skill.[13]

Finally, I would suggest that some Christian ethicists have found what they take to be adequate grounds for sitting loose to theoretical discussions in the embargoes which have been launched from both the philosophical and the theological camps. Thus, for all his philosophical prowess, Kant's insistence that an imperative may not be deduced from an indicative has tempted some Christians, who are properly insistent upon the fact that doctrine and ethics are integral to one another, to dismiss moral philosophy as irrelevant. Newman Smyth has not been alone in complaining that Kant was the chief representative of those moral philosophers whose efforts resulted in the disengagement of ethics from history: 'In his critical hands moral science was emptied of actuality.'[14] Other Christians have understood Barth as, in the interests of the Word of God, minimising the importance of rational ethical reflection on the part of human beings as such. To this latter point I shall return.

It is one thing to lament a theoretical lacuna, but how is the gap to be filled? Before turning to that question, and with a view to gaining perspective upon it, a brief sampling of the relations between Christian ethics and moral philosophy is in order, and to this I now turn.

I

To cut a long story disgracefully short, we may say that while Augustine construed the Platonist understanding of virtue in terms of the perfect love of

---

[13] A. C. Ewing must surely be among the most perceptive and productive ethicists of his generation not to have received a university chair.
[14] Newman Smyth, *Christian Ethics*, Edinburgh: T. and T. Clark, 3rd edn, 1916, 2.

God, and Aquinas laid an ethic heavily influenced by Aristotelian categories alongside his dogmatic utterances, neither allowed Christian doctrine its full weight in the formulation of Christian ethical theory.[15] For Luther and Calvin the ethical dimension of dogmatics was important, but a separate discipline of Christian ethics did not develop under their hands. Indeed, in early Reformed university circles the Lutheran Melanchthon's practice of regarding ethics as a matter of commentating upon Aristotle's ethics with scriptural corrections as appropriate was adopted, significant exceptions being Daneau's ethics which he sought to base upon Scripture and not upon Aristotle or dogmatics as such; and Keckermann's, a philosophical ethic of virtue which was adversely criticised by William Ames in his *Medulla Theologiae* (1627) for making moral good an external matter and spiritual good internal. For his part Ames promoted what came to be the classical Puritan relationship of faith and works *within* dogmatics at large — in which matter Johannes Wollebius, with his *Christianae Theologiae Compendium* of 1626 preceded him by one year.[16] Thomas Watson and John Gill, from whom I set out, followed suit, as did many others.

It is generally agreed that the Englishman who did more than any other to elicit dogmatically-independent ethical discussion was Thomas Hobbes, whose insistence that human beings are bound to seek their own individual ends in accordance with their desires seemed alien to Platonism, Aristotelianism and Christianity alike, and called for an alternative analysis of human nature by way of rebuttal. Hence the writings of those like Henry More, Cudworth, Cumberland, Clarke and Wollaston, whose emphasis upon reason was intended to refute Hobbes's subjectivism; and those like Shaftesbury, Hutcheson and Butler, who emphasised the affective aspects of human nature and produced alternative accounts of self-love to that of Hobbes.[17] As far as I have been able to discover, it was Henry Grove (1683–1738), tutor at Taunton Dissenting Academy, who, while not separating morality from God, was the first Englishman to divide his curriculum in such a way that ethics was henceforth taught separately from dogmatics.[18] While attacked by the high Calvinist Presbyterian John Ball of Honiton for elevating reason above Scripture, Grove

---

[15] See further, N. H. G. Robinson, *The Groundwork of Christian Ethics*, London: Collins 1971, 18–19; J. Burnaby, *Amor Dei*, London: Hodder & Stoughton 1938, 49.

[16] See further, Donald Sinnema, 'The discipline of ethics in early Reformed orthodoxy,' *Calvin Theological Journal*, XXVIII no. 1, April 1993, 10–44.

[17] See further, W. Bernard Peach, 'Human nature and the foundation of ethics,' *Enlightenment and Dissent*, IV, 1985, 13–34.

[18] See further, Alan P. F. Sell, *Dissenting Thought and the Life of the Churches. Studies in an English Tradition*, Lampeter and Lewiston, NY: Edwin Mellen Press, 1990, ch. 5; and see ch. 5 above. Schleiermacher's later view that Christian doctrine and Christian ethics were distinct but related disciplines, and that Christian ethics and philosophical ethics were independent sciences concerned with duty did not immediately influence British moral philosophers and theologians.

was not, like his contemporaries at Yale, rebuked by Cotton Mather for 'Pelagianism' and 'Stoicism', and reprimanded for 'employing so much time upon Ethik in College, a vile form of paganism'.[19]

Once the ethical jack was out of the dogmatic box there was no putting it back. Christian ethics began a life of its own, and henceforth had to make its way *vis à vis* dogmatics on the one hand and moral philosophy on the other. As the latter became increasingly secularised, the divorce of Christian ethics from moral philosophy, which it is the purpose of this paper to lament and to heal, became increasingly possible. The divorce was not, however, immediate, and of the many possible permutations in the relationship between Christian ethics and moral philosophy I shall note three. I take soundings at roughly fifty-year intervals from English Dissent. I select this Christian tradition because its authors were not beholden to pre-Reformation thought to the degree that practitioners of moral theology were; and because it is always interesting to see the variations possible within one tradition. It is not without significance to observe that the first of the three selected authors, George Payne, was an Englishman educated within Glasgow University's philosophical tradition, Oxford and Cambridge being closed to him; the second, Robert Mackintosh, was a Scot educated in the same place; the third, Sydney Cave, was an Englishman, who could have gone to Oxford, but in fact trained at Hackney College, London, under P. T. Forsyth, an alumnus of Aberdeen University.

George Payne (1781–1848),[20] born at Stow-on-the-Wold, educated at Hoxton Academy and Glasgow, became theological tutor at Blackburn Independent Academy in 1823, following ministerial service in Leeds, Hull and Edinburgh. He proceeded to the Western Academy on its removal in 1829 from Axminster to Exeter, and moved with the Academy on its relocation between Exeter and Plymouth in 1846. There he remained until his death. On the appearance of Payne's *Lectures on Christian Theology* in 1850, Evan Davies declared that 'Since the year 1763, the Church has not been furnished with the Theological Prelections of any Professor among the English Nonconformists. In that year — the twelfth after his lamented death — the first edition of Dr Doddridge's Lectures was issued from

---

[19] So G. Stanley Hall, 'On the history of American college text-books and teaching in logic, ethics, psychology and allied subjects,' *Proceedings of the American Antiquarian Society*, N.S. IX, 1894, 147.

[20] For George Payne see Memoir by John Pyer, Interment Address by H. F. Burder and Reminiscences by Ralph Wardlaw — all prefixed to George Payne, *Lectures on Christian Theology*, London: John Snow, 1850, I; ODNB; *The Evangelical Magazine*, August 1848, pp. 393–8, 415–16; *The Scottish Congregational Magazine*, 1850, 289–96; William D. McNaughton, *The Scottish Congregational Ministry 1794–1993*, Glasgow: Congregational Union of Scotland, 1993, 124; Alan P. F. Sell, *Philosophy, Dissent and Nonconformity*, passim; *Dictionary of Nineteenth-Century British Philosophers*, Bristol: Thoemmes Press, 2002.

the press.'²¹ But Payne had already made a name for himself with his *Elements of Mental and Moral Science; Designed to Exhibit the Original Susceptibilities of the Mind*, which was first published in 1828, and achieved its fourth edition in 1856.

Payne was greatly influenced by the metaphysics of Thomas Brown, in which Scottish common sense philosophy was blended with French sensationalism, but he departed from him in ethics, regretting, among other things, the way in which Brown's elevation of the feeling of moral approval into a criterion of rectitude caused him to forget the distinction between what is, and what ought to be: 'How was it possible for this acute writer to avoid perceiving, that he has no more right to take for granted the rectitude of the feeling of moral approbation, than the rectitude of any other feeling?'²² Indeed, 'It is necessarily involved in Dr Brown's principles, that there might be virtue in a nation of atheists'.²³ With this remark we come to the methodological point which is crucial to our purpose here. Writing of himself in the third person Payne declares that while there is a connection between some doctrines of mental science and some theological doctrines, the writer 'is not aware that his Theology has influenced his philosophical opinions,'²⁴ and this, he thinks, is as it should be. On the other hand, Payne invokes Scripture, and clearly cannot keep the Most High God out of his argument. Thus, for example, he writes, '[V]irtue, as it regards man, is the conformity or harmony of his affections and actions with the various relations in which he has been placed — of which conformity the perfect intellect of God, guided in its exercise by his infinitely holy nature, is the only infallible judge.'²⁵ The closing words of the fourth edition are even blunter: '[A] person might fulfil all the claims of all *men* upon him, yet, if he practically forget the claims of *God* upon him, in no way can he be designated, with consistency and truth, but as an immoral and a bad man.'²⁶

In Payne, then, we have what is intended as a system of ethics uninfluenced by theological considerations, yet the theistic assumption is made throughout, and Scripture is resorted to with deference. Fifty years on we find Robert Mackintosh (1858–1933) in his prime. After a Congregational pastorate in Dumfries he became Professor at Lancashire Independent College, Manchester²⁷

---

[21] Evan Davies, Preface to George Payne, *Lectures on Christian Theology*, iii.
[22] G. Payne, *Elements of Mental and Moral Science*, London: B. Holdsworth, 1st edn, 1828, 486.
[23] Ibid., 489.
[24] Ibid., xi.
[25] Ibid., 511.
[26] Ibid., 4th edn, 1856, 428.
[27] For Robert Mackintosh see ODNB; *Who Was Who, 1919–1940*; *The Congregational Year Book*, 1934, 269; W. D. McNaughton, op. cit., 92; Alan P. F. Sell, *Robert Mackintosh: Theologian of Integrity* (ch. 5 concerns 'Theology and Ethics') Bern: Peter Lang, 1977; idem, *Dictionary of Scottish Church History and Theology*, Edinburgh: T. and T. Clark, 1993; idem, *Dictionary of Nineteenth-Century British Philosophers*.

If Payne thought that ethics could proceed in a manner innocent of theology and then inconsistently invoked a theistic conclusion, Mackintosh was convinced that Christian ethics are distinct from secular ethics, yet engaged in both with little attempt to foster theoretical commerce between them. Whereas philosophers as such are in no position to say, 'The love of Christ constrains us,' 'Christian ethics,' he declares, 'will be a view of the Christian life from the inside, while it is still in progress and unfinished ... Christian ethics are ethics for Christians.'[28] After all, 'The Christian [ethical] motive is thankfulness for redeeming love. And personal love to our Lord incorporates love towards all the great principles for which he stands.'[29]

Mackintosh does not, however, deny the existence of common ground between Christians and others. On the contrary, he invokes the principle of natural law as a bulwark against undue subjectivism in ethics. But he is prevented from presenting a Christian construction of natural law by the psychological-motivational gulf which is fixed between Christians and others. On the other hand, Mackintosh does not hesitate to take moral philosophers to task on their own ground. But Christian doctrine does not supply him with overt principles of criticism. Instead, for example, Mackintosh contends against idealism and naturalism on the ground that they inhibit freedom and construe logical necessitation as physical compulsion. 'If we cannot repel this combined attack,' he contends, 'it is idle to talk about values'.[30] In *From Comte to Benjamin Kidd* Mackintosh takes up the cudgels against naturalism in ethics. He reviews Comte's doctrine of altruism, concluding that 'it is destitute of exactness, or, one might even say, of truth;'[31] he regards Spencer's 'social organism' as nothing more than a phrase with him; he undermines the evolutionary ethics of Alexander and others; and concludes that since science as applied to physical nature is incompetent to 'guarantee the world against moral paralysis', there is room for the Christian testimony that in Christ alone we have the pledge that 'the great career' will at last terminate in that 'one far-off divine event to which the whole creation moves'.[32] In *Hegel and Hegelianism* Mackintosh casts a critical eye over Hegelian ethics. Finding little to choose between Hegel's contention that 'the real is the rational' and the old superstition that 'whatever is is right,' he charges Hegel with landing us in a remorseless naturalism, wryly adding, 'It was doubtless to him and others a comfortable faith that all dissatisfaction with the present is due to philosophical incompetence'.[33]

---

[28] R. Mackintosh, *Christian Ethics*, London: T. C. and E. C. Jack, 1909, 8, 10, 15.
[29] Ibid., 86.
[30] Idem, *Values. A Bird's Eye Survey*, London: Independent Press, 1928, 73.
[31] Idem, *From Comte to Benjamin Kidd*, London: Macmillan, 1899, 54.
[32] Ibid., 280–81.
[33] Idem, *Hegel and Hegelianism*, Edinburgh: T&T Clark, 1903, 211.

A further fifty years on we have the publication in 1949 of Sydney Cave's *The Christian Way*.³⁴ Cave (1883–1953) had taught in India, ministered in Bristol, served as President of Cheshunt College, Cambridge, and by now was Principal of New College, London, with which his *alma mater*, Hackney, had merged in 1924. He published widely in Christian doctrine and world religions, and was noted for the clarity and accuracy of his teaching. His one ethical work is subtitled 'A study of New Testament ethics in relation to present problems', but he does make space to reflect upon the relations between Christian ethics and moral philosophy.

On his very first page Cave articulates his general stance: 'In Christ's words and deeds, in His Cross and Resurrection, there is disclosed the nature of God's character and rule, and so the secret of this mysterious universe. It is the task of Christian Theology to explore these great redemptive facts. Christian Ethics is derivative; it asks, Since God has so acted, what ought men to do?'³⁵ He later elaborates upon this: 'The world into which Jesus came was not lacking in moral philosophy or ethical admonition, and the uniqueness of the Christian Gospel is not to be found in the nobility of its ideas but in its story of what God has done for men in Christ's Life and Death and Resurrection.'³⁶ Jesus summons people to life in the Kingdom, and goes behind legalism to an exhortation to be like God; for this, as the epistles make plain, the motivation is not 'the reiteration of the commands of Jesus but ... the recital of what Christ was, of what He suffered and of what God had done in Him'.³⁷ Hence, 'it is not possible to speak adequately of Christian Ethics except in relation to Christian facts'.³⁸ When these are seen for what they are, it is not surprising that 'the lovely little' Heidelberg Catechism 'deals with the whole sphere of Christian Ethics under this one head of Gratitude'.³⁹

Where does this leave moral philosophy? Cave maintains that 'Christian Ethics does not make Moral Philosophy superfluous, for the concepts of ethics need to be scrutinised and their validity discussed. Yet Christian Ethics and Moral Philosophy inevitably differ in method and approach. Christian Ethics is a deduction from Christian theology and expresses in the imperative mood what theology states in the indicative'. In other words, the *didache* depends upon the *kerygma*.⁴⁰

---

[34] For Sydney Cave see ODNB; *The Congregational Year Book*, 1954, 506–507; Alan P. F. Sell, 'Sydney Cave,' in Trevor Hart, ed., *The Dictionary of Historical Theology*, Carlisle: Paternoster Press, 2000; Ronald Bocking, 'Sydney Cave (1883–1953), missionary, principal, theologian,' *The Journal of the United Reformed Historical Society*, VII no. 1, October 2002, 28–35.
[35] S. Cave, *The Christian Way* (1949), London: Nisbet, 1950, 13;
[36] Ibid., 97.
[37] Ibid., 98.
[38] Ibid., 98–9.
[39] Ibid., 132 n. 2.
[40] Ibid., 105.

It may by now seem that Cave is becoming a convert to Barthianism. In fact, however, he regards Barth as a 'fierce advocate' of the view that, as a result of human depravity, outside the Christian sphere there is no goodness and no right discernment of good, and from this position he strongly dissents, with reference to Barth's infamous 'Nein!' to Emil Brunner in connection with natural theology.[41] He is willing to agree with Barth that Christian ethics are theological ethics, but the Christian ethicist 'cannot be content to survey the human conflict from an ivory tower, nor can he restrict moral insight to those who understand and accept the affirmations of Christian faith. The history of Christian Ethics shows how much the church's ethical teaching has needed to be criticised, and the teacher of Christian Ethics, even of Christian Ethics, needs to take note of such criticism… It is right that there should be a Moral Philosophy, scrutinising ethical principles and motives, and Christian Ethics cannot be established only by authority'.[42]

Sadly, however, Cave does not address the challenge posed to, Christian ethics by ethical emotivism deriving from the logical positivism of A. J. Ayer; he does not treat of the implications for Christian ethics of the discussion of the naturalistic fallacy, which theme G. E. Moore had famously re-introduced. There is no reference to the intuitionism of Prichard, Carritt or Ross, to Joseph's critique of deontology, or to Field's teleological ethics.[43] Thus, while not ruling moral philosophy out of court — indeed, while valuing it and welcoming its critique of Christian ethics, Cave pays no heed to its then current expression in the relevant section of his ethical volume.

---

[41] Ibid., 106. Cf. the Brunner *versus* Barth debate in *Natural Theology*, London: G. Bles 1946. It is not fanciful to see the continuing influence of P. T. Forsyth upon Cave at this point — as also upon Forsyth's younger pupil, H. F. Lovell Cocks (for whom see Alan P. F. Sell, *Commemorations. Studies in Christian Thought and History*, Cardiff: University of Wales Press, and Calgary: University of Calgary Press, 1993; Eugene, OR: Wipf & Stock, 1998, ch. 13). P. T. Forsyth has sometimes been branded 'a Barthian before Barth,' but this needs to be qualified by the fact that in two respects: his greater openness to the apologetic enterprise (to which, admittedly, he did not make a large contribution, but he did not rule it out) and the kerygmatic as distinct from trinitarian shape of his theology, Forsyth was more a 'Brunner before Brunner'. His two pupils reflect this stance. See further, John Thompson, 'Was Forsyth really a Barthian before Barth?', in Trevor Hart (ed.), *Justice the True and Only Mercy. Essays on the Life and Theology of Peter Taylor Forsyth*, Edinburgh: T. and T. Clark, 1995, 237–55; N. H. G. Robinson, *Christ and Conscience*, London: Nidbet, 1956, 132–43.

[42] Ibid., 106–107.

[43] See A. J. Ayer, Language, Truth and Logic, London: Collancz, 1936; G. E. Moore, *Principia Ethica*, Cambridge: CUP, 1903; H. A. Prichard, *Moral Obligation. Essays and Lectures*, London: Oxford, 1949; E. F. Carritt, *The Theory of Morals*, London: CUP, 1928; W. D. Ross, *The Right and the Good*, London: OUP, 1930; idem, *The Foundations of Ethics*, London: OUP, 1939; H. W. B. Joseph, *Some Problems in Ethics*. Oxford: The Clarendon Press, 1931; G. C. Field, *Moral Theory. An Introduction to Ethics*, London: Methuen, 2nd rev. edn., 1928.

As a result of the above brief soundings we find that Payne seeks a theologically innocent ethic, but fails to keep theism and Scripture out of it; Mackintosh believes that Christian Ethics is distinct from general ethics, but while he deals sometimes trenchantly with the latter he confronts it on its own ground and does not offer a critique from a specifically Christian vantage-point; Cave, by contrast, agrees with Mackintosh that Christian ethics are distinctive, grants moral philosophy its rightful place, but does nothing about it at all. Such is the variety of ethical approaches within one ecclesiastical tradition.

II

What, then, is required? A further fifty years on (roughly), and from the same ecclesiastical tradition, I shall make four suggestions, taking my cue for the first three from each of the ethicists I have reviewed (though taking them in reverse order), and adding a final suggestion of my own.

First, Cave raises the questions of the nature of Christian ethics as theological, and of its relation to moral philosophy. I have already agreed that the Christian life is a response to redeeming grace, that Christian ethical behaviour is a response to God's revealed, active, victorious, saving love; and that the supreme motive in Christian ethical behaviour is gratitude to God for the new life — life in Christ by the Spirit — which he gives. I endorse the words of Arthur Dakin: '[T]he good life is the progressive appropriation of the life that is possible in God. As sin is traced to a relationship that has failed to mature or gone awry, so the good life is the living truly in this relationship, now restored.'[44] I am quite in accord with those who dissent from the view of A. B. D. Alexander that 'Christian Ethics is a branch of general Ethics.'[45] It does not, however, follow that Christian ethics and moral philosophy have nothing to say to one another. If Christian ethicists have a firm grasp upon those parts of theology which deal with creation and with the Spirit's blowing where he will, we ought to expect them to be concerned with reflection upon the deliverances of moral experience from whatsoever quarter they come, and to have the requisite skills for analysing these deliverances. Such is the close tie between theology and ethics that it would be a failure in *theology* and not simply in ethics were Christian ethics to become ghettoized.

Opponents of my view might say that it is precisely because of doctrine — in particular the doctrines of sin and total depravity — that commerce between

---

[44] Arthur Dakin, 'Evangelical ethics,' in *Studies in History and Religion Presented to Dr H. Wheeler Robinson, M.A., on his Seventieth Birthday*, ed. Ernest A. Payne, London: Lutterworth Press, 1942, 201.

[45] A. B. D. Alexander, *Christianity and Ethics*, London: Duckworth 1941, 22.

N. H. G. Robinson is among the dissenters. See his *The Groundwork of Christian Ethics*, 27; cf. 171.

Christian ethicists and moral philosophers is precluded. But, as John Baillie reminded us, a totally depraved person could not sin, for he or she would not be open to the making of moral choices between good and evil;[46] and John Whale pointed out that the doctrine of total corruption never did mean that the stream of human history is solid mud, but that it is 'corrupted in every part of its course'.[47] None of which prevented Barth from declaring that theology must repudiate all human answers to ethical questions in deference to the answer which is given in Jesus Christ.[48] Not surprisingly, N. H. G. Robinson concluded that 'radical Protestantism is radical authoritarianism in the sphere of religion, but it is so because it is first of all and primarily radical *empiricism* in theology, if this word may be used to indicate a reliance upon that which is given and not just upon that which is given to sense'.[49] However, in a different sense of 'empirical', Ronald Preston felt that Barth was not empirical enough. Barth insisted upon moving directly from the Bible to ethical deliverances and accorded no status in his writings to empirical knowledge of the world as it currently is. He is therefore 'a very unsafe guide in Christian Ethics'.[50] Preston continues, 'One example of his influence on the study work of the World Council of Churches can be seen in the pamphlet *Christians and the Prevention of War in an Atomic Age*, which attempts to move direct from Scripture to the problems of nuclear warfare by arguing that God's purposes for men are discriminate, therefore men must not be indiscriminate. One could equally argue the opposite, that because God send his rain indiscriminately on the just and the unjust, men are entitled to drop bombs equally indiscriminately upon them!'[51]

It really does seem that whether we are confronted by the Word of God, whether we are under agapaestic obligations, no matter what ethical theoretical baggage we bring with us, we have to decide what to do in the world as it is. In this connection I must express my surprise at an assertion by the evangelical theological ethicist Donald Bloesch, who writes, 'Christian ethics is neither utilitarian — appealing to the consequences of an action — nor deontological — appealing to a universal moral rule. Instead it is revelational — submitting to the divine commandment, which is always concrete and particular.'[52] But is the revelation, and are its recipients, abstracted from the world? May not God

---

[46] John Baillie, *Our knowledge of God*, London: CUP, 1939, 33.
[47] John Whale, *Christian Doctrine* (1941), London: Collins Fontana, 1957, 40.
[48] K. Barth, *Church Dogmatics*, Edinburgh: T. and T. Clark, 1957, II.2, 509.
[49] N. H. G. Robinson, *Christ and Conscience*, London: Nisbet, 1956, 95.
[50] Ronald Preston, 'The study of Christian ethics,' *Theology* LXVII, April 1964, 147.
[51] Ibid.
[52] Donald G. Bloesch, *Freedom for Obedience. Evangelical Ethics in Contemporary Times*, San Francisco: Harper & Row, 1987, 22. This is nevertheless an illuminating volume — not least because of the way in which the author weaves his way through numerous ethical contributions from the 1950s to the present.

address us through human reflection upon obligations, goals and empirical circumstances? As Robinson said, 'The Christian is certainly in some sense a new creature, but that clearly means, not another species altogether, but a creature, a man transformed or renewed, whose transformation and renewal cannot be articulated apart from some understanding of his existence as a creature independently of that renewal.'[53] Christians should not be unduly surprised, therefore, if they find themselves weighing deontological and teleological considerations in relation to the facts of the situation as they perceive them, and as they are enabled by the Spirit. No doubt Christian ethical decisions and actions will always be those of the sinful, but they need not and should not be those of the witless.

Secondly, those who would remove Christian ethics from the sphere of general moral debate by identifying theology and ethics serve theology ill by depriving it of ethical criticism. Barth warns against any attempt 'to set up general ethics as a judge, and to prove and justify theological ethics before it'. This is because theological ethics is one of grace, and God's will can be done only within the sphere of grace.[54] But (a) there is biblical evidence to suggest that the 'unsaved' may do the will of God unawares — and, indeed, that they will sometimes make a better job of it than the 'religious'; and (b) theology can take wrong turnings and go bad, and when this happens the ethical critique of it is urgently required. Unless there is a distinction between theology and ethics this would be a circular affair were it attempted at all. In fact, what often happens within the church is that ethical actions which have been inspired by bad theology are rebuked by ethical insights derived from better theology. I would suggest the theology of apartheid and its theological correction as an example of this.[55]

In all of this I am echoing Robert Mackintosh's belief that 'Part of the business of Christian ethics is to keep doctrine ethical'.[56] With this his contemporary, Newman Smyth, agreed: 'Old theology,' he wrote, 'is always becoming new in the vitalising influence of ethics.'[57] Mackintosh himself knew how personally costly this activity could be, for it was his ethical wrestling with the confessional theology of the Free Church of Scotland in which he was reared which eventually made him a self-styled 'refugee' to Congregationalism. In his day

---

[53] N. H. G. Robinson, *The Groundwork of Christian Ethics*, 16.
[54] K. Barth, *Church Dogmatics*, II.ii, 524, 539.
[55] See further, Alan P. F. Sell, *Aspects of Christian Integrity*, Louisville: Westminster/John Knox and Calgary: University of Calgary Press, 1990; Eugene, OR: Wipf & Stock, 1998, ch. 3; idem, *A Reformed, Evangelical, Catholic Theology. The Contribution of the World Alliance of Reformed Churches 1875–1982*, (1991), Eugene, OR: Wipf & Stock, 1998, 18, 233–4.
[56] Robert Mackintosh, *Christian Ethics*, 11.
[57] N. Smyth, *Christian Ethics*, 11.

and context the ethical corrective was called for in relation to atonement theories which maligned the Father and the Son by suggesting that 'there is no grace in God until Christ's death has "satisfied justice"'.[58] Related to such theories was that concerning the predestinated elect. Mackintosh was convinced that *'God's unmotivated or secret will, used as the masterkey* — always works for the disintegration both of theology and of faith ... It is time that Christian theology should cease to dabble in blasphemy'.[59] Note that Mackintosh is saying of untoward atonement theories what Christians later were to say about apartheid — not only that the doctrines were intellectually unsound, but that in the light of the Gospel they were immoral doctrines which ought not to be believed, proclaimed and lived by.

But it is too easy to raise our hands in horror about distant ills and untoward doctrines of atonement. from a past age. We may well feel that some current ways of interpreting the atonement, such as that which finds God the Father guilty of child abuse against the Son, leave something to be desired.[60] One does not need to be 'anti-women' — as I am not — to conclude that such a view is biblically and theologically inept — even morally offensive; or to regard such expressions as indicative of the perils we encounter if we elevate particular kinds of human experience into absolute norms of theological interpretation.[61]

Be all that as it may, I submit that in our own time one area of Christian doctrine which urgently needs ethical attention is ecclesiology. Let me state in summary form the high, catholic doctrine of the Church to which I subscribe: The Church compromises all in every age who, on the ground of Christ's finished work, have been called by God's gracious Spirit through the Word, engrafted into Christ, and hence given to one another in a fellowship which knows no barriers of class, race or sex. Over his redeemed community Christ reigns as the only Lord;[62] so he is confessed; and his will only is to be sought and done.

If this is the case any imposition of 'new circumcisions' will strictly be immoral and will yield sectarian results, for what God in Christ has made one will be rent asunder, and the unity which God. has given to his Church will be

---

[58] R. Mackintosh, *Essays Towards a New Theology*, Glasgow: Maclehose, 1889, 122.

[59] Idem, *Historic Theories of Atonement*, London: Hodder & Stoughton 1920, 155.

[60] The example given would seem to fly in the face of Paul's conviction that 'God was in Christ reconciling the world to himself' (II Corinthians 5: 19). If such a text fails to discourage those who would drive a wedge between Father and Son it is difficult to discern what else would suffice.

[61] See Alan P. F. Sell, *Commemorations*, 54.

[62] Hence, for example, the importance of that credal assembly, the Church Meeting — Congregationalism's gift to the church at large (albeit a gift sometimes neglected and misunderstood by those who have inherited it). See further Alan P. F. Sell, *Commemorations*, ch. XIV, especially 349–361 and n. 87 (second part).

obscured. Yet such behaviour occurs all the time. It occurred when on 12 June 1984 the present Pope, in an address to the international bodies which occupy the Ecumenical Centre in Geneva, said this: 'To be in communion with the bishop of Rome is to give visible evidence that one is in communion with all who confess [the, catholic faith of the ages] ... That is our Catholic conviction, and our fidelity to Christ forbids us to give it up.'[63] I was there; I was not surprised; but (as one deeply involved in the international bilateral dialogue between the Reformed family and the Roman Catholic Church) because of the negative implication of the first sentence quoted, and because of my conviction that church membership affords visible evidence of catholicity, I was deeply saddened. But I am no less concerned when Strict Baptists almost become a mirror image of the papacy (of which some of them are otherwise highly suspicious) by saying, 'Unless you have been baptized by immersion on profession of faith you may not come to the Lord's table in our church.'[64]

Sadly, it is not difficult to multiply examples from several quarters: 'Unless you are a five-point Calvinist..., Unless you are a biblical inerrantist ..., Unless you have the ministry and orders of which we approve ..., Unless you can speak in tongues ..., Unless you do theology in our way ..., Unless you adopt our socio-political platform ... we cannot have full fellowship with you.'[65] If my 'high, catholic' statement of the nature of the Church is true and complete these assertions betoken 'another Gospel which is no Gospel at all' (Galatians 1), and should, as a moral requirement be repudiated on the ground that they are sectarian postures. If my statement is untrue, or only partially true, or incomplete, it is a moral requirement that convincing theological arguments be adduced to demonstrate this and to show either that the present divided state of the Church is justifiable and tolerable, or to name the real culprits and call them to repentance. Until this is done I shall continue to affirm that those whom God has claimed and grafted into one family, and who confess Christ as Lord, may not justifiably be sundered at the Lord's Table by any 'new circumcision', whether ecclesiologically, doctrinally, ethically, racially or sexually inspired. To the extent that there may be convergence on this matter in the future it will be a moral requirement that fresh understandings are accompanied by genuine reconciliation of memories in the way of past maltreatment of one another.

---

[63] John-Paul II, Address given in the Ecumenical Centre, Geneva, on 12 June 1984. The text is printed in John J. McDonnell, *The World Council of Churches and the Catholic Church*, Lewiston, NY: The Edwin Mellen Press, 1985, 356.

[64] The literature is vast, but, for example, this conviction runs through Peter Naylor's *Picking Up a Pin for the Lord. English Particular Baptists from 1688 to the Early Nineteenth Century*, London: Grace Publications, 1992. See my review of this book in *The Baptist Quarterly*, XXXV, no. 5, January 1994, 257–8.

[65] For further remarks on theological and ethical sectarianism see Alan P. F. Sell, *Commemorations*, ch. II, especially 46–59.

Please note that nothing I say should be construed as repudiating the need of order and discipline within the Church, or as implying that a restorationist view of Scripture will suffice, or that the deliverances of the Christian heritage are redundant.[66] But positive convictions on these points ought not, for example, to encourage those of my tradition (blessed word!) to 'buy into' sectarian ministries by 'reordination' — a term which, it may gently be suggested, is, like 'rebaptism' and 'unicorn', a non-instantiated concept. Neither should the Reformed seek to retract from that part of the Gospel with which we have all too belatedly — and not yet universally — caught up, namely that from his one, barrier-free family God has the right to call whom he will to be his ministers — even if they be women.

Thirdly, Christian ethicists would do well to take seriously the metaphysical underpinnings of their discipline. Here I regress to George Payne. In the Preface to the second edition of his *Elements*, Payne wrote, 'The writer has long been of the opinion that ethical and theological systems are modified to a greater degree than is frequently imagined, by the views which those who advocate them take of the nature and laws of the mind.'[67] He further explains, 'Mental Philosophy is the anatomy of human nature: is it possible, then, to exhibit the rationale of Morals, if we are ignorant of this species of anatomy?' The several emotions are 'the springs of human conduct'.[68] Again, in 1892 Newman Smyth enumerated the philosophical postulates of Christian ethics, namely, 'that human nature is constituted for moral life', and that 'Christian Ethics assumes the sense of obligation, or the authority of conscience.'[69] In our own time Henry Stob has claimed that since all ethics assumes that people ought to be good, the ethicists are committed to the view that they are members of a free world which legislates for them. But these are metaphysical claims. Hence, 'Every obligation demands ultimate validation. There is no genuine "ought" that does not need the whole universe to back it.'[70] For his part, Professor T. A. Roberts has said that 'The Christian must claim that the essential basis for his morality is the metaphysical view of the nature of man as a rational, social being who is also the child of God, created in the image of God.'[71]

To recall my earlier reference to Cumberland, Hutcheson and others, in 1748 Hume referred to his immediate ethicist predecessors and said, 'There has been

---

[66] See further, ibid., ch. 1.
[67] G. Payne, *Elements of Mental and Moral Science*, 4th edn, p. v.
[68] Ibid., 1st edn., p. 9.
[69] N. Smyth, *Christian Ethics*, 27, 28.
[70] Henry Stob, *Ethical Reflections. Essays on Moral Themes*, Grand Rapids: Eerdmans, 1978, 26.
[71] T. A. Roberts, 'Moral theology or Christian ethics?' *Church Quarterly Review*, CLXV 1964, 208.

a controversy started of late ... concerning the general foundation of Morals; whether they be derived from Reason, or from Sentiment; whether we attain knowledge of them by a chain of argument and induction, or by an immediate feeling and finer internal sense; whether like all sound judgments of truth and falsehood, they should be the same to every rational intelligent being; or whether, like the perception of beauty and deformity, they be founded entirely on the particular fabric and constitution of the human species.'[72] Hume here neatly summarises a variety of options, but in so far as the theories described are not dormant yet, they exemplify potential challenges to theological ethics with which Christian ethicists would do well to wrestle. In particular, we seem here to be verging upon territory which, theologically, impinges upon the doctrines of creation and humanity. How do these bear up in face of the ethical alternatives outlined by Hume? As for some philosophers nearer our own time, do Christian ethicists need to be concerned about the seemingly endless debate, of which H. A. Pritchard's article, 'Does moral philosophy rest on a mistake?' was the catalyst, over the question whether reasons can be given for our acting in ways we feel obliged to act, or whether, as he thought, the intuitionist position was correct, namely, that 'The sense of obligation to do, or of the rightness of, an action of a particular kind is absolutely underivative or immediate.'[73] And ought not Christian ethicists to probe the often tacit metaphysics, whether positivist, naturalist, deconstructionist, of those who overtly oppose metaphysics and claim personal freedom from it? So many other questions might be posed: 'Is God's love necessarily expressed as a moral requirement on all occasions?' 'Are the actions of Christians distinct from those of others, and if so, in which ways?' This last question takes us back to the matter of ethical common ground which I found Robin Gill posing at the outset of this paper. I cannot pursue these questions here, but trust that I have succeeded in providing pertinent examples of those metaphysical enquiries which ought to be the stock in trade of the Christian ethicist.

I come, fourthly and finally, to the challenge posed to Christian ethicists by the analytical philosophy of recent decades. It will be clear by now that my suggestions do not fall within categories which are mutually exclusive; and certainly this concluding suggestion, concerning the challenge to adequate conceptual analysis, ought to be practised by Christian ethicists whatever their special fields of interest. I can do no more than randomly illustrate the need for this metaethical, work. The need is as likely to arise from the writings of other

---

[72] D. Hume, *Enquiries Concerning Human Understanding and Concerning the Principles of Morals*, eds L. A. Selby-Bigge and P. H. Nidditch, Oxford: The Clarendon Press, 1975, 170.

[73] H. A. Prichard, 'Does moral philosophy rest on a mistake?' *Mind*, 1912; reprinted in his posthumous *Moral Obligation and Duty and Interest*, London: CUP, 1968, 7.

ethicists as from the discourse of Christians who are not professional ethicists. Thus, from professionals come such statements as the following: 'There is no room in morality for commands, whether they are the father's, the schoolmaster's, or the priest's. There is still no room for them when they are God's commands.'[74] Graeme de Graff's point is that if we substitute obedience to orders for morality we no longer have morality. But what if I *ought* to obey a command and freely choose the path of obedience? Again, when James Gustafson expounds his concept of moral fittingness and asks, 'What is God enabling and requiring us, as participants in the patterns and processes of interdependence of life in the world, to be and to do?'[75] we need to ask what is the analysis of 'God's enabling and requiring', and of 'the patterns and processes of interdependence of life in the world'? When these questions have been answered we then need to ask how far such patterns and processes can be the basis of ethical discernment. The importance of this analytical work — and Gustafson himself patiently undertakes the task — is clear, for if we wish to claim that Christian ethical judgments are susceptible to truth or falsity we must at the very least be clear what the terms in which they are expressed mean or refer to. On the other hand if we were to remove Christian ethical judgments from the sphere of the true or the false, we should at the very least need to show what functions we take them to serve in our discourse. Quite apart from judgments, there is a wide range of Christian ethical assertions which are made by professionals and others alike, which employ such terms as sin, grace, redemption, holiness. There is much analytical work to be done on these. But we should not confine ourselves to the *quasi*-technical terms of Christian ethical discourse. Very often the most intriguing cases are those in which an everyday term, like 'guidance', consorts with a theological term, like 'Holy Spirit'. I conclude this section by illustrating the point.

In an illuminating paper I. John Hesselink writes on 'Governed and guided by the Spirit. A key issue in Calvin's doctrine of the Holy Spirit'. He presents Calvin as teaching that over and above Scriptural injunctions and the role of Christ as model, 'Calvin submits that we are given not only faith and assurance by the Holy Spirit but also both general and specific wisdom and direction for our lives quite apart from any explicit instruction in the Scriptures or preaching of the gospel. In short, the Spirit at times gives seemingly independent and secret guidance. The Spirit gives a sort of suprarational insight and

---

[74] Graeme de Graaff, 'God and morality,' in *Christian Ethics and Moral Philosophy*, ed. I. T. Ramsey, London: SCM Press, 1966, 34.

[75] James M. Gustafson, *Ethics from a Theoretical Perspective. II Ethics and Theology*, Chicago: University of Chicago Press, 1984, 146.

understanding'.⁷⁶ What are we to make of the notion of the guidance of the Spirit — a notion with significant ethical implications?

I once heard a retired army officer testify to the effect that when on one occasion he was in utter moral perplexity, the Holy Spirit came like a dove, rested upon his shoulder, and whispered guidance into his ear. This was recounted as if it were a matter of straightforward fact. It was intended as an empirical claim. But would the most sophisticated photographic equipment have produced an image of the Spirit, or the most advanced recording device have reproduced the whisper? If not, the officer's claim is more complicated than he appeared to think.

It seems to me that if we would understand the claim of another to the effect that on such and such an occasion he or she was guided by the Holy Spirit ' we must attend to the world view — that conglomeration of biblical, confessional and experiential standpoints and attitudes — against the background of which the person speaks. Even then, we still have to analyse 'guidance' in this context. It will become clear that the analogy of guide dog and blind person will not do, for the Spirit is said to be personal. The image of a man with a lamp standing on the shore in a dark night, guiding a boat to harbour is nearer the mark, but the factor of distance is disruptive, for the Spirit is said to be within. The picture of an experienced mountain guide roped to a novice is better in so far as it emphasises the dependence of the novice, the closeness of the relationship, the frequent difficulty of the path to be traversed. But these analogies will always operate at one remove from the alleged reality which they purport to illuminate, and none of them is entirely satisfactory. They may, however, be, the best the Christian can manage in a situation in which the guidance spoken of is by definition supernatural. In any case, the proof of the pudding will be found in what the Christian does with the guidance he or she claims to have received.

The plot thickens when the Holy Spirit appears to offer different guidance to different Christians — over pacificsm, teetotalism, the appropriate political party. the propriety of the ecumenical movement, and other such boulders in the Christian ethical millpond. Ought Christians to claim absolute certainty in these matters? How far is it possible to mistake the Spirit's guidance? What seems clear on the basis of traditional logic, and on the theological assumption that the Spirit does not speak with a forked tongue, is that if Christian A says 'The Spirit has advised me that pacifism is the only proper option for Christians in the time of war,' while Christian B says 'The Spirit has advised me that pacifism is not the only proper option for Christians in time of war' both maybe mistaken as to the

---

⁷⁶ I. John Hesselink, 'Governed and guided by the Spirit. A key issue in Calvin's doctrine of the Holy Spirit,' in *Reformiertes Erbe. Festschfift für Gottfried W. Locher zu seinem 80. Geburtstag*, eds H. A. Oberman *et al*, Zürich: Theologischer Verlag, 1992, II, 163.

Spirit's actual view, one or the other may be mistaken, but they cannot both accurately be expressing the Spirit's mind.[77]

Again, what of the situation in which A, B, C, and D all decide to perform the same action, but A attributes his decision to the guidance of the Holy Spirit, B to the guidance of spirit doctors, C to the guidance of the stars, and D to the fact that he had a hunch that it was the right thing to do? Can all of these attributions be correct? Do the first two assertions properly refer? How might the third claim effectively be countered? Is the fourth claim adequate as an explanation? If we were to say that they are all meaningful locutions when placed within a coherent world view, what of the fact that numerous coherent systems might be devised which were entirely imaginary? If we wished to say that one only of A, B, C and D is uttering a true proposition, on what basis should we make our choice? Would our judgment be in the nature of a leap of faith? Would it be based upon an appeal to authority? But if it were either of these the line of questioning would simply be moved one step further back, and the viability of faith claims and of authorities would now be at issue. Or should we privatize truth along the line that that is true' which is true *for me* — taking in our stride the breakdown of rational discussion and the anarchy which might then ensue? Or should we save ourselves a great deal of trouble by opting for a species of postmodernism, thereby obviating the necessity of the rational grounding of ethical decisions altogether? You can readily see how much more of this kind of fun can be had in Christian ethics; but I must close.

III

Christian ethics is a growth area, of that there is no doubt. It also displays certain characteristics of a bomb site. In this paper I have suggested that as well as sitting with scientists, medical personnel, lawyers, economists and others, it would serve Christian ethics well if more of its practitioners sat more regularly with moral philosophers. It is legitimate to maintain that Christian ethics are theological ethics, but illegitimate to construe this as meaning that they are isolated from all other ethical thinking. In the ever-changing intellectual context the relations between Christian ethics and moral philosophy require ever fresh examination. If theology and ethics are distinct yet clearly related, it is also true that non-theological ethics is entirely viable, and that morally inadequate theology needs to hear and to heed its challenge. The metaphysical underpinnings of Christian ethics require constant exploration, while the critical

---

[77] For these remarks upon guidance, I plunder and modify a few pages in my Nottingham University doctoral thesis of 1967.

analysis of Christian ethical presuppositions and discourse — both in its more technical and its more popular forms — is something continually needed.

I do not, of course, deny the urgency of socio-ethical questions. We must not press the theoretical-applied distinction too far. But while some are delivering themselves upon fashionable topics in glamorous televisual contexts, we need to ensure the preservation of that threatened species, the Christian ethical theorist. With which ecological consideration I desist, lest this 'impractical' divine become far too useful!

CHAPTER 10

Reformed Theology : Whence and Whither?

The term 'Reformed theology' is slippery indeed. Some know only too well what it means – it is encapsulated in the five points of Dort, for example – and they measure all claimants to the description 'Reformed' against their chosen doctrinal criterion. Others, many Lutherans among them, profess to find the Reformed family puzzling because, in contrast the unifying force of the *Augsburg Confession*, the Reformed have many confessions – indeed, in some quarters they are still writing them; and the way in which they are held varies from the most casual acknowledgement that, as it happens, these documents are part of the heritage, to sincere and lively attachment to the *Helvetic, Belgic* or *Westminster Confessions*, and to the *Heidelberg* or *Westminster Catechisms*. It further transpires that while some non-Reformed Christians – notably a percentage of Baptists and Anglicans – understand themselves as embracing Reformed theology, some theologians who are Reformed in terms of ecclesiastical allegiance may be far from the stricter sect of Calvin's sons and daughters. There are nowadays Reformed scholars, whether biblical or philosophical or church historical, from whose works one would not – indeed, should not – be able to infer their confessional allegiance simply because that issue is not germane to the practice of their discipline; and there are also Reformed Christians who, having imbibed certain church growth principles, hide their confessional lights under such bushels as those proclaiming 'Community Church' in order not to dissuade the sensitive or leave the child care facilities and gymnasia, whether physical or emotional, empty.

The Term 'Reformed' as descriptive of a Christian world communion is equally puzzling to many. Whether we think in terms of doctrines espoused, attitudes to Scripture, ways of worship, church order and polity, the Reformed family as it actually exists is diverse. It has spawned upholders of the penal substitutionary theory of the atonement and convinced Abelardians; biblical inerrantists and the most liberal of biblical critics; its worship is on a continuum with exclusive unaccompanied psalmody at one end and the Disney-style celebrations of the Crystal Cathedral at the other; in some parts there are ministers and deacons; in others ministers, elders and deacons; in still others, ministers, elders, deacons and doctors, to which, in Hungarian-speaking circles are added bishops; there are churches which espouse a consistorial polity, others which are congregational in government, and some in which the two styles are blended. Some Reformed churches are free churches, others are established churches, some, whether established or free, are the folk churches of their region.[1]

Confronted by such incontestable facts, Reformed Christians may be inclined to grope for some such poetic phrase as 'a richly variegated tapestry.' If, on the other hand, there existed any Reformed Christians of a cynical turn of mind, they might be tempted to wonder, 'At what point does a richly variegated tapestry become a dog's breakfast?' Rather than resorting to the wanton use of labels, I prefer to try, in a discriminating way, to ask, What are some of the factors which have brought us to our present position?

The first claim I wish to make is that there has been theological variety within the Reformed family since its inception. This is not unconnected with the fact that one of the advantages of the family is that it is not named after anyone. From the outset a variety of pastors and theologians were reflecting on the Bible in relation to their understanding of the Gospel and the circumstances in which God had placed them. Nor should we forget that 'the outset' is not a date in the sixteenth century, but encompasses the 'first Reformation' associated with such names as Valdes and Hus, to whom look back, respectively, the Waldensians of Italy and the Evangelical Church of Czech Brethren. The first Reformation emphasis upon the Sermon on the Mount and the life of Christian simplicity flowed down and mingled with the theological contributions of Zwingli, Calvin, Knox, Bucer, Farel, Bullinger, Viret, Beza and Ursinus, all of whom were singing in the same choir if not taking exactly the same part. To these we must add (to mention only the most significant) John Owen in England, Jonathan Edwards in North America, and the 'father of modern theology', Schleiermacher, in Germany.

Many of these theologians were involved in drafting and publishing confessions of faith – more than sixty in the sixteenth century alone. While the early confessions display a considerable degree of unity – an unsurprising fact given the commuting between Reformed centres, and the ability of all to consult through the medium of Latin – there were significant confessional variations as time went on. The *Westminster Confession's* affirmation of the federal theology was suggested by contextual considerations prevailing at the time of its composition, while the Congregationalists of the *Savoy Declaration* (1658), who adopted the bulk of Westminster, nevertheless thought it appropriate to add a paragraph in which, over against hyper-Calvinism, they advocated the

---

[1] On Reformed variety see further, Alan P. F. Sell, 'The Reformed family today: some theological reflections,' in Donald K. McKim, ed., *Major Themes in the Reformed Tradition*, Grand Rapids: Eerdmans, 1992, 433–41. For empirical evidence see Jean-Jacques Bauswein and Lukas Vischer, eds., *The Reformed Family Worldwide*, Grand Rapids: Eerdmans, 1999.

proclamation of the Gospel to all.² A later dispute over this latter point lasted for about two hundred years (echoes of it may be heard to this day in certain circles), and Reformed protagonists were to be found on both sides: the Presbyterian turned Independent Joseph Hussey being staunchly opposed to the free offer, and Ralph Wardlaw, the Scottish Congregationalist in favour of it, for example.³ As for the confessions which the Reformed family has produced in the second half of the twentieth century, the term 'predestination' is generally conspicuous by its absence, and in a number of declarations the concept is not present; the Pope is no longer branded Antichrist nor the Anabaptists anathematized; and the fragility of the created order, and peace and justice are among topics which many of today's confessors, unlike their predecessors, feel bound to emphasize in their confessions.⁴

The political circumstances of the time influenced not only the directions in which the Reformed movement spread, but the ecclesiastical shape it took. With some princes and dukes opting for Lutheranism, others for the Reformed way, it would have been difficult for the Reformed in continental Europe to have escaped baptism as established churchpeople. In any case, their experience of Anabaptists, some of whom were excitable enough, as well as of even wilder sectaries, made them psychologically unwelcoming to the free church idea. By contrast, in England and Wales non-Anglican Reformed Christians had no option but to work out their polity in face of an establishment which, to the early Separatists, spoke of nothing so clearly as Antichrist, and which to their less threatened successors seemed nevertheless to be a compromised Church, having one foot in Scripture, the other in a particular national constitution.

Among many social influences upon the Reformed tradition to which one might point are the changing ideas concerning slavery in the nineteenth-century, and concerning women in the later nineteenth and twentieth centuries. Thus far Reformed churches have universally embraced the former, whereas a continuing witness needs to be made to a number of Reformed churches regarding the latter. In both cases the Reformed, like other Christians, have found themselves having to catch up with the Gospel according to which all are

---

[2] *The Savoy Declaration of Faith and Order*, ed. A. G. Matthews, London: Independent Press, 1959, ch. 20.

[3] See J. Hussey, *God's Operations of Grace but no Offers of Grace*, 1707; R. Wardlaw, *Systematic Theology*, ed. James R. Campbell, 1857, II, 549. For this and related matters see Alan P. F. Sell, *The Great Debate. Calvinism, Arminianism and Salvation*, (1982), Eugene, Oregon: Wipf & Stock, 1998.

[4] See further A. C. Cochrane, *Reformed Confessions of the 16th Century*, Philadelphia: The Westminster Press, 1966; Lukas Vischer, ed., *Reformed Witness Today*, Bern: Evangelische Arbeitsstelle Oekumene Schweiz, 1982; Alasdair I. C. Heron, *The Westminster Confession in the Church Today*, Edinburgh: The Saint Andrew Press, 1982.

one in Christ; and their theologies – especially their doctrines of the church and the ministry – have had to be revised.[5]

Time would fail even to scratch the surface of the many factors in the intellectual environment which have resulted in theological adjustment. I think, for example, of a positive benefit of the Enlightenment – a phenomenon too easily lambasted by some theologians today who forget that God can work through Cyrus. We owe to the deists among others that protest in the interests of morality against God presented as a wrathful Father who could not be merciful until he had killed his obedient Son. Thus Thomas Paine refers to 'the outrage offered to the moral justice of God by supposing him to make the innocent suffer for the guilty, and the loose morality and low contrivance of supposing him to change himself into the shape of a man in order to make an excuse to himself for not executing his supposed sentence on Adam.'[6] It is not fanciful to suppose that McLeod's Campbell's insistence in *The Nature of the Atonement* (1856) that the first word of the Gospel is grace is at least an implicit endorsement of such charges, as well as a more general impetus towards the later nineteenth-century emphasis upon the Fatherhood of God which, when in some circles it was running out into a bland humanism, was corrected by P. T. Forsyth and others with the insistence that it is holy Fatherhood with which we have to do.[7]

The Romantic movement's influence, especially when coupled with post-Hegelian immanentist thought, likewise prompted significant changes in the formulation of Reformed theology. We may recall, for example, the Mercersburg theology of John Williamson Nevin and Philip Schaff, which did well to remind those who needed to be reminded that the Reformed share in the entire catholic heritage of Christian faith, and that the witness did not fizzle out at the end of the New Testament to be rekindled only at the Reformation;[8] but which tended

---

[5] It is only fair to point out that a number of the Reformed churches which do not yet ordain women are inhibited by cultural rather than biblical or theological considerations. This does not, of course, alleviate the pain of those women who, in the churches concerned, feel called to ministry. Some of these churches have yet to reach their centuries. It ill behoves us, who took nineteen-hundred years to brace ourselves to ordain women to wax too impatient with our friends, though we ought continually to encourage them to see what we have belatedly tumbled to.

[6] T. Paine, *The Age of Reason*, (1794, 1796), London: Watts, 1938, 35.

[7] For Campbell see G. M. Tuttle, *So Rich a Soil. John McLeod Campbell on Christian Atonement*, Edinburgh: The Handsel Press, 1986. For Forsyth see Trevor Hart, ed., *Justice the True and Only Mercy. Essays on the Life and Theology of Peter Taylor Forsyth*, Edinburgh: T. & T. Clark, 1995; Alan P. F. Sell, ed., *P. T. Forsyth, Theologian for a New Millennium*, London: The United Reformed Church, 2000; and ch. 7 and 8 above.

[8] I like to think that this lesson has largely been learned, though as late as 1957 the philosopher and Anglican, H. A. Hodges, could write of the English Free Churches that among them 'there is no real awareness of anything in Christian history or tradition that is earlier than the sixteenth century.' See his *Anglicanism and Orthodoxy. A Study in Dialectical Churchmanship*, London: SCM Press, 1957, 29. The charge was too sweeping even when he wrote it.

to emphasize the organic model, the idea of continuity and the doctrine of the Incarnation to such an extent that sinful humanity's rescue at the Cross seemed to J. H. A. Bomberger and others in the German Reformed Church to be played down in a quite unPauline way.[9]

The rise of modern biblical scholarship was a further significant factor for theology at large, and for Reformed theology, with its formal elevation of the Bible as the supreme rule of faith and order, in particular. On the one hand it yielded the so-called Princetonian scholastics – Charles Hodge and Archibald Alexander, debtors to Turretin's *Institutio Theologiae Elencticae*, in which was propounded a doctrine of biblical inerrancy according to which the Bible is inerrant not only where doctrinal or moral matters are concerned, but also regarding 'statements of facts, whether scientific, historical, or geographical.'[10] Later versions of this theory, powerful to this day in some quarters, have been a ground of more than one inner-Reformed secession. On the other hand the new approach to Scripture yielded Robert Mackintosh, that delightfully sardonic self-styled refugee from the Free Church of Scotland to Congregationalism who, in a pamphlet provocatively entitled *The Obsoleteness of the Westminster Confession of Faith*, made merry with the proof texts which the Westminster divines were required to supply after the Confession was completed. At the end of a splendidly teasing paragraph he writes, 'Finally – and I specially recommend this to supporters of the Establishment principle – the proof that the civil magistrate may lawfully summon religious synods is found in the fact that Herod consulted the chief priests in order to plot more successfully how to murder the infant Jesus. Comment on these citations could be nothing but a feeble anti-climax. Let us treasure them up in our hearts.'[11]

Coming closer to our own time I simply list the way in which some have followed Barth, others Brunner on the issue of natural theology; the embracing by some theologians of the principles of process thought; the several contextual theologies – black, liberation, feminist, Minjung; the growth of conservative evangelical theology; and the concern of many for a theology of religions: all of these have, severally or in combination, been embraced by Reformed theologians among others, and as a result recastings of Reformed theological positions, ranging from the subtle to the violent, have been proposed. So much,

---

[9] See further, Alan P. F. Sell, *Commemorations. Studies in Christian Thought and History*, Calgary: University of Calgary Press and Cardiff: University of Wales Press, 1993; Eugene, OR: Wipf & Stock, 1998, ch. 11.

[10] C. Hodge, *Systematic Theology*, New York: Scribners, 1871, I, 163.

[11] R. Mackintosh, *The Obsoleteness of the Westminster Confession of Faith*, bound with his *Essays Towards a New Theology*, Glasgow: Maclehose, 1889, 48. I am pleased to observe that some years after I attempted a 'resurrection' for Mackintosh (*Robert Mackintosh, Theologian of Integrity*, Bern: Peter Lang, 1977), his works are beginning to be cited by other scholars – for example, by Dale A. Johnson, *The Changing Shape of English Nonconformity 1825–1925*, New York: OUP, 1999.

very sketchily, for the 'Whence' of my title. What, now, of the 'Whither'? I shall make three points each of which encompasses a positive declaration and one or more cautionary words.

I

First, as we go forward we should do well to remember that Reformed theology is catholic in intention, but ever at risk of affording hospitality to the sectarian demon. A moment ago I spoke of recastings of Reformed theological positions. But what are these positions? Whatever they are, they are not positions which are exclusively the possession of the Reformed. For Reformed theology is catholic in intention. The Reformers did not set out to devise novel sets of doctrines, or to invent new churches. Rather their objective was to reform the one Church according to the Word of God. The unity of the Church is God's gift to his people.[12] It is the possession of those who are 'in Christ', who 'abide in Christ,' who are branches of the vine, saints by calling, limbs of the body of Christ, members of the household of faith, the priesthood of believers.[13] The classical Reformed confessions bear witness to this fact, and Dr. Krafft summed up their testimony in a paper submitted to the First General Presbyterian Council in these terms:

> We acknowledge and confess one Catholic or Universal Church, which is a communion of all believers, who look for their whole salvation in Jesus Christ alone, who are cleansed by his blood, and sanctified by his Spirit; that his holy Church is confined to no special place, or limited to special persons, but is scattered over the whole earth, and yet is united in one and the same spirit by the power of faith.[14]

I should myself prefer to say that the Church is united by the grace and calling of God, to which our faith is the enabled response; and I miss here a reference to the Church triumphant in heaven. But that the Reformed have traditionally conceived of the Church as catholic is quite clear. Turning to our own century, we find that the same point is made in *A Declaration of Faith* (1967) of the Congregational Church in England and Wales:

> We worship God through Jesus Christ within the Christian Church. This Church is the whole company of believers, drawn from all humanity

---

[12] See further Alan P. F. Sell, 'Reformed identity: a non-issue of catholic significance,' *Reformed Review*, LIV no. 1, Autumn 2000, 17–27; idem, *A Reformed, Evangelical, Catholic Theology. The Contribution of the World Alliance of Reformed Churches, 1875–1982*, (1991), Eugene, OR: Wipf and Stock, 1998, ch. 3.

[13] II Cor. 5: 19; John 15: 5; Rom. 1: 7; I Cor. 12: 27; Gal. 6: 10; Eph. 2: 19; I Pet. 2: 5, 9.

[14] *Report of the Proceedings of the First General Presbyterian Council*,Edinburgh: Thomas and Archibald Constable, 1877, 46.

> irrespective of nation, colour, race or language ... The Church is founded upon Jesus Christ ... God creates the Church to be one, holy, catholic and apostolic ...[15]

To say that the Reformed affirm the catholicity of the Church does not mean that there are no doctrinal emphases which the Reformed have traditionally wished to make.[16] Over and above their witness to the general Reformation watchwords, Grace alone, Faith alone, Christ alone, Scripture alone, the Reformed have emphasised the initiative of God and the work of the Spirit in salvation, the sovereignty and providence of God, the inescapability of the Church and the necessity of its right ordering, the true presence of Christ at his Supper, and the work of the exalted Christ as prophet, priest and king. But they have propounded these teachings not because they believed that they were in some exclusive sense Reformed, but because they regarded them as important, and in some quarters overlooked, aspects of catholic truth given in Scripture.

To return for a moment to the Congregationalists of 1967: having affirmed the catholicity of the Church, they go on at once to say that 'the Church as Christians know it is not yet as God would have it be ... '.[17] Such statements of the obvious have not always characterized Reformed confessions, but they are none the less true. The empirical Church, as is well known, is riddled by sectarian division; we do not appear to be, in Paul's words, 'one person in Christ Jesus.'[18] The question of the degree of doctrinal or ethical tolerance properly to be allowed within the Church is one which has perplexed the Church in every generation; friction has been caused, parties have been formed, secessions have taken place. For their part the Reformed in various times and places have not been slow to detect the sectarian spirit in Christians of other traditions. If the Pope thinks that he must not accept invitations to the Lord's Table in our churches, we say that is because he espouses a sectarian doctrine of ministry and sacraments; if a high Anglican ecumenical drafter proposes a fudge which will enable those who wish to believe that re-ordination is occurring when the overall desire is to reconcile ministries, we say that he is a sectarian; if a Strict and Particular Baptist bars us from communion because we have not been immersed, we say the same thing. How easy it is to see when others are being sectarian!

The sad truth is that the Reformed harbour a sectarian demon in their own bosom. Our history is full of examples of inner-family division. Time would fail

---

[15] *A Declaration of Faith*, London: Congregational Church in England and Wales, 1967, 26–7.

[16] See further, for example, John H. Leith, *Introduction to the Reformed Tradition: A Way of Being the Christian Community*, Richmond, VA: John Knox Press, 1977; Donald K. McKim, 'The "heart and center" of the Reformed Faith,' *Reformed Review*, LI no. 3, Spring 1988, 206–19.

[17] Ibid., 27.

[18] Gal. 3: 28.

me to tell of the Relief Church, the Reformed Presbyterians, the Old Light Burghers, the New Light Burghers, the Old Light Antiburghers and the New Light Antiburghers, all of whom, together with those who departed during the 'Lifter controversy' of 1783, were separately active in Scotland during the eighteenth century; and it is almost impossible to keep up with the Presbyterians of South Korea who, when last I enquired, were to be found in approximately one hundred denominations. It is also true that within the Reformed family there have been occasions of ecclesiastical healing, and there are even some transconfessional unions in which those of the Reformed heritage share. Neither do I deny that very often those who have led secessions have been in effect, and sometimes quite vociferously, passing judgment upon a church deemed to have gone off the doctrinal rails or fallen into non-evangelistic slumber. But there have also been occasions when the sectarian spirit, which unchurches those who do not adhere to our way of expressing the truth, has prevailed. Not indeed that secession is the necessary consequence of the sectarian spirit: in a way it is more painful when it is not. Thus, in our own time we have caucuses and politicized pressure groups within churches which can seem on occasion to elevate their particular way of doing theology, or their preferred set of ethical stances above the Gospel which has made us one, so that if we do not all look exactly up their periscope we are somehow traitors to the cause or less than *bona fide* believers. This is the Galatian heresy, and it is sad.[19] It is my conviction that our favoured ways of worship, our church polities, our doctrinal convictions, and our ethical stances may not be raised to the position of principles on the basis of which we exclude from fellowship any who sincerely confess the Lordship of Christ. So to wield them would be legalistically to elevate our customs, formulae and behaviour above the Gospel of God's grace, and to divide those whom God has already made one in Christ.

Where the Reformed sectarian prescibing of doctrine is concerned I often feel that if those who claimed to stand to strongly by the confessions would only read some of the prefaces to the confessions, where the authors profess themselves open to change if any can show how they have departed from Scripture, they would understand that even the authors realised that they were *interpreting* Scripture – what else could they do? What else can any of us do? Again, there is a moral in the way God teased his Presbyterians of Old Dissent in England and Wales during the eighteenth century. For a variety of reasons – the fact that their forebears had been the majority party among those who compiled the Westminster Confession notwithstanding – most of them had become

---

[19] See further, Alan P. F. Sell, *Aspects of Christian Integrity*, ch. 4; idem, Commemorations, ch. 2; 'Reformed Identity.'

unitarian by the century's close.[20] To repeat, when once we fall into the trap of thinking that people are saved by adherence to our confessional formulae, or that confessions as such guard the faith, we have left saving grace behind, and have fallen into a new legalism; and if on this basis we proceed to unchurch others, or withhold fellowship from them, we have adopted a posture which is clearly sectarian in spirit and in result. For making this point so strongly, some of the Arian Presbyterian divines of the eighteenth century, so frequently maligned for their doctrinal conclusions, deserve our gratitude. Said one of them, John Taylor of Norwich, 'a popish, anti-Christian Spirit I will ever oppose, as God shall enable me'[21] – and he said it not against Rome, but in opposition to the Independent James Sloss of Castle Gate church, Nottingham, who wished a church member, Joseph Rawson, who was accused of consorting with 'heretics', to answer a test question couched in orthodox trinitarian terms. Rawson replied in biblical terms, but this was deemed insufficient, so the church meeting banished him from the Lord's Table. When he resolved to present himself at communion in any case he was threatened with civil action. John Taylor rose in defence of freedom of conscience and in opposition to the 'popish' imposition by dissenters of credal tests.[22]

But even if we take the point concerning the peril of elevating our formulae above the Gospel, we are not yet out of the wood. The following words of the Unitarian Joseph Priestley will help me make to the point. He writes in 1783:

> ... though the *Calvinistic Dissenters* are frequently losing the younger, the more thoughtful and inquisitive part of their congregations, numbers of the more illiterate people are continually joining them; and societies of *Calvinistic Baptists* are readily formed, and easily extend themselves; so that of late years their numbers are very considerably increased. This is, in some measure, owing to the zeal of those who hold such tenets; a zeal which is easily accounted for, from the stress which they have been led to lay upon them; imagining that men's future happiness depends upon their holding the right faith: whereas the *Rational Dissenters* do not think that the future state of any man will depend upon his opinions, but only on his disposition of mind and his conduct of life. They have, therefore, naturally less zeal for all matters of opinion than the Calvinists have, and for the same reason they are less solicitous about making converts.[23]

To the extent that Priestley challenges those who think that salvation comes to others when their own set of tenets, expressed in their way, is embraced, he

---

[20] For an attempt to tell this complicated tale see Alan P. F. Sell, *Dissenting Thought and the Life of the Churches. Studies in an English Tradition*, San Franciso: Edwin Mellen Press, 1990, ch. 5.

[21] J. Taylor, *A Further Defence of the Common Rights of Christians*, 1738, 78.

[22] See further, Alan P. F. Sell, *Dissenting Thought*, ch. 7.

[23] *The Theological and Miscellaneous Works of Joseph Priestley*, ed. J. T. Rutt, 1817–1831, XXI, 480.

underlines the point I have been trying to make. But when he says that a person's future state turns upon disposition of mind and conduct of life, he might seem to be sitting loose to the question of truth. Does it matter what we believe so long as we are of a pleasing mental disposition and act morally? Priestley, of course, thinks it does matter greatly: not for nothing did he resent the way in which some were lumping Unitarians together with deists. But he could more easily assume widespread faith in God and the desirability of commitment to Jesus (however understood) than we can. Hence for us his words taken just as they stand, when transposed into our present-day context, pose clamantly the question of truth.

I conclude this section with two further remarks concerning Reformed catholicity. First, when we articulate our catholic theology in dialogue with Christian traditions other than our own we frequently find that a helpful way of approaching classical doctrinal disputes is to ask, 'In expressing things as they did, what were the "other side" trying to guard against?' Thus, for example, the evangelical Arminians of the eighteenth century stoutly opposed a Calvinist scholasticism according to which human salvation was resolved into a matter of God's eternal, inscrutable will. Where is grace? they properly enquired. Positively, they wished to assert the importance of the human being's free response to that same grace. On the other hand, the Calvinists wished to exalt God's sovereignty in salvation, and loathed any position which seemed to suggest that God cannot quite save us unless we give him permission, or otherwise assist by an act of decision. The international Reformed-Methodist dialogue commission concluded that both had a point, that the dire perils perceived on both sides were rightly to be avoided, and that this hoary dispute, while people may still sincerely take up either side of it, should no longer be regarded as church dividing. The commission's report declares that 'we have found that the classical doctrinal issues we were asked to review ought not to be seen as obstacles to unity between Methodists and Reformed.'[24]

Two other international dialogues between the Reformed and others have reached similar conclusions following the discussion of hitherto neuralgic issuess. That with the Lutherans, building upon earlier consultations in Europe and the United States declares that 'nothing stands in the way of church fellowship,' and that, accordingly, the way is clear for 'full puplit and altar/table fellowship, with necessary mutual recognition of ministers ordained for word

---

[24] *Reformed and Methodists in Dialogue. Report of the Reformed/Methodist Conversations (1985 and 1987)*, Geneva: World Alliance of Reformed Churches, 1988, 14. Among other papers contributed to these coversations are Geoffrey Wainwright, 'Perfect salvation in the teaching of Wesley and Calvin,' in idem, *Methodists in Dialog*, Nashville: Kingswood Books, 1995, ch. 8; Alan P. F. Sell, 'Some reflections on Reformed-Methodist relations,' in idem, *Dissenting Thought and the Life of the Churches*, ch. 21.

and sacrament';[25] while that with the Disciples of Christ affirms that 'there are no theological or ecclesiological issues which need divide us as churches.'[26] These developments, I suggest, ought to mean that when in the future systematic theologies are written by Reformed, Lutherans, Methodists and Disciples, account is taken of the positions reached. It too frequently happens that systematicians proceed in apparent ignorance of doctrinal steps taken by the traditons to which they belong. For example, we might expect that henceforth Disciples theologians will write ecclesiology in the light of the agreement that there can (and do) exist church orders in which both paedobaptism and believers' baptism are alternatively available.[27] Even if theologians should wish to protest that official dialogue reports of the kind to which I have referred have moral authority only, they ought at least to acknowledge their existence, expound their contents, and present grounds for disagreeing with them if that is their desire.

Secondly, by way of summary, I should like to quote my own attempted definition of catholicity:

> On the ground of the finished work of Christ the Son, the Father graciously and freely calls out by his Spirit a people for his praise and service; he enables their confession of Christ's Lordship and, in drawing them to himself, he gives them to one another in a fellowship in which all barriers of race, sex and class have been broken down; this people, whose membership encompasses heaven and earth, we call the Church catholic.[28]

II

My second affirmation is that as we go forward we should remember that Reformed theology has a comprehensive sweep in principle and manifests certain lacunae in practice. That is to say, the theological vision embraces the whole of life, whilst at the same time manifesting certain blind spots. I shall attempt to illustrate this claim by reference to practical theology, ethics and apologetics.

It is supremely in the practice of the liturgy of Word and sacrament that theology is anchored for the people of God as a whole. Here the Word is

---

[25] *Toward Church Fellowship. Report of the Joint Commission of the Lutheran World Federation and the World Alliance of Reformed Churches*, Geneva: LWF and WARC, 1989, 28.

[26] *Towards Closer Fellowship*, Geneva: World Alliance of Reformed Churches, 1988, 14.

[27] The international Baptist-Reformed dialogue invited the members of the Baptist World Alliance and the World Alliance of Reformed Churches to consider the possibility of such an order, grounded in a fresh understanding of the *process* of Christian initiation. See *Baptists and Reformed in Dialogue*, Geneva: WARC, 1984; Alan P. F. Sell, *A Reformed, Evangelical, Catholic Theology*, 142–6.

[28] Alan P. F. Sell, 'Reformed identity,' 19.

proclaimed in such a way that its claim on the whole of life is made plain; here sinners who are also saints by calling adjust their sights to the challenge of God's holy love, and, by the Spirit's help, resolve to amend their ways and engage with enthusiasm in God's mission. Here the saints offer praise and thanksgiving to the One who has so loved them. Even from this brief and incomplete statement of principle concerning worship as the *locus* of theology we can see that, for good or ill, what actually takes place in worship itself makes a theological statement.[29] Is the emphasis more upon sin than upon grace? Does the Good News which is proclaimed tell of an atonement which is open to us because it has first met the needs of God, or are we (perhaps sentimentally) led to think that the Cross concerns humanity – even me – alone? Is Christ presented primarily as teacher, master, elder brother, or saviour? Will the congregation perceive that the primary objective is to bring them into the presence of the holy one, or will they think that it is to make them feel good? Are the prayers the prayers of the people, or of the pastor? Do the hymns, taken altogether, tend in the direction of praising God or coddling us? Over the course of the weeks do we feel that we are being nurtured in holy living, equipped for mission, and prepared to face the issues of life – including death? Or is death something mentioned only at funeral services – by which time it is too late for the deceased? So one might go on; but enough has been said to indicate that as the gathering of the people under the Word of God, worship is a theological *locus*; and also that the content of worship, and the manner in which it is conducted together make a theological statement.[30]

I wish to pursue a little further a point I have just made – the one concerning the equipping of the saints for what used to be called a godly walk. My limited experience suggests that on the one hand many are craving for serenity, seeking guidance for life, desirous of 'finding themselves'. Hence courses on spirituality, the popularity of counselling sessions, and the like, many of which are quite unrelated to Christian theology (I do not adversely judge them, I simply state a fact). On the other hand we have the mushrooming of seminary courses in practical theology, many of which seem to be more practical than theological. I do not deny the usefulness of some of these. Depending upon one's context it may be very important to know something about survival techniques in the jungle; or how to create a website for your church; or (though this is not a problem which perplexes many British ministers) how to electronically tag the

---

[29] So, too, does the architectural setting of worship, where one of the challenges is to design and construct buildings which at one and the same time speak of the 'high and holy' one, and of the God in the midst of his people. Not, indeed, that there can be no worship without special buildings. But if we build the buildings they will 'say' something, and it is well that what they 'say' undergirds our theology.

[30] See further, Alan P. F. Sell, *Aspects of Christian Integrity*, 142 ff.

church's children lest they get lost on, or are illicitly enticed from, the church campus. Again, it can be informative and instructive – even at times necessary – to reflect upon the impact of Romanticism on nineteenth-century hymnody, or to inquire into the doctrine of humanity which is presupposed by the counselling techniques of Carl Rogers.

My point is that, perhaps aided and abetted by ideas concerning the professionalization of the ministry, the mushrooming and modularization of theological courses, and the laicizing of theological education, there is in many quarters – not least Reformed ones – a bifurcation between systematic-cum-doctrinal theology and practical theology. Similarly, there has grown up a bifurcation between systematic-cum-doctrinal theology and Christian ethics. As far as I have been able to discover the latter began in England in the eighteenth century, when Henry Grove, the Dissenting academy tutor at Taunton, separated ethics from dogmatics in the curriculum of the academy.[31] In view of such current pressing issues as third world debt, genetic engineering and the like, it is not surprising that there is intense and frequently highly-specialized activity in the field of applied ethics – sometimes at the expense of consideration of the presuppositions of Christian ethics and of the analysis of the logic of Christian ethical utterance.[32] But ought not the Reformed ideals of theological comprehensiveness and a Gospel for the whole of life prompt us to query such bifurcations at the level of underlying principle? Certainly within our own tradition – especially in the Puritan parts of it, we have some models to challenge and help us. It is quite clear that when the Puritans and those in their tradition wrote their bodies of practical divinity, they were under no illusion that they were writing manuals on how to shoe a horse, helpful though such knowledge may have been. Rather, in many cases the same divines who could see off Arminianism or antinomianism or Socinianism or deism to their own satisfaction could also offer such works as *A Lifting up for the Downcast* (William Bridge, 1648), *Precious Remedies against Satan's Devices* (Thomas Brooks, 1652), and *The Saint's Everlasting Rest* (1650). The last, by the seventeenth century's Reformed pastor par excellence, Richard Baxter, epitomises the seamless robe of biblical-cum-doctrinal-cum-pastoral theology. These divines could encourage the saint, reprove the sinner, handle topics such as guilt and assurance, and write at length on the nature of, and resources for, the godly walk. Of course they did not have to reckon with modern biblical criticism. They could make assumptions which we no longer can. But the questions press: Have we lost the skill? Have we lost the language? Have we lost the experiences? To the extent that we have lost these, does it matter? I suggest that it does if it is the

---

[31] See Alan P. F. Sell, *Dissenting Thought and the Life of the Churches*, ch. 6; ch. 5 above.
[32] See ch. 9 above.

theologian's task to be first a servant of the Word of God and secondly one who can encourage the saints to live their lives in the presence of God.

But as well as loving God with heart and soul and strength, Christians are challenged to love him with all their mind. In the nineteenth century the Reformed were to the fore in Christian apologetics – not least in Scotland. Flint, Bruce, Iverach, Orr – these are just a few of the theologians who were engaged in coming to terms with agnosticism, materialism, naturalism, evolutionary thought, and idealistic philosophy, and all against the background of modern biblical criticism and the devastation by Hume and Kant of the classical theistic arguments.[33] I have elsewhere gauged the swift demise of such apologetic activity by reference to the concerns of the World Presbyterian Alliance and the International Congregational Council (the forebears of the World Alliance of Reformed Churches, 1970) as expressed in their proceedings and other literature. Until about 1920 they frequently discussed their theology in relation to the intellectual climate of the day, but since that time this theme has been conspicuous by its absence from the literature.[34] It is partly that we are unsure where to start with those beyond our circles who are still sufficiently interested to ask for a reason for our hope. But it is partly that some of our giants have been telling us that the effort should not be made – cannot be made, with which conclusion, though on quite different grounds, many postmodernists are in hearty accord. At the heart of the problem is the question of starting points. For example (and here I must plead brevity as the excuse for crudity), if, as with Butler against the deists, we occupy the rationalistic ground of our opponents we shall not – as Butler himself fully realised[35] – be able to introduce certain considerations which are germane, even vital, to Christian faith. On the other hand, if we allow ourselves to become imprisoned in what has been called the circle of revelation, how shall we get out of it to meet enquirers at all? Is there what Mr. Tony Blair might call a third way? I very much hope so, not least because, in my now rather lengthy experience as an homiletic vagrant I find time and again that many of those still in the pews have questions concerning the faith which trouble them, and which they feel they cannot – or dare not – articulate either because they pick up no clues to suggest that their questions would receive adequate attention, or because they fear being slapped down by the godly on the ground of their alleged faithlessness. But not to address the honest intellectual concerns of the church member is a failure in practical theology; not to address the honest intellectual concerns of 'outside' critics

---

[33] See Alan P. F. Sell, *Defending and Declaring the Faith. Some Scottish Examples 1860–1920*, Exeter: Paternoster Press and Colorado Springs: Helmers & Howard, 1987.

[34] See *A Reformed, Evangelical, Cathloic Theology*, ch. 5 – the shortest main chapter.

[35] Joseph Butler, *The Analogy of Religion*, (1736), London: Ward Lock, n.d., 192.

whether hostile or benign, is a failure in mission. Not to consider the question of common ground – whether epistemological or ethical – on which we can stand with those who do not share our faith is a failure in ecumenism, the objective of which is the whole inhabited earth giving glory to God. I do not say that every Christian is competent to rise to the more technical aspects of these tasks – to say this is not to be élitist in a nasty sense, it is simply to recognize that there are diversities of gifts; but it would be reassuring to feel that church members might know who can handle such matters, just as they might know who has a pastoral ear, who can sing a solo, who can teach the young, who is good at flower arranging, who can maintain the churchyard; and it would be even more reassuring to feel that every church member felt able, when the opportunity arose, to speak with confidence, joy and humility of the things he or she has seen and heard.[36] Just as Calvin sought a Geneva reformed according to the Word of God, so many Reformed theologians properly emphasize that the eschatological vision is of the whole inhabited earth glorifying God. Accordingly, they heed their several contexts, they advocate the cause of the poor and the downtrodden, they seek justice for all and devote themselves to pressing ethical issues. If I am brief at this point it is simply because this kind of activity is not something to which we need to be recalled. I would simply utter the cautionary word that one of the ways of ensuring the rootage of such activity in the Gospel is to ask from time to time the questions, What do we do or say that rightminded humanists do not? Are our motivations identical with those of the Ethical Society? This is not to deny that we should, where issues of peace, justice, human need and the like are concerned, stand together with those whose beliefs may differ from our own. It is simply to invite Christians to reflect upon the ground and inspiration of their witness, and to relate their social action to their worship. As Nicholas Wolterstorff has written,

> It is because our fellow human beings are joined irrevocably with us in mirroring God's glory, especially God's wisdom and goodness, that we are to treat them with justice. But it is also God's glory, including God's wisdom and goodness, that grounds our worship with praise and adoration and blessing and thanksgiving. Worship and justice are thus joined in being two ways of acknowledging God's glory. So united are they, that to worship and not practice justice is to worship inauthentically ... and to practice justice and not worship is to practice justice inauthentically, or in blindness to God's glory all about us.[37]

---

[36] I have given some thought to the question of Christian apologetic method in a trilogy published in Cardiff by the University of Wales Press: *Philosophical Idealism and Christian Belief*, 1995; *John Locke and the Eighteenth-Century Divines*, 1997; *Confessing and Commending the Faith: Historic Witness and Apologetic Method*, 2002.

[37] N. Wolterstorff, 'Worship and justice,' reprinted in Donald K. McKim, ed., *Major Themes in the Reformed Tradition*, 316.

III

So to my third and final claim: as we go forward we should take full account of the fact that the Reformed have a theological method which is integrally related to their pneumatology and to their *completed* ecclesiology, but which is open to abuse in more than one way. The positive thesis is that at our best the Reformed have understood that the Word of God, which is addressed to the people of God, is discerned by the Spirit through the Bible within the fellowship of the Church. In this context 'the Church' embraces both the local fellowship and the heritage of faith to which it is heir.

In two directions at least that principle is vulnerable. First, in the course of our history wedges have sometimes been driven between Spirit, Bible and Church in such a way that we have spawned individualistic spirituals on the one hand and biblical fundamentalists on the other – neither of whom, have much of an eye to the fellowship as corporate hearer and student of God's Word. Secondly, in practice it has too frequently been only a part of the Church which has assumed the right to, or been expected to, discern the Word. With this I come to the explanation of my term 'completed ecclesiology': I do believe that through their study of the Bible in the context of their political situation, the English and Welsh orthodox Dissenters and their American heirs completed the polity of the Reformed tradition by embracing the whole people of God in the priestly governance of the body. Calvin, that is to say, left matters hanging with the elders and deacons; the Congregationalists and Particular Baptists rooted the polity in the whole people of God.[38] Hence the importance of Church Meeting, where, under the leadership of the one called to minister the Word and sacraments, the saints gather to acknowledge the Lordship of Christ over the entire life and witness of the church, and to seek unanimity (not majority rule) in him. There are problems here, of course. It is possible for the local churches to become isolationist and to elevate autonomy above the Gospel. But all church polities have their pitfalls – there can be heretical bishops, recalcitrant presbyteries and ungodly Church Meetings. But at their best these Calvinist-Puritan spirits knew that to be a member of the Church catholic is to be anchored as a member among the saints in a given place. Clearly, the polity turns upon knowing who the saints are. This has implications for ecclesiastical discipline – in many places today a lost art; but it also presupposes that there is a distinction of eternal significance between those who are in Christ and those

---

[38] See Alan P. F. Sell, *Saints: Visible, Orderly and Catholic. The Congregational Idea of the Church*, Geneva: World Alliance of Reformed Churches and Allison Park, PA: Pickwick Publications, 1986.

who are not.[39] Is this something which we still wish to maintain, or ought to maintain? Again, the polity implies an adverse criticism not only of the polity of the established Church of England but of continental Reformed state church polities as well. In a word, it is critical of lingering Constantinianism. While maintaining that Church and state have mutual obligations towards one another, it will not confuse their respective powers or suppose that the state can determine the worship, ordering and witness of the Church.[40] It cannot equate the concept of catholicity with that of ecclesiastical monopolism within a state. And it cannot allow that one becomes a Christian – still less one of a particular brand – simply by virtue of being born in a particular place. There are matters here which need urgent attention within the Reformed family, especially if we wish realistically to claim that ministry is the task of the whole people of God – that is, of the people of God as church,[41] and not just as individuals each shining in his or her corner and offering his or her talent; and if we believe, as I do, that theologizing is too important to be left to the theologians who, perhaps more than most, need the checks and balances supplied by the fellowship of saints. Moreover, if the Reformation was in part a protest against the peoples' having religion done to them by the priests, it is a poor exchange if in our circles they now have it done to them by the presbyteries – or even by autocratic 'princes of the pulpit.' Note that in none of this do I employ the language of democracy in the sense of 'one person, one vote' and government by the majority. My concern is with the lordship of Christ in his Church, and with the mutuality of *episcope as between the several foci* of churchly life.[42]

---

[39] In this connection it is interesting to note that unlike those who composed the sixteenth-century Reformed confessions, those who framed the *Westminster Confession* (followed largely by the Congregational *Savoy Declaration* of 1658 and the *Second London Confession* of 1677 and 1688 of the Particular Baptists) introduced a chapter on adoption. Though the majority of the Westminster divines were Presbyterians, it was the Particular Baptists and the Congregationalists who drew out the implications of adoption for polity.

[40] H. A. Hodges makes no bones about it. Writing of the English Reformation he declares, 'The continuation of the hierarchy, on which so much depends, was made possible by the co-operation of the Crown with the Church's leaders.' See his *Anglicanism and Orthodoxy*, 30. See Alan P. F. Sell, *Dissenting Thought and the Life of the Churches*, ch. 22; *Commemorations*, ch. 4; 'Reformed identity'; and ch. 11 below.

[41] The World Council of Churches document, *Baptism, Eucharist and Ministry*, Geneva: WCC, 1982, emphasizes the importance ministry of the whole people of God. However, relatively few churches make provision in their polity for the real participation of all members *together*. Some local churches belonging to traditions which might, historically, have been expected to do so have memberships so large that church meeting is a practical impossibility; elsewhere, where the excuse of numbers cannot be advanced, Church Meeting is, nevertheless, in too many cases moribund.

[42] See further, Alan P. F. Sell, *Commemorations*, ch. 14; idem, 'By the Spirit, through the Word, within the fellowship,' *Touchstone*, VI no. 3, September 1989, 33–41.

From the membership of the Church we may continue to hope and pray that there will be raised up those who shall teach the flock and educate the ministry. I cannot here embark upon the question of theological education,[43] but I should like to say that in addition to theological competence, professional theologians need two further things. First, the understanding that, as Forsyth put it, the theologian 'represents the rights of the laity. He defends their only *locus standi*. He stakes Christianity on something that can be verified not indeed by human nature, or by natural religion, but by a universal experience of grace, where preacher and theologian are all laymen, yet all experts, alike.'[44] Secondly, if theologians are to give God glory in their work – and this, I repeat, should be the primary objective of Reformed theologians – we need that humility which understands that we can take no credit for our message: we have received it as a gift of grace. Neither can we tie all the loose ends or devise the absolutely copper-bottomed theological system; for what we have received has come from One whose nature and love far surpass our powers of comprehension. Yet again, we see that theology is a great leveller. Which brings me back to where I started: Reformed theology is concerned with catholic truth; to this I now add that the students and practitioners of it are the Church catholic.

IV

Whence Reformed theology? I have attempted briefly to remind you of the diversity of the Reformed family's theological roots, and of the many ways in which our theological and doctrinal positions have been articulated in relation to political, social, intellectual and other influences. To such influences Reformed theologians have responded positively, or negatively, and with, or sometimes without, due discrimination.

Whither Reformed theology? It would be foolish to deny that there have been doctrinal emphases which have characterized the Reformed family, but I have suggested that in intention Reformed theology is catholic. At the same time our history is riddled with sectarianism which has frequently led to inner-family secessions. But the catholicity of our doctrines and of our ecclesiology ought to prompt us to work for the healing of the one body of Christ, ever remembering that ecumenism, like charity, begins at home. Furthermore, we ought, when doing our theological-ecumenical work, to draw upon those doctrinal accords which have been attained.

I next sought to show that, consistently with the comprehensive sweep of Reformed theology, Reformed theologians might give more thought in the

---

[43] For some reflections on this see ch. 1 above.
[44] P. T. Forsyth, *The Church, the Gospel and Society*, London: Independent Press, 1962, 80.

future to the Church's worship as a theological *locus,* and to the content and manner of worship as making a theological statement. Against this background further reflection might follow on the presuppositions of that godly living which is a response to the Gospel of God's grace, and on those apologetic questions which clamour for attention if we are to love God with all our mind. In both cases the question of common ground with those who do not hold our faith is clamantly raised.

Finally, I suggested that the Reformed have a theological method which is integrally related to their pneumatology and ecclesiology. It turns upon the conviction that we discern the mind of God (insofar as we do discern it) by the Spirit, through the Scriptures, within the fellowship of the Church. We are challenged, I think, to reflect further on this method; but, more importantly, to practise it. This means that we shall ensure that our polity facilitates the ministry of the whole people of God, a significant part of which ought to be their theologizing. In this connection I believe that the established church idea which is found in some parts of the Reformed family is a dissuasive, whereas the Congregational idea, properly practised and fertilized by consistorial arrangements adopted because they are right and not simply because they are useful, is a decided advantage. But the latter throws into relief the question, Who are the Church? When we think we know who they are, we can be waylaid into a falsely pietistic, isolationist ghetto; on the other hand, if we do not know who they are we face the possibility that the church has become so identified with the society in which it lives that it is quite unable to be either a witness or a prophet to it.

So much for some of the things Reformed theologians might be pondering in the coming years. As to the manner of our theologizing, allow me in conclusion to quote myself a second time:

> It is no bad thing for the Reformed, whose path has been strewn with intellectual battles within and without, to recall that the Bible says more about letting our light shine than about keeping our pencils sharp. No doubt the Reformed will ever wish to attend to the latter as a means to the former, but let them beware of sharp pencils and dim lights.[45]

---

[45] Alan P. F. Sell, 'The Reformed family today,' 441.

CHAPTER 11

The Dissenting Witness: Yesterday and Today[1]

I have sometimes half-jokingly said that in the unlikely event of my one day having a grave stone, I should like it to be inscribed thus: 'Minister of the Gospel', followed by a footnote numeral; and at the bottom: footnote one, 'Of the Dissenting sort'. My motive in this would not be querulous, but catholic. The argument of this present paper is that for the sake of ecumenism in this country the Dissenting witness needs to be made, heard and pondered, because it drives to the heart of the Gospel of God's free, Church-convoking grace. The aspect of that witness with which I am especially concerned here is the Dissenting testimony in regard to the establishment principle. I shall suggest that when the subject is raised at all today by members of the Church of England the main points are frequently missed or, if perceived at all, are silently shelved in the interests of sundry contextual matters, some of which can be dressed up theologically or missiologically, but which are not central; while on the other hand, Free Churchmen too easily come to think that the cause is won because they are permitted to bury their own dead and graduate from Oxbridge. (I am well aware of the variety of church establishments elsewhere in Europe, but in this paper I am concerned only with the sole Anglican establishment, namely, that of England).

The discussion of establishment has sometimes been referred to a future which never seems to come. Thus in a report on churchly reunion presented at the Fourth International Congregational Council in 1920 by a committee including such forward-looking stalwarts as S. M. Berry, A. E. Garvie and W. B. Selbie, we read that 'In all these discussions ... one element of difficulty seems to have been left out of account and will need to be reckoned with before any practical steps can be taken. We refer to the question of Establishment ... So far, the question has been shirked but it will need to be faced in the not very distant future.'[2] Sixty-four years on, in the report of the international bilateral dialogue between the Anglican Consultative Council and the World Alliance of Reformed

---

[1] An abbreviated version of this paper, 'Establishment as a theological issue: the Dissenting witness,' was published in *Theology*, CVI, July-August 2003, 237-49.

[2] *The influence of Congregationalism in promoting Christian unity, and the lines upon which it should use that influence*, in Proceedings of the Fourth International Congregational Council, 1920, 483.

Churches the establishment is cited as a matter requiring further attention, and is implicit in five of the appended questions for discussion.[3]

Against the background of such shelving it almost comes as a shock to observe the fairly large press which establishment has received during the last ten years, though it would be too much to claim that this renewed interest has had its origin either in Dissenting zeal or in broader ecumenical debate. The antics of some members of the royal family and the reform of the House of Lords seem to have been among the main efficient causes of debate. Nevertheless the matter is in the air, and it would seem that the views of some prominent Christians are moving relatively swiftly. Thus, for example, while in 1993 the then Archbishop of Canterbury was warning that disestablishment 'would take spirituality off the national agenda,' and in 1994 was declaring that establishment affords an opportunity for the Church 'to share the Christian faith with our nation and to be a service to people,' in 1999 he supported an ecumenical gathering at which establishment was aired, and in 2000 he declared that there is a 'real argument' to be pursued on the Church-state question.[4] Perhaps significantly, between the George Carey of 1993 and the George Carey of the turn of the century, the report of Churches Together in England, *Called to be One*, had declared, 'The issue of the effect of the establishment on the nature of the Church, and more particularly the establishment ethos and attitude, require further ecumenical discussion.'[5] Not, indeed, that all subsequent discussion has been ecumenical, as witness turn-of-the-century contributions to the Anglican journals, *Modern Believing* and *Theology*.[6]

Since the establishment question is now on the table it is appropriate that the Dissenting voice be heard. I believe that it would be a signal failure on the part of those who inherit the Dissenting tradition were they to remain silent at this juncture. But what ought they to say? The answer to this question will become clear if we remind ourselves briefly of the heritage of testimony which has been offered, however spasmodically and sometimes ambiguously, over the past 450 years. The period of time is significant, for when I speak of the Dissenting witness I am being quite precise. I refer to those whose *raison d' être* was evangelical and hence ecclesiological, and not to the broader ranks of Nonconformity in which stand the Methodists of the eighteenth, the Brethren and Salvation Army of the nineteenth, and the Pentecostal and black led churches of the twentieth centuries, all of whose original testimonies (however

---

[3] See *God's Reign and Our Unity*, London: SPCK and Edinburgh: The Saint Andrew Press, 1984, 7, 84.
[4] See reports in *The Observer*, 4 April 1993, 11; *The* Times, 11 July 1994, 2; The *Sunday Times*, 10 January 1999; *The Observer*, 24 December 2000, 2.
[5] *Called to be One*, London: CTE (publications), [1996], 12.
[6] Reference will be below made to some of these contributions.

much they may subsequently have aligned themselves with Dissent) were prompted by issues other than the nature of the Church, and none of whom have English martyrs directly in their memories.

I

By way of taking our bearings, let us hear Bernard Lord Manning who, almost seventy years ago to the day, referred to the English Baptists, Congregationalists and Presbyterians, and addressed the Protestant Dissenting Deputies in these terms:

> We of the Three Dissenting Bodies never 'left the Church.' From the moment when, at the Reformation, the mediaeval Church began to split up, there were churchmen who stood in this country for a Church after the Calvinistic pattern, and hoped to make such a Church the Church of England ... From the beginning of modern history we have put up an alternative notion of what the Church is, and what churchmanship is; and when in 1662 it became clear that we could not practise our churchmanship inside the Establishment we continued to practise it outside ... We still stand for that other conception of the Church, of the Ministry, of the Grace of God, and the Means of Grace: a conception (as we think) less legalistic and less Judaic than that of the Anglican body.[7]

Let us take a few soundings from the history by way of illustrating Manning's declaration.

We must first ask, What is that 'other conception of the Church? Quite simply, it is that the Church comprises the regenerate, the saints. Such are what the Separatist harbingers of Dissent and their heirs would have called 'the matter' of the Church.[8] John Robinson, the pastor to the Pilgrims, spoke for many when he said that the term *ecclesia* 'denoteth an assembly of persons called out of the state of corrupt nature into that of supernatural grace, by the publishing of the gospel.'[9] They have had 'faith and repentance wrought in them to the obtaining of forgiveness of sins, and promising of life eternal, and to sanctification and obedience.'[10] Note that in the first place the saints are called out of 'the world', not out of the Church of England. The clear implication of this is that one does not become a Christian by being born in a so-called Christian country. John Greenwood, one of the martyrs of 1593, made the point

---

[7] B. L. Manning, address of 4 November 1931, in *Essays in Orthodox Dissent*, (1939), London: Independent Press, 1953, 132-3.

[8] For the views of John Smyth the se-Baptist on this, see his *Works*, Cambridge: CUP, 1915, I, 253.

[9] J. Robinson, *Works*, ed. R. Ashton, London, 1851, III, 33. See further, R. Tudur Jones, *John Robinson's Congregationalism*, London: The Congregational Memorial Hall Trust, 1987.

[10] Ibid., II, 96.

clearly when arraigned before the Lord Chief Justices on 24 March 1588/89. The interrogation proceeded as follows:

> *Question*: Doe yow not hold a parish the church?
> *Answer*: If al the people were faithful, having God's law and ordinances practised amongst them, I doe.
> *Question*: Then yow hold that the parish doe not make it a church?
> *Answer*: No, but the profession which the people make.[11]

The point is underlined in a tract of 1588, which may have been jointly written by Greenwood and his fellow martyr, Henry Barrow:

> The true planted and rightlie established church of Christ is a companie of faithful people; separated from the unbelevers and heathen of the land; gathered in the name of Christ, whome they trulie worship, and redily obey as thier only king, priest and prophet; joyned together as members of one bodie; ordered and governed by such officers and lawes as Christ in his last will and testament hath thereunto ordeyned ... [12]

To the Separatist mind, the problem was that 'the world' had been allowed into the Church by law established: it was what they called a 'promiscuous company' of the saved and unsaved; wheat and tares were growing together in such a way that the Gospel could not but be compromised. As if this were not enough, the established Church was by definition one in which the laws of men compromised the law of God by presuming to order the Church, thereby constricting its full liberty under the Gospel. Concerning this liberty M. Dorothea Jordan wrote:

> The liberty which the first Independents preached was most certainly NOT based by them upon any theory that men have a natural right to worship GOD as they think fit – a doctrine of the later seventeenth century which would have amazed most sixteenth century Englishmen. Nor yet was it founded on faith in democracy, if democracy implies the right of an adult commuity to govern itself as it chooses. For the Independents of the first generation were quite as incapable as their compatriots of even conceiving such an idea: to them, as to practically every Englishman of their day, it came naturally to think and speak of 'the Prince' as the ruler of the State. It was no RIGHT to liberty, no RIGHT to become a member of a self-governing body, that they preached, but the DUTY of refusing a blind obedience to man which hampered the soul' s endeavour to learn and to do the will of Christ. The DUTY of living in subjection to the admonitions and censures of the

---

[11] Leland H. Carlson, ed., *The Writings of John Greenwood, together with the Joint Writings of Henry barrow and John Greenwood*, London: Allen & Unwin, 1962, 27. See further Alan P. F. Sell, *Saints: Visible, Orderly and Catholic. The Congregational Idea of the Church*, Geneva: World Alliance of Reformed Churches and Allison Park, PA: Pickwick Publications, 1986, ch. 2.

[12] Ibid., 98.

saints. Resistance to man was the outcome of the humbling desire to submit to Christ ... [13]

In a word, the Separatists could not accept with Whitgift and Hooker that the English Church was coterminous with the English nation, and hence that the state had any right to order the life and worship of the Church. As Robert Browne put it, the true Church is under 'the Lordshipp of Christ in the communion of his offices: wherby his people obey to his will, and haue mutual vse of their graces and callings, to further their godliness and welfare.'[14] The refrain echoes down the Dissenting ages. To R. W. Dale, the idea that 'The members of a Christian Church should be Christians ... was the *fons et origo* of the whole Congregational movement;'[15] or, in the words of Nathaniel Micklem, 'This ... sense of the utter and eternal difference between the man who is in Christ and the man who is not, gave to Browne, Greenwood and Barrow their high doctrine of the Church.'[16] As if recalling the Separatists' description of the Church of England as 'antichrist', W. B. Selbie, the second principal of Mansfield College, Oxford, waxed lyrical: 'Congregationalists have their own doctrine of the Church, a doctrine so high, so scriptural, and so inspiring, that beside it the idea of a State Church is like an evil dream.'[17]

It must be granted, however, that although the line so far expounded has become standard in Dissent, there has been ambiguity at certain points in the story.[18] As already indicated, Greenwood could have conceived of a parish-Church equation if all the parish had been godly. Again, while some Separatists eschewed all relations with the Church of England, others, among them Henry Jacob, were ready to grant that within that Church some *bona fide* Christians were to be found.[19] For his part John Robinson who, according to Cotton Mather, ' had been in his younger time ... *sowred* with the most rigid principles

---

[13] M. D. Jordan, 'The early Independents and the visible Church,' *Congregational Historic Society Transactions*, VIII no. 6, October 1923, 303–304.

[14] A. Peel and Leland H. Carlson, eds., *The Writings of Robert Harrison and Robert Browne*, London: Allen & Unwin, 1953, 253.

[15] R. W. Dale, *Essays and Addresses*, London: Hodder and Stoughton, 1895, 185.

[16] N. Micklem, *God's Freemen*, London: James Clarke, [1922], 141.

[17] W. B. Selbie, 'The religious principle of Congregationalism,' in *Mansfield College Essays*, London: Hodder and Stoughton, 1909, 35.

[18] For a somewhat fuller account of the history see Alan P. F. Sell, *Dissenting Thought and the Life of the Churches. Studies in an English Tradition*, Lewiston, NY: The Edwin Mellen Press, 1990, ch. 22.

[19] See, for example, H. Jacob, *Reasons taken out of God's word and the best humane testimonies proving a necessitie of reforming our churches in England*, 1604, 55. See further, Patrick Collinson,' Towards a broader understanding of the early Dissenting tradition,' in C. Robert Cole and Michael E. Moody, *The Dissenting Tradition. Essays for Leland H. Carlson*, Athens, Ohio: Ohio University Press, 1975, 3-38; John von Rohr, 'The Congregationalism of Henry Jacob,' *Congregational Historical Society Transactions*, XIX no. 3, October 1962, 107-17.

of *separation*,'[20] came to believe that 'The Spirit of God in one of his people will own itself in another of them though disfigured with many failings, especially in outward orders, and ordinances.'[21] Yet again, most of the ministers who emigrated to Massachusetts after 1630 sought to plant churches which would both comprise the establishment and be godly. When some of them were accused of being Separatists on the slippery slope to Anabaptism, they replied ' That they were neither Separatists nor Anabaptists; that they did not separate from the Church of England, nor from the ordinances of God there, but only from the corruptions and disorders of that Church...'[22] To Roger Williams, who did adopt Baptist views and was banished to Rhode Island, and to certain Quakers, it soon became clear that toleration was not a necessary constituent of godliness as far as the saints of the Congregational establishment were concerned. Indeed, Congregationalism did not lose its established status in Connecticut until 1818 or in Massachusetts until 1834.

In mid-seventeenth-century England, too, such Congregational Dissenters as those who participated in the Westminster Assembly and those who prepared the *Savoy Declaration* of 1658 were quite persuaded of the propriety of the state' s having the duty to encourage and promote religion and to protect professors of the Gospel,[23] provided that one brand of the faith only were not favoured above all others, and that the magistrate had no jurisdiction within the Church. They wished the Protestantism as delivered in the Bible to be the religion of the country, and under the Instrument of Government of 1653, and with their variously Baptist, Congregational and Presbyterian convictions intact, they accepted parochial appointments. It was only when, after the Restoration of the monarchy in 1660 it became clear that the Anglican-episcopal backlash was going to require them to go against consciences, notably by requiring them under the Act of Uniformity of 1662 to give their 'unfeigned assent and consent' to the *Book of Common Prayer* and to use it exclusively in worship, that nearly two thousand of them withheld consent and were ejected from their livings.[24] Even then some of their number, more particularly older Presbyterians, Richard Baxter among

---

[20] C. Mather, *Magnalia Christi Americana*, (1702), reprinted from the 1852 edn., London: The Banner of Truth Trust, 1979, 47.

[21] J. Robinson, *Works*, III, 108.

[22] C. Mather, op.cit., 73.

[23] See *The Savoy Declaration*, xxiv.III. See further, John Huxtable, 'National recognition of religion,' *The Congregational Quarterly*, XXXV no. 4, October 1957, 297-310; John H. Taylor, 'Church and state,' in *1662 and its Issues*, supplement to *Congregational Hisorical Society Transactions*, April 1962, 15-22.

[24] See further, Jeremy Goring, 'Some neglected aspects of the Great Ejection of 1662,' *Transactions of the Unitarian Historical Society*, XIII no. 1, October 1963, 1-8. Another provision of the Act was that all ministers of the Church of England should be episcopally ordained. This was too much for some of those ordained during the Cromwellian period – not least for John Howe, despite the entreaties of his friend Seth Ward, Bishop of Exeter. See E. Calamy, *Memoirs*

them, continued to entertain the increasingly forlorn hope of a Presbyterian establishment until the turn of the seventeenth century. It must, however, be noted that such a character as that 'peculiar Man', William Dell, rector of Yelden who resigned his living in 1660, took a different view of Church-state relations, and saw no point in removing episcopacy only to replace it with Presbyterianism. 'What wild and woful work do men make,' he thundered, 'when they will have the Church of God thus and thus, and get the power of the magistrate to back theirs ... as if the New Jerusalem must of necessity come out of the Assembly of Divines at Westminster.'[25] By the end of the century, and much more soberly, John Locke was promoting voluntarism, arguing that 'No body is born a member of any Church; otherwise the Religion of Parents would descend unto Children, by the same right of Inheritance as their Temporal Estates ... than which nothing can be imagined more absurd;'[26] and with this he set the tone for many of the eighteenth-century discussions of Church-state relations.

Lest we be misled into thinking that older Presbyterians alone were open to establishment ideas we should note the interestingly different views expressed in the first half of the eighteenth century by the Independents Isaac Watts and Philip Doddridge. It was Doddridge, the younger of the two, who in a letter to Thomas Sherlock, Bishop of London, was, according to taste, ecumenically open or ingratiating almost to the point of obsequiousness: 'I have always pleaded for the reasonableness of submitting to a majority here, and of our being obliged, though we are Dissenters, to do our part towards maintaining that clergy which the authority of our country in general has thought fit to establish ...'[27] He would have supported a civil establishment of religion provided it were able to accommodate a diversity of polities, memories of the Sacheverell riots and of attempts, as, for example, in the Schism Bill of 1714, to retract some of the

---

of the Life of the Late Revd. Mr. John Howe, M.A.., 1724, 39; Geoffrey F. Nuttall, 'The first Nonconformists,' in G. F. Nuttall and Owen Chadwick, *From Uniformity to Unity 1662-1961,* London: SPCK, 1962, 149-87.

[25] Quoted by John Brown, *John Bunyan. His Life Times and Work,* London: Wm. Isbister, 1885, 79. For Dell see A. G. Matthews, *Calamy Revised,* (1934), Oxford: Clarendon Press, 1988. Dell seems to have caused distress in numerous ways: by permitting Bunyan to preach in his pulpit, by neglecting to administer the sacraments for a period of twelve years. He was against paedobaptism, but had his own children baptized; he preached against universities whilst holding the Mastership of Caius College, Cambridge, and he opposed tithes whilst taking £200 p.a. at Yeldon.

[26] J. Locke, *A Letter Concerning Toleration,* 1689, Indianapolis: Hackett, 1983, 28. For Locke's developing view of toleration see Alan P. F. Sell, *John Locke and the Eighteenth-Century Divines,* Cardiff: University of Wales Press, 1997, ch. 5.

[27] Doddridge to Sherlock [14 May 1751], reproduced (albeit incorrectly dated 1753 – Doddridge died in 1751) by John Waddington, *Congregational History 1700-1800,* London: Longmans, Green, 1876, 424. Cf. Geoffrey F. Nuttall, *Calendar of the Corresondence of Philip Doddridge DD (1702-1751),* London: HMSO, 1979, no. 1729.

advantages of the Toleration Act of 1689 notwithstanding. Watts, on the other hand, was not so inclined, and neither was his Presbyterian contemporary at Moorfields academy and lifelong friend, Henry Grove. The latter, no lover of controversy, nevertheless opined that 'among Protestants whoever make the Christian Religion, or any part of it, an engine of State, seem either to mistake, or not duly consider, the nature of Christ's Kingdom ... ;'[28] and because of remarks in *An Humble Attempt towards the Revival of Practical Religion among Christians* (1731) which suggested that Dissenters had the edge over Anglicans where godliness was concerned, was the unwitting perpetrator of a debate between the Anglican John White, who responded to Watts in three letters *To a Gentleman Dissenting from the Church of England* (1743, 1745, 1745), and the Presbyterian Micaijah Towgood. Towgood's tract, *The Dissenting Gentleman's Answer to the Reverend Mr. White's three letters; in which a separation from the Establishment is fully justified; the Charge of Schism is refuted; and the Church of England and the Church of Jesus Christ, are impartially compared, and set in Contrast, and found to be Constitutions of a quite Different Nature* (1746) supplied many Dissenters with anti-establishment ammunition until well into the nineteenth century. As so often happens with eighteenth-century pamphlets, the case is set out in the title, and the word 'impartially' may gently be queried. Towgood insists that the constitution of the Church is found in the Bible, whereas that of the Church of England is found in the statute book; and among his arguments is one to the effect that the only sovereign and head of the Church is Christ, not the monarch – a matter on which he approaches apoplexy when he thinks of Queen Anne: 'Behold here, Sir, a Woman exercising spiritual ecclesiastical Authority over the Man!'[29] In his Second Letter of 1747 Towgood makes it clear that the allegiance he properly owes to the King in no way implies subjection to the Church of England, 'from whom I receive no protection, enjoy no Benefit or Advantage, and in Communion with which I by no means consent to live.'[30]

That the Particular Baptists were in general sympathy with Towgood's line is clear from the case of Mr. Baskerville of the Unicorn Yard church, London. He protested his right under the Occasional Conformity Act to take communion in the Church of England with a view to appointment as a councillor. His minister, Thomas Flower, sought advice from the Baptist Board of Ministers, whose reply was unambiguously opposed on the grounds that 'a church that owes its

---

[28] *Henry Grove: Ethical and Theological Writings*, with an Introduction by Alan P. F. Sell, Bristol: Thoemmes Press, 2000, II, 128; see ch. 5 above.

[29] M. Towgood, *The Dissenting Gentleman's Answer*, 32.

[30] Idem, *The Dissenting Gentleman's Second Letter*, 1747, 85. See further Alan P. F. Sell, *Dissenting Thought and the Life of the Churches*, ch. 7; Robert D. Cornwall, 'Advocacy of the independence of the Church from the state in eighteenth century England: a comparison of a Nonjuror and a Nonconformist view,' *Enlightenment and Dissent*, XII, 1993, 12-27.

constitution, its officers, its discipline, and many of its modes of worship, merely to human policy and power ... and that indulges in its bosom multitudes of people of the most corrupt principles, and the most immoral and profligate lives' is not to be communed with.[31] Unrepentant, Baskerville was removed from the membership roll in 1743. Fifty years on, Robert Hall was stoutly in the line of his Baptist forebears: 'Turn a Christian society into an established church, and it is no longer a voluntary assembly for the worship of God ... I have used the term great Head of the church, by way of distinction from that *little* Head which the Church of England has invented ... '[32]

A number of factors helped to re-focus the discussion of the establishment question in the nineteenth century. Of these I shall mention just two. First, there was the impetus from Scotland, where the voluntary question had been much debated, and from whence an increasing number of prominent ministers were joining the ranks of English Dissent.[33] At the same time some English Congregational ministerial candidates had, from the beginning of the century been beating a path to the Scottish universities. In 1804 a trio arrived in Glasgow, all of whom subsequently taught in English theological colleges: Joseph Fletcher at Blackburn, Henry Foster Burder at Wymondley, Hoxton and Highbury, and Hackney, and George Payne at Blackburn, Exeter and Plymouth. Since they became bosom friends of Ralph Wardlaw,[34] then in the second year of his ministry at North Albion Street, Glasgow; and since Payne's third pastorate pastorate was at Albany Chapel, Edinburgh (1812-1823), during which period, in 1817, Wardlaw had a public disputation on the matter with Thomas Chalmers, it is inconceivable that he and Wardlaw did not discuss the Church-state question, or that they were unaware of their respective writings on the subject. Payne's contributions were two. In 1834 he published *The Separation of Church and State calmnly considered, in reference to its probable Influence upon the Cause and Progress of Evangelical Truth in this Country*. The nub of his case is that:

---

[31] Joseph Ivimey, *A History of the English Baptists*, 4 vols. London, 1811-1830, III, 231. Flower was ordained at Unicorn Yard on 29 April 1836, and remained there for about eight years. 'He then betook himself to the trade of a corn-factor, which procured him the appellation of "Worldly-minded Flower." He, however, acquired a handsome subsistence ...' So Walter Wilson, *The History and Antiquities of Dissenting Churches and Meeting Houses, in London, Westminster, and Southwark*, London, IV, 1814, 235.

[32] R. Hall, *Collected Works*, ed. O. Gregory, London, 1831, III, 145, 192.

[33] See further, David M. Thompson, 'Scottish influence on the English churches in the nineteenth century,' *The Journal of the United Reformed Church History Society*, II no. 2, October 1978, 30-46.

[34] See R. Wardlaw, *Reminiscences of the late Rev. George Payne, LL.D.*, appended to John Pyer's *Memoir* of Payne prefixed to the latter's posthumous *Lectures on Christian Theology*, London: John Snow, 1850, I, cxxxiii-cxxxiv.

> The Church, as it is called by courtesy, *i.e.* the Episcopalian denomination is now the spouse of the State (we think she ought to be the spouse of Christ only); – our anxiety is simply to obtain a writ of divorce. If our opponents will continue to represent this as a desire to put the bride to death, the public must judge whether the defect is in our statements, or in their perceptions.[35]

Two years later Payne returned to the matter, and showed himself far removed from the position of Doddridge a century earlier:

> The all-engrossing question ere long will become – 'Is it compatible with the rights of conscience – with the principles, and laws, and spirit of Christianity, – and is it the best mode of providing for the religious instruction of a country, for the State to take any denomination of Christians into union with itself, to employ the ministers of that denomination as its agents in teaching religion to the nation at large, and to compel all its inhabitants to contribute to their support?' ... It is the duty of all who have come to a decision to avow it; – *of the Churchman* to show, if he can, that the alliance of Church and State is scriptural and expedient; – no less so, *that of the Dissenter* to prove, if he be able, that it necessarily brings the former into vassalage to the latter, – corrupts her principles, mars her purity, defaces her glory, and paralyzes her influence.[36]

That the young John Stoughton was similarly minded is evident from the statement he gave at his ordination in 1833: 'The true Church of Christ is formed of spiritual elements, and incapable of an alliance with earthly power and royal edicts and proclamations. Every departure from the primitive model I consider dangerous; a union between Church and State goes to destroy the spirituality of religion.'[37]

Secondly, in the wake of the Evangelical Revival, and with increasing industrialization, there were numerical and geographical gains to Old Dissent, no less than to newer Methodism. Thus, for example, Robert Vaughan, who had been the first president of Lancashire Independent College, was able, in the wake of the 1851 census, to declare that 'Nonconformity, judging from the numbers who attend public worship, has come by degrees to be as national as Conformity.'[38] Not surprisingly, many felt that growing prestige would assist in removing anti-Nonconformist disabilities once and for all. J. Guinness Rogers spoke for many when he said, 'The inequalities of nature and grace we meekly accept, the inequalities of culture we regret, the inequalities of holy Christian

---

[35] Quoted in *Memoir*, lxx.
[36] Ibid., lxxv-lxxvi, quoting the appendix to G. Payne, *The Operation of the Voluntary Principle in America*, Exeter, 1836.
[37] [Georgina King Lewis], *John Stoughton DD. A Short Record of a Long Life. By his Daughter*, London: Hodder and Stoughton, 1898, 17.
[38] R. Vaughan, *The Church and State Question as settled by the Ministry of Our Lord and of the Apostles*, 1867, 165.

service we will, with God's blessing, seek to redress; but against the inequalities which the State creates we protest as unrighteous, as contrary to the law of Christ, and as hindrances to the spread of His Kingdom.'[39] By the time those words were written Nonconformist muscles had been flexed in a variety of ways. Prominent among these was the Congregationalist Edward Miall's British Anti-State-Church Association, founded in 1844 and rebaptized the Liberation Society in 1853. Miall used *The Nonconformist* to propagate his views, while the equally Congregationalist John Campbell lambasted Miall's Society in the British Banner. In all of this the generation gap played a part, as witness the opposition to Miall articulated by John Angell James of Carrs Lane, Birmingham, and the support of him forthcoming from R. W. Dale, James's assistant and successor.[40]

The changes were rung on the themes specified in numerous books and pamphlets as the century wore on, and we need not indulge in endless repetition. Two concluding observations on the nineteenth century may, however, be made. First, many Dissenters, John Stoughton among them – and no one was less a firebrand than he – persuaded themselves that in pressing for disestablishment they were doing the Church of England a favour. Said he, 'that the law of England must ever treat a Church established and endowed by the State differently from what it does a Church not so endowed, and that it will withdraw a portion of liberty in exchange for State patronage, national property, and exclusive position, seems so exceedingly plain, that it is wonderful indeed, when any one with a practical mind does not see it in a moment.'[41] Secondly, the advocates of Dissent on occasion strained every homiletic nerve – even to the point of invoking the positively spooky – in making their case. Said Alexander Mackennal, 'the magic has never yet been discovered which can transmute a nation into a church;' and he continued: 'Frankenstein sought to make a man; he gathered together simples of nature, chemical compounds, portions of living beings, scraps from the charnel-house; and into the body he so constructed he somehow infused life. But it was an incomplete life, a treacherous gift; he had made a monster and not a man.'[42]

Since I shall shortly have cause to refer to a number of twentieth-century contributions to the establishment debate it will suffice at present to make one or

---

[39] J. G. Rogers, *The Church Systems of England in the Nineteenth Century*, London: Hodder and Stoughton, 1881, 448.

[40] For a further example of the taking of sides locally on this issue see Joseph Thompson, *Lancashire Independent College 1843-1893*, Manchester: J. E. Cornish, 1893, 86 and n. See further, William H. Mackintosh, *Disestablishment and Liberation. The Movement for the Separation of the Anglican Church from State Control*, London: Epworth Press, 1972.

[41] J. Stoughton in H. R. Reynolds, ed., *Ecclesia*, 1st series, London: 1870, 35.

[42] A. Mackennal, 'The witness of Congregationalism,' in D. Macfadyen, ed., *Constructive Congregational Ideals*, London: H. R. Allenson, 1902, 163.

two very brief comments on the century just past. As that century opened, Joseph Parker of London's City Temple, was found laying it on the line in no uncertain terms:

> We ought never to forget that it is no more the business of the State to denounce religion than to patronise it. The State must keep its hands off at both ends ... As Nonconformists we are more than merely willing to hail Edward the Seventh as King of Great Britain and Ireland, as Emperor of India, and as the Sovereign of self-governing colonies ... but we will never hail him as head of the Church or defender of the faith. There is one head of the Church; He will defend the faith. If we let go that central doctrine our Nonconformity is a pretence, and sooner or later it will die in shame.[43]

At a later point in his address he contemplates a question too preposterous to take seriously: 'may not God convert a dissenter into a national churchman? Never. Our God is not a God of backwardness. He converts Saul into Paul, He never converts Paul into Saul. He converts fools into wise men, He never converts wise men into fools. A transcendental "CANNOT" guards the eternal throne.'[44] No less definite, and even more lyrical, was William Edwards, principal of the Baptist College in Cardiff, who in the same year contended that the establishment principle is 'the child of the Dark Ages,' and that in any case it is alien to the Welsh nation *qua* Nonconformist.[45]

The 1902 Education Act prompted a closing of the Nonconformist ranks. It was strongly felt by many that the proposal to fund Anglican schools from public funds unfairly discriminated against Nonconformists, and the Baptist leader, John Clifford, led a Passive Resistance campaign which drew support from many Free Churchpeople. In this context the Congregationalist P. T. Forsyth warned that 'The spirit that would capture our schools would close our pulpits, as it denies our Church.' But his underlying principle was that 'You will never establish the Cross without disestablishing the Church.'[46] R. F. Horton proposed a more practical test: 'The pressing question, the key to the whole problem,' he wrote, 'is this: Are English Churchmen prepared ... to recognise that, as a matter of fact, Christ has not owned their exclusive conception of the Church, but that, outside their artificial limits, He has wrought to the conversion of souls, and built up believers on their most holy faith, and supplied a ministry which He could use?'[47]

---

[43] J. Parker's address of 22 April 1901 to the Congregational Union of England and Wales, in his *Two Addresses on The United Congregational Church*, London: CUEW, n.d., 2, 3.
[44] Ibid., 12.
[45] W. Edwards, *A Handbook of Protestant Nonconformity*, Bristol: W. Crofton Hemmons, 1901, 200, 206.
[46] P. T. Forsyth, *Missions in State and Church*, London: Hodder and Stoughton, 1907, 91.
[47] R. F. Horton, *The Dissolution of Dissent*, London: Arthur H. Stockwell, 1902, 106.

As the years went on a number of Dissenting leaders, anxious that their tradition play its full part in society, sought to smooth the rougher edges of its testimony. Peter Shepherd has found this true of J. H. Shakespeare, the architect of the Baptist Union in its modern aspect.[48] Nevertheless when in May 1921 the Free Churches replied to *An Appeal to All Christian People* from the Lambeth Conference of the preceding year they affirmed that ' Free Churchmen cannot be asked to consent that the civil power – which within its own sphere is called to be the servant of God – has any authority over the spiritual affairs of the Church.'[49] The Baptist scholar Henry Townsend was among those who feared that the pass was being sold, and in 1949 he published a substantial work in which he argued that the principle of utility, on which much of the establishment case as advanced by Anglicans rested, was an inadequate foundation. To this point I shall return. Three years later Ernest Payne, General Secretary of the Baptist Union, was more emollient in tone. In *The Free Churches and the State* he argued that it was not opportune to raise the establishment question because of the prevailing uncertain political situation; because discussions of the nature of the Church are in process; and because it would be ' disastrous' to raise the matter at the beginning of a new reign.[50] There the matter has more or less rested for the last half century. Not, indeed, that a few Free Churchmen have not from time to time published on the matter; not indeed, as I have already indicated, that the establishment question has not from time to time been noted in ecclesiastical – even ecumenical – discussions as something to be discussed at a future date. But it is only in the past ten years that the issue has come to the fore. Since, as I believe, the issue has arisen in such a way as to cloud if not altogether to obscure the Dissenting witness, the question, What ought we to be saying? arises clamantly.

II

Or does it? It may be that even some heirs of historic Dissent, not to mention the wider Free Church fold, query the necessity of 'flogging a dead horse' . After all, they may say, the Church of England is no longer altogether as it was. From the Enabling Act of 1919 onwards its government, especially through its Synod, has been much more in its own hands and, as the Methodist scholar J. T. Wilkinson remarked, ' The establishment of the Parochial Roll is so far a recognition that

---

[48] See P. Shepherd, *The Making of a Modern Denomination. John Howard Shakespeare and the English Baptists, 1898-1924*, Carlisle: Paternoster Press, 1999, 46.

[49] Quoted by Henry T. Wigley, *The Distinctive Free Curch Witness Today*, Wallington: The Religious Education Press, 1949, 64. See further, E. K. H. Jordan, *Free Church Unity. History of the Free Church Council Movement 1896-1941*, London: Lutterworth, 1956, ch. 11.

[50] See E. A. Payne, *The Free Churches and the State*, London: Independent Press, 1952, 28.

the Church is not the nation, nor yet the baptized citizens.'[51] Again, relationships between Anglicans and Free Churchpeople have on the whole greatly improved during the past fifty years, and this not only in the context of bilateral dialogues and ecumenical enterprises of various kinds, but at the grass roots in a number of Local Ecumenical Projects. Moreover, many Free Churchpeople would nowadays readily grant that however it may be with establishment as such, the state *recognition* of religion other than that of the Church of England is not only desirable, but has actually been accorded – officially, if not always practically by those on the 'Church' side of the traditional 'Church/chapel' divide – since the Toleration Act of 1689.[52] To be recognized by the state is far more than acquiescence in trust laws and the like on the ground that we own property. It is to have received religious liberty, something which is not universally enjoyed by religious believers to this day.

In view of all this, and above all because the disabilities under which our forebears laboured have almost entirely been removed, the heirs of Old Dissent may be tempted to silence on the establishment question. Happily, it is about four hundred years since our last martyr, and the struggle of our predecessors against legislation ranging from the punitive to the irritating has largely been won. The Conventicle and Five Mile Acts were repealed in 1812; Unitarians secured freedom under the law in 1813; the Test and Corporation Acts were repealed in 1828; the impediments to the marriage of Nonconformists according to their own rites were removed in 1828; Church Rates were abolished in 1868; the degrees of Oxford, Cambridge and Durham universities (though not the divinity degrees and professorships) were opened to Dissenters in 1871; and by the Burial Act of 1880 Nonconformists could be buried in parish churchyards by religious leaders of their own choice.[53]

What more, it might be asked, do Dissenters desire? Whatever they desire, it may be suggested that one of the things they need is a restoration of their historical memory, and this for ecumenical reasons. As long ago as 1943 George Phillips of Lancashire Independent College lamented that 'we have forgotten the forces of arrogance, intolerance and tyranny with which the old Dissenters had to contend. To our great detriment we have almost lost historical sense, which is one of the more serious causes of our weakness.'[54] Over a century

---

[51] J. T. Wilkinson, *1662 and After*, London: Epworth Press, 1962, 198 n.

[52] Thus the ecclesiastical recognition that the idea that church and commonwealth are one is obsolete is earlier than the nineteenth-century political recognition of the same idea which is implicit in the advent of Dissenters in parliament – a fact to which A. R. Vidler refers in *Soundings*, 256.

[53] See further on the position of Dissenters in the wake of the Toleration Act of 1689, Alan P. F. Sell, *Commemorations*, ch. 5.

[54] G. Phillips in *The Fourth Freedom*, London: Independent Press, 1943, 41.

earlier the eirenic John Stoughton said, 'on calm reflection, that, looking back on the way in which Nonconformity was treated for more than two hundred years, the wonder is that so much forebearance has been manifested and such measured language has been used by those who, generation after generation, have endured a cruel oppression.'[55] Our Dissenting forebears did not have to wait for the Minjung theologians of twentieth-century South Korea to learn something about 'the underside of history': here they were it. This thought should not, however, encourage their successors in the direction of sanctimony. It is said that on one occasion C. H. Spurgeon announced to his congregation that his Church ' had never persecuted, and was the only one which never had. The statement was received with applause. But Mr. Spurgeon, although he was a great preacher, was a very honest man. "Shall I tell you why? (he asked). Because it has never been in its power to do so."'[56] I have already mentioned occasions on which Dissent *qua* established overstepped the mark when it had the power to do so.

But everything turns upon the motive for remembering our history and the spirit in which we do it. I urge it only so that there may be such a reconciliation of memories as between the Church of England and the heirs of Old Dissent that healing leading to renewed common proclamation of the Gospel may result. Certain it is that too many have died for nothing to be done.[57]

However, it is not enough that the past be dealt with. Has Dissent a positive point for the future? Long ago Bernard Lord Manning rightly declared that 'Our Free Church life cannot go on living as a protest against injustices that have been removed and errors that are dying.'[58] My conviction is that precisely because almost all the disabilities have been removed and the ecumenical climate is more cheerful we have the opportunity of driving to the positive heart of the

---

[55] *John Stoughton DD*, 29.

[56] Related by Alfred Fawkes, 'The Church as a divine institution,' *The Modern Churchman*, XIX nos. 6, 7, 8, September-November 1929, 387.

[57] It is entirely likely that most Anglicans (not to mention most Free Churchpeople) are, literally, innocent of all of this. It may be hoped, however, that enough of them have sufficient historical knowledge to see the point of my remarks. Not indeed that I plead for breast-beating, liturgy-and morality-confusing confessions on the part of those who were not objectively morally responsible for acts committed before they were born. The notion of collective moral responsibility can be grossly abused. See further, Alan P. F. Sell, *Aspects of Christian Integrity*, (1990), Eugene, OR: Wipf & Stock, 1998, 65-8. As an example of what is required the international Reformed-Mennonite dialogue may be cited. The dialogue began with a united service of reconciliation in Zurich Cathedral on 5 March 1983, just yards from the river in which the Reformed drowned some of the Anabaptist forebears of the Mennonites. See Ross T. Bender and Alan P. F. Sell, eds., *Baptism, Peace and the State in the Reformed and Mennonite Traditions*, Waterloo, ON: Wilfrid Laurier University Press, 1991, ch. 1.

[58] Quoted by A. J. Grieve in *Congregationalism Through the Centuries*, London: Independent Press, 1937, 101.

Dissenting witness in an intellectual environment less impeded than ever before. In other words, there is a deeply theological Dissenting testimony to be made which would have needed to be made even if no Dissenter had been killed or subjected to adverse legislation.[59] It is a word which, to repeat what I said at the outset, directly relates the Gospel of God's free grace with the inescapably catholic nature of the Church. It concerns the matter of the Church; the catholicity of the Church; and Christ's sole Lordship over the Church.

Before briefly elucidating these points it will be well to clear away some less than weighty arguments which have been deployed on both sides of the establishment question. As we proceed we shall do well to remember not only that there is more than one kind of religious establishment, and that there are many folk churches, from Orthodox to Congregational, which are not established; that our concern is with the Church of England *qua* established; and that just as the situation of Dissent has changed over the centuries, so has that of the Church of England, whose ties to the apparatus of the state have been loosened in important if not root and branch ways as the centuries have rolled by.[60]

III

Some who are opposed to the establishment have enquired whether Prince Charles is fit to be the temporal head of the Church of England. Writers in the tabloid newspapers have from time to time made merry with this theme, and the Archdeacon of York, George Austin, has mused along similar lines.[61] It takes little theological acumen to appreciate that this line of argument represents a sublime missing of the point; for even if all monarchs had lived morally impeccable lives, the question whether the Church is the kind of body which can have a monarch as its temporal head would still be there.

An analogous reponse may be made to Tony Benn's rhetorical question, 'How can a Church preserve its spiritual integrity when its Prayer Book may

---

[59] A remark of that faithful Scottish episcopalian, Donald MacKinnon, comes to mind (Anglicans may be trusted to judge its accuracy). He speaks of the 'extent to which the Anglican approach to [other Christians], on the official level, not only expresses a bland forgetfulness of the insults of the past but also shows itself almost incurably intellectually pragmatic, hopelessly in bondage to the illusion that it is by the method of some sort of institutional arrangement that the moral and spiritual hurt of the people will find, if not healing, at least a kind of temporary and possibly permanent anaesthesia.' See his *The Stripping of the Altars*, Collins Fontana, 1969, 77-8.

[60] See further, Wesley Carr, 'A developing establishment,' *Theology*, CIII, January-February 1999, 2-10; Paul Avis, ' Establishment and the mission of a national Church,' ibid., CIII, January-February 2000, 3-12.

[61] See *The Observer*, 12 December 1993, 10.

still, in theory, be amended, or a new one rejected, as in 1928, by a parliament composed of members who are not required to be Anglicans or even Christians.'[62] This may seem, and actually be, odd; but the point is that even if all Members of Parliament were practising communicant members of the Church of England, the theological question of the propriety of parliamentary concern with a Church's liturgical affairs worship would remain.

Again, some have urged that an established Church cannot speak a prophetic word to the nation because it is so closely intertwined with it. But the evidence of individuals such as G. K. A. Bell during World War II and Robert Runcie in the aftermath of the Falklands War, as well as of the Church of England's corporate voice in such reports as *The Church and the City*, suggests that this argument requires serious qualification.

Then there are those who contend that the existence of an established Church violates the principle of religious equality. Undeniably this argument was deployed by Nonconformists during the nineteenth century[63] when, as we have seen, a number of restrictions – from their point of view adverse – were in force.[64] But down to our own time the anti-privilege point has been made by a variety of people. Thus the columnist Melanie Phillips has asked, 'Is it appropriate for the Church of England to enjoy a special place in a pluralist, multio-ethnic state? The immediate answer would appear to be no. It offends against our commitment to equality.'[65] John Huxtable, a prominent ecumenist of the United Reformed Church, having regard to the to multi-racial character of present-day Britain, threw the question even wider and said that we must ask 'how long it is right that one religion [not simply one Church], albeit the traditional religion of the land for many centuries, should hold a privileged position at all.'[66] Chris Bryant, of the Christian Socialist Movement, has declared that the Church of England's constitution is 'based on privilege, patronage and political power,' and that this leads 'to the effortless Anglican presumption of seniority over other faiths and denominations,'[67] a view with which, it would

---

[62] T. Benn, 'A case for the disestablishment of the Church of England,' in Donald Reeves, ed., *The Church and the State*, London: Hodder and Stoughton 1984, 69.

[63] See G. I. T. Machin, *Politics and the Churches in Great Britain 1869 to 1921*, Oxford: Clarendon Press, 1987. See also the interesting letter of 29 November 1875 from Dr. Magee, the Bishop of Peterborough, to John Stoughton. The Bishop does not claim that the Church of England is superior in all respects to Dissent, but only in respect of its suitability to be in alliance with the state. He therefore prefers the term 'ecclesiastical equality' to 'religious equality'. See *John Stoughton*, 159.

[64] For some Methodist reflections on the theme from the turn of the nineteenth century see J. Courtney James, *The Philosophy of Dissent. Analytical Outlines of some Free Church Principles*, London: James Clarke, 1900, 252-74.

[65] M. Phillips, 'Soupy defender of the ouija board,' *The Observer*, 3 July 1994.

[66] J. Huxtable, *A New Hope for Christian Unity*, Glasgow: Collins, 1977, 79.

[67] Quoted by Martin Wroe, *The Observer*, 25 January 1998.

seem, Rowan Williams, Archbishop of Canterbury, is in accord,[68] as is Simon Barrow, who has spoken of the 'benign superiority which still hampers the creativity of the Church of England.'[69] On the other hand, Owen Chadwick would be distressed if bishops were chosen otherwise than by the Queen, for then they would not have ' that primacy of honour which is attached to a regius chair.'[70] While we may raise an eyebrow at the thought of any Church of the towel-taking servant Christ desiring primacy of honour in any respect, and while the heirs of Dissent may, according to taste, find Anglican pretensions irritating or hilarious, the question of equality construed in social terms is not of primary importance. Equality in Christ is, however, and the question, Who are in Christ? or , Who comprise the 'matter' of the Church? will face us shortly.

First, however, we must dispose of a few less than conclusive arguments advanced by supporters of the establishment. Many Anglicans stand in the line of Cyril Garbett, who claimed that 'the Church of England far more fully than any other religious body makes spiritual provison for the people of the nation,' – indeed, it 'still in many ways represents the religious aspect of the nation.'[71] But establishment is not necessary to the supply of spiritual provision, as witness the United States, where such provision in great – sometimes disconcerting – variety is available, and is partaken of by a greater proportion of the population than in England; and the Church in Wales which, according to some, has become much more of a people's Church since disestablishment. Hastings Rashdall was not the first Anglican to point out that 'A State which has no established Church is not necessarily godless;'[72] while from the other side Robert Vaughan, countering those who support the establishment on the ground that the alternative is a godless or atheistic state, retorted that 'there are no such enemies to godliness as the men who would substitute the semblance of it in the place of the reality.'[73]

---

[68] See the report by Gaby Hinsliff, *The Observer*, 24 December 2000, 2. Though he made the point when he was Archbishop of Wales.

[69] See his letter in *Theology*, CII, May-June 1999, 231. From the other side H. F. Lovell Cocks writes, 'If to the English palate the moral tonic of Nonconformity has seemed unnecessarily bitter, it must be remembered that Anglican arrogance was one of its ingredients.' See his *The Nonconformist Conscience*, London: Independent Press, 1943, 16.

[70] O. Chadwick, 'The link between Church and state,' in *The Church and the State*, 43.

[71] C. Garbett, *The Claims of the Church of England*, London: Hodder and Stoughton, 1947, 188, 189.

[72] H. Rashdall, *Ideas and Ideals*, Oxford: Blackwell, 1928, 36. It is interesting to note that while at first Philip Schaff, nurtured in the state churchism of Europe, was dismayed by the multi-denominationalism of America when he first went there in 1844, following a return visit to Europe in 1853-1854 he concluded that 'American denominationalism was succeeding better in churching the United States than the state church system was doing in Europe,' and this despite sectarian rivalries. See John M. Koehnlein, 'Theology on a crooked line: Philip Schaff' s understanding of evangelical catholicism,' *The New Mercersburg Review*, XIX, Spring 1996, 36.

[73] R. Vaughan, *The Church and State Question*, 146.

A related argument concerns the parochial availability of Church of England ministries to all without discrimination. 'We are appointed,' wrote A. C. Headlam, not to minister to one section of the people or to those who are most anxious to receive our ministrations, but to the whole of the people in the parish to which we are assigned, and we should never allow the interests or tastes of a section of the people to hide from us our duty towards the whole.'[74] A quarter of a century on D. L. Edwards declared that 'Historically, it has been its state connection which has maintained the Church's comprehensive welcome'[75] – though we may hope that he does not wish us to infer that had there been no establishment there would have been no welcome. When, for more than three hundred years, it has been possible for Dissenters to decline, with varying degrees of politeness, the ministrations of the Church of England; and when today we have people of other faiths in our midst who would be surprised to think that the Vicar is their spiritual guide; and when, above all, increasing numbers of people, religious or not, are welcoming what, to use the familiar blanket term, may be described as post-Constantinianism, this claimed pastoral concern for all, however well intentioned and sincerely entertained, can be, and sometimes is, perceived as patronising. More to the point, there is no reason whatsoever why members of any Christian church may not show pastoral care and appropriate concern to those amongst whom they are set. John Habgood has suggested that established churchpeople are in a different position on this matter from non-established church folk: 'For members of non-established churches there is always a prior question to be asked: What are my grounds for being concerned with this or that person? For members of an established church the sense of responsibility is instinctive.'[76] To this is is necessary only to reply that the Good Samaritan was precisely not of the establishment, and that his motive, that of being a good neighbour to the wounded man, should be the primary instinctive response of established and non-established Christian alike.

It is well known that on these matters members of the Church of England are themselves divided. For every one who thinks that establishment assists the Church's mission by affording it a place in spheres of influence, there is another who denies this on the ground that present arrangements sadly turn the Church into the 'top people's' Church and further alienate it from the masses. At which point Donald MacKinnon's quip comes to mind: 'Where England is concerned, the passing of Establishment as we have known it would surely lead to a day in which episcopal lawn sleeves would cease to flutter in the breeze as their wearer

---

[74] A. C. Headlam, *The Church of England*, London: John Murray, 2nd edn. 1925, 191-2.
[75] D. L. Edwards, *Not Angels but Anglicans*, London: SCM Press, 1958, 50.
[76] J. Habgood, *Church and Nation in a Secular Age*, London: Darton, Longman and Todd, 1983, 97.

bestowed the diocesan blessing upon the latest Polaris submarine. Here we should find sheer gain without any loss at all.'[77]

Sooner or later the question of endowment looms in establishment discussions, and J. S. Bezzant is but one of many to have been disturbed by the consequences of disestablishment in this respect. Indeed he feared that it 'would cede the first place to the Church of Rome,'[78] and he even invoked the fact of endowment as justifying the state's right to select from the priesthood the principal officers of the Church.[79] Less hysterically, David Edwards noted the material benefits accruing to an established Church. These, 'while being separable from the legal fact of its establishment by the state, come more plentifully when a Church is regarded as the Church of the nation.'[80] He gives no indication of distress at this point.

Finally, there is the straightforward claim that the thing works. As Garbett wrote, 'Never in the whole of my ministry have I felt hindered in its exercise by the fact that I belong to an established Church, while I have become conscious of greater opportunities given to me both at home and overseas as one of the representatives of the national Church.'[81] Even if Garbett was not too pleased – or complacent – that this should be so, the retort of P. T. Fosyth to the general attitude expressed is understandable: 'However Establishment may seem to work at a given time, *the thing is wrong.*'[82] There is evidence that prominent Anglicans are coming around to this view, among them David Jenkins, who, believing that disestablishment is inevitable, recommends that it 'should be initiated by a group of Christians who relate it to ecumenical action together, so that we get a new coalition of churches. I think it would be healthy for the Church in pluralistic times and make it realise that it gets its title from its faith and its gospel alone.'[83] With this we leave less than adequate pro- and anti-establishment arguments, and are returned to the heart of the matter.

IV

The three fundamental questions are: Who are the Church – that is, who comprise the 'matter' of the Church? Is the concept of a national Church true to

---

[77] D. M. MacKinnon, *The Stripping of the Altars*, 32; cf. 34.
[78] J. S. Bezzant, 'Establishment and alternatives,' *The Modern Churchman*, XIX nos. 6-8, September-November 1929, 455.
[79] Ibid., 454.
[80] D. L. Edwards, *Not Angels but Anglicans*, 50.
[81] C. Garbett, *The Claims of the Church of England*, 199.
[82] P. T. Forsyth, *The Charter of the Church*, London: Alexander and Shepheard, 1896, 32.
[83] Report by Martin Wroe, *The Observer*, 10 July 1994.

the nature of the Church? How may we best honour the sole Lordship of Christ in his Church? Let us consider each question in turn.

Who are the Church? The Separatists and their heirs were, as we have seen, quite clear, positively, that the Church comprises the regenerate and, negatively, that it does not include all those who happen to have been born in a particular country. The point was reiterated in the second half of the nineteenth century – the period which saw the greatest volume of anti-establishment theologizing. Thus, for example, Robert Vaughan taught that 'Jesus restricts membership in his Church to spiritual men;' he warned against the possibility that 'the slow process of bringing souls into the Church by conviction and conversion' will be replaced by 'the more ready policy of declaring men Christians by royal edicts, by the law of senates, or by mere boundary regulations'; and he insisted that ' godliness comes from conviction, and cannot be made to be inherent in State forms, or in State law.'[84] Vaughan was also alive to the church disciplinary implications of his stance. If the Church is to be 'a communion of the devout ... it pertains to the Church, the existing body of communicants, to decide, in its judgment and charity, as to who are persons of that character, and who are not.'[85]

R. W. Dale, one of the most notable Dissenters of the second half of the nineteenth century, was in complete accord from the time of his ordination onwards. At his ordination he explained his dissent from the Church of England. His positive point is that 'the visible church of Christ is "a congregation of faithful men"', whereas 'a national church cannot be a congregation, nor can there be any adequate security for all its members being faithful ... I cannot admit that the heterogeneous mass of godly and godless people who equally belong to the National Establishment, constitute a Christian Church.'[86] Elsewhere he said that *'formally* a religious society ceases to be a Church when it ceases to require personal union with Christ as the condition of communion with itself, and when it consciously, voluntarily, and of deliberate purpose, includes within its limits what John Robinson ... calls "a mingled generation of the seed of the woman and the seed of the serpent."'[87] To put it otherwise we might say that what we generally call a local congregation is normally larger than the ' congregation of the saints' which is within it. Heirs of Dissent cannot deny that many of their congregations (in the former sense) are nowadays of this kind: indeed, some local churches serve as *quasi* parish churches. So far Dissenters can agree with A. R. Vidler that 'Non-religious

---

[84] R. Vaughan, *The Church and State Question*, 61, 78, 93; cf. 140. Vaughan's student, J. Guinness Rogers, followed in his teacher's wake. See his *Church Systems*, 644.
[85] Ibid., 179.
[86] See *The Ordination Services of the Rev. R. W. Dale, M.A.*, 1854.
[87] Idem, *Essays and Addresses*, London: Hodder and Stoughton, 1899, 91; cf. 139.

Christians, semi-detached believers, and semi-detached agnostics, so far from being excluded, are welcome in so far as they wish to be.'[88] Conversely, it would seem that the question of the 'church within the church' disturbs some Anglicans too. John Habgood, for example, has noted the 'very real dilemma' that 'By concentrating on the committed, and by raising the barriers against nominal allegiance, [parish clergy] effectively unchurch large numbers of people who still think of themselves ... as part of a Christian society.'[89] Indeed, it would seem that Anglicans have their own special way of being 'church within a church'. As George Phillips pointed out, the Anglican

> kind of comprehensiveness can only be gained at the expense of spiritual power and purity. It inevitably drives the Church to distinguish among its own membership a pale within which its special powers and privileges are resident. A truly national Church is therefore almost compelled to be hieratic in character – that is, the ministry and spiritual activity of the community and also the governing body will be concentrated in the hands of some select body, which constitutes a kind of spiritual aristocracy. The great majority of the membership must be reduced to an inactive and submissive role.[90]

With this we may compare the experience of the ecumenist John Huxtable:

> When Anglicans talk of the nature of the Church they almost always give the impression of meaning the hierarchy and the priesthood, almost as if the laity were little more than a necessary background to the labours of bishop, priest and deacon ... A Congregational minister and his people are so closely knit that he cannot function without them; and this is an indication of the belief that Church acts are indeeed acts of the Church and not simply of Church officials: the Church, *not the minister*, celebrates the Eucharist. This is epitomised in the Church Meeting, that characteristic feature of Congregationalism.[91]

For his part, P. T. Forsyth perceived in the establishment 'a fatal severance between the idea of the Church and the idea of Redemption.'[92] He continued:

> If we ask indeed why England is not Pagan to-day, the grateful answer must be: Because of the Church. But if we go on to ask why she is but half Christian, the answer, if critical and honest, must still be: Because of the Church, and especially because of the Establishment.[93]

---

[88] A. R. Vidler, 'Religion and the national Church,' in *Soundings. Essays Concerning Christian Understanding*, Cambridge: CUP, 1963, 260.
[89] J. Habgood, *Church and Nation in a Secular Age*, 89. Cf. idem, *Making Sense*, London: SPCK, 1993, 148.
[90] G. Phillips in *The Fourth Freedom*, 59.
[91] J. Huxtable, 'Introduction' to John Owen, *The True Nature of a Gospel Church*, London: James Clarke, 1947, 15.
[92] P. T. Forsyth, *Rome, Reform and Reaction*, London: Hodder and Stoughton, 1899, 162.
[93] Ibid., 163.

The nub of the problem is that 'A Church established by grace is forbidden by its free nature to be established by law.'[94]

One may hope that Christians of an ecumenical turn of mind may increasingly come to see the point of earnest discussion, in our ideologically diverse culture, of the 'matter' of the Church in relation to church discipline and God's grace in redemption.

V

The second major question is, Is the concept of a national Church true to the nature of the Church? Many defenders of the establishment would side with Donald Maclean of the Free Church of Scotland who complained that Voluntaryism 'denied the State the liberty and privilege of doing homage to the King of Kings; it denied the State the right of an avowal of the Christian religion, thus reducing it to creedlessness.'[95] Specifically with regard to the English Church J. S. Bezzant explained that 'The Establishment by law means that to the Church's formulations of belief, of worship and of law, the State has added its sanction, thereby ratifying and confirming, not as true but as conditions of Establishment, what was done by the Church [in breaking with Rome].' [96] Forsyth's reading of the matter was significantly different, however: 'It was a national church that slew the universal Christ. You will note that it is one thing to have a church established in law, and another thing to have religion established in a nation's heart.'[97]

What then of the companion point that the existence of a national church makes clear Christ's claim over the life of the nation?[98] A. R. Vidler argued that a national church, by which he meant 'a church built into the constitution as a

---

[94] Idem, 'The evangelical basis of Free Churchism,' *The Contemporary Review*, LXXXI, January-June 1902, 685.

[95] G. N. M. Collins, *Donald Maclean, D.D.*, Edinburgh: Lindsay, 1944, 33-4. It will be recalled that the Free Church of Scotland maintains the establishment principle, regarding itself as the Church of Scotland, Free.

[96] J. S. Bezzant, 'Establishment and alternatives,' 450.

[97] P. T. Forsyth, *The Charter of the Church*, 10.

[98] From the Dissenting side that wise man H. F. Lovell Cocks, a pupil of Forsyth, mused thus: 'Perhaps there is some value, after all, in the public acknowledgement of Christ's claim over the national life, provided that in regard to the counter-claim of the State the national church is ceaselessly vigilant and uncompromisingly nonconformist. To be truly obedient to the Word of God, such a national church would have to be as free from control by the worldly interests of her members as from the intrusions of dictators or parliaments in the high concerns of her faith and worship. To such a church Nonconformists might return. Her victory over them would be their victory too; for they would have won their case.' See his *The Nonconformist Conscience*, 93-4. It is a pity that Cocks's Baptist contemporary, Ernest Payne, distorted Cocks's view by quoting only the first words and omitting the crucial proviso, in his *The Free Church Tradition in the Life of England*, London: Hodder and Stoughton, revised edn., 1965, 146.

complement and counterpoise to the state and to civil government – is a standing witness to the fact that man, every man, is a twofold creature with a twofold allegiance': to a temporal state and to the eternal realm.[99] But Vidler would have been the first to recognize the necessary modification of Richard Hooker's ideal that 'one and the self-same people are the Church and the Commonwealth;'[100] though as late as 1929 J. M. Creed was found making – and italicizing, the point: *'The Church of England is the nation viewed as a religious community.'*[101] Maintenance of this view, he thought, would counter the danger that the Church was an institution having a particular shape. On the other hand, Creed's contemporay, Rashdall, observed that 'Even where [Church and state] are actually composed of the same persons, practical convenience may render a differentiation of function between its different organs extremely desirable.'[102] Not that this satisfied Dissenters and, presumably, the declaration of John Moses, Dean of St. Paul's, that establishment is an 'acknowledgement of the meeting of the sacred and the secular'[103] does not satisfy them either, for they would argue that at certain neuralgic points, notably those concerning worship and the appointment of church officers, the secular usurps the sacred – a point to which I shall return.

The reason for Dissenters' dissatisfaction is, as the Baptist Townsend saw long ago, that most of the arguments for an established/national Church so far considered in this section are unashamedly based upon pragmatic considerations. Indeed, it is not unjust to say that a strong strand of pragmatism has been present from the earliest days of what might be called 'establishment theology', for a prominent objective at the time of the Anglican Settlement was to secure a united nation against foreign (Roman Catholic) threats, and to require religious uniformity as a cementing agent. Cyril Garbett was quite open about it: 'The central idea of a National Church is that it should manage its ecclesiastical affairs without external interference: it is the result of the demand for freedom from foreign dictation.'[104] Such an approach does not drive, theologically, to the nature of the Church.[105] It is not altogether surprising,

---

[99] A. R. Vidler in *Soundings*, 262.

[100] R. Hooker, *Laws of Ecclesiastical Polity*, VIII. iii.6.

[101] J. M. Creed, ' The idea of a national Church,' *The Modern Churchman*, XIX nos. 6-8, September-November 1929, 427-8.

[102] H. Rashdall, *Ideas and Ideals*, 46.

[103] Report of a confidential meeting on the establishment of the Church of England, *The Tablet*, 16 January 1999, 96.

[104] C. Garbett, *The Claims of the Church of England*, 182-183.

[105] This is not to deny that from time to time doctrine has been invoked both for and against the establishment. Thus A. R. Vidler declares that 'It is an advantage to the Church of England that it has ill-defined or archaic standards of doctrine,' while J. Guinness Rogers holds that 'A national Church must include all doctrines, which practically means that it must exclude all.'

therefore, that in our own time John Habgood deliberately selects a pragmatic-empirical-sociological method which precludes such a theological enquiry: 'My defence of establishment,' he writes, 'was based fundamentally on an assessment of the needs of the nation, and a view of the church as not confined to those whose religious commitment is most explicit and most ready to express itself in overt religious activity.'[106] He does, however, allow that there may arise circumstances in which it would be appropriate to review the disestablishment question. A Dissenter might reply that the circumstances have been ripe for fundamental theological discussion of the matter for the past 450 years, but that the time has never been more opportune than now, when almost all the anti-Dissenter disabilities have been removed and the need of a concerted Christian witness to the nation is clamant.

Dissenters have made two further points against the idea of a state Church. Especially at the period when Nonconformity was in the ascendant they fairly frequently gave the impression that by appealing for disestablishment they were assiting the Church of England out of a prison of its own making. Were it disestablished it could be free as never before in and for the Gospel – just as the Free Churches are. To A. M. Fairbairn, ' An Established Church is more of a static, but a Free Church more of a dynamic force in society ... '[107] Here, it might seem, is utilitarianism, mingled with a dash of Nonconformist triumphalism, from the other side: disestablishment will free the Church and make it more useful. But at the deepest level the case is that such freedom is demanded by God's grace in the Gospel. Hence the remark of Fairbairn's pupil, the pioneer modern ecumenist A. E. Garvie: 'Establishment or Endowment of the Church by the State brings it into a servitude which, however light the yoke may be made, is a restriction and deprivation of that freedom in grace which consecration to the purpose of God in Christ demands.'[108]

Compatible with this is the Dissenting argument that the Church as such knows no territorial boundaries and, therefore on grounds of catholicity it cannot be regarded as co-terminous with the nation. John Whale put the point bluntly:

See, respectively, *Soundings*, 258 and *Church Systems*, 473. Norman Sykes pointed out that 'Leaders of the successive religious revivals in the Church, alike evangelical, catholic and broad church, have found shelter and protection from episcopal and clerical persecution in the circumstances of State establishment.' See his 'The actual position in England today,' *The Modern Churchman*, XIX nos. 6-8, September-November 1929, 449. Here is more ecclesiology-skirting utilitarianism

[106] J. Habgood, *Church and Nation in a Secular Age*, 176.

[107] A. M. Fairbairn, *Studies in Religion and Theology. The Church in Idea and History*, New York: Macmillan, 1904, 104.

[108] A. E. Garvie, 'Freedom of the Church in Christ,' *The Congregational Quarterly*, XX no. 2, April 1942, 110.

> To us a State Church is a contradiction in terms ... There can be no such thing as territorial Christianity, as though the faith were like the English language or English Common law – an aspect or function of our national life. To us, State control of the deepest things by which Christendom lives would be a blasphemous betrayal of the Crown Rights of the Redeemer.[109]

To the question of the Crown Rights of the Redeemer I shall return: it is, after all the most important point of all in the Dissenting case. But first we should observe that some Anglicans have urged the Church as national on the humble ground that this dissuades the Church of England as an organization from identifying itself with the Church Catholic. Says J. M. Creed, 'It is plausible to identify the Papal Church with the Church Catholic. It is not plausible to identify the Church of England with the Church Catholic.'[110] But, surely, this is to think too much in terms of particular structures, the sway of one of which happens to be more territorially restricted than the other. But if territory is not the primary ingredient of catholicity, which it is not – especially when the Church triumphant in heaven is in view, then the argument is vitiated.

It follows that 'a church which insists on being tied to ... a nation-state just makes itself look provincial and sectarian.'[111] There is a long line of anti-sectarian Dissenting testimony along this line. As long ago as 1834 the Congregationalist Thomas Binney argued that 'An exclusive political establishment is necessarily and in principle schismatical,' and the Church of England's 'connection with the state has injured its catholicity.'[112] Later in the same century R. W. Dale gave a political twist to the same argument: 'A Church forgets its own Idea when by its very polity is confirms national isolation ... the Church is a supernatural society and exists for supernatural purposes; it is in relation to these that its polity must be judged.'[113] Few were more swingeing than P. T. Forsyth: 'What we protest against is not the abuses but the existence, the principle, of a national Church.'[114] Again, 'Christianity is not national in spirit. Its conception is catholic and universal, transcending and submerging national differences, "elect from every nation, yet one o'er all the earth ... Christ said His Kingdom was not of this world. The Established Church, *qua* established, is. Let us secure the principle, and the true comprehension will

---

[109] J. S. Whale, 'Commemoration sermon' in *Congregationalism Through the Centuries*, London: Independent Press, 1937, 106.
[110] J. M. Creed, 'The idea of a national Church,' 430.
[111] Clifford Longley, 'Manacled to a spiritual corpse,' *The Times*, 2 December 1989.
[112] T. Binney, *Dissent not Schism. A Discourse delivered in the Poultry Chapel, December 11, 1834, at the Monthly meeting of the Associated Ministers and Churches*, London: Joseph Ogle Robinson, Junr., 1835, 57, 59.
[113] R. W. Dale, *Essays and Addresses*, 114-15.
[114] P. T. Forsyth, ' The evangelical basis of Free Churchism,' 693.

automatically settle itself."'[115] At the opposite pole to the catholic Church is what Forsyth calls the monopolist Church:

> No church has a right to the name Catholic if it insists on unchurching all others which are not episcopal or established by the State. It is only *Monopolist*. The true catholicity is to recognise the Church in every community where the pure word of the Gospel is preached and the sacraments duly administered as its expressions. 'Grace be with all who love the Lord Jesus Christ in sincerity and truth.' It is an Apostolic benediction. Why do we hear it so seldom from the Apostles' successors? Why is the validity of Paul's sacramental grace so often denied?[116]

Here is a deeply theological point, tellingly expressed in some of the language of the 'opposition' (validity, sacramental grace), and the adverse implications of the monopoly were forthrightly spelled out by that Congregational lover of the Church of England, Bernard Lord Manning, in these terms: ' When in the sixteenth century Englishmen ceased to be of one mind about religion, it was – we always said so and we must go on saying so – a monstrous piece of impudence and injustice that kings, parliaments, courtiers, and politicians should decide which part of the flock of Christ in these islands should enjoy what hitherto all had enjoyed.' It is, he says, even more to be regretted when the 'episcopal sect' is no longer a national institution.[117] Is it, or is it not, the case that:

> The saints on earth and all the dead
> But one communion make;
> All join in Christ, their living head,
> And of his grace partake?[118]

If it is the case, what are the implications for the Church *qua* established and national? Is the current ecumenical climate sufficiently open for these questions graciously to be discussed in a theological and not simply an utilitarian/pragmatic way? Our understanding of the nature and catholicity of the Church is at stake.

---

[115] Idem, *The Charter of the Church*, 49, 101.

[116] Ibid., 39.

[117] B. L. Manning, *Essays in Orthodox Dissent*, 137. Thomas Hooper earlier made the point thus: '[I]mmediately the State begins to support religion, it must define what form of religion it supports, what creeds, formularies, ceremonies, and ministerial dress it approves. To do that is to sectionalise religion, and to make a part of the Church a branch of the Civil Service. The State has no right to coerce its citizens in matters of religion; neither has it a right to patronise a section of its citizens at the expense of the others.' See his, *The Story of English Congregationalism*, London: Independent Press, 1907, 146.

[118] Isaac Watts.

If such discussion is to proceed the chosen methodology must be appropriate. While the empirical situation presses, it must not be permitted to determine the shape and course of the debate. When discussing establishment, Norman Sykes stated, 'The principle which I should wish to establish is that ... the problem should be studied by reference to known historical statutes and uses, not to theoretical speculations concerning the nature and rights of a church.'[119] This sad disjunction, if it became the procedure followed in discussion between the Church of England and Dissent, would not reach the heart of the matter. It might also gently be suggested that there was nothing exclusively theoretical or speculative about being martyred with the approval of bishops on account of one's ecclesiology. The positive point is that while, living as we do on our side of modern biblical criticism, we cannot find the blueprint of any one current church polity in the Bible, this does not preclude recourse to Scripture altogether. And on the specific point at issue John Marsh truly said that 'the New Testament gives no precedent whatever for thinking of a "nation" as a "church".' [120] Is this witness altogether to be ignored?

VI

It is time to come to the most important question of all: How may we best honour the sole Lordship of Christ in his Church? In 1532 the King was proclaimed the Church's 'single protector, the sole and sovereign lord, and, in so far as the law of Christ allows, supreme head.' From that day to this there have been Anglicans who have been happy to regard 'the Queen in Parliament [as] the ultimate source of all authority and jurisdiction in spiritual matters relating to the church of this nation.'[121] Similarly, from that day to this the Dissenters have raised the logical point that the phrase, 'in so far as the law of Christ allows' begs a huge question. They may be even more disturbed by the fallacy of incomplete enumeration perpetrated by a Protestant Anglican thus: 'If we once admit the propriety of a connexion between the church and the state, and at the same time deny the supremacy of the pope, it seems to follow of necessity that we should admit the supremacy of the sovereign.'[122] Not so: all we need do (without necessarily becoming republican – as most Dissenters have not been) is to uphold the supremacy of Christ as ruler of his Church. For 'When "by one blast of Queen

---

[119] N. Sykes, 'The actual position in England to-day,' 433.

[120] J. Marsh, 'Obedience to the Gospel in terms of churchmanship and church order,' in J. Marsh, ed.,*Congregationalism To-day*, London: Independent Press, 1943, 48.

[121] So David N. Samuel, 'The Protestant succession to the throne,' *Churchman*, XCIII no. 4, 1979, 299.

[122] Ibid.

Elizabeth's trumpet" [the reference is to Elizabeth I] all Englishmen were made members of the national Church, and were required under penalty to attend its services, the complaint of the Congregationalists was not that the Queen had trampled on the personal rights and violated the freedom of the English people, but that she had usurped the authority of Christ.'[123] Those in accord with this will be flabbergasted by Cyril Garbett's remark, 'I for one do not yet feel able to ask for Disestablishment, though I am prepared to accept it without opposition if the State demands it.'[124] At least this is an archbishop's testimony that establishment is not of the *esse* of the Church; but the idea that one should respond without opposition to a state's preferred polity is not the way of those in the line of the ecclesiological martyrs. And when J. S. Bezzant declares that 'The only question of principle is this: What measure of State control is compatible with the Church's absolute duty of loyalty to the Headship of Christ?'[125] We have a further begging of the question and, in the the light of our knowledge of totalitarian regimes – a knowledge considerably and distressingly increased since Bezzant wrote in 1929 – we have a disconcerting use of the term 'control'. The contrasting Dissenting view was ably expressed by J. Guinness Rogers in these terms. Speaking of the Church he said,

> The power it possesses no prince or prelate can confer, and none can take away. It is a power which does not accrue from some natural right belonging to its members separately, or in their corporate capacity, but comes directly from the presence of Christ Himself in accordance with His own promise. Christ is wherever His saints meet in His name, and the presence of Christ makes the Church, and gives its decision validity and force.[126]

Convictions of this kind lie behind the claim that the Church and not Parliament should (consistently with the maintenance of public order) have full rights over its worship and polity. It is such convictions which render Dissenters dumbfounded when, as happened after Parliament, in 1984, rejected a measure concerning the appointment of bishops sent to it by the Synod of the Church of England, a commentator could say that 'the measure does not touch upon doctrine or worship but on man management ... ;'[127] and Lord Fletcher could aver 'I think it is a healthy part of our constitutional arrangements that the wishes

---

[123] R. W. Dale, *Essays and Addresses*, 217.
[124] C. Garbett, *The Claims of the Church of England*, 198.
[125] J. S. Bezzant, 'Establishment and alternatives,' 452.
[126] J. G. Rogers, 'Clericalism and Congregationalism,' in *Jubilee Lectures: A Historical Series delivered on the occasion of the Jubilee of the Congregatioanl Union of England and Wales*, London: Hodder and Stoughton, 1882, II, 235.
[127] 'The way bishops are made,' *The Times*, August 1984.

of the General Synod cannot be enacted without Parliament's approval.'[128] On the question of such appointments John Habgood expressed the opinion that since 'the only people who know how the system works at first hand, seem satisfied with it. I do not see ... that there are any *pragmatic* grounds for alarm.'[129] That there may be theological grounds for alarm is not, in context, his concern.

By now some members of the Church of England may be wondering why I should be so concerned with their polity: to each his own. First, it is clearly right for Christians to address one another in love concerning neuralgic theological points, especially where the Lordship of Christ and the catholicity of the Church are at issue. Secondly, I am a member of the state, and am thus in some sense responsible for what the state does. Conversely, I am irresponsible if I do not raise objection when it makes an arrangement with a Church which I believe to be questionable.[130] The crucial point is that 'neither the Prince nor Premier shall be head, or even be called head, of the Church; but only Jesus Christ, in His direct access by the Spirit to the soul of the Church in the souls of the faithful.'[131] Hence the words of *A Statement concerning the Nature, Faith and Order of the United Reformed Church*:

> The United Reformed Church declares that the Lord Jesus Christ, the only king and head of the Church, has therein appointed a government distinct from civil government and in things spiritual not subordinate thereto, and that civil authorities, being always subject to the rule of God, ought to respect the rights of conscience and of religious belief and to serve God's will of justice and peace for all men.[132]

VI

It will be clear from the foregoing argument that nothing I have said denies the necessity of the recognition of the Church by the state.[133] As Forsyth perceived, 'An absolute separation and neutrality between Church and State is impossible.'[134] I do, however, think it advisable in the interests of clarity to distinguish carefully between recognition and establishment where 'establishment theology' is in view. Thus, where A. C. Headlam says that 'as a

---

[128] Letter of 30 July 1984 to *The Times*.
[129] J. Habgood, *Church and Nation in a Secular Age*, 104. My italics.
[130] For a fuller development of this argument see Henry W. Clark, *History of English Nonconformity*, London: Chapman and Hall, 1913, II, 409-10.
[131] P. T. Forsyth, *The Charter of the Church*, 50; cf. idem, *Theology in Church and State*, London: Hodder and Stoughton, 1915, 208.
[132] *A Statement concerning the Nature, Faith and Order of the United Reformed Curch*, para. 8, in *The Manual* published by the Church, London, 1973
[133] See further, Alan P. F. Sell, *Commemorations*, ch. 4.
[134] P. T. Forsyth, *Theology in Church and State*, 123.

matter of fact, every religious body in the country that holds property is to a certain extent established,'[135] and where John Huxtable agrees,[136] it would be preferable and less ambiguous to speak of recognition, because a socio-legal point is being made, not a theological one. That is to say, it is precisely not being said that the non-Anglican churches espouse establishment theology according to which the monarch is the temporal head of the Church, and Parliament has rights over the Church's spiritual life and polity. Sixty years on the plea of the Free Church Federal Council stands: 'We should welcome a thorough examination of the forms in which ... State recognition of the Church may be accepted without impairing in any way the independence of the Church in the discharge of its proper functions.[137] The further words of Forsyth are worthy of consideration: 'Disestablishment is but ending a wrong relation of the Church to the State; we have yet to establish the right relation.'[138] What he sought was ' not a severance so much as a moving of the two far enough apart to give them room to act, and to grow, and to be themselves.'[139] Thus far we may agree with Paul Avis that most churches 'welcome some sort of partnership between church and state for the benefit of society.'[140] But it must also be possible for the Church, in the name of the Gospel, to oppose to the death an evil regime without self-destructing. Were such dire circumstances ever to overtake England we may suspect (and one bishop has already publicly predicted) that Anglicans would find a way of coping without an establishment.

I have noted, but have not elevated, some less than conclusive arguments for and against church establishment: there is surely more to it than the maintenance of pageantry on the one hand and the reform of snobbish manners on the other. Rather, I have sought to draw attention to the three major questions: Who are the Church? How may we best understand the catholicity of the Church? And 'By which polity is the Lordship of Christ in his Church best honoured?' which clamour for ecumenical attention. On the grounds that many nonconformist churches nowadays serve as *quasi* parish churches, and that the Church of England has shed many of its establishment features, David Thompson has wondered 'whether a continuing separate [nonconformist] identity is necessary.'[141] I believe that until the three theological questions specified have been earnestly addressed and satisfactorily disposed of, the

---

[135] A. C. Headlam, *The Church of England*, 194.
[136] J. Huxtable, *A New Hope for Christian Unity*, 78.
[137] G. K. A. Bell, *Documents on Christian Unity*,London: OUP, III, 1948, 111.
[138] P. T. Forsyth, *Faith, Freedom and the Future*, (1912), London: Independent Press, 1955, 318.
[139] Idem, 'The evangelical basis of Free Churchism,' 681.
[140] P. Avis, 'Establishment and the mission of a national Church,' 11.
[141] D. M. Thompson, 'The Free Churches in Modern Britain,' in P. Badham, ed., *Religion, State, and Society in Modern Britain*, Lewiston, NY: The Edwin Mellen Press, 1989, 115.

witness of Dissent is vital. One may hope that were such intensive and sincere discussion to take place the way would open for such a reconciliation of memories as between Dissent and the Church of England as would inspire the witness of the churches to the state and renew their common mission to the nation. Meanwhile Dissenters may ponder, and members of the Church of England may overhear, an epilogue from Thomas Binney:

> I am a dissenter because I am a catholic; I am a separatist, because I cannot be schismatical; I stand apart from some, because I love all; I oppose establishments, because I am not a sectarian; I think little of uniformity, because I long for union; I care not about subordinate differences with my brother, for ' *Christ* has received him, and so will I ... [142]

---

[142] T. Binney, *Dissent not Schism*, 65.

CHAPTER 12

From Union to Church: Autobiographical Recollections of Congregational Ecclesiology in the 1960s[1]

By comparison with other themes announced in the programme of this conference: politics, Abraham Lincoln, education, Cardinal Newman, I am concerned with a minor footnote in Congregational history. I was, however, asked to introduce a theological theme, and it seemed appropriate to reflect upon the doctrine of the Church as expressed within Clyde Binfield's own tradition. The following autobiographical reflections are those of one among a number who, in the 1960s, had theological reservations concerning certain proposals which were put before the Congregational *Union* of England and Wales but who, following intense discussion, were reassured and proceeded into the Congregational *Church* in England and Wales and thence into the United Reformed Church. Whereas the story of those who did not thus proceed has been told,[2] this paper represents, so far as I am aware, the first account of one in the category of the initially anxious but subsequently reassured.

It is not too much to say that for most of my life I have been haunted by ecclesiology. When I was four years of age I met Jimmy in the ice cream shop. He also was four. A month or two ago a Solemn Mass was held in celebration of the fortieth anniversary of the ordination of Father James (as he has since become). He has never deviated from the highest of High Anglicanism. When other boys would be arguing over whether Burnley were robbed when Charlton Athletic beat them 1–0 in the 1947 F. A. Cup Final, Jimmy and I would be arguing the toss about the apostolic succession, the propriety of extempore prayer, the place of bishops, and the like. On our many cycle tours of churches within a ten mile radius of our homes he always had the advantage in that when it was raining we could shelter in his buildings, mine always being firmly locked.

I was baptized in Godalming Congregational church, but by the time I met Jimmy we had moved to Cranleigh. Apart from a non-union Baptist church and

---

[1] With this paper I seek to honour Clyde Binfield in general for his valuable contribution to historical studies and, more particularly, for his grasp and practice of Congregational catholicity – both words carrying equal weight. Other contributions to this conference will refer to ecclesiology in its original sense, namely, the study of church buildings and decoration. I here use the term, as has become customary, as shorthand for 'the doctrine of the Church'.

[2] See notes 96 and 98 below.

an Evangelical Free Church there were no Dissenters around. My maternal grandparents, however, were there. They were members of the Methodist church, and that is how I fell among the Methodists. By one of those turnings of the circle so frequent in church life, Godalming Congregational (now United Reformed) church is today locally united with the Hugh Price Hughes Memorial Methodist church in that town – the very building on whose behalf my grandfather, when a young man, had gone from his home in Devonshire on fund-raising singing tours in South Wales. I attended the Cranleigh Methodist Sunday School, later joined the youth fellowship, found my way around the organ, and became what was called a junior church member. It was not long before I felt an inescapable call to the Christian ministry, something which was utterly incomprehensible to my Headmaster who, under 'Aptitudes' on my School Leaving Report wrote, 'Philosophical and abstruse.'

Of more concern to me than my Headmaster was the question, How should I fulfil my calling – and amongst whom? I was happy with the Methodists, and I clearly remember the ministers who came to our village: Howard Belben, F. G. Healey, Brian Boshier, Frederick Bagshaw, Francis Case, Fred Russell, Herbert Harris and Charles Venn – all of these in nine or ten years, and this was one of my problems. I had the idea that ministers should live longer amongst those they served: this on grounds both of pastoral care and efficient edification. It seemed to me that the Methodist system of those days, as we received it in our village, militated against that depth and continuity of fellowship between pastor and people which seemed important to me.

My other query concerned the church members. The ministers came to us, we knew not how; indeed, the members did not gather in fellowship as a whole, though class meetings were held.

I resolved to take no hasty action, and instead gave rein to my already burgeoning research instinct. I spent most of my pocket money in Thorp's secondhand bookshop in Guildford. I ransacked the place for books on the polity of the several nonconforming denominations, and what I could not find there I sought from the public library and from denominational offices. Much later I discovered that the eminent John Stoughton, who served Kensington Congregational Church with distinction from 1843 to 1875, went through the same exercise as a young man.[3] Like Stoughton, I concluded that 'on the whole' the Congregational system 'came nearest to the principles laid down in the New Testament.'[4] In particular, as far as I was concerned, it provided for consistent ministry and Church Meeting. I therefore explained myself to the understanding

---

[3] *John Stoughton. A Short Record of a Long Life*, by his daughter (Georgina King Lewis), London: Hodder and Stoughton, 1898, 15–16.

[4] Ibid., 16.

Methodists and, following a period of cycling to Godalming to church, became a member of Worplesdon Congregational Church when my family removed to that area.

To this day I continue to regard the relation of pastor and people as sacred: the analogy drawn by John Robinson, pastor to the Pilgrims, that that relationship is comparable with the relation of husband and wife in marriage does not seem to me to be at all inappropriate.[5] There are many ramifications of this which I cannot pursue here, but I should like to mention just one. Over fifty years ago Alexander Grieve, a former principal of my college, Lancashire Independent, pleaded among other things that the 'Exposition' be restored 'to its old place in Ordination and Induction services – as instruction for our own folk rather than as apologia for outsiders.'[6] The reason, of course, is that the pastoral relationship is rooted in the Gospel to which personal and not merely formal testimony is made. I fear, however, that far from restoring the Exposition, it is not even present as an option in the latest Ordination and Induction orders of the United Reformed Church.

As for Church Meeting, I believe more strongly than ever in its importance as the years go by, and I have sought to commend it to Anglicans and Presbyterians when I have had opportunity.[7] It is the point at which the congregationalists of England and Wales, whether Congregational or Baptist, completed the Reformation from the point of view of polity. Where Calvin stopped at elders, they, undeniably influenced by the socio-political circumstances in which they found themselves, brought matters down to the priesthood of believers corporately conceived; and I have always warmed to John Robinson's protest against any undue clericalism in the church which would lead to a situation in which 'Simon the saddler, Tomkin the tailor, Billy the bellows-maker must be no churchmen, nor meddle with church matters.'[8] Incidentally, another of Robinson's remarks might be taken as a challenge to the builders of megachurches in our own time: 'a particular church under the new testament, ought to consist of no more members than can meet together in one

---

[5] See J. Robinson, *Works*, London: John Snow, 1851, II, 396–7. This conviction has fuelled my critique of the uncritical adoption of the corporate model by churches, whereby the doctrine of vocation becomes a casualty. See, for example, chs. 1 above and 13 below. See further R. Tudur Jones, *John Robinson's Congregationalism*, London: The Congregational Memorial Hall Trust, 1987.

[6] Quoted by Charles E. Surman (his son-in-law), *Alexander James Grieve, M.A., D.D. 1874–1952*, Manchester: Lancashire Independent College, 1953, 47.

[7] See further, Alan P. F. Sell, *Commemorations. Studies in Christian Thought and History*, Calgary: University of Calgary Press and Cardiff: University of Wales Press, 1993; reprinted Eugene, OR: Wipf & Stock, 1998, ch. 14.

[8] J. Robinson, *Works*, II, 390.

place.'⁹ I readily concede that, like all polities which are operated by saints who are also sinners, Church Meeting is not always all it might be. I can understand something of R. F. Horton's frustration when forced to admit after an unusually long ministry at Hampstead, 'They do not know what a Church Meeting is. In fifty years I have failed to teach them.'[10] Certainly, if it is at least democratic, it should be much more than democratic. 'The true church,' wrote Lovell Cocks, 'is constituted by believers whom the Holy Spirit has gathered and over whom Christ presides; yet the believers constitute the church not as an aggregate of "saved" individuals, but as a living fellowship or commonality which seeks in all its acts of worship and witness to acknowledge the sovereign authority of its Lord.'[11] Applying this to Church Meeting he elsewhere declared, 'It is our understanding of the Gospel that makes [it] indispensable. It is not a convenient form of organization, but a way of Gospel obedience.'[12] Hence, of course, the close association of Church Meeting with the church's worship: it is a credal assembly where the Lordship of Christ is proclaimed, his will sought, and where those who by grace are one in him seek, by the Spirit, to be one in their decisions and judgments.[13] Moreover, it is not simply the local church gathered. Expecting the answer, 'Yes', Samuel Davidson of Lancashire College asked in 1848, 'Does not every church-meeting present a miniature image of the church universal?'[14] Thus, whereas to the present Pope 'to be in communion with the Bishop of Rome is to give visible evidence that one is in communion with all who confess that same faith ... ,'[15] to those who stand in, or are heirs of, the Congregational Way, the Church Meeting – or, indeed, any service of worship, yields visible

---

[9] Ibid., III, 12–13.
[10] Albert Peel and J. A. R. Marriott, *Robert Forman Horton*, London: Allen & Unwin, 1937, 186.
[11] H. F. Lovell Cocks, 'The Gospel and the Church,' in John Marsh, ed., *Congregationalism To-day*, London: Independent Press, 1943, 37. For this unduly neglected theologian see Alan P. F. Sell, *Commemorations*, ch. 13. Cf. Bernard Lord Manning, *Essays in Orthodox Dissent*, (1939), London: Independent Press, 1953, 99: 'We Congregationalists and Baptists have never been able to conceive of a churchless Christianity, a private sect, a Christian experience that is not also an ecclesiastical experience. We have always associated the grace of our Lord Jesus Christ with the communion of saints.'
[12] Idem, 'The foundation of a Congregational church,' typescript/ms in the Lovell Cocks papers, Dr. Williams's Library, London, 7.
[13] See Wilton E. Rix, 'The inner workings of a Congregational church,' in John Marsh, ed., op.cit, 64–5; Alan P. F. Sell, 'The worship of English Congregationalism,' in Lukas Vischer, ed., *Reformed Worship, Yesterday and Today*, Grand Rapids: Eerdmans, forthcoming.
[14] S. Davidson, *The Ecclesiastical Polity of the New Testament Unfolded, and its Points of Coincidence or Disagreement with Prevailing Systems Indicated*, London: Jackson and Walford, 1848, 409.
[15] This remark, delivered in the course of a sermon preached in my hearing in the Ecumenical Centre, Geneva, is taken from the text of the sermon translated from the French by the World Council of Churches, 1984.

evidence at once more impressive and more catholic (because less sectarian) of rootedness in the faith of the ages. I cannot restrain myself from echoing R. W. Dale's well-known testimony to Church Meeting:

> [T]o be at a Church meeting – apart from any prayer that is offered – any hymn that is sung, any words that are spoken, is for me one of the chief means of grace. To know that I am surrounded by men and women who dwell in God, who have received the Holy Ghost, with whom I am to share the eternal righteousness and eternal rapture of the great life to come, this is blessedness. I breathe a Divine air. I am in the new Jerusalem which has come down out of Heaven from God, and the nations of the saved are walking its streets of gold. I rejoice in the joy of Christ over those whom He has delivered from eternal death and lifted into the light and glory of God. The Kingdom of God is there.[16]

Having become a Congregationalist by conviction my call to ministry was tested in the usual ways, and although from the 'deep South', I sought entry to Lancashire Independent College, which would enable me to take advantage of three years of Arts prior to Theology, and enable me to sit at the feet of Manchester's then distinguished group of theological teachers. It would also give me plenty of preaching experience in places very strange to me. I read the texts set for the entrance examination in Congregational history and polity: Albert Peel's *Brief History* and E. J. Price's *Handbook,* and found on entering the College that I had landed among teachers – Gordon Robinson, George Phillips and Eric Hull – each of whom in his distinctive way represented the best traditions of English Dissent. My ordination took place in 1959, and in that same year the Congregational Union took a decision of considerable importance, which provoked my next series of ecclesiological excitements.

I

In 1957 Howard Stanley, the General Secretary of the Union had begun to promote the idea of a review of the entire life of the denomination from the point of view of administrative and other practicalities. Suggestions were welcomed, and at the Council Meeting of 17–18 November 1958, it was resolved to submit to the next Assembly a plan under the heading, 'The Next Ten Years'. The idea was to establish eight commissions which, between them, would examine all aspects of the denomination's life. Howard Stanley was a dynamic leader of forthright opinions bluntly expressed. Although he had a sense of humour (something which of which I was unaware until I read his obituary,

---

[16] R. W. Dale, 'The evangelizing power of a spiritual fellowship,' address to the Congregational Union of England and Wales, 1886, in D. Macfadyen, ed., *Constructive Congregational Ideals,* London: H. R. Allenson, 1902, 136.

wherein the fact is clearly stated), he really could look quite terrifying on occasion.[17] His saving graces were his enthusiasm, his deep Christian commitment, and his ability to change his mind – and admit that he had done so. Thus, in 1947, he had led the opposition to the union talks with the Presbyterian Church of England, and the project foundered.[18] For this reason John Huxtable, his successor as Union secretary, was among those who opposed Stanley's candidature for that post.[19] But Stanley's views changed, and he became the one who did more than any other to set Congregationalism on its way towards the very union he had once opposed. Again, when he first pondered a review of the denomination's life, he had practicalities in mind – not least funding; but at the Council Meeting at which he introduced 'The Next Ten Years' he declared that events had taken what, for him, was an unexpected turn, and that his proposals were now 'more theological than practical; more concerned with the why than the how; less a call to action than a call to clear and brave thinking.'[20]

This was a most significant change of direction. It gave the promise that while practical concerns and the signs of the times constituted the occasion for the review, the discussions would be grounded in the theology, and especially the ecclesiology of Congregationalism. To a considerable degree the promise was fulfilled. P. T. Forsyth would have rejoiced. Reflecting upon J. H. Shakespeare's determined efforts in the early years of the twentieth century to pull the Baptist Union into shape he referred to Shakespeare's quest of 'practical unity' and declared, 'There is but one thing that can overcome the inertia he has to meet, and that is the kind of faith, creed, and passion that makes a Church great in spite of us. For Church union ever to come about we must be more ruled by a

---

[17] *The United Reformed Church Year Book*, 1977, 272. Stanley's dates are 1901–75.

[18] The executive committee of the Lancashire Congregational Union, of which Stanley was then secretary (a post he combined with that of provincial moderator for Lancashire, Cumberland and Westmorland), appointed a special committee, whose members included Gordon Robinson, George Phillips, Kathleen Hendry and T. T. James. Their Report on the Congregational-Presbyterian union was published proposals in 1948. The unanimous special committee submitted its Report to the executive committee, two of whose members abstained from voting upon it. Among others who expressed reservations in print was C. J. Cadoux, *The Congregational Way*, Oxford: Basil Blackwell, 1945, 30–35. One wonders whether Independent Press declined to take the tract – an unsanctified suspicion, no doubt. Of those who produced the abortive *Joint Conference Report*, London: Independent Press, 1947, Gordon Robinson only was a member of the Lancashire special committee.

[19] J. Huxtable, *As it Seemed to Me*, London: The United Reformed Church,1990, 37. For Huxtable (1912–90) see also ODNB; *The United Reformed Church Year Book*, 1991/92, 229.

[20] Quoted by Norman Goodall, 'Congregationalism looks at itself. A Momentous session of the Union Council,' *The Christian World*, 17 November 1958, 7.

faith of power than by a fear of fizzling out ... [T]he Church can be unified only by the faith, insight, and passion of the same Gospel as made it.'[21]

On 12 May 1959 Howard Stanley introduced and enthusiastically commended the eight-commission scheme to the Union Assembly, which body committed itself to the task ahead.[22] While I am most concerned here with Commission I on the relations of local churches to their counties and to the national Union, church unity and oversight, it is well to list the themes of the other seven Commissions in order to show the way in which their work was theologically informed. Commission II was responsible for preparing a *Short Confession of Faith*, and a more substantial *Declaration of Faith*;[23] Commission III concerned church extension, while Commission IV examined the local church's nature, purpose, worship and practice (including the Church Meeting construed as 'part of the worship that we offer to God'),[24] the Christian use of Sunday, the place of the church in local ecumenical life, and the pattern of church organisations. Commission V considered the Church's missionary obligation; Commission VI, recruitment for the ministry, the nature of the ministry and the meaning of ordination; Commission VII the moral influence of local churches and the Union; and Commission VIII the Union itself.

There can be no doubt that while local churches and individuals responded to all of the interim reports, which were faithfully distributed to them, it was Commission I on the nature of the church, the relations between the churches and the Union, and oversight, which hit the headlines. Some smelled the burning rubber of connexionalism, and, unlike Howard Stanley, by no means all had adjusted their principled opposition to union with the Presbyterians – a matter which had been intermittently on the table since the mid-nineteen-thirties.[25] From their point of view it was almost certainly not the most tactful

---

[21] P. T. Forsyth, *Church, Ministry and Sacraments*, bound with J. Vernon Bartlet and J. D. Jones, *The Validity of the Congregational Ministry*, London: Congregational Union of England and Wales, n.d., 34. For a comprehensive account of Shakespeare's efforts see Peter Shepherd, *The Making of a Denomination. John Howard Shakespeare and the English Baptists, 1898–1924*, Carlisle: Paternoster Press, 2001. See especially Shepherd's comment (p. 48) on the growing tendency to refer to the 'Baptist Church' (as distinct from 'Union'): 'For Shakespeare, this development had more to do with pragmatism than with any question of principle. If Baptists were going to use their ministerial and financial resources efficiently to meet the challenge of twentieth-century urban society, they needed to organise themselves effectively.' See also p. 178.

[22] His address was published as *The Next Ten Years*, London: Congregational Union of England and Wales, 1959.

[23] Published in 1967, the *Declaration* remains one of the most substantial twentieth-century productions of its kind from any branch of the Reformed family. For essays on the *Declaration* see Roger Tomes, ed., *Christian Confidence*, London: SPCK, 1970.

[24] *Third Interim Report of Commission IV*, London: Independent Press, May 1961, 4.

[25] See Ronald Bocking, 'The United Reformed Church: background, formation, and after,' in Clyde Binfield, ed., *Reformed and Renewed 1972–1997. Eight Essays. Supplement to The Journal of the United Reformed History Society*, V (Supp. No. 2), September 1997, 8–9.

thing to set up the Joint Committee with the Presbyterians in 1963, in the midst of the debate over Commission I, and three years before the Congregational Union became a Church. A representative query from the grassroots is that of Michael Taylor of the Bolton and Farnworth group of Congregational churches. In 1962 he reflected upon the proposal to change from 'Union' to 'Church', and asked, 'are the demands from the World Council of Churches or Presbyterians being anticipated too strongly?'[26] There can be no question that the support which many Congregationalists gave to the findings of Commission I was motivated at least in part by the conviction that union with the Presbyterians would thereby be facilitated, or that some Presbyterians who were suspicious of union with Congregationalists felt that the Congregational transition to 'Church' was nothing more than a cynical ploy designed to mask obdurate independency.

II

It would be quite wrong to leave the impression that the matter of the relations between local Congregational churches and the wider fellowship did not surface until the middle of the twentieth century. On the contrary, the question had been discussed intermittently from the days of Congregationalism's Separatist harbingers onwards. Thus while Robert Browne declared that 'The Church planted or gathered, is a companie or number of Christians or beleeuers, which by a willing couenant made with their God, are vnder the government of god and Christ, and kepe his lawes in one holie communion,'[27] he also had a place for synods; and his synods were to be gatherings of whole churches, not of representatives only: 'A Synode is a Ioyning or partaking of the authoritie of manie Churches mette togither in peace, for redresse and deciding of matters, which can not wel be otherwise taken vp.'[28] Elsewhere, in connection with church practice and discipline, he advocated 'seeking to other churches to haue their help, being better reformed, or to bring them to reformation ...'[29] Some Separatists, however – Francis Johnson among them, resolutely declined any guidance from other churches, maintaining that the local church was omnicompetent in all matters of faith and practice. This, however, was a

---

[26] M. Taylor, 'A call for restraint,' *Group Life* (Bolton and Farnworth Congregational Group Churches), no. 37, May 1962, 3.

[27] R. Browne, *A Booke which sheweth the life and manners of all true Christians*, in A. Peel and L. H. Carlson, *The Writings of Robert Harrison and Robert Browne*, London: Allen & Unwin, 1953, 253. For a fuller study of the history of the congregational polity see Alan P. F. Sell, *Saints: Visible, Orderly and Catholic. The Congregational Idea of the Church*, Geneva: World Alliance of Reformed Churches and Allison Park, PA: Pickwick Publications, 1986.

[28] Ibid., 271.

[29] Idem, *A True and Short Declaration*, ibid., 423.

minority opinion. Many others, including Richard Mather and Jeremiah Burroughes contended for synods, while in the most concise statement of all Thomas Hooker declared that consociation was 'not only lawful, but very useful also.'[30] The *Cambridge Platform* of 1648 underlined the point and specified a number of duties, including prayer, financial aid and assistance in times of division, which the churches owed to one another. Ten years later the *Savoy Declaration of Faith and Order* followed suit. Although in chapter XXVI of *Savoy* the *Westminster Confession* is modified in such a way as to make it clear that 'the visible Catholique Church of Christ ... is not intrusted with the administration of any ordinances, or have any officers to rule or govern in, or over the whole Body,' the appended paragraphs on church order, while stating that 'there is not instituted by Christ any Church more extensive or Catholique entrusted with power for the administration of his Ordinances, or the execution of any authority in his name' than particular churches, nevertheless enjoin communion between the churches, and admit consultative and advisory synods or councils whose determinations have moral authority only.[31] To the mind of John Owen, the leading theological light behind the *Declaration*, synods, though not expressly commanded by Christ, are entirely in accordance with the Lord's mind. Indeed, 'the *end* of all particular churches is the edification of the *church catholic* unto the glory of God in Christ.'[32] Synods are to be composed of representatives from local churches (not of whole churches as in Browne's scheme), and their powers are, firstly, '*declarative*, consisting in an authoritative teaching and declaring of the mind of God in the Scripture; the second is *constitutive*, appointing and ordaining things to be believed; and, thirdly, *executive*, in acts of jurisdiction towards persons or churches.'[33] The findings of synods 'are to be received, owned and observed on the evidence of the minds of the Holy Spirit in them, and on the ministerial authority of the synod itself.'[34]

With greater or lesser regard to the principles thus sketched, the Congregationalists co-operated with one another in manifold ways as time went on. There were associations of ministers in various counties, among them the London Board of Congregational Ministers, founded in 1727. By the end of the eighteenth century there was the London Missionary Society (1795), the

---

[30] T. Hooker, *A Survey of the Summe of Church Discipline, Wherein the Way of the Churches of New England is warranted out of the Word*, 1648, IV, 1.
[31] *Savoy Declaration of the Institution of Churches, and the Order appointed in them by Christ*, paras. XV, XXVI-XXVII.
[32] J. Owen, *The True Nature of a Gospel Church and its Government*, (1689), in *Works*, ed. W. H. Goold, (1850–1853), London: The Banner of Truth Trust, 1968, XVI, 196.
[33] Ibid., 205.
[34] Ibid., 208.

Congregational Society for Spreading the Gospel in England,[35] as well as the earliest county unions of Congregational churches, and the Home Missionary Society (1819).

By 1831 there were thirty-four county unions, and to many the time seemed ripe to inaugurate a national union. Earlier attempts from 1806 onwards had failed owing to suspicions regarding the possible usurpation of the rights of the local church, and despite the powerful advocacy of a number of prominent ministers, among them John Angell James, whose book of 1822, *Christian Fellowship; or the Church Member's Guide*, was widely circulated. The *Eclectic Review* lent its weight to the cause, as did the *Congregational Magazine*, founded in 1818 and edited by John Blackburn.[36] John Morison, who was to edit the *Evangelical Magazine* for thirty years, published a lecture 'On the best Methods of promoting an effective Union among Congregational Churches, without infringing on their Independence.' While agreeing that the New Testament sanctioned no such thing as a national church, he argued that 'there existed among all the apostolic churches (though complete in themselves in point of government), an unbroken sympathy of fellowship; such a sympathy as that if "one member suffered all the members suffered with it; or, if *one member was honoured, all the members rejoiced with it.*"'[37] In 1831 the *Congregational Magazine* published contributions, many of them anonymous, for and against a national union. 'Roffensis' warned that 'Hierarchies have sprung from the most inconsiderable beginnings,' and declared, 'It is our glory that hitherto we have been no sect. We subscribe to no creed. We submit to no synod or conference. We are not properly a body. We recognize but two definitions of the term church. It designates the separate assembly of believers united together for the observance of religious ordinances; and it designates the whole number of the redeemed.'[38] To the definition of 'church' we shall return shortly. From John Nelson Goulty, a high Calvinist of the old Independent school, there came dire warnings. He saw in the projected Union 'a Trojan horse full of mischief; predicted the rise of spiritual assumption; suspected the approach of a controlling money power; deprecated the perils of centralization; and strove to

---

[35] For this largely forgotten body see R. F. G. Calder, 'The Congregational Society for Spreading the Gospel in England 1797–1809,' *Congregational Historical Society Transactions*, XIX no. 6, May 1964, 248–52.

[36] For Blackburn see Charles E. Surman, 'The Rev. John Blackburn (1792–1855), pioneer statistician of English Congregationalism,' *The Congregational Quarterly*, XXXIII no. 4, October 1955, 352–60.

[37] Quoted by A. Peel, *These Hundred Years. A History of the Congregational Union of England and Wales 1831–1931*, London: Congregational Union of England and Wales, 1931, 41. I am indebted to this book for much of the information in the present paragraph.

[38] Quoted by A. Peel, ibid., 54.

hark back his brethren from deceitful bye-ways to the well and wisely trodden paths of the old Dissent.'[39]

Suspicions and hesitations notwithstanding, the proposal for a Congregational Union of England and Wales was promulgated in May 1831, and the Union was consummated on 11 May 1832. It was made very clear that the Union was to be 'founded on the broadest recognition of their own distinctive principle, namely, the scriptural right of every separate church to maintain perfect independence in the government and administration of its own particular affairs.'[40] It followed that the Union had no legal authority over the churches, and that its objectives were to foster co-operation between them, to promote evangelism to raise funds for new buildings, to gather accurate statistics, and to work for the removal of the remaining disabilities under which Protestant Dissenters chafed. The moderate Calvinist *Declaration of Faith and Order*,[41] promulgated in 1833, declared it 'the duty of Christian churches to hold communion with each other.'[42] However, the fact that at the Autumnal Assembly held at Devonport in 1845 the Union's secretary, Algernon Wells, was still finding it necessary to insist that the Union claimed no Scriptural authority for its constitution and plans, but was a voluntary, human and legitimate expedient for accomplishing the purposes for which it had been established, suggests that some were finding reasons for their less than enthusiastic embracing of the duty.[43] In a word, at its inception the Union's basis (and, no doubt the only means by which it could have been achieved) was that whereas the local church had Scripture behind it, the Union as such did not. This point was to be reiterated during the 1960s.

As the nineteenth-century moved on it became increasingly clear that modern biblical criticism would no longer countenance the idea, on which many Congregationalists had hitherto relied, that there was one polity only sanctioned by the New Testament, namely theirs. Forsyth made no bones about it, referring to the double fallacy, 'first, that the polity in the New Testament is sole and

---

[39] So John Stoughton, *Reminiscences of Congregationalism Fifty Years Ago*, London: Hodder and Stoughton, 1881, 71–2.
[40] From the motion of May 1831 in support of the idea of a Union. It was moved by John Angell James and seconded by J. Baldwin Brown. See A. Peel, ibid., 62–3.
[41] Prepared by George Redford, one of my predecessors at Angel Street, Worcester.
[42] Clause X.
[43] It would seem that like Howard Stanley after him Wells was able to change his mind; for Thomas Binney remarked in his funeral oration for his friend that 'When the Congregational Union was first projected, he did not feel quite sure that it was allowable or safe!' Quoted by John Stoughton, *Reminiscences of Congregationalism Fifty years Ago*, 60. Samuel Davidson took a intermediate position regarding consociations. They were legitimate, he thought, but should not be called too frequently – indeed, only 'in cases of great difficulty.' He faulted the New England Congregationalists in this connection, and, against them, thought it was not the business of councils to license preachers of the Gospel, or deliberate on their removal from one pastorate to another, or depose them. See *The Ecclesiastical Polity of the New Testament*, 343.

sacrosanct; and, second, that the polity was Independency. History has shown that neither is true. Neither is true for any Church.'[44] For his part, John Stoughton, while believing that extreme Puritan restorationism was 'one of those unguarded positions into which ardent minds are betrayed by a blind consistency,' nevertheless upheld 'the principle of the authority and unchangeableness of a revealed Church polity.'[45] As to the nature of the Church – and here we return to a point alluded to earlier – modern New Testament scholarship clearly revealed that in the New Testament 'church' refers to the local congregation and to the whole body of believers only (understand: not to an intermediate 'denominational' body). In making this point a number of Congregationalists appealed to the researches of the distinguished Anglican scholar, F. J. A. Hort, which were published as *The Christian Ecclesia* in 1897.[46] Not, indeed, that some Congregationalists were prevented from continuing to regard their polity as most consonant with the New Testament. If, half a century before Hort, William Bengo Collyer, who ministered at Peckham from 1800 to 1853, could say, 'I cannot but consider Congregational churches most consonant with the constitution of primitive churches',[47] others, among them A. J. Grieve, were saying much the same thing same thing half a century after Hort. In an address on 'The Congregational tradition' delivered at Carrs Lane church, Birmingham on 1 June 1948, Grieve warned:

> Do not ... be misled by any assertion that all derive from and broke away from Episcopacy. Both it and Presbyterianism are offshoots from us and from the New Testament Church. The Early Church Universal was a Congregational type. Two points are decisive: (i) the exercise of discipline as the act of the whole body of church members – a point on which our fathers in the sixteenth century laid the greatest stress; (ii) the manner in which the ministry of the church was conceived and applied. Each Congregational 'bishop' or pastor was elected by the whole people ... [48]

A further fifty years on, it is not altogether idle to speculate that the occasional Nonconformist historian in receipt of a *festschrift* may be of a similar mind.

Reverting to the Victorians, we may first note Charles Berry's address delivered to the Union in May 1896. He took as his title, 'Congregational

---

[44] P. T. Forsyth, *Congregationalism and Reunion*, London: Independent Press, 1952, 63.

[45] J. Stoughton, 'Primitive Ecclesia: its authoritative principles and its modern representations,' in H. R. Reynolds, ed., *Ecclesia*, first series, London, 1870, 24.

[46] D. Macfadyen was one who thus referred to Hort. See *Constructive Congregational Ideals*, 293–4. He does not, however, have in mind the ideal of 'Church' as used of a denomination, but rather two things which the New Testament excludes: '(1) any use of the word which makes the Church equivalent to the "clergy"; (2) any use of the word which makes political or geographical boundaries natural boundaries for a spiritual society.'

[47] Quoted by J. Stoughton, *Reminiscences*, 69. For Collyer see DNB.

[48] Quoted by C. S. Surman, *Alexander James Grieve*, 48.

churchmanship: its principles, its privileges, its obligations.' 'Congregationalists,' he declared, 'are churchmen, as opposed to individualists. We are living members of an organism, not loose atoms wandering in eternal isolation.'[49] Pursuing a line that was to be followed from Forsyth to Daniel Jenkins, he continued,

> A Congregational Church is not a club, in which membership depends upon pew rents. Neither is it a theological society, the purpose of whose existence is to discuss speculative questions and to attempt the settlement of am philosophy of religion. It is more even than an association of admirable people, met for the promotion of ethical culture and philanthropic enterprise. Clubs and societies are makeable and manageable by men. Churches are the creation and instrument of the Holy Ghost. Christ in the heart of each, Christ in the midst of all is the spiritual factor which translates a mere human association into a Christian Church.[50]

Secondly, we should note the curiously oscillating position of Joseph Parker. In his address to the Union of 1876, Parker was highly critical of the Congregational Union and, by implication, of its then secretary, Alexander Hannay. The union, he felt was becoming autocratic, and Congregationalism was under threat. In 1901, without offering any explanation of his change of heart, he gave two addresses, complete with a draft constitution, in which he argued for the constitution of The United Congregational Church. While stoutly affirming that 'We are not contemplating the destruction of Congregationalism, but its perfection. The individual Church is the primary and indestructible unit of Congregationalism,' he declared, 'I wish to take part in the creation and full equipment of an institution to be known and developed as the United Congregational Church.'[51] Invited to comment upon Parker's scheme under the title, 'The Congregational Church', R. F. Horton began, 'The title, which is not of my choosing, is one which would never occur to a Congregationalist.'[52] As late as 1898, when Parker wrote the Preface to his autobiography, he was still contending against those who wished for a more tightly structured Congregationalism, branding Hannay 'my chief opponent'.[53] In the fifth edition

---

[49] Quoted by James S. Drummond, *Charles A. Berry, D.D., A Memoir*, London: Cassell, 1899, 139. The idea of the Church as an organism grew in popularity under the influence of post-Hegelian idealism. The Mercersburg theologians, Nevin, Schaff and others, majored on the theme, but I have no evidence that Berry was influenced by them, his American connections notwithstanding.

[50] Ibid., 140.

[51] J. Parker, *Two Addresses on The United Congregational Church*, London: Congregational Union of England and Wales, 1901, 10, 8.

[52] Quoted by Peel and Marriott, *Robert Forman Horton*, 143.

[53] J. Parker, *A Preacher's Life. An Autobiography and an Album*, London: Hodder and Stoughton, 5th edn., 1903, 258–61.

of the autobiography (1903), the passage stands unaltered, Parker's 1901 crusade for The United Congregational Church notwithstanding. Meanwhile Parker had died in 1902, but the dates 1898 and 1901 do indicate the relatively brief time which it took him to effect his startling ecclesiological about-face.

A somewhat closer relationship between local churches and the Union was secured by the adoption of the latter's new constitution of 1904, the preamble to which specified the powers and duties' of local churches and the 'duties and responsibilities' which concern Congregational churches as a whole. A further step towards the recognition of mutual responsibility was taken when the scheme of provincial moderators became a reality in 1919. As might be expected by now, a number of voices were raised against the project, of which surely the most hysterical was that of the Assembly speaker who opined that this was simply a devious plot to push bishops down our throats behind our backs! But even the most sophisticated, W. B. Selbie among them, were at pains to point out that 'The work of Moderators is purely consultative and advisory. They have no sort of authority over the churches ... '.[54] E. J. Price had invoked the same considerations in 1924, but with respect to the Union as such: 'like the county unions, it possesses no legislative authority. It is a voluntary association with no power to override the autonomy of its members.'[55]

During the next thirty years we begin to breathe a different air. Nathaniel Micklem, Lovell Cocks and various members of the Church Order Group began to emphasize the catholicity of Congregationalism (though just to show that they did not have a monopoly on the term A. J. Grieve asserted that 'It is one of the divine paradoxes that separatism and catholicity meet in the Congregational way').[56] Lovell Cocks went so far as to weigh the celebrated R. W. Dale's *A Manual of Congregational Principles* (1884) and find it wanting: 'Why does he equate Congregationalism with the autonomy of the local church to the point of making it seem that ... outward-looking concerns and compassions are optional rather than obligatory? ... Dale establishes to his own satisfaction, if not to ours, that the New Testament churches were Independent in their polity; but in the course of his argument the koinonia of those churches in Christ drops out of sight.'[57] Lovell Cocks welcomes the way in which the term 'covenant' was coming back into Congregational usage, but now with respect to the wider

---

[54] W. B. Selbie, *Congregationalism*, London: Methuen, 1927, 186–7. Cf. R. K. Orchard, 'The place of church councils,' in *Congregationalism Today*, 86–7.

[55] E. J. Price, *A Handbook of Congregationalism*, London: Independent Press, 1924, 31–2.

[56] Quoted by C. S. Surman, *Alexander James Grieve*, 47.

[57] H. F. Lovell Cocks, 'Where two or three,' *World Congregationalism*, III no. 8, May 1961, 31–2. The Presbyterian T. W. Manson quotes H. Cunliffe-Jones who, in an address to the Yorkshire Congregational Union (see *The Yorkshire Congregational Union Year Book*, 1947–1948, 15) found Dale wanting at the same point. See his *The Church's Ministry*, London: Hodder and Stoughton, 1948, 94.

family of churches, and not in relation to the local church alone. Indeed, he goes so far as to say 'Atomistic Independency is dead or dying. But the Congregational pattern of two or three gathered in Christ's name is the very hall-mark of true catholicity. We have come to see that what has made us a denomination will not let us stay a denomination, as the tides of the Spirit sweep the divided communions of Christendom towards a deeper understanding of one another ... '[58] In somewhat more down to earth fashion, Joseph Figures, Howard Stanley's successor as Lancashire moderator, blending theology, history and administrative pragmatism, asked 'what we mean by Congregationalism when we think of it in a corporate or denominational sense.'[59] He pointed to the indispensability of the county unions, regretting that they were grounded in expediency rather than doctrine, and arguing that 'the attitude and relationship of a local church to the Union and its reactions to decisions of the Union should be precisely the same as the attitude and relationship of a church member to his church.'[60]

With this we return to 'The Next Ten Years' and in particular to that aspect of Commission I's work which concerns the relations between the local churches and the national union.

III

The fourteen members of Commission I met under the chairmanship of John Huxtable, with Charles Haig as vice-chairman and John Buckingham as secretary. Daniel Jenkins and Aubrey Vine were the best-known theologians on the panel, while the two women were the Reverend Kathleen Hendry and Mrs. H. S. Stanley. An interim report entitled *Oversight and Covenant* was presented to the Council of the Union in November 1960. The document opens thus:

> Christ is both Lord and Shepherd of His people. Christian oversight (episcope) is the attempt to express His rule and care through the offices and officers of His Church. This oversight is exercised through the Minister and deacons and the Church Meeting, and also through Councils, Synods, and Assemblies, and men called to serve them in positions of leadership, for example Secretaries and Moderators.[61]

Leaving on one side the fact that neither those who commended the Commission's report nor those who queried or opposed it batted an eyelid at the assumption that those called to be in positions of leadership would be men –

---

[58] Ibid., 39.
[59] J. A. Figures, 'Corporate Congregationlism,' *The Congregational Quarterly*, XXXV no. 1, January 1957, 44.
[60] Ibid., 54.
[61] *Oversight and Covenant*, 1960, 4.

notwithstanding that women had been ordained since 1917 and Elsie Chamberlain had occupied the Chair of the Union in 1956–1957, we can see at once the point at which guardians of the Congregational Way, whether evangelical or liberal, would plunge the dagger in. The opening statement begs the question whether the oversight exercised through the minister, deacons and Church Meeting is similar in kind to that exercised by the other bodies and persons specified: indeed, whether the latter is properly called 'oversight' at all. The entire thrust of the document, however, is that oversight as described is actually experienced within the denomination, and that what is needed is the recognition of the fact. This recognition, it is argued, will best be expressed if the churches of the Union dip into their heritage for the term 'covenant' but apply it now to the fellowship as a whole. The covenant of 1946 entered into by the saints at Banstead is printed as an example of such a document,[62] and the conviction is expressed that it is 'necessary for Congregational churches to covenant with one another for the purpose of their distinctive Churchmanship.'[63] Presumably in anticipation of the objection that the move from Union to Church would further, and unhappily, entrench denominationalism in an increasingly ecumenical age, the commissioners explain that

> The churches thus associated have no wish to appear as a Denomination in distinction from other Denominations, or to weaken their own sense of ecumenicity; but since it is not at present possible to gather all Christians into one Church Order it is necessary that Congregational churches should express in some corporate form their belonging together which is so plainly a fact of their experience.[64]

They therefore propose that the churches enter into a national covenant. They state their unanimous view that the name 'Congregational Union of England and Wales' no longer adequately describes the present relationship of the churches, but they note that while twelve of their number are content that the new body be known as the Congregational Church in England and Wales, two commissioners (afterwards revealed as John Buckingham and Daniel Jenkins) felt that this would be too great a departure from tradition. Accordingly the options presented were, 'The Congregational Church in England and Wales', or, 'The Synod of the Congregational Churches in England and Wales.'[65]

---

[62] This, of course, was a *local* covenant. According to the then minister at Banstead, the Reverend Eric Allen, he and other members of the Banstead church regretted that their covenant, originally prepared under the guidance of Daniel Jenkins, was 'de-contextualized' when used as an example by the commissioners. They felt that a covenant for the denomination as a whole would necessarily be different in kind.

[63] *Oversight and Covenant*, 5.

[64] Ibid., 6.

[65] Ibid., 7.

A two-page insert accompanied the interim report. In it John Huxtable defines 'synod' and writes briefly on the use of covenants in Congregationalism, though some were soon to pounce upon what they perceived as the *non sequitur* between the traditional local covenants and any kind of national covenant. The New Testament scholar George Caird contributes a note on the term 'Church' in the New Testament. He explains that, fundamentally, there is one Church, the people of God, the new Israel; but there is also the church of the Laodiceans as well as the church in Nympha's house in Laodicea. In a word, he concludes, reasonably enough, to fluidity of useage, though some objectors (some of them only very selectively restorationist in habit) were shortly to point out that not even Caird could find 'Church *qua* denomination' in the New Testament. A pamphlet bearing the title, *A Bible Study on 'Covenant'* was also circulated on behalf of Commission I. It was anonymous, the author in fact being Gordon Robinson, not himself a member of the Commission. It is characteristically lucid and informative, but, strictly true to its title, it does not stray from biblical texts or draw any inferences from them regarding later churchly practice. However, Robinson also contributed an article to *The Christian World* of 8 June 1961 entitled, '"Covenant relationship" its history in Congregationalism.' He here sought to remind Congregationalists of the place of covenants in their tradition, whilst admitting that if they recaptured the historic idea, they would be prepared for 'the next step – which is informed consideration of the *newer* idea of the covenanted relationship of Congregational churches with each other.'[66]

John Huxtable introduced the report to the November Council meeting, and underlined the fact that the Commission's intention was to begin from the state of affairs actually pertaining: the denomination has 'in fact accepted a notion of oversight which is not confined to the local church; and the Commission has started from this fact.'[67] The point was reiterated at the following May Meetings, and the churches began to consider the report for themselves. A considerable discussion ensued in the religious press, notably in *The Christian World* (until its demise on 7 December 1961) and *The British Weekly*. Thus, for example, in his column, 'Answers to your questions', the respected minister, John Murray, explained that:

> My own reason for supporting Commission I is that I think that, through it, we are now seeking to give theological and churchly expression to so much that has been happening to us over recent decades. The face of

---

[66] W. Gordon Robinson, '"Covenant relationship": its history in Congregationalism,' *Christian World*, 8 June 1961, 7. My italics. I am very pleased to have been able to contribute a short biography of my college principal, W. Gordon Robinson (1903–1977) to the *Oxford Dictionary of National Biography*.

[67] Quoted in 'Congregationalism: Union or Church? Council debates an "historic" report,' *The Christian World*, 17 November 1960, 7.

> Congregationalism has changed, and many of our fathers would be astounded if they sat in the May meetings today and heard of all that the Union does, and saw the extent to which we have 'grown together,' so that we are no longer a loose-knit association of churches, but one fellowship ordering a common life and the many agencies needed in it. One has only to mention the Moderatorial system, the Home Churches Fund, the denominational action to recruit candidates for the minister, the nation-wide ordering of training for lay preachers and lay pastors, to be reminded of the striking extent to which we have been drawn together, and have set ourselves to do things together.[68]

In writing as he did, Murray had in mind three published letters of Sydney Myers.[69] With regard to the expressed intention of the leadership that the work of Commissions I and V should be regarded as indivisible in order that mission be brought fully into the life of the Church, Myers argued that precisely because Congregationalists were able to do all that they were doing as a Union, they could integrate the missionary work forthwith, whether or not they eventually became a covenanted Church – an outcome, he felt, which was not a foregone conclusion. With reference to the Home Churches Fund, Lovell Cocks found it necessary to endorse Murray's point, if more impishly, eleven years later in connection with the proposed scheme of union with the Presbyterians:

> Listen to this rule of the Congregational Union – you'll find it in the Year Book for 1912 or thereabouts. 'In the interest of the Aided Churches it is required as an absolute condition of grant that no invitation be given to any person to accept the pastorate, or even to supply the pulpit with a view to the pastorate, without the approval of the Executive of the County Union.' You won't find anything in the Scheme of Union half as grimly peremptory as that! What has happened to the absolute autonomy of the two or three gathered in Christ's name? Some churches it seems are more independent than others. Absolute autonomy costs more money than our aided churches can afford. If Independency means financial dependence, then anyone looking for New Testament warrant for that won't find it – though he seek it diligently and with tears.[70]

John Huxtable was indefatigable in commending the findings of Commission I. In September 1961 he acquainted the wider family of Congregationalists with the covenant proposal, and at the same time attempted to allay some of the fears at home. 'We do not envisage,' he said, 'that the local Church will be told what to do.' Rather, 'we should recognise that there are, in fact, three spheres at least in which we are made aware of receiving the guidance of the Holy Spirit, the

---

[68] J. Murray, Ibid., 5 October 1961, 8.

[69] Ibid., 20 July 1961; 17 August 1961; 14 September 1961. Norman Goodall replied to Myers on 3 and 31 August 1961; 21 September 1961.

[70] H. F. Lovell Cocks, Sermon preached at the Congregational Council Meetings, Argyle Church, Bath, on 14 March 1972, 2. Typescript in the Lovell Cocks papers.

local Church, the County Union and the National Union.' Moreover, these three spheres are equal in importance, no hierarchy is envisaged.[71]

It is interesting to note in passing that the idea underlying Commission I's report was not original to its authors, as the following quotation proves: 'Our chief Constitutional doctrine – the independence of the particular Church – remaining untouched substantially (although certain definitions and practical implications of it, which have not been uncommon, may have to be set aside), we might, quite well, if we will, put our *external relations* under some common law, to which we should all be subject. We might be as dependent mutually, as we are independent singly.' These words appear in an address entitled 'Questions and duties of the time', delivered by Alexander Raleigh to the Congregational Union in 1868.[72]

Returning to the 1960s, a further dimension was added to the debate by twenty-seven self-styled evangelical ministers who disseminated a twelve-point *Statement* almost as sombre as Zechariah's flying scroll. Among their number were Gordon Booth and Edward Guest, later to be prominent in An Evangelical Fellowship of Congregational Churches, and Gilbert Kirby of the Evangelical Alliance. It is at least mildly interesting that the twenty-seven came into the Congregational ministry by the following collegiate/non-collegiate routes:

Brecon/Swansea	7
CUEW Examinations	5
New	4[73]
Paton	4
Mansfield	2
List B	2
Cheshunt	1
Western	1
? layman	1

The fact that Lancashire/Yorkshire United/Northern and Bala-Bangor Colleges are absent from the list should not prompt unsanctified suspicions concerning the 'soundness' or otherwise of their alumni.

---

[71] J. Huxtable, 'A covenant fellowship of churches,' *World Congregationalism*, III no. 9, September 1961, 14.

[72] See *The Congregational Year Book*, 1869, 70.

[73] The four from New College were ordained in the same year, 1950. When contemplating succeeding Sydney Cave as principal of New College in 1953, John Huxtable recalls that he sought Nathaniel Micklem's advice. Micklem cautioned him not to make the mistake he himself had made on coming to Mansfield, namely, that of thinking that the battle against fundamentalism was over. Huxtable comments, 'I found out later not only how wise that judgement was; I also discovered how much Cave had suffered himself from the arrogance of those who would not, or could not, learn.' See *As It Seemed to Me*, 30–1.

In response to what they call a 'serious crisis' facing the Congregational churches the evangelicals first set down the gist of their faith in five affirmations:

(a) There is one God, in three Persons, Father, Son, and Holy Spirit, each being fully God.
(b) Man has fallen and is in a lost condition before God.
(c) Salvation is only through the atoning death of Christ and is received by faith.
(d) Conversion is necessary and, in this, the work of the Holy Spirit is indispensible [sic].
(e) The Scriptures of the Old and New Testaments are divinely inspired and of supreme authority.[74]

The co-signatories claim that these doctrines are consistent with those specified in the Savoy *Declaration* of 1658, the Congregational Union *Declaration* of 1833, and with the trust deeds 'which originally governed the vast majority of our churches and Congregational foundations.' They continue in paragraphs four and five:

We hold these doctrines to be essential to the truth of the Gospel, yet we know there are ministers and churches in the Congregational Unions which, by statement and practice deny them.

We therefore declare that to enter into any proposed covenant with such ministers and churches would, we believe, seriously compromise witness to the Gospel.

They tell us that they have studied Commission I's report, and have noted Huxtable's address, and they are in no doubt that where the findings are accepted 'the full autonomy of the local church would be lost', with the result that Congregationalism would not be modified, but abandoned.[75]

Under the headline, 'Evangelical veto,' *The Christian World* reported the circulation of the *Statement*, and uttered its first 'reaction of regret ... that these ministers should have contemplated what must be called a new form of separatism within the "separatist churches".'[76] The following week 'Nemo' observed against the evangelicals' strong plea for uninhibited local autonomy, that 'An independency that will not listen to testimony as to what Christ is saying to the churches has always been a false Congregationalism.'[77] In the same issue John Ticehurst presumed to find the evangelicals' statement of faith an

---

[74] *A Statement*, privately circulated, para. 3.
[75] Ibid., paras. 7, 8.
[76] *The Christian World*, 5 October, 1961, 1.
[77] Ibid., 12 October 1961, 2.

'emasculated affair which does not, for example, mention the Manhood of our Saviour,' and he boggled at their non-Congregational fondness for a credal test on the basis of which they will decide the Christian status of others and agree to covenant only with those who think as they do. He cheekily noted that the signatories were located in various parts of the country and thus were not a Church Meeting, and hence, on their own premisses, could be divinely guided; and as for their call to others to urge the rejection of Commission I's proposal in County Union meetings, this, he declared, 'seems to smack of casting out devils by the Prince of Devils.'[78] In a circular letter to his co-signatories Edward Guest wrote, 'We have been accused of being strong in our Statement. Well – we were sounding an alarm, not crooning a lullaby. Enough dreamers around already!'[79]

Meanwhile there were stirrings in the most north-westerly parts of the Yorkshire Dales (as they then were); and here I revert to autobiography. A Congregationalist by conviction, and less than two years into my first pastorate at Sedbergh and Dent, I attended the annual Dales Conference at Hawes on 29–30 May 1961. On the evening of 30th Norman Beard, secretary of the Yorkshire Union, introduced Commission I's report and, according to my diary, I made some critical comments, with which Norman Beard agreed.[80] Later in the year, on Saturday 28 October, a special meeting of the Dales churches was held at Hawes, with Norman Beard again present. Two days previously the Dales ministers had held a fraternal at which, to quote my diary again, 'we planned our campaign for Saturday.' It transpired that the general feeling among the Dales churches was that the Commission's proposal could not be endorsed until certain matters had been clarified – if then. In view of the Dales discussions and the wider debates in the press, I was by now increasingly concerned on the one hand that there were ecclesiological issues which had yet to be adequately

---

[78] J. Ticehurst, 'The new separatists,' *The Christian World*, 12 October 1961, 2. Letters for and against the evangelicals were published, ibid., 19 October 1961; and on 26 October Charles Haig published 'An open letter to the evangelicals' in which he addressed them (knowingly using the 'language of Canaan'?) as 'My dear brothers in Christ.' On 2 November ten evangelicals signed an article in reply to Haig. It is thus surprising that one of the evangelical signatories, Walter H. Denbow, should begin the second of four privately-circulated pamphlets with the remark that 'the publishing facilities of both Independent Press and Christian World are reserved exclusively for the support of the Commission Reports. Both definitely decline to publish criticisms of the Reports, direct or implied, while they are before the Churches.' Unlike the evangelical *Statement*, Denbow's pamphlets major on autonomy rather than more general doctrine. Indeed, having regard to the evangelicals' doctrinal criterion of fellowship, it is faintly ironic that in the second pamphlet (p. 2) he can write in block capitals, 'COVENANT WILL NO MORE BIND OUR CHRISTIAN CONDUCT THAN CREED WILL BIND OUR CHRISTIAN BELIEF.'

[79] Quoted by Gordon Booth, 'Winds of change in Congregationalism,' *The Christian*, 23 February 1962, 8.

[80] For J. Norman Beard (1910–96) see *The United Reformed Church Year Book*, 1997, 270.

addressed and, on the other hand, that claims were being made by the defenders of Congregationalism which seemed to me to be spurious. Accordingly, I wrote a draft article under the title, 'A Dales view of Commission I,' and went up to the Manse at Ravenstonedale to discuss it with my senior colleagues, George Curry and Arnold Mee.

These two colleagues could not have been more different from each other, or from myself, though I suppose that we could all consistently have labelled ourselves 'evangelical' had that word not been so sadly hijacked, and provided that we could also call ourselves liberal, catholic and Reformed. George Curry (1901–1991), a larger-than-life Greatheart from the north-east, who had been raised among the Methodists and who, after an engineering apprenticeship, had served as a circuit rider in deepest Saskatchewan, finally returning to his native parts via a two-year sojourn on the Isle of Wight, had become a Congregationalist by conviction. By now he was the Dales minister, enjoying his roving ministry over a vast tract of country extending from Newton-in-Bowland to Keld, and from Sedbergh to Richmond. He faithfully tended his extensive patch in all weathers, and it cannot in truth be said that the winding, undulating roads were made less terrifying by the presence of his hurtling Mini upon them. At the time of our little crusade he was chairman of the Yorkshire Union.[81]

Arnold Mee (1901–1966) was a life-long Congregationalist, raised in Leeds under the celebrated ministry at Salem of Bertram Smith and Francis Wrigley. Never robust in health, he eventually went blind, and to those who looked on this was a particularly cruel blow upon one who was a fine scholar, not least of Hebrew. For a period Arnold had served with great success as tutor at Yorkshire United College, but failing eyesight dictated that the rest of his ministry would be in rural pastorates. A man of deep faith, sharp yet kindly wit, and no mean poet, Arnold Mee was a blessing to all who met him.[82]

These were the two who cast their eye over my draft article. To my considerable surprise they approved it without amendment and said that they would happily endorse it should it appear in *The Christian World*. On 31 October 1961 I wrote to the editor to ask if he would accept the piece, pointing out that my co-signatories and I felt that 'out of our bewilderment arise certain questions which have not so far been raised in the columns of your paper.' By the same post I sent a copy of the article to John Huxtable, whom I had never met, assuring him that 'there is no connection between the submission of our effort today, and Luther's action [in nailing up his theses] 444 years ago today!!'

---

[81] For his obituary see *The Congregational Year Book 1991/1992*, Nottingham: Congregational Federation, 30–31.

[82] See further, Joan W. Moody [daughter], *Arnold Francis Mee 1901–1966*, privately printed; *The Congregational Year Book 1966–1967*, 460–61.

Huxtable replied by return. He felt that we had not sufficiently considered the actual state of current Congregationalism, and that we had made too much of the proposed change of name. Indeed, he pointed out that 'we make no recommendations about it at all if you look at the document carefully. We state the fact that some of us think that we might as well call ourselves a church and be done with it, since, in fact, we are functioning as one, and that a small minority thought that the word "synod" would cover the matter better ... '.[83] I circulated Huxtable's letter to my colleagues, and could not forbear to point out to them that even if the name 'Church' were not, technically, the subject of a Commission recommendation, it could not be denied that the alternatives of 'Church' and 'synod' had formally been proposed for consideration by the commissioners themselves.

The burden of the Dales article, which on publication was re-titled, 'Commission I: from the camp of the "bewildered",'[84] was that there was more theological work to be done before final decisions could be made. The first question was that of the relative authority of the several *foci* of churchly life. Secondly, the statement in the Commission's report to the effect that national covenanting was a necessity 'for the purpose of [our] distinctive Churchmanship'[85] was queried as to the nature of the 'necessity' involved: 'It cannot be logical necessity,' I boldly declared, 'for we are not covenanted at present and yet believe that we have a distinctive Churchmanship. Surely the implication is not that if we do not covenant we shall have a distinctive Churchmanship no more?' Thirdly we sought more guidance on the nature and implications of the covenant sought, noting that dissatisfaction with the term 'Union' had not adequately been explained, 'For the people behind the Report obviously do not subscribe to the erroneous belief that the only factor which provides our present sense of fellowship is the payment of an affiliation fee. If they did believe this, they could hardly employ the "regularising of what already obtains" argument.' Finally, we sought a stronger theological justification of the use of the terms 'Church' or 'Synod' with reference to the national body. 'What's in a name?' we asked in conclusion: 'In this case the answer is "Our doctrine of the Church." And that is why the matter is so important.' Our position thus was that we could not vote for or against the proposal until further illumination had been granted.

The article drew a gracious response from Charles Haig, in which he reiterated the Commission's line, sought to reassure us that 'We are interested in forming a Congregational Church, not any other sort' (though he was deficient

---

[83] Huxtable to Sell, 1 November 1961.
[84] See *The Christian World*, 9 November 1961, 8.
[85] *Oversight and Covenant*, 5.

in the detail), and was even prepared to believe that the term 'covenant' may not be the best to express what the Commission has in mind – albeit it was difficult to think of an adequate alternative term.[86]

To my very great surprise I began to receive letters from many quarters, mostly from people whom I had never met. All unwittingly I found myself in the position of a communications channel which involved much correspondence, and this at a time when I was writing two sermons and an evening lecture every week, serving on the local Council, and finishing my MA thesis. The first response was from Hugh Kember, one of the twenty-seven evangelicals, who had given the charge at my Ordination, and with whom I continue in close friendship. The next was from Principal Maurice Charles of Paton College,[87] with whom George Curry and I were to work closely over the next few months. Through him we came into contact with Reginald Cleaves a successor of P. T. Forsyth at Clarendon Park, Leicester.[88] The correspondence continued to flow, and on 25 November 1961 the Dales trio decided to support a petition to the Congregational Council urging that in view of the serious division of opinion among Congregationalists over Commission I's proposal, any resolution assuming that churches are ready to make a final decision in May 1962 be postponed. R. W. Cleaves sent the letter to Howard Stanley on 5 January 1962, with copies to C. J. Buckingham, secretary of Commission I, Norman Goodall of Commission V, and the press. There were twenty-one signatories, and no overlap between this list and the evangelical one. Indeed, Cleaves wrote in his letter to Stanley, 'The signatories are not members of any organised group, nor have they met at any time to deliberate on the matter in question.'

The petition duly appeared in *The British Weekly* of 22 February 1962, under the headline, 'Anxious Congregationalists advise delay.' Thereafter we were labelled, and further letters were published for and against the petition, including one from Charles Haig, who felt that the petitioners were overestimating the degree of divided opinion among Congregationalists.[89]

To some of the points raised in correspondence the Dales trio replied. Haig had suggested that the way to see how great the division of opinion was was to have a full-scale debate in the assembly, with a view to testing the 'main principle.' We felt that since the materials had been circulated to every church, every church should be permitted to submit the finding of its Church Meeting as data for consideration by the Assembly. We countered that the division of

---

[86] C. A. Haig,'Commission I: a word to the bewildered,' *The Christian World*, 23 November 1961, 8. For Haig (1910–1986), who came to the ministry from the law, see *The United Reformed Church Year Book*, 1986/87, 197.
[87] For Maurice Charles (1903–1964) see *The Congregational Year Book*, 1964/5, 436–7.
[88] For R. W. Cleaves (1915–1980) see *The Congregational Year Book*, 1980/81, 154.
[89] *The British Weekly*, 1 March 1962.

opinion between the supporters of the Commission's proposals and, for example, the evangelical signatories was great. And we pressed again the fundamental point that many were still unclear as to what the 'main principle' was, and that a theological justification be given of the leap from our present (welcome) degree of unity to an assertion concerning the nature of the Church which we had not hitherto made – namely, that a denomination is a Church. We were concerned lest we should be 'undermining part of our distinctive testimony to the essential oneness of the Church, by making it appear that we think there is more than one Church.'[90]

Once it became known that a motion was to be put at the May Meetings urging that 'a serious attempt be made to implement the main findings of Commission I,' and to appoint 'a fully representative committee' with that end in view, a meeting was convened at Paton College on 24 April 1962. George Curry and I went down from the Dales, and there I met not only Maurice Charles and Reginald Cleaves for the first time, but also Gordon Booth, one of the evangelical signatories. The upshot of the meeting was that an amendment to the Council's motion was prepared consistent with our wish for further consideration of the theological principles prior to a final vote. Our amendment was 'That a serious attempt be made to consider the implementing of the main findings of Commission I ... '. It was signed by fifteen ministers (all that could be mustered in the time available) duly published in *The British Weekly* on 10 May, as was a letter expressing the opposition of thirty evangelicals. Early in May I received a letter from Gordon Booth in which he pledged the support of what he called the evangelical 'Resistance Movement'.[91] I rushed a note to the editor of the *British Weekly*, which he appended to our letter. In it I said that a group of evangelical ministers was prepared to support the amendment: 'I do not know their precise reasons for this, and it would be unjust to give the impression that our motives necessarily coincide. The fact of this support, however, confirms my opinion that the introduction of the word "consider" into the original proposition, which is what our amendment suggests, would have a valuable therapeutic effect.'

On 7 May Reginald Cleaves agreed to move the amendment. To my very great surprise, others having been approached and being unavailable, I found myself in the position of seconding it. So it came to pass that on 16 May 1962, in a packed Westminster Chapel, Hubert Cunliffe-Jones, the proposer of the official resolution, asked in the name of himself and his seconder, John Huxtable, for permission to substitute the the phrase 'work out the implications of ... ' for the word 'implement'. This was not allowed, so the motion as published was moved

---

[90] Ibid., 8 March 1962, 6.
[91] Booth to Sell, 3 May 1962.

and seconded: 'That a serious attempt be made to implement the main findings of Commission I ... ' Then Reginald Cleaves moved our amendment proposing the introducton of the words, 'consider implementing' in place of 'implement'. His speech emphasised the Congregational heritage and especially the autonomy of the local church. I, having first pointed out that I had never before addressed so large a congregation, adduced four reasons for the introduction of the word 'consider'. First, it would make sense of the resolution; for 'If we really want a fully representative, ungagged, committee, the word 'consider' must be in.' Secondly, 'The word "consider" is needed so that more homework will be encouraged.' In particular, more work is needed on the so-called 'third Church' subsisting between the local church and the great Church; a fuller statement of our doctrine of the Church is required – in the year of the tercentenary of the Great Ejectment of all years; and we should learn from recent merger history, especially in America, the folly of undue haste. Thirdly, 'The word "consider" is desirable because it will help to heal. Many of the anxious and many evangelicals can support the amendment.' Finally, 'further consideration will enable us to discover what is our distinctive contribution for the sake of the Great Church.' Let us not confuse dying in order to live with committing suicide. I concluded, 'Mr. Chairman, I second the amendment because it makes better sense of the original propositon, it will encourage more homework, it will help to heal, and it is for the good of the whole Church.' Cleaves and I were then asked in the puplit whether we could accept the phrase, 'work out the implications of ... '. I thought that this was ambiguous: was it assumed that we knew what the implications were, and all we had to do was to put them into effect? Or, did we need to work out what the implications were? I could be happy with the latter. Cleaves addressed the Assembly again, arguing that the words 'work out the implications of' meant the same as 'consider', to which those gathered responded 'Yes' in chorus. Cunliffe-Jones's wording carried the day; at least it was preferable, even in its ambiguity, to the original; and assurances were given that the points raised in the debate would be addressed by the representative committee. As I came down the steps of the enormous pulpit, Norman Goodall was passing at the bottom. He said, 'I hope we shall hear more of you.'

Geoffrey Beck's report of the debate in *The British Weekly* of 24 May was so compressed as to be misleading, and in response to a request from Cleaves,[92] the official minute was published in the paper on 7 June, over the signatures of John Huxtable, H. A. Hamilton, the Union chairman, and Howard S. Stanley. The minute stated that Cleaves and I withdrew our amendment. However, we did

---

[92] Cleaves to Sell and Curry, 31 May 1962.

not; we accepted Cunliffe-Jones's wording as an interpretation of it – a point which Cleaves made to Huxtable and Hamilton in a communication of 11 June.

Meanwhile on 18 May I wrote to John Huxtable expressing my pleasure at the way things had gone in the Assembly, reiterating my hope that the theological issues would receive due consideration, and reminding him that in his letter responding to the Dales article he had said that 'It would be much easier to discuss this in conversation.' I requested a meeting, and on 28th we met in his office. We then had lunch together, and our conversation continued in a taxi heading for an up-market gents outfitters, where he was to purchase a black Homburg in anticipation of a junket with the Archbishop of Canterbury. I was thus able to put my two main points directly to him: the first concerning the importance of oversight conceived mutually as between the several *foci* of churchly life; the second concerning the need, on ecumenical grounds, of admitting that the use of the term 'Church' for 'denomination' is biblically and theologically irregular. The main outcome of the meeting from my point of view was his reiteration of the assurance that the theological work would be done, and that he was on the representative committee to ensure that it would be.

The committee duly went to work, and in May 1963 a *Draft Constitution* together with *A Commentary* on it written by Robert Latham was presented to that Assembly and remitted to the churches for consideration.[93] It is most unfortunate that in his resumé of the events leading to the drafting of the Constitution Latham, in an otherwise able exposition, should have quoted the *original* that the main findings of Commission I be implemented, as if it were the Assembly's final resolution. I wrote to Hubert Cunliffe-Jones about this and in reply he said,

> I am sorry there is a misstatement in Robert Latham's Commentary. But I don't think there is anything sinister in this. This has been done in a great hurry and the resolution may have been copied wrongly by the typist. By all means write to Howard Stanley, call his attention to the misstatement and I think he will cancel it publicly. He likes to have things correctly stated.
>
> On the point of substance, we are not going to implement anything that we do not agree to. I am sorry that this mistake has occurred at a point where there is, understandably enough considerable feeling.[94]

---

[93] John Marsh contributed a balanced article, 'Understanding the Draft Constitution' to *The British Weekly*, 9 May 1963, 3.

[94] Cunliffe-Jones to Sell, 4 May 1963. For Cunliffe-Jones (1905–91) see *The United Reformed Church Year Book*, 1991/2, 226–7.

IV

How far was I reassured by the *Draft Constitution*? The strategy adopted was that the question of the name of the denomination should not be considered unless and until the principle of a national covenant had been agreed. There was thus no discussion of the definition of 'Church' in the documents. There was, however, a clear statement of the mutuality of *episcope* as between the local and wider *foci* of churchly life: 'Both the local church and this covenanted body are under the same authority – the Lordship of Christ. Both are pledged to discern the mind of Christ for themselves and to listen to the testimony of others as to what the mind of Christ is ... '[95] This I greatly welcomed, because it seemed to me to honour that catholic thrust which had ever been inherent in Congregationalism, but which had too frequently been obscured by restrictive understandings of local autonomy. Moreover, only along the lines of mutual *episcope* could due weight be accorded to the remark (sadly, one of relatively few remarks published) of my teacher of doctrine, the much loved George Phillips: 'The active presence of the Holy Spirit is ... the principle of Church unity rather than any form of external authority ... Hence the imposition of an external authority upon the Church of Christ seems to us, as to our fathers, a humiliation, and a usurpation of the sole right of the Divine Spirit.'[96] I took further encouragement from Commission I's report on *The Nature of Christian Unity and its Challenge to our Churches*, which was submitted to the 1963 Assembly of the Union:

> Neither man nor party, nor Church Meeting nor Assembly can arrogate the right to be considered the sole authoritative interpreter of the Mind of the Spirit. It is not possible to exclude the possibility of error, even when a Council or Asembly of the Church has spoken. Nor, on the other hand, can a minority or dissident individual make good the claim to be the sole medium of the Spirit's guidance. Majorities may be arrogant, but minorities can be self-willed.[97]

It is difficult to conceive that the transition from Union to Church would have been made at all had the principle of mutual *episcope* not clearly been written into the Draft Constitution. As it was, the transition was not accomplished without a parting of the ways.

---

[95] *Draft Constitution*, London: Congregational Union of England and Wales, 1963, 8. Cf. the pamphlet, *Some Questions and Answers*, para. 6. This was published to accompany Commission I's Interim Report.

[96] G. Phillips, 'Freedom in religious thought,' in *The Fourth Freedom*, London: Independent Press, 1943, 51. George Phillips was raised among the Strict Baptists.

[97] *The Nature of Christian Unity and its Challenge to our Churches*, 5.

By now I was feeling increasingly that the labels attached to Congregationalists: 'Commission supporters', 'bewildered', 'anxious, 'evangelical' were obscuring more than they revealed. I was able to see the point of Nathaniel Micklem's assertion that while the local church has a 'faith structure' in that the final appeal is to the authority of Christ, 'Our denomination has an expediency-structure, not a faith-structure.'[98] I felt that some of those alongside whom I had pressed for further theological clarification were more concerned with local autonomy as such, than with the idea that the local church is an expression of the Church catholic, with all that that means in terms of wider fellowship not on grounds of expediency or utility, but of right. I was not surprised, therefore, when Reginald Cleaves and George Curry subsequently became leaders of the Congregational Federation.[99] Again, while a number of evangelicals were willing to support those who appeared to be striving for local autonomy – in their case because they did not wish to be unequally yoked with those whose understanding of Scripture differed from their own, they knew and I knew that their credal criteria appeared to many as a 'new circumcision' on the basis of which they would judge the Christian status of others. The sensitivity of my ecclesiastical antennae to evangelical sectarianism did not, of course preclude me from agreeing with Robert Mackintosh, who said that 'The body of Congregationalism might continue to exist for a season, though it had ceased to be an expression of evangelical faith and life; but the soul which has animated it would be gone. And a body without

---

[98] N. Micklem, *Congregationalism and the Church Catholic*, London: Independent Press, 1943, 30.

[99] See R. W. Cleaves, *Congregationalism 1960–1976. The Story of the Federation*, Swansea: John Penry Press, 1977. It is to be feared that some statements herein are tendentious. For example, of those who eventually became part of the United Reformed Church it is said that 'For them, Historic Independency no longer mattered and was thrown to the wind', p. 9. This is a libel, and one suspects that it is not how some uniting Presbyterians, trying to get their minds around the idea of Church Meeting, viewed matters. See also the review of the book by F. R. Tomes in *The Journal of the United Reformed Church History Society*, II no. 1, April 1978, 25–6. It should be noted, however, that in his Presidential Address to the Congregational Federation, 'Jesus is Lord,' delivered to the 151st Congregational Assembly on 8 May 1982, John C. Travell sought to place some of the 'autonomy' talk in its theological context: 'May I confess that it makes me uneasy that our Year Book states that the Foundation Principle of our Federation is "the scriptural right of every separate Church to maintain perfect independence in the government and administration of its affairs" ... [T]he reason *why* this Assembly or the Federation shall not assume legislative authority is because Christ alone is head of his Church. That is our true distinctive principle and the reason why we believe in the independence of the local church is so that it may be free more directly to be obedient to its Lord. It is not a matter of rights but of faith,' 1. See also J. C. Travell, 'The Congregational Federation 1972–1997,' in *Reformed and Renewed*, 29–42.

a soul is a corpse.'[100] In due course a number of the evangelicals constituted An Evangelical Fellowship of Congregational Churches.[101]

While so far reassured, I continued to feel that it was ill advised to discuss the nature of a covenanted body apart from its name, for the one could not really be divorced from the other. I argued along this line at the Dales Conference on 2 November 1963. Speaking for the Commission was Martin Shepherd, the Yorkshire moderator and member of the representative committee.[102] In responding to my paper he, according to my diary, 'got a bit overwrought.' In all of this I was hoping for the recognition that to call our national body a Church was a departure from our tradition, and a development of New Testament teaching, which could be countenanced only on the grounds that it was an interim usage given the divided state of the whole Church.[103] I did not wish us to become a sectarian bloc – a consideration which did not seem to weigh so heavily upon some of my 'anxious' and 'evangelical' friends. Embedded in the Sedbergh church's response of 28 February 1964 to the *Draft Constitution*, submitted to Howard Stanley, is the following sentence: 'if we become a churchly body (as though we believed that there are numerous Churches), may we not be surrendering a part of our historic witness too soon – i.e. outside the context of a truly representative round-table conference of churchmen? Or, alternatively, has it been found already that nobody will listen to us on this point and that we are destined to be eternally out on a limb unless we amend our views?' It is true that Commission I's original report had declared that 'The churches thus associated have no wish to appear as a Denomination in distinction from other Denominations, or to weaken their own sense of ecumenicity; but since it is not at present possible to gather all Christians into one Church Order it is necessary that Congregational churches should express in some corporate form their belonging together which is so

---

[100] R. Mackintosh, 'The genius of Congregationalism,' in A. Peel, ed., *Essays Congregational and Catholic*, London: Congregational Union of England and Wales, [1931], 125.

[101] For a brief account of *An Evangelical Fellowship of Congregational Churches* see that body's Year Book, 1990–1991, 21; Alan Tovey, 'An Evangelical Fellowship of Congregational Churches 1972–1997,' in *Reformed and Renewed*, 42–50; E. S. Guest, *Wandering Pilgrims. Whatever Happened to the Congregational Churches?* Beverley: The [sic] Evangelical Fellowship of Congregational Churches, 1998. The difference in attitude between the founders of the Federation and the evangelicals is captured by Gordon Booth in an article entitled, 'Continuing Congregationalists,' published in *Evangelical Times*, June 1972, 10, in the wake of the constitution of the Congregational Federation on 13 May 1972. There are in addition some independent Congregational churches which, in order to receive their due from the assets of the Congregational Church in England and Wales, were designated Unaffiliated by the Charity Commissioners. Their story is told by John Franks, *Stewards of God's Bounty. The History of the Unaffiliated Congregational Churches Charities*, June 1996.

[102] For M. Shepherd (1902–72) see *The United Reformed Church Year Book*, 1973/74, 281–2.

[103] See further, Alan P. F. Sell, *Saints: Visible, Orderly and Catholic*, 115.

plainly a fact of their experience.'[104] But how this bore on the doctrine of the Church to be espoused was not, in the initial stages of the debate, clear.

As the discussion proceeded, however, encouraging comments from various quarters began to coalesce. I have already mentioned the principle of mutual *episcope* which was built into the Constitution, and, consistently with this, the witness to the local church as an expression of the Church catholic. This latter point was underlined in the *Declaration of Faith* produced by Commission II and finally adopted in 1967.[105] In addition, members of Commission I began more frankly to endorse the truth that the New Testament knows nothing of a 'third Church' between the local church and the whole Church. Thus, for example, John Huxtable declared that the proposed use of 'Church' of the denomination as a whole 'certainly has no literal warrant in scripture.'[106] He reiterated the point elsewhere, but asked, 'in the present unhappily divided state of the Church, in which Anglicans, Presbyterians and Methodists can speak of Churches, might we not, without too great a damage to language, so describe ourselves?'[107] It is not without interest that, according to its secretary, Martin Cressey, the exegetical point was conceded by the Joint Committee of Presbyterians and Congregationalists who were preparing the *Basis of Union* of the United Reformed Church, and that to call a denomination a Church is to demonstrate 'that the failure and weakness of the Church have in particular been manifested in division which has made it impossible for Christians fully to know, experience and communicate the life of the one, holy, catholic, apostolic Church.'[108] What seems undeniable is that the covenanting together of the Congregational churches in 1966 as the Congregational Church in England and Wales facilitated the eventual constitution of the United Reformed Church in 1972. The theological tasks sufficiently done, I happily accepted both decisions, believing that the insights of Congregational catholicity had been preserved in a church order which emphasised the *mutuality* of *episcope* as between the local and wider *foci* of churchly life, and that the anomalous, interim, denominational

---

[104] *Oversight and Covenant*, 6.

[105] See *A Declaration of Faith*, 34.

[106] J. Huxtable, *Proceedings of the International Congregational Council*, X, 1966, 33.

[107] Idem, *As It Seemed to Me*, 38. Among earlier stalwarts in denying the 'third Church' idea was C. J. Cadoux. See his *The Congregational Way*, 18–19; 'Congregationalism the true catholicism,' in *Essays Congregational and Catholic*, 69–70. John Marsh, on other matters significantly apart from Cadoux, reiterated the point in 'Obedience to the Gospel in terms of churchmanship and church order,'*Congregationalism To-day*, 48–9. Erik Routley was among more prominent authors who in the 1960s queried the proposed application of 'Church'. See his *Congregationalists and Unity*, London: Mowbray, 1962, 31-3. He preferred to think of Congregationalism as 'an order within the church catholic,' 34. For a 'classical' statement on the matter see R. W. Dale, *A Manual of Congregational Principles*, 212.

[108] *Basis of Union*, para. 7, quoted by M. Cressey, 'The theology of union,' in *Reformed and Renewed*, 22.

use of the term 'Church' was a stimulus to work to render it redundant.[109] Indeed, in that spirit I spoke in the Union Assembly debate on 19 May 1965, when the motion to change the Congregational denomination's name from 'Union' to 'Church' was successful. The consummation came one year later in a Service of Thanksgiving and Dedication held on 22 May 1966 at Whitefield Memorial Church, London.

V

I little thought, during the ecclesiological excitements of the early 1960s, that twenty years on I would be regularly engaged in international bilateral dialogues on largely ecclesiological issues as Theological Secretary of the World Alliance of Reformed Churches, or that forty years on I would still be summoned as a consultant to such dialogues. That is another chapter, but it is all part of the story which began when I met Jimmy in the ice cream shop in 1939.

---

[109] R. W. Cleaves was thus mistaken in implying that all those who has earlier been labelled 'anxious Congregationalists' found their way into The Congregational Association. See his 'The Congregational Association,' *Congregational Monthly*, June 1969, 4. I corrected the error in ibid., July 1969, 14, concluding that in my opinion 'what is of value in Congregationalism is to be found within the C[ongregational] C[hurch in] E[ngland and] W[ales].'

CHAPTER 13

Reminiscence, Reflection, Reassurance

In the course of a vagrant ministry my wife and I have found it a privilege to live amidst a variety of cultures, and to visit many more, each with its own attractions, traditions and challenges. But Wales take the prize for the proliferation of tales of ministers of yesteryear, who seem to be as much remembered for their eccentricities as for anything they might have had to say about the Gospel. During the past nine years I have been regaled with many such stories, and they never lose anything in the telling. Today I take my revenge. I introduce this Davies Lecture by referring to a minister from my own native tradition.

John Stoughton was born in Norwich on 18 November 1807, and died in London on 24 October 1897. After training at Highbury College and graduating in the University of London he ministered first at Windsor (1832–1843) and then from 1843 to 1875 he conducted a distinguished ministry in Kensington. From 1872–1884 he was professor of historical theology at New College, London. He was honoured with the DD of the University of Edinburgh, and occupied the Chair of the Congregational Union of England and Wales in 1856. At many points I feel a certain kinship with this giant of the past. Not only was he an inveterate scribbler, but when he was a child 'He was never interested in athletic sports, but amused himself by making a little theatre and writing plays'[1] – just as I myself did. But above all I empathize with his firm commitment to the principles of his denomination, coupled with his catholic, non-sectarian spirit, which yielded him friends from across the Christian spectrum.

Of all his many books, the one from which I take my cue is entitled, *Reminiscences of Congregationalism Fifty Years Ago*. It was published in 1881, and in it Stoughton looks back across half a century to the 1830s, comparing and contrasting those years with the present. He ponders the changes in theological thought, the style of preaching, the ecclesiastical scene, home life, mentioning along the way the increasing political influence of the Nonconformists and the growing friendship between them and the Church of England. I shall refer to some of the things he says as we proceed. My point at present is that as I re-read this short but most informative book, it struck me that the year 2002 would see the fiftieth anniversary of my first public sermon. I did not suppose that that

---

[1] *John Stoughton DD. A Short Record of a Long Life*, by his daughter (Georgina King Lewis), London: Hodder and Stoughton, 1898, 8.

anniversary will occasion widespread rejoicing, and I hoped it would not become a time of widespread lament. But the thought of it prompted me to muse, Stoughton-like, in a 'then and now' way. Hence the theme of this lecture. I propose to recall the Church and the world of fifty years ago with a view to reflection on the contemporary situation, and to utter that most necessary word of reassurance which alone motivates and sustains Christians in their faith and service in any age. The biblical-theological justification of my method is that the present witness of those who stand in the Judaeo-Christian tradition has ever been informed and inspired by the grateful remembrance of God's providence in times past, by confidence in his grace and mercy in the present, and by a good hope for the future – themes which for Christians are nowhere more dramatically telescoped than at the Lord's Supper.

I

When thinking of the Church I think first of its primary obligation, the worship of God. The first question in the *Westminster Shorter Catechism* of 1648 is, 'What is the chief end of man?' The answer (subsequently purloined and modified for use as the final clause of the Presbyterian Church of Wales's *Short Confession*) is, 'Man's chief end is to glorify God, and to enjoy him for ever.' It is not difficult to find examples of those who would utterly repudiate the *Catechism*'s answer. Henry Braverman, for example, in his classic work on management and capitalism, contended that work constitutes humanity's central purpose, and is the primary factor in motivating individuals.[2] And even if some allow, as has been pronounced from many a pulpit, that human beings are so constituted that they must worship something, they clearly do not all worship the same thing. As long ago as 2 December 1836 the *Philadelphia Public Ledger* famously declared that 'The almighty dollar is the only object of worship.'

But my concern today is not with the ends proposed for human life by others; or with the many possible objects of worship before which people may bow down. My question is how far we ourselves are honouring the profession we make. The *Catechism* rightly proclaims that worship, literally, the declaration of God's worth, is the business of the whole of life. In general terms, therefore, everything I shall say in this lecture concerns worship. But I also wish to be specific, and so I ask, first, What of the Sunday act of worship?

As long ago as 1928 the Anglican A. H. Clutton-Brock proffered some homely advice on the subject. Like the curate's egg, it is good in parts. He writes:

---

[2] H. Braverman, *Labour and Monopoly Capitalism*, New York: Monthly Review Press, 1974.

> The chief purpose of worship is to draw us into the fellowship of spiritual experience; and it is a useful rule of decorum that people should not fan themselves in church or eat chocolates or look at their noses in a bag-mirror. They know that in church such behaviour would prevent the fellowship of spiritual experience. But unfortunately there is another, more servile motive for decorum in church. We must behave ourselves there lest God be offended; and so churchgoers put up with much in their services that cannot produce any spiritual experience, because they think they acquire merit by being bored ... We must apply this test to [services]: Do they produce in us a common spiritual experience? Not always, for the failure may be in ourselves, but at least sometimes. Otherwise we are on the way to the prayer wheels of Tibet, or to the miner who wrote up his prayers over his bed and every night jerked his thumb towards them and said, 'My sentiments.'[3]

Of course a certain decorum facilitates the worship of all; certainly we do not earn merit by going to worship (though we ought to go); still less do we earn more merit the more boring the proceedings are. Undoubtedly worship should be more than a tedious routine. But is Clutton-Brock correct in saying that 'The chief purpose of worship is to draw us into the fellowship of spiritual experience?' And is he right to say that the test of the worth of a service of worship is whether it produces a common experience? It seems to me that his emphasis is too instrumentalist and anthropocentric; even that he may be on that slippery slope as the bottom of which is that 'feel good' religion so professionally packaged and ardently sought by some in our present-day Western consumerist societies. Surely the first purpose of worship – and I couch the point deliberately in trinitarian terms – is the praise of the Father who in his Son came to seek and to save the lost, and who, by his Holy Spirit, calls out a people for his praise and service. In such a service the Word is proclaimed and Christ is present at his table no matter what the individual Christian or the entire congregation may feel about it all. We might almost say that if that is truly our objective in worship the sense of spiritual fellowship will take care of itself. But, to repeat, the first thing is not what we may or may not experience during the service; it is what God has done and our gratitude for it. The primary thing in the worship of God is the worship of God. As the pithy Puritan, Thomas Watson, put it when commenting upon the *Shorter Catechism's* first question and answer, 'Praise is the quit-rent we pay to God: while God renews our lease, we must renew our rent.'[4] Small wonder that when pondering the evils that

---

[3] A. Clutton-Brock, 'Spiritual experience,' in B. H. Streeter, ed., *The Spirit. God and his Relation to Man considered from the standpoint of Philosophy, Psychology and Art*, London: Macmillan, 1928, 301.

[4] T. Watson, *A Body of Divinity*, (from *A Body of Practical Divinity*, 1692), London: The Banner of Truth Trust, 1965, 15.

distressed him most in worship John Elias placed first, 'Losing sight of *God in his greatness and purity as the object of my adoration.*'[5]

II

What thoughts come to mind as I reflect upon the worship in which I shared half a century ago? Picture first the village chapel at Worplesdon, in the midst of Surrey heathland. According to the 1950 *Congregational Year Book* it seats 150 people – an utter impossibility, though by 1954 the more realistic figure of 90 is given. It has a springy floor, not because it was built like a dance hall but because the joists below are under attack. There are thirty-one church members and, on occasion – it might be Sportsman's Sunday when the cricket team comes along – the congregation swells to the mid-fifties.

There is a choir among whose anthems the chartbuster is Joseph Barnby's, 'O Lord, how manifold are Thy works.' The front row on the right is fully occupied by gracious elderly ladies, dressed in dark clothes from head to toe, all of whom were greeting one another with an holy kiss long before liturgical whizz-kids began foisting the kiss of peace upon the unsuspecting. There are teenagers, a few professional and business people, some tradesmen, some workers on the land, some retired. The children, who outnumber the church members, meet in a separate afternoon Sunday School and are well drilled in Bible stories until confirmation time approaches. Many then depart to the Parish Church, some of their parents being not uninfluenced by the fact – more potent then than now, perhaps, that the Rector is a cousin of the Princesses Elizabeth and Margaret.

The service book, used as a resource by the minister, though not slavishly followed, is *A Manual for Ministers*. It is an intriguing amalgam which might almost have been put together with the express purpose of giving liturgical purists ulcers. It contains suggestions for morning and evening worship, for the ordinances and offices of the church, for some of the Christian festivals (though not for Ascensiontide or Trinity Sunday); and in a section on ordination and dedicatory services there is an order for 'The opening of a bazaar or sale of work.' The order of worship at Worplesdon is straightforward and simple. It is what is sometimes somewhat pejoratively described as a 'hymn sandwich'. The Lord's Supper is observed as an 'after service', some members of the congregation leaving before it starts, the minister bidding them farewell at the door. In some churches the interval between the services was filled by the wrapping up of flowers and the counting of the offering, but not at Worplesdon. The minister and the people know what they are there to do, and there is no

---

[5] J. Elias, Letter of 15 April 1802 to Miss Rogers, afterwards Mrs. Davies, in Edward Morgan, *John Elias, Life, Letters and Essays*, Edinburgh: The Banner of Truth Trust, 1973, 298.

mistaking the sincerity of the proceedings, the presence of God, and, *hence*, the warmth of the fellowship.

The minister is the saintly George Sydney Morgan, schooled in the believing liberalism of W. F. Adeney, W. H. Bennett and Robert Mackintosh at Lancashire Independent College, Manchester. His walk with God is close; he is the friend of all; and his sermons, based upon the Bible, are straight-forward messages, illustrated by tales from the mission field, by the wonders of natural history, and by the witness of Christian heroes and heroines past and present. These are edifying sermons designed to foster devotion and godly living, and they bring Christ close. At the age of eighty-one, having finally retired a year before, he set off to preach at Uckfield. He intended to preach on a theme in which his pastoral care and abiding hope were alike rooted: 'We love God because he first loved us.' Instead, he died on the platform at Lewes station.[6]

Come now to Guildford, the nearest town. Here is the historic North Street chapel, Congregationalism's local 'cathedral'. Here too is its 'bishop', Dr. James Alfred Kaye, one of the last of the princes of the pulpit, rightly described in his obituary as a 'Great Heart'.[7] He is great in all respects, as I can personally testify; for on his sudden death aged seventy-four, his wife passed on to me his cassock (the wearing of such a garment being one of a number of follies committed in my early ministry), and it hung on me like a bell tent until a sizeable chunk of material was removed from it. Dr. Kaye is known affectionately as the Congregational bishop of Guildford, his church having over the years spawned others, of which nine are continuing in 1950. Trained at Harley College, established by the Bibles side of the Bibles and brewing Guinness family, he has a sonorous voice well suited to the proclamation of an evangelical message, and although his entire ministry has been in England, he has never lost his pronounced Scottish borders accent, which is never more pronounced than when he is beginning one of his prayers, 'Eternal and ever-blessed God ... ' Then you know that you are in the presence of the Almighty – in fact, of both of them! When he sweeps into the lay preachers class the preachers stand and we all address him as 'Sir'. As might be expected in a prominent town church of 388 members there is a fine choir which can take on Handel's *Messiah* – and such soloists as Hervey Allen – with no difficulty whatsoever; and when Mr. F. W.

---

[6] For G. S. Morgan see *The Congregational Year Book*, 1962, 466–7. For the Worplesdon church see Alan P. F. Sell, *Congregationalism at Worplesdon 1822–1972*, printed for the chapel, 1972; Anne Philps, 'Perry Hill chapel' in *Worplesdon: A Tale of Four Villages*, a millennium project published by the Parish Council, 2000.

[7] See *The Congregational Year Book*, 1959, 424–5; Alan P. F. Sell, *Commemorations. Studies in Christian Thought and History*, (1993), Eugene, OR: Wipf & Stock, 1998, 298–300. For the Guildford Congregational 'diocese' see Joyce Reason, *A Fellowship of Churches, 1662–1962*, privately printed, 1962.

Danzelman, ARCO, lets the mighty organ rip you cannot help wondering how the dead could do anything else but be raised in-corr-uptible. But for all the affluence, the numbers, the larger-than-life preacher, the choir and the oratorios, the order of worship differs not at all from that in the village.

III

Between those days and our own, remarkable shifts have taken place in the public worship of God. Separate Sunday schools have largely vanished in favour of family worship. The liturgical renewal movement spread from continental Europe to many parts of Britain, and its influence is to be seen in many places, not least in our service books. True, it is still possible to find ministers whose proudest boast is that they do not use a book. At best this is a testimony to that charismatic emphasis which is so important a part of our tradition. At worst it betokens arrogance or laziness. But those who manage without devotional aids need to work hard if the people's worship, which they are called to lead, is not to become stale and impoverished, even banal. At the very least they should constantly ask themselves whether they are depriving their flocks of aspects of worship which ought to be present. Please do not think that I am pleading for liturgical fuss-pottery. I do not think that the Parousia will be delayed if we put the epiclesis in the wrong place (though it is disturbing when, in some of our more extempore communion services, one hunts in vain for the epiclesis). My plea is for freedom within order, and for as comprehensive a coverage as possible of the several dimensions of worship. Indeed, were I to articulate a general maxim it would be this: the freer the worship the more imperative it is that those leading it be disciplined and unselfish, resisting the temptation to fasten exclusively upon their favourite hymns, their favourite biblical passages and, in prayer, their passing moods.

As for the order of worship: it would take more than fifty years of service books to dislodge the hymn sandwich. But at least the point has been grasped in many places that Word and Sacrament belong together, and that to put them asunder is to destroy the flow of the liturgy, for both bear witness to God's saving grace in Christ. Consistently with this many have come to see that the shape of the service of Word and Sacrament (which is not the only legitimate form of worship), which moves through the Approach, the Ministry of the Word of God, and the Response in the offertory[8] (divorced from announcements!) and

---

[8] In many churches the offertory is the most abused aspect of the liturgy. In this connection few were more devastating than H. F. Lovell Cocks when he thundered (albeit with a twinkle in his eye) against those who inform the congregation that the stewards will now wait upon them for their kind gifts: '"God so loved the world that He gave His Only-begotten Son" –

either the Lord's Supper or, if the sacrament is not being observed, the prayers of thanksgiving, not only represents a liturgical convergence of some ecumenical significance, but actually contributes to the intelligibility of the proceedings. It also has the decided advantage of positioning the reading of Scripture adjacent to the exposition of it in preaching.

My recollection of the prayers offered in worship fifty years ago by ministers and lay preachers alike is that many of them were in the style of free, or conceived prayer, some were extempore. Some of the latter were utterly sincere; some were so formulaic – especially in their Cook's-tour-intercessions, that they might as well have been read from a book. While in no way despising the sincere utterances of a humble, self-taught lay preacher, Gordon Rupp was not altogether out of place when he observed that 'the dialogue with the Eternal and Almighty ought not to be as a man speaketh with the milkman.'[9] And did not the American theologian Cornelius Van Til, who had no particular liking for set forms of prayer, nevertheless declare that if a minister used published prayers at least Van Til would not be so likely to hear anything silly?

Concern for modes of prayer goes back a long way in our broad nonconforming traditions. As early as 1812 the authors of *A New Directory for Nonconformist Churches* lamented that 'there are many respectable persons ... who are partial to the Preaching of some dissenting ministers, and occasionally attend it, but are dissatisfied with their *Prayers* ... '.[10] The moral would seem to be that if we would honour our rich heritage of free prayer and practise the art and craft faithfully, we must understand the correlation between what comes out in free prayer and what has previously gone in, in terms of the devotional life and the pastoral concern of the one leading the prayers.[11] How John Stoughton lamented the low state of personal devotion among ministers. In one of his addresses he quoted an unnamed colleague as saying that the absence of private prayer on the part of ministers '"stains the glory" of everything else; it renders worthless their genius, talents, and acquisitions, obstructs their own spiritual prosperity, impedes their usefulness, and blasts their success.'[12]

"Love so amazing, so divine, demands" – *our kind gifts*.' See his address to the Congregational Union of England and Wales, *A Church Reborn*, London: Independent Press, [1950], 14–15. For this unduly neglected theologian see Alan P. F. Sell, *Commemorations*, ch. 13.

[9] Gordon Rupp, 'Assessing the new liturgies, 3. A too comparable liturgy?' *Epworth Review*, VIII no. 3, September 1981, 43. He was commenting upon the then new Methodist service book.

[10] *A New Directory for Nonconformist Churches*, London, 1812, 103–104.

[11] See further, *Our Heritage of Free Prayer*, London: Congregational Union of England and Wales, n.d., but 1950s. This anonymous pamphlet was in fact written by W. Gordon Robinson, principal of Lancashire Independent College, whose biblically rooted and ever fresh prayers in college chapel revealed the high degree to which he had mastered the art and craft of free prayer.

[12] John Stoughton, 236–7.

Whether prayers are read, conceived or extempore, they are the prayers not of the one leading worship, but of the people. With reference to the wider priesthood of believers properly construed corporately and not in the sense that anyone in the church can do anything, P. T. Forsyth argued that 'The ministry is the organ of the Church's priestliness even more than of its prophetic power. And when I say "more than" I mean this. It preaches *to* the Church what it does not receive from the Church – directly at least; but it prays *with* the Church and *from* it.' He proceeds to ask some searching questions: 'Have we taken our priestly work as seriously as our prophetic?' 'Does our prayer express more of the idiosyncracy of the minister than of the consecration of the Church?' He concludes, 'in free prayer we do not wish the minister to lay bare the recesses of his private soul. He prays as a "common person".'[13]

Few things are more likely to discipline the minister in regard to public prayer than due attention to the several parts of prayer. As I recall, fifty years ago many preachers paid careful attention to adoration, confession, supplication, intercession, thanksgiving – not forgetting thanksgiving for the faithful departed. But when a church member says to me at the end of a service I have conducted, as one did not so long ago, 'It is a long time since we heard a prayer of confession' we have more than a liturgical deficiency on our hands; we have a pastoral failure.

In John Stoughton's view, 'It is one of the perils of Nonconformity that we are tempted to think more of preaching than of worship.'[14] It comes out even in our language: we go to church to hear someone. Even so, preaching is to be taken with due seriousness. We need not demote the prophetic role of the preacher of the Word whilst we restore the pastor's priestly function. I have already spoken in general terms of two of the preachers I remember from half a century ago. Neither of them disturbed us with the latest pronouncements of Barth or Bultmann, and neither of them treated us to the word studies which were in vogue in the biblical theology of the day. They did not take a biblical book and expound it systematically over many weeks – even months – as some in the more tribalist evangelical tabernacles did. And they never finished with an altar call, the fact that Billy Graham was then beginning his rounds notwithstanding. They did, however, cover the main Christian doctrines. Above all the Cross was central to their preaching, even though their styles were very different, with Sydney Morgan wooing us to the Cross and Alfred Kaye urgently directing us there. It is at this point that I query our present state.

Nearly a century ago Thomas Lewis, another alumnus of Lancashire Independent College and at the time principal of the Memorial College, Brecon,

---

[13] P. T. Forsyth, *Congregationalism and Reunion*, London: Independent Press, 1952, 74–5.
[14] J. Stoughton, *Reminiscences of Congregationalism*, 89.

surveyed the homiletic scene. He concluded, 'The power of the Welsh pulpit in the future will be determined by the ability of its occupants to deal intelligently with all the problems that constitute the burden of Biblical criticism, and by their enlightened adhesion to, and earnest presentation of, the central verities of our Faith.'[15] As to biblical criticism: the pulpit is not the place for extended disquisitions on this subject; but there can be no question that our people need help to understand the Bible which, in the most basic sense is a collection of ancient oriental literature far removed from their daily experience of life. We shall never know how many people have silently drifted away from our churches during the last fifty years because they could not integrate their immature understanding of the Bible with the rest of their developing knowledge, and they found none to help them. They thought they were expected to believe what they could not believe; and what they could not believe most of the ministers did not believe either, only they never said so. In the pulpit integrity must take precedence over over silent avoidance. Were this not an august Davies Lecture I might be tempted to recall Johnny Speight's monstrous television creation, Alf Garnett, the right-wing, monarchist, racist bigot who, if memory serves, was one day arguing about the Bible with his Liverpudlian son-in-law. Garnett was advocating the fundamentalist literalist attitude: It's in the Book! The son-in-law was advocating the equally fundamentalist attitude of scientism: It's all fairy stories: it doesn't fit the empirical methods to which we are exclusively predisposed.[16] (I have tidied up what he actually said, but that is what he meant). And when their voices attained their loudest volume Mrs. Garnett, piously raising her eyes heavenwards, interjected, 'If you two don't keep your voices down He'll drop a thunderbolt on you!' Here we have a telling epitomization of three immature attitudes entertained by adults, examples of which – sometimes more, sometimes less sophisticated – are still with us.

As for what Lewis called the 'central verities of our Faith,' it is not a new problem. In 1855 the Mercersburg theologian Philip Schaff sought to encourage his students to pay heed to the Christian Year with a view to ensuring that the major doctrines were covered in their preaching. 'If you have no *Church year*,' he said, 'you will have no assurance that these important subjects will be preached at all – or it will be left to the caprice of every single one to touch on these when he pleases. They should be bound to some order and not as Dr. Berg who preached against stingyness or something of the kind on Ascension Day.'[17]

---

[15] T. Lewis, 'Higher criticism and Welsh preaching,' in T. Stephens, ed., *Wales: To-day and To-morrow*, Cardiff: Western Mail, 1907, 27.

[16] For a perceptive critique of scientism see Mary Midgley, *Science and Poetry*, New York: Routledge, 2000.

[17] Quoted by George Shriver, *Philip Schaff, Christian Scholar and Ecumenical Prophet*, Macon, GA: Mercer University Press, 1987, 37.

It is a question of comprehensiveness, and of surrounding our people with the ingredients out of which they may forge their Christian view of the world. In 1891 D. W. Simon, the principal of Edinburgh Theological Hall, lamented that 'out of upwards of 450 discourses by Congregational ministers printed during the last five years or thereabouts in *The Christian World Pulpit*, scarcely thirty were properly doctrinal.'[18] The problem has not gone away with the passage of time. I have sometimes asked students, When was the last time you heard a sermon on the Trinity or the Second Coming? The question has too frequently been greeted with blank stares. This suggests a gappiness in proclamation – one almost certainly exacerbated in a system in which so much reliance is placed upon itinerant preachers – which almost makes one wish for enforced lectionary use. Not that I should like to belong to a church which did enforce such use; but I cannot resist the feeling that if more ministers and lay preachers voluntarily paid some heed to the lectionary the hungry sheep in our pews would receive a more balanced diet. As John Stoughton roundly declared, 'when, instead of a full exhibition of the redeeming love of God in the gospel of Christ, only "a faint shadow of Christian sentiment" and graphic sketches "touched with Christian tints" appear, there must be loss – grievous loss.'[19] Mine is not an argument for rooting ourselves in past formulations of doctrine. Of course we have to address people where they are in our time – and do it as those who stand in the apostolic succession: that succession of those who tell out the apostle's Gospel of redemption through Christ. Indeed, we may need to be prophets to the age as well; and we shall not maintain the distance required for that task unless we have learned the lesson of Dean Inge's words, 'The Church which marries the spirit of the age in one generation will be a widow in the next.'[20]

IV

It is difficult to resist the conclusion that some Christians at the present time are failing to heed the Dean's warning. And it must be said that there are some signs that they are meeting with success not least in their pursuit of the young. Consider some evidence. Betty De Berg of the University of Northern Iowa has directed a study of *The Teaching and Practice of Religion in Selected American Colleges and Universities*. In an explanatory interview she says,

---

[18] D. W. Simon, 'The present direction of theological thought in the Congregational Churches of the several countries represented by the Council,' in *Proceedings of the First International Congregational Council*, London: Congregational Union of England and Wales, 1891, 78.

[19] J. Stoughton, *Reminiscences*, 87.

[20] For further reflections upon preaching in relation to pastoral care and catechetics see Ch. 3 above.

I was surprised by how important contemporary Christian music was to undergraduates. It makes me wonder how Christian campus ministries out of liturgical traditions can compete for attendance at large worship group events. Related to this, I was struck by how closely worship services run by para-church groups such as Campus Crusade resembles the Sunday morning worship services I attended at a nearby Evangelical 'megachurch'. Students' experience in Campus Crusade would prepare them perfectly for the worship life in such a congregation. On the other hand, the worship experience offered by the Presbyterians and Methodists, for example, was very different than typical Sunday morning worship in those denominations. Would these Presbyterian and Methodist student leaders find the transition to congregations difficult? Maybe. But maybe they would be a source of creative renewal in congregations after graduation if they could find a congregation they like.[21]

We may note in passing the consumerist attitude which seems to be taken for granted in the assumption that graduates will shop around for a congregation they like. On both sides of the Atlantic people, when pondering what Americans call a 'church home' are increasingly moved more by the music and the facilities than by denominational principle. But what I wish to focus on is the importance of a particular kind of music, and to point out that enthusiasm for it is not confined to the young. I understand that in some of our own churches there is now, during the service, a period of what is called praise, during which simple 'modern' choruses (many of which are already thirty years old) are endlessly repeated, often to the accompaniment of guitar and rhythm section (and they sometimes tell us that other styles of worship are boring and repetitive!). Somebody has characterized this practice as 'four words, three notes, and two hours'.[22] If the motive is to make the Gospel accessible, it is worthy. But is it always the Gospel which is made accessible? Some of these ditties have much more to do with how the singer is feeling than with anything which the sovereign Lord has done. Small wonder that Hughes Oliphant Old criticized those who set out to attract in these terms: 'In our evangelistic zeal we are looking for programs that will attract people. We think we have to put honey on the lip of the bitter cup of salvation. It is the story of the wedding at Cana all over again but with this difference. At the crucial moment, when the wine failed we took matters into our own hands and used those five stone jars to mix up a batch of Kool-Aid instead.'[23] Ian Bradley has rightly contended that,

---

[21] B. De Berg, 'Research Briefing,' *Religious Studies News, AAR Edition*, XV nos. 3–4, October 2000, 20.

[22] D. G. Hart, who quoted this phrase, has an entertaining piece entitled, 'Post-modern evangelical worship,' *Calvin Theological Journal*, XXX no. 2, November 1995, 451–9.

[23] H. O. Old, *Worship*, Atlanta: John Knox Press, 1984, 177.

> By and large, hymns are not written to entertain or boost the audience ratings. They have an altogether nobler and higher purpose, being intended to praise or petition God, convert sinners, sustain the righteous, guide the perplexed, comfort the downhearted, challenge the complacent, wrestle honestly with doubt, celebrate the wonders of creation, teach the basic doctrines of the faith or penetrate the mystery of holiness.[24]

Bradley's phrase concerning the role of hymns in comforting the downhearted should not be too quickly passed over. 'In the last year,' reports Carl Trueman of the University of Aberdeen, 'I have asked three very different evangelical audiences what miserable Christians can sing in church. On each occasion the question has elicited uproarious laughter, as if the idea of a broken-hearted, lonely, or despairing Christian was so absurd as to be comical – and yet I posed the question in all seriousness.'[25] The happy-clappy types need to remember that their very gaiety can alienate those who need to hear good news. They need to remember both that some Christians are in pain, and that other Christians can be a pain in the neck. The variety in the book of Psalms – from heartfelt praise to anguished laments – may serve to assist them in their reflections.

Again, a regular diet of emotional 'highs' can have the result (even when the result is not specifically sought) of cocooning the participant against the world – not least the intellectual world – into which the risen Lord would drive us in his name. Let us be cautioned by that wise philosopher W. G. De Burgh whose words of 1937 bear repeating now:

> It is fashionable in these latter days for religious writers to idealize the irrational in human nature at the expense of reason and to believe that in stressing the emotional factor in religion, they are vindicating its independence from scientific and historical criticism. They should beware of the allurement. A religion that severs its faith from intellectual truth may flourish for a generation or even for a century, but it is doomed to eventual extinction.[26]

In support, De Burgh quotes A. N. Whitehead's remark that Methodism 'is the first decisive landmark indicating the widening chasm between the theological tradition and the modern intellectual world.'[27]

Above all, we can even be cocooned against the idea that it is the holy One with whom we have to do. Listen to these words of the distinguished minister, J. H. Jowett, who having ministered successively at St. James's, Newcastle, Carrs Lane, Birmingham, Fifth Avenue Presbyterian Church, New York and

---

[24] I. Bradley, *Abide with Me: The World of Victorian Hymns*, London: SCM Press, 1997, xv.
[25] C. Trueman, 'What do miserable Christians sing?' *Themelios*, XXV no. 2, February 2000, 2.
[26] W. G. De Burgh, *Towards a Religious Philosophy*, London: Macdonald & Evans, 1937, 39.
[27] Ibid., quoting A. N. Whitehead, *Adventures of Ideas*, Harmondsworth: Penguin Books, 1942, 28–9.

Westminster Chapel, London, died in 1923. He had in mind what he called the 'light and lilting, tripping strains' of such hymns as 'The glory song':

> We leave our places of worship, and no deep and inexpressible wonder sits upon our faces. We can sing these lilting melodies, and when we go out into the streets our faces are one with the faces of those who have left theatres and the music halls. There is nothing about us to suggest that we have been looking at anything stupendous and overwhelming! Far back in my boyhood I remember an old saint telling me that after some services he liked to make his way home alone, by quiet by-ways, so that the hush of the Almighty might remain on his awed and prostrate soul. That is the element we are losing, and its loss is one of the measures of our poverty, and the primary secret of inefficient life and service.[28]

I have not been pleading for boring, dull worship. That is easily achieved by a lack of preparation, pondering, prayer and pastoral concern on the part of the one leading worship. Worship should be a joyous celebration of the God of all grace, who is high and lifted up, the holy one, who yet deigns to dwell in our midst and can meet our every need.

V

If the worship of almighty God truly is the first task of the Church, what are the implications for our understanding of the ministry? I in no way play down the ministry of the whole people of God. I strongly assert that the one ministry in which all are called to share is that of the risen and ascended Lord. But here I am thinking especially of those whom we call ministers or pastors. And I am thinking of them because of something like a sea-change which our understanding of ministry has undergone over the past half-century.

Fifty years ago we knew what the ministers were for. They were to lead us in the worship of God, to teach us the faith, to offer pastoral care, and to encourage us out into the world for the Lord's sake. We understood that they had been called first by God and then by ourselves for these purposes. They were not our employees: we spoke of a stipend, not a salary, and a stipend was intended to free them from the necessity of earning a living in order that they could exercise their ministry in our midst.

Then came the decade of the swinging sixties, and with it something of a crisis of confidence in the ministry. Theology was at sixes and sevens: the *Honest to God* debate, the Death of God theologians, secular theology, and the Calvinist-Puritan reaction underlying the formation of the Banner of Truth Trust. Some

---

[28] Quoted in Arthur Porritt, *John Henry Jowett, C.H.,M.A.,D.D.*, London: Hodder and Stoughton, [1924], 97.

ministers wondered just what they could preach – a question reinforced by some of the educational theory of the times which seemed to call in question any attempt to teach children about God because they had no concept of him yet. Perhaps not surprisingly, a number of ministers from many denominations took themselves off to social work and other useful employments.

In some ways more menacing has been the way in which, during the last thirty years, the managerial-corporate model has come into its own in many churches – not all of them in the West.[29] The ministry has become a job; people speak of hiring and firing pastors; and an advertisement like the following (which I quote exactly) can appear in the 'Employment Opportunities' column of the respected magazine, *Christianity Today:*

> EXECUTIVE PASTOR
> Trinity Church is a new, programmatically innovative, seeker-sensitive church located in Greenwich, CT – 35 miles north of New York City – that is searching for an Executive Pastor who can relate well to affluent, 'fast-track' commuters and their families. We are a rapidly growing church with 350 in weekly attendance that needs a highly relational, self-motivated individual who can develop and motivate leaders, design and build infrastructure, envision and create ministry delivery teams, oversee staff, and direct operations. Seminary degree unnecessary and a business background preferred.[30]

I was teaching in North America when this advertisement appeared last year, and I suggested to my class that they might care to write to the editor of *Christianity Today* to say how very much they had enjoyed the spoof advertisement which had appeared in his journal. I fear they did not respond.

Before we lapse into thanking God that we are not like other men, or even as those Americans, let us be aware that the corporate model is working its way through our churches here. It is not, of course, that we can learn nothing from best business practice. But in an age of rampant managerialism we need to take care lest we inappropriately apply criteria and use language which may be appopriate in other spheres to the work and ministry of the Church. In some places the trend towards the corporate model is dictated by the considerable size of congregations. In some parts of Britain, however, it is more likely that ministers take on more administrative roles because the helpers are fewer than once they were. Certainly recent research in this country shows that the bulk of the minister's time is taken up with tasks which may be accommodated under the heading of 'Management'. Not surprisingly the same researcher finds that the 'rag end' of ministers' time is devoted to their devotional life.[31] What will

---

[29] See further, Alan P. F. Sell, *Aspects of Christian Integrity*, (1990), Eugene, OR: 1998, ch. 6.
[30] *Christianity Today*, 22 May, 2000, 107.
[31] Research by Malcolm Clarke. See *Free Church Chrinicle*, LIII no. 2, November 2000, 11.

churches do to free ministers to do the work to which they have called them? When will churches and ministers themselves resist the idea that ministers are the ones who must increase the size of the congregation, keep the whole show on the road, and conjure up ways of keeping the church ahead of the competition from other denominations?[32] When shall we organize our pastorates so that vibrant ministry and eager mission become possible? In the absence of creative answers to such questions as these, we hear increasingly of ministerial burnout, and of the refusal of some young people to candidate for ministry at all.

The supremely important question underlying all of this is, What has happened to our doctrine of ministerial vocation? Of John Stoughton it was said, 'To undertake the sacred office as a profession was to him simple presumption – indeed, profanity.'[33] If the first duty of the Church is to worship God, those called to the high office of leading such worship ought to be very humble about it. They may need many gifts, but the first thing they need, to borrow Thomas Carlyle's phrase, is to know God 'otherwise than by hearsay.'[34] And the God they need to know is the God of holy love who, in his Son, ever seeks and saves the lost. Then they need to love those to whom they have been called. Far from being just one more job, far from the minister's being an employee, the relation of pastor to people is a sacred one. Listen to John Robinson, pastor to the Pilgrims: 'The bond between the minister, and people is the most strait, and near religious bond that may be, and therefore not to be entered but with mutual consent, any more than the civil bond of marriage between the husband, and wife.'[35]

So awesome is the work that the sense of call of would-be ministers needs the most kindly and rigorous testing. In my circles fifty years ago candidates were required to have had a minimum of two years of lay preaching before beginning ministerial training. The college entrance examinations included one on the denomination's history and theology. This necessitated the reading of set texts, and its objective was to discover why, granted the genuineness of the call, and given the fact of the fragmented nature of the empirical Church, the candidate wished to enter the ministry of one denomination rather than another. It was assumed that candidates would have made a principled decision on this matter, and to have answered 'I wish to serve here because this is where I was brought up, or feel at home' would not have been deemed sufficient. This question, I

---

[32] See further, Marva Dawn and Eugene Peterson, *The Unnecessary Pastor: Rediscovering the Call*, Grand Rapids: Eerdmans, 2000.

[33] *John Stoughton*, 15.

[34] Quoted by Alan Flavell, 'The place of the evangelical in the Church of today,' *The Monthly Record of the Free Church of Scotland*, January 1969, 14.

[35] *The Works of John Robinson*, London: John Snow, 1851, II, 396.

believe, is still important, and it is not anti-ecumenical to say so.[36] On the contrary, we ought to believe that in his providence God has been leading the several strands of his one Church through the ages, imparting to them gifts and insights which ultimately are for the good of the whole body. If this is so, then the last kind of ecumenism we need is that into which people tumble because they do not believe anything in particular. To his inaugural lecture delivered at Mercersberg in 1846 Philip Schaff appended no fewer than 112 *Theses for the Time*, the penultimate one of which reads as follows:

> What we most need now is theoretically a thorough intellectual theology, scientifically free as well as decidedly believing, together with a genuine sense for history; and practically, a determination to hold fast the patrimony of our fathers, and to go forward joyfully at the same time in the way in which God's Spirit by providential signs may lead, with a proper humble subordination of all we do for our own denomination for the general interest of the One Universal Church.[37]

The other question – the supremely important one – addressed to ministerial candidates, then as now, was, Why do you wish to candidate for the ministry rather than to serve as a layperson? The answer expected would have related to the primary task of the Church: the leading of the worship of God and the announcement of the Gospel of his grace. An answer restricted to a general desire to be helpful or useful in society – as any decent humanist might be – would have prompted anguished twitching of venerable eyebrows.

It goes without saying that our ministers deserve the best training we can give them. I know well enough that theological colleges can never do all they ought. I am well aware that the defensive reaction of some recently ordained ministers when they first encounter crusty elders, or are asked by a child, 'Will I see my rabbit in heaven?' is to turn accusingly on their college and mutter, They did not prepare me for this! But I have also noticed that when the same ministers have been at the pastoral 'coal face' for thirty years or so a haze of sentiment envelops them, and they spend the rest of their days lovingly recounting the eccentricities of such as myself to the rising generation. Be that as it may, my point is that the content of ministerial education needs to be shaped by a deep understanding of the nature of ministry as a vocation, and when the chips are down for the institutional Church – as they are for the churches of western Europe, it will take more than a few extra courses in church administration or a placement in a kibbutz to put matters right. Invaluable though I found my

---

[36] Cf. J. Stoughton, *Reminiscences*, 21.
[37] Quoted by George Warren Richards, *History of the Theological Seminary of the Reformed Church in the United States 1825–1934, Evangelical and Reformed Church 1934–1952*, Lancaster, PA: Theological Seminary of the Evangelical and Reformed Church, 1952, 516.

academic courses to be, and rigorous though I think every ordinand's theological course ought to be, the fact is that we need to form men and women, not simply inform them. We need ministers who know how to pray, who know their Bibles, and who will be fit to lead the saints to the throne of grace. That is their essential task. Not the least valuable part of my own theological training were the two Bible examinations we had to sit each term: on the first and last Saturday mornings. These examinations were additional to the university courses, and they were compulsory. If you were there for six years, as I was, you were tested on the content and background of every book in the English Bible. It was a superb discipline, and one for which I continue to be grateful. Conversely, I have always found it hard to understand those ordinands who limit their Bible reading to the texts set for degree examinations. Consider the amount of time medical students devote to learning the bones in the foot. Ought not prospective ministers to know where to find Obadiah – and even to have read him?

In the last resort, and despite the final examination question I used to set, we do not need ministers who can merely parrot the main doctrinal findings of the Council of Chalcedon of 451. We need ministers who see the whole of their work in the context of the worship of God, and who view the entire work of the church in theological and missiological perspective. In this connection the words of the Canadian theologian Douglas John Hall constitute a solemn charge to all ministers:

> Any congregation that wants to make it into the new millennium by more than two or three decades has got to become more serious about [the] faith – knowledgeable, thoughtful, engaged. For this to occur, however, preachers themselves are going to have to work harder than they are at theology, biblical exegesis, history, literature, and all the other beneath-the-surface struggle that is the requisite to real preaching.[38]

Perhaps Douglas Hall includes apologetics under the 'beneath-the-surface struggle.' However apologetic issues are sufficiently clamant for that discipline to be specifically noted.

VI

What now of the wider relations of the local church? Fifty years ago we would from time to time welcome a missionary home on furlough from some far-flung mission field. These good folk would travel many miles on deputation, carrying their photographs and artifacts with them. We felt that they were out there in

---

[38] Quoted by Stephen R. Graham, 'The Protestant principle and the Catholic substance: Philip Schaff speaks to the Church of the 21st century,' *The New Mercersburg Review*, XXVII, Autumn 2000, 97.

our name, and they made our endless quest of pennies for the John Williams ships which plied the South Seas seem worthwhile.

What a dramatic change has come about in the intervening years in our understanding of mission. We have come to see that mission is the task of the whole Church not of a few enthusiasts, and that church budgets should reflect the fact. Because of the vision of those who drew the historic London Missionary Society (1795), the Commonwealth Missionary Society (1836) and others into the Council for World Mission (1973), we no long think simply in terms of sending churches and receiving churches. On the contrary, we see ourselves as partners in mission, receiving or sending Christian workers as appropriate. During the same period the balance of Christians in the world has significantly shifted in that whereas the Christian majority used to be found in Europe and North America, it now occupies Latin America, Africa and Asia. At the same time our own land, though traditionally an amalgam of Celtic, Anglo-Saxon, Norman and other ethnic groupings, has become more religiously pluralist in character, as well as in many ways thoroughly secularized on the one hand, and with significant numbers of spiritual seekers on the other. However we may characterize our present society it is undeniable that we do not need to go anywhere else to find a mission field.

It would not be too great an exaggeration to say that half a century ago we village worshippers knew more about what was going on in Western Samoa or parts of India than about the affairs of other Christian churches within our neighbourhood. The Church/chapel distinction was alive and well in many places, and it had social as well as religious implications. Moreover, the fact that Nonconformists of the more 'respectable' sort chafed under Anglican airs of superiority did not prevent some of them from looking down from a great height upon the 'tin tabernacles' of the more ostensibly evangelical groups. As for the Roman Catholics: where I lived we had no churchly contact with them, and we hardly knew any of them. When I was growing up we would occasionally see seminarians in black from their Homburgs to their shoes out for a walk in threes – very mysterious, we thought; and sometimes when youthful misdemeanours were reported the fallacy of the false cause would be committed as one irate adult would exchange a knowing look with another and explain, Of course, they're Roman Catholics. Here again there has been a sea-change. Not, indeed, that there were no good inter-denominational relations prior to the formation of the World Council of Churches in 1948. Indeed the establishment of that body was built upon Life and Work and Faith and Order and Mission movements from earlier in the century; and these in turn were fertilized by contacts made between the major Christian world communions and in such para-church organizations as the British and Foreign Bible Society, the Evangelical Alliance, and many more.

But what should also be recalled is that it was the Roman Catholic Church which, following its Second Vatican Council of 1962–1965, did as much as any other Christian world communion, and more than most, to foster bilateral conversations between themselves and those whom they were by now calling separated brethren rather than heretics. Their impetus was a major force in stimulating the setting up of bilateral dialogues, both internationally and regionally, between representatives of other Christian world communions.[39] Over a number years it has been my privilege to participate in many of these dialogues as a representative of the Reformed family. In such gatherings has been done some of the theological spadework which has led churches to draw closer together, and even in some cases to unite, on the ground. In this connection the agreement in both the international Reformed-Methodist and Reformed-Disciples of Christ dialogues to the effect that any differences of opinion over theology and church order should no longer be regarded as church dividing was significant – Calvinism and Arminianism having been traditional stumbling-blocks in the former case and, from the side of the Disciples, believers' baptism in the latter; and the reconciliation of memories with the Mennonites, some of whose Anabaptist forebears our people had drowned in the river in Zurich, was something which had to happen, and, having happened, the international dialogue with that family of historic peace churches moved forward in creative ways. The question of Christian initation was, understandably enough, prominent in the discussions with the Baptist World Alliance. The major proposal that Christian initiation might be viewed as a process in which baptism, nurture, regeneration, profession of faith and admission to the Church were moments, and that if these constituents were present the time at which they came into focus in an individual's life may not be so important, has yet to receive the attention it merits around the world, though that general line has successfully been pursued in the United Kindgom and elsewhere – hence, for example, the union in 1981 of most of the Churches of Christ with the United Reformed Church. Some dialogues do not have church union within even their middle distance sights: that with the Orthodox churches is, for example, much more concerned with how far we are in accord as to the major Christian doctrines. It is unfortunate that the constructive dialogue with the Anglican Consultative Council has not as yet led to any reconciliation of memories between the Church of England and the heirs of historic Dissent over the question of the sixteenth-century martyrs and subsequent punitive

---

[39] See further, Alan P. F. Sell, 'The role of bilateral dialogues within the one ecumenical movement,' *Ecumenical Review*, XLVI no. 4, October 1994, 453–60; idem, *A Reformed, Evangelical, Catholic Theology. The Contribution of the World Alliance of Reformed Churches 1875–1982*, (1991), Eugene, OR: 1998, ch. 4.

legislation; but it is encouraging that the Lutheran-Reformed dialogue report proposes that the way is clear for full pulpit and table fellowship, entailing the recognition of ministries, between those major Reformation traditions.[40]

It may even be that some of the work done in the dialogues I have mentioned so far has filtered down to the groups appointed to consider The United Church of Wales, though not having been party to those conversations, I have no direct knowledge of the proceedings. It is, however, reassuring that, according the the discussion document, *The Way Forward*, the motivation of the plan is not that specified by Dr John Edward Williams in a letter to the *Methodist Recorder*. He writes, 'Within a generation or less, the seepage of members (from nonconformist churches in Wales) will reduce them to small sects lacking any national presence or influence. The proposal to unite the four nonconformist denominations is an attempt to confront the crisis.'[41] That the situation is one of challenge cannot be denied. That Christians sometimes do not do the right thing until the roof falls in is also true. But if the primary motive is that the churches should regain, or gain, national presence and influence, no union scheme deserves to succeed. The Church is not in business for its own aggrandisment. The primary motive is the compulsion of the Gospel and the desire to manifest the unity of Christ's one Church. It would be right to work for that even if no higher profile or greater influence followed. If they did, it would be a bonus – perhaps even a sign of God's blessing upon the union consummated. P. T. Forsyth was right: 'For Church union ever to come about we must be more ruled by a faith of power than by a fear of fizzling out ... [T]he Church can be unified only by the faith, insight, and passion of the same Gospel as made it.'[42]

Why do otherwise sober and intelligent persons engage in such time-consuming work at such great expense? Speaking, as far as I am able, for the Reformed family, it is because of our evangelicalism and our catholicity. What is the Gospel, the evangel? It is, as I said at the outset, that on the ground of Christ's finished work the Father calls out by the Spirit a people, reconciled to himself and to one another, for his praise and service. In other words, the evangel is inherently catholic: God does not call out many churches, but one Church, and it comprises all those in heaven and on earth who, by grace, are in Christ.[43] Calvin, Richard Baxter, John Owen, and many others in our Reformed

---

[40] For the international bilateral dialogues in which the World Alliance of Reformed Churches has been involved from the 1970s to 1992 see *Bilateral Dialogues* (Studies from the World Alliance of Reformed Churches, 24), Geneva: WARC, 1993; Alan P. F. Sell, 'The Alliance in dialogue 1970–2002: retrospect and reflections,' *Reformed World*, LIII no. 4, December 2003.

[41] Quoted in the *Free Church Chronicle*, LIII no. 2, November 2000, 12.

[42] P. T. Forsyth, *Church, Ministry and Sacraments*, bound with J. Vernon Bartlet and J. D. Jones, *The Validity of Congregationalism*, London: Congregational Union of England and Wales, n.d., 34.

[43] See further Alan P. F. Sell, 'Reformed identity: a non-issue of catholic significance,' *Reformed Review*, LIV no. 1, Autumn 2000, 17–27.

heritage understood this very well. The Reformers did not set out to create new churches, but to reform the one Church of the Lord Jesus Christ. Moreover this Church is supposed to be an earnest, a foretaste, of that reconciliation which God wills for the whole inhabited earth, the *oikoumene*. Insofar as the Church visible is divided, supremely at the Lord's table, we are in an hypocritical situation – preaching on Paul's words that we are one body because we all partake of the one loaf, when we know quite well that in practice we do not. We undermine our witness and, what is worse, we succumb all too often to the sectarian spirit. The history of our Reformed family is littered with secessions, and enhanced by a few comings together. It is my commitment to the catholicity inherent in the evangel which has fuelled my striving against sectarianism wherever it rears its head, and which makes the stance of some who take either the label 'evangelical' or the label 'catholic' to themselves whilst shunning moves to realize the unity which God has already given us in Christ incomprehensible to me.

By 'sectarianism' I mean that spirit which is exemplified by the Galatian heresy. You will recall that Paul trounced the Galatians (whoever and wherever they were) for concocting a so-called gospel which was no Gospel at all. It was as if they were saying, 'Salvation is by Christ plus circumcision, and only those who have come by our route are true Christians.' Extrapolating from this we can see that whenever Christians impose conditions over and above the confession of Christ as Lord and Saviour, they are elevating their interpretations of Scripture or their favoured practices above the Gospel. And if they then refuse fellowship with those with whom they disagree, they have fallen into sectarianism. It can happen in so many ways. Some appear to say, 'Salvation is by Christ plus our favoured ministerial orders; or by subscription to our preferred creed or statement of faith;[44] or our particular slant on biblical inerrancy; or the code of ethics of which we happen to approve – you know what I mean: Don't go to the dance hall because it's a sink of iniquity, but if you're a racist in your heart nobody will know ... '[45] Salvation is by God's grace

---

[44] As an aside we may note the observation of the conservative evangelical scholar F. F. Bruce: 'A sense of security with regard to the foundations of faith and life encourages a spirit of relaxation with regard to many other matters. I am sure that an inner insecurity is often responsible for the dogmatism with which some people defend positions which are by their nature incapable of conclusive proof ... ' See his *In Retrospect. Remembrance of Things Past*, London: Marshall Pickering, 1983, 172–3.

[45] Cf. the observation of the Quaker philosopher, D. Elton Trueblood in his book, *Signs of Hope in a Century of Despair*, London: SCM Press, 1950, 51–52: 'Many persons who are not guilty of fornication or gluttony, and who may actually have no serious temptations in these directions, may develop sins of the spirit that are far more damaging to themselves and others than these can ever be. They may seek to destroy reputaitons and to spread slander; they may struggle cruelly for position and power. It has often been noted that such sins sometimes

in Christ plus nothing. At this point some who profess to be on the evangelical wing may be inclined to retort, 'But fellowship must be fellowship in the truth', and what they frequently have in mind is a collection of doctrinal formulae to which they have given their seal of approval. They do not seem to see that all of us interpret Scripture and doctrine and we shall never all agree on all points: the quest of absolute uniformity of expression and of church order is an unrealistic goal which has nothing to to with ecumenism intelligently understood. What has made Christians one is the fact that by grace they are in Christ – unity is not secured by their work of defining a doctrinal position. The immediate question is, Are our disagreements within the context of overall confession of Christ as Saviour and Lord, or are we going to tumble into that sectarianism which, as Philip Schaff said long ago results from 'a one-sided false subjectivity, sundered from the authority of the objective'?[46] The fundamental question is, Is it the case that in Christ God has acted once and for all to create one family in which the barriers between male and female, bond and free, sick and well, employed and unemployed, congenial and downright cussed and – dare I say it? – Welsh and English are broken down? If that is what the evangel is; if that is what God in Christ has actually done, then we need to press on with our ecumenical work of manifesting this reality, ever remembering the accurate diagnosis of that wise Puritan, John Howe: 'Without all controversy, the main inlet of all the distractions, confusions, and divisions of the Christian world hath been by adding other conditions of Church communion than Christ hath done.'[47]

Two illustrations of the sectarian spirit will suffice. The second phase of the international dialogue between ourselves and the Roman Catholic Secretariat for Promoting Christian Unity considered the crucial question, Is there a specific church order given in and with the Gospel? The report of that dialogue clearly sets down the divergent positions of the Roman Catholics and the Reformed on the matter. We made it clear that to us it seems that the Roman Catholics place their church order above the Gospel, while we seek to place our churchly life under the challenge and judgment of the Gospel. From their stance flows their position on ministry and sacraments – a position which to us seems sectarian. We have not been afraid to express this view, politely but firmly. Imagine the dismay in many parts of the Reformed world – indeed, in many parts of the Christian world at large, not least in some Roman Catholic quarters too, when last year Cardinal Ratzinger declared in paragraph 17 of the document *Dominus*

---

appear vividly among prominent churchmen, who may be truly ascetic in their physical existence, but absolutely ruthless in seeking to dominate others.'

[46] P. Schaff, *The Principle of Protestantism*, (1845), Philadelphia: United Church Press, 1964, 155.

[47] J. Howe, *Works*, ed. Henry Rogers, 1862–1863, V, 226. See further, Alan P. F. Sell, *Aspects of Christian Integrity*, ch. 4.

Iesus, that 'the ecclesial communities which have not preserved the valid episcopate and the genuine integral substance of the eucharistic mystery are not churches in the proper sense (*sensu proprio Ecclesiae non sunt*); however, those who are baptized in these communities are, by baptism, incorporated in Christ and thus are in a certain Communion, albeit imperfect.' This is a blunter statement of what some have felt to be implied in Vatican II documents themselves where the phrase 'churches and ecclesiastical fellowships' is used. Professor Pàolo Ricca of the Waldensian Faculty in Rome is not alone in having wondered whether the term 'ecclesiastical fellowship' is understood by Roman Catholics more in a sociological than a theological sense.[48]

Reactions were swift. *Dominus Iesus* was published just one week before a session of the third phase of dialogue between the World Alliance of Reformed Churches and the Secretariat for Promoting Christian Unity was due to take place on the theme of the Church as a 'community of common witness' to the kingdom of God. The irony was not lost upon the Alliance's general secretary, Setri Nyomi, who wrote at once to the Secretariat to express 'disappointment and dismay' at the document. Indeed, the Alliance considered calling off the dialogue session, but persisted with it in view of its commitment to ecumenical co-operation.[49] The Pope visited the dialogue participants and reaffirmed his view that 'the commitment of the Catholic Church to ecumenical dialogue is irrevocable.'[50] In his comment on *Dominus Iesus* the communications director of the Alliance declared that 'what is written is clear: we are second-class citizens in the household of God ... Those of us who believe that the church of Jesus Christ is found wherever his gospel is truly preachers and his sacraments rightly admitinstered have a duty continually to challenge this sectarianism ... We must hope that the sound we hear is that of Cardinal Ratzinger locking the stable door after the horse of openness and ecumenism has irretrievably bolted.'[51]

From the Roman Catholic side Kilian McDonnell sought to address the question whether *Dominus Iesus* represented a return to pre-Vatican II theology. He couched his negative answer in terms of the wider context of the *Dominus Iesus*: it was intended as a document for internal consumption in the Roman Church – a watchdog's bark from Ratzinger's department, warning against deviations from the faith in an increasingly relativistic age. Nevertheless he could not deny that it did reaffirm the 'bottom line', namely, that 'there is no bypassing of the communion of churches gathered around Peter. The Catholic church has the fullness of the theological reality, *elements* of which are found in

---

[48] See further, Alan P. F. Sell, *A Reformed, Evangelical, Catholic Theology*, 132–3.
[49] *Update*, X no. 4, December 2000, 3–4.
[50] *Greeting of the Holy Father to the participants at the third phase of the international dialogue between the World Alliance of Reformed Churches and the Catholic Church*, 18 September 2000.
[51] Páraic Réamonn, 'Comment,' *Update*, X no. 4, December 2000, 4.

other Christian communions.'⁵² Less restrained was an editorial in the respected Roman Catholic paper *The Tablet*, which called *Dominus Iesus* 'a public relations disaster' which reiterated the 'intransigent approach' of Ratzinger's department to 'sister churches'.⁵³ Much more than that, it denied the Gospel of Christ which has made us one, whether we like it or not. Commenting on Paul's greeting, 'Grace be with all men that love the Lord Jesus Christ in sincerity,' the genial John Stoughton exhorted the hearers of a lecture he gave in these terms: 'Let the sentiment of the Apostle be cherished by us all; and while others boast of the name, let us cultivate and display the spirit of catholicity.'⁵⁴

But (and here is my second illustration) before we yet again seek false consolation: this time that we are not like other people, or even as those Roman Catholics, let us not forget those mirror images whom we have nurtured who have left a sectarian inheritance which has vitiated Christian witness at home and abroad. Who was it, for example, who refused the 1966 invitation of the Billy Graham Evangelistic Association to chair the first World Congress on Evangelism because he disapproved of the theological position and church allegiance of some other members of the platform party? It was not Cardinal Ratzinger. It was Martyn Lloyd-Jones.⁵⁵ The ecclesial consequences of the one full, perfect and sufficient sacrifice of Christ upon the Cross are a standing challenge to all such sectarianism. How one sympathizes with the general tenor of the Puritan Thomas Brooks's outburst: 'Ah, Christians! Can Turks and Pagans agree? Can Herod and Pilate agree? Can Moab and Ammon agree? Can bears and lions, can wolves and tigers, agree? Yea, which is more, can a legion of devils agree in one body? And shall not the saints, whom heaven must hold at last, agree?'⁵⁶

VII

Back in Worplesdon fifty years ago the saints took seriously that aspect of their church polity which continued their worship and linked them to the world. I refer to Church Meeting, that credal assembly in which the Lordship of Christ is proclaimed over the entire life and work of the church, and where those who

---

⁵² Kilian McDonnell, 'The unique Mediator in a unique Church. A return to pre-Vatican II theology?' *The Ecumenical Review*, LII no. 4, October 2000, 544.

⁵³ *The Tablet*, 9 September 2000, 1179. For some of the correspondence engendered by this editorial and by *Dominus Iesus* see ibid., 16 September 2000, 1222. For further comment see ibid., 21 October 2000, 1403.

⁵⁴ *John Stoughton*, 51.

⁵⁵ See I. H. Murray, *D. Martyn Lloyd-Jones: The Fight of Faith, 19391981*, Edinburgh: The Banner of Truth Trust, 1990, 440–3.

⁵⁶ T. Brooks, *Heaven on Earth. A Treatise on Christian Assurance*, (1654), London: The Banner of Truth Trust, 1961, 12–13.

have heard the Word proclaimed and received the bread and wine at the Lord's table gather to face the question, How are we to witness to this Gospel in the world around us? This was the question embracing all the agenda, and what was sought was not democratic majority rule, but the mind of Christ and unanimity in him.[57] The true spirit of Church Meeting was nowhere better captured than by John Robinson when writing to doubting Richard Bernard:

> I tell you, that if ever I saw the beauty of Sion, and the glory of the Lord filling his tabernacle, it hath been in the manifestation of the divers graces of God in the church, in that heavenly harmony, and comely order, wherein by the grace of God we are set and walk: wherein, if your eyes had but seen the brethren's sober and modest carriage one towards another, their humble and willing submission unto their guides, in the Lord, their tender compassion towards the weak, their fervent zeal against scandalous offenders, and their long-suffering towards all, you would, I am persuaded, change your mind ... [58]

But what changes have taken place in the world Robinson contemplated, and even the world we contemplated fifty years ago, and the one in which we are called to witness now! The early fifties marked a period of post-war austerity. Food rationing was not abolished until 1954. The National Health Service was getting under way, and comprehensive education was coming in. In 1951 Winston Churchill became prime minister again, Margaret Roberts (later better known as Mrs. Thatcher) failed to win the Dartford seat, and the Goons erupted on the wireless. Then came the Festival of Britain on the South Bank of the Thames, and soon those relatively few who were fortunate enough to have television could see the coronation of Elizabeth II in their own homes. University students wore soberly-coloured suits to lectures, while Teddy Boys in drainpipes and long jackets roamed the streets. Lou Preager played for thousands of dancers per week at the Hammersmith Palais, while Billy Graham held forth at the White City. Johnnie Ray cried and stopped the traffic in Manchester, and Louis Armstrong's All Stars further encouraged such home grown traditional jazz devotees as Humphrey Lyttelton and Chris Barber. Lonnie Donegan took to skiffle. More seriously, the Cold War between the USSR and the West was in full swing; Joseph McCarthy was seeking our the 'Reds under the bed' in the United States; there was war in Korea; the Hungarian uprising and the Suez crisis of 1956; and the cry for independence from colonial powers was being heard around the world, the Mau Mau of Kenya helping the British on their way. There was great concern over the atom bomb, and the Campaign for Nuclear Disarmament grew from strength to strength. When in

---

[57] See further, Alan P. F. Sell, *Commemorations*, ch. 14.
[58] J. Robinson, *Works*, ed. R. Ashton, London, 1851, II, 223.

1952 the first wave of immigrants from the West Indies were invited over to assist with post-War development, the 'colour bar' was soon erected. As far as the socio-ethical witness of the churches was concerned, while the traditional opposition to alcohol and divorce and the advocacy of Sunday observance were continued, the churches began to sound the prophetic note, not least in connection with nuclear weapons and racism.

Ethical pronouncement by the churches was not a new thing, of course. As long ago as 1876 Joseph Parker addressed the Congregational Union assembly in words which may still strike a chord with some of us today:

> What an amazing amount of so-called 'business' we have to do! We have to disestablish the Church [of England], modernize the Universities, rectify the policy of School Boards, clear the way to burial-grounds, subsidize magazines, sell hymn-books, play the hose upon [the Anglican] Convocation, and generally give everybody to understand that if we have not yet assailed or defended them, it is not for want of will, but merely for want of time.[59]

Undeterred, the denominations gave due thought to such matters, and many local churches became institutionalized to the point of providing a range of social services and all-age activities, many of which we would nowadays expect national and/or local government to supply. Insofar as the churches sought to serve the needy for the Gospel's sake, they were right. To the extent that secular authorities came to take on a bulk of the burden, they were right. But if the churches had thought that by engaging in caring ministries they would increase their memberships they were mistaken, for we can now see that that decline set in from the first decade of the twentieth century (it was not a product of the First World War), and nothing the churches did could prevent it.[60]

When we view the world of our own time, what do we see? To over-simplify we might say that whereas fifty years ago it was not so obvious that our fortunes were as directly linked to those of other parts of the world as we know them to be today, we did a least have many of the supportive social structures – whether of church, trade union, marriage – which are, for an increasingly changing society with a more mobile population, frequently lacking today. Robert D. Putnam, the Malkin Professor of Public Policy at Harvard University, has recently drawn attention to the way in which societal fellowship, as we might call it, is in decline. He has shown that while more people than ever before go bowling in America, they go as individuals: the number of bowling leagues has

---

[59] Quoted by Albert Peel, *These Hundred Years. A History of the Congregational Union of England and Wales*, London: CUEW, 1931, 264.

[60] See further, Peter Shepherd, *The Making of a Modern Denomination: John Howard Shakespeare and the English Baptists, 1898–1924*, Carlisle: Paternoster Press, forthcoming, 171.

decreased by two thirds in the past twenty-five years. The decline in civic responsibility has been comparable, and mainstream church attendance has dramatically fallen across Europe as well as in America. One American sociologist's diagnosis is as follows:

> American religion is a welter of contradictions. American boomers want community, but on strictly individual terms. They want human closeness without feeling cramped or obligated. They want a personal God who doesn't ask much personally. They want mystery, but in a controlled, non-disruptive way. They want a faith that's fulfilling, practical, earthy, tolerant, transcendent, fun, empowering, morally serious without being morally demanding, a faith that restores wonder and deepens intimacy, and they want it not to cost too much or take up a lot of time.[61]

Others have pointed out that while through the internet we can be in touch with people around the world, we can do it all without direct human contact, and for this as for other reasons – long hours of work among them, many are becoming socially withdrawn to the detriment of their own health. Unlike some pundits, Putnam declares that in this situation the churches have a vital role to play in creating community.[62] But, of course, churches can only begin where they are, and in many of our churches with their high average ages, it may be that we must seek more urgently to minister to that ever-increasing proportion of the population who are over retirement age and who, if recent studies are to be believed are increasingly turning the tables on the long-cherished view that the older people get the more religious they become.[63] They – or should I say we – are going to need more than testimony and dominoes; we are going to need to have our skills utilized and our minds convinced.

It is in this paradoxical world of isolation yet togetherness that the churches must address the clamant issues of the time. They must do this if they believe that the Gospel is for the whole person and not just for the individual soul. They must do this if they take with any seriousness at all Jesus's concern for the hungry, the outcast, the despairing. It is to the eternal credit of the many liberation theologies, whether Latin American, feminist, black, Minjung,

---

[61] Mark Buchanan, 'We're all syncretistic now: not religious, just spiritual,' *Books and Culture*, January-February 2000, 9. Cf. Wade Clark Roof, *A Generation of Seekers: The Spiritual Journeys of the Baby-Boom Generation*, San Francisco: Harper, 1993; idem, *Spiritual Marketplace: Baby Boomers and the Remaking of American Religion*, Princeton, NJ: Princeton University Press, 1999; Robert Wuthnow, *After Heaven: Spirituality in America since the 1950s*, Berkeley: University of California Press, 1998.

[62] See R. D. Putnam, *Bowling Alone: the Collapse and Revival of American Community*, New York: Simon & Schuster, 2000.

[63] See Ben Summerskill, 'Elderly lose faith in religion,' *The Observer*, 3 September 2000, 5 – a discussion of a report to be presented to the annual conference of the British Society of Gerontology. Cf. Tom Kirkwood's 2001 Reith Lectures, 'The end of age.'

Coconut, that for all their occasional internal contradictions, exaggerations and one-sidedness, they have clamantly raised the consciousness of the theological world as far as the needy and oppressed are concerned. More particularly, they have made it much more difficult for the 'haves' to hide behind the unjust structures which oppress the 'have nots', for we see as never before that these structures are erected and held in place by people who are accountable to others and ultimately to God our common creator. Theirs has been a prophetic voice recalling the appeal of the eighth-century BC prophets for justice and for care of the widows and orphans, and bringing vividly to our attention the ministry of active compassion which Jesus exercised – a ministry one significant aspect of which was his challenge to the unjust authorities of his day.

It would not be difficult to present a long litany of concerns which do, or should, exercise all Christians who are concerned with the Gospel in all its fullness. Almost at random one can refer to the warnings surrounding global warming and our stewardship of the created order in general; the AIDS epidemic which, for example, has left 200,000 orphans in Botswana alone, out of a total population of only 1,600,000, and which has resulted in one in four pregnant women and one in nine of the total population carrying the virus in South Africa;[64] the violence and bloodshed spawned by older and newer ethnic and nationalistic tensions; the challenges posed by developments in genetic engineering;[65] the power of frequently unaccountable multi-national corporations, many of whose monetary value exceeds that of many developed countries together, and in face of whom particular governments often seem powerless. So one could go on. But the pressing question is what is to be done in face of these challenges? In particular, what can the churches do? I have three suggestions.

First, as part of their Christian education of all age-groups, local churches can examine some of these pressing issues with a view to seeing first what the nature of a Christian response might be, and secondly, how far their members may take action. Both parts of the task are important, for what is called for is Christian witness. We need not expect that our neighbours will necessarily guess the connection between our actions and our beliefs, and if we cannot explain our stance we have not shown how we differ from many a right-minded humanist. Suppose a native American were to say, 'We must treat the earth aright.' We might be tempted to dismiss this as one of those platitudinous statements to which all can assent; or, we might suspect that the person were

---

[64] For the situation in South Africa see *The Times Higher Education Supplement*, 13 April 2001, 17.

[65] See John F. Kilner, Paige C. Cunningham and W. David Hager, eds., *The Reproduction Revolution: A Christian Appraisal of Sexuality, Reproductive technologies , and the Family*, Grand Rapids: Eerdmans, 2000.

simply making the prudential calculation that if we abuse the earth this season we shall imperil next year's harvest. But what a native American actually said was this: 'The drum represents the cycle of life. It's made of an animal skin and wood, the Creator's gifts to us, and you have to heat it up near fire for it to sound good. There's a real power behind it. The drum brings people together and awakens something. When you hear it and dance, it's a way of expressing yourself, rejoicing. You realize you have this powerful connection between yourself, the Creator, and everyone else.'[66] Now that is a witness in line with the deepest insights of native American spirituality. What might the Christian doctrine of creation have to say concerning ecology, land use, global warming, human togetherness? The question is, Given what we believe, what should our lifestyle be? But in attempting to answer this question let us beware of falling into that sectarian legalism which contents itself with specifying negatives and quite fails to emphasize the joy of a Christian life which receives good at God's hand, and in fellowship with him freely responds in grateful, stewardly, living. As Second Isaiah reminded his hearers long ago, our religion is supposed to carry us along; we do not have to trundle it around.[67]

Secondly, as a development of the point just made, the churches need to equip those of their members who occupy positions of influence in government, industry, business, education, so that they can bring a Christian view of the world to bear upon the kind of issues I have listed. So often we have told people from the pulpit that they must make a Christian witness at work, but how often we have left them to it. The kind of activity I am encouraging is one in which the churches will need to listen much more carefully than they sometimes have done to their members who are, as it were, at the front line. Only then will they be able to articulate pertinent responses. I heard an honest scientist say on television that in about four years time he would be able to apply a technique currently used on rats to human beings – but he had no idea whether it would right to do so. Let us thank God for scientists humble enough to recognize that some of the judgments which their work calls for transcend scientific methodology as such. Hence the ethical committees in hospitals, industry, and elsewhere. The churches here and in many parts of the world still have gifted members who can make more than a technical contribution in such spheres. Let us help them to do so. If they are to be helped we shall need to take with full seriousness a number of current intellectual trends, of which I shall mention a few.

---

[66] Quoted by George W. Lyon, *Community Music in Alberta. Some Good Schoolhouse Stuff*, Calgary: University of Calgary Press, 1999, 131/134.
[67] Isaiah 46.

We shall need to tackle that aspect of postmodern culture which denies that there are intellectual and ethical foundations, and seems to lead to relativism in ethics. As the philosopher Hugo Meynell has asked,

> Are we really to believe that there is no more 'foundation' for the proposition that the moon largely consists of silicon, than that it is made entirely of green cheese? Is the truism that it is wrong to burn to death lonely old persons who own black cats, no better 'founded' than the view that this is quite a commendable practice? Is it not in fact obvious, to almost anyone but a professional philosopher, that if there are no better 'foundations' for any judgment of fact or value than for its contradictory, then 'anything goes'?[68]

Again, there are signs in the popular press of a resurgence of naturalism, which is being invoked in such a way as to explain sexual promiscuity as natural and monogamy as unnatural.[69] I more than suspect that we shall not be able satisfactorily to make our Christian witness in the ethical sphere until we enable our suitably placed members to expose and counter the frequently tacitly held adverse philosophical ideologies and doctrines of humanity which prompt ethical stances and decisions.

Thirdly, we must counter the pessimism regarding religion which has been expressed by Will Hutton, normally a perceptive commentator on events and ideas. He writes: 'religion has been losing the battle against science, humanism and the march of the rational for more than 300 years – and it will not triumph in the argument over stem-cell research. That does not mean there are not fundamental moral questions raised by where science is leading, but religion is not going to be able to provide the answers. We have to find the answers ourselves.'[70] Though it would take me too far afield to offer a full response here, I may, perhaps, be forgiven for pontificating Hutton-style: it is not inevitable that there should be a battle between religion and science: indeed, the rise of modern science was to a considerable extent prompted by the desire of appropriately skilled religious believers to explore God's handiwork; to pronounce in advance that religion will not be able to offer anything of worth to current moral debate, and accordingly to disregard it, is tantamount to censoring a vast quantity of ethical reflection, and repudiating a considerable amount of ethical experience accumulated over many centuries in a way which is unbecoming in a liberal-minded person; and it further tacitly and without argument implies the superiority of a non-religious stance. The sooner we understand that in intricate socio-ethical matters we are dealing with often

---

[68] Hugo A. Meynell, 'Lonergan's search for knowledge,' *The Literary Review of Canada*, February 1993, 14.
[69] See, for example, Robert Wright, 'Our cheating hearts,' *Time*, 15 August 1994, 44–52.
[70] W. Hutton, 'Losing the way of Winning [a pun on the Cardinal's name]' *The Observer*, 20 August 2000, 29. The entire article is peppered with confusions, I fear.

unarticulated, frequently conflicting, and sometimes even unacknowledged world views, the sooner we shall bring reality to ethical debate and be impelled to seek such common moral ground as there may be.

Yet again, the churches in their regional, national and international expressions can deliberate upon pressing issues and directly approach those in a position to take action. Let it clearly be understood that this is highly skilled work. The churches need to inform themselves as fully as they can upon the issue concerned. It is useless to churn out resolutions which are so platitudinous that nobody would disagree with the sentiments expressed – or take any action concerning them; or which are so technically specific that the recipients of the messages may dismiss them on the ground that the Church is sounding off beyond its competence.[71]

Again, the wider the base, the more difficult it is to frame resolutions which will really represent the views of those in whose name they are delivered; and there is nothing more counter-productive than a grandly phrased churchly resolution which is passed at an assembly only to be repudiated by large numbers of the constituency after the event. When the resolution is one which hopes to command international churchly support the matter is more complicated still, given the time it takes for issues to be taught in around the world, and the differing cultural contexts in which the members live. And yet I believe that in the providence of God the international agencies of the Christian churches – both the Christian world communions and the inter-confessional groupings – have become established at precisely the time when so many of the challenges facing humanity are global in nature: AIDS, crime, ecology, economic exploitation and so many more – all of these are international in scope, and they call for concerted Christian responses.

Are such responses really possible? I believe that they are, and I cite one example which is by now a classic. For more than twenty years the World Alliance of Reformed Churches discussed and pleaded with its white Dutch South African member churches concerning the policy of apartheid. Then in 1982 the *Resolution on Racism and South Africa* was adopted at the General Council meeting in Ottawa. It was overwhelmingly supported there and among the member churches around the world and, on the testimony of a number of South Africans on all sides, it was one of a number of initiatives which encouraged those working for the changes of which we are all now aware. But note the character of the Resolution. It sets out with a strong biblical and theological statement concerning the one family that God in Christ has made – a family in which the barriers of race are broken. In the light of that it affirms that apartheid is a sin, and that any attempt to justify in on biblical or theological

---

[71] See Alan P. F. Sell, *Aspects of Christian Integrity*, 68–71.

grounds is heretical. It then takes action by suspending the erring members, whilst at the same time specifying what they will have to do to be restored to full fellowship – as the larger of the two now has been. And it urges all its member churches around the world to deal with the racism in their midst. My point is that this was not simply hot air. It was Christian witness. The groundwork was carefully laid down; action was taken; and further developments were provided for. I believe that that Resolution is a model of the kind of careful and effective corporate Christian witness which is achievable in this threatened, divided, and challenging world.[72]

As a footnote to the general line I have adopted, and not at all by way of offering an excuse to Christians who may wish to opt out of their socio-ethical witness, I would point out that there may be occasions on which the correct stance for the churches is to maintain silence. This will generally be concerning those issues, such as pacifism *versus* non-pacifism which have, in my view rightly, been traditionally seen by most churches as matters on which Christians may sincerely differ without dividing the church. Clearly, the question of the permissible degrees of tolerance within the Church applies as much to ethical as it does to doctrinal and biblical issues.

VIII

To repeat: the challenges are daunting. *The Times Higher Education Supplement* published a special Millennium magazine in December 2000, from the cover of which I take the following facts: two thirds of the world's population will be living in severe drought conditions by 2025; about 20% of the world's population lacks access to safe drinking water; almost one third of all children are under-nourished; a conservative estimate of the number of people in slavery in 1999 was 27 million; some three billion people live in extreme poverty, and of the 1.3 billion poorest, only 30% are male and 70% are female. Where predictions are concerned, people have been shown to be wrong before. In the mid-nineteenth century someone contemplated the huge number of horses on the streets and speculated that if things went on as they were, a century hence London would be under four feet of horse manure. It did not happen; the motor

---

[72] For the text of the Resolution see *Proceedings of the Twenty-second Council of the World Alliance of Reformed Churches*, Geneva: WARC, 1982, 177. Cf. Alan P. F. Sell, *A Reformed, Evangelical, Catholic Theology*, 233–4; idem, *Aspects of Christian Integrity*, ch. 3. The Alliance is currently devoting much attention to the relations between economic injustice and ecological destruction. See, for example, *Processus Confessionis*, Geneva: WARC, 1998, and *Consequences of Economic Globalization*, Geneva: WARC, [2000]. From the same publisher see also the pamphlet designed to assist members churches in their reflections: *The Gospel confronts Economic Injustice and the Destruction of the Earth. A Call to Confess our Faith*, n.d. but post 1997. See also Noreena Hertz, *The Silent Takeover*, London: Heinemann, 2001.

car was invented (with its attendant problems), and horses largely left the streets. But let us not be too sanguine that predictions may fail; and certainly let us heed the statements of fact to which I have just referred. And lest any think that dire facts apply only far away from ourselves (as if that would be a legitimate reason for ignoring them), let me remind you that one in three criminals in our country under the age of 25 owns, or has access to, a gun; that one in three children in our land are officially classed as living in poverty; and that after allowing for population increase, crimes of violence in England and Wales have increased by 46% since 1946.[73] So one could go on ... In the name of the Gospel we are right to be concerned; because of the Gospel we should not be paralysed. I do not hold out any Utopian vision before you; I do not know how or when it will all end, but I think I can see some of the things we need to be doing if we sincerely profess to proclaim Christ's Gospel, and I have suggested what these are.

Any reassurance we may feel as we proceed with our witnessing cannot in the end come from any prospects of success we may have. Nor can it come simply from such welcome facts as the burgeoning of church life in central and eastern Europe in the wake of forty years of communism, or the rapid numerical growth of the Church in many countries. Just as there is nothing in the Bible to suggest that God cannot bring his purposes to pass unless and until we have packed everybody into our pews, so there is no guarantee that our socio-ethical witness will succeed. Rather, the Bible has much to say about the faithful remnant – a remnant which is called to witness, even to the death, against great odds. I can understand those elderly folk who have said to me, in despair, that despite the faithful witness of themselves and their friends over many years, the world seems no better now than it was when they came into it. But what they and we need to remember is that the final outcome turns not upon what we do, but upon what God in Christ has already done. Let us ever remember, with P. T. Forsyth, that 'We live ... in a redeemed world, not in a world which is only being redeemed as the number of believers grow.'[74] With this I come to my conclusion.

I have sought to reminisce; to take my sights from my experience of the churches I knew best fifty years ago; to reflect upon the present situation; and to speak a word of reassurance as we proceed further into this new millennium. You may be thinking that I have left it rather late to bring in the reassurance, but in fact it has been there all the time. For I first spoke of the Church's worship –

---

[73] I find these random illustrations in *The Observer*, 3 September 2000, 7; *The Free Church Chronicle*, Autumn, 2000, 12, 5.

[74] P. T. Forsyth, *Revelation Old and New. Sermons and Addrsses*, London: Independent Press, 1962, 37.

worship inspired by God's redeeming act in his Son at the Cross. I spoke of ministers who are called as their primary duty to lead that worship and to proclaim the word of the Cross. I spoke of the urgency of the ecumenical challenge whereby the churches might increasingly manifest that unity into which they have been brought by the grace of God in the Gospel. And I spoke of the world in which we have to proclaim and act out the message of the Cross in *all* its dimensions of caring concern. Why this constant emphasis upon the Cross? Precisely because of the Christian conviction that therein lies the hope of the world.

Not the least of the pitfalls in our Christian witness is that of inadequately grasping what God in Christ has done. Not, indeed, that we shall ever fully plumb the mystery of the Cross, and mercifully the Church has never formally defined the doctrine of the atonement. But the most casual glance at the history of proclamation will show that at times the Church's testimony has been sadly skewed. For example, there has been a tendency for preachers and others to set out from human sin rather than from the good news of God's grace, and to do this in such a way that Benjamin Jowett's mid-nineteenth-century charge was justified: 'God is represented as angry with us for what we never did; he is ready to inflict disproportionate punishment on us for what we are; He is satisfied by the sufferings of His Son in our stead.'[75] At worst the claim was made that God could not be gracious until his Son had died. This view can still be heard – and not only from some American tele-evangelists. It is thoroughly offensive; it drives a wedge between the Father and the Son; and it completely overlooks Paul's great affirmation, 'God was in Christ reconciling the world to himself.'[76] As P. T. Forsyth roundly declared, 'The atonement did not procure grace, it flowed from grace ... We must renounce the idea that [Christ] was punished by the God who was ever well pleased with his Son.'[77]

On the liberal swing of the doctrinal pendulum there came to be proclaimed in some quarters a genial, sentimental notion of God's love. God is our Father and we are brothers and sisters, and all is well. This drew that stern rebuke of H. Richard Niebuhr, 'A God without wrath brought men without sin into a Kingdom without judgment through the ministerations of a Christ without a cross.'[78] If the former view overlooked the priority of grace, this one played down the fact that God's love is holy love, and that he is the merciful One who is righteous.

---

[75] B. Jowett, 'On atonement and satisfaction,' quoted by B. M. G. Reardon, *Religious Thought in the Victoorian Age*, London: Longmans, 1971, 334.

[76] II Corinthians 5: 19.

[77] P. T. Forsyth, 'The distinctive thing in Christian experience,' *The Hibbert Journal*, VI, 1908, 486.

[78] H. R. Niebuhr, *The Kingdom of God in America*, Hamden: The Shoe String Press, 1956, 193.

The balance of these exaggerated views can be adjusted, and it frequently has been; but very often only in regard to the individual's salvation. But it is not enough that we think of the atonement as having reference only to God's grace and to our sin and reconciliation. If this is all we proclaim we are preaching only half a doctrine of atonement. The first thing done at the Cross is done for God, not for us. It is to the eternal credit of Anselm that, long ago, he saw that God's holy love, outraged by sin, must be satisfied. Every sinner ought to render such satisfaction declares Anselm, but God's grace is such that Christ does it on our behalf. It is because, at the Cross, God's holy love has been vindicated and our sins forgiven that we can go forward in Christian witness, confident that because the crucial battle has been fought and won the end is assured, though it is not yet. It is not just that the believer's life in Christ is secure now and eternally, though that is wonderfully true; it is that what Paul calls the principalities and powers have been defeated. I have sometimes jokingly said that if ever any over-sensitive hymnal editor wishes on grounds of archaism to delete Bunyan's 'hobgoblins and foul fiends' from his fine hymn, 'Who would true valour see', I shall pack my bags! I need to know that the hobgoblins and foul fiends are done for. And they are. Let us not so individualize or privatize the Gospel that we forget or obscure its cosmic dimension which, as John the Seer reminds us, concerns a new heaven and a new earth.[79] In thundering language P. T. Forsyth underlines the point: 'The evil world will not win at last, because it failed to win at the only time it ever could. It is a vanquished world where men play their devilries. Christ has overcome it. It can make tribulation, but desolation it can never make.'[80]

As we go forth in the Saviour's name into a threatened, divided, and needy world our confidence resides in the fact that although the end is not yet, the final victory of the purposes of God is assured. For by his sovereign grace the God of holy love has, in the person of his Son already defeated at the Cross all the forces that would seek to defy him; and by his Spirit he grants us new life, informs our testimony, and empowers our witness.

Long ago John Stoughton endorsed a friend's observation that one of the losses of the times was 'a diminished sense of sin, and therefore a diminished

---

[79] We should not delude ourselves that the principalities and powers do not on occasion stray into the Church. As long ago as 1856 Robert Halley asked the Congregational Union of England and Wales: 'Is the spirit of the world becoming strong in our midst?' And he went on to warn in sepulchral tones that 'If our sanctuaries are the resorts of world-minded men, who affect our administration and discipline by their influence; and if we have not power, by our preaching and prayers to overthrow the tables of the money-changers, and to cast out the unclean spirit, our mission is over, and the hour of our bondage is come upon us.' *The Congregational Year Book*, 1856, 51.

[80] P. T. Forsyth, *The Justification of God. Lectures for War-time on a Christian Theodicy*, (1917), London: Independent Press, 1957, 223.

conviction as to the need of an Atonement.'[81] If that was true in 1881, it is no less true today. While many may feel depressed, elated, in despair, they do not see themselves as sinners. So a Gospel couched solely in terms of individual salvation from sin will not reach them. Indeed, I do not think that any of us really understands what sin is until we have seen something of the costliness of God's act in Christ to deal with it. But most of the people to whom I refer are not hearing that good news either. This is where we need the whole Gospel, and a doctrine of atonement which is as concerned with God's holy love as with human sin. Given that so many in our society have been out of earshot of the Gospel for generations, it may be that as the Church, in the name of, and with explicit reference to, the holy One, addresses, prayerfully and theologically, those ills which the least perceptive person can see as problems – the last gasps of the principalities and powers, the ground will be prepared in which personally appropriatable seeds of grace may take root.

However that may be, I leave you with a charge drawn from a sermon by the Scottish divine, Thomas Boston (1676–1732):

> Learn and hold fast the Gospel principles in your heads; keep up a Gospel frame in your hearts, and have a Gospel practice in your walk. Learn the art of living by faith, believing the promise, and on the credit of the promise going out in duty. Let love constrain you to obedience, and be strict and tender in the whole of your walk, and so adorn the profession of the Gospel.[82]

---

[81] *Reminiscences*, 90.
[82] T. Boston, *The Duty and Advantage of Cleaving to the Lord and His Way in a Declining Time*, Grand Rapids: Inheritance Publishers, n.d., 24.

Index of Persons

Abelard 106
Adeney, W. F. 9, 321
Alexander, Archibald 237
Alexander, A. B. D. 222
Alexander, Samuel 219
Allen, Daniel 56
Allen, Eric S. 300
Allen, Hervey 321
Alston, William 16
Ames, William 216
Amory, Thomas 91, 95, 97, 99–100, 105,
  108, 112, 113–14
Anderson, Marvin 146
Andrews, Jessie Forsyth 144
Angus, Joseph 67, 69
Anne, Queen 92, 260
Anselm 351
Aquinas, Thomas 216
Aristotle 155, 174, 216
Arminius, Jacobus 4
Armstrong, Louis 341
Ashley, Timothy R. 119
Ashton, R. 255, 341
Aspland, Robert 134
Aspland, R. Brook 134
Athanasius 6, 120
Auden, W. H. 1
Augustine 47, 179, 215
Austin, George 268
Avis, Paul 268, 283
Ayer, A. J. 221

Bagshaw, Frederick 286
Baillie, John 223
Baird, Charles 25
Balguy, John 112
Ball, John 105, 216
Ball, William 105
Banks, Charles W. 65
Barber, Chris 341
Barnby, Joseph 320
Barrow, Henry 19–21, 256
Barrow, Simon 270
Barth, Karl 7, 18, 27, 140, 157, 214, 215,
  221, 223, 224, 237, 324
Bartlet, J. Vernon 9, 163, 203, 291, 336
Baskerville, Mr. 260–61
Bauswein, J-J. 234

Baxter, Richard 37–40, 43–7, 103, 127,
  193, 245, 258, 336
Bayes, Thomas 112
Beard, J. Norman 305
Beard, J. R. 57
Beasley-Murray, Paul 73
Beck, Geoffrey 310
Beddome, Benjamin 61, 92
Beeke, Joel R. 17
Begbie, Jeremy 145, 173
Belben, Howard 286
Bell, G. K. A. 269, 283
Belsham, Thomas 119, 128
Bender, Ross T. 267
Benn, Tony 268–69
Bennett, James 24, 94
Bennett, W. H. 9, 321
Berg, Joseph F. 325
Bernard, Richard 15, 341
Berry, Charles 296
Berry, S. M. 253
Beverley, James A. 68
Beza, T. 234
Bezzant, J. S. 272, 275, 281
Biddle, John 120, 127
Binfield, [J.] Clyde [G.] 198, 285, 291
Binney, Thomas 24, 25, 278, 284, 295
Blackburn, John 294
Blair, Tony 246
Bligh, Michael 57
Bliss, Philip H. 57
Bloesch, Donald 223
Bocking, Ronald A. H. 220, 291
Boff, Leonardo 5
Bogue, David 24, 94
Bolam, C. G. 102
Bold, Samuel 127
Bomberger, J. H. A. 180, 183, 237
Bonhoeffer, Dietrich 13, 214
Booker, Henry 57
Booth, Gordon 303, 305, 309, 314
Boshier, Brian 286
Boston, Thomas 352
Boswell, James 116
Brackney, William H. 51
Bradley, F. H. 212
Bradley, Ian 327–8
Bradley, W. L. 144, 149, 157, 198

Bratt, James D. 192
Braverman, Henry 318
Brewer, Samuel 24
Bricker, George M. 173
Bridge, William 245
Briggs, John H. Y. 49, 51, 73, 77
Brine, John 61–3
Broad, C. D. 212
Brooks, Thomas 245, 340
Brown, J. Baldwin 295
Brown, John (of Haddington) 7, 9
Brown, John (of Bedford) 259
Brown, Raymond 56, 62, 75
Brown, Robert McAfee 154
Brown, Thomas 218
Browne, Robert 20, 257, 292
Bruce, A. B. 246
Bruce, F. F. 337
Brunner, Emil 221, 237
Bryant, Chris 269
Bucer, M. 234
Buchanan, Mark 343
Buckingham, John 299, 300, 308
Buffard, Frank 57, 66
Bullinger, H. 234
Bultmann, Rudolf 324
Bunyan, John 259, 351
Burder, H. F. 217, 261
Burgersdyck, Franco 93
Burke, E. 174
Burnaby, John 216
Burn, Edward 121
Burns, Dawson 68
Burrage, Champlin 19, 20
Burroughes, Jeremiah 293
Busher, Leonard 81
Butler, Joseph 159, 216, 246

Cadoux, C. J. 26, 290, 315
Caffyn, Matthew 52–6, 65, 72
Caird, Edward 147, 172
Caird, George 301
Caird, John 172
Calamy, E. 258
Calder, Ralph F. G. 294
Calvin, John 4, 33, 181, 216, 229, 234, 242, 247, 248, 287, 336
Cameron, N. M. de S. 121
Campbell, Alistair 75
Campbell, James R. 235
Campbell, John 263
Campbell, John McLeod 135, 236

Campbell, R. J. 155, 174
Carey, George, 254
Carlson, Leland H. 20, 256–7, 292
Carlyle, Thomas 146
Carr, Wesley 268
Carritt, E. F. 221
Case, Francis 286
Catherine of Genoa 203
Cave, Sydney 9, 26, 144, 217, 220, 303
Chadwick, Owen 259, 270
Chalmers, Thomas 261
Chamberlain, Elsie 300
Chambers, R. F. 57
Charles, Maurice 308–9
Charles, Prince 87, 268
Churchill, Winston, 341
Cicero 37
Clark, Henry W. 282
Clark, J. C. D. 119
Clarke, Malcolm 330
Clarke, Samuel 102, 109, 110, 216
Cleaves, Reginald W. 309–11, 313
Clements, Keith 76, 80
Clifford, John 49, 68, 73, 83, 264
Clutton-Brock, A. H. 318–9
Cochrane, A. C. 235
Cockain, George 21
Cocks, H. F. Lovell 9, 28, 139, 140, 161, 169, 174, 221, 270, 275, 288, 298, 302, 322
Coffey, David 73
Coggins, James R. 52
Cole, C. Robert 257
Collier, Arthur 110
Collier, Thomas 58
Collins, G. N. M. 275
Collyer, William Bengo 296
Coltman, Constance M. 41, 166
Conser, Walter H., Jr. 192
Cook, Henry, 50, 69–70, 75, 78, 84, 87
Cooper, Christopher 53
Cornish, William 97–8, 100, 105, 108, 113
Cornwall, Robert D. 260
Cox, Martin L., Jr.188
Cradock, Walter 43–4
Cramp, J. M. 58, 61
Creed, J. M. 276, 278
Cressey, Martin H. 315
Crosby, Thomas, 4
Crosley, David 58
Cross, Anthony R. 28
Cudworth, Ralph 216

INDEX

Cumberland, Richard 93, 216, 227
Cunliffe-Jones, Hubert 28, 298, 309–11
Cunningham, Paige C. 344
Cunningham, William 136
Cupitt, Don 5
Curran, Charles 5
Curry, George 306, 308–9, 313

Dakin, Arthur 69, 70, 78, 84, 222
Dale, R. W. 25, 26, 145, 257, 263, 273, 278, 281, 289, 298, 315
Daneau, Lambert 216
Danzelman, F. W. 321–2
Darch, Robert, 96
Darracott, Risdon 98
David, Francis 124
Davidson, Samuel 288, 295
Davies, Evan, 217, 218
Davies, Horton 22, 23, 24
Davies (née Rogers), Mrs. 320
Dawn, Marva 331
De Berg, Betty 326–7
De Burgh, W. G. 328
Defoe, Daniel 94
Dell, William 259
Demosthenes 37
Denbow, Walter H. 305
Densham, W. 98
Derodon, David 93
Descartes, R. 96, 112
Deweese, Charles W. 72, 77
DiPuccio, William 175
Dix, Kenneth 60, 62–3
Dockery, David S. 62, 119
Doddridge, Philip 23, 92, 169, 217, 259, 262
Doggett, John 60
Dorner, I. A. 182–4, 193, 195, 200
Drummond, James S. 297
Dulles, Avery 32
Dummett, Michael 16
Duthie, Charles S. 169
Dye, Alfred 65

Eames, John 97
Eckersley, Rachel 119
Edward VII 264
Edwards, David L. 271–2
Edwards, Jonathan 234
Edwards, William 83–4, 264
Elias, John 320
Elizabeth I 281

Elizabeth II 341
Elizabeth, Princess 320
Emerson, R. W. 155
Emlyn, Thomas 127
Emmet, Dorothy M. 215
Epictetus 37
Erskine, Thomas 135
Escott, Harry, 23
Eustacius de Saint-Paul 93
Evans, Caleb 51
Evans, Owen E. 8
Evershed, John J. 52
Ewing, A. C. 215
Fackre, Gabriel 37
Fairbairn, A. M. 9, 145, 277
Falding, F. J. 9–10
Farel, G. 234
Fawkes, Alfred 267
Ferguson, J. P. 102
Fiddes, Paul S. 51, 77
Field, G. C. 221
Figures, Joseph A. 299
Finney, C. G. 192
Fitz, Richard 19
Flavell, Alan 331
Flavel, John 127
Fletcher, Joseph 261
Fletcher, Lord 281
Flint, Robert 246
Flower, Thomas 260–61
Floyd, Richard L. 38
Forsyth, P. T. 2, 4, 5, 9, 26, 28, 37–8, 40–43, 45–7, 50, 66–7, 87, 137, ch. 7, ch. 8, 217, 221, 236, 250, 264, 272, 274–5, 278, 279, 282, 283, 290, 291, 295, 296, 297, 308, 324, 336, 349–51
Foskett, Bernard 51
Fox, George 54
Franks, John 314
Franks, Robert S. 9
Fuller, Andrew 63–4, ch. 6
Fuller, J. G. 51

Gadsby, William 63–4
Gale, Richard 16
Gale, Theophilus 94
Garbett, Cyril 86, 270, 272, 276, 281
Garvie, A. E. 9, 28, 140–41, 160, 165, 169, 208, 253, 277
Geddes, Alexander 121
Gee, Henry 86
George, Timothy 62, 119

Gibbons, Thomas 168
Gill, John 4, 57, 61, 62, 160, 211, 216
Gill, Robin 213, 214, 228
Gillard, Daniel 58
Gilmore, A. 71, 73, 75, 77, 79, 80
Gisburne, John 134
Goodall, Norman 290, 302, 308, 310
Goodwin, Thomas 146, 168
Gordon, Alexander 52, 53, 56, 59, 72, 93, 94, 96, 97, 102, 114
Goring, Jeremy 258
Goulty, John Nelson 294
Graff, Graeme de 229
Graham, Billy 324, 340–41
Grant, John W. 71
Green. T. H. 145, 172
Greenwood, John, 20, 255–7
Gregory, Olinthus 68, 77, 83, 261
Grieve, A. J. 267, 287, 296, 298
Griffioen, Arie J. 175, 180, 203
Grigge, William 59
Grove, Edward 91
Grove, Henry ch. 5, 216, 245, 260
Grove, Elizabeth 98
Grützmacher, F. 144
Guest, E. S. 303, 305, 313
Guinness family 321
Gunnemann, Louis H. 172, 197
Gustafson, James 229

Haakonssen, Knud 91
Habgood, John 271, 274, 277, 282
Hager, W. David 344
Haig, Charles, 299, 305, 307–8
Hall, Douglas J. 333
Hall, G. Stanley 217
Hall, Robert 77, 82, 83, 261
Hallett, Joseph, Jr 110–12
Halley, Robert 351
Hamilton, Harold 143
Hamilton, H. A. 29, 310–11
Hamstra, Sam, Jr. 175, 180, 199, 206
Hannay, Alexander 297
Harbaugh, Henry 183
Hardy, E. Bruce 66
Hardy, William J. 86
Hare, R. M. 212, 215
Harnack, Adolf 7, 144, 155
Harrald, J. W. 62
Harris, Herbert W. 286
Harris, Howel 92
Harrison, Jonathan 215

Harrison, Robert 20, 257, 292
Harson, Daniel 101, 104, 117
Hart, D. G. 327
Hart, Trevor A. 38, 145, 171, 173, 198, 220, 221, 236
Hartmann, J. R. Edouard von 145
Haskoll, Farnham 103
Hayden, Roger 51
Haykin, Michael A. G. 60
Haymes, Brian 76, 80
Headlam, A. C. 271, 282–3
Healey, F. G. 286
Hegel, G. W. F. 154, 155, 172–5, 177, 178, 219
Helwys, Thomas 52, 76, 77, 81
Hendry, Kathleen M. 290, 299
Henry, Matthew 119, 137
Heron, Alasdair I. C. 235
Herrmann, W. 145, 173
Hertz, Noreena 348
Hesselink, I. John 229–30
Hetherington, H. J. W. 5
Hill, G. B. 116
Hinsliff, Gaby 270
Hobbes, Thomas 112–16, 216
Hodge, Charles 237
Hodges, H. A. 236, 249
Hoffman, Melchior 53
Honeysett, B. J. 64
Hooker, Richard 174, 257, 276
Hooker, Thomas 293
Hooper, Thomas 279
Hopkins, William 127
Hort, F. J. A. 296
Hort, Josiah 94
Horton, R. F. 264, 288, 297
Hoskyns, Edwyn C. 143
Howe, John 96, 110, 127, 258–9, 338
Hughes, John 94
Hughes, T. Hywel 140
Hull, [John Howarth] Eric 289
Hume, David 15, 227, 228, 246
Hunt, Jeremiah 94
Hunter, A. M. 143
Huntington, William 63
Hus, J. 234
Hussey, Joseph 61, 235
Hutcheson, Francis 216, 227
Hutton, Will 346
Huxtable, [W] John [F] 24, 28, 29, 173, 174, 258, 269, 274, 283, 290, 299, 301, 302–4, 306–7, 309, 310, 311, 315

Inge, W. R. 326
Iverach, James 246
Ivimey, Joseph 261

Jackson, Alvery 61
Jacob, Henry 257
James, John Angell 263, 294–5
James, J. Courtnay 269
James, Stephen 96–7
James, T. S. 96, 98
James, T. T. 290
Jebb, John 127
Jenkins, Daniel T. 28, 33, 297, 299–300
Jenkins, David 272
Jennings, David 126
Jimmy (see Rhodes-Wrigley, James)
John Paul II 226
Johnson, Dale A. 237
Johnson, Francis 292
Johnson, John 62
Johnson, Samuel 116
Jones, Henry 5
Jones, J. A. 168
Jones, J. D. 28, 163, 203, 291, 336
Jones, John Morris 5
Jones, R. Tudur 255, 287
Jordan, E. K. H. 265
Jordan, M. Dorothea 256–7
Joseph, H. W. B. 221
Jowett, Benjamin 350
Jowett, J. H. 328–9

Kähler, Martin 144, 146
Kant, Immanuel 2, 145, 146, 159, 172, 174, 215, 246
Kaye, J. Alfred 321, 324
Keach, Benjamin 56
Keckerman, B. 216
Kember, Hugh 308
Kensett, Emily 74
Kentish, John 126, 128–30, 131, 133, 134, 136
Kershaw, John 63
Key, Mark 56
Kieffer, Elizabeth C. 200
Kierkegaard, S. A. 145, 155
Kilner, John F. 344
Kippis, Andrew 128
Kirby, Gilbert 303
Kirk, Robert 21
Kirkwood, Tom 343
Klaassen, Walter 53

Kliever, Lonnie D. 52, 213
Knox, J. 234
Koehnlein, John M. 270
Krafft, W. L. 238
Küng, Hans 5

Lardner, Nathaniel 127
Latham, Robert O. 311
Layman, David 180
Le Clerc, Jean 93
Leith, John H. 239
Lessing, G. E. 174
Lewis, Donald M. 119
Lewis, Georgina K. 262
Lewis, Thomas 324–5
Light, Alfred W. 94
Lincoln, Abraham 285
Linden, F. O. zur 53
Lindsey, Theophilus 119, 124
Lloyd-Jones, D. Martyn 340
Locke, John 69, 93, 96, 105, 106, 109, 113, 173, 247, 259
Longley, Clifford 278
Lover, Samuel 52
Lucas, Richard 96
Lumpkin, William L. 50, 51, 53, 54, 59, 71–2, 77, 78, 79, 89
Luther, Martin 6, 214, 216, 306
Lyon, George W. 345
Lyttelton, Humphrey 341

McCarthy, Joseph 103, 341
McCurdy, Leslie 38, 144, 171
McDonnell, John J. 226
McDonnell, Kilian 339–40
Macfadyen, D. 263, 289, 296
Macguire, Leonard J. 57
Machin, G. I. T. 269
Mackennal, Alexander 263
Mackenzie, Robert 7, 9
McKim, Donald K. 234, 239, 247
MacKinnon, Donald M. 268, 271–2
Mackintosh, Robert 4, 9, 26, 141, 143, 217, 218, 219, 222, 224, 225, 237, 313, 321
Mackintosh, William H. 263
McLachlan, Herbert 9, 91, 96
McLachlan, H. John 52
Maclaren, Alexander 88
MacLean, D. 21, 275
McNaughton, William D. 217, 218
Magee, W. C. 269

Manning, Bernard Lord 26, 28, 255, 267, 279, 288
Manson, T. W. 8, 298
Marcion 142
Margaret, Princess 320
Marriott, J. A. R. 288, 297
Marsh, John 9, 28, 29, 280, 288, 311, 315
Marshall, David B. 11
Martineau, James 9, 24, 146, 156
Mather, Cotton 217, 257, 258
Mather, Richard 293
Matthews, A. G. 21, 22, 91, 235, 259
Maurice, F. D. 145
Maurice, Matthias 61
Maxwell, Jack Martin 193, 200, 210
May, William 99
Mayor, Stephen H. 20
Meadley, Thomas D. 168
Mee, Arnold F. 306
Melanchthon, P. 216
Meynell, Hugo A. 16, 346
Miall, Edward 263
Micklem, E. Romilly 29
Micklem, Nathaniel 22, 28, 257, 298, 303, 312–3
Midgley, Mary 325
Milner, Thomas 95
Mitchell, Basil 16, 211, 215
Monk, Thomas 54
Moody, Michael E. 257
Moody, Joan W. 306
Moon, Norman 51
Moore, G. E. 212, 221
More, Henry, 216
Morgan, Edward 320
Morgan, G. Sydney 321, 324
Morison, John 294
Moses, John 276
Mozley, J. K. 139, 142, 143, 161
Muirhead, J. H. 172
Mullins, Mrs. 101
Mullins, Samuel 101
Munckley, John 99
Munckley, N. 99
Murch, J. 99
Murray, I. H. 340
Murray, John N. 301–2
Murton, John 81
Myers, Sydney 302

Naylor, Peter 62, 226
Neal, Daniel 94

Nettles, Thomas J. 62
Nevin, J. W. Ch. 8, 236, 297
Newman, J. H. 154, 285
Newton, Isaac 96, 116
Nichols, James H. 198, 200
Nidditch, Peter H. 109, 228
Niebuhr, H. Richard 350
Niebuhr, Reinhold 157
Nielsen, Kai 16
Nowell-Smith, P. H. 212
Nuttall, Geoffrey F. 9, 22, 29, 61, 259
Nyomi, Setri 339

Oberman, H. A. 230
Ogle, J. 98
Old, H. O. 327
Oliver, Robert 62–3
Orchard, W. E. 27
Orr, James, 246
Overend, Frederick 58
Owen, John 22, 28, 44–5, 187, 200, 234, 274, 293, 336

Packer, Brian A. 56, 58, 74
Paine, Thomas 119, 126, 236
Palmer, Samuel 95
Parker, Irene 91
Parker, Joseph 264, 297–8, 342
Pascal, B. 145
Paul, Robert S. 81, 197
Paul, S. F. 64
Payne, Ernest A. 49, 51, 63, 66–7, 75, 78–9, 86, 275
Payne, George 217–19, 222, 227, 261–2, 265
Payne, John B. 176, 204
Peach, W. Bernard 216
Peake, A. S. 141
Peel, Albert 20, 26–7, 257, 288, 292, 294–5, 297, 313, 342
Penelhum Terence M. 16
Penzel, Klaus 172, 176, 188, 196, 198, 201, 204
Peterson, Eugene 331
Pfizenmaier, T. C. 102
Phillips, George 27, 266, 274, 289–90, 312
Phillips, Melanie 269
Philpot, J. C. 63, 65
Philps, Anne 321
Plantinga, Alvin 16
Plato 37, 179
Popham, J. K. 64–5

Porritt, Arthur 329
Powell, L. F. 116
Powicke, F. J. 102
Preager, Lou 341
Preston, Ronald 213, 223
Price, Ernest J. 28, 298
Price, Richard 97, 121, 127
Prichard, H. A. 221, 228
Priestley, Joseph 97, 119–26, 136, 241–2
Putnam, Robert D. 342–3
Pyer, John 217, 261
Prior, A. N. 212
Pyle, Andrew 95
Pythagoras 179

Quicke, M. J. 49

Raleigh, Alexander 303
Ramsbottom, B. A. 64
Ramsey, I. T. 229
Ramsey, Paul 214
Randall, Ian M. 28
Rashdall, Hastings 270, 276
Ratzinger, J. 338–40
Rauch. F. A. 171
Rawson, Joseph 241
Ray, Johnnie 341
Réamonn, Páraic 339
Reason, Joyce 321
Redford, George 295
Rees, Abraham 128
Rees, Fred A. 144
Rees, Thomas 61
Reynolds, H. R. 25, 263, 296
Reynolds, W. 60
Ricca, Paolo 339
Richards, George W. 195, 332
Ridgley, Thomas 151, 160
Rippon, John 60
Ritschl, Albrecht 145–6, 149, 172, 174, 177
Rix, Wilton E. 288
Roberts, Phil 119
Roberts, T. A. 227
Robertson, Connie 1
Robinson, H. Wheeler 70, 71, 73, 75, 80, 87, 222
Robinson, John 14, 15, 255, 257–8, 273, 287, 331, 341
Robinson, N. H. G. 216, 221, 222–4
Robinson, Robert 82
Robinson, W. Gordon 29, 32, 289–90, 301, 323

Rodgers, John H. 143, 156–7
Rogers, Carl 245
Rogers, Henry 338
Rogers, J. Guinness 25, 262–3, 273, 281
Rogers, John 127
Rohr, John von 257
Roof, Wade Clark 343
Roper, Frances H. 116
Ross, W. D. 212
Rothe, F. 144
Routley, Erik 315
Rowe family 91, 99
Rowe, Benoni 94
Rowe, John 91, 94
Rowe, Thomas 94–6
Rowe, Thomas (1687–1715) 94
Rowland, Daniel 92
Rowland, John 57
Runcie, Robert 269
Rupp, E. Gordon 323
Russell, Fred 286
Russell, Stanley H. 145, 173
Rutt, J. T. 120, 126, 241
Ryland, John 63
Ryland, John Collett 51, 72, 80, 82, 87

Sacheverell, Henry 259
Samuel, David N. 280
Savage, Samuel Morton 126, 140, 164
Say, Samuel 94
Schaff, Philip 6, 171, 172–3, 175–6, 178, 188, 191, 193, 194–6, 197, 198, 201, 202, 204, 205, 208, 236, 270, 297, 325, 332, 333, 338
Schleiermacher, F. D. E. 146, 216, 234
Schmiedel, Paul W. 144
Seeberg, Reinhold 144
Selbie, W. B. 253, 257, 298
Selby-Bigge, L. A. 228
Sell, Alan P. F. 1, 4–5, 13–17, 20, 22, 26, 28, 33, 38, 40, 46, 51, 57, 61, 63, 65, 69, 71, 76, 78, 83–4, 88, 91–2, 97–8, 102, 105, 109, 113, 119, 134, 136–7, 139, 151, 153, 162, 172–4, 180, 183, 197–8, 200, 212, 214, 216–18, 220–21, 224–6, 234–8, 240–51, 256–7, 259–60, 266–7, 282, ch. 12, ch. 13
Sellers, Ian 68
Seneca 37
Servetus, Michael 124
Shaftesbury (Anthony Ashley Cooper) 216

Shakespeare, J. H. 265, 290, 291, 342
Shepherd, Martin 314
Shepherd, Peter 265, 291, 342
Sherlock, Thomas 259
Short, John 28
Shriver, George H. 6, 325
Sidgwick, Henry 212
Simmonds, John 57
Simon, D. W. 11, 326
Singer, Elizabeth 94
Sinnema, Donald 216
Skepp, John 61
Slater, David, 75, 78, 80
Sloss, James 241
Smart, Mr. 55
Smith, Bertram 306
Smith, John 127
Smyth, John 52, 69, 81, 255
Smyth, Newman 215, 224, 227
Socinus, F. 105, 119, 124, 127
Socrates 37
Solly, Henry 68
Speight, Johnny 325
Spencer, Herbert 161, 219
Spinks, Bryan D. 22, 25, 27, 29
Spurgeon, C. H. 44, 57, 58, 60, 61, 62, 267
Spurgeon, Susannah 62
Stanger, John 74
Stanley, Howard S. 289–91, 295, 299, 308, 310, 311, 314
Stanley, Mrs. H. S. 299
Stennett, Joseph 56, 62
Stepelevich, Lawrence S. 175
Stephens, T. 325
Stevens, John 62, 64
Stevens, William 57
Stewart, M. A. 97
Stirling, J. H. 172
Stob, Henry 227
Stoughton, John 262–3, 267, 269, 286, 295–7, 317–8, 323, 324, 326, 329, 331, 332, 340, 351
Strauss, D. F. 5
Streeter, B. H. 319
Strong, James 98, 99, 117–8
Summerskill, Ben 343
Surman, Charles E. 287, 294
Swanson, R. N. 28
Swinburne, Richard 16
Sykes, Norman 277, 280
Sylvester, M. 38

Taylor, A. E. 212
Taylor, Dan 57
Taylor, John 241
Taylor, John H. 258
Taylor, Michael 292
Temple, William 87
Thames, Shad 56
Thatcher (née Roberts), Margaret 341
Thomas, D. O. 119
Thomas, G. F. 212
Thomas, Roger 102
Thompson, David M. 261, 283
Thompson, John 221
Thompson, Joseph 8, 263
Ticehurst, John 304–5
Todd, James 29
Tomkins, Martin 102
Torbet, Robert G. 56, 71
Toulmin, Joshua 93–4, 124, 126, 127–33, 135, 137
Toulmin, S. E. 212
Tovey, Alan 313
Towgood, Micaijah 98, 260
Towgood, Stephen 98
Townsend, Henry 84–6, 265, 276
Travell, John C. 313
Trenchard, John 116
Trueblood, D. Elton 337
Trueman, Carl 328
Turretin, Francis 237
Tuttle, G. M. 236

Underwood, A. C. 54, 56, 58
Ursinus, Z. 234

Valdes, P. 234
Van Til, Cornelius 323
Vaughan, Robert 7, 24, 262, 270, 273
Venn, Charles H. 286
Vidler, A. R. 266, 273, 274, 275–6
Vine, Aubrey R. 299
Vine, Thomas 57
Viret, P. 234
Vischer, Lukas 30, 234, 235, 288
Vowell, Benjamin 98

Waddington, John 259
Wainwright, Geoffrey 242
Wallin, Benjamin 60, 73
Walton, R. C. 75
Warburton, John 63
Ward, John 118

Ward, Seth, 258
Wardlaw, Ralph 217, 235, 261
Warren, Matthew 93, 95–7
Warschauer, Joseph 141
Watson, Thomas 211–12, 214, 216, 319
Watts, Isaac 23, 29, 37, 45, 94–5, 259–60, 279
Watts, Michael R. 92, 102
Weaver, John 70
Weller, John 55
Wells, Algernon 295
Wells, James 63
Wentz, Richard E. 192
Wernle, P. 144
Wesley, John 92, 173, 242
West, W. M. S. 49, 73, 75, 79
Whale, John S. 9, 28, 223, 277–8
Whitby, Daniel 62
White, B. R. 51, 75, 78, 80
White, John 260
Whitefield, George 57
Whitehead, A. N. 328
Whitehouse, W. A. 28
Whitgift, John 257
Whitley, W. T. 55–6, 58, 69, 78
Wigley, Henry T. 265
Wileman, William 64
Wilkinson, J. T. 265–6
Williams, John 334
Williams, J. B. 119, 137
Williams, John E. 336

Williams, Roger 81, 258
Williams, Rowan 270
Wilson, John 94
Wilson, Joshua 97
Wilson, Robert S. 119
Wilson, Walter 61, 94, 96–7, 99, 102, 164, 168, 261
Winchester, Elhanan 57
Wogaman, Philip 212
Wollaston, William 110, 216
Wollebius, Johannes 216
Wolterstorff, Nicholas 247
Wood, Ralph C. 157, 173
Wooden, R. Glenn 119
Wright, George 59
Wright, Joseph 55
Wright, N. G. 78
Wright, Robert 346
Wright, T. 63
Wrigley, Fancis 306
Wroe, Martin 269, 272
Wuthnow, Robert 343
Wykes, David L. 91, 97, 126

Yolton, John 109
Yrigoyen, Charles, Jr. 173

Zahn, Theodor 144
Zeman, Jarold K. 68
Zeno 37
Zwingli, U. 234

General Index

Aberdeen University 140, 143, 151, 164, 169, 172, 217, 328
Act of Uniformity 91, 93, 258
adoption 249
agnosticism 2, 147, 152, 246
AIDS 344, 347
An Evangelical Fellowship of Congregational Churches 303, 313
Anabaptists 27, 29, 52, 53, 134, 235, 258, 267, 335
Anglican Consultative Council 253, 335
Anglicans 47, 86, 92, 203, 206, 233, 260, 265–72, 274, 278, 280, 283, 287, 315
see also Anglo-Catholicism; Church of England; Church in Wales
Anglo-Catholicism 19, 24–5, 30, 40, 201, 207
antinomians 51, 58, 66, 245
apartheid 6, 347–8
apologetics 16–17, 47, 52, 153, 160, 243, 246, 333
architecture 24
Arianism 53, 55, 57, 59, 97–8, 103, 121, 151, 206, 241
Arminianism 11, 40, 51, 57–9, 61–3, 66, 92, 242, 245, 335
atheism 121
atonement, *see* Cross
Augsburg Confession 233
authority 188–98, 213, 231
Axminster 217
Aylesbury 54

Bala-Bangor Independent College 303
Banstead 300
baptism 20, 25–7, 29, 30, 33–4, 40, 45, 49, 66, 72–4, 76, 79, 101, 204–5, 235, 243, 259, 335, 339
Baptist College, Cardiff 264
Baptist Missionary Society 119
Baptists 11, 44, 47, ch. 4, 92, 134, 233, 243, 255, 261, 285, 287–8, 290, 291
　Fellowship Baptists 68
　General Baptists 50, 53–7, 59, 60, 65–6, 68, 72, 74, 79–80, 81–2
　Gospel Standard Baptists 63–7
　Johnsonian Baptists 62
　New Connexion Baptists 57, 63, 66, 68

Particular Baptists 27, 51, 53, 56, 57–60, 62, 63–6, 69, 71, 74, 79, 80, 83, 248, 249, 260
Reformed Baptists 78
Southern Baptists 76
Strict and Particular Baptists 57, 60, 62–3, 67, 70, 73–4, 226, 239, 312
Unitarian Baptists 57–8
Baptist Union of Great Britain and Ireland 49, 63, 68, 70, 73, 265, 290
Baptist World Alliance 49, 243, 335
Barmen Declaration 6
Belgic Confession 233
Bessels Green 57, 74
Bible 2–3, 6, 9, 11, 19, 20, 30–31, 32, 69, 72, 77, 85, 88, 104, 108, 111, 113, 120, 125–6, 130, 135, 140, 142–3, 146, 153–4, 158, 163, 186, 188–9, 220, 223, 234, 237, 239, 243, 245, 248, 251, 258, 260, 280, 295, 301, 304, 315, 319, 320–21, 325, 333, 349
Biddenden 56
Billingshurst 74
Birmingham 29, 121, 126, 128
Bishops Hull 98
Blackburn Independent Academy 217, 261
black led churches 254
black theology 343
Brighton 57
Bristol 51
British and Foreign Bible Society 334
Burial Act 266

Calvinism 11, 40, 56, 59, 60, 62, 63–4, 74, 92–3, 103–5, 119, 122–5, 128, 132–3, 135–6, 141, 155, 211, 216, 226, 234, 241–2, 249, 255, 294, 335
Cambridge Platform 293
Cambridge University 217, 266
Campaign for Nuclear Disarmament 341
Canterbury 270
catechetics 39, 45–7, 54, 193
catholicity 28, 79, 169, 193, 194, 202, 204, 208–9, 226, 239, 242–3, 257, 277, 282–3, 297, 298–9, 315, 317, 336, 340
Chalcedonian Formula 147, 185
charismatic movement 13

Cheshunt College 220, 303
Christendom 46
Christian Endeavour 75
Christian Socialist Movement 269
Christian Year 29, 46, 151, 325
Christology 42–3, 52–3, 59, 64–5, 102–3, 120–21, 124–5, 128–30, 131, 135, 147–9, 152–3, 155, 162, 169, 179–85
Church
   and the incarnation 194–6, 201, 207
   and ministers 34
   and state, 80–81, 116–17, 164, 249, ch. 11
   as authority 186
   as missionary 152, 166
   as preacher 41–6, 186
   discipline 5, 22, 56–7, 68, 79, 248, 275
   growth 32, 76–7
   H. Grove on 107–8
   its foundation 193
   its nature 31, ch. 4, 69–80, 107–8, 163, 187–8, 191–202, 208–9, 239, ch. 11, ch. 12
   its theological task 7, 11
   membership 67, 72–4, 250
   necessity of 187, 191
   unity of 13, 14, 165
Churches of Christ 335
Church in Wales 270
Church Meeting 26, 32–4, 40, 50, 70–71, 74–8, 80, 196–7, 209, 225, 248, 274, 287–9, 299–300, 305, 308, 312–13, 340–41
Church of England 19, 21, 30, 40, 85–7, 91, 116, 134, 164, 192, 201, 249, ch. 11, 317, 335
   see also Church and state; establishment
Church of Scotland 83
Church Order Group 28, 298
Civil War 43, 92
coconut theology 344
Cold War 341
Colyton 126
common sense philosophy 173, 218
Commonwealth Missionary Society 334
Congregational Association 315
Congregational Church in England and Wales 285, 291, 300
Congregational Federation 313–14
Congregational Fund Board 126

Congregationalism/ists 17, ch. 2, 38, 40–41, 44, 50, 71, 76, 92, 94, 98, 140–41, 163–4, 169, 171, 196–7, 224–5, 237–9, 248, 255, 257, 258, 263, 264, 274, 281, ch. 12, 321
   see also, Church Meeting
Congregational Union of England and Wales 25, 26, 29, 34, 285, 289–91, 296, 300, 304, 307, 317, 342, 351
conscience 114, 156, 158, 227, 241
contextualism 46, 237, 247
Conventicle Act 266
conversion 40, 106, 207, 304
Council for World Mission 334
covenant 25, 34, 40, 69, 72, 299–301, 304–5, 312, 314
Coward Trust 126
Cranbrook 56, 58
Cranleigh 285
creation 345
creeds 22, 25, 39, 51, 54, 68, 104, 189–90, 208, 210, 241
Cross 2, 12, 42–3, 47, 60, 106, 124, 136, 141–3, 146, 161–2, 164–7, 171, 181–6, 189–91, 194, 203, 205, 208, 220, 237, 244, 324, 340, 350–51

Daventry Academy 128
Declaration of Faith 30, 238, 291, 315
deism 111, 121, 125–6, 132, 135, 236, 245, 246
Dent 305
dialogues 242–3, 335–6
Disciples of Christ 243, 335
Dissenting academies 91–4
Ditchling 57
Dominus Iesus 339–40
Dort 233
Dover 58
doctrinal development 67
Downgrade Controversy 68
Dumfries 218
Durham University 266
duty faith 60–66

ecology 347
Edinburgh 217, 261
Edinburgh University 317
Education Act 264
Enabling Act 265
Enlightenment 3, 13, 15, 40, 173, 236

establishment 50, 69, 82–7, 192, 237, 253, ch. 11
   see also, Church and state; Church of England
eternal Sonship 64–5
Ethical Society 247
ethics 4, 96–8, 167, ch. 9
   history of 216–17
   social 343–8
Evangelical Alliance 303, 334
Evangelical Church of Czech Brethren 234
Evangelical Free Church 286
Evangelical Revival 25, 35, 40, 262
evolutionary thought 246
Exeter 98, 128

federal theology 234
feminist theology 343
Festival of Britain 341
Five Mile Act 266
Folkestone 56
Free Church Federal Council 283
Free Church of Scotland 83, 224, 237, 275
Frittenden 56
Fullwood 98

Geneva 247, 288
Glasgow 261
Glasgow University 217
Godalming 285, 287
Göttingen University 172
Great Ejectment 88, 258, 310
Grundisburgh 60
Guildford 321

Hackney [Congregational] College 38, 171, 220, 261
Hackney [Unitarian] College 128
Hammersmith 58, 341
Hampstead 288
Harley College 321
Harvard University 342
Hawes 305
Headcorn 58
Heidelberg Catechism 6, 233
Helvetic Confession 233
Highbury College 261, 317
historical development 175–6
holy love 42, 140, 146, 159, 161, 167–9, 185, 244, 351–2

Holy Spirit 3, 7, 13, 17, 18, 45, 47, 54–5, 64, 65–6, 69–72, 80, 106, 131, 151–3, 163, 166, 189, 196, 198, 200, 209, 224, 229–31, 239, 244, 248, 251, 289, 293, 302, 304, 312, 319, 332
Home Missionary Society 294
Honiton 105, 216
Horsham 52–3, 74
Hoxton Academy 126, 140, 217, 261
Hull 217
hymns 22–3, 244, 327–9
Hythe 56

idealism 172–5, 178, 219
Ilminster 98
immortality 109, 111, 116
Incarnation 13, 180–85, 209
   see also, Christology
Independents, see Congregationalism/ists
individualism 13, 25, 33, 40, 78, 149, 163, 187–8, 194, 197, 204, 208, 297
International Congregational Council 246, 253

Jews 21, 92

Keld 306
Kensington 317
Kidderminster 39

Lambeth Conference 265
Lancashire Independent College 218, 262, 266, 287–9, 303, 321, 323
Leeds 217, 306
Leicester 308
liberalism, theological 135–6, 153–6, 178–9, 183–4, 190, 195, 205, 321
Liberation Society 263
liberation theology 343
liberty 80–88, 112, 113, 163–4, 256
Lifter Controversy 240
Liverpool 62
Llanvaches 43
London 43, 55–6, 128, 259–60, 316–17, 348
London Confession 59, 79, 81
London Missionary Society 293, 334
London University 317
Lord's Supper 20, 22–30, 33, 34, 73, 77, 79, 100–101, 150, 189, 202–5, 210, 239, 318, 320, 323

Lutherans 87, 233, 235, 242–3, 336

Maidstone 55
Manchester Baptist College 85
Mansfield College 303
materialism 109, 113, 246
Memorial College, Brecon 303, 324
Memorial College, Swansea 303
Mennonites 267, 335
Mercersburg theology ch. 8, 236, 297, 325
Methodism/ists 86, 122, 134, 242–3, 254, 262, 286–7, 306, 315, 335
Milborne Port 98
ministers
   absent 44
   as pastors 44–5
   education of 7–10, 144, 244–6, 250, 331–3
   H. Grove on 96–8
   priestly role of 41, 200, 206
   their vocation 14–15, 46, 331
   threefold 165
   women 17, 41, 166, 235–6
ministry, nature of 198–202, 209, 324, 332
Minjung theology 267, 343
mission 152, 244, 247, 333–4
moderators 298–9
monism 143, 157, 163, 177–8
Moorfields Academy 94, 97, 260
morality 112–15, 130–3, 146, 159, 216–17, 227, 236
Moravians 127
Muggletonians 53
music 327–9
mysticism 174

National Health Service 341
naturalism 219, 246, 346
natural law 219
natural theology 46, 153, 221, 237
New College, London 169, 220, 303, 317
Newington Green Academy 94
New Light Antiburghers 240
New Light Burghers 240
Newton-in-Bowland 306
Northern Congregational College 303
Norwich 317

Occasional Conformity Act 260
Old Light Antiburghers 240
Old Light Burghers 240

ordination 17, 150, 200–201, 209, 239, 262, 291, 308
Orthodox churches 335
Ottawa 347
Oxford 54
Oxford University 52, 93, 217, 266

Paton Congregational College 303, 308–9
Pentecostalism 13, 254
pessimism 346
Peterborough 269
pietism 173–4
piety 44, 101
Pinhoe 91
Pitminster 98
Plymouth 128
prayer 20–24, 27–8, 30–32, 39, 41, 44, 160, 205–7, 244, 323–4
postmodernism 346
preaching 21, 26, 30, 32, ch. 3, 96, 163, 243–4, 317, 323, 324, 331
predestination 136, 235
Presbyterian Church of England 290
Presbyterian Church of Wales 318
Presbyterian Church USA 45
Presbyterians/ism 15, 17, 37–8, 45, 57, 92–4, 96, 105, 116, 126, 216, 235, 238, 240, 246, 255, 258–60, 292
priesthood of believers 25, 75, 196, 198, 238, 287, 324
primitive Methodists 44
process thought 155, 237
Puritans 21–2, 94, 119, 123, 168, 178, 187, 189, 193, 198, 202, 211, 245, 296, 319

Quakers 27, 29, 59, 92, 203, 258

Rational Dissenters 241
Ravenstonedale 306
reason 93, 100, 101, 104, 106, 108, 111–12, 125, 156, 158, 228,
Reformation 10, 28, 33, 154, 187, 234, 239, 249, 336
Reformed family 3–4, 12, 15, 31, 37, 40, 47, 197, 226, 230, ch. 10, 291, 335–7
Reformed Presbyterian Church 240
Reformed theology ch. 10
Relief Church 240
republicanism 87, 280
revelation 2, 108, 111, 121, 135, 145, 153–8, 161, 163, 172, 177–8
   general 153, 157

Richmond 306
Roman Catholicism 24, 40, 92, 108, 192, 226, 276, 334–5, 338–40

sacraments 165–6, 186, 196, 202–5, 207, 209, 239, 248
  see also, baptism; Lord's Supper
Salters' Hall Conference 51, 102, 151
Salvation Army 254
Sandemanians 119
Savoy Declaration of Faith and Order 234, 249, 258, 293
Schism Bill 92, 259
Scottish Congregational College 140, 169
Scottish Episcopal Church 21
Second Coming 326
Second London Confession 51, 79, 249
Second Vatican Council 335
sectarianism 3–4, 132, 137, 188, 191, 201, 226, 250, 313, 337–40
Sedbergh 305, 306, 314
Separatists 19–22, 235, 257, 273, 292
service books 29
Sherborne 98
Short Confession 318
six principles 74
Smarden 56
Socinianism 52–3, 93, ch. 6, 245
Soham 134
Somerset Confession 58, 71
soul 109
Standard Confession 51–3, 71, 74, 82
Stoicism 114–15
Stow-on-the-Wold 217
Stradbroke 59
Sunday schools 29, 286, 320, 322

Taunton 91, 93, 118, 126, 245
Taunton Academy 93, 96
Test and Corporation Acts 122, 266
theodicy 162, 207
theology ch. 1
Toleration Act 92, 260, 266
total depravity 223
Trinity 12–13, 29, 34, 50, 52, 54, 56, 66, 102, 121, 151, 152, 326
Tuam 94

Uckfield 321
Unaffiliated Congregational Churches 314
Unitarians/ism 21, 57, 66, 68, 92, 97, ch. 6, 141, 146, 206, 241
United Church of Christ 171, 197, 209
United Reformed Church 30, 269, 282, 285–7, 313, 315, 335
Universalism/ists 57, 61, 119
Ursinus College 183

vocation 14–15, 46, 331

Waldensians 234, 339
Western Academy 217
Western College 303
West Hatch 98
Westhill College 29
Westminster Assembly 21, 47, 103, 258
Westminster Confession 160, 233, 249, 293
Westminster Larger Catechism 11, 160
Westminster Shorter Catechism 318
Wicken 134
Windsor 317
Wivelsfield 57
Women 16–17, 41, 166, 235–6, 260
World Alliance of Reformed Churches 17, 246, 253–4, 316, 339, 348
World Congress on Evangelism 340
World Council of Churches 15, 49, 249, 292, 334
World Presbyterian Alliance 246
Worplesdon 287, 320–21, 340
Worship 12, 14, ch. 2, 41–4, 76–8, 100, 122, 132, 202–7, 233, 240, 249, 251, 261, 269, 288, 318–29, 331–4, 340, 350
Wymondley Academy 261

Yale College 217
York 268
Yorkshire United Independent College 303, 306

Zurich 267